What Others Have Said About *Wheel*

"Wheelchair users of Florida . . . exult! Your passport to less ten-
tative travel is a recent paperback book that has a fairly comprehensive rundown of the wheelchair-friendly attractions and their
nearby accommodations . . ."
— Ingrid L Kohler, *St Petersburg Times*

". . . helps remove barriers for those traveling with a wheelchair
and opens doors to activities ranging from swimming to sky diving. . . It's the authors' attention to detail that makes the guide so
valuable."
— Margo Harakas, *Fort Lauderdale Sun-Sentinel*

"My mother uses a cane and sometimes a walker. Thank you
Wheelchairs on the Go! You made our trip to Florida a great
success."
— Clarice Wiza, Muncie, Indiana

". . . outstanding access guide for visitors but a must for those of
us who are active Florida residents."
— Pat Carson, Disabled American Veterans

"It's about time someone decided to help the handicapped find the
kinds of vacation spots . . . and resorts easily accessible by wheelchair."
— Ken Moore, *Naples Daily News*

"I've discovered a great book . . . *Wheelchairs on the Go* helps disabled people know great places to go and fun things to do."
— Joyce M Rost, Saftey Harbor, Florida

Wheelchairs on the Go

Accessible Fun In Florida

Michelle Stigleman & Deborah Van Brunt

Access Guide Publishing, Inc

Wheelchairs on the Go

Accessible Fun In Florida

Michelle Stigleman & Deborah Van Brunt

To order books, visit www.wheelchairsonthego.com, e-mail wheelchairsonthego@yahoo.com or call 727-573-0434/888-245-7300.

Published by:
Access Travel Guide Publishing, Inc
14060 Egret Lane
Clearwater, FL 33762-4511 USA

Cover Design: John Atkinson
Wheelchair compliments of Custom Mobility
Graphic Production: Heather Nicoll
Additional Art: Laura Stigleman

Library of Congress LCCN 2002091721
ISBN 9664356-5-6
First Edition 2002

WHAT'S INSIDE?

If you like to enjoy life and you ride a wheelchair or otherwise have limited mobility, here's a book for you! Reflecting the range of people's interests and abilities, this guide describes accessible fun in Florida, from popular tourist spots and typical leisure activities to high adventures and wilderness expeditions. You'll find minimally accessible to fully ADA-compliant operations as well as lodging both *on* and *off the beaten path*. Descriptions include potential barriers and what means, if any, are available to overcome those barriers. The appendixes are jammed with additional useful resources on travel and recreation in general and in Florida.

Please, take nothing for granted. Unfortunately we could not visit and personally explore every site in this book. In these cases, we have typically relied on owners, management and/or staff to describe their operations and facilities. We have verified and re-verified that information in writing and by phone. However, we cannot absolutely guarantee the information in each entry. So *please*, before you go to a place or activity described here call to make sure the operation works for you. Also, find out if weather, construction or other forces have altered access since this book came out. For more risky activities, go observe and talk with the staff to decide for yourself if you can participate safely and comfortably. We accept no responsibility for any injury or inconvenience you sustain while using this book.

We'd like to hear from you. If you would like to receive e-mail notice of additions or updates to this book and/or similar future online and in-print publications, please register at our web site www.wheelchairsonthego.com. If you have suggestions, discover a neat spot or opportunity that we've missed, or you have a negative experience with one of the listings, please contact us. If we use your input in our next edition, we'll thank you by acknowledging you in the credits and sending you a free copy of the next edition. Reach us by e-mail at wheelchairsonthego@yahoo.com.

Use this guide in good health and have fun!

TABLE OF CONTENTS

USING THIS GUIDE

For the sake of space, we use several abbreviated terms that are explained below. Here you'll also find tips and additional information on many of the activities listed in this book.

■ OVERALL

Beneath some activities, other sites with related activities are cross-referenced by category and name. For example, under *Canoeing*, you may see *Parks: John Pennekamp*, meaning you'll also find canoeing described at John Pennekamp State Park under Parks within the same geographic area.

If no barrier is described in an entry, assume the place or activity is readily accessible. If a feature is universally designed, we use *ADA* to describe it. For example, *ADA picnic tables* and *ADA playgrounds* are designed to be used by wheelchair riders while *picnic tables* and *playgrounds* are not.

Near the end of each entry is a list of additional features, such as accessible amenities, activities for able-bodied people in your party or important notes such as reservations are necessary.

In noting the hours of operations, *wkdy* refers to Monday through Friday and *wknd* to Saturday and Sunday. For hours of operations, we did not repeat the opening or closing hours for subsequent days of the week if they are the same. For example, *wkdy 9-5* and *wknd -8*, indicates the operation opens at 9:00am and closes at 5:00pm Monday through Friday and closes at 8:00pm on Saturday and Sunday.

City names are not repeated in the addresses for those operations that are located in the major city listed as the section title. After the address, we often give rather cryptic directions so you can find the spot on a local map.

■ ABBREVIATIONS USED

WC	wheelchair
ECV	electric convenience vehicle or scooter
HC	handicapped as in handicapped parking or permits
Rr	ADA men's and women's restrooms
Rr, not ADA	gender specific restrooms that are accessible but do no meet ADA standards
CRr	ADA companion or large unisex restroom
AC	air-conditioned
$	admission fee (or charge) when fees are not routine for an activity
$D	donations are welcome
✢	beach wheelchair is available for loan

■ ACCOMMODATIONS

ADA accommodations comply with the standards of the Americans with Disabilities Act. *WC-friendly* accommodations are somewhat accessible but not adapted for wheelchair riders; in such cases, inaccessible features are described. For example, you can get into a WC-friendly accommodation but perhaps may not fit through the bathroom doorway. We have included some minimally accessible accommodations because in some areas even WC-friendly lodging is unavailable, or because the lodging is particularly interesting and perhaps worth the inconvenience to some readers.

Descriptions of accommodations indicate after the bed size in parentheses ( ) the bed height from the floor to the top of the mattress and whether the mattress is on an open frame where a portable lift can be used or on a platform. *Full kitchens* are equipped with pots, utensils, plates and so forth. Descriptions of bathrooms indicate *seats* where shower seats are available; usually you must request one be brought to your room.

Toward the end of each lodging entry is a list of additional amenities. *Free brkfst* indicates a continental breakfast is included. *Pool* indicates the pool area or deck is accessible; we clearly celebrate the few motel pools that are actually accessible. *Full restaurant* refers to one that serves breakfast, lunch and dinner. Some items, such as *golf courses*, are listed for able-bodied persons in your party.

Too often motel clerks miss the notation that you need an ADA or accessible room. Call the day you plan to check in and confirm the correct unit will be available.

Toll-free numbers at the end of entries are to that specific location; the toll-free numbers for the national chains are listed in the Appendix on page 410. For B&B/Inns and Motels, nightly charges are designated: $ for under $60; $$ between $60 - $100; and $$$ for over $100.

■ BASKETBALL
The NWBA, or National Wheelchair Basketball Association sponsors women's, men's, intercollegiate and junior teams all over the United States and Canada. Check out the web site www.nwba.org/teams2.htm or call Roger Davis 407-654-4315.

■ BEACHES
Don't expect the boardwalks at beaches to take you close to the water. Unless described otherwise, they simply lead over the dunes or a short distance onto the beach. A few communities allow vehicles on the beach. While this policy certainly enhances access and usually means hard-packed sand for easier use of a standard wheelchair, it also means you have to be cautious about the traffic as you go to the water's edge.

■ BEACH WHEELCHAIRS
Increasingly, many public beaches loan beach wheelchairs with large tires to traverse the sand more easily. An asterisk (*) indicates places where you can borrow a beach wheelchair. Most beach wheelchairs, unless described as *self-propelling*, must be pushed from behind; even self-propelled beach wheelchairs can be difficult for the rider to wheel on soft sandy beaches. Some beach wheelchairs

have *swing-away*, *removable* or *no arms* or armrests, that make transfers easier; others have *fixed arms*, meaning you cannot remove or swing the armrests away. Few beach wheelchairs can go in the water, although the PVC ones can often go to the edge of the water so you can get your feet wet. Some beach wheelchairs have extra features such as umbrellas or drink holders.

■ BOATING

Whether you are considering boats for rent, tours or fishing, call ahead to make sure the operation can accommodate you. Be aware, when we indicate that the operator can lift or *help* others in your party lift you aboard that your weight and your type of wheelchair may exceed the operator's capability to do so. Often extra staff must be arranged beforehand to lift wheelchairs aboard. If you ride an ECV or scooter, explore renting a manual WC for a day of boating; check WC Resources at the beginning of the section or Travel Resources in the Appendix (pg 406). Ask the operator if high or low tides can ease or compound boarding in a wheelchair. Even where tides may not be relevant, Florida can experience severe droughts that can render docks at inland waterways difficult for boarding in wheelchairs. *Floating docks* that rise and lower with the water level are usually easier than *fixed docks* for boarding in a wheelchair.

The width of the gate or opening is noted for pontoon boat rentals so you can determine if you can roll aboard. Where the opening is too narrow, sometimes the operator can help your friends or get staff to lift you over the railing in your WC or lift you and your WC aboard separately. Unless otherwise noted, pontoon boats used for boat tours in this book have gates wide enough to accommodate wheelchairs.

For your own safety and comfort, bring a portable seatbelt and tie-down when boating. Portable seatbelts are sold at automotive stores. Bolt the ends to each other so it only opens by the buckle in front then secure yourself in your WC or a boat seat. Ratchet tie-downs (with hooks on both ends) are sold in discount stores' automotive departments. Run the straps through your back wheels then secure the hooks to the boat or something solid so can keep your WC stationary.

■ BOWLING

The bowling alleys listed in the book have either have flat entrances to the lanes or are ramped for access. Many bowling alleys offer *bowling ball ramps* or adaptive devices on which you place your bowling ball and then aim the ramp in the direction of the pins. A simple nudge gets the ball moving off the ramp and down the lane. *Bumpers* are often available to keep the ball out of the gutters, at least for most of the way down the lane. For more information, visit the web site of the American Wheelchair Bowling Association www.awba.org or call Earl Annis at 727-734-0023.

■ CANOEING/KAYAKING

We indicate if a canoe instructor has an Adaptive Paddlers Endorsement from the *ACA* or the American Canoe Association. Such persons are certified by the ACA as instructors and also have been specifically trained to help paddlers with disabilities.

A *sit-on* kayak has a very low back support; this type of kayak is easier to board since you don't have to slide into it, but you need to have good balance. A *sit-in* kayak has more support but requires you to wriggle down inside. Descriptions specify solo (1-person) or tandem (2-person) kayaks.

■ DISC GOLF
This game involves tossing a Frisbee or disc on a course similar to a golf course. Instead of hitting a tiny ball into a small hole in the ground, you aim your Frisbee at a goal or basket hanging from a pole on the green.

■ FISHING CHARTERS/PARTY BOATS
Fishing charters are private arrangements for a captain (and boat) where the captain serves as a personal guide to your group of anglers. If you do not have enough anglers in your group, charter captains can sometimes *split* your trip (and costs) with another party. Ask the captain if it is possible to board from a floating dock. Don't forget to bring a seat belt and tie-downs and be aware that your weight may exceed the operator's capacity to help lift you aboard; see Boating above.

Party boats are open to the public, carry large numbers of people and are comparatively inexpensive. Mates can usually help bait your hook and untangle crossed lines. Because the boat has lots of anglers and flying hooks, wear clothing to protect your skin from the accidental snag.

Charters and party boats include rod/reel, tackle, bait and fishing licenses. Often operators carry a cooler with ice to keep your drinks and food cold. Sometimes you can bring your own cooler. Some party boats sell lunch or snacks onboard.

■ FISHING LICENSES
Any person under 16 and residents (with proof of age and residency) over 64, do not need fishing licenses in Florida. Florida residents do not need licenses to fish from a shore or pier. You do not need a license to fish from a charter boat or party boat; the captain's license covers you.

Florida residents certified as permanently disabled by the Veterans Administration, the Armed Forces or Social Security can obtain a free license by applying at the county tax collector's office.

You can purchase licenses at the county tax collector's office, bait/tackle shops, sporting goods and discount stores. If you catch a fish in brackish water, you can keep it only if you have the pertinent license for the salt- or freshwater fish.

■ GOLF
Several golf courses in Florida have adaptive golf carts to enable someone with a mobility impairment to play. The 1-person cart has hand controls, a bag carrier in front and a swivel seat from which you take your swing. As pointed out in the individual entries, courses have different rules about driving the carts in bunkers and on greens. Florida Adaptive Golf is an organization that sponsors instruction with adaptive equipment, identifies courses and practice areas for members and schedules

tournaments with adaptive carts. Call Paul Goodlander; office 941-957-0310; home 941-365-3809.

■ HANDCYCLES

Handcycling, sometimes called crank-cycling, is growing as a recreational and competitive sport. Two different designs are currently used. One design is a single wheel that attaches to and raises the front wheels of a manual wheel-chair. The other, more common design is a 3-wheel bike into which you transfer. You *pedal* both types by hand or arm and both incorporate hand brakes; adaptations can be made for quads. For more information visit the US Handcycling web site www.ushf.org.

■ HORSEBACK RIDING

The *NARHA* or North American Riding for the Handicapped Association has a network of riding centers with specially trained and certified instructors who practice hippotherapy with physically disabled persons. Some centers also offer recreational riding. Sessions are free or very inexpensive. NARHA can provide you the most current list of certified centers at 800-369-7433 or www.narha.org.

■ HUNTING

You can purchase hunting licenses at the county tax collector's office, bait/tackle shops, sporting goods and discount stores. An adult must accompany any hunter under age 16. Any person under age 16 and residents (with proof of age and residency) over 64 do not need hunting licenses.

Disabled hunters who live in Florida and are certified as permanently disabled by the Armed Forces, Veterans, Railroad or Social Security Administrations can currently get applications for no-cost Disabled Person's Hunting & Fishing Certificates at their county tax collector's office. Florida's Fish & Wildlife Conservation Commission (FWC) issues the certificate, informally called a disabled hunting license, renewable at 5 years.

FWC also issues Disabled Off Road Vehicle (DORV) Permits for hunters with mobility impairments to hunt in a particular wildlife management area from vehicles on designated service roads not open to the public. Request an application from the regional FWC office over the wildlife management area where you wish to hunt. Find the address at www.floridaconservation.org or from FWC (850-488-3831). Along with the completed application, you must include a copy of your Disabled Person's Hunting Certificate and a letter from your doctor describing your permanent disability and how it impedes your walking. Non-residents can also obtain these permits that are good for one year. Be aware, that any hunter can hunt from a vehicle as long as the engine is not running.

FWC sponsors 3-day Mobility-Impaired Hunts each year at 4 wildlife management areas described in this book. To qualify, you must first obtain a Mobility Impaired Certification card, good for 5 years. Get an application from the FWC, Dept of Quota Hunts, 620 S Meridian St, Tallahassee, FL 32399 (850-488-8573).

A physician must sign off on your application. Once you receive certification, you can apply for Mobility-Impaired Hunts at specific management areas. These MI Hunt applications are generally available from the FWC on July 1; completed applications must be received by late July. Participants are selected by random drawings for each site. You are notified by mail if your application was selected, told of the orientation (usually the night before the hunt) and given directions to these remote locations. In most cases, an able-bodied person may accompany you but not hunt. General gun rules allow modern and primitive firearms and archery equipment. During MI Hunts, all participants may drive vehicles off roads; in some areas ATVs are allowed. Non-residents can also apply for MI Hunts.

A few mobility-impaired hunts are held at areas owned or managed by other entities. Generally the same rules apply as for the FWC MI Hunts.

For more information, contact the Florida Disabled Outdoors Association at 850-668-7323/fdoa@nettaly.com or Florida Fish & Wildlife 850-488-4676/www.floridaconservation.org.

■ PICNICKING
An *ADA picnic shelter* is accessible and has at least one ADA picnic table. *ADA picnic tables* are designed so wheelchair riders can roll under and eat comfortably from the table. Some picnic tables that are not necessarily ADA have extended ends where you can roll under the table. *Grill* indicates a standup grill.

■ POOLS
If a pool is ramped, we indicate if a submersible wheelchair is available. If a pool has a lift, we indicate the type of seat on the lift. *Sling* seats usually are nylon and hang from chains at the front and back of the seats; you can use the chains to steady yourself however, most wheelchair riders need help transferring because the seats are not stationary and the chains can get in the way. Lifts with *fixed* seats generally have hard, molded plastic seats that are stationary but have no armrests. Staff operates the lift even if they cannot help you transfer into the seat.

■ QUAD RUGBY
Originally quad rugby was called *murderball* because of the rough and tumble nature of the game. Players must have both upper and lower extremity impairments to be eligible to participate. This international sport has more than 45 teams in the USA. Check out the web site www.quadrugby.com or contact John Bishop 561-964-1712.

■ SCUBA/SNUBA
Some dive shops offer *resort dives*, generally meaning that you can spend the morning learning the basics of scuba and can go out on an afternoon dive with your instructor in open water down to 50 feet. Some dive shops offer training required to get certified in diving that includes written work, pool sessions and four open water dives with your instructor. Other shops only offer dive trips to those who are already certified.

The *HSA* or Handicapped Scuba Association trains and certifies dive instructors to work with and teach divers with physical disabilities. HSA can provide you a current list of local instructors with HSA certification at 949-498-4540 or www.hsascuba.com. You may also want to check web site www.diverlink.com/training/handicapped.htm for more information on dives for disabled persons.

Another option that somewhat falls in between scuba and snorkeling is called *SNUBA* where you are connected by a long hose to a compressed air source above the water. You have more time to explore the underwater without coming to the surface as in snorkeling, but don't have to go through the training required for scuba certification or carry tanks on your back. To date, we've only found SNUBA operators in the Keys.

■ TENNIS
The United States Tennis Association has an active wheelchair-tennis component. For an updated list of programs, camps or tournaments, contact USTA, Florida Section at 954-968-3434 x 214 or www.usta-fl.com. Where this book lists tennis at the end of a description for example, for a park or motel, the courts are hard surfaced.

WHEELCHAIR EVENTS

Many of these events are open to all persons with disabilities. Locations and dates may change over time. Contact the person or phone number at the end of each description to register and/or ascertain the location and schedule.

JANUARY

Miami
Rolex-Miami Olympic Class Regatta pits able-bodied sailors against disabled sailors who are trying to qualify for the Paralympic Games; teams are rated to equalize physical abilities. Sailors compete in Sonar 23', 3-person keelboats and 2.4-meter, 1-person keelboats. Held at several sailing centers on Biscayne Bay. (Katie Richardson 401-683-0800)

Tampa Bay
Coveen International Quad Rugby Tournament is the largest rugby tournament before nationals involving the 8 strongest US teams and 4 strongest international teams. Fri-Sun. Venue varies. (Justin Stark 813-719-6151)

W Palm Beach
Knock & Roll Quad Rugby Tournament, sponsored by Palm Beach County Parks & Recreation Department, features the top 8 Division 2 teams from around the country. Fri-Sun. Venue varies. (John Bishop 561-964-1712; Parks Dept 561-963-7379)

FEBRUARY

Miami
Mid-Winter International Regatta, sponsored by Shake-A-Leg and open to the public, features teams of 1 able-bodied and 2 disabled sailors in 20' boats. Races are available for novice and experienced sailors. 4 days. Biscayne Bay. (Shake-A-Leg Water Sports Center, 2600 S Bayshore Dr; 305-858-5550)

Sarasota
Sarasota Smash Quad Rugby Tournament features Division 2 teams from the northeast US and Canada. Fri-Sun. Timing and venue may change. Cardinal Mooney High School, 4171 Fruitville Rd. (Patrick O'Conner 941-751-1176)

Tampa
Loren Vandermark Classic is sponsored by the Florida Wheelchair Bowling Association and open to members who are also members of the American Wheelchair Bowling Association. 2 days. Terrence Sports Bowling Center, 5311 E Busch Blvd. (Earl Annis 727-734-0023)

MARCH

Gainesville   **National Women's WC-Basketball Tournament** is a national women's event with 8 teams from around the country. Winners of this event represent the US in international competitions. Thu-Sat. Santa Fe Community College, 3000 NW 83 St. (Dug Jones 352-395-5269)

Jacksonville   **Gate River Run** is a National Championship for American Runners sponsored by the Jacksonville Track Club. WC riders start 15 min before other runners in this 15K race. A 5K event is also open to runners, walkers and WC riders. No electric WCs, handcylces or crank-cycles are permitted. 1 day. Altel Stadium, Stadium Dr at I-95 and Union St. (Bob Hawkes 904-744-1174)

Miami   **Ericson Open WC-Tennis Tournament**, along with the tournament for able-bodied players, is USTA-sanctioned. Crandon Park Tennis Center, 7300 Crandon Blvd; 305-365-2300. (FL USTA 954-968-3434x214)

Tampa   **Gulf Coast Trapshoot,** sponsored by the Paralyzed Veterans of America and open to the public with advanced registration, includes 5 trapshooting events with prizes. A practice day is followed by 2 days of competition. Silver Dollar Trap Shoot Club, 17202 Target Way, Odessa; 813-920-3231. (Paul Wolbert 813-935-6540; 800-397-6540)

Tampa   **Open WC-Tennis Tournament,** sponsored by the Tampa WC-Tennis Foundation, the city of Tampa and area businesses, is a USTA-sanctioned event and a good warm up for players competing in the Boca Florida Open. Hillsborough Community College; 3901 W Tampa Bay Blvd. (Tracy Wilkerson 813-672-2573)

Tampa   **National Wheelchair Poolplayers Association Tournament** is open to 32 national and international players in WCs who are earning points to qualify for the US team. 3 days. Planet 9-Ball, 11236 W Hillsborough Ave. Visit the National Wheelchair Pool Players web site www.nwpainc.com. (Ken Miller 813-818-7665)

APRIL

Boca Raton **Florida Open International WC-Tennis Championships,** sponsored by the USTA, is one of the largest WC-tennis competitions in the country. Patch Reef Park Tennis Center, 2000 NW 51 St; on Yamoto Rd, just W of Military Tr; 561-997-0881. (Bruce or Verena Karr 561-655-4930)

Gainesville **Gator Invitational Sports Ability Games** are sanctioned track and field events for physically challenged persons with classes from novice to professional. Events include 20-meter to 1-mi track, a weave course for power WCs, an obstacle course for all WCs, softball throw, shot put, discus and relay races. 1 day. Kiwannis Challenge Playground, 2131 NW 39 Ave; behind the girls club. (Claudia Siders work 352-955-6701; home 386-462-4880)

Sanford **Bass Fishing Tournament,** sponsored by the Florida Paralyzed Veterans of America and open to the public, has divisions for fishing from the banks and from boats on Lake Monroe. Boating participants are paired with a captain; crew can lift you into the boat seat from your WC. 2 days. Monroe Harbor Marina, 531 N Palmetto Ave; 407-322-2910. (407-328-7041)

Tampa Bay **Fishing Has No Boundaries** hosts a non-competitive fishing event whereby novices fish from a boat with an experienced angler. 2 days. Venues vary (Brad Stigleman 727-573-7955)

MAY

Gainesville **GatorSport Exploration Camp** is for adults with spinal cord injuries and lower extremity amputations, to explore and learn sports, including WC basketball, tennis, racing, amputee racing, quad rugby, swimming, fencing and golf. 2 days. University of Florida. (Dr Carolyn Hanson, Dept of Occupational Therapy 352-846-1023)

Tallahassee **Sports Ability,** sponsored by the Florida Disabled Outdoors Association, offers the disabled public an opportunity to try out various sports and recreational activities, from water skiing and horseback riding to basketball, depending upon local resources. You can also check out demonstrations and displays of specialized products, services and programs. 2 days. Venues vary (David Jones 850-668-7323)

Tampa	**State Wheelchair Bowling Tournament** is sponsored by the Florida Wheelchair Bowling Association and open to members who are also members of the American Wheelchair Bowling Association. 3 days. Location varies. (Earl Annis 727-734-0023)

AUGUST

Orlando	**National/World Disabled Water Ski Championship** is sponsored by the USA Water Ski and the City of Altamonte Springs. Winners go on to represent the USA in the subsequent World Championships. 4 days (including 2-day clinics open to the public). Cranes Roost Park, Shorecrest & Northlake Blvds, Altamonte Springs. (US Water Ski 800-533-2972; Jerrey Thurston 407-468-7958; Bill Bowness WSDA@unlimitedskiing.org)

SEPTEMBER

Jacksonville	**Sports Ability**, as described above under May, Tallahassee, occurs sometime in the autumn. (David Jones 850-668-7323)

OCTOBER

Dade City	**Dade Battle of Brilliance** is a bicycling and handcyling competition in downtown and includes some of the area's top amateurs and the nation's best cyclists. Handcyclists of all levels and all ages compete in a 20-min race. 1 day. (David Hevia 352-567-2378 or Ellen Kast 813-885-2473/800-724-9686)

NOVEMBER

Daytona/ Ft Lauderdale	**Florida Fall Classic** is sponsored by the Florida Wheelchair Bowling Association and open to members who are also members of the American Wheelchair Bowling Association. 2 days. Locations alternate. (Earl Annis 727-734-0023)
Ft Lauderdale	**Sunshine Sectional WC-Tennis Tournament** is a USTA-sanctioned event for players world wide. 3 days. Maxwell Park, 1200 SW 72 Ave, Pembroke Pines; 954-986-5021. (Nancy Horowitz 954-435-6759)

DECEMBER

Jacksonville   **Jacksonville Marathon**, sponsored by the Jacksonville Track Club, is a 26.3-mi qualifying race for the Boston Marathon with a WC Division that gets a 1-min downhill head start. 1 day. Altel Stadium, Stadium Dr at I-95 and Union St. (Bob Hawkes 904-744-1174)

Miami   **Jr Orange Bowl Sportsability Games** includes sailing, swimming and track and field events for physically challenged kids age 8-18 from all over the world. 3 days. 3 different venues (James Daley 305-724-3322)

Tampa   **WC Derby**, sponsored by the Hillsborough County Parks & Recreation Department, includes races for all ages and abilities on a 2.2-mi paved loop road. Categories range from electric carts to 3-wheelers and from kids to masters. 1 day. Hillsborough River State Park, 15402 US 301 N, Thonotosassa; 12 mi N of Tampa. (813-987-6771)

W Palm Beach   **The Mosquito Open** WC-tennis tournament, sponsored by the Palm Beach County Parks and Recreation Department, is a USTA-sanctioned event. 2 days. Carlin Park, 400 S SR A1A, Jupiter. (Kristen Karon 561-963-7379)

W Palm Beach   **Holiday Showcase**, sponsored by Vision Strength Artistic Expression and Palm Beach County Parks & Recreation Department, features music, dance and other performances by local talent with a variety of abilities. Palm Beach Community College, Duncan Theater, 4200 S Congress Ave, Lake Worth. (561-964-4822)

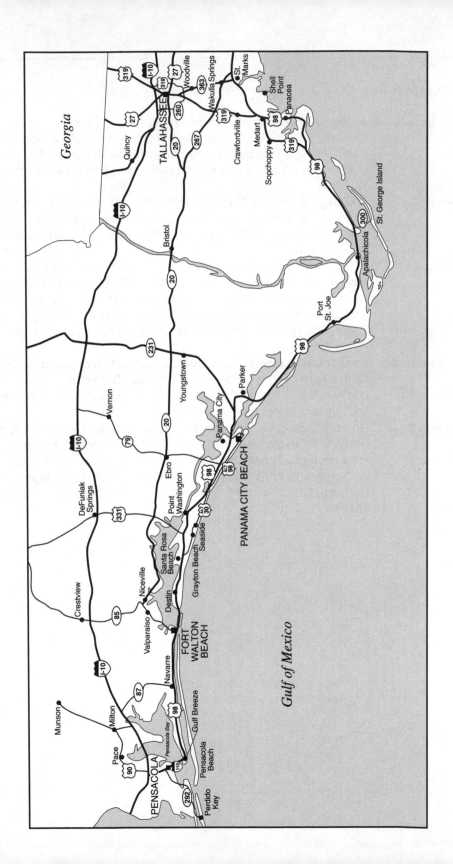

PANHANDLE

FORT WALTON BEACH
Crestview, Destin, Grayton Beach, Niceville, Santa Rosa Beach, Seaside, Valparaiso

Here's the place to enjoy miles of relatively uncrowded, sugar sand beaches with awesome sunsets, beach wheelchairs and fine surf fishing. Nearby Destin is renowned for its deep-sea fishing. US 98 is also called Miracle Strip Parkway and SR61 is called Thomasville Road.

Tourist Info
Okaloosa County Visitors Bureau: 1540 US 98 E, 32549; 850-651-7122; 800-322-3319
Web Sites: www.destin-fwb.com

Transportation
Okaloosa Coordinated Transportation services the county with lift-equipped vans Mon-Sat 6am-11pm. You must go to the office (weekdays 7:30-5) to complete an application. Reservations must be made by noon the day before, with priority for medical appointments. (207 Hospital Dr; 850-833-9168)

WC Resources
Island Sports Shop rents and delivers beach WCs for the day or longer. The De-Bug beach WC (no arms; umbrella, drink or fishing-pole holders) can be self-propelled or pushed from behind. (1688 E Old Hwy 89, Destin; 850-650-9126)

ACTIVITIES

■ ATTRACTIONS
Gulfarium presents four 20- to 25-min shows starring sea lions, dolphins and human scuba divers in 4 different venues every 30 min. The 2-story tank for the Dolphin Show has 2 flights of stairs, but you can watch from the sidewalk through the tank's large windows at ground level. The indoor Living Seas show features divers in a 60,000-gal tank of sharks, sea turtles and tarpons; WC seating is front and

center. The other 2 shows are ramped and under cover. For a small fee, take home a photo of you and a friendly sea lion. Covered sidewalks take you past habitats and tanks of otters, penguins, sharks, eels and other sea life; only the rookery where seals are trained is inaccessible. For an extra charge, you can have a 40-min Dolphin Interaction in a waist-deep pool where you hand-feed and signal commands to dolphins; advance reservations are needed for the therapist to accompany you. The JF Dolphin Project is a 1- to 2-wk therapeutic program for kids with a range of disabilities; call 850-217-0099. Snack bar; gift shop; Rr. $/WC guests free. May-Sep 9-6; Oct-Apr -4; shows begin at 10 (1010 US 98; 850-243-9046)

Sasquatch Zoo is the 22-acre home to more than 250 animals representing 50 species from 27 countries. A hard-packed 1200' path loops through the park where animals roam in natural settings. Staff carries baby animals, birds and reptiles that you can pet. Bring your own picnic. Picnic tables; drinks; gift shop; Rr. $. Wed-Sun 9-4 (5262 Deer Springs Dr, Crestview; 7 mi E of Crestview off US 90; 850-682-3949)

■ **BEACHES**

*Grayton Beach State Park, with its 1-mi stretch of soft sand along the Gulf, is one of the top 10 beaches in the USA. To borrow a beach WC (fixed arms) sign a release at the entrance; staff will bring it to you in the beach parking lot. Both Western Lake and the boat ramp are inaccessible. See Campgrounds. ADA picnic shelter; grills; outdoor showers; Rr. $. 8-dusk (357 Main Park Rd, Santa Rosa Bch; E off CR 30A, S of US 98; 850-231-4210)

*Henderson Beach State Park has 208 acres of woods, dunes and beach along the Gulf. Ask at the ranger station to borrow a beach WC (removable right arm; umbrella) that is kept at the ramp to Eastern Beach. The entrance station

has a video of the hilly, sandy, 1-mi nature trail through a coastal scrub. Surf fishing is allowed. See Campgrounds. ADA picnic shelters; grills; outdoor showers; Rr. $. 8-dusk (17000 US 98, Destin; 850-837-7550)

*Marler Memorial Park is a 10-acre county park on the bayside of Okaloosa Island where you can borrow a beach WC (fixed arms; umbrella). Call ahead so staff can meet you with the WC that you can take into the shallow, roped-off swim area. Surf fishing is allowed. Lifeguards in summer; ADA picnic shelters; grills; outdoor showers; Rr. 6am-8:30pm (1111 N Santa Rosa Blvd; 850-830-5505)

*Okaloosa County loans beach WCs (fixed arms; umbrellas) at 3 Gulf beaches: Beasley Park (1540 US 98; 1 mi E of Santa Rosa Blvd), Seashore Beachwalk (552 Santa Rosa Blvd; just W of US 98) and Blue Dolphin Beachwalk (376 Santa Rosa Blvd; 1 mi W of US 98). Call so staff can meet you with the WC at the beach of your choice. Each has boardwalks to the beach. Lifeguards in summer; ADA picnic tables; outdoor showers; Rr. 6am-8:30pm (850-830-5505/651-7299)

*Topsail Hill State Preserve has over 1600 pristine acres, including a gorgeous 3-mi beach. Ask at the ranger station to borrow the beach WC (removable arms). A WC-accessible tram travels between the parking lot, campground and beach with a 700' ADA boardwalk. See Campgrounds. ADA picnic shelters; Rr. Dawn-dusk (7525 W Scenic CR 30A, Santa Rosa Bch; 850-267-0299)

■ **BOAT RAMPS**

Beaches: Marler. Parks: Liza Jackson

■ **BOAT RENTALS**

Adventure Pontoons rents 10- to 16-person boats (30" entry) for half/full days or for 2 hrs at sunset on the Santa Rosa Sound or Choctawhatchee Bay. Staff can help you roll down the 28" wide dock and aboard. Restaurant & Rr at marina (East Pass Marina, 288 E US

98, Destin; 850-837-3041)

Harbor Cove Charters rents pontoon boats (31" entry) for use on the sound, Destin Harbor or the bay for half/full days for up to 14 people. Staff can help you board. Bait shop nearby; Rr in AJ's. May-Sep (AJ's Club Bimini, 116 E US 98, Destin; 850-837-4703; 877-527-4511)

Pontoon Rentals for up to 13 passengers (28" entry) are available for half/full days on the sound, bay or Intracoastal. Staff can help lift you aboard in your WC from the fixed dock. (54 SE US 98; 850-664-0039)

■ **BOAT TOURS**

AJ's Seablaster offers 90-min daytime and 2-hr sunset cruises on a 73' speedboat through the Destin Harbor and into the Gulf. Add dolphins, music and kids to co-captain the boat! Crew can lift you from your WC into a boat seat. Free beer, wine & soda; Rr in AJ's (AJ's Club Bimini, 116 E US 98, Destin; 850-837-4703; 877-527-4511)

Dolphin Cruises are narrated, 2-hr daytime or sunset tours aboard a 79' glass-bottom boat. Board by ramp; there's a 4" lip to the cabin. Snack bar onboard; restaurants & Rr in marina. Feb-Oct (Harborwalk Marina, 76 E US 98, Destin; 850-837-774; 888-424-7217)

Emerald Queen is a huge paddlewheel boat that can take you on 2 1/2-hr narrated dinner cruises in Destin Harbor. Roll aboard the gangplank to the accessible 1st deck, including the AC cabin. Choose prime rib or chicken and enjoy music and dancing. Rr in marina. Schedule varies (Harborwalk Marina, 76 E US 98, Destin; 850-837-2930)

Snorkel Destin has 2-hr sunset cruises from Destin Harbor to the Gulf aboard the open-decked, 50' Reef Runner. The fixed dock is ramped and staff can help you board. Reservations; snack bar onboard; restaurants & Rr in marina. Apr-Sep Mon-Sat (Harborwalk Marina, 76 E US 98, Destin; 850-654-4655)

■ **BOWLING**

Shoal River Bowling Center has ramped lanes and bowling ball ramps. Every other Fri afternoon, local disabled residents gather to bowl; Special Olympics teams also train here. Game room; snack bar; Rr. Hrs vary (5204 S Ferdon Blvd, Crestview; I-10 exit 56, 1 mi S; 850-682-1310)

White Sands Bowling Center has ramped lanes and a bowling ball ramp. Game room; karaoke on Wed & wknd nights; Thunderball Fri & Sat mdnt-2am; snack bar; Rr. Hrs vary (653 Beal Pkwy NW; 850-863-2193)

■ **FISHING CHARTERS**

Adventure Charter Service can take you and 5 friends on 4- to 12-hr deep-sea trips in the Gulf. The sport fishing boats range from 38'-55', some with accessible AC cabins. Four anglers can take trips in the back bays. Crew can lift you aboard in your WC. Private/split charters; restaurant & Rr at marina (East Pass Marina, 288 US 98 E, Destin; 850-654-4070)

Flat Out Charters offers 4-hr trips in early mornings or late afternoons on the back bays and bayou. The 25' flats boat can take up to 4 anglers for fly-fishing or light tackle. With advance notice, crew can lift you aboard in your WC. Restaurant & Rr at marina (East Pass Marina, 288 US 98 E, Destin; 850-654-1106)

Harbor Cove Charters offers deep-sea and bay fishing trips on a variety of boats from 40'-65' long, some with accessible AC cabins. Crew can lift you aboard in your WC. Bottom fishing, trolling and sport fishing trips range from half day to overnight. Food can be included for an extra charge. Private/split charters; Rr in AJ's (AJ's Club Bimini, 116 US 98 E, Destin; 850-837-2222; 877-527-4511)

Just in Time has deep-sea trips in the Gulf from 4 hrs to overnight. Crew can help lift you in your WC aboard the 50' sport fishing boat that holds 18 anglers. The AC cabin has a small step at the entrance. Lunch can be included for an extra charge. Restaurants & Rr in marina (Harborwalk Marina, 76 US 98 E,

Destin; 850-837-2930)

■ FISHING-PARTY BOATS

New Florida Girl goes out for half/full-day deep-sea trips. Roll aboard the 90' boat and around the shaded deck but the AC cabin has a 6" lip. Full galley. Hrs vary (Capt Dave's Marina, 310 US 98 E, Destin; 850-837-6422)

■ FISHING PIERS

Parks: Eglin AFB, Ft Walton Landing, Liza Jackson

Okaloosa Island Pier is a 1262' lighted, cement pier on the Gulf. Snack/bait shop; Rr. $. 24 hrs (1030 US 98 E; 850-244-1023)

■ HUNTING

Eglin AFB hosts a 2-day, white-tailed deer and feral hog hunt on the 1st weekend of Feb for mobility-impaired hunters using modern or primitive firearms or archery equipment. Call Eglin for an application for the hunt that must be returned by mid-Dec. You must have Mobility-Impaired Certification; see p 13. The 50 selected hunters are notified by mail, advised of the orientation the night before and given directions. You can hunt from a vehicle, ATV or many concrete paths. (Eglin AFB, Natural Resources Branch, 107 SR 85 N, Niceville, 32578; 850-882-4164)

■ MUSEUMS

Air Force Armament Museum explains the history and development of Air Force armaments from WW I onward. Exhibits include restored aircraft from WW II through the Vietnam War, an antique pistol collection and armaments such as missiles, rockets and smart bombs. Learn about Eglin AFB in a continuous 30-min video. Many aircraft are outside. Gift shop; Rr. 9:30-4:30 (100 Museum Dr, Eglin AFB; off SR 85, S of SR 189; 850-882-4062)

Emerald Coast Science Center is a children's museum with interactive fun for the whole family. Call for special events and workshops. Gift shop. $. Wkdy 10-4; wknd 11-4 (139 Brooks St; 1 blk S of US 98; 850-664-1261)

Heritage Museum tells the history of Okaloosa and Walton Counties from 10,000 BC onward. Sign up for classes in quilting, tatting, bobbin lace and basketry. Gift shop; Rr. Tue-Sat 11-4 (115 Westview Ave, Valparaiso; 850-678-2615)

Indian Temple Mound Museum depicts 10,000 yrs of Native American history and European exploration and settlement in NW Florida. The museum houses a major collection of prehistoric ceramics. The temple mound, just outside, was constructed in 1400 AD and has been restored. Tours; gift shop; Rr. $. Wkdy 11-4; Sat 9-4 (139 US 98; 850-833-9595)

■ PARASAILING

Emerald Coast Watersports, with advance notice, can arrange for extra staff to help with transfers at a dock that best suits your needs. Staff can lift you from your WC onto the boat's bench seat and then onto the launch platform. Schedule for early morning or late afternoon when the operator has more time to spend with you. Mar-Sep (1310 US 98; 850-664-0051/302-0021)

Harbor Cove Charters offers 1- to 3-person parasail trips over the Gulf. Call ahead to reserve a boat large enough for WCs. Don the 3-way harness and crew can lift you onto the launch platform; you must have upper body strength. Staff is experienced with WC parasailors and promises smooth take-offs and landings. Rr in AJ's. May-Sep (AJ's Club Bimini, 116 E US 98, Destin; 850-837-9766; 877-527-4511)

■ PARKS

Eglin AFB Reserve has a .5-mi boardwalk with interpretive signage and a 25' fishing pier in the Anderson Pond Area. Boardwalk from parking; ADA picnic shelters. $. Dawn-dusk (SR 85; just N of Niceville; 850-882-4164)

Ft Walton Landing is a lovely 6-acre park with a 700' boardwalk and 60' fishing pier along the shady shores of the Santa Rosa Sound. Community festivals and concerts are held here throughout the year. Dawn-11pm (131

Brooks St; 1 blk S of US 98; 850-833-9576)

Liza Jackson Park sits on 14 acres on Santa Rosa Island along the Sound. Sidewalks lead to boat ramps with fixed docks and a 120' lighted fishing dock. ADA picnic shelters; grills; Rr. Dawn-11pm (318 US 98; 850-833-9576)

Rocky Bayou State Park is 357 acres of sand pine forest and wetlands along a bayou off the Choctawahatchee Bay. At the boat ramp is a small fixed dock that generally requires a big step down to a boat. Three nature trails have roots and sandy spots. See Campgrounds. ADA picnic shelters; playground; Rr. $. 8-dusk (4281 SR 20; 5 mi E of Niceville; 850-833-9144)

■ **PERFORMING ARTS**

Civic Auditorium offers performances by local and regional groups from the Stage Crafters Community Theater (850-243-1106) to the NW Florida Ballet Company (850-664-7787). The auditorium is ramped and WC seating is in back on the right. (107 US 98; 850-833-9583)

■ **SCUBA/SNORKELING**

Panama City: Scuba: Al Lewando

Snorkel Destin can take you out for 2-hr snorkel trips aboard a 50' open-decked boat. The fixed dock is ramped and staff can help you roll aboard. To get out of the water after snorkeling, you need upper body strength to pull yourself up the boat's lower steps so crew can help lift you onto the boat. Reservations; equipment & instructions included; snack bar onboard/BYO; restaurants & Rr in marina. Apr-Sep Mon-Sat (Harborwalk Marina, 76 E US 98, Destin; 850-654-4655)

■ **SHOPPING**

Boutiques can be found in downtown Ft Walton Beach (along US 98), in the Market at Sandestin (US 98; 8 mi E of Destin) and at Destin's Harborwalk (US 98 E, foot of Destin Bridge; 850-654-6500).

Malls: Santa Rosa Mall (300 Mary Esther Blvd, Mary Ester; 1 blk N of US 98); Manufacturers Outlet Center (US 98)

■ **TENNIS**

USTA WC-Tennis instructional programs are held for beginning and advanced players Tue at 6pm. To register call Rene Grifol 850-206-1277. (Univ of West Florida, 11000 University Dr)

ACCOMMODATIONS

■ **B&B/INNS**

Josephine's French Country Inn is a lovely place in the heart of the new Victorian community of Seaside, where bikes are the main transportation and all shops and restaurants are WC-friendly. The ADA guestroom has a king and 2 twin beds (open frames), a wet bar, small refrigerator, microwave and coffeepot. The private bathroom has a raised toilet and a shower. Gourmet breakfast; accessible dune crossovers to the beach. $$$ (Seaside; E of the town common; 850-231-1940; 800-848-1840)

The Pensione is a new old-world inn, from its Venetian plaster ceilings and chenille bedspreads to elevators. Every room has a Gulf view; the ADA 1BR suite has a queen bed (open frame) and a bathroom with a raised toilet, roll-under sink and roll-in shower with a hand-held sprayer. Another room has identical features but no grab bars. Nearby is an accessible dune crossover where you can enjoy the view or access the beach. Free breakfast. $$$ (78 Main St, Rosemary Bch; 45 mi E of Ft Walton Bch, off CR 30A/Main St; 850-231-1790)

■ **CABINS/CAMPGROUNDS**

*Grayton Beach State Park has 37 RV/tent campsites with water/elec on very soft terrain in a pine scrub forest. ADA sites 31, 33 and 35 have ADA picnic tables and raised ground grills. Sidewalks lead from these sites to the ADA bathhouse with raised toilets, roll-under sinks and roll-in showers. Thirty 2BR cabins are fully equipped; each has 2 queen beds (open frames) and a screened porch. ADA cabins 9A and 9B have bathrooms with raised toilets, roll-under sinks and roll-in showers. The full kitchens have lowered counters and just outside, ADA picnic tables and grills. The park loans a beach WC; see Beaches. Campfire program in summer (357 Main Park Rd, Santa Rosa Bch; E off CR 30A, S of US 98; 850-231-4210)

*Henderson Beach State Park has 60 sites for RV/tents with water/elec, ADA picnic tables, grills and fire pits. Paved paths lead to an ADA bathhouse with raised toilets and roll-in showers. The park loans a beach WC; see Beaches. Campfire program in summer (17000 Emerald Coast, Destin; 850-837-7550)

Rocky Bayou State Park has 42 RV/tent sites with water/elec, grills, fire pits and picnic tables. ADA sites 9, 10 (no elec) and 11 have cement pads and sidewalks to the ADA bathhouse with raised toilets, roll-under sinks and roll-in showers. See Parks. (4231 SR 20; 5 mi E of Niceville; 850-833-9144)

*Topsail Hill State Preserve/Gregory E Moore RV Resort has 156 RV campsites in a 140-acre campground. All sites have paved pads and full hookups. Paved paths lead to an ADA bathhouse with raised toilets, roll-under sinks and roll-in showers. A WC-accessible tram goes between the campground and beach and a beach WC is available; see Beaches. Camp store; heated pool; clubhouse downstairs (7525 W Scenic CR 30A, Santa Rosa Bch; 850-267-0299; 877-232-2478)

■ **CONDOS**

Abbott Resorts has a variety of WC-friendly condos. Call to describe your specific needs and preferences. (2700 US 98 E, Destin; 850-837-4853; 800-336-4853)

Resorts at Pelican Beach, on the Gulf in the heart of Destin, has 10 ADA condos with full kitchens and, in the living

rooms, queen sofa beds. Each 1BR unit has a king bed (open frame) while each 2BR unit has a king and queen bed (Room T102 has 2 twin beds). Bathrooms have roll-under sinks and hand-held sprayers; rooms T102, 518 and 1217 have roll-in showers; others have tubs or step-in showers. Pool; lounge; restaurant for brkfst & lunch; accessible walkway to the beach (1002 US 98 E, Destin; 850-654-1425; 888-735-4226)

■ **MOTELS**

Best Western has 4 ADA rooms, each with a king bed (24" high/platform), refrigerator and coffeepot. Bathrooms have roll-under sinks; room 118 has a roll-in shower with a hand-held sprayer and seat; others have tubs. Free brkfst; pool; laundry. $$-$$$ (14047 Emerald Coast Pkwy, Destin; 850-650-8003)

Country Inn & Suites has 3 ADA rooms and an ADA suite. Each room has 2 queen beds. The suite has a king bed (23" high/open frame), sofa bed in the living room, a refrigerator and microwave. All units have coffeepots. Room 116 has a roll-in shower; others have tubs/step-in showers with hand-held sprayers. Free brkfst; pool; fitness room; laundry. $$-$$$ (4415 Commons Dr E, Destin; 850-650-9191)

Econo Lodge, on the Intracoastal, has 3 ADA rooms with a king, a full or 2 full beds (platforms). Bathrooms have raised toilets and roll-under sinks; one room has a roll-in shower with a hand-held sprayer and seat; others have tubs. Fishing dock; free brkfst; laundry. $-$$ (1284 Marler Ave; US 98 at NE end of bridge; 850-243-7123)

Hampton Inn has 4 ADA rooms and 1 ADA suite. Each unit has a king bed (platform). The suite also has a sofa bed in the living room and full kitchen. Bathrooms have raised toilets and roll-under sinks; units 113 and 308 have roll-in showers; others have tubs. Free brkfst; pool. $$-$$$ (1625 US 98 E, Destin; 850-654-2677)

Sheraton Four Points Hotel has 6 beachfront and 3 courtyard ADA rooms, each with a king bed, micro-wave, refrigerator and coffeepot. Bath-rooms have toilet extenders and roll-under sinks; rooms 107 and 235 have roll-in showers with hand-held sprayers and seats; others have tubs. The board-walk is a great spot to overlook the beach, but stairs lead down to the sand. Heated pools; tiki hut; seasonal enter-tainment poolside & in lounge; full res-taurant; fitness room; hot tub; gift shop; laundry. $$$ (1325 US 98; 850-243-8116)

Panama City Beach
DeFuniak Springs, Ebro, Panama City, Parker, Point Washington, Port St Joe, Vernon, Youngstown

While the coastal strip in Panama City Beach is crowded with hotels, condos and tourist schmaltz, uncrowded stretches along this incredibly beautiful beach do ex-ist. Because of fragile dunes, private ownership and limited parking, check below for accessible public dune crossovers. Three sources rent beach wheelchairs so you can truly enjoy the beaches here. Rish Park, in Port St Joe, loans a beach wheelchair for its barrier-free beach and also has a ramped pool, accessible miniature golf and shuffleboard. Try out the area's rich opportunities for boating, fishing and snorkel-ing or diving. Alt 98 is also called Miracle Strip Parkway and Front Beach Road; US 98 is also called Panama City Beach Parkway.

Tourist Info
Panama City Beach Visitors Bureau: 17001 US 98, 32413; at SR 79; 850-233-6503; 800-722-3224
Panama City Beach Chamber: 415 Beckrich Rd, Suite 200, 32407; 850-234-3193/235-1159
Bay County Chamber: 235 W 5 St, Panama City, 32401; 850-785-5206
Web Sites: www.800pcbeach.com; www.pcbeach.org

Transportation
Baytown Trolleys, all with lifts, operate 6am-6pm in Panama City, Lynn Haven, Springfield and along Alt 98 in Panama City Beach. (850-769-0557)
Bay Transportation provides curb-to-curb service in vans with WC lifts (wkdy 8-5) anywhere in Bay County not serviced by the trolley. Make reservations the day be-fore. (850-784-9360)

WC Resources
Island Sports Shop in Destin rents and delivers beach WCs as far E as Panama City for the day or longer. This De-Bug beach WC can be self-propelled or pushed from behind and comes with an umbrella, drink or fishing-pole holder and no arms. (850-650-9126)
Option Medical rents and, with advance notice, delivers standard and beach WCs (removable arms). (1830-A Lisenby Ave, Panama City; 850-872-0046)
Vital Aire/Inhome Medical rents standard and beach WCs (fixed arms) for a day or longer. Fee for delivery. Wkdy 8-5 (2405 SR 231, Panama City; 850-747-8070; 800-321-3508)

ACTIVITIES

■ **ATTRACTIONS**

Chautauqua Winery offers 20-min tours that end in a wine tasting. Rr. 9-5 (US 331, DeFuniak Springs; just N of I-10; 850-892-5887)

Coconut Creek Gran Maze is a 300' maze that tests your logic and instincts against time. Validate your ticket at 4 checkpoints before clocking out. WC guests bypass the stairs at each checkpoint. $. Summer 9am-11:30pm; winter hrs vary (9807 Alt 98; 850-234-2625)

Eden State Gardens, formerly the 10-acre estate of an early timber magnate, has moss-draped live oaks and magnificent gardens overlooking the Choctawhatchee Bay. You must negotiate grass lawns and gravel roads. The Greek Revival manor has a WC lift to the 1st floor and a video of the 2nd floor. The home is only open for hourly guided tours Thu-Mon 10-3. You can fish from a dock here. ADA picnic tables on grass; small ramped CRr. $. 8-dusk (CR 395, Point Washington; off US 98 W; 850-231-4214)

Gulf World Marine Park has shows presenting dolphins, sea lions, parrots and scuba divers as well as shark and turtle feedings; WC seating is in front. You can view the shark tank from above, but you must go down several steps to pass through the tank. WC guests can enjoy other exhibits, including the dolphin petting zoo and tropical fish tanks. For an extra fee you can swim with dolphins. The 90-min program includes classroom instruction with the trainer and about 30 min in the water. Staff can help lift you into the 3' deep dolphin pool where, if you prefer, you can sit in a plastic chair rather than swim. Call to discuss your needs. Reservations; WC rental; gift shop; snack bar; Rr. 9-7:30; summer -9:30 (15412 Alt 98; 850-234-5271)

Water Planet is a unique research operation that offers 4-hr and 3-day programs for the public to learn about and interact with dolphins. Start with a video and instructional session then roll aboard a pontoon boat for your dolphin encounter and perhaps a visit to Shell Island. Snorkel gear, including a floatation device, is provided; you can use a water scooter as well. Staff can lift you (150-lb limit) from your WC into the water. The Institute can arrange WC-friendly lodging for the 3-day program. 15-day advance reservations; Rr in restaurant (open at 5pm). Apr-Oct (5711 N Lagoon Dr; behind Hamilton's Restaurant; 850-230-6030; 866-449-5591)

Zooworld is home to more than 300 species, many endangered, from around the world. Learn about birds, reptiles and primates and meander through the botanical gardens. The petting zoo is on wood chips. Gift shop; snack bar; CRr. $. 9:30am-closing varies (9008 Alt 98; 850-230-1243)

■ **BEACHES**

See WC Resources for beach WCs. Parks: St Joseph Peninsula, Rish

County Pier (or MB Miller Pier) has an ADA ramp down to a large overlook above the beach. Outdoor showers; snack bar; Rr. 24 hrs (12213 Alt 98; 850-236-3034)

Mexico Beach has 2 dune crossovers along the 1-mi open beach on St Andrews Bay. (10 St & Beck Ave, Panama City)

Panama City Beach has an ADA ramp from parking to the beach. (Alt 98; at Alf Coleman Rd)

Rick Seltzer Park has an ADA ramp and boardwalk from a reasonably hard-packed parking lot to a beautiful, 4.5-acre county beach on the Gulf. Outside showers; Rr. Dawn-dusk (7419 Thomas Dr; just E of Creek St at the E end of the city)

■ **BIKE TRAILS**

A 6.5-mi, level, paved trail runs parallel to CR 30A from Inlet Beach (where CR 30A diverges from US 98) westward to Sea Grove Beach. This pleasant sunny ride through non-commercialized beach communities has no facilities.

■ BOAT RAMPS

Parks: St Josephs

Lake Powell Park has steep boat ramps and a wide fixed dock. This tidal saltwater lake leads to the Gulf through Phillips Inlet. Fish cleaning sink; Rr (23104 Lake View Dr; off Lake Powell Rd, N of US 98 at the W end of the city)

■ BOAT RENTALS

The Entrance, at the entrance of St Joseph Peninsula Park, rents deck boats (20" entry) that carry up to 8 people for half/full days on the bay. With advance notice, crew can lift you over the gate and aboard in your WC. Bait/snack shop. Mar-Jan 8am-9pm (8048 Cape San Blas Rd, Port St Joe; 850-227-7529)

Shell Island Boat Rentals has 12-person pontoon boats (29" entry) for half/full days on the Grand Lagoon. Staff can help you from the gravel parking lot to the fixed dock where, depending on the tides, staff can help lift you aboard in your WC. Rr (3605 Thomas Dr; behind Treasure Ship Restaurant; 850-234-7245; 800-227-0132)

You're the Captain rents pontoon boats (23"-34" entries) for 8-12 people for half/full days on the Grand Lagoon or St Andrews Bay. Resident dolphins are very friendly with boaters. Depending on tides, staff can help lift you aboard in your WC from the ramped fixed dock. Apr-Oct (5711 N Lagoon Dr; behind Hamilton's Restaurant; 850-230-3440)

■ BOAT TOURS

Capt. Anderson III is a glass-bottom boat for 3-hr narrated trips and a 75-min evening dolphin encounter on St Andrews Bay. Crew can help you board by ramp and over the lips in the doorways on the accessible 1st deck. On the 3-hr trips, the boat makes a 1-hr stop at Shell Island where disembarking in a WC is not feasible. Snack bar; restaurants & Rr in marina. Mar-Oct 1 & 5:15; summer also 9am (5550 N Lagoon Dr;

at Thomas Dr; 850-234-3435; 800-874-2415)

Glass-Bottom Boat offers 3-hr sightseeing and educational trips with 50-min stops at Shell Island. A narrow door renders the cabin, with the glass bottom, inaccessible. But staff can lift you aboard in your WC to the covered rear of the boat where you can see and learn about sea life caught in a shrimp net, view dolphins and enjoy the narrated tour of the Grand Lagoon and jetties. At Shell Island you can take the boardwalk to the beach on the Gulf. Park in front of the marina at the bow of the big treasure ship. Snack bar; restaurant & Rr in marina. Call for schedule. (3605 Thomas Dr; behind Treasure Ship Restaurant; 850-234-8944)

Sea Dragon Pirate's Cruise is a 2-hr journey with swashbuckling, sword-fighting pirates, blasting cannons and loads of fun. Staff can help WC passengers up 2 steps to the ramp for boarding. Drinks on board. Ticket booth opens at 10; cruises at 1 & 4; Tue-Sun also 5; winter hrs vary (3601 Thomas Dr; behind Treasure Island Restaurant; 850-234-7400)

Sea Screamer, reportedly the world's largest speedboat, takes you on a leisurely 1-hr, narrated cruise of the Grand Lagoon past Shell Island looking for dolphin, manatee and other marine wildlife. The cruise ends with a thrilling high-speed ride back to the dock. The ramp to the boat is only 24" wide but staff can lift you in your WC over the short span to the boat. Restaurant & Rr in marina. Mar-Oct schedule varies (Slip#41, 3601 Thomas Dr; behind Treasure Ship Restaurant; 850-233-9107)

■ BOWLING

Bowlarama has ramped lanes and bowling ball ramps. Snack bar; game room; Rr. Open bowl 3:30-6pm & 9-11pm; Sat 12:30pm-mdnt (2300 W 15 St, Panama City; 850-763-2972)

Hickory Lanes has 2 ramped lanes. Snack bar; game room; Rr. Hrs vary (5420 Hickory St, Parker; 950-769-7443)

■ CANOEING/KAYAKING

Parks: St Josephs Peninsula

Cypress Springs rents canoes for the 3.5-mi, roughly 2-hr paddle on Holmes Creek that slowly winds past high sandy banks and lush swamps. With advance notice, staff can help your WC across the sand and lift you into the canoe at the water's edge. Staff can bring your WC to the take-out and lift you into the shuttle van or someone in your party can take the shuttle back to the launch and return with your vehicle. (1 Cypress Springs Rd, Vernon; off SR 79; 850-535-2960)

Econfina Creek Canoe Livery rents canoes and solo sit-on and tandem sit-in kayaks for 1 1/2- to 3 1/2-hr trips past several crystal clear springs and unspoiled natural beauty. The launch site is sloped hard ground with rocks and roots but, with advance notice, staff can help with transfers. When you make reservations, ask if staff can shuttle your vehicle or bring your WC to the take-out; or, a companion can take the shuttle and return with your vehicle. Rr. May-Sep; Oct-Apr only by reservation (5641A Porter Pond Rd, Youngstown; 850-722-9032)

■ DINNER CRUISES

Lady Anderson Dining Yacht is a 135' luxury vessel with 3-hr dinner-dance cruises on Mon, Wed, Fri and Sat and dinner cruises with gospel music on Tue and Thu. Take the ramp aboard the 1st deck where all activities occur. Rr. Mar-Oct board at 6:30pm (Capt Anderson's Marina, 5550 N Lagoon Dr; at Thomas Dr; 850-234-3435; 800-360-0510)

■ FISHING CHARTERS

Bob Zales Charters has 4 fishing yachts (from 44' to 54') for up to 6 anglers. Sport fishing and offshore trolling trips run half day. With these large engines, you get to great fishing spots in minutes. All cabins have AC (except the Aquarius) and a microwave. Staff can lift your WC down the 2 steps to the dock and onto the boat. Tired of fishing? The capt can take you sightseeing.

Restaurant & Rr at marina (3605 Thomas Dr; behind Treasure Ship Restaurant; 850-763-7249)

Box Full Charters offers 4- to 8-hr flyfishing or light tackle trips inshore or offshore. From the floating dock, Capt Buddy can help lift you aboard the 26' center console or the 18' flats boat. Feb-Nov (Baypoint Marina, 3824 Hatteras Ln; 850-896-8371/235-3257; marina 850-235-6911)

Capt Anderson can take you on 1- or 2-day charters on request Mar-Nov and Dec 26-31. Crew can help lift you in your WC onto the gangplank, down the step into the boat and over the lip into the AC cabin. Snack bar onboard; restaurants & Rr in marina (5550 N Lagoon Dr; 850-234-3435; 800-874-2415)

Cool Breeze Charters offers 4- to 8-hr trips both inshore and offshore for up to 4 anglers. With advance notice, the capt can use a wider dock where crew can lift you in your WC aboard the 26' open sport fisherman. A canvas top provides some shade. (Sun Harbor Marina, 5505 Sunharbor Rd, Panama City; off US 98; 850-819-4209; 850-871-0534)

■ FISHING-PARTY BOATS

Capt Anderson offers 4- to 12-hr deep-sea trips day and night. Crew can help lift you in your WC onto the gangplank, down the step into the boat and over the lip into the AC cabin. Of the fleet, the Capt Anderson X and Gemini have the widest decks for easy mobility. Snack bar onboard; restaurants & Rr in marina. Mar-Nov & Dec 26-31 (Capt Anderson's Marina, 5550 N Lagoon Dr; at Thomas Dr; 850-234-3435; 800-874-2415)

■ FISHING PIERS

Attractions: Eden Gardens. Parks: St Andrews, Rish

County Pier (or MB Miller Pier) is a lighted 525' wood pier on the Gulf. Snack bar; bait shop; Rr. 24 hrs (12213 Alt 98; 852-236-3034)

Dan Russell Pier (or City Pier) is a lighted 1642' pier on the Gulf across the street from Aaron Bessant Park. Parking across street; bait/snack shop; outdoor shower; CRr. $/free for seniors & disabled anglers. 24 hrs (16101 Alt 98; 850-233-5080)

■ **FITNESS TRAILS**
Parks: Bay Memorial, Under the Oaks

■ **HELICOPTER TOURS**
Paradise Helicopters can take 2 passengers on scenic flights, 5 to 30 min long, over the glorious beaches here. Staff can lift you from your WC into the copter seat. Hrs vary (15726 Alt 98; 850-230-2080)

■ **HUNTING**
Florida Northwest Water Management Area, along the Econfina Creek, holds the state's only quota permit mobility-impaired hunt during which your able-bodied buddy can also hunt. This area is closed to hunting except during these special hunts so the wildlife is particularly abundant. Three-day hunts for small game and deer are offered 1 weekend in November, 3 weekends in Jan and during the 1st week of Feb. Weekend hunts for turkey occur in Mar and Apr. You can hunt from an ATV or any vehicle. Tent/RV camping is allowed in a grassy area with Rr port-a-lets near the hunting grounds; otherwise, under Motels see Ebro Motel (15 mi E) or Comfort Inn (20 mi S). Call 850-539-5999 for an application that must be returned by Oct 1 for the random drawing. (SR 20 at Econfina Creek; 8 mi E of Ebro; 850-539-5999)

■ **MISC FUN**
Noahs Ark Snowbird Club hosts activities such as craft making and card games Nov-Mar. Seasonal membership is required. Rr. 9-9 (12902 Alt 98; 850-234-6062)

Senior Center is a hub for folks age 60 and over who enjoy educational and recreational activities such as ceramics, sketching, quilting, crafts, bingo and bridge. Lunch is available with advance notice. Rr. Mon-Thu 9-5; Fri 9-2 (1116 Frankford Ave, Panama City; 850-769-3468)

■ **MUSEUMS**
Constitution Convention State Museum commemorates St Joe where Florida's Constitution was drafted in 1838. Between a yellow fever epidemic and a hurricane, St Joe was wiped out by 1844. The museum recreates the chambers of the constitutional convention and displays artifacts from the 1840's. Rr. $. Thu-Mon 9-12 & 1-5 (200 Allen Memorial Way, Port St Joe; off US 98; 850-229-8029)

Museum of Man in the Sea is devoted to the history of diving from 1500 onward. You can see creatures in a 500-gal saltwater tank, a video of shipwreck salvaging, early scuba gear and treasures from shipwrecks. Gift shop; CRr. $. Mon-Sat 9-5 (17314 W US 98; 850-235-4101)

Visual Arts Center occupies the old City Hall, jail and fire station and hosts rotating exhibits of national and local works of art. A hands-on art space encourages children to explore concepts of design, color, form and texture while learning art techniques. Classes, lectures and workshops are offered for all ages; demonstrations are given by visiting artists and crafts people. Gift shop; Rr. $. Mon-Sat hrs vary (19 E 4 St, Panama City; at Harrison Ave; 850-769-4451)

■ **PARI-MUTUELS**
Ebro Greyhound Park has live races Jan-Oct and simulcast greyhound and thoroughbred racing year round. Poker is played in a card room. Reservations are needed for WC seating on the top tier of the covered open-air box seats and on the 2nd level of the AC mezzanine. Outside seating is besides the bleachers. Or, enjoy a buffet while you watch the races live or from a tabletop TV. (6558 Dog Track Rd, Ebro; from SR 20, N on SR 79; 850-234-3943)

■ **PARKS**
Bay Memorial Park has a paved, 1-mi walking/fitness trail through its 13 acres. You can take a sidewalk across a moat to the Veterans Memorial and, if

you don't mind rolling over grass, you can fish in the moat. (Garden Club Dr, Panama City; 850-872-3199)

St Andrews State Park is 1260 acres of beach, pine forest and marsh at the eastern tip of Panama City Beach. The day use area by the 450' lighted pier on the Gulf is the most readily accessible. A 12' wide ramp leads from parking to the beach and a sidewalk goes to ADA picnic shelters and the pier. Or, over grass is a 120' fishing pier and picnic tables on the Grand Lagoon. The 2-mi loop road through the park is popular for cycling. A very sandy nature trail, fishing from the jetties and Shell Island (where hourly shuttles run) are not accessible. See Campgrounds. Camp/snack/bait store Mar-Oct; Rr. $. 8am-dusk (4607 State Park Ln, Panama City; from US 98, S 5 mi on CR 3031/Thomas Dr; 850-233-5140)

St Josephs Peninsula State Park is a 2516-acre spur from the mainland with the Gulf to the W and St Joe Bay to the E. It is an excellent birding area with over 200 species sighted. To view migrating birds, the dunes and tidal marsh, try the 400' stretch of boardwalk on the Maritime Hammock Trail and the 1800' boardwalk between the 2 campgrounds. Or, rent a canoe for a paddle on the bay. Staff can help you down the steep slope and sandy grass to the canoe launch and help you into the canoe. High dunes guard the beach here, but at the Shady Pines Campground (where, as a day-use guest, you need an HC permit) you can take a boardwalk to the sugar sand beach. Cyclists make good use of the paved park roads with little traffic. The boat ramp has a ramped fixed dock. Sandy terrain makes the campground virtually inaccessible. ADA picnic tables in Bayview picnic area; Rr. $ Dawn-dusk (8899 Cape San Blas Rd, Port St Joe; 850-227-1327)

+Rish Park is a 100-acre barrier-free state beach on the pristine Cape San Blas that can be used only by Florida residents with physical or developmental disabilities (and their families and caregivers). Extensive boardwalks and ramps run along and to the sugar sand beach. You can borrow a beach WC (removable arms). An Olympic swimming pool, miniature golf course, shuffleboard courts and social hall are all ramped. You can fish from piers over St Joe Bay. See Campgrounds. ADA picnic tables; WC loaners; Rr. $. 8-4:30 (6773 CR 30E, Port St Joe; 2 mi S of St Joseph Peninsula State Park; 850-227-1876)

Under the Oaks is a 9-acre county park with ADA picnic tables, including some under a gazebo. Roll across the hard-packed terrain for a pretty view of East Bay. A hard-packed fitness trail runs around the park perimeter and to a playground. Dawn-dusk (5843 E US 98, Parker)

■ **PERFORMING ARTS**

Kaleidoscope Theatre is a community group performing musicals, comedies and drama. WC seating in 1st row; Rr (207 E 24 St, Lynn Haven; 850-265-3226)

Marina Civic Center hosts local events and national touring companies, including a Broadway series. WC seating is in the orchestra section, center rear and along the aisles. HC parking left of building; Rr (Panama City Marina, 8 Harrison Ave, Panama City; 850-763-4696)

Martin Theater, a 1936 movie theater, now presents musicals, concerts and one-person shows. A community theater group performs Sep-Apr and the St Andrew Bay Orchestra has performances Oct-May. WC seating in 1st row; street parking & behind theater; Rr (409 Harrison Ave, Panama City; 850-763-8080)

Ocean Opry presents family entertainment, including comedy and country music shows with some guest appearances by Nashville stars. WC seating on aisles; snack bar; Rr. Hrs vary (8400 Alt 98; 850-234-5464)

■ **POOLS**

Parks: Rish

■ **SCUBA/SNORKELING**
Campgrounds: Vortex Spring
Al Lewando, certified by HSA, offers private instruction for certification including 4 classroom sessions, 4 pool dives and 5 open water dives on weekends. Open water dives are usually at Vortex Spring (see Campgrounds) where a dock with wide steps has been designed for access; people are available to help you in the water from the dock and out of the water by the steps. Other sites vary but Al can help with transfers. Call to discuss your abilities and set up a schedule. (Home 228-864-6171; work 228-813-1067)
Hydrospace Dive Shop offers wreck and reef dives, half-day resort dives for non-certified divers, 2-wk scuba certification courses and 3-hr snorkeling trips (on which you're likely to meet some dolphin). Usually you can roll aboard the ramp to the canopied back deck of the 3 dive boats; if tides are unusual, crew can lift you aboard in your WC. Crew can help your companion lift you from your WC to the dive platform in back and then into the water. Rr at dock. 9-5 (3605-A Thomas Dr; also 6422 W US 98; 850-234-3063; 800-874-3483)
Panama City Dive Center makes 4-hr trips to wreck sites, and 6- to 8-hr trips that go farther offshore with dives down to 100' where you encounter larger marine life. Request the Tropical Sun, a roll-aboard boat designed with WC divers in mind. Crew can help you in and out of the water. Restaurant & Rr at marina (Dive shop: 4823 Thomas Dr; 850-235-3390. Dock: Sun Harbor Marina, 5505 Sun Harbor Rd; E end of the Hathaway Bridge)
You're the Captain offers 2 1/2-hr snorkel trips in St Andrews Bay where you are likely to spot dolphins. The trip makes 2 stops: the 1st is over grass flats, 3'-5' deep, to get acclimated; the 2nd spot depends on weather. Depending on tides, crew may need to lift you in your WC aboard the pontoon boat. Call ahead if you need the crew to lift you (150-lb limit) from your WC into the water. Gear included. Apr-Oct (5711 N Lagoon Dr; behind Hamilton's Restaurant; 850-230-6030)

■ **SHOPPING**
Boutiques: Alt 98 along the beach has numerous tourist shops and downtown Panama City has a restored area (along Harrison Ave up from the Panama City Marina) with some specialty shops.
Malls: Panama City Mall (2150 Cove Blvd; US 231 at SR 77; 850-785-9587)

ACCOMMODATIONS

■ **B&B/INNS**
Turtle Beach Inn has a WC-friendly 2BR cottage where you can rent the 1st floor alone or the 2-story house. On the 1st floor is a bedroom with a queen bed (open frame), full kitchen, living room with a twin sofa bed, a screened porch with a Gulf view and a bathroom with grab bars and a tub (seat available). The 2nd floor has a bedroom with a king bed and standard bathroom. On the B&B plan, breakfast is delivered to the cottage. The Inn, on an often-deserted Gulf beach where loggerhead turtles are known to nest, is 7 mi from the barrier-free Rish Park; see Parks. $$-$$$ (140 Painted Pony Rd, Port St Joe; 850-229-9366)

■ **CABINS/CAMPGROUNDS**
+Rish Park is a barrier-free state park with 2 ADA 2BR family cottages and 6 ADA dormitory-style cabins located on a beach specifically for state residents with physical or developmental disabilities (and their families or caregivers). The cottages have AC, full kitchens, living rooms, TVs, 2 queen beds (open frames) and 4 bunk beds. The private bathrooms have raised toilets, roll-under sinks; 1 cottage has a roll-in shower with a hand-held sprayer and a step-in shower; the other has a step-in shower

and a tub. The dorms sleep up to 19 and have only privacy curtains to the bathrooms with raised toilets, roll-under sinks and roll-in showers with hand-held sprayers. Three of the dorms have stoves. Park amenities include a ramped pool and a beach WC; see Parks. (6773 SR 30E, Port St Joe; 2 mi S of St Joseph Peninsula State Park; 850-227-1876)

St Andrews State Park has 176 RV/tent sites, 3 are ADA sites with water/elec, fire pits and ADA picnic tables. Paved paths lead from these sites to a bathhouse with a roll-in shower. As a camper you can enjoy the lighted fishing pier on the Gulf 24 hrs; see Parks. Reserve 11 mos in advance for Mar-Sep. (4607 State Park Ln, Panama City; from US 98, S 5 mi on CR 3031/Thomas Dr; 850-233-5140)

Vortex Spring, a private campground on 360 acres of rolling hills and majestic pines, is a treasure for snorkelers, scuba divers and underwater cave-certified divers. A dock with wide steps has been designed for access; people are available to help you in the water from the dock and out of the water by the steps. There is a fee to dive in the crystal clear, 50' deep spring basin and the 115' deep limestone cavern. Sixteen grassy and somewhat shady RV/tent sites have water/elec, picnic tables, grills and fire rings. Sites 5, 6 and 8A are closest to the ramped, WC-friendly bathhouse that has stalls with wide doors and step-in showers. Camp/dive store (1517 Vortex Spring Ln, Ponce DeLeon; 5 min N of I-10; 850-836-4979)

■ **CONDOS**

St Andrews Bay Resort Management Company rents several condos and houses that are WC friendly. (850-235-4075; 800-621-2462; www.panamabeachrentals.com)

■ **MOTELS**

Beachcomber by the Sea has 4 ADA rooms and 3 WC-friendly suites all with Gulf front balconies. Each room has a king bed (24" high/platform), refrigerator, microwave and coffeepot. Bath-

rooms have raised toilets, roll-under sinks and tubs with hand-held sprayers and seats; room 209 has a roll-in shower. Suites have 2 extra-long full beds (24" high/platforms), living rooms and full kitchens. Bathrooms have tubs with hand-held sprayers and seats. The heated pool has a huge shallow end with a 24' long support bar in the center of four 15' wide by 6' deep steps that gradually enter deeper water. From the pool deck are steps to the beach. Free brkfst; laundry. $-$$$ (17101 Alt 98; 850-233-3622; 888-886-8916)

Beach Tower has 2 ADA rooms with a king or 2 full beds (20" high/platforms) and bathrooms with raised toilets, roll-under sinks and a tub or step-in shower. The ADA ramp to the beach on Alt 98 at Alf Coleman Rd is nearby. Pool. $-$$ (12011 Alt 98; 850-235-0089; 800-446-8694)

Comfort Inn has 4 ADA rooms, each with a queen bed (22" high/platform), refrigerator and microwave. Bathrooms have raised toilets, roll-under sinks and tubs with hand-held sprayers and seats. Free brkfst; pool; outside entrance. $$-$$$ (1013 E 23 St, Panama City; 850-769-6969)

Ebro Motel has 1 WC-friendly room with 2 full beds (platforms) and a large bathroom with grab bars. The other rooms are also on the ground floor but have smaller bathrooms. $ (5312 Capt Fritz Rd, Ebro; 850-535-2499)

Hampton Inn has 2 spacious ADA rooms and an ADA 1BR suite, all with microwaves, refrigerators and coffeepots. Each room has 2 queen beds (23" high/open frames) and the suite has a king bed and a king sofa bed in the living room. Bathrooms have raised toilets, roll-under sinks and tubs; room 124 has a roll-in shower with a hand-held sprayer and seat. Free brkfst; pool; Jacuzzi; exercise room; interior entrance. $$-$$$ (2909 Thomas Dr; 850-236-8988)

Sleep Inn has 3 ADA rooms with a queen bed (23" high/open frame) and a bathroom with a raised toilet, roll-under sink and a roll-in shower with a hand-held sprayer and seat. Free brkfst; pool. $$ (5126 W US 98, Panama City; 850-763-7777)

PENSACOLA
Gulf Breeze, Milton, Munson, Navarre, Pace, Pensacola Beach, Perdido Key

Known as the City of Five Flags for the five nations that have claimed it, Pensacola offers history, sugar sand beaches and plenty of outdoors fun from canoeing to fishing. Beach wheelchairs, available for rent from 2 sources and for loan at 3 parks, make this 40 miles of shoreline more accessible than most.

Tourist Info
Pensacola Beach Visitors Info: 735 Pensacola Beach Blvd, Pensacola Bch, 32561; 850-932-1500; 800-635-4803
Pensacola Visitors Center: 1401 E Gregory St, 32501; 850-434-1234; 800-874-1234
Santa Rosa Visitors Center: 8543 Navarre Parkway, Navarre, 32566; 850-939-3267; 800-480-7263
Web sites: www.pensacolabeachchamber.net; www.visitpensacolabeach.com; www.visitpensacola.com; www.navarrefl.com; www.beaches-rivers.com

Transportation
ECAT buses, serving Pensacola and surrounding area, and the green trolleys, in the downtown business district, all have lifts. The free tropical trolleys have lifts and run along Pensacola Beach on weekends, holidays and daily in the summer. (850-595-3228)
Intelitran offers curb-to-curb service in Escambia and Santa Rosa Counties for those who cannot use ECAT. You must complete an application and be pre-approved. Make reservations by 4:30 the day before. (850-484-7770)

WC Resources
Center for Independent Living has a loan closet of adaptive items. (3600 N Pace Blvd; 850-595-5566)
Deming Designs rents and delivers beach WCs in Pensacola Beach as far E as Navarre. The De-Bug beach WC can be self-propelled or pushed from behind (no arms; umbrella, fishing-pole or drink holder). (850-478-5765)
Island Sports Shop in Destin rents and delivers beach WCs as far W as Navarre for the day or longer. The De-Bug beach WC can be self-propelled or pushed from (no arms; umbrella, fishing-pole or drink holder). (850-650-9126)

ACTIVITIES

■ ATTRACTIONS
Historic Pensacola Village is a state-run complex of early 19th to early 20th century buildings. Three museums have ramps and elevators. The TT Wentworth Jr Florida State Museum, in the restored City Hall, contains exhibits about the human and natural history of western Florida, a children's museum and Coca Cola memorabilia. The Museum of Commerce contains full-scale replicas of a print shop, gas station, train depot, trolley and stores of the early 1900's. The Museum of Indus-

try captures the 19th century industrial boom in west Florida with displays on the fishing, brick-making and lumber businesses. The restored 1879 Old Christ Church is open to the public. The historic houses of Lavalle, Dorr and Lear-Rockeblave are on pier foundations, but with advance notice, staff can help lift you. Costumed docents lead tours through the houses twice a day depending on the season. Craft demonstrations in summer; gift shop; Rr. $/free for WC riders. Tue-Sat 10-4 (330 S Jefferson; 850-595-5985)

Wildlife Sanctuary treats and houses or releases injured and orphaned wildlife. Exhibits are outside along sidewalks. Rr. $D. Wed-Sat 12-3:30 (105 North S St; 850-433-9453)

The Zoo is home to more than 700 animals and lush botanical gardens. View a 30-acre preserve from a boardwalk 12' above gorillas, chimps and other animals. A carousel of wild animals includes stationary animal compartments where WCs can be locked in for the ride. The Safari Line Train is inaccessible. Weekend animal encounters; WC rental; gift shop; restaurant; Rr. $/discount for WC riders. 9-4; summer -5 (5701 US 98; 14 mi E of Gulf Breeze; 850-932-2229)

■ **BEACHES**
Parks: Fort Pickens, Navarre

+Big Lagoon State Park has almost 700 acres along the Big Lagoon stretch of the Intracoastal. Ask at the front gate to borrow the beach WC (no arms; can be self-propelled) and staff will bring it to your destination. You may choose to have it pushed from behind on the sugar sand beach but you can probably roll it yourself on the sandy trails that delight birders. The Yaupon Trail, that takes you near the water, is fairly hard-packed except for one sandy break for vehicles. The park has many boardwalks. One leads from parking to ADA picnic shelters among the dunes and to the beach. Others include the short Long Pond Trail from the campground to W Beach and one through a coastal dune and a pine ridge with interpretive signage. A boat ramp with a fixed dock is on the lagoon. Fish from the dock or surf cast from the beach. The amphitheater features occasional concerts. The observation tower, canoe rental and launch are inaccessible. Call for the schedule of guided walks, campfires and other events. See Campgrounds. ADA playground at W Beach; Rr. $. 8-dusk (12301 Gulf Beach Hwy/SR 297; 10 mi SW of Pensacola; 850-492-1595)

+Perdido Key/Gulf Islands National Seashore loans a beach WC (fixed arms) to enjoy this 7.5-mi stretch of gloriously uncrowded beach. May-Sep, get the beach WC from the lifeguards; in off-season, call the visitor center (850-934-2600). The Rosamond Johnson Beach has sidewalks to a pavilion with a snack bar (Mar-Labor Day), picnic tables, outdoor showers and Rr. $/free with Golden Access. Beach: May-Sep 7am-mdnt; Oct-Apr -10pm (from SR 292, W on Johnson Beach Rd; 850-492-0912)

+Perdido Key State Park is a 247-acre barrier island on the Gulf with boardwalks from parking to the sandy beach and to ADA picnic shelters along the dunes. With advance notice, rangers can bring a beach WC from Big Lagoon State Park so you can get down to the water's edge for swimming or fishing. Rr. 8-dusk (SR 292; 15 mi SW of Pensacola; 850-492-1595)

■ **BIKE TRAILS**
Blackwater Heritage State Trail is a 7-mi paved trail along a former railroad bed running N from downtown Milton to the E gate of the Whiting Field Naval Air Station. The terrain is quite flat and beyond Milton, the trail passes through wooded areas, crossing several creeks. The Milton trailhead has Rr (S side of US 90 & Stewart St; 850-983-5363). At MM 1.5 (Alabama St), a visitors center has parking, a concession stand, gift shop, water fountain and Rr. You can also park by the gate at Whiting Station.

Pensacola Beach Trail is an 8' wide paved path parallel to and separated from SR 399 that runs from the Bob Sikes Bridge W to Fort Pickens and E to the most eastern Gulf Islands National Seashore area.

■ **BOAT RAMPS**

Beaches: Big Lagoon. Fishing Piers: Carpenters

Hurricane Lake, a 318-acre lake in the Blackwater State Forest, has a boat ramp in the N campground with low fixed docks. 24 hrs (N Hurricane Lake Entrance Rd; off SR 4, 9 mi from Munson; 850-689-7838)

Russell Harber Landing has boat ramps and floating docks on the Blackwater River near the mouth of the Blackwater Bay. ADA picnic tables. 24 hrs (5229 Old River Rd, Milton; 850-983-5400)

■ **BOAT RENTALS**

Adventure Perdido rents 10- and 12-person pontoon boats (27" entries) for half/full days along the oak-lined coasts of Perdido Bay or the white beaches of Big Lagoon. You can roll aboard from the floating dock. Captains are available for hire. (13726 Ole River Rd, Perdido Key; 850-492-9321; 888-492-9321)

■ **BOAT TOURS**

Adventure Perdido Sailing Charters offers sailing cruises on the Perdido Bay or Gulf for a minimum of 2 hrs. Crew can lift you aboard from a floating dock onto a bench seat next to the captain who is also a trauma nurse. After some instructions and with good upper body strength and balance, you may get a chance to captain. (13726 Ole River Rd, Perdido Key; 850-492-9321; 888-492-9321)

Yellow Crab Water Taxi has a 2-hr narrated cruise on Big Lagoon to view dolphins, islands, antebellum forts and more. Roll aboard the catamaran's front gate from a floating dock. Sunset cruises are available. (13726 Ole River Rd, Perdido Key; 850-492-9321; 888-492-9321)

■ **BOWLING**

Avalon Bowling Center has ramped lanes and bowling ball ramps. Game room; pool tables; snack bar; Rr. 10am-mdnt (2986 Avalon Blvd, Milton; 850-995-4006)

■ **CANOEING/KAYAKING/TUBING**

Adventures Unlimited rents canoes, tubes and solo/tandem sit-on kayaks for use on the 3mph Coldwater Creek. Follow the shuttle to the launch; staff can drive your car back to the take-out. The launch has some soft sand but staff can help you to the water's edge and into your craft. Tube trips are 4 mi; canoe and kayak trips are 4, 7 or 11 mi. This company provides shuttle service for a fee if you bring your own boat/tube. See Accommodations. (8974 Tomahawk Rd, Milton; SR 87 12 mi N of Milton, E at sign for 4 mi on Neal Kennington Rd that becomes Spring Hill Rd; 850-623-6197; 800-239-6864)

Blue Dolphin Kayak Tours has solo/tandem sit-on kayaks for trips geared to experienced or novice kayakers, including instructions. With advance notice, appropriate trips and help with transfers can be arranged. Guided trips are also available along the Santa Rosa Sound where the water is shallow and you paddle back to the launch. Light snack provided (3164 Wells Beach Rd, Navarre; 850-939-7734)

Bob's Canoe Rental rents canoes, tubes, and solo/tandem sit-on kayaks for the clear waters of the Coldwater Creek. Trips leave hourly beginning at 9. The 5-mi trip takes 2 hrs; the 12-mi trip takes about 4 hrs. Staff cannot shuttle your car but may be able to lift you onto the front seat of a pickup truck to take you to the launch. With advance notice, staff can help with transfers into your craft. (7525 Munson Hwy; from Milton take SR 87 N, then E for 7 mi on CR 191; 850-623-5457; 800-892-4504)

■ **FISHING CHARTERS**

Beach Marina can set you up with a guide for an inshore or offshore trip. Deep-sea or bottom-fishing trips range 4-12 hrs. Crew can lift you aboard in your WC. (655 Pensacola Blvd; 850-932-0304)

Performer offers full-day bottom fishing in the Gulf on a 45' boat that holds up to 20 anglers. Staff can lift you aboard in your WC from the ramped, floating dock. Restaurant & Rr at marina (Seville Harbor, 600 Barricks St; 850-434-7533)

■ **FISHING-PARTY BOATS**

Beach Marina offers half/full-day deep-sea fishing trips in the Gulf on a variety of boats. Crew can lift you aboard in your WC. BYO food & drink. Hrs vary (655 Pensacola Blvd; 850-932-0304)

See Saw Charters offers 6- and 8-hr deep-sea fishing trips in the Gulf. Crew can lift you aboard in your WC and over the 4" lip into the AC cabin. BYO food & drink. 7am (13700 Ole River Rd, Perdido Key; 850-944-5269; 800-806-7889)

■ **FISHING PIERS**

Parks: Fort Pickens, Navarre

Bear Lake is a 107-acre lake in the Blackwater State Forest with a 60' T-shaped, lighted pier. The ramp for non-motorized boats has no boarding dock. See Campgrounds. 7am-dusk (SR 4; 2 mi E of Munson; 850-957-6140)

Bob Sikes Fishing Bridge is lighted and spans the 1.5 mi across the Santa Rosa Sound between Gulf Breeze and Pensacola Beach. You can park on the bridge; the entrance is on the N side of the bridge. 24 hrs (Pensacola Beach Rd)

Carpenters Park sits on 22 acres along the Blackwater River with a 60' fishing pier in a lighted area. Boat ramps have fixed docks and low tide can mean a 3' drop to the boat. Picnic shelters; playground on sand. 7am-10pm (Broad St & Munson Hwy/Oliver St, Milton; 850-983-5400)

Carsick Lake is a 65-acre lake in the Blackwater State Forest with a 60' T-shaped lighted pier. 24 hrs (CR 189; 8 mi N of Baker; 850-957-6140)

Gulf Breeze Municipal Pier is a 1.5-mi former vehicular drawbridge on the Pensacola Bay, now used only for fishing. You can park on the bridge. Bait/snack shop; CRr port-a-let. $/free for 100% disabled veterans. 24 hrs (1 US 98, Gulf Breeze; 850-934-5147)

Hurricane Lake is a 318-acre lake in the Blackwater State Forest with a 60' T-shaped, lighted pier in the N campground. 24 hrs (N Hurricane Lake Entrance Rd; 9 mi from Munson off SR 4; 850-689-7838)

Navarre Beach Fishing Pier is a 1000' T-shaped pier on the Gulf. Bait shop; Rr. Dawn-dusk (8525 Gulf Blvd, Gulf Breeze; 850-936-6188)

Pensacola Bay Fishing Bridge is a lighted, 1.5-mi chance to catch white trout, speckled trout, redfish, sheepshead and more. Park on the bridge. Covered picnic tables in nearby Wayside Park at Gregory St & 17 Ave; bait/snack shop; CRr. $ Dawn-mdnt (1750 Bayfront Pkwy; 850-444-9811)

■ **MISC FUN**

Bayview Senior Center is a place to meet new friends and play bingo, billiards, chess, bridge, bunco and dominoes. The building sits on a hill, so you may want to be dropped off at the entrance. Call for schedule. Rr. Wkdy 8-5 (20 Ave & Lloyd St; 850-436-5190)

■ **MUSEUMS**

Attractions: Historic Pensacola Village

Civil War Soldiers Museum houses artifacts, memorabilia and letters from the Civil War. Dioramas depict battlefield medicine. Street parking; gift shop; CRr. $. Tue-Sat 10-4:30 (108 S Palafox St; 850-469-1900)

National Museum of Naval Aviation, one of the world's largest air and space museums, chronicles American naval aviation from wood and fabric biplanes to Skylab. Among the 150 historic aircraft on display are WW II fighters, the first trans-Atlantic flying boat and the Skylab Command Module. Vietnam War POW items are among the memorabilia. The IMAX theater presents films every hour. When in town, the Blue Angels practice here on Tue at 8:30 am. Flight simulators are not accessible. Docents, many of whom are retired avia-tors with personal stories to share, lead 1 1/2-hr tours. WC loaners; gift shop; Rr. 9-5 (US Naval Air Station, 1750 Radford Blvd, Perdido Key; 850-452-3604; 800-327-5002)

Pensacola Historical Museum, in the 1882 Arbona Building, tells the history of the Gulf coast through artifacts from the Native American and Colonial eras to the Civil War and the present. Ramped entrance; street parking; CRr. ⊅. Mon-Sat 10-4:30 (115 E Zaragosa St; 850-433-1559)

Pensacola Museum of Art changes ex-hibits every 6 wks. Permanent collec-tions include European and American glass, African artifacts and 20th century paintings. The WC entrance is on the side by the parking lot. Gift shop; Rr. ⊅. Tue-Fri 10-5; wknd 12-4 (407 S Jefferson St; 850-432-6247)

■ **PARASAILING**
Key Sailing is experienced with disabled parasailors. Staff can pull your WC over the 75' beach, onto the dock and aboard the boat. You don the harness and are lifted onto the launch platform from where you sail 1000' into the air. Call ahead so an extra deck hand can be scheduled to help. 9-6 (500 Quietwater Beach Rd, Pensacola Bch; 850-932-5520)

■ **PARI-MUTUELS**
Pensacola Greyhound Track features year-round live and simulcast racing with WC seating on the top level where you enter. Restaurant; Rr. Wed-Sat at 7; wknd 1 (951 Dog Track Rd/SR 297; off US 98 W; 850-455-8595)

■ **PARKS**
Blackwater River State Park occupies 700 pristine but often soggy acres with limited access other than several board-walks and a ramp to a soft sand beach. This beautiful, sand-bottom river is popular with canoeists but the high eroding banks make WC access diffi-cult. See Campgrounds. ADA picnic shelters; Rr. ⊅. 8am-dusk (7720 Deaton Bridge Rd, Holt; off US 90, 15 mi NE of

Milton; 850-983-5363)

⁺Fort Pickens/Gulf Islands National Sea-shore sits on the W end of Santa Rosa Island, guarding the Pensacola Bay since the 1829. Drive 7.5 mi from the park entrance to a sidewalk that loops through the fort. From the fort, either drive (and park by the seawall) or take the long sidewalk W of the fort parking lot to a museum that tells the area's natural and human history. From the parking area by the seawall is an uphill sidewalk to a lighted, 320' L-shaped fishing pier on the bay. If you are an overnight camper or if you have a Golden Access Pass (and purchase a special night owl pass from the Ranger Station), you can fish throughout the night. The 2 lookout towers E of the fort are inaccessible. Fort Pickens, Langdon Beach and Perdido Key are the only areas with boardwalks to the sand. You can borrow a beach WC (remov-able arms) for use at Langdon Beach and, with permission, on trails. From May-Sep, borrow the beach WC from the lifeguards at Langdon; Oct-Apr, ask at the Entrance Station or call the visi-tors center (850-934-2635) to reserve. Just W of Langdon, at Campground A, is the Dune Nature Trail, a .5-mi board-walk with interpretive signage. The 4-mi bike trail is hard-packed shell with sandy stretches. In the summer guided tours occur daily and on weekends in the evening also. An auditorium (with WC seating throughout) features mov-ies and other events. Call for the sched-ule of outdoor and indoor programs. See Campgrounds. Picnic shelters; camp store; Rr at pier & Langdon Beach. ⊅/ free with Golden Access. Park: May-Sep 7-mdnt; Oct-Apr -10pm. Visitor center: May-Sep 9:30-5; Oct-Apr 8:30-4 (Fort Pickens Rd; 9 mi W of SR 399 on Pensacola Bch; 850-934-2600)

Gulf Islands National Seashore is a mo-saic of 10 National Park areas along 150 mi of barrier islands from the Okaloosa Area, by Ft Walton Beach, westward into Mississippi. Many areas are undeveloped beaches and marshes that help protect the mainland from violent Gulf storms. The Florida areas that offer the most recreational opportunities to WC riders are Fort Pickens (described immediately above) and Perdido Key (see Beaches). A great starting point is the visitor center at Naval Live Oaks where a 10-min film describes the role of the National Seashore. See Campgrounds. Picnic area; Rr. 9-5 (1801 US 98, Gulf Breeze; 850-934-2600)

Hitzman/Optimist Park is a 16-acre sports complex with an ADA playground. Snack bar; Rr. Dawn-dusk (Langley Ave & Buford St; 850-435-1770)

Krul Recreation Area, in the Blackwater State Forest, has a 3000' boardwalk through wetlands. Swimming at Krul Lake is minimally accessible. From campground #2, take the sloped boardwalk to a long swimming pier where friends can lift you to the edge of the pier for you to drop in. To get out, swim to the shallow water by the small sandy beach; you may need help getting across the soft sand and back to the boardwalk. See Campgrounds. Picnic tables; Rr. 24 hrs (SR 4; 2 mi E of Munson; 850-957-6140)

Navarre Park is a lovely 5-acre park and beach with a .5-mi wood/brick nature walk along the Santa Rosa Sound. A sidewalk leads to the 220' fishing pier, butterfly house and overlook on a pond where ducks and swans swim. ADA picnic table; picnic gazebo; Rr. Dawn-dusk (8543 US 98, Navarre Bch; at the bridge from Navarre; 850-623-1569)

Veterans Memorial Park has 5.5 waterfront acres to honor veterans of all wars. This private park contains the *Wall South*, a half-scale replica of the Vietnam Veterans Memorial in Washington, DC. 24 hrs (Bayfront Park Place at 9 Ave)

■ **PERFORMING ARTS**

Bayfront Auditorium hosts anything from big-name concerts to wrestling matches. Seating is in folding chairs that can be moved to accommodate WCs. (900 S Palafox St; 850-444-7696)

Milton Opera House, dating back to 1912, has the Imogene Theater on the 2nd floor, where periodically community dinner theater and concerts occur. Park on the side and use the elevator entrance; folding chairs can be moved to accommodate WCs. Notify the usher to access the Rr on the 1st floor in the museum. (6868 Caroline St, Milton; 850-626-9830)

Pensacola Civic Center features arena-type shows such as concerts, ice shows and rodeos. WC seating varies with shows. Rr (201 Gregory St; 850-432-0800x224)

Pensacola Little Theater is a community theater performing musicals, dramas and children's plays. WC seating in front on aisle; HC parking on street; Rr. Sep-Jun (Pensacola Cultural Center, 400 S Jefferson St; 850-432-2042)

Saenger Theatre is a restored 1926 theater with performances by the Pensacola Symphony (850-435-2533), Pensacola Opera (850-433-6737) and, Oct-May, professional touring companies. WC seating in rear; street parking; Rr (118 S Palafox St; 850-444-7686)

■ **POOLS**

Pensacola Junior College offers to students a heated indoor pool with a lift (fixed seat). You can sign up for Recreation and Leisure Swimming at the college for the semester. Locker room; Rr. Mon-Sat hrs vary (Building 3, 1000 College Blvd; 850-484-1311)

Salvation Army has a heated indoor pool with a lift (fixed seat). Staff can help with transfers. Open swim is usually from 1 to 2 and you can register for various water aerobics classes. Locker room; Rr. ϟ. Mon-Sat hrs vary (1501 N Q St; 850-432-1501)

■ **SCUBA**

Panama City: Scuba: Al Lewando

Scuba Shack offers dive trips in the Gulf to different sites with sunken vessels or a giant artificial reef awash with marine life. Crew can lift you in your WC aboard the 50' boat that leaves from a dock behind the shop. Crew can also lift you into and from the water. With advanced notice, a dive master can be hired as your personal partner. (711 S Palafox St; 850-433-4319)

■ **SHOOTING RANGES**

Champion International Shooting Range has a 100-yd rifle range, a 50-yd pistol range, shotgun pads for shooting clays and an archery range. The 15-station sporting clays course is wide and graded. Sidewalks lead to the ranges. Drinks; Rr. $. Wed-Fri 9-5; wknd 8-5 (6850 Quinette Rd, Pace; 850-995-9377)

■ **SHOPPING**

Antiques: Go gallery-hopping and antiquing in Pensacola's Palafox Place, Quayside Art Cooperative and Seville Square (along Palafox St).

Boutiques: Harbourtown Shopping Village has some neat shops and the ambience of a New England village (913 Gulf Breeze Pkwy, Gulf Breeze). The Quietwater Beach Boardwalk has fun, touristy shops, restaurants and entertainment (400 Quietwater Beach Rd).

Flea Markets: The Flea Market is outside, ramped, on pavement and under roofs. Paved HC parking; snack bars; Rr. Wknd 9-5 (5760 Gulf Breeze Pkwy, Gulf Breeze; 850-934-1971). The Pea Ridge Flea Market has over 100 vendors, most on pavement and under cover. Snack bar; Rr. Wknd 8-4 (5186 US 90, Pea Ridge; between Milton & Pace; 850-994-8056). The T Street Flea Market covers 10 acres from T to W St, is paved and partially covered. Street parking; snack bars; Rr. Thu-Sun dawn-dusk (7171 N Davis Hwy; at I-10; 850-433-4315)

Malls: Cordova (5100 N 9 Ave; 850-477-5563); University Mall (7171 N Davis Hwy; at I-10; 850-478-3600)

■ **SPECTATOR SPORTS**

Ice Hockey Pensacola Ice Pilots play Oct-Apr. WC seating is at the top of the lower level. Rr (Pensacola Civic Center, 201 E Gregory St; 850-432-7825)

ACCOMMODATIONS

■ **B&B/INNS**

Adventures Unlimited has an ADA guestroom in the 1926 Schoolhouse Inn on an 88-acre wooded preserve along Coldwater Creek. The room has a kitchenette, queen bed (open frame) and a bathroom with a raised toilet, roll-under sink and tub. Able-bodied companions can enjoy the ropes course here; WC paddlers can enjoy the river; see Canoeing. $$ (8974 Tomahawk Rd, Milton; SR 87 12 mi N of Milton, E at sign for 4 mi on Neal Kennington Rd that becomes Spring Hill Rd; 850-623-6197; 800-239-6864)

Marsh House, right in historic downtown, has a WC-friendly guestroom on the 1st floor. The room has a queen bed (30" high/open frame) and a bathroom with a 30" entry, raised toilet and step-in shower with a seat. From parking on the side of the house, enter by ramp into the kitchen. Continental brkfst. $$-$$$ (205 Cevallos St; 850-433-4866)

■ **CABINS/CAMPGROUNDS**

Adventures Unlimited has 1 group cabin and 2 RV/tent sites that are ADA. The ramped cabin sleeps up to 27 people on bunk beds and has a bathroom with a raised toilet and roll-under sinks (no showers). The campground is on flat, hard-packed ground with no paved road or paths. All campsites have water/elec, grills, fire pits and picnic tables. Campsites 7 and 8 have ADA picnic tables and are close to the ramped ADA bathhouse with raised toilets, roll-under sinks and roll-in showers. Able-bodied companions can enjoy the ropes course here; WC paddlers can enjoy the river; see Canoeing. (8974 Tomahawk Rd, Milton; SR 87 12 mi N of Milton, E at sign for 4 mi on Neal Kennington Rd that becomes Spring Hill Rd; 850-623-

6197; 800-239-6864)

Bear Lake, in the Blackwater River State Forest, has 20 RV sites with water/elec, paved pads, picnic tables and fire pits. Six tent sites have running water. Sidewalks lead from the paved camp road to a bathhouse with grab bars. See Fishing Piers. (11650 Munson Hwy, Milton; 1.5 mi E of Munson on SR 4850-957-6140)

⁺Big Lagoon State Park has 75 RV/tent sites along a pine ridge. ADA campsites 7 and 8 have water/elec, grills and ADA picnic tables. Sidewalks lead to an ADA bathhouse with raised toilets, roll-under sinks and roll-in showers. Boardwalks lead to beaches where you can borrow a beach WC and, as a camper, you are covered for admission at Perdido Key State Park, 5 mi W; see Beaches. Sat night campfires in summer (12301 Gulf Beach Hwy/SR 297; 10 mi SW of Pensacola; 850-492-1595)

Blackwater River State Park has 30 RV/tent sites with water/elec, ADA picnic tables and fire rings. Campsites 5, 6 and 19 are closest to the bathhouse with raised toilets, grab bars, roll-under sinks and roll-in showers. Paths are natural. See Parks. No reservations (7720 Deaton Bridge Rd, Holt; off US 90, 15 mi NE of Milton; 850-983-5363)

⁺Fort Pickens, part of the Gulf Islands National Seashore, has 200 RV/tent sites. In Loop E, ADA sites 58 and 59 have water/elec, paved pads, grills and ADA picnic tables. These sites have paved paths to a nearby bathhouse that has a step at the entrance but is equipped with grab bars, roll-under sinks and roll-in showers with seats. This park has a beach WC to enjoy fabulous beaches and great fishing; see Parks. Laundry (step at entrance); camp store (Mar-Oct). (9 mi W of SR 399 on Pensacola Bch; 850-934-2635; 800-365-2267)

Krul Recreation Area, in the Blackwater River State Forest, has 50 RV sites with water/elec, picnic tables and fire pits; 4 tent sites have water. Sidewalks lead from the paved camp road to a bathhouse with grab bars and step-in showers; 6 campsites are nearby. See Parks. (SR 4; 2 mi E of Munson; 850-957-6140)

■ **CONDOS**

Privately-Owned Condo that is WC-friendly and on the beach can be rented for a minimum of 3 nights. The 1500 sq ft, 2BR condo is on the top floor of an 8-story building with a large balcony and great views of the Gulf. The 2BR unit has a king and queen bed (open frames), a sofa bed in the living room, full kitchen. Both bathrooms have step-in showers. Outside, a path leads to the beach. Guest laundry (13333 Johnson Beach Rd, Perdido Key; owners: the Hurleys, 3710 Tanglewood Dr NW, Atlanta, GA 30339; 770-435-2875)

Soundside Holiday Beach Resort, along the Intracoastal, has 4 WC-friendly 2BR condos. Each has a king and 2 twin beds (24" high/platforms), a full kitchen, queen sofa bed in the living room and a washer/dryer. The master bath is large with a step-in shower and Jacuzzi; the other bath has a tub with a hand-held sprayer. A paved walkway leads across sand to the Intracoastal and a fishing pier with steps. Restaurants nearby. (19 Via DeLuna Dr, Pensacola Bch; 850-934-2500; 800-874-0402)

■ **MOTELS**

Beachside Resort has 4 ADA rooms, each with a king bed (open frame), microwave and refrigerator. Bathrooms have roll-under sinks; room 107 has a roll-in shower; others have tubs. Full restaurant; lounge; pool. $$-$$$ (14 Via DeLuna, Pensacola Bch; 850-932-5331; 800-232-2416)

Best Western has 8 ADA rooms, each with 2 full beds and coffeepots. Bathrooms have raised toilets, roll-under sinks and roll-in showers with hand-held sprayers and seats. Free brkfst; pool; laundry. $$ (8240 N Davis Hwy; just off I-10 exit 13; 850-479-1099)

Clarion Suites Resort has 5 ADA rooms,

each with a queen bed (24" high/open frame), microwave, refrigerator and queen sofa bed. Bathrooms have roll-under sinks and roll-in showers with hand-held sprayers and seats. Free brkfst; pool; laundry. $$-$$$ (20 Via DeLuna, Pensacola Bch; 850-932-4300; 800-874-5303)

Hampton Inn has 9 ADA rooms with Gulf views. Each has a king or 2 full beds (24" high/platforms), microwave and refrigerator. The rooms with king beds also have recliners. Bathrooms have raised toilets and roll-under sinks; rooms 112, 212, 312 and 412 have roll-in showers with hand-held sprayers and seats; others have tubs. A walkway leads to the Gulf. Free brkfst; pool; laundry; Sep-Mar free happy hour. $$-$$$ (2 Via DeLuna, Pensacola Bch; 850-932-6800; 800-320-8108)

Holiday Inn has 3 ADA rooms, each with a queen bed (platform), coffee-pot and, upon request, a microwave and refrigerator. Bathrooms have raised toilets and roll-under sinks; rooms 103 and 105 have roll-in showers with hand-held sprayers and seats; others have tubs. Pool; laundry; fitness room; restaurant for brkfst & dinner. $$ (7200 Plantation Rd; off I-10 exit 13; 850-474-0100)

LaQuinta has 6 ADA rooms, each with a king bed (open frame), microwave, refrigerator and coffee pot. Bathrooms have raised toilets and roll-under sinks; room 132 has a roll-in shower with a hand-held sprayer and seat; other rooms have tubs. Free brkfst; pool; laundry. $$ (7750 N Davis Hwy; just off I-10 exit 13; 850-474-0411)

TALLAHASSEE

Apalachicola, Bristol, Crawfordville, Medart, Panacea, Quincy, St George Island, St Marks, Shell Point, Sopchoppy, Wakulla Springs, Woodville

Florida's state capital, with 2 major colleges, has the cultural agenda of a large city, yet the charm of a small Southern town. You'll find some unique recreational opportunities here. WC athletes can enjoy the annual Sports Ability Day in May (see WC Events), as well as year-round horseback riding, swimming, track, tennis and basketball. You can borrow a handcycle and tour some wonderful bike trails both in and out of the city. Wakulla Springs has a vehicle that is a cross between a beach wheelchair and a boat that you can take across sand and out into the water. Or, try skydiving with a company experienced with disabled jumpers! And, outside of city limits is some great fishing. We use SR 263 for Capitol Circle that serves as a beltway around the city.

Tourist Info

Visitors Bureau: 106 E Jefferson St, 32301; 850-413-9200; 800-628-2866
Visitors Center: New Capitol Bldg, 400 S Monroe St, 32301; 850-488-6167
Apalachicola Chamber: 99 Market St, Suite 100, 32320; 850-653-9419
Web sites: www.talchamber.com; www.co.loen.fl.us\visitors\index.htm

Transportation

TalTran City Bus has lift-equipped buses within the city limits. (850-891-5200)
Old Town Trolley has lifts and provides free service in downtown weekdays 7-6. (850-891-5200)
Dial-a-Ride provides curb-to-curb service in vans with lifts for those unable to access the city buses. You must pre-qualify and make reservations 1 day ahead. Wkdy

6:30-6:30; limited wknd (850-891-5199)
Yellow Cab has ramped mini vans. (850-580-8080)

WC Resources
Center for Independent Living of North Florida has a loan closet and can refer you to various services in the area. (572-C Appleyard Dr; 850-575-9621)

ACTIVITIES

■ **ATTRACTIONS**
Florida State Capitol Complex includes the 22-story New Capitol where the public can view on the 5th floor either the Senate or House in session Mar-Apr. Visit the top floor art gallery and lounge with a 360-degree view of the city and countryside. HC parking is by the N loading zone off Jefferson St; a ramped entrance is on the E side of the building. Rr. Hourly tours (Duval St; 850-488-6167) Right in front is the Old Capitol, a low-lying antebellum structure restored to its 1902 heyday. In addition to the former Governor's office, Supreme Court and legislative chambers, there's an extensive timeline of Florida from pre-history to the present. Use the entrance in back of the building, left of the stairs, where you can take an elevator to the 1st floor for the rotunda and to the 2nd floor for the displays. Self-guided tours; volunteers, who can give an overview, are usually in the rotunda. Wkdy 9-4:30; Sat 10-4:30; Sun noon-4:30 (400 S Monroe St; at Apalachee Pkwy; 850-487-1902)
Governor's Mansion is a Southern plantation house patterned after Andrew Jackson's home, the Hermitage, and features antique furnishings, gifts from foreign dignitaries and a collection of silver. A 40-min tour includes the state rooms where the governor entertains and holds meetings. Rr. Mon, Wed & Fri (when the Legislature is in session) 10-11:30am (700 N Adams St; 850-488-4661)
Gulf Specimen Marine Lab is a chance to see and learn about the smaller sea creatures, such as the seahorse, not often a focus at large aquariums. Touch tanks allow you to handle sea anemones, urchins, starfish, sea pansies and more. Enjoy the 25,000-gal marine aquarium and demonstrations. Some tanks have a step. Gift shop; Rr. Wkdy 9-5; Sat 10-4; Sun 12-4 (222 Clark Dr, Panacea; off US 98; 850-984-5297)
Mission San Luis is a 53-acre hilltop site of a partially restored 17th century Spanish-Indian village where archeologists are still at work. Take one of 2 alternatives to the very steep path up the hill. With advance notice, staff can open a gate for WC visitors to be dropped off. Or, if you can transfer into a golf cart (fixed arms), staff can meet you in the parking lot and take you on a tour. The visitor center has a 10-min orientation video, displays and gift shop. The reconstructed village has sidewalks and ramped entrances into the mission church, council house, Spanish colonial home and other buildings. Demonstrations by costumed craftsmen occur monthly (3rd Sat); call for tour schedule. ADA picnic tables; Rr behind visitor center. Tue-Sun 10-4 (2020 W Mission Rd; between White Dr & Ocala Rd; 850-487-3711)
■ **BASKETBALL**
Tallahassee Tornadoes, a NWBA team, invites you to watch, scrimmage or try out for the team. Games Oct-Feb; practice begins in Aug. Contact Sunny Patel 850-921-1520/877-5311. Rr (Dade Street Community Center, 1115 Dade St; 850-891-3910)
■ **BEACHES**
*****St George Island State Park** has a self-propelling beach WC (fixed arms). Ask at the entrance and staff will deliver it to you in the day use area. ADA picnic

shelter; Rr. See Campgrounds. (1900 E Gulf Beach Dr/CR 300, St George Island; 850-927-2111)

■ **BIKE TRAILS**

Parks: Ochlockonee

Azalea Park has a 2935' lighted paved trail. Picnic tables; Rr (N of Crawfordville on US 319)

St Marks Historic State Trail is a 16-mi paved trail parallel to SR 363 from just S of the Capitol building, through part of the Apalachicola State Forest, to the village of St Marks near the Gulf. The terrain is flat through varied scenery, including wooded and remote areas. At the N trailhead (SR 363; just S of SR 261 SE) is parking, Rr and bike rental/repair. Water fountains along trail; near the S trailhead are cafes with Rr. 9-5 (850-922-6007)

■ **BOAT RAMPS**

Parks: Ochlockonee

Halls Landing has a ramp with a floating dock and a fishing platform on the 8800-acre Lake Talquin. ADA picnic shelter; Rr (Luther Hall Landing Rd; off SR 20 W)

Joe Budd Wildlife Management Area has a boat ramp and fixed dock on the 12-mi, 8800-acre Lake Talquin. You can also access a T-shaped, 200' ADA pier. Be aware, this is a popular hunting ground! Picnic tables (CR 268; 3 mi W of Midway, S on Peters Rd, when it becomes dirt, go E on High Bluff Rd for 2.5 mi)

Marshes Island Park has a ramp and floating dock as well as a 210' fishing pier over the Ochlockonee Bay. Rr (S of Panacea; take SR 372 E off of US 98)

Newport Park has a boat ramp and fixed dock on the St Marks River. Rr (7928 US 98; W of St Marks)

■ **BOAT TOURS**

Fishing Charters: Florida Light Tackle. Parks: Wakulla Springs

Capt Tony offers tours for up to 6 along the Apalachicola River or on the Bay and Gulf, depending on the time you want to spend. Crew can help you over the shell parking lot up the fixed dock

and can lift you in your WC onto the 23' boat. Along the river expect to see gators; bayside you can stop at Little St George or St Vincent Islands. See Fishing Charters. Rr in marina (Scipio Creek Marina, 400 Market St, Apalachicola; 850-653-3560)

■ **BOWLING**

Seminole Bowl has ramped lanes and a bowling ball ramp. Snack bar; game room; Rr. Sun-Thu 12-12; Fri & Sat -2am (1940 W Tennessee St; 850-561-0894)

■ **CANOEING/KAYAKING**

Parks: Ochlockonee River

TNT Hideaway rents tandem kayaks and canoes for the cypress-lined, slow moving Wakulla River. The 6-mi round trip through heavily wooded residential areas takes about 3 hrs. The river is teeming with wildlife and you may see manatees May-Oct. Depending on the water level, the launch has a 5' gentle slope to the water's edge. With advance notice staff can arrange for someone to help your companions lift you into a boat. Dirt parking (6527 US 98, Crawfordville; 850-925-6412)

■ **FISHING CHARTERS**

Capt Jerry Alexander offers half/full-day inshore trips on a 21' Carolina Skiff for 2 on the flats of the Apalachee Bay. With advance notice, extra crew can lift you aboard in your WC from the floating dock. Restaurant with Rr near marina (Shell Point Marina, 78 Beaty Tafs Dr, Shell Point; 30 mi S of Tallahassee; capt 850-926-1768; marina 850-926-7162)

Capt Tony offers 4- and 6-hr offshore and bay fishing trips for up to 4 people on a 23' boat. Crew can help you over the shell parking lot to the fixed dock and can lift you aboard in your WC. Rr in marina (Scipio Creek Marina, 400 Market St, Apalachicola; 850-653-3560)

Florida Light Tackle & Sport Fishing offers half/full-day inshore trips for 2 anglers on a 24' flats boat. With advance notice, Capt Jody Campbell can arrange for extra crew to help lift you aboard in your WC from the floating dock. If you prefer sightseeing, he offers 2- and 3-hr, sunset and full-day cruises. (34 Connie Dr, Shell Point; 850-926-1173)

■ **FISHING PIERS**
Boat Ramps: Halls Landing, Joe Budd, Marshes Island. Parks: Maclay, Ochlockonee, San Luis Mission, Tom Brown, Trout Pond
Battery Park has a 1000' lighted pier on the bay. 24 hrs (Bay Ave at 6 St, Apalachicola)
Lafayette Park has a 1000' lighted pier on the bay. 24 hrs (180 Ave B, Apalachicola)
Lake Miccosukee is a 6300-acre lake with a 300' ADA pier. (US 90; 15 mi W of Tallahassee)

■ **HANDCYCLING**
Center for Independent Living loans a handcycle with V-shaped handles. You must be able to transport it. Wkdy 8:30-5 (572-C Appleyard Dr; 850-575-9621)

■ **HUNTING**
St Marks National Wildlife Refuge holds a 2-day Mobility-Impaired general gun hunt at the Panacea Unit in mid-Dec for does, bucks, hogs and bearded turkeys. You must have Mobility-Impaired Certification; see p 13 on Hunting. You can hunt from vehicles, including ATVs, on refuge roads and fire lanes. Get an application from St Marks in early Jul; applications must be returned by early Aug for the random drawing. The 35 hunters selected are notified by mail, advised of the orientation the night before the hunt and given directions. Your able-bodied companion may not hunt. For suggestions on camping, call Jay Leonard at 850-926-2821. (PO Box 68, St Marks, 32355; 850-925-6121)

■ **MISC FUN**
Senior Center offers craft and foreign language classes, bingo and card games for adults age 55 and over. Lunch available; Rr. Wkdy 9-7; Sat –2 (1400 N Monroe St; 850-891-4000)

■ **MUSEUMS**
Black Archives Research Center & Museum contains African-American artifacts, photographs, manuscripts, art and oral history tapes. Only the 1st floor is accessible. With advance notice, staff will unlock a gate so you can park in the adjacent employee parking lot. Rr. Wkdy 8-5 (Florida A & M Univ, Carnegie Library, M L King Blvd & Gamble St; 850-599-3020)
John Gorrie State Museum honors the physician and inventor of a cooling system for yellow fever patients. He later invented a machine that made ice, which led to today's modern refrigeration and air-conditioning. Gift shop; Rr. $. Thu-Mon 9-12 & 1-5 (46 6 St, Apalachicola; 850-653-9347)
Knott House Museum was a private home built in 1843; in 1928, the Knott family furnished it with Victorian pieces and attached poems to the furniture. You can see an 8-min video on the *House that Rhymes* and take a 1-hr guided tour. An elevator goes to all floors. WC guests can park in driveway and use the side entrance. Gift shop; Rr. Tours hourly Wed-Fri 1-3, Sat 10-3 (301 E Park Ave; 850-922-2459)
Mary Brogan Museum of Art & Science features national traveling art and interactive science, math and technology exhibits for all ages. Family-focused science demonstrations and various programs occur each Sat. Parking garage beneath the bldg; gift shop; Rr. $. Mon-Sat 10-5, Sun 1-5 (Kleman Plaza, 350 S Duval St; 850-671-5001)
Tallahassee Museum of History & Natural Science is a 52-acre potpourri of nature and historical exhibits. A boardwalk takes you through woods and swamp to view a Florida panther, black bear and other indigenous animals and reptiles. A wood chip trail leads to an 1880's farm complex where the buildings are not ramped. The Discovery Center has hands-on exhibits, the Phipps Building has rotating exhibits and the aviary houses birds of prey. The 1st floor of Bellevue, the historic antebellum plantation home of Princess Catherine Murat, is accessible. All paths

are either hard-packed dirt or wood chips. Programs & demonstrations wknd; gift shop; snack bar; picnic areas; Rr. $. Mon-Sat 9-5; Sun 12:30-5 (3945 Museum Dr; 850-575-8684)

■ **PARKS**

Downtown Chain of Parks has sidewalks connecting 7 beautifully landscaped parks that often host art shows, festivals, farmers' markets and live Saturday jazz concerts (spring and summer). ADA picnic tables (Park Ave)

J Lewis Hall Park has an ADA tot playground and a standard youth playground, both on accessible surfaces. Picnic tables; Rr. 8-dusk (7575 SR 363, Woodville; 850-488-0221)

Lake Jackson Mounds State Archaeological Site has several earth mounds where Native Americans flourished in 1200. A mulched trail, steep in spots, allows a view of the area and the remains of a gristmill. Stairs lead to the top of some mounds. ADA picnic table; Rr. $. 8-dusk (3600 Indian Mounds Rd; 850-922-6007)

Leon Sinks Geological has a .5-mi trail to the Gopher Hole Sinkhole that is hard-packed and mostly level other than the slope down to the sinkhole. Under an overhanging rock is a window into Florida's critical aquifer. The rest of the trails are soft and steep. ADA picnic tables by parking lot; Rr. $. 8-dusk (Apalachicola National Forest, US 319; 7 mi S of Tallahassee; 850-926-3561)

+Maclay State Gardens are ornamental gardens overlooking Lake Hall; visit Jan-Apr for peak blooms. A ranger can take guests with mobility impairments on a tour through the gardens on a golf cart that holds 4. The trails through the garden are brick, pine mulch or packed earth. To enter the Maclay house, you must go up several steps. Down an incline is a dock for fishing in the lake. Ask at the ranger station to use the beach WC for the sandy beach with a swim area. ADA picnic tables; WC loaner, Rr. $. Gardens 9-5; park 8-dusk (3540 Thomasville Rd; 850-487-4556/

487-41115)

Medart Park is a 36-acre park with a 1-mi paved trail and a playground with a ramp to a play station. Rr. 8-dusk (23 Recreation Dr; N of Medart off CR 375)

Ochlockonee River State Park is a 392-acre scenic pine woods at the confluence of the Ochlockonee and Dead Rivers. Nestled between the Apalachicola National Forest and St Marks National Wildlife Refuge, this place is teeming with wildlife (and mosquitoes during the summer). Both fresh and saltwater fishing is excellent here. You can fish from the grassy banks of various ponds or from the fixed dock on Tide Creek. From the boat ramp with a floating dock, you can go 5 mi downstream to the Ochlockonee Bay and the Gulf of Mexico. The park rents canoes for paddling Tide Creek and the rivers with currents mild enough that you can paddle back to the launch site. With advance notice, staff can put the canoe in the boat ramp and lift you into it. The two 1-mi bike/hike trails, which are hard packed but rough in spots, start at the boat ramp and end at the picnic area. One trail runs along the river, the other goes through a pine forest and scrub. Or, take the 3-mi scenic loop drive. Call ahead and rangers will plan an accessible trail for the regularly scheduled guided walks. See Campgrounds. Campfires in summer; ADA picnic shelter; grill; Rr in campground. $. 8-dusk (429 State Park Rd; 4 mi S of Sopchoppy off US 319; 850-962-2771)

St Marks National Wildlife Refuge is divided into 3 sections; most activities are in the St Marks Unit where a visitor center has exhibits, bookstore and Rr. The Plum Orchard Pond Trail behind the center is a short limestone trail (difficult if wet) where you can view native plants. Other trails in the area are sandy. You can fish off the bank at the Mounds Pool or picnic by Picnic Pond. On the Gulf is a boat ramp with a fixed dock. ADA picnic tables; Rr. $. Dawn-dusk (1200 Lighthouse Rd, St Marks;

850-925-6121)
San Luis Mission Park is a 68-acre city park with a boardwalk from which you can fish in a 10-acre lake. ADA playground; ADA picnic tables. 8-dusk (San Luis Rd; between Tharpe St & Mission Rd)

San Marcos De Apalache State Historic Site has a short, mulched trail where you can view the remains of a wood fort circa 1500, a 1739 stone fort and a military cemetery. In the middle of the trail are steps, but if you backtrack you can view the other half by restarting at the trail exit. At the museum you can learn local history through artifacts found from the different eras of occupation. An observation deck overlooks the confluence of the Wakulla and St Marks Rivers. ADA picnic area; gift shop. $. Thu-Mon 9-5 (148 Old Fort Rd, St Marks; 850-925-6216)

Tom Brown Park is a 255-acre city park with a boardwalk from which you can fish in a lake. A 2-acre enclosed area invites your dog to run off leash. ADA playground; ADA picnic tables; Rr. 8-dusk (Capital Cir SE & Easterwood Dr)

Trout Pond is currently closed for renovations but has a 700' looped paved trail through the woods to a boardwalk and a 50' ADA fishing pier over the 10-acre lake. ADA picnic tables; Rr. $. Call first. (CR 373; 7 mi S of SR 263; 850-926-3561)

*Wakulla Springs State Park is a 4800-acre home to the state's largest freshwater spring and lots of accessible fun. The ramp down to the waterfront is paved. One river tour boat has a WC platform in front where you can roll aboard for a 40-min guided tour to see gators and plenty of birds. When the water is clear, the 30-min glass-bottom boat tour is a chance to see marine life in the spring. For WC passengers, staff puts a ramp over the entry stairs so you can roll up to the glass viewing area. At the waterfront office you can borrow an aquatic device that is a cross between a beach WC and a 1-person boat

on which you can get across the small grassy sand beach and into the water. Staff can help with transfers. The diving tower by the swim area is at ground level and about 5' above the water's surface; from there it's a short swim to the shallow water at the beach. The 3-mi looped nature trail is level and composed of compact sand and chips. The 1937 lodge has a dining room, soda fountain, gift shop; see Inns. ADA picnic tables; Rr. $. 8am-dusk (SR 267, Wakulla Springs; between SR 61 & SR 363; 850-224-5950)

■ **PERFORMING ARTS**

FAMU Essential Theater offers 4 performances annually from drama to comedy. The Charles Winter Wood Theater has WC seating in back on the aisle. (Tucker Hall, Gamble St; between Railroad & M L King Blvd; 850-561-2425)

FSU School of Music presents opera, chamber music and symphony concerts in 2 halls on the FSU campus. The Opperman Music Hall is in the KMU Music Building and has WC seating in back on the aisles. The Ruby Diamond Auditorium is in the Westcott Building with WC seating in the aisles on the main floor. Rr (Fine Arts Ticket Office, Copeland & Call Sts; 850-644-6500)

FSU School of Theater presents a wide range of works including Shakespeare, Broadway and classical and modern drama. The Main Stage Theater has WC seating in the back row on the aisle. The Lab Theater has WC seating in the front row. Rr (Fine Arts Ticket Office, Copeland & Call Sts; 850-644-6500)

Ruby Diamond Auditorium is home to the Tallahassee Symphony Orchestra which performs a Masterworks Series, holiday concerts and youth concerts and the Tallahassee Ballet that offers 3 performances a year. WC seating is in the aisle on the main floor. Rr (Fine Arts Ticket Office, Copeland & College Sts; 850-644-6500; Symphony: 850-224-0461; Ballet: 850-222-1287)

Tallahassee Civic Center offers a Broadway Series as well as concerts and other entertainment. WC seating is at all levels and ticket prices. Elevators; Rr. (505 W Pensacola St; 850-222-0400; 800-322-3602)

Tallahassee Little Theater and **Theater A La Carte** are community groups performing Broadway shows, musicals, classics and avant-garde pieces. The best WC seating is in the 4th row where staff can remove standard seats but you can also find WC seating in the front row. CRr (1864 Thomasville Rd; at Betton Rd; 850-224-8474)

■ **POOLS**

The following pools have lifts (fixed seats) and Rr. Lifeguards can help with transfers. Call individual pools for information on water aerobics and swim lessons: **Forest Meadows** Jun-Aug daily and May & Sep wknd 12:30-5:30 (4750 N Meridian; 850-891-3927). **Hilaman Pool** Jun-Aug daily and May & Sep wknd 10-5. Restaurant (2737 Blairstone Rd; 850-891-3937). **Levy Pool** Jun-Aug Mon-Sat 12:30-5:30 (625 W Tharpe St; 850-891-3950). **Robinson Trueblood Pool** Jun-Aug Mon-Sat 12:30-5:30. Or, try the zero-depth pool into which you can roll into the water. (1115 Dade St; 850-891-3911). **Wade Wehunt Pool** is heated and covered in the winter. Hrs vary (907 Myers Park Dr; 850-891-3985). **Walker Ford Pool** Jun-Aug Mon-Sat 12:30-5:30 (2301 Pasco St; 850-891-3973)

■ **SCUBA**

Panama City: Scuba: Al Lewando

■ **SHOPPING**

Antiques & Boutiques, in Havana and Quincy, are connected by SR 12 and are part of the North Florida Art Trail. The best place to start exploring is Havana (15 mi NW of Tallassee on US 27), known for shops with unique treasures, galleries and antique stores within 4 blocks of Main St. Travel W towards Quincy and stop at the Nicholson Farmhouse where you can have a meal, listen to live country music and shop for crafts. In Quincy browse fine works

from local artisans.

Specialty Shops: Find renowned shellfish in the historic fishing village of Apalachicola. (US 98/SR 30; at the W end of the John Gorrie Memorial Bridge)

Malls: Governor's Square Mall (1500 Apalachee Pkwy); Tallahassee Mall (2415 Monroe St)

■ **SHOOTING RANGES**

Apalachicola National Forest Shooting Range has rifle and pistol ranges from 25- to 100-yd long with sidewalks. No shotguns allowed. Dawn-dusk (FR 305; from SR 267, 8 mi E of Bloxham, watch for small sign then N 5 mi on dirt road; 850-265-3676)

■ **SKYDIVING**

School of Human Flight offers tandem jumps for quads and paras. First you don the harness in your WC, then staff lifts you (170-lb limit) and carries you by the harness up the steps into the plane where you sit on the floor. Your knees are strapped to your chest so you don't hit on landing and when you jump you are in the lap of an instructor. Staff on the ground softens your landing. A strong steady breeze is best. You can hire a photographer to jump with you. Allow 4 hrs, including the 25-min airplane ride, the 1-min free fall and the 5- to 7-min ride by parachute. (Quincy Airport, SR 12; 1.5 mi E of Quincy; 850-627-7643)

■ **SPECTATOR SPORTS**

Arena Football is played at the Tallahassee Civic Center where WC seating is at all levels and ticket prices. Elevators; Rr. Apr-Sep (505 W Pensacola St; 850-222-0400; 800-322-3602)

■ **TENNIS**

WC-Tennis classes are offered through USTA for beginning through advanced players. To register talk to Dusty Smith. Rr (Forest Meadows Park Tennis Center, 4750 N Meridian Rd; 850-891-3920)

■ **TRACK**

Achilles Track Club meets Sat mornings at the St Marks Historic Trail and is open to folks with any type of disability. Come train for marathons or just for fun and exercise. Volunteers can accompany and assist you on the trail. Call for the schedule. The N trailhead (SR 363; just S of SR 261/Capitol Cir SE) has HC parking and Rr. Near the S trailhead are cafes with Rr. 9-5 (Lydia Burnes 850-421-4852; Phil Yon 850-671-1599)

ACCOMMODATIONS

■ B&B/INNS

Allison House Inn, an English country B&B in the heart of historic Quincy, has an ADA guestroom with a full bed (21" high/open frame) and a bathroom with a toilet extender, a roll-under sink and tub. Enjoy nearby antique shops and restaurants. $$ (215 N Madison St, Quincy; 20 mi W of Tallahassee; 850-875-2511; 888-904-2511)

Coombs House Inn, in historic Apalachicola, is an elegant Victorian mansion with 2 ADA units. Room 4, in the main house, has a king bed (open frame), an entrance off the veranda and a bathroom with a raised toilet, roll-under sink and tub. Room 14, in Coombs House East (close to the main house), has a queen bed (open frame) and bathroom with a raised toilet, roll-under sink and ramped shower. Gourmet continental breakfast is served in the dining room and, on weekends wine receptions are served in the parlor. $$-$$$ (80 6 St, Apalachicola; 850-653-9199)

Sweet Magnolia Inn, in the quiet fishing village of St Marks, has 1 ADA guestroom with 2 full beds (25" high/open frames) and a bathroom with a roll-under sink and roll-in shower with a hand-held sprayer and seat. Relax in the lovely garden or on ground-floor covered porches. Full breakfast is served in the dining room. $$ (803 Port Leon Dr, St Marks; 850-925-7670)

Wakulla Springs State Park Lodge recalls the elegance of its conception in the 1930's. An old timey elevator can take you to 12 large WC-friendly rooms, with either 2 twins, a queen or 2 full beds (24"-29" high/open frames). The standard bathrooms have 27" wide entries; rooms 28 and 29 have raised toilets. The lodge has a dining room, soda fountain and gift shop. $$ (550 Wakulla Park Dr, Wakulla Springs; 15 mi S of Tallahassee near SR 267 & SR 61; 850-224-5950)

■ CAMPGROUNDS

Ochlockonee River State Park is a remote wilderness area with 30 RV/tent sites. ADA site 24 has water/elec, a raised grill, ADA picnic table and paved ramp to the ADA bathhouse with raised toilets, roll-under sinks and roll-in showers with seats. This park offers great fishing and canoeing; see Parks. (429 State Park Rd; 4 mi S of Sopchoppy on US 319; 850-962-2771)

*St George Island State Park is a very popular spot with a beach WC and fishing from the shore; see Beaches. The 60 RV/tent sites have water/elec, grills and picnic tables. Sites 34, 35, 39, 48, 49 and 51 are close to the boardwalks to ADA bathhouses with roll-under sinks and roll in showers. Boardwalks to the beach; campfire programs on request (1900 E Gulf Beach Dr/CR 300, St George Island; 850-927-2111)

Wright Lake Campground, on the W side of the Apalachicola National Forest, has 24 RV/tent sites under oak and cypress trees and spread out along the spring-fed lake. Sites are on aggregate surfaces and have water, ADA picnic tables, grills and fire pits. Campsites 3, 5, 9, 16 and 19 are closest to the ADA bathhouse with raised toilets, roll-under sinks and roll-in showers with seats. Paths to the bathhouse are level but sandy. Trails are maintained and generally hard packed. The campground has a small beach with a swim area and flat, open spots for fishing. A boat ramp (with no dock) at nearby Hickory Landing primitive camp area opens onto Owl Creek and ultimately the Apalachicola River. No reservations (FR 101; from Sumatra take SR 65 S for 2 mi, W on FR 101 for 2 mi, then N; 850-643-2282)

■ MOTELS

Best Western Apalachicola Inn has 2 ADA rooms with a king or 2 queen beds (platforms) and bathrooms with raised toilets, roll-under sinks and a tub or step-in shower with hand-held sprayers and seats. Free brkfst; pool. $$-$$$ (249 US 98, Apalachicola; 850-653-9131)

Comfort Inn has 4 ADA rooms, each with a king bed. Bathrooms have raised toilets, roll-under sinks and roll-in showers with hand-held sprayers and seats. Free brkfst; pool; laundry. $-$$ (2727 Graves Rd; near I-10 & US 27; 850-562-7200)

Doubletree Hotel is downtown close to the State Capitol and museums. Seven ADA rooms have either a king or 2 full beds. Bathrooms have raised toilets, roll-under sinks; 3 rooms have roll-in showers with hand-held sprayers and seats; others have tubs. Pool; laundry; full restaurant. $$-$$$ (101 S Adams St at Park Ave; 850-224-5000)

Hampton Inn has 5 ADA rooms, each with a king bed (platform) and bathroom with a raised toilet, roll-under sink and tub with a hand-held sprayer; one room has a roll-in shower. Free brkfst; pool. $$ (3210 N Monroe St; I-10 exit 199, N 1 block; 850-562-4300)

Hilton Garden Inn has 4 ADA rooms, each with a king bed. Bathrooms have raised toilets and roll-under sinks; room 129 has a roll-in shower; others have tubs; all have hand-held sprayers and seats. Pool; restaurant for brkfst; hot tub; fitness room; laundry. $$-$$$ (3333 Thomasville Rd; off I-10 exit 203; 850-385-3553)

La Quinta South has 6 ADA rooms, each with a king bed and coffeepot; some have refrigerators and microwaves. Bathrooms have raised toilets and roll-under sinks; 1 room has a roll-in shower; others have tubs; all have hand-held sprayers and seats. Free brkfst; pool. $$ (2850 US 27; 850-878-5099)

Microtel Inn & Suites has 4 ADA rooms, each with 1 or 2 queen beds (open frames), and an ADA suite with a queen bed and full sofa bed. The suite also has a refrigerator, microwave and coffeepot. Bathrooms have roll-under sinks; room 133 has a roll-in shower with a hand-held sprayer and seat; others have tubs. Free brkfst. $-$$ (3216 N Monroe St; I-10 exit 199, N 1 blk; 850-562-3800)

Sleep Inn has 4 ADA rooms, each with 2 queen beds (platforms) and a bathroom with a raised toilet, roll-under sink and tub with a seat. Close to airport; free brkfst; pool. $-$$$ (1695 Capital Cir NW; I-10 exit 196, go S; 850-575-5885; 877-669-2241)

Rr means ADA or handicapped restrooms; CRr stands for companion or unisex restrooms.

Look for ADA picnic tables which have the bench cut away or an elongated top at one end so you can roll underneath instead of sitting sideways.

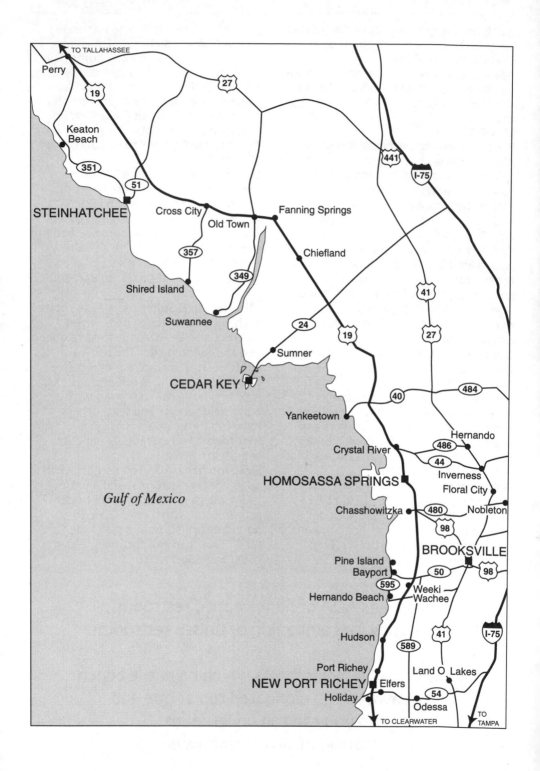

NORTHWEST GULF COAST

BROOKSVILLE
Bayport, Hernando Beach, Nobleton, Pine Island, Weeki Wachee

What variety for a rural area: beach wheelchairs at a riverside and a Gulfside beach, two fabulous bike trails, llamas, mermaids and year-round Christmas shopping!

Tourist Info
Hernando County Tourist Info: 30305 Cortez Blvd, 34602; 352-754-4405
Web sites: www.co.hernando.fl.us/tourdev

ACTIVITIES

■ **ATTRACTIONS**
Boyett's Citrus Grove has a souvenir shop with citrus products, a small aquarium with fresh- and saltwater creatures, including a shark, and a wildlife park with gators, llamas and monkeys. Rr. 9-5 (4355 Spring Lake Hwy; 352-796-2289)
Weeki Wachee Spring is famous for its underwater theater with 30-min live performances by mermaids; WC seating is in back. The 30-min dog and cat show has WC seating in front. To board the 30-min wilderness cruise boat, you must take 3 steps down and transfer into a boat seat. Rr. $. Wed-Sun 10-closing varies (US 19 at SR 50, Weeki Wachee; 352-596-2062)
■ **BEACHES**
Parks: Hernando Beach, Rogers

*McKeathan/Pine Island Park is a 3-acre county beach with a beach WC (fixed arms). Ask at the entry gate and staff will bring the WC to you at HC parking where a paved path leads to a ramp onto the soft sand about 50' from the water's edge. A paved path also leads to a ramped observation deck overlooking the Gulf. Lifeguards in summer; concession stand; ADA picnic shelters; grills; outdoor showers; ADA playground on sand; Rr. $. Dawn-dusk (10800 Pine Island Dr/CR 595, Pine Island)
■ **BIKE TRAILS**
Suncoast Trail is a paved, 12' wide bike and pedestrian path through a landscaped corridor along the Suncoast Parkway/SR 589. Ultimately the trail will run 42 mi S from the Hernando/

Citrus county line to N Hillsborough County; currently 21 mi are complete, from SR 50 (W of Brooksville) S to the future Ridge Rd exit (W of Port Richey in Pasco County). You can access the trail from all county and state roads intersecting the parkway; parking and Rr are at the trailhead just S of SR 50, W side of the parkway. Along the trail are interpretive and rest areas. Contact the Suncoast Parkway at 813-558-1117. Dawn-dusk

Withlacoochee State Trail is a paved, fairly flat, rails-to-trails path running 46 mi from just S of Dunnellon south through Citrus and Hernando Counties to Trilby in N Pasco County. In Hernando County the trail follows the Withlacoochee River and goes through the Withlacoochee State Forest (where hunting seasons occur Oct-Apr; call for schedule and wear fluorescent orange at those times). The only steep grade on the trail is the bridge over SR 50 at Ridge Manor. Hernando County access points, with parking, Rr and water, include: Lake Townsen Park (.5 mi W of trail; CR 476; just E of CR 39 & Nobleton), Silver Lake Park (1 mi E of trail; from SR 50, N 3.5 mi on Croom Rital Rd; 352-754-6896) and Ridge Manor Trailhead (at US 98/SR 50, just E of I-75). Order the Trail Guide with a mile-by-mile history, recreational sites and businesses through Rails-to-Trails of the Withlacoochee. (Box 807, Inverness, 34451; 352-726-2251)

■ **BOAT RAMPS**
Parks: Hernando Beach, Rogers
Bayport Park has 2 boat ramps, floating docks and a lighted, 300' fishing pier on the Gulf. A long boardwalk along the water is planned. ADA picnic shelters; grills; Rr. 24 hrs (4140 Cortez Blvd/CR 595, Bayport)

■ **BOWLING**
Louie's Bowling Center has a 2" lip to each lane and a bowling ball ramp. Rr. Hrs vary (1691 E Jefferson St; 352-799-1987)

■ **CANOEING**
Nobleton Boat Rental rents canoes for 5-, 8- or 10-mi trips along the very mellow Withlacoochee. Staff can lift you into the shuttle or you can follow in your vehicle to the put-in. Staff can also help lift you from the concrete launch into a canoe. Snack bar & Rr at shop. 8-dusk (CR 476/ Lake Lindsey Rd, Nobleton; next to the river bridge; 352-796-7176)

■ **FISHING PIERS**
Boat Ramps: Bayport. Parks: Hernando Beach, Lake Townsen

■ **MUSEUMS**
Hernando Heritage Museum is a ramped home furnished with items from the 1860's to the 1930's. Only the 1st floor is accessible. $. Tue-Sat 12-3 (Jefferson St & May Ave; 352-799-0129)

■ **PARKS**
Hernando Beach/Jenkins Creek Park are adjacent county parks, occupying 36 acres along Jenkins Creek. At Hernando Beach, a boardwalk leads from HC parking to paved paths across the soft-sand beach to a ramped floating dock with a ladder into the swim area by a spring. Lifeguards in summer; ADA picnic shelters; grills; ADA playground on grass; outdoor showers; Rr. Dawn-dusk. Across CR 595 is Jenkins Creek Park with a lighted, 300' fishing pier and a boat ramp (for small boats/canoes) with a floating dock. Across the creek is a 30' pier next to an observation tower, ramped to the 8'-high 1st level from which you can watch manatees in winter. Both piers have sidewalks from HC parking. ADA picnic tables; grill; Rr. 24 hrs (6400 Shoal Line Blvd/CR 595, Hernando Bch)

Lake Townsen/Withlacoochee Riverside Community Park is a lovely 175-acre shady park with a 150' fishing pier over the lake. Drive along a rough dirt road and park by the ramped pier; after heavy rains, the road can be impassable. The boat ramp has no dock.

You can access the Withlacoochee State Trail from here; see Bike Trails. ADA picnic shelters; grills; ball fields; ADA playground on mulch; Rr, by picnic area. Dawn-dusk (28011 Lake Lindsay Rd/CR 476; just E of CR 39 & Nobleton; 352-754-4027)

+Rogers Park, a 3-acre county park, has a paved path with a railed ramp into the spring-fed water of the Weeki Wachee River. In summer, ask lifeguards to borrow a beach WC (fixed arms). The boat ramp (open 24 hrs) has fixed docks. Lifeguards in summer; ADA picnic shelters; outdoor showers; vending machines; ADA playground on sand; Rr. $ in summer. Dawn-dusk (7244 Shoal Line Blvd/CR 595; W of Weeki Wachee)

Withlacoochee Forest-McKeathan Lake has a 2-mi, paved road good for cycling around a lake being filled in by Mother Nature. Picnic and bird watch in a beautiful hardwood hammock. A 2-mi, relatively hard-packed nature trail can be a challenge for most WC riders. Rr. 8-dusk (US 41; 7 mi N of Brooksville; 352-754-6896)

■ **SHOPPING**

Roger's Christmas House Village is made up of 5 buildings, each with a different emphasis, from Christmas decorations or crystal to country cottage. Rr. 9:30-5 (103 Saxon Ave; 352-796-2415)

ACCOMMODATIONS

■ **MOTELS**

Best Western has 2 ADA rooms, each with a king or 2 full beds (open frames) and bathroom with a roll-under sink and roll-in shower. Pool; full restaurant. $$ (US 98; at I-75 exit 301, 12 mi E of Brooksville; 352-796-9481)

Comfort Inn has 3 ADA rooms, each with a king bed (platform) and bathroom with a roll-under sink and roll-in shower with a seat. The pool area has 1 step. Free brkfst; laundry. $$ (9373 Cortez Blvd, Weeki Wachee; 352-596-9000)

Days Inn is near the Withlacoochee State Trail (see Bike Trails). It has 6 ADA rooms, each with a king bed (platform), refrigerator, microwave and bathroom with a raised toilet. Five rooms have roll-in showers with hand-held sprayers and seats; the other has a step-in shower. Pool; laundry; lounge; full restaurant (open 24 hrs; 10% discount). $-$$ (6320 Windmere Rd; 352-796-9486)

CEDAR KEY
Chiefland, Fanning Springs, Sumner, Yankeetown

Cedar Key includes some 100 undeveloped wildlife refuge islets. Take a 4-mile causeway to the main island, where you'll find great seafood, galleries, shops and excellent sports fishing. However, when Cedar Key advertises that you'll step back into the 19th century, it unfortunately also describes access. Much of the architecture is old and because it is a flood-prone area, many buildings have several steps. (In downtown, accessible restrooms are in the Seabreeze and the Captain's Table.) Furthermore, many of the natural areas are sandy or wet. ADA lodging is non-existent on the island. But, if you can cope with these limitations, Cedar Key is a wonderful window on an old, tranquil Florida.

Tourist Info
Cedar Key Chamber: Fire Station, 2 St, Box 610, 32625; 352-543-5600; open

Mon-Wed & Fri 9-1pm; Sun 10-2
Greater Chiefland Chamber: 17 N Main St, Box 1397, Chiefland, 32626; 352-493-1849
Web sites: www.cedarkey.org; www.visitcitrus.com

ACTIVITIES

■ **BIKE TRAILS**
Nature Coast State Trail is a 32-mi, rails-to-trails, paved bike path that parallels US 19 from Chiefland N to Cross City with a 7-mi jaunt from Fanning Springs State Park E to Trenton. The trail is flat with gentle grades; just NW of Fanning Springs, the trail goes across a bumpy, but scenic, historic trestle bridge over the Suwannee River. Along US 19 are plenty of parking spots and small towns with Rr; the trek to Trenton has few facilities. Each trailhead has parking at an old railroad depot, some under restoration to include Rr. For a trail map, call Manatee Springs (352-493-6072) or Fanning Springs (352-463-3420) State Parks.
■ **BOAT RAMPS**
Fishing Piers: City Dock. Parks: Lower Suwannee
■ **BOAT RENTALS**
Island Hopper rents 24' pontoon boats for up to 12 persons for 4, 6 or 8 hrs. Roll onto the front of the boat from the floating dock. (City Dock, Dock St; 352-543-5904)
■ **BOAT TOURS**
Island Hopper offers 1 1/2-hr tours of nearby islands on a 24' deck boat. Roll onto the front of the boat from the floating dock. There's a 20-min stop at an inaccessible island. Hrs vary (City Dock, Dock St; 352-543-5904)
Lower Suwannee Wildlife Excursions designs custom ecotours from 1 hr to a few days along the local islands, the coast and/or the backwaters of the Suwannee and Wacasassa Rivers. Roll aboard the pontoon boat from the ramped floating dock; or crew can help lift you from your WC into a seat in a 23' skiff. For overnight trips, accessible camping or lodging is arranged. (City Dock, Dock St; 352-

543-5580)
■ **CANOEING**
Parks: Manatee Springs
■ **FISHING CHARTERS**
Capt Collins has a fairly roomy 21' Carolina Skiff for 5- to 8-hr trips around the islands or coastal flats. With advance notice, the capt can select an accessible dock near where the fish are running and help lift you aboard in your WC or onto a boat seat. (352-543-9102)
■ **FISHING PIERS**
Parks: Fanning, Lower Suwannee, Manatee Springs. Tours: FWC
City Dock has a ramp with a floating dock and a long, ramped, lighted fishing pier, with 6 finger piers and lowered railing for some fine fishing in the Gulf. Bait shop at hardware store (Dock St; off 1 St, 1st stop sign left of SR 24)
■ **KAYAKING**
Fishbonz rents solo/tandem kayaks for half/full days among nearby islands. You can slide 1' into a kayak from the floating dock or seawall; at higher tide, you may be able to cross the narrow beach to the water's edge. Staff can help with boarding. Shop is upstairs; snack bar (509 3 St; 352-543-9922)
Wild Florida offers a range of 4-hr guided kayak tours along the coastal flats and estuaries around Cedar Key and the Waccasassa and Suwannee Rivers. Launch sites vary from flat shorelines to a paved boat ramp; guides can help lift you from your WC into a solo sit-on or tandem sit-in kayak. You must have upper body strength and a companion. The married guides combine professional ecology and ACA Instructor certification, so you can anticipate a fascinating

and safe expedition, daytime, sunset or full moon. Trips include lunch or snacks; during breaks you can remain in your kayak or guides can help lift you out. Call to discuss your abilities and which tour works best for you. (352-373-6047; 877-945-3928)

■ MUSEUMS

Cedar Key Historical Museum covers the island's social and architectural history and keeps local genealogical records. Rr. $. Hrs vary (SR 24 & 2 St; 352-543-5549)

Cedar Key State Museum depicts the island's colorful history from the 1840's, through its boom time as a logging center after the Civil War, the ignominious destruction of the nearby town of Rosewood and onward. On the 18-acre grounds is a short, interpretive trail, mostly hard packed with some sandy spots, and a ramped, refurbished home from the 1920's (to open by 2003). Rr. $. Thu-Mon 9-5 (12150 SW 166 Ct; off SR 24; 352-543-5350)

■ PARKS

Cedar Key Scrub State Reserve comprises 4000 acres of diverse habitat, from tidal marsh to scrub. With over 10 mi of trails on grassy, but relatively hard-packed service roads, here's a chance to see scrub jay, gopher tortoises and other threatened species. Trails 1, 2 and 3 are drier and more WC-friendly, although Trail 3 has a steep grade in one area. ADA picnic tables; Rr in picnic area. 9-dusk (SR 24; 6 mi E of Cedar Key; 352-543-5567)

Fanning Springs State Park has a relatively WC-friendly swim area in the spring that feeds into the Suwannee River, popular with manatees. Roll down the paved path to the swim area, then either get out of your WC and work your way down the shallow steps or take a steep ramp into the 73-degree water. Boats and canoes can tie up (for a fee) at a floating dock. Plans are underway for canoe rentals. Currently the steep, paved canoe launch is usable but in bad repair. A 550' boardwalk takes you from parking to the launch. You will be able to rent a canoe here and paddle 10 mi downstream to Manatee Springs where a shuttle returns to Fanning. The 1-mi nature trail is wide and hard packed, except when wet, and passes a series of sinkholes. Ranger programs on winter weekends include boardwalk tours and riverside talks. Lifeguards in summer; ADA picnic shelters; ADA playground on mulch; ball field; Rr. $. 8-dusk (US 19/98, Fanning Springs; 352-463-3420)

Lower Suwannee National Wildlife Refuge offers 53,000 unspoiled acres with accessible features in 3 different areas. Near Shell Mound (from SR 24, 5 mi from Cedar Key, turn N onto CR 347, then W on CR 326) is a boat ramp, without a dock, and a wood, 40' fishing pier on a salt marsh. From CR 326, go 6 mi N on CR 347 to the Refuge's S Entrance for a scenic 9-mi Loop Road to the N Entrance; interpretive signage is planned. Near the N Entrance is the refuge headquarters with Rr and, across the road, River Trail, a ramped 400' boardwalk along the river (no fishing here). The 3rd area is N of the Suwannee River in Dixie County (from US 19 in Old Town, go SW on CR 349 then NW on Dixie Mainline Rd). The 9-mi Mainline Rd has interpretive signs as you drive through cypress forest, hardwood floodplains, pine forest and marsh to Shired Island on the Gulf. Off Mainline Rd, just N of CR 349, is Salt Creek with a 50' fishing pier over a salt marsh. Wkdy 7:30-4 (352-493-0238)

Manatee Springs State Park comprises 2444 acres of swamp and forest around the spring from which crystal clear water runs daily into the Suwannee River and, 23 mi downstream, the Gulf. Near the springhead, swimming is permitted and a shallow area has been terraced.

Friends, and possibly rangers, can lift you onto that terraced area to enjoy the 72-degree water. A 900' boardwalk takes you close to the springhead and to a floating dock for fishing along the river. A boat ramp by the dock is steep when water levels are low, but can be used for motor boats and non-motorized craft; only non-motorized boats are allowed up the spring run. The park offers canoe rentals (summer daily; winter wknds) and, with 2-wk notice, staff can help lift you into the canoe. While the river is quite mellow, the current in the spring run is stronger; but you can paddle back to the put-in. The 8.5-mi N End Trail and the Sink Trail are dirt and sand service roads, fine for motorized and all-terrain WCs. Rangers periodically offer a variety of tours and slide shows; check for the schedule. See Campgrounds. Bait shops outside entrance; snack bar summer daily & winter wknds; ADA picnic table; playground; Rr in campground. $. 8-dusk (SR 320; 6 mi W of Chiefland; 352-493-6072)

■ SHOPPING

Cedar Key shops and galleries generally have steps at the entrance, but several are accessible, including the Keyhole and The Natural Experience. The Dilly Dally Gally, an artsy gift shop, has a steep ramp where most WC riders need a push. The Rustic Woods and Suwannee Triangle Gallery, by City Dock, are accessible once you get over the high curb. Diagonally across the street is the Wild Women Gallery to which you can take the ramp by the City Dock onto the narrow sidewalk and into the ramped entrance.

Dakotah Vineyards & Winery invites you to taste wines before your purchase. Mon-Sat 10-5; Sun 12-5 (14365 NW US 19, Chiefland; 352-493-9309)

■ TOURS

FWC, the Florida Fish and Wildlife Conservation Commission's field lab, may, with advance notice, be able to lead an informal tour of the various marine research facilities housed in the blue building on stilts (with a ramp and elevator). Picnic table; Rr. Wkdy 9-4 (11350 SW 153 Ct; from SR 24, turn left after 1st bridge to Cedar Key, turn left again; 352-543-9200) Past the FWC, at the end of the road is a wood, 150' fishing pier.

ACCOMMODATIONS

■ B&Bs

Cedar Key B&B, built in 1880 for mill employees, has been painstakingly restored under a canopy of live oaks and has a WC-friendly guest room. The entrance is ramped. The front room, Miss Verona's, has wide doors, a king bed (26" high/open frame) that can be pulled apart into 2 twins and a roomy private bath with grab bars, a roll-under sink and step-in shower with a hand-held sprayer and seat. Homemade breakfasts and afternoon teas round out this gracious little place. $$ (Corner of 3 & F Sts; 352-543-5050; 877-543-5051)

■ CAMPGROUNDS

Manatee Springs State Park has 93 RV/tent sites on hard-packed terrain in a beautiful forest. Four ADA sites (#12, 13, 89, 90) have water/elec, ADA picnic tables and fire pits. The ADA bathhouse has raised toilets, roll-under sinks and roll-in showers with a seat. This park offers good fishing and somewhat accessible swimming; see Parks. (SR 320; 6 mi W of Chiefland; 352-493-6072; 800-326-3521)

Rainbow Country Campground is about 5 mi from Cedar Key and 7 mi from the Gulf in a lovely, wooded area. The 65 RV/tent sites include 55 with full hookups; some have concrete pads, grills and fire pits; all have picnic tables. Paved paths lead to 2 ADA bathhouses with roll-under sinks and roll-in showers. Camp store; laundry; lounge; game & TV rooms (11951 SW Shiloh Rd, Sumner; from US 19/98, 14 mi W on SR 24; 352-543-6268)

■ **CONDOS**

Seahorse Landing has WC-friendly 2BR/2BA ground floor condos built on an 18' bluff over the Gulf. Each master bedroom has a king or queen bed (23" high/open frame); the 2nd bedroom has a full or 2 twins beds; some living rooms have full sofa beds. Unit 301 has a master bath with grab bars, a roll-under sink and tub with hand-held sprayer and seat; the 2nd bath has a step-in shower. Units have full kitchens and linens. Enjoy a 200' pier for fishing or watching spectacular sunsets. Pool (4050 G St; 352-543-6801; 888-733-4853)

■ **MOTELS**

Cedar Inn has a room on the ground floor with a 31" entry, 2 full beds (22" high/open frames) and a bathroom with a 22" entry, roll-under sink and grab bars at the toilet and tub with a seat. $ (410 2 St; 2 blocks left of SR 24; 352-543-5455)

Holiday Inn Express has 4 ADA rooms, each with a king bed (open frame), twin sofa bed and bathroom with a raised toilet and tub; room 106 has a roll-in shower with a hand-held sprayer and seat. Free brkfst; pool; laundry. $$ (809 NW 21 Ave, Chiefland; 352-493-9400)

Osprey Motel has roomy 1BR efficiencies on the ground floor with 2" steps at the 32" entries. Standard bathrooms have 21" doorways; showers, with a 5" lip, are large enough for a stool or companion. Units have 2 full or twin beds (23" high), living rooms and full kitchens. The private dock on the Gulf has a deck and fish cleaning facilities. Hard-packed gravel parking lot; 2 RV hookups available. $ (SR 24; 352-543-9743; 800-890-8327)

Park Place Hotel has 10 WC-friendly efficiencies, each with a small lip at the entry and a kitchenette. Unit 121, with a king bed (open frame) and a queen sofa bed, has more floor space in the standard bathroom and a grab bar at the tub. Other units have 2 queen beds. A ramp leads from the loose rock parking lot. $$ (211 2 St; 800-868-7963)

HOMOSASSA SPRINGS

Chassahowitzka, Crystal River, Floral City, Hernando, Inverness

Book boat tours, rentals and snorkel trips in advance for the peak manatee-watching season from Jan to May. For a drier view of manatees, check out Homosassa Springs State Park. An unexpected delight is the Rock Crusher Canyon Music Park, where you can camp and enjoy a big-name concert.

Tourist Info

Citrus County Chamber: 208 W Main St, Inverness, 34450; 352-726-2801; 28 NW US 19, Crystal River, 34428; 352-795-3149

Homosassa Springs Chamber: 3495 S Suncoast Blvd, Box 709, 34447; 352-628-2666

Web sites: www.homosassachamber.com; www.visitcitrus.com; www.gminet.com/crystalr

ACTIVITIES

■ **ATTRACTIONS**

Crystal River State Archaeological Site

is a ceremonial center and mound complex built by Native Americans between BC 200 and AD 1400. The visitor center houses artifacts of these pre-Columbian mound builders and an interpretive video. Along the .5-mi, paved trails through the mounds are sound posts with historical information; Mound A has steps and Mound H has a steep incline. Picnic tables; Rr. $. 8-5 (3400 Museum Pt; 2.5 mi W of US 19, N of Crystal River; 352-795-3817)

Power Place has displays, videos and lectures on electrical generation today and for the future. WC entrance on E side of the bldg; Rr. Wkdy 9:30-4 (Florida Power Energy Complex, Crystal River; from US 19, W on Power Line Rd, 3.8 mi to Site Admin Bldg; 352-563-4490)

■ **BIKE TRAILS**

Withlacoochee State Trail is a paved, fairly flat, rails-to-trails path running 46 mi from Dunnellon S through Citrus and Hernando Counties to Trilby in N Pasco County. In Citrus County, the trail parallels US 41 and has access points with parking, Rr & water at: the N terminus, Gulf Junction Trailhead (Magenta Dr; off N Ocean Dr, 4 mi S of Dunnellon), Citrus Springs (S Citrus Springs Blvd), Inverness (Trail Shop, N side of N Apopka Ave), Wallace Brooks Park (Park Ave & Dampier St, Inverness), Fort Cooper State Park (3100 S Old Floral City Rd, Inverness; from US 41, E on Eden Dr, then N) and Floral City (off SR 48). Order the Trail Guide with a mile-by-mile history, recreational sites and businesses through Rails-to-Trails of the Withlacoochee. (Box 807, Inverness, 34451; 352-726-2251)

■ **BOAT RAMPS**

Eden Park has a boat ramp and floating dock with access to Little Lake Spivey and adjoining lakes. Small fishing pier; picnic tables; grills; playground. Dawn-dusk (614 Park Lake Ter, Inverness; 352-527-7620)

Fort Island Trail Park has a boat ramp with floating docks and a ramped, T-shaped, wood pier on the Crystal River. ADA picnic shelters; bait shops on US 19; Rr. Dawn-dusk (12073 W Fort Island Tr/SR 44, Crystal River; 5 mi W of US 19; 352-795-2202)

Hernando Park has a boat ramp and floating dock on Lake Hernando. ADA picnic tables; Rr. Dawn-dusk (3650 E Lake Pl, Hernando; 352-527-7620)

Pete's Pier has 2 boat ramps and a floating dock with access to Kings Bay, Crystal River and the Gulf. 7-6 (1 SW 1 Pl, Crystal River; off Kings Bay Dr, .6 mi W of US 19; 352-795-3302)

■ **BOAT RENTALS**

American Pro-Dive rents pontoon boats (30" entry) for 8 people on Crystal River. Most WCs can roll aboard from the ramp; if tides are extreme, staff can help lift you aboard in your WC. Bait shop; Rr in restaurant (10432 W Halls River Rd; 352-628-3595; 800-291-3483)

Crystal River Dive Center rents 24' pontoon boats (21" and 31" entries) for up to 9 by the hr to snorkel or dive in Kings Bay. Roll aboard from the floating dock; staff can help. (Best Western Hotel, 614 NW US 19, Crystal River; 352-795-6798; 800-444-1919)

Plantation Inn Marina rents pontoon boats (28" entry) for up to 12 people on Kings Bay, 1-hr minimum. Roll aboard from the floating dock; staff can help. (Plantation Inn, 9301 W SR 44, Crystal River; 352-795-5797; 800-632-6262)

Port Hotel & Marina rents pontoon boats (24" entry) for up to 12 along with dive and snorkel gear for use on Kings Bay. Or, you can take a dive/snorkel trip with staff, experienced with disabled persons, who can lift you into the water. The marina also offers customized tours aboard pontoon boats. Roll aboard from the ramped floating dock; staff can help. Rr in hotel. 8-6 (1610 SE Paradise Cir, Crystal River; off US 19 W on Paradise Point; 352-795-7234)

River Safaris rents pontoon boats (26"-30" entries) for use on the

Homosassa River. Boats hold 5-20 people. Roll aboard from a ramp off the fixed dock; staff can help. 8-5 (10823 Yulee Dr; 3 mi W of US 19; 352-628-5222; 800-758-3474)

■ **BOAT TOURS**

Boat Rentals: Port Hotel

American Pro-Dive offers 1 1/2-hr sightseeing trips on a pontoon boat along the Crystal River. Roll aboard from the fixed dock; if tides are extreme, staff can lift you aboard in your WC. Winter 6-6; summer 7-6 (821 SE US 19, Crystal River; 352-563-0041; 800-291-3483)

Chassahowitzka River Tours offers 2 1/2- to 3-hr ecotours aboard a 31' pontoon boat through a 30,000-acre wildlife refuge accessible only by boat. 9-6 (Public boat ramp at the Chassahowitzka River Campground, 8600 CR 480, Chassahowitzka; W of US 19, 9 mi S of Homosassa; 352-382-0837)

Crystal River Dive Center offers 1-hr sightseeing tours on a pontoon boat or airboat in Kings Bay. Roll aboard the pontoon boat from the floating dock; the airboat is too narrow for WCs, but staff can help lift you onto a seat. (Best Western Hotel, 614 NW US 19, Crystal River; 352-795-6798; 800-444-1919)

Glass-Bottom Boat goes out along the Chassahowitzka River and Wildlife Refuge for 2 1/2-hr tours with up to 6 passengers on a 24' boat. The fixed dock is ramped; with advance notice, staff can help lift you in your WC down the step into the boat. Capt Karen can also pick you up at the Chassahowitzka River Park (see Campgrounds). Roll right up to the 5' glassed viewing area. Reservations; cooler provided; snacks for sale at dock; Rr at marina. Usually 9, 12 & 3 (Bait House, 8501 Miss Maggie Dr, Chassahowitzka; off US 19, 6 mi S of Homosassa; behind Jake's Bar & Grill; 352-382-3968)

River Safaris offers 75-min tours of the spring to see manatees or the back waters of the Homosassa River; 2 1/2-hr trips cover both areas. Roll aboard the pontoon boat from a ramp off the fixed dock; staff can help. 8-5 (10823 Yulee Dr; 3 mi W off US 19; 352-628-5222; 800-758-3474)

Scott Faulkenberg's Manatee Tours are morning rides for 6-12 people to observe and learn about manatees. Roll aboard the pontoon boat from the floating dock. (Pete's Pier, 1 SW 1 Pl, Crystal River; off Kings Bay Dr, .6 mi W of US 19; 866-352-7946)

■ **BOWLING**

Neffer Lanes, with advance notice, can ramp a lane for WC bowlers. Game room; snack bar; sports bar; Rr. Noon-mdnt (3655 S Suncoast Blvd; 352-628-3552)

Sportsmen's Bowl has a ramped entrance and staff can help a WC bowler down the 2 steps to the lanes. Bowling ball ramp; lane bumpers; game room; snack bar. 9am-varies (100 N Florida Ave, Inverness; 352-726-2873)

■ **CANOEING/KAYAKING**

Parks: Fort Cooper

Port Hotel & Marina rents canoes and tandem sit-on kayaks for Kings Bay. Staff can lift you from your WC on the floating dock or you can get out of your WC, sit on the edge of the boarding barge and slide 14" into the boats. Rr in hotel. 8-6 (1610 SE Paradise Cir, Crystal River; off US 19 W on Paradise Point; 352-795-7234)

■ **FISHING CHARTERS**

Capt Andrews is experienced with WC anglers and, with advance notice, can help lift you in your WC onto his bass boat. He specializes in fishing local rivers for bass and can meet you at an accessible dock. Let him know the type reel you prefer. (352-726-4748)

Galley Wench Charters fishes the flats, offshore reefs and wrecks. Try half/full days aboard a 24' T-Craft for up to 4 anglers or all-day offshore trips on a 34' Crusader for up to 6. Crew can lift you in your WC aboard either boat. Lunch can be arranged. (Capt John

Rogers 352-628-2421; cell 352-634-5257)

River Safaris can take you out for half/full-day fishing trips on a pontoon boat. Roll aboard from a ramp off the fixed dock; staff can help. 8-5 (10823 Yulee Dr; 3 mi W of US 19; 352-628-5222; 800-758-3474)

■ **FISHING-PARTY BOATS**

Apollo Deep-Sea Fishing offers full-day trips. With advance notice, crew can lift you aboard in your WC and reserve the more accessible fishing spots on deck. Drinks sold. Days vary 7:30-5 (1340 NW 20 Ave, Crystal River; 352-795-3757)

■ **FISHING PIERS**

Boat Ramps: Eden, Ft Island

SR 44 Park has a ramped, T-shaped, wood pier on the Crystal River. ADA picnic shelters; bait shops on US 19; Rr. Dawn-dusk (12073 W SR 44, Crystal River; 5 mi W of US 19; 352-795-2202)

Wallace Brooks Park has a wood, 140' pier on the Tsala Apopka Lake. ADA picnic tables; ADA playground; Rr. 7-dusk (Dampier St, Inverness; 352-726-3913)

■ **MUSEUMS**

Coastal Heritage Museum has historical displays such as a 1920's jail cell and doctor's office. You'll find some narrow passages to negotiate. $D. Tue-Fri 10-2 (532 Citrus Ave; 352-795-1755)

Ted Williams Museum celebrates the achievements of this famous Red Sox player with game footage and memorabilia. The Hitters Hall of Fame honors the game's greatest batters. Rr. $. Tue-Sun 10-4 (2455 N Citrus Hills Blvd, Hernando; off SR 486; 352-527-6566)

■ **PARKS**

Fort Cooper State Park, a 710-acre area around the spring-fed Lake Hoathlikaha has .5-mi paved paths through a shaded picnic area. The 1-mi Dogwood Trail and 2-mi Fort Site Trail are hard packed and have excellent birding. Except during droughts, the

170-acre lake offers canoeing and swimming. Staff can help you over the 50' of soft sand to the launch and help lift you into either a canoe or 2-person paddleboat. Traversing the 150', soft sand beach to the swim area is difficult in most WCs. Primitive tent camping is available on hard-packed terrain with water and an ADA port-o-let. ADA picnic tables; Rr. $. 8-dusk (3100 S Old Floral City Rd, Inverness; 2 mi S of Inverness, off US 41 S, E on Eden Dr, then N; 352-726-0315)

Homosassa Springs State Wildlife Park, formerly a private tourist attraction, is now a 180-acre habitat zoo and animal rehab center renovated to near state-of-the-art access. At the park entrance, the visitor center houses a large nature display, Manatee Education Center, unique gift shop and Rr. An elevator takes you up to a restaurant or down to a dock where you can roll aboard a pontoon boat for a 20-min narrated ride to the Wildlife Park (last ride at 4pm). At the W entrance to the Wildlife Park is a cafe and gift shop for children. The Children's Education Center has an interactive environmental exhibit and ongoing activities. Outside, able-bodied guests go down steps to an observatory below the water's surface to see manatees year-round; WC riders can see them from above. A 1-mi trail of elevated boardwalks, paved paths and crushed stone, takes you past crocodiles, gators, bobcats and other indigenous wildlife, not to mention the hippopotamus left over from tourist attraction days! Interpretive talks are throughout the day. $. 9-5:30 (9225 W Fish Bowl Dr; off US 19; 352-628-5343)

■ **PERFORMING ARTS**

Rock Crusher Canyon Music Park has a natural amphitheater among limerock cliffs and a concert hall where national and regional stars perform anything from Big Band and swing to country and jazz. General admission for the amphitheater is on a huge field; paved paths lead to WC seating on a raised area about midway to the stage. VIP seating is roped off front and center; staff can lift you from your WC onto a golf cart, transport you and lift you back into your WC in the VIP area. Generally gates open 2 hrs before performances; no reserved seating in either area. The Garden Pavilion is an inside hall with buffet dining and smaller shows; seating is cafe-style. VIP tickets to the amphitheater include dining at the Garden Pavilion. See Campgrounds. Rr, including port-a-lets at the amphitheater (275 S Rock Crusher Rd, Crystal River; from US 19, 2 mi E on W Venable St; 352-795-1313; 877-722-2696)

■ POOLS

Bicentennial Park is a 148-acre county park with a Jr Olympic pool. Lifeguards can help you transfer into the park's submersible WC and roll down a ramp into the water. A 1-hr Water Wellness Program (wkdy 12-1) is designed for folks with disabilities. Ball fields; tennis; playground; Rr. $. Apr-Oct hrs vary (501 N Baseball Pt, Crystal River; off US 19 E on Godfrey Ln, S on Lindbergh; 352-795-1478)

Whispering Pines Park has a Jr Olympic pool with a lift (fixed seat); lifeguards can help you transfer. Water aerobics classes; ADA playground; locker room; Rr. $. May wknds; Jun-Labor Day daily (SR 44 & Forest Dr, Inverness; 352-726-1995)

■ SCUBA/SNORKELING

Boat Rentals: Port Hotel

American Pro-Dive, experienced with disabled snorkelers and certified divers, offers 3-hr guided trips on which you may get close to manatees. Meet at the shop to get your gear, then drive to the dock in Homosassa where you can board by ramp or crew can lift you aboard in your WC. Crew can also lift you in and out of the water. Nov-May 6:30am & 9am (821 SE US 19, Crystal River; 352-563-0041; 800-291-3483)

Crystal River Dive Center has experience certifying disabled divers. Advance at your own speed. Staff lifts you from your WC in and out of water for the classes that are given in the springs. Speak to the manager, Darren Wilks, when making reservations. (Best Western Hotel, 614 NW US 19, Crystal River; 352-795-6798; 800-444-1919)

ACCOMMODATIONS

■ CAMPGROUNDS

Parks: Ft Cooper

Camp 'n' Water Campground has 6 acres with 73 WC-friendly RV/tent sites with pads, full hookups, picnic tables and grills. Sites 77A and 78A are nearest the bathhouse with grab bars, raised toilets and step-in showers. Cabins have 4 steps to enter. The marina has boat slips, a boat ramp and fixed dock on the Homosassa River, 5 mi from the Gulf. The park also rents canoes; WC paddlers can board from the boat ramp; staff may be able to help lift you aboard. Laundry; lounge; pool deck has 3 steps; playground on hard-packed dirt (11465 W Priest Ln,

Homosassa; from US 19 go W on W Halls River Rd/CR 490A, then S on Fishbowl Dr for 3 mi, SW on Mason Creek Rd, then 4 blocks N on Garcia; 352-628-2000)

Chassahowitzka River Campground is a county park with 40 shady acres along the river. It has 88 RV/tent sites; 40 have full hookups, 16 have water/elec only and the rest are primitive; all have picnic tables and grills on hard-packed terrain. The ADA bathhouse has raised toilets, roll-under sinks and roll-in showers with seats. There are fixed docks from which you can fish and, on the other side of the boathouse, a boat ramp near the

Chassahowitzka Spring. Staff can help lift you into a rental canoe, johnboat or 2-person paddleboat from the paved launch. Laundry; camp store; rec hall (8600 W Miss Maggie Dr/CR 480, Chassahowitzka; 1.8 mi W of US 19; 352-382-2200)

Encore Super Park has 30 acres with 250 RV sites; 5 are WC-friendly with pads, full hookups, picnic tables, fire pits and paved paths to the ramped bathhouse with wide doors, grab bars, raised toilets and step-in showers. You can fish from the banks of a canal and private lake or from the fixed and floating docks by the boat ramps. Rent a pontoon boat for up to 8 for half/full days; from the canal you can get onto Crystal River. Pool; laundry; rec room; tennis; playground on grass; camp store (11419 W Fort Island Tr/SR 44, Crystal River; 4 mi W of US 19; 352-795-3774; 888-783-6763)

Rock Crusher Canyon RV & Music Park has 400 wooded RV/tent sites with full hookups and picnic tables on level, hard-packed terrain. Paved paths lead to ADA bathhouses with roll-under sinks and roll-in showers with hand-held sprayers. Sometimes ticket packages are available for campers to weekend concerts or shows at the amphitheater and Garden Pavilion; see Performing Arts. A lake, once a quarry, has a 40' stretch of sandy beach to a swim area where the slope is gradual; paddleboats can be rented. You can also fish off the lake's flat banks. Hiking trails are planned for the 250-acre grounds. Pool; laundry; restaurant for shows at music park; camp store (275 S Rock Crusher Rd, Crystal River; from US 19, 2 mi E on W Venable St; 352-795-1313; 877-722-2696)

■ COTTAGES

American River Rendevous has 4 WC-friendly, ramped 2BR cottages, each with 2 full beds or 1 full and 2 twin beds (30" high/open frames), a full kitchen and full sofa bed in the living room. Standard bathrooms have wide doors, roll-under sinks and step-in showers. Next door, American Pro-Dive has pontoon boat rentals and fishing docks; see Boat Rentals. Glassed-in porch; linens included; picnic tables & grills; lounge; full restaurant (10386 W Halls River Rd; 352-628-2551; 800-291-3483)

■ MOTELS

Best Western Crystal River Resort has 4 ADA rooms, each with a king bed (20" high/platform), coffeepot and refrigerator. Rooms 2101 and 4107 have raised toilets, roll-under sinks and roll-in showers with hand-held sprayers and seats; others have tubs. A marina is on the property; see Boat Rentals, Boat Tours and Scuba. Pool; full restaurant/tiki bar. $$-$$$ (614 NW US 19, Crystal River; 352-795-3171; 800-435-4409)

Days Inn has ADA rooms, each with 2 full beds (22" high/open frames) and a bathroom with a raised toilet, roll-under sink and roll-in shower with a hand-held sprayer and seat. Free brkfst; pool; laundry; lounge. $-$$ (2380 NW US 19, Crystal River; 352-795-2111)

Plantation Inn has 7 ADA rooms, each with 2 full beds (23" high/open frames), a coffeepot, refrigerator and bathroom with a raised toilet and roll-under sink. Rooms 111 and 113 have roll-in showers with hand-held sprayers and seats; others have tubs. This resort lies along the Crystal River where you can fish from the seawall, use the boat ramp with fixed and floating docks and rent pontoon boats. Pool; tiki bar; full restaurants; marina. $$-$$$ (9301 W Fort Island Tr/SR 44, Crystal River; 352-795-4211; 800-632-6262)

Three Rivers Motel has 1 ADA room (#7) with a full bed (23" high/platform), full futon and bathroom with a raised toilet and roll-in shower with a hand-held shower and seat. It is next to the Homosassa Springs State Wildlife Park. $ (4891 S Suncoast Blvd; 352-628-6629)

NEW PORT RICHEY

Elfers, Holiday, Hudson, Land O'Lakes, Odessa, Port Richey

At Jay B Starkey Park, you can rent an accessible primitive cabin. You can also enjoy 3 pools with lifts, drive a horse-drawn cart, ride horseback, go sky diving and take a tour of a working cattle ranch.

Tourist Info
West Pasco Chamber: 5443 Main St, 34652; 727-842-7651

ACTIVITIES

■ BIKE TRAILS
Suncoast Trail is a paved, 12' wide bike and pedestrian path through a landscaped corridor along the Suncoast Parkway/SR 589. Ultimately the trail will run 42 miles S from the Hernando/Citrus county line through Pasco County to N Hillsborough County; currently 21 mi are complete, from SR 50 (W of Brooksville in Hernando) S to the future Ridge Rd exit (W of Port Richey). You can access the trail from all county and state roads intersecting the parkway. In Pasco, parking and Rr are at Crews Lake Park; see Parks. Along the trail are interpretive and rest areas. Contact the Suncoast Parkway at 813-558-1117. Dawn-dusk

■ BOAT TOURS
Miss Daisy offers 2-hr tours along the coast and out into the Gulf where dolphins are frequent companions. Roll up to the 40' deck boat where the capt can lift you in your WC up the step and onboard. Reservations; snacks & soda sold onboard; Rr in restaurant at dock. 10:30, 1 & sunset (4927 US 19 S; behind Leverocks; 727-819-1754)

■ FISHING CHARTERS
Mijoy Adventures customizes trips for up to 4. Fish offshore or inshore in the Gulf and, if you like, take some time for swimming and picnicking. The husband and wife team can help lift you in your WC aboard the 28' boat and choose a dock that best suits your needs. (727-842-7605)

■ FISHING-PARTY BOATS
Miss Virginia Deep-Sea Fishing takes full-day trips on the Gulf. Crew can lift you from your WC aboard the 58' boat then back into your WC. There's an open area toward the back where crew can secure your WC. Crew can also help you over the 6" lip into the cabin and into booth seats for lunch, sold onboard. Reservations; cooler available for snacks. 8-4 (Port Richey Marina, 4932 Limestone Dr, Port Richey; 1st left on US 19 N of bridge crossing Cotee River; 727-862-5516)

■ FISHING PIERS
Parks: Crews Lake
Anclote Gulf Park is a 31-acre county park with a lighted, 400' ADA pier over a bay. ADA playground; ADA picnic tables; bait shop nearby; Rr. 24 hrs (2305 Baillie's Bluff Rd, Holiday)

■ HORSEBACK RIDING
Quantum Leap Farm specializes in horseback riding for adults, age 16-75, with a range of disabilities. An NARHA-certified riding instructor leads warm-up sessions (with therapeutic goals), lessons, trail rides and even polo lasting from 15 min to 1 hr. Staff can help you mount from a mounting ramp. Or, you can drive a horse-drawn cart. If you like, help groom your steed. You must submit a medical release from your physician. Reservations; Rr. Mon, Wed, Fri & Sat (10504 Woodstock Rd, Odessa; from SR 54, S on Gunn Hwy, W on Crescent

Rd .8 mi then W to the end of Woodstock; 813-920-9250)

■ **KAYAKING**

Adventure Kayak rents kayaks for half/full days and offers 3-hr guided trips on the bays and rivers throughout the region. See Tampa Bay: Clearwater: Kayaking pg 79 (5446 Baylea Ave, Port Richey; 727-848-8099)

■ **PARKS**

Crews Lake Park is a 111-acre county park with a wood, 400' pier over the lake and a paved, .5-mi bike trail. A mulched, 2.5-mi, marked nature trail leads to an observation tower ramped to the 3'-high 1st level. Just outside the park, you can access the Suncoast Trail; see Bike Trails. ADA picnic shelters; Rr. Dawn-dusk (16729 Crews Lake Dr, Shady Hills; from US 19, go E on SR 52, N on Shady Hill Rd, then E; 727-861-3038)

Jay B Starkey Wilderness Park is an 8069-acre park with a paved, 3.5-mi bike trail and a 1-mi loop road, both good for cycling. See Campgrounds. ADA picnic shelters; ADA playground; Rr. Dawn-dusk (10500 Wilderness Park Rd; 727-834-3247)

■ **PERFORMING ARTS**

Show Palace Dinner Theater features Broadway musicals with an optional buffet. WC seating on the sides; Rr. Matinee & evening performances vary (16128 US 19, Hudson; 727-863-7949; 888-655-7469)

■ **POOLS**

The county operates the following outdoor, Jr Olympic pools with lifts (sling seats), all open noon-7pm from Memorial Day-Labor Day and Sep weekends. Lifeguards cannot help you transfer, but will lower you into the pool. All have ADA picnic tables and locker rooms with roll-in showers and Rr.

Grove Park Community Center (4145 Fairmont Dr, Elfers; 727-834-3285)

Land O'Lakes Recreation (3032 Collier Pkwy, Land O'Lakes; 813-929-1222)

Veteran's Memorial Park (14333 Hick Rd, Hudson; 727-863-3033)

■ **SHOOTING RANGES**

Silver Dollar Trap Shoot Club has skeet, 5 stand and a trap-shooting course. Gun rental; restaurant; Rr. Closed Aug; Oct-Apr Wed-Sun; May-Sep Wed & wknd; 10-5 (17202 Target Way, Odessa; 813-920-3231

■ **SKYDIVING**

Skydive City offers tandem jumping for quads and paras who are in good physical condition with normal blood pressure, no cardiac conditions or osteoporosis. T K Hayes, General Manager, recommends you come observe so you can determine together whether you can safely jump. (Zephyrhills Airport, 40440 Chancey Rd, Zephyrhills; 800-404-9399)

■ **TOURS**

Flatwoods Adventures offers 2-hr tours of the Anclote River Ranch, a 2900-acre, working cattle ranch in operation since the early 1900's. Board the shaded safari bus (with lock downs) by ramp. Discover how pioneers lived from the land as well as the history of cracker cowboys and today's cattle ranch techniques. Included is a stroll through a cypress swamp on an elevated boardwalk. Horseback tours (Wed, Fri & Sat) are available for able-bodied guests. Reservations; gift shop; picnic shelter; CRr. Mon-Sat hrs vary (12959 SR 54, Odessa; 9 mi E of US 19, 16 mi W of I-75; 813-926-1133; 877-734-9453)

ACCOMMODATIONS

■ **CABINS/CAMPGROUNDS**

Jay B Starkey Wilderness Park has a primitive, ramped cabin (#6) with 4 bunk beds to sleep 8 and the bare necessities: a table, chairs and light. Outside are paved paths to a private patio with table, grill and fire pit and to an ADA bathhouse with roll-under sinks

and large step-in showers. Bring linens
and utensils. Tent sites 12-14 are fairly
flat, closest to the bathhouse and have
picnic tables, grills and fire pits. (10500
Wilderness Park Rd; 727-834-3247)
■ MOTELS
Holiday Inn Express has 5 ADA rooms,
each with a king or 2 queen beds (30"

high/open frames) and a bathroom
with a raised toilet. Two rooms have
roll-under sinks and roll-in showers
with hand-held sprayers and seats;
others have tub/showers. Free brkfst;
pool. $-$$ (10826 US 19 N, Port Richey;
727-869-9999)

STEINHATCHEE
Cross City, Keaton Beach, Old Town, Perry, Shired Island, Suwannee

Peak season in the Steinhatchee area is summer when people come to snorkel
for scallops. But year-round you can fish, boat and even hunt for exotic African
animals. Another unusual treat in this rural area is a tearoom in Perry. Local
lodging ranges from rugged camping to upscale cottages with not much ADA in
between.

Tourist Info
Dixie County Chamber: Box 547, Cross City, 32628; 352-498-5454
Perry/Taylor County Chamber: 428 N Jefferson St, Box 892, Perry, 32347; 800-
257-8881
Web sites: www.dixiecounty.org

ACTIVITIES

■ BIKE TRAILS
Nature Coast State Trail is a 32-mi,
rails-to-trails, paved bike path that
parallels US 19 from Chiefland N to
Cross City with a 7-mi jaunt from Fanning Springs State Park E to Trenton.
The trail is flat with gentle grades; just
NW of Fanning Springs, the trail goes
across a bumpy, but scenic, historic
trestle bridge over the Suwannee
River. Along US 19 are plenty of parking spots and small towns with Rr; the
trek to Trenton has few facilities. Each
trailhead has parking at an old railroad
depot, some include Rr. For a trail
map, call Manatee Springs (352-493-
6072) or Fanning Springs (352-463-
3420) State Parks.
■ BOAT RAMPS
Gornto Spring has a boat ramp and
floating dock, popular with canoeists
and anglers, in a small, rural county
park next to the Suwannee River. The

banks of the swim area at the spring
are steep and inaccessible. See Campgrounds. 24 hrs (E end of CR 353; E off
CR 349, 12 mi N of Old Town)
Hinton Landing has a boat ramp and a
floating dock on the Suwannee River.
This is a 2-acre, wooded county park
where people canoe, fish and swim off
the floating and fixed docks. See
Campgrounds. Rr. 24 hrs (CR 317; from
Old Town, go 3 mi S on CR 349, E 2 mi
on CR 346A, then S)
Horseshoe Beach is a Gulfside county
park with a boat ramp (no dock)
popular with canoeists. Due to many
storms, there is no longer a beach, but
there are picnic shelters with lovely
views. Rr. 24 hrs (8 Ave, Horseshoe
Bch; off CR 351, 15 mi S of Cross City)
Jenna, a Dixie County boat ramp has a
floating dock at the mouth of the
Steinhatchee River. Park alongside the
road. 24 hrs (W end of CR 358)

Keaton Beach has a lighted, county boat ramp with a floating dock on the Gulf. 24 hrs (20131 Beach Rd, Keaton Bch)

Miller's Marine has a boat ramp and floating docks on the Suwannee River. Bait shop & Rr, not ADA, at marina. $. 7:30am-7pm (Big Bradford Rd, Suwannee; W end of CR 349 S, 23 mi S of US 19/98; 352-542-7349)

■ **BOAT RENTALS**

Pace's Cottages rents pontoon boats, with bimini tops, for up to 8 people for a day on the Gulf and Steinhatchee River. Roll aboard from the floating dock at Sea Hag Marina. Bait shop; Rr, not ADA, at dock. 7-5 (321 Riverside Dr; 352-498-0061)

River Haven Marina rents a 23' deck boat and a 21' pontoon boat, with a 40hp motor, for use along the Gulf flats (2-hr minimum). The entry gates are too narrow for standard WCs, but with advance notice, staff may be able to lift you aboard from your WC on the floating dock and return you to your WC onboard. Bait shop; convenience store; Rr, with 29" doorway. 7-5 (1110 River Side Dr; 352-498-0709; 877-907-0709)

■ **FISHING CHARTERS**

Capt Brooke has a 25' flats boat and offers 8-hr trips for up to 4 anglers and 5-hr flyfishing for 2. From the floating dock, roll aboard the front deck of the boat, then the capt can help you down the step where you can sit in front of the center console. Cooler provided; Rr (Palm Grove Fishing Lodge, 810 SR 51 N; 352-498-3721; 800-498-5057)

Capt Cronk offers half/full-day offshore grouper or inshore trout and redfish trips for up to 4 anglers. The capt can help lift you from your WC on the floating dock and into a boat seat on the 25' boat. Rr, not ADA, at marina (Capt 352-498-7317; Sea Hag Marina, 322 Riverside Dr; 352-498-3008)

Capt Shearin offers offshore grouper/ snapper charters for up to 6 in a 31' Morgan with a 12' x 12' fishing cockpit. The capt can help lift you aboard in your WC from the floating dock. 10% discount to disabled anglers; Rr, not ADA, at marina (Capt 912-897-2706; Sea Hag Marina, 322 Riverside Dr; 352-498-3008)

Lite-Line Charters specializes in light tackle and flyfishing in the saltwater flats for half/full days. Capt LeNeave can help lift you from your WC on the floating dock and into a seat aboard the skiff. Rr, not ADA, at marina (Capt 352-374-4003; Sea Hag Marina, 322 Riverside Dr; 352-498-3008)

River Haven Marina can arrange for a guide who can take you out for fishing trips along the Gulf flats and is able to board you in your WC from the floating dock at the marina. (1110 River Side Dr; 352-498-0709; 877-907-0709)

■ **FISHING PIERS**

Parks: Lower Suwannee

Hodges Park, a county beach, has a ramped, 700', wood pier along a deep canal as it empties into the Gulf. Picnic shelter; Rr. Dawn-dusk (21275 Keaton Bch Dr, Keaton Bch; 17 mi S of Perry)

■ **HUNTING**

Dixie Sportsman Hunting Lodge offers hunting on a 1000-acre private ranch from a swamp buggy not only for trophy deer and wild hog, but also African game and American bison! You can roll by ramp onto the 11'-high hunting platform on the roof of the buggy, parked in a deep ditch for boarding. Hunting blinds are also accessible. If you choose, stay in the cracker-style 3BR lodge that sleeps up to 6, with a queen, 2 bunk and 2 twin beds (20" high/open frames), wide doors, AC, kitchen, laundry and a bathroom with a raised toilet and step-in shower. Meals are included. Staff also offers guests night fishing trips and airboat tours along the Suwannee River or in the Gulf. (SR

358; E of US 19, 6 mi N of Cross City;
352-498-3809)

■ KAYAKING

Wild Florida offers 4-hr guided kayak
tours along the coastal marshes near
the mouth of the Steinhatchee River.
The launch site is a flat shoreline
where guides can help lift you from
your WC into a solo sit-on or tandem
sit-in kayak. You must have upper
body strength and a companion. The
married team of guides combines professional ecology and instructor certification, so you can anticipate a fascinating and safe expedition, daytime,
sunset or full moon. Trips include
lunch or snacks; during breaks you can
remain in your kayak or guides can
help lift you out. Call to discuss your
abilities and decide which tour works
best for you. (352-373-6047; 877-945-
3928)

■ MUSEUMS

Forest Capital Museum has dioramas
and exhibits on the forestry and turpentine industries in the old and
nowadays. Down a pine-needle path
you can get to a cracker-style homestead from 1900 where staff can help
lift you up 3' to the front porch. A
Florida Forest Festival is held here
each Oct. ⚲. Thu-Mon 9-5 (204 Forest
Park Dr, Perry; 850-584-3227)

■ PARKS

**Lower Suwannee National Wildlife
Refuge** includes 29,000 unspoiled
acres on the N or Dixie County side of
the Suwannee River. The 9-mi Dixie
Mainline Rd has interpretive signs as
you drive through cypress forest,
hardwood floodplains, pine forest and
marsh to Shired Island on the Gulf. Off
Mainline Rd, just N of CR 349, is Salt
Creek with a 50' fishing pier overlooking a salt marsh. Wkdy 7:30-4 (from
US 19 at Old Town, go SW on CR 349
then NW on Dixie Mainline Rd; 352-
493-0238)

Shired Island Park is a lovely, remote,
2-acre, soft sand county beach on the
Gulf surrounded by wetlands. There is
no path to the beach, but you can
park next to 6 picnic shelters with
great vistas. A boat ramp (no dock) is
on the Gulf. See Campgrounds. Rr. 24
hrs (end of CR 357, Shired Island; 11 mi
S of CR 351)

■ SHOPPING

Sister's Mercantile is a historic building housing a Tearoom & Gallery, with
home decor and gourmet foods, and
gege's Emporium, a baby shop. The
Tearoom (Tue-Fri 11-4; Sat 11-2) serves
light and high tea. Rr. Tue-Fri 10-6;
Sat 10-3 (121 E Green St, Perry; 850-
838-2021)

ACCOMMODATIONS

■ CAMPGROUNDS

Hinton Landing has 20 wooded RV/
tent sites on hard-packed grass, each
with non-potable water and a picnic
table; some have elec. Bring drinking
water. See Boat Ramps. No reservations; Rr, no showers (CR 317; from
Old Town, go 3 mi S on CR 349, E 2 mi
on CR 346A, then S; 352-498-1206)

Miller's Marine has 60 RV/tent sites
with full hookups and picnic tables on
level, hard-packed terrain along a river
marsh or canal to the Suwannee River.
The ramped bathhouse has step-in
showers (with 4" lips) large enough

for a seat. Houseboats (with 24" entries to the interior) and 13' Whalers
are rented at the marina where there
are floating docks. (Big Bradford Rd,
Suwannee; W end of CR 349 S, 23 mi S
of US 19/98; 352-542-7349)

Shired Island Park has 10 RV/tent sites
on hard-packed grass along the Gulf,
each with non-potable water/elec, picnic table and grills. Campers often pull
alongside the picnic shelters. Bring
drinking water. See Parks. No reservations; Rr, no showers (W end of CR
357, Shired Island; 11 mi S of CR 351;
352-498-1206)

■ COTTAGES

Pace's Cottages has 2 WC-friendly units, each with wide doorways, 2 full beds and 1 twin bed (24" high/open frames), a microwave, refrigerator, coffeepot, porch and bathroom with a raised toilet and step-in shower with grab bars. The wooded grounds are across the street from Sea Hag Marina with pontoon boat rentals and fishing charters. $$-$$$ (321 Riverside Dr; 352-498-0061)

River Haven Marina & Motel has a 2BR cottage with 2 full beds (open frames), a standard bathroom (21.5" entry) with a tub, a full sofa bed in the living room, portable twin bed and full kitchen. There are also 4 motel rooms, each with a 6" step at the entry, 2 full beds and a standard bathroom with a 21.5" entry and tub. The marina offers fishing charters, pontoon boat rentals and fishing off the docks. Picnic tables are on the back porch of the marina shop. $ (1110 Riverside Dr; 352-498-0709; 877-907-0709)

Steinhatchee Landing Resort has 3 ADA cottages (and a WC-friendly unit) under pines and moss-draped oaks along the Steinhatchee River. The 2BR/2BA Cottage (#21) is ramped and has a king and 2 full beds (21" high/open frames), a living room, full kitchen, porch with a Jacuzzi and master bathroom with a roll-in shower with a hand-held sprayer. Two honeymoon cottages (#22 and 24) are ramped and have twin beds (open frames), full kitchens and bathrooms with hand-held sprayers in the tub/shower. In the Victorian-style main house is a ramped, WC-friendly 2BR/2BA condo (#8), with a king and 2 full beds (23" high/open frames), a living room, full kitchen, porch and roomy bathrooms with 26" wide doors and tub/showers. The resort rents pontoon boats (28" entries) that you can roll aboard from the floating dock and take 3 mi to the Gulf of Mexico. You can also fish from the dock. Free brkfst; pool; canoe rentals; gourmet restaurant for dinner; tennis; playground. $$$ (CR 51; 8 mi W of US 19; 352-498-3513; 800-584-1709)

■ MOTELS

Days Inn has 2 ADA rooms, each with 2 full beds (22" high/open frames), a refrigerator, microwave and bathroom with a raised toilet and tub. Pool; laundry; restaurant nearby. $ (2777 S Byron Butler Pkwy, Perry; 850-584-5311)

Steinhatchee River Inn has 8 ground-floor suites, each with a step at the door, 2 full beds (open frames), and in the living room a queen sofa bed, small refrigerator and coffeepot. Bathrooms are standard; room #101 has a grab bar in the tub/shower. This hotel is across from River Haven Marina and is affiliated with Steinhatchee Landing where you can rent canoes and a pontoon boat. Pool; picnic area with grills. $-$$ (Riverside Dr; 352-498-4049)

We want to hear from you!
Your comments and suggestions
are important to us.
If you find something new,
please tell us about it.
If you've had a disappointing experence,
we'd like to know that too.

You can either e-mail us at:
wheelchairsonthego@yahoo.com

Or send your comments to:
Wheelchairs on the Go
14074 Egret Lane
Clearwater, FL 33762

As a service to our readers only,
you can access updates at
www.wheelchairsonthego.com/pages/2/updates

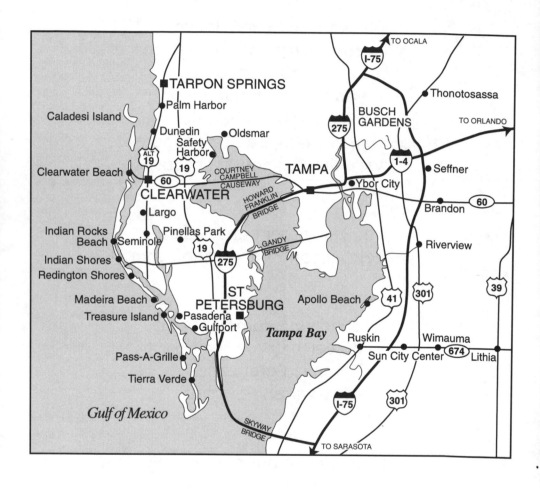

TAMPA BAY

CLEARWATER
Clearwater Beach, Dunedin, Indian Rocks Beach, Largo, Palm Harbor, Safety Harbor

Clearwater is a great destination point for WC riders. You'll find beach wheelchairs at Clearwater Beach, Sand Key Park and the spectacular Caledesi and Honeymoon Islands; check out the private tours at the last two parks. You can also enjoy a wonderful sailing program, swimming pools, numerous boat tours, fishing, horseback riding, even parasailing and walleyball. Both Safety Harbor and Dunedin have charming downtowns with galleries and artsy shops. Dunedin's Scottish legacy is best evidenced by the Highland Games and Scottish Festival held here every spring (727-736-5066).

Tourist Info
Clearwater/Pinellas Suncoast Welcome Center: 2001 Ulmerton Rd/SR 688, 33762; 727-573-1449; 888-425-3279
Dunedin Chamber: 301 Main St, 34698; 727-733-3197
St Pete/Clearwater Visitors Bureau: 14450 46 St N, Suite 108, 33762; 727-464-7200
Hotline for entertainment (727-825-3333) is a 24-hr phone line with taped information on current and upcoming artistic and cultural events.
Web sites: www.floridasbeach.com; www.visitClearwaterFlorida.com; www.clearwater-fl.com

Transportation
PSTA buses have lifts and run 5am-10pm. (727-530-9911)
Demand Response Service has lift-equipped vehicles for folks who need door-to-door service and are pre-qualified. If you are visiting and are certified at home, you can take 21 trips through this service. (727-530-9921)
The Trolley, with lifts, runs every 20-30 min along the beach on Gulf Blvd, 5am-10pm, from the Hurricane Restaurant in Pass-a-Grille N to Sheraton at Sand Key. From 11-11, trolleys run from the beach to BayWalk and the Pier in downtown St

Pete. Some stops are also on PSTA bus routes. (727-530-9911)
Clearwater Yellow Cab has a van with a lift serving all of Pinellas County. (727-799-2222)
The Limo can take you to and from the airport, with 24-hr notice, in a lift-equipped van. (727-572-1111; 800-282-6817)

WC Resources
Custom Mobility repairs WCs. Wkdy 8-4:30 (12345 Starkey Rd; 727-539-8119)

ACTIVITIES

■ ATTRACTIONS
Clearwater Marine Aquarium is a marine wildlife rehab and education center with presentations every 30 min at the dolphin, otter and sea turtle exhibits. Examine the mangrove exhibit and a tank of sharks and stingrays. See Boat Tours. Rr. $. Wkdy 9-5; Sat 9-4; Sun 11-4 (249 Windward Passage, Clearwater Bch; just W of downtown, from Memorial Cswy/ SR 60, N on Island Way, then W; 727-441-1790)
Pier 60 elevates evenings to an art form Thu-Mon at dusk with magicians, jugglers, musicians and craftspeople. (W end of SR 60, Clearwater Bch)

■ BASEBALL
Challenger Baseball has experienced coaches who offer instruction and fun, scoreless games for kids, age 5 through high school students with a range of disabilities. Buddies can help players in all aspects of the game and drop-ins are welcome. Call Jim Scheuerman 727-441-9047. Mar-May Sat 9-11 (Sid Lickton Field, 714 Saturn Ave; off Drew St)
Spirited All Stars are a team of kids, age 5 through high school students with a range of disabilities, who compete in fun games against age-appropriate, able-bodied kids. Drop-ins are welcome. Call Dan Martin 727-397-8157. Mar-May Fri 6:30-8pm; Sat 9-11 (Seminole Jr Warhawks Athletic Assn Complex, 11500 125 St N, Largo; next to Walsingham Park)

■ BEACHES
*Caladesi Island is a 600-acre barrier island state park accessible by private boat and ferry (hourly starting at 10am from Honeymoon Island or downtown Clearwater; 727-734-5263). Board and disembark by ramp and floating dock. Take boardwalks from the picnic shelters by the docks, to an undeveloped soft sand beach. With 24-hr notice (727-469-5942), you can borrow a beach WC at Honeymoon Island for an excursion to Caladesi. Snack bar; Rr. $. 8-dusk (Dunedin, 727-469-5918)
*Clearwater Beach loans self-propelling beach WCs (removable arms; attachable umbrellas) at the lifeguard stand (9:30-4), just S of Pier 60. If possible, park by Pier 60 with a paved path to the pier for fishing, a large ramped picnic shelter and easy access to the beach WC. Concessions; beach shop; Rr here & at the South Beach Pavilion (W end of SR 60, Clearwater Bch; 727-462-6963)
Eldorado Ave, in a residential area, has 3 short boardwalks to decks ramped to the sand; each is a great spot for sunset. No facilities (W end of SR 60, Clearwater Bch; W off Mandalay Ave onto Bohemia Cir that ends at Eldorado Ave, continue N)
*Honeymoon Island is a 400-acre state park on a barrier island connected by causeway to the mainland. At the drawbridge on the N side of the causeway, is a concrete platform (protected from cars that park along the causeway shoulders) for fishing in the Intracoastal. Call 24 hrs in advance to reserve the beach WC (removable arms). On the island is a hard-packed sand nature trail with some soft spots. Fish from a ramped seawall by the Bird Observation Area. ADA picnic tables; bath-

house; Rr. $. 8-dusk (W end of Curlew Rd/SR 586, N of Dunedin; 727-469-5942)

Indian Rocks Beach has a boardwalk to the beach. Bathhouse; restaurants nearby (1700 Gulf Blvd, Indian Rocks Bch; between 17 Ave & 18 Ave)

Mandalay Park Public Beach has a 20' wide, elevated concrete overlook on the beach. Restaurants nearby (Rockaway St, Clearwater Bch; W off Mandalay Ave)

*Sand Key Park is a 95-acre county beach with beach WCs (swing-away arms; drink holders) that can be borrowed at the lifeguard stand (9:30-4) on the sand. If you are alone, ask any park employee to get the WC for you. From parking you can access a boardwalk that takes you about 450' from the water's edge. ADA picnic shelters; grills; vending machines; umbrellas & chair concessions; $ parking; outdoor showers; Rr. 7-dusk (1060 Gulf Blvd, Clearwater Bch; just S of Clearwater Pass Bridge; 727-588-4852)

■ **BIKE TRAILS**

St Pete: Handcycles

Dunedin Causeway has a 2.5-mi, paved trail from the Pinellas Trail (at Curlew Rd/SR 586) over the causeway to Honeymoon Island State Park; see Beaches. The trail is separated from the road but is close as the causeway goes over drawbridges. Along the way you'll see sunbathers, wind surfers and more. Find parking & Rr at Honeymoon and at Publix supermarket on Curlew Rd/SR 586.

East-West Trail is a 4.5-mi paved trail undergoing many improvements and linking several sports complexes with lovely parks. Presently the most convenient stretch is the 1.5 mi between the Long Center (1501 N Belcher Rd) heading E under US 19 to Fairwood Ave where you can enjoy Moccasin Lake Nature Park (see Parks). Both parks have parking and Rr. East of Fairwood Ave, before McMullen Booth Rd/CR 611, is a long steep slope that you can bypass using the sidewalk along Drew St. By Oct 2003, a bridge will cross the busy McMullen Booth Rd. From Cooper's Bayou N through Philippe Park in Safety Harbor is a lovely meander along Old Tampa Bay. By 2005, the trail will link to the Pinellas Trail and by 2007, to Clearwater Beach. See Handcycles. Call Jon Russell at Clearwater City Parks 727-562-4811.

Pinellas Trail extends 34 mi from St Pete N to Tarpon Springs along an abandoned railroad route parallel to Alt US 19. The best WC access points for hassle-free parking and room for transfers to a handcycle in Clearwater are: Seminole City Park at 7464 Ridge Rd, Seminole, 727-391-0204; and Taylor Park at 1100 8 Ave SW, Largo, 727-584-7448. In Dunedin use Publix supermarket (on the NE corner of Curlew Rd/SR 586 & Alt US 19) or Youth Guild Park (604 Buena Vista Dr N; just W of Hammock Park); see Parks: Hammock. See St Pete: Bike Trails. (Trail Supervisor, 12020 Walsingham Rd, Largo; 727-549-6099)

■ **BOAT RAMPS**

Disc Golf: Cliff Stephens. Misc: Clearwater Rec. Parks: John Chestnut, Philippe Park

Belleair Boat Ramp has a floating dock on the Intracoastal. Bait shop; Rr. 24 hrs (3900 West Bay Dr; 727-586-3474)

Clearwater Marina does not have a ramp but does have a WC lift for private boaters at the fuel dock in the SE corner of the marina. You must stand to make the transfer or friends must lift you into the lift's fixed seat on chains; staff lowers you aboard into a boat seat or your WC (6:30-6:30). Or you can bring the seat, chains and hook from your own lift and attach them. After hours, you need a hook on a pole to unzip the cover of the lift. Rr. (25 Causeway Blvd, Clearwater Bch; 727-462-6954)

Dunedin Marina has a paved boat ramp, fixed docks and WC hoists on the Intracoastal. Contact the Harbormaster (8-5) to help with the WC lifts (sling seats); at dock-level is a bell to his 2nd floor office. The end of the pier, with day boat slips, is reserved for fishing. Nearby is the 4-acre Edgewater Park with an ADA playground and Rr. $. 24 hrs (51 Main St, Dunedin; 727-298-3030)

Seminole St Boat Ramp has a floating dock on the Intracoastal. Picnic tables; bait shop. $ (Seminole St; 727-443-6011)

Walsingham Park has a ramp and floating dock on the Walsingham Reservoir. No gas motors are allowed. (12615 102 Ave, Largo; 727-549-6142)

■ **BOAT TOURS**

Capt Memo's Pirate Cruise aboard a swashbuckling, 70', bright red pirate ship is probably the most surprising sight in the Intracoastal. Staff can help you board by ramp. The 2-hr cruises run 4 times daily with great pirate schmaltz and frequent dolphin sightings. Rr. 9-5 (Clearwater Bch Marina, 25 Causeway Blvd, Clearwater Bch; 727-446-2587)

Encounters with Dolphins runs 1 1/2- to 2-hr trips several times a day to dolphin watch in the Gulf. Roll aboard the 1st level of the covered deck boat. Reservations. 10-5 (Clearwater Bch Marina, 25 Causeway Blvd, Clearwater Bch; 727-466-0375)

Sea Life Safari is a 2 1/2-hr cruise narrated by a Clearwater Marine Aquarium biologist who discusses the sea creatures pulled up in a trolling net and the wildlife at island bird sanctuaries. Staff can help you roll aboard by ramp. The trip stops for 15 min to shell at the inaccessible Compass Island. Rr in Aquarium. 12:45 & 3:30 (249 Windward Passage, Clearwater Bch; take Memorial Cswy/SR 60 W of downtown, N on Island Way, then W; 727-462-2628)

Sea Screamer offers 1-hr trips that combine sightseeing along the beaches and a 40-mph thrill ride. If the weather is warm, the capt will be sure to get you wet! Roll up a ramp and staff takes you down 3 steps into the boat. 12, 2 & 4 (Clearwater Bch Marina, 25 Causeway Blvd, Clearwater Bch; 727-447-7200)

Show Queen resembles a Mississippi paddleboat and offers daily 2-hr lunch and dinner cruises. The 1st deck, including an outside area, is accessible. Rr. 9-5 (Clearwater Bch Marina, 25 Causeway Blvd, Clearwater Bch; 727-461-3113)

Starlite Majesty offers lunch, dinner and dance cruises, from 2 to 3 1/2 hrs long. If you cannot go up a flight of stairs, advise the reservationist to seat you at tables on the 1st deck where the dance floor is located. 9-5 (Clearwater Bch Marina, 25 Causeway Blvd, Clearwater Bch; 727-462-2628)

■ **BOWLING**

Liberty Lanes has bowling ball ramps, bumper bowling, glow-in-the-dark bowling, game room, restaurant, bar and Rr. 9am-closing varies (11401 Starkey Rd, Largo; 727-397-3947)

■ **DINNER THEATERS**

Bill Irle Early Bird Dinner Theater offers luncheon matinees Thu and Sat at 11 and dinner shows Thu-Sun at 4. Buffet service and all tables are accessible. Rr (1411 N Ft Harrison Ave; 727-446-5898)

Mystery Dinner Theater is an audience participation mystery with dinner, no stage and lots of corny fun. Rr. Fri-Sat (Belleview Biltmore Hotel, 25 Belleview Blvd, Clearwater Bch; 727-584-3490)

■ **DISC GOLF**

Cliff Stephens Park has paved paths and an accessible fitness trail winding under huge oaks. An 18-hole disc golf course is on grass and hard-packed terrain. Use the boat ramp to launch non-motorized boats onto Alligator Lake for some good fishing and plenty of gators. Or, fish off a dock on either side of Fairwood Ave. ADA picnic tables; Rr. Dawn-dusk (801 Fairwood Ave; next to Moccasin Lake Nature Park)

■ **FISHING CHARTERS**

Capt Blackmore can accommodate 2 able-bodied and 2 WC anglers on his 22' center console boat for inshore and near-shore trips using light tackle. If you like, spend some time sightseeing as well. The capt can help lift you aboard in your WC at an accessible dock. (813-831-8987)

Gulf Stream II is a 51' diesel with an AC

cabin that offers half/full-day deep-sea fishing charters for up to 4 anglers. Capt Foster and crew can lift you aboard in your WC or you can use the lift at the marina (see Boat Ramps). (Slip 34, Clearwater Bch Marina, 25 Causeway Blvd, Clearwater Bch; 727-442-6339)

Need Two offers 4- to 8-hr fishing trips using spin tackle, bait casting or fly rods for up to 3 anglers in an 18' flats boat on the flats and back bays. Full-day trips are split, 4 hrs in the morning and 4 hrs in the evening, to take advantage of the best fishing times. You can board by electric davits. (Clearwater Bch Marina, 25 Causeway Blvd, Clearwater Bch; 727-449-2449)

■ **FISHING-PARTY BOATS**

Double Eagle offers 4-hr trips (at 1 and 5) and 8-hr trips (at 9) on the Gulf. Crew can lift you aboard in your WC and over the lip into the cabin with a snack bar. (Clearwater Bch Marina, 25 Causeway Blvd, Clearwater Bch; 727-446-1653)

Queen Fleet has a 90' boat that goes out on 4-hr trips (at 8 and 1) and 8-hr trips (at 9). Depending on tides, you can roll aboard or crew can lift you aboard in your WC and over the lip into the cabin with a snack bar. (Clearwater Bch Marina, 25 Causeway Blvd, Clearwater Bch; 727-446-7666)

■ **FISHING PIERS**

Beaches: Honeymoon. Disc Golf: Cliff Stephens.

Pier 60 is an 1100', lighted, steel pier for fishing on the Gulf. Bait shop; Rr. 24 hrs (W end of SR 60, Clearwater Bch)

Safety Harbor Pier is a 650', lighted wood pier on Old Tampa Bay. Rr, dusk-dawn. 24 hrs (750 Main St, Safety Harbor)

■ **FITNESS TRAILS**

Disc Golf: Cliff Stephens

■ **HANDCYCLES**

St Pete: Handcycles

■ **HORSEBACK RIDING**

Medicine Horse, a member of NARHA, offers disabled folks leisure riding, long-term hippotherapy and trail riding with able-bodied family members, all by appointment. A rider must be strong enough to sit up, remain balanced and help with mounting. Staff can lift children onto the horse. Adults use a ramped mounting block and transfer from WC to saddle. (4550 Ulmerton Rd/SR 688; 727-323-3454)

■ **KAYAKING**

Adventure Kayak rents kayaks for half/full days and offers 3-hr guided trips on the bays and rivers throughout the region. Choose solo or tandem, sit-in or sit-on kayaks. With advance notice on rentals, staff may be able to transport kayaks to the launch site of your choice and pick up the boats at an agreed upon hour. Explain your abilities and interests so staff can suggest appropriate trips. Staff can help lift you into the kayak. (3011 Alt US 19, Palm Harbor; 727-784-6357)

■ **MISC**

Clearwater Recreation Center offers a range of activities for youth and adults, from art and billiard lessons to cards and dances. Outside you can fish off a seawall and use a boat ramp with a floating dock on the Intracoastal (24 hrs). Paved paths to ADA picnic tables; fitness room; game room; lighted tennis; basketball courts; ball fields; Rr. Wkdy 7am-8:45pm; Sat noon-3:45 (69 Bay Esplanade, Clearwater Bch; 727-462-6138)

SCION is the Spinal Cord Injury Network that holds guest lectures, discussions, social events and activities each month. Call Sherri Bastress for schedule. (Health South Rehabilitation, 306 Indian Rocks Rd S, Largo; 727-586-2214)

Spirited All Stars are a group of kids, 5-year olds through high school students with a range of disabilities, who participate in different activities, from baseball to putt-putt golf, depending on the season or holiday. Drop-ins are welcome. Call Scott Malone 727-709-6186.

■ **MUSEUM**

Parks: Highlander

Dunedin Historical Museum, an old railroad depot off the Pinellas Trail in downtown, rotates exhibits of the old days. Rr. $D. Tue-Sat 10-4 (349 Main St, Dunedin; 727-736-1176)

■ **PARASAILING**

Parasail City staff, experienced with physically disabled parasailors, can lift you aboard from your WC and help in take-off and landing. (The marina also has a WC lift that you may use to board; see Boat Ramps.) You must be physically fit and have enough balance to sit on the boat without back support. Choose to get wet or stay dry. Reservations. 9-dusk (Clearwater Marina, 25 Causeway Blvd, Clearwater Bch; 727-449-0566)

■ **PARKS**

Florida Botanical Gardens has paved paths through 200 acres of natural and formal gardens and greenhouses of native plants and exotic tropicals. Call for horticultural assistance, classes and special events or to arrange a tour. Cafe; picnic tables; gift shop; Rr. 7-6 (Pinewood Cultural Park, 12175 125 St N, Largo; S off Ulmerton Rd/SR 688; 727-582-2200)

Hammock Park is a 75-acre city nature park with plenty of trails. The 1-mi, hard-packed shell Cedar Trail leads to a hard-packed access road, then boardwalk and footbridge over Cedar Creek to Youth Guild Park and 3 ADA picnic shelters. Here you can link to the Pinellas Trail (see Bike Trails) or loop back to ADA picnic shelters in Hammock Park. At high tide, you can also fish from the footbridge. Rr. Dawn-dusk (1900 San Mateo Dr, Dunedin; NW end of the road, just N of San Salvador Dr)

Heritage Village is a 21-acre wooded history park with 23 structures from Pinellas County's pioneer days where costumed volunteers describe and demonstrate traditional crafts. The museum, an orientation theater (with a video tour of all the buildings) and a few historic buildings are accessible with brick or hard-packed paths. Elsewhere paths are pine straw. Rr. $D. Tue-Sat 10-4; Sun 1-4 (Pinewood Cultural Park, 11909 125 St N, Largo; S off Ulmerton Rd/SR 688; 727-582-2123)

Highlander Park is a 70-acre city nature and sports park. The Nature Center has ecology displays and nature programs (wkdy 9-5; 727-298-3271). Paved paths lead through a butterfly garden and a sensory garden with interpretive signage about plants you can touch and smell. The Fine Art Center has 2 galleries with rotating art exhibits, a children's art museum, art classes, a gift shop and Rr (wkdy 10-5; Sat 10-2; Sun 1-4). Next door is a ramped pavilion where you can fish in a pond. See Pools. Lighted tennis; ball fields; Rr (903 Michigan Blvd, Dunedin; just W of Pinehurst Rd)

John Chestnut Park is a 255-acre county park at the SE tip of Lake Tarpon. Fish from the shore, or a boat dock behind shelter #7. Enjoy over 2 mi of packed shell and boardwalk nature trails; the lookout tower is not accessible. Bring a canoe for Lake Tarpon and a .5-mi canoe trail through marshland. Boat ramp with floating dock; ADA picnic shelters; grills; Rr. 7-dusk (2200 East Lake Rd, Palm Harbor; off McMullen Booth Rd/CR 611; 727-669-1951)

Moccasin Lake Nature Park is a 51-acre city park with a 1-mi, loop boardwalk and hard-packed shell path. The nature center has displays of amphibians, solar energy and conservation and an aviary for injured birds of prey. A path links the park to the East-West Trail; see Bike Trails. ADA picnic shelters; Rr. $. Tue-Fri 9-5; wknd 10-6 (2750 Park Trail Ln; from US 19, go W on Drew St, then N on Fairwood Ave; 727-462-6024)

Philippe Park is a beautiful county park meandering along Old Tampa Bay. It has an Indian mound with a very steep ramp on the W side. You can fish from a footbridge at the S end of the park or from a seawall. A 1-mi path follows the shore to the Safety Harbor Spa and connects to the East-West Trail; see Bike Trails. Boat ramp with floating dock & HC parking; ADA picnic shelters; Rr, at shelter #2 is most readily accessible. 7-dusk (2525 Philippe Pkwy, Safety Harbor; 727-669-1947)

Taylor Park is a county park with grassy level areas for fishing in a lake and comfortable access to the Pinellas Trail. Picnic shelters; ADA playground; Rr. 7-dusk (1100 8 Ave SW, Largo)

■ **PERFORMING ARTS**

Eight O'Clock Theatre hosts a variety of plays by community actors as well as a jazz series, children's theater and performances by the Summit Orchestra and the Suncoast Singers. Rr. (105 Central Park Dr, Largo; at Seminole Blvd & East Bay Dr, behind the library; 727-587-6793)

Francis Wilson Playhouse offers 6 mainstage community productions of musicals and family shows. WC seating is on the side aisles in the front and rear. Rr. Sep-May (302 Seminole St; 727-446-1360) ·

Ruth Eckerd Hall, seating over 2000, is one of the major performing arts centers in Tampa Bay. Internationally and nationally acclaimed artists, as well as superior local artists perform here. WC seating is toward the front on either side and also in the back row. Several other seats are available if you can transfer from your WC. A smaller, upstairs theater presents a variety of shows. When you make reservations, ask which entrance to use for your seats. Elevator; Rr (1111 McMullen Booth Rd/CR 611; 727-791-7060)

■ **POOLS**

Clearwater Family Aquatic Center has a 75' pool with a zero-depth ramp and submersible WC. A play area in the pool has an accessible raindrop umbrella, a frog slide (with 3 steps) and an inaccessible 5' slide. Lifeguards can help with transfers. Lap lanes; classes; Rr with roll-in showers. $. Mar-Oct hrs vary (51 Bay Esplanade, Clearwater Bch; 727-462-6020)

Highlander Community Pool is a 25-meter, heated pool with a ramp (no submersible WC); in winter, the pool is under a bubble roof. Locker room with roll-in shower & Rr. $. Hrs vary (1937 Ed Eckerd Dr, Dunedin; off Michigan Blvd; 727-298-3266)

Long Center has a 50-meter pool with a lift (fixed seat) and a 25-meter pool with a ramp and submersible WC (fixed arms). Both indoor pools are heated. Lifeguards can help with transfers. Call for classes. Rr. $. Wkdy 8am-8:45pm; Sat 9-4:45 (1501 N Belcher Rd; 727-726-2181)

■ **SAILING**

Sailability has *access dinghies* for 1 or 2 people. These small, center-weighted boats cannot tip over and can be steered with an electric joystick while the sailor sits in a hammock-type seat. Sailability offers a basic recreational course, after which you can participate in the monthly open sail. Regattas are also hosted here. Staff can help you transfer into the lift (sling seat) and onboard. Call Alder Allensworth 727-327-0137. (Clearwater Community Sailing Center, 1001 Gulf Blvd, Clearwater Bch; across from Sheraton Sand Key; 727-462-6368)

■ **SCUBA**

Our Ocean Dreams have HSA-certified Instructors who offer lessons at your home or any pool with a lift. Lessons are performance-based but usually run about 16 hrs of pool and class work plus a weekend of open water dives where staff can lift you in and out of the boat. Kevin and Kari, a medical rehab physician, can also work with you on adaptive equipment and barrier-free dive resorts. (727-578-3095)

■ **SHOPPING**

Antique, art shops and boutiques can be found in downtown Clearwater and along Main St in Safety Harbor. Dunedin has a charming Main St lined with unique shops, antique shops, galleries and several intimate and fine restaurants. Streets have wide, well-graded curb cuts.

Malls: Bay Area Outlet Mall (US 19 N at Roosevelt Blvd; 727-535-2337); Country-side Mall (27001 US 19 N at SR 588; 727-796-1079); Northwoods Plaza (3030 Enterprise Rd; off McMullen Booth Rd/CR 611; 727-725-7405)

Specialty shopping includes Orange Blossom Groves with freshly squeezed juice and other citrus products. (18200 US 19 N; 727-536-3588 & 5800 Seminole Blvd; 727-392-1277)

■ SOCCER

Tops is a team of kids, 5-year olds through high school students with a range of disabilities, who complete in fun soccer games against age-appropriate, able-bodied kids. Drop-ins are welcome. Call Linda or Steve Siesel 727-595-7752. Nov-Feb Fri 6:30-7:30pm (Seminole Jr Warhawks Athletic Assn Complex, 11500 125 St N, Largo; next to Walsingham Park)

■ SPECTATOR SPORTS

Auto Racing Sunshine Speedway offers the roar of the crowd and the engines with mini-stocks, school bus demolitions, figure eights, even blindfold races. The main grandstand is ramped; WC seating is to the right by the flagger's stand, to the immediate left of the ramp and further left in the family section (alcohol-free); companion seating is in the row behind. Rr. $. Wed & Fri 6; Mar-Nov Sat 6 (4500 Ulmerton Rd/SR 688; 727-573-4598/4660)

Baseball Philadelphia Phillies train and play exhibition games in Mar. The mi-nor league Clearwater Phillies play Apr-Sep. WC seating is on the 1st level. Rr (Jack Russell Stadium, Seminole St & Greenwood Ave; 727-442-8496)

Toronto Blue Jays have spring training games in Mar; Dunedin Blue Jays play Apr-Sep. WC seating behind home plate; Rr (Grant Field, 373 Douglas Ave, Dunedin; N of SR 588; 727-733-9302)

■ TOURS

It's Our Nature offers 1 1/2- to 5-hr walking tours throughout the area at parks and beaches. Many tours are accessible; some beaches loan beach WCs, with 24-hr notice. At Caladesi Island, learn about its 3 ecosystems and the family that once inhabited the island. The trail is hard packed with tree roots and a slight elevation. At Honeymoon Island, explore the beach along the mangroves and sea oats where wading birds stop to feed. For the beach WC, see Beaches: Honeymoon Island. (727-441-2599; 888-535-7448)

■ WALLEYBALL

Largo Recreation SW Complex hosts WC-walleyball games, an adaptation of volleyball played on a racquetball court with a low net between 2 teams of 2-3 players. Each team is allowed 2 bounces before getting the ball over the net. You need good arm movement (for protection) and a manual WC. Games open to everybody, even able-bodied friends as long as they bring their own WCs. $ (13120 Vonn Rd, Largo; 727-518-3125)

ACCOMMODATIONS

■ CONDOS

Surfside Villas, on the Gulf, has luxurious 2BR and 3BR ADA condos to sleep up to 8 for a minimum of 1 wk. Units have beachside balconies, beds on open frames, full kitchens and bathrooms with tubs or step-in showers. Heated pool; laundry; covered parking. (11 Idlewild St, Clearwater Bch; 727-461-1123)

■ MOTELS

Adam's Mark has 10 ADA rooms, each with a king or 2 full beds (open frames), some with a sofa bed in a living room, all with coffeepots. Bathrooms have raised toilets and roll-under sinks. Rooms 520, 522 and 523 have roll-in showers; others have tubs; all have hand-held sprayers and seats. A short sidewalk gets you onto the motel beach. Pool; laundry; lounge; poolside entertainment; full restaurant. $$$ (430 S Gulfview Blvd, Clearwater Bch; 727-443-5714; 800-444-2326)

Best Western Yacht Harbor Inn has an ADA room, overlooking St Joseph's Sound, with 2 full beds (23" high/platforms), kitchenette and bathroom with a roll-under sink and tub/shower with a seat. At the end of the hotel's parking lot is the Dunedin Marina; see Boat Ramps. Free brkfst; lounge; restaurant for lunch & dinner. $$-$$$ (150 Marina Plaza, Dunedin; 727-733-4121)

Candlewood Suites has 6 ADA rooms and 2 ADA 1BR suites, each with a queen bed (open frame), full kitchen and bathroom with a raised toilet and roll-under sink. Units 103, 111, 134 and 133 have roll-in showers; others have tubs or step-in showers; all have hand-held sprayers and seats. Each suite has a full sofa bed in the living room. Laundry; convenience store. $$-$$$ (13231 49 St N; 727-573-3344)

Courtyard Marriott has 2 ADA rooms, each with a king or full bed (24" high/open frame) and bathroom with a raised toilet, roll-under sink and either a tub or roll-in shower with hand-held sprayer and seat. Pool; laundry; lounge; restaurant for brkfst. $$$ (3131 Executive Dr; 727-572-8484)

Days Inn has 5 ADA rooms, each with a queen bed (21" high/open frame), full sofa bed, refrigerator, microwave and coffeepot. Rooms 120 and 123 have roll-in showers with seats; others have tubs; all have hand-held sprayers. Free brkfst; pool; laundry. $-$$ (3910 Ulmerton Rd/SR 688; 727-573-3334)

Fairfield Inn has 5 ADA rooms with either a king or 2 full beds (21" high/open frames) and bathrooms with raised toilets and roll-under sinks. Room 123 has a roll-in shower with hand-held sprayer and seat; others have tubs. On request, you can have a refrigerator and microwave in your room. Free brkfst; pool; fitness room. $$ (3211 Executive Dr; off Ulmerton Rd/SR 688; 727-572-4400)

Four Points Sheraton, on Lake Tarpon, has ADA rooms, each with a full bed (22" high/open frame), waterfront patio or balcony, coffeepot and bathroom with a raised toilet; room 115 has a roll-in shower with a hand-held sprayer and seat. Pool; laundry; lounge; restaurant for breakfast & dinner. $$$ (37611 US 19 N, Palm Harbor; 727-942-0358)

Hampton Inn has 8 ADA rooms, each with a king bed, coffeepot and bathroom with a raised toilet and roll-under sink; 2 units have roll-in showers with hand-held sprayers and seats. Free brkfst; pool; laundry. $$ (21030 US 19 N; 727-797-8173)

Hilton Resort has 4 ADA 1 BR suites, each with a king or 2 full beds (open frames). Rooms 440 and 438 have roll-in showers with hand-held sprayers; others have tubs. The Hilton is next door to Clearwater Beach that loans a beach WC; see Beaches. Pool; full restaurant. $$$ (400 Mandalay Ave, Clearwater Bch; 727-461-3222; 800-753-3954)

Holiday Inn Express has 7 ADA rooms, each with a king or full bed (26" high/open frame) and a bathroom with a raised toilet and roll-under sink. Two rooms have roll-in showers; others have tubs; all have hand-held sprayers and seats. Free brkfst; pool. $$-$$$ (1365 Icot Blvd; 727-536-7275)

Homewood Suites has 4 ADA 1BR and 2 ADA 2BR suites, each with either a king and/or 2 full beds (24" high/platforms), a queen sofa bed in the living room, full kitchen and bathroom with a roll-under sink. Units 102 and 129 have roll-in showers; others have tubs or step-in showers; all have hand-held sprayers and seats. Free brkfst; wkdy socials with light meals & beer/wine; pool; laundry; lounge. $$$ (2233 Ulmerton Rd/SR 688; 727-573-1500)

Inn on the Bay has an ADA room with a queen bed (open frame), balcony and bathroom with a raised toilet, roll-under sink and roll-in shower with hand-held sprayer. If you want a suite, this room can be opened up to an adjoining one with a kitchen. Tiki deck; heated pool; fishing dock; next to Pinellas Trail; restaurant. $-$$ (1420 Bayshore Blvd, Dunedin; 727-734-7689; 800-759-0972) **Ramada Inn Gulfview** has 4 ADA rooms, each with a king or 2 full beds (22" high/open frames) and a bathroom with a roll-under sink. Rooms 307 and 407 have roll-in showers; others have tubs or step-in showers; all have hand-held sprayers and seats. You can fish from the pool deck or seawall behind the hotel. Clearwater Beach, where you can borrow a beach WC, is nearby; see Beaches. Pool; laundry; lounge; entertainment; full restaurant; salon. $$$ (521 S Gulfview Blvd, Clearwater Bch; 727-447-6461; 800-776-6461) **Red Roof Inn** has 4 ADA rooms, each

with a king bed (24" high/open frame) and bathroom with a raised toilet and roll-under sink; room 127 has a roll-in shower, others have tubs, all with hand-held sprayers and seats. Heated pool. $-$$ (32000 US 19 N, Palm Harbor; 727-786-2529) **Safety Harbor Resort** & Spa has 4 ADA rooms, each with 2 queen beds (open frames), a coffeepot and bathroom with a raised toilet and roll-under sink. Rooms 253 and 255 have roll-in showers with hand-held sprayers and seats; other units have tubs. The spa is not modified for WC riders, but the resort is on Old Tampa Bay with lovely grounds near the Safety Harbor Pier and an artsy downtown. Laundry; lounge; full restaurant. $$-$$$ (105 N Bayshore Dr, Safety Harbor; 727-726-1161; 888-237-8772)

St Petersburg

Gulfport, Indian Shores, Madeira Beach, Pasadena, Pass-A-Grille, Pinellas Park, Redington Shores, Seminole, Tierra Verde, Treasure Island

St Pete is a vacation spot to please all in the family. Beach wheelchairs at Treasure Island and soon at Fort De Soto Park enable all to enjoy the Suncoast's primary allure. Cultural events and a B&B with an ADA guestroom appeal to many. For the outdoors enthusiast in a wheelchair, St Pete has an active sailing program, handcycles for diverse bike trails, four pools with lifts and varied sports opportunities thanks to a busy Therapeutic Recreation office.

Tourist Info

Gulf Beaches Chamber: 6990 Gulf Blvd, St Pete Bch, 33706; 727-360-6957
St Pete Area Chamber: 100 2 Ave N, Suite 150, 33701; 727-821-4069
St Pete/Clearwater Visitors Bureau: 14450 46 St N, Clearwater, 33762; 727-464-7200; 800-345-6710
Entertainment Hotline (727-825-3333) is a 24-hr taped message on current and upcoming artistic and cultural events.
Web sites: www.floridasbeach.com; www.gulfportfl.com; www.stpete.com; www.tampabaybeaches.com; www.trekflorida.com

Transportation

See Clearwater.

WC Resources

Caring & Sharing Center for Independent Living provides support services, including a loan closet where you can borrow manual WCs and other equipment. (1130 94 Ave N; 727-577-0065)

ACTIVITIES

■ **ATTRACTIONS**
St Pete Pier, a 5-story, inverted pyramid at the end of an 1800' roadway on Tampa Bay, has been a downtown landmark since 1973. It features a small aquarium, outdoor observation deck, food court, restaurants and touristy shops. Currently, regularly scheduled activities include Big Band dances, family entertainment and rock to jazz concerts; call for times. Outside is a bait shop (6am-10pm; 727-821-3750) and plenty of fishing. HC parking next to building; free trolleys with lifts shuttle from parking at the end of the pier; Rr (800 2 Ave NE; 727-821-6164)
Suncoast Seabird Sanctuary, the nation's largest wild bird hospital, is a chance to see our injured, feathered friends up close. Paths are crushed shell and gravel. $D. 9-dusk (18328 Gulf Blvd, Indian Shores; 727-391-6211)
Sunken Gardens was a private tourist attraction since 1935 with more than 6 acres of exotic flowers, plants and a butterfly garden. The city has taken it over and increased the educational thrust with horticultural presentations, guided tours and reptile and bird shows; call for times. Rr; snack bar. $. Wed-Sun 10-4 (1825 4 St N; 727-551-3100)
■ **BASEBALL**
Challenger Baseball has experienced coaches who offer instruction and fun, scoreless games for kids, age 5 through high school students with a range of disabilities. Buddies can help players in all aspects of the game and drop-ins are welcome. In Pinellas Park, games are played at Youth Park (4100 66 Ave N); call Bruce Mallon 727-393-6200. In St Pete, games are played at Azalea Park (1600 72 St N); call Lee Fulmer 727-345-7407. Mar-May Sat 9-11
■ **BASKETBALL**
St Pete Thunder is the local NWBA team, age 13 and up, that plays late Oct-Feb. Visitors are welcome to watch,

scrimmage or try out for the team! Sports WCs are available for players; travel is involved for regional competition. Call St Pete Therapeutic Recreation 727-893-7899.
■ **BEACHES** (from north to south)
Parks: Fort De Soto
Redington Shores Beach has a boardwalk to the beach. Restaurants nearby; Rr (Gulf Blvd at 182 Ave, Redington Shores)
Madeira Beach has a boardwalk to the beach. Restaurants nearby; Rr (15100 Gulf Blvd, Madeira Bch)
***Treasure Island Beach** loans beach WCs (fixed arms; umbrellas) at the concession stand (9-4:30). In case someone is waiting, you may have to check in every hour. Picnic tables; grill; Rr (11260 Gulf Blvd, Treasure Island; 727-360-3278)
Upham Beach has boardwalks onto the beach and a Seaside Grille (8-4). Rr (Beach Plaza, Pasadena; 1 block W of Gulf Blvd between 67 Ave & 69 Ave)
St Pete Beach has 2 ramped boardwalks to the beach; the ramp N of the bathhouse has easier WC access. Rr (4700 Gulf Blvd, St Pete Bch)
Pass-A-Grille Beach Park has a Seaside Grille surrounded by a cement deck with picnic tables, popular for sunset. Just S is a ramp with a 6" drop to the sand. N of the Grille are boardwalks to the beach. HC parking at Grille; restaurants nearby; Rr (800 Gull Way, Pass-A-Grille)
■ **BIKE TRAILS**
Parks: Boyd Hill, Fort De Soto
Friendship Trail is the old Gandy Bridge, once used by vehicles to cross Tampa Bay between Tampa and St Pete. The 2.5-mi lighted span has a steep hump roughly midway that offers a rigorous climb and potentially dangerous descent. You can also fish (24 hrs) from a lighted catwalk that runs along the bridge. See Handcycles. Bait shop nearby; Rr port-o-let. Dawn-dusk (Gandy Blvd)

Pinellas Trail is a 34-mi paved trail from St Pete to Tarpon Springs along an abandoned railroad route that parallels Alt US 19. It passes many points of interest, parks and wonderful secluded spots for picnics. However, it does cross busy intersections, some with steep overpasses, others with only stop signs. The best spots in St Pete for hassle-free parking and transfers to a handcycle are: Trailhead Park (Fairfield Ave between 37 & 40 Sts S), Azalea Park (1600 72 St N; 727-893-7150) and Taylor Park (1100 8 Ave SW, Largo; 727-584-7448). See Handcycles. Get a mile-by-mile trail guide at most bike shops, local tourist info sites or the Trail Supervisor. (12020 Walsingham Rd, Largo, 33778; 727-549-6099)

■ **BILLIARDS**
9 Ball WC Billiard League plays every Thu 1-4:30. Call Ken Horgen 727-596-7361. Rr (Side Pocket Billiards, 7570 Starkey Rd; 727-388-0890)

■ **BOAT RAMPS**
Parks: Fort De Soto
Gandy Bridge Marina has a boat ramp on Tampa Bay. There's a step to the floating dock. Bait shop. $. Wkdy 8-6; wknd 7-6 (13060 Gandy Blvd; next to Banana Boat Restaurant; 727-576-5117)
Park Blvd Boat Ramp is lighted and has a floating dock on the Intracoastal. 24 hrs (18651 Gulf Blvd, Indian Shores; at Park Blvd; 727-549-6165)
War Veterans Memorial Park, a 122-acre county park, has a lighted boat ramp and floating dock (24 hrs) on Boca Ciega Bay. You can also fish off the seawall here and enjoy the quiet roads and trail through the woods. Bait shop; ADA picnic shelters; Rr. Dawn-dusk (9600 Bay Pines Blvd; 727-549-6165)

■ **BOAT RENTALS**
Gandy Bridge Marina rents pontoon boats (24" & 36" entries) to carry up to 6 or 8 people on the Tampa Bay within a 2-mi radius. Staff can help you over the step to the floating dock and aboard. Bait shop. Wkdy 8-6; wknd 7-6 (13060 Gandy Blvd; next to the Banana Boat Restaurant; 727-576-5117)
Resort Boat Rentals rents a pontoon boat (36" entry) by the hour or day for up to 15 people on the Intracoastal. You can also rent fishing boats, center consoles, bow riders and deck boats that can go into the Gulf. Staff can lift you aboard in your WC from the floating dock. Bait shop; restaurant; Rr. 9-5 (Tierra Verde Resort Marina, 200 Madonna Blvd, Tierra Verde; I-275 exit 4, W on Pinellas Bayway/SR 682 then S on Pinellas Bayway S/SR 679 1.5 mi; 727-906-8686)

■ **BOAT TOURS**
Hubbard's Sea Adventures offers 2-hr, dolphin watching or ecocruises on a catamaran in the Intracoastal and nearby estuaries. Crew can help you board over the step onto the catamaran. (Johns Pass Village, 12901 Gulf Blvd E, Madeira Bch; 727-398-6577)
Shell Key Sunset Cruises depart evenings for 1 1/2-hr sightseeing cruises through residential waterways and pristine barrier islands. Call to find out if you can handle the tight turn to get onto the boarding ramp. Mon-Sat 10-4 (Merry Pier, 801 Pass-A-Grille Way, Pass-A-Grille; 727-360-1348)

■ **BOCCE**
St Pete Therapeutic Recreation offers instruction, fun competition and adaptive equipment for team and individual bocce ball. Parents must stay with participants under 12. Call St Pete Therapeutic Recreation 727-893-7899. Mon 6:30pm-8pm (Azalea Middle School Gym, 7855 22 Ave N)

■ **BOWLING**
Southland Lanes has leagues on Mon afternoons and Thu evenings with teams of WC and stand-up bowlers. Staff can help or give lessons with adaptive equipment including snap handle balls and bowling sticks especially designed for WC bowlers, including quads. Call team captain Jim Sullivan 727-586-1785. (10001 66 St; 727-545-0943)

■ **CANOEING/KAYAKING**

Parks: Weedon Island

Canoe Outpost rents canoes, tandem sit-in and solo sit-on kayaks for the waters around Fort De Soto Park. Use the descriptive map on the 2.5-mi, roughly 2-hr, marked trail in Mullet Key Bayou. Staff can help you cross the 20' stretch of hard-packed sand to the water and can lift you aboard your craft. A tour group, It's Our Nature (727-441-2599; 888-535-7448), offers 2- to 3-hr guided trips around the mangrove islands. (Fort De Soto Park, 3500 Pinellas Bayway S/SR 679; from park entrance, turn right at stop sign, 1 mi to outpost on right; 727-864-1991)

■ **FISHING CHARTERS**

Capt Blackmore can accommodate 2 WC and 2 able-bodied anglers on his 22' center console boat for inshore and near-shore trips using light tackle. If you choose, the capt can take you sightseeing and can help lift you aboard in your WC. Depending on where the fish are running, the capt can suggest an accessible dock. (813-831-8987)

Fish-On! Sport Fishing Charters has a 32' boat for up to 6 anglers on 4- to 14-hr trips. Capt Hayes specializes in blue water bottom fishing and guarantees 100 lbs of fish on all-day charters. Crew can lift you aboard in your WC from the floating dock. Rr at marina (Tierra Verde Resort Marina, 200 Madonna Blvd, Tierra Verde; I-275 exit 4, go W on Pinellas Bayway/SR 682, then S on Pinellas Bayway S/SR 679 1.5 mi; Capt 727-866-8927; 813-340-8600)

Light Tackle Fishing offers half/full-day charters for inshore saltwater fishing with light tackle or flyfishing gear on 18'-21' boats. Board by ramp from a floating dock. The boat deck is roomy enough for 1 WC angler and 2 able-bodied anglers. From Fort De Soto Park, you fish in the mouth of the Tampa Bay. This group also offers charters from Tampa and Tarpon Springs. (813-249-5224; 800-972-1930)

■ **FISHING-PARTY BOATS**

Hubbard's Marina Fishing Fleet offers half/full-day and 2-day/2-night trips going up to 100 mi offshore to the Florida Middle Ground. Board by a 36" wide ramp; crew can help you board and over the step into the AC cabin with a full galley. Crew can clean your catch and the nearby Friendly Fisherman Seafood Restaurant can cook it. Because WC anglers fish in the stern where the boat is most stable, reservations are advised, for overnight trips at least 1 month in advance. 5:30am-7:30pm (Johns Pass Village, 12901 Gulf Blvd E, Madeira Bch; 727-393-1947)

■ **FISHING PIERS**

Attractions: St Pete Pier. Bike Trails: Friendship Trail. Boat Ramps: War Veterans. Parks: Fort De Soto, Weedon Island

Merry Pier is a small wood, rather rickety looking, lighted pier on Boca Ciega Bay. You can also fish off a very wide sidewalk that runs along the bay. Bait shop with rod rentals (7-6); Rr. 24 hrs (801 Pass-A-Grille Way, Pass-A-Grille; 727-360-6606)

Redington Shores Long Pier is a 1020' lighted wood pier on the Gulf with a steep incline at the entrance. Bait shop; no HC parking; Rr. $. 24 hrs (17490 Gulf Blvd, Redington Shores)

Skyway Fishing Piers are the remains of either end of the old Skyway Bridge that was damaged by a barge in 1980. The North Skyway Pier extends .5 mi and the South Pier 2.5 mi into the mouth of Tampa Bay. Both piers are lighted, have bait shops with rentals, snacks and Rr. $. 24 hrs (from St Pete, take the last exit off I-275 before crossing Skyway Bridge for the N Pier 727-865-0668; take the 1st exit after the bridge for the S Pier; 941-729-0117)

Williams Pier is a 600' lighted pier on Boca Ciega Bay. 24 hrs (S Shore Blvd, Gulfport)

■ **HANDCYCLES**

St Pete Therapeutic Recreation rents ($1/day) 2 handcycles for children and 3

for adults for the day and overnight. Transport is easiest in a pickup truck. (1400 19 St N; 727-893-7899)

■ **HORSEBACK RIDING**

Horses & the Handicapped, an NAHRA center, offers therapeutic riding with a certified instructor for adults and kids during the school year on Sat mornings at no charge. Three trained volunteers work with each rider to mount and ride in the ring up to 45 min. Applications must include a physician's release. (Seminole Vocational Education Center, 125 St N; at 90 Ave, in field behind school; 727-539-0455)

■ **MISC**

Coliseum is a marvelous old ballroom, notable as the site of Don Amiche's break dancing in the movie *Cocoon*. Enjoy anything from Big Band and rock to tearoom and ballroom dancing. Snack bar; BYOB (534 4 Ave N; E of I-275, off US 375; 727-892-5202)

Gulfport Casino is landmark dance hall on Boca Ciega Bay where everybody, from line dancer to ballroom dancer, has a night. (5500 Shore Blvd S, Gulfport; S end of Beach Blvd; 727-321-7288)

Physically Challenged Expressions offer a range of events, sports training and social activities for adults with physical disabilities. Call St Pete Therapeutic Recreation 727-893-7899.

■ **MUSEUMS**

Florida Holocaust Museum displays photographs, artifacts and personal histories in a moving memorial to one of history's saddest episodes. Elevator; Rr. $D. Wkdy 10-5; wknd noon-5 (55 5 St S; 727-820-0100)

Florida International Museum, an affiliate of the Smithsonian, features traveling and 2 permanent exhibitions: the Kennedy Collection and the Cuban Missile Crisis. Rr. $. Mon-Sat 10-5; Sun 12-5 (100 2 St N; at 1 Ave N; 727-822 3693)

Great Explorations is a hands-on museum with challenging puzzles, interactive displays and experiential workshops for kids and adults. Only the 90' pitch black, Touch Tunnel, a maze through which people crawl on hands and knees, is inaccessible. By spring 2003, this museum moves to Sunken Gardens; see Attractions. Rr. $. 10-8; Sun 11-6 (St Pete Pier 3rd floor, 800 2 Ave NE; 727-821-8992)

Museum of Fine Arts has a fairly comprehensive international collection and a special gallery of Steuben glass. Rr. $/ Sun free. Tue-Sat 10-5; Sun 1-5 (255 Beach Dr NE; at the entrance to St Pete Pier; 727-896-2667)

St Pete Museum of History offers a browse through local history and a look at the Benoist airboat that launched commercial aviation in 1914. Rr. 10-5; Sun 1-5 (335 2 Ave NE; just W of St Pete Pier; 727-894-1052)

Salvador Dali Museum is home to the world's largest collection of Dali's works and is one of St Pete's cultural gems. Even if you think you don't care for his art, try a guided tour! HC parking is at the front entrance, N of the building, and in the main parking lot in back. Rr. $. Tue-Sat 10-5; Sun-Mon 12-5 (1000 3 St S; from I-275, E on US 175, then S; 727-823-3767)

■ **PARASAILING**

Johns Pass Parasail is experienced with quad- and para-parasailors. Don a special harness that keeps you in a comfortable sitting position, then staff can lift you aboard the boat from your WC. If you have a balance problem, staff can sit on either side of you for support. The boat has a winch that makes takeoff and landing gentler. Talk to either Linda or Dan when making reservations so extra staff is available. Calm weather is required. (110 Johns Pass Boardwalk, 12901 Gulf Blvd E, Madeira Bch; 727-391-7738)

■ **PARI-MUTUELS**

Derby Lane offers live greyhound-racing Jan-Jun and all year a card room and simulcast racing. WC seating is throughout the stands. The dining room, the Derby Club, is terraced but WCs can access the top level easily or a lower level via the kitchen. Enjoy great roast beef while you watch races through huge windowed walls or on tabletop monitors. (10490 Gandy Blvd; 727-576-1361)

■ **PARKS**

Boca Ciega Millennium Park is the county's new 182-acre nature preserve on Boca Ciega Bay. Enjoy a .5-mi paved trail from the entrance to the first picnic shelter. An observation tower, ramped to a 13' high deck, has a wonderful view of the coastal area. An ADA boardwalk runs .5 mi along the shore and loops back through an oak hammock. Interpretive signage is planned for a short hard-packed dirt loop trail; watch for tree roots. Over grass is a steep canoe launch made of honeycomb block that makes WC access difficult. ADA picnic shelters; playground on ADA surface; Rr. 7am-dusk (12410 74 Ave N, Seminole; E of 125 St, S of Old Oakhurst Rd; 727-588-4882)

Boyd Hill Nature Center is the city's 245-acre oasis of unspoiled natural habitat. Use a flora and fauna checklist as you follow 3 mi of paved and crushed-shell trails and boardwalks through several Florida ecosystems. Paved paths lead past cages of injured birds of prey. Staff can help you transfer into a tram for a daily, guided 1-hr tour at 1pm. Rangers offer regular hikes that focus on birds, wildflowers and even night wildlife. Picnic shelters; grills; Rr. $. 9-5; Apr-Oct Tue & Thu - 8pm (1101 Country Club Way S; from I-275, E on 54 Ave S, N on 9 St S, then W; 727-893-7326)

*Fort De Soto Park, the county's southernmost park, is actually 5 connected islands with stunning beaches, a taste of history, scenic picnicking and plenty of access. The Park plans to obtain beach WCs to make its beautiful beaches even more enjoyable. The huge N and E beaches have paved paths from parking to the soft sand; the furthest N beach has a footbridge to a long, palm-lined strip of sand with a calm, gently sloped swim area. Historic Trail leads from HC parking to a Trailhead at the S entrance of the Spanish-American War fort, for which the park is named. The fort's lower level is accessible; guided tours occur Sat 10am or pick up a self-guiding brochure at the trailhead. The trail also leads to the Quartermaster's Storehouse Museum (9-4), an ADA replica of the 1898 supply officer's building, where wall panels and a touch screen computer depict local history from indigenous inhabitants through the Civil, Spanish-American and World Wars to today's role as a port. The Arrowhead Picnic Area, across from N beach, has lovely, secluded spots under trees and along the shore, with grills and picnic tables on sand. A sunny 6.5-mi paved recreational trail runs along the park road, from Bunces Pass Bridge at the park entrance to E and N beaches. A .5-mi paved nature loop starts at park headquarters and has audio stations that describe the ecology as you go through a palm hammock, along a canal and near dunes. Check out the 2 paved, lighted fishing piers (24 hrs): the 500' Bay Pier is E of the fort and has a bait shop (727-864-3345) and Rr; the 1000' pier on the Gulf is just S of the fort. Canoe rentals and guided trips are also available here; see Canoeing. Near the canoe rental you can take the hard-packed dirt Soldiers' Hole Trail for either a .5 or 1.25 mi through palm hammock and mangroves. From the paved boat launch with ramped floating docks, just S of Bunces Pass Bridge, boaters can access Tampa Bay or the Gulf. Near the Bay Pier is Paw Playground, a fenced-in dog park including 150 yds of beach, where dogs can run off leash. See Campgrounds. Lifeguards in summer; ADA playgrounds at both beaches & campground; snack bar/gift shop just N of fort; ADA picnic shelters at N beach; Rr. $. Dawn-dusk (3500 Pinellas Bayway S/SR 679, Tierra Verde; I-275 exit 4, W on Pinellas Bayway/SR 682, then S; 727-582-2267)

Sawgrass Lake Park is a 400-acre county nature park with 3 trails and a nature center with a 300-gal freshwater aquarium and displays. The Sawgrass Trail is an ADA boardwalk through a maple swamp to an observation tower, ramped to the 1st level and overlooking the lake. The Maple Trail goes from the swamp through an oak hammock. Together these trails run just over a mile. The .5-mi Hammock Trail is sandy in dry weather and has tree roots. WC loaner; large ADA picnic shelter; ADA picnic tables; Rr. 7-dusk (7400 25 St N; N off 62 Ave N; 727-217-7256)

Weedon Island Preserve is a relatively undiscovered island favored by birds, fish, canoeists and WC riders. Over 9000' of boardwalk link the .5-mi paved Upland Trail and the Getting Memorial Trail through marshy wetlands and a mangrove jungle to an observation platform, with a ramped 20' high deck. Bring a canoe or kayak (or rent one just outside the park entrance) and use the paved launch and marked canoe trails. A 163' wood fishing pier extends over the bayou. Make reservations for the weekly ranger-led hikes on Sat 9am. ADA picnic tables; Rr. 7-dusk (1500 Weedon Island Dr; from Gandy Blvd, S on San Martin Blvd/CR 823; 727-217-7208)

■ **PERFORMING ARTS**

American Stage offers professional mainstage productions throughout the year, Shakespeare in the Park Apr-May and outstanding children's programs. WC seating in front; Rr (211 3 St S; 727-822-8814)

Bayfront Center includes the Mahaffey Theater, a performing arts center with world-class ballet, theater and the Florida Symphony. WC seating is available in box seats, in front at the right and left of the stage and in row W. The Times Arena that features large productions, such as the circus and ice shows, has WC seating at all ticket prices; Rr (400 1 St S; 727-892-5767)

Catherine Hichman Theater offers a variety of performances from big band concerts to plays. It is also home to the Gulfport Community Players (727-322-0316) WC seating is in the front center section and in the rear. (5501 27 Ave S; Gulfport; 727-893-1070)

Palladium Theater, a renovated 1925 church, hosts varied performances from classical concerts to plays and dance recitals, generally by local, non-profit groups. WC seating is in the center of the 5th row and in the back on the sides. Enter by ramp on the NW side of the building along 3 St; an attendant there can go to the lobby for your ticket and operate the elevator to the theater. Parking on the E side; Rr. Oct-Aug (253 5 Ave N; 727-822-3590)

St Petersburg Little Theater is a community theater offering comedies, musicals and dramas. WC seating in back; Rr. Sep-Jun (4025 31 St S; 727-866-1973)

■ **POOLS**

The following outdoor pools have lifts (fixed seats) and locker rooms with roll-in showers and Rr. Lifeguards can operate the lifts but cannot help with transfers. $: **E H McLin Pool** Summer hrs vary (Campbell Park Center, 602 14 St S; 727-893-7635); **Fossil** Summer hrs vary (Willis Johns Center, 6739 9 St N; 727-893-7740); **Walter Fuller Pool** is heated. Hrs vary (7883 26 Ave N; 727-893-7636); **North Shore Community Pool** is heated and lifeguards can help with transfers. Wkdy 9-4; Sat 9-4; Sun 1-4 (901 N Shore Dr NE; 727-893-7727)

■ **SAILING**

Sailing Alternatives is a wonderful program to empower disabled sailors for leisure and competition. Classes and racing are open to physically disabled sailors, age 8 and older, beginning to advanced. Sailors need only some level of hand movement, not the ability to grasp. The Sailing Center has ramps to floating docks. Sailors can board by lift (sling seat) either solo or crew boats, none of which can capsize or sink even in extreme weather. In summer, Fri evening races occur with usually 3-4 boats of disabled sailors competing against able-bodied sailors. Call St Pete Therapeutic Recreation 727-893-7899 or Sailing Alternatives 941-377-4986. (St Pete Municipal Marina, Demen's Landing Park; downtown Bayshore Dr, S of St Pete Pier)

■ SCUBA

Clearwater: Scuba

■ SHOOTING RANGES

Wyoming Antelope Club has a plinking pit and target ranges for almost any gun you want to shoot, from pellet rifles and pistols to black powder rifles and high speed handguns. Call about safety classes, NRA certification, qualifications and training/competitions for a variety of disciplines. Vending machines; Rr. $. Wed-Thu 9-1; Fri-Sun 9-5 (3700 126 Ave; from Ulmerton Rd/SR 688, S on 34 St N, then W; 727-573-3006)

■ SHOPPING

Antiques and antique-wannabes are plentiful in downtown along Central Ave (6 to 20 Sts) and along 4 St N (near 12 Ave).

Art Galleries in downtown include the St Pete Art Center (719 Central Ave), Florida Craftsman (501 Central Ave) and P Buckley Moss Gallery (190 4 Ave NE), across from the Fine Arts Museum. Also check out downtown Gulfport.

Entertainment Complexes: Baywalk is an upscale entertainment/shopping complex with restaurants and a stadium-seating movie theater. Rr (3 Ave N at 1 St).

Flea Markets: Wagon Wheel has more than 3000 vendors. Wknd 7:30-4 (7801 Park Blvd; 727-544-5319)

Johns Pass Village has touristy shops, restaurants and open-air bars along a boardwalk by the docks (12901 Gulf Blvd E, Madeira Bch; 727-399-9633).

Malls: Tyrone Square (6901 22 Ave N; 727-347-3889); Park Side Mall (US 19 & Park Blvd; 727-527-7241)

Specialty Stores include Haslam's, an expansive family-owned bookstore (2025 Central Ave); Bill Jackson's, an upscale sporting goods store (9501 US 19, Pinellas Park); and fine shops at each of the museums.

■ SOCCER

St Pete Chargers welcomes spectators and newcomers with power chairs to practice and play Wed 6:30pm-8. Call St Pete Therapeutic Recreation 727-893-7899. (Azalea Middle School, 7855 22 Ave N)

■ SPECTATOR SPORTS

Baseball Tampa Bay Rays, the region's long sought-after major league baseball team, plays in the fully accessible Tropicana Field. Apr-Sep (1 Tropicana Dr; US 175, just E of I-275; 727-825-3250)

ACCOMMODATIONS

■ B&Bs

Inn at the Bay, built in 1910 but renovated to 21st century standards and comfort, has an ADA guestroom, the Manatee, on the ground floor. The room has a 4-poster king bed (30" high/ open frame), sitting area and private bathroom with a roll-under sink and roll-in shower with a hand-held sprayer and seat. The home is ramped in back near parking. Enjoy a full gourmet breakfast in the dining room, the quiet of a lovely garden and, within walking distance, St Pete's downtown waterfront. $$$ (126 4 Ave NE; between 1 St N & Beach Dr; 727-822-1700; 888-873-2122)

■ CABINS/CAMPGROUNDS

Fort De Soto Park has a wooded and waterfront campground with 235 RV/ tent sites on shell and sand terrain, with water/elec. Camp roads are dirt and, after rains, can be difficult to navigate. Each camp area has an ADA bathhouse with raised toilets, roll-under sinks and roll-in showers with hand-held sprayers and fold-down seats; bathhouse #5 also has an ADA washer/dryer. Request a site with an ADA picnic table. See Parks. (3500 Pinellas Bayway S/SR 679, Tierra Verde; I-275 exit 4, W on Pinellas Bayway/SR 682, then S; 727-582-2267)

St Pete Resort KOA is a delightful campground on the Boca Ciega Bay and next to the Pinellas Bike Trail. Five rustic, WC-friendly cabins have electricity and AC and are near ADA bathhouses. The ramped cabins have 1 or 2 rooms and a full bed (on platform) against the wall, allowing transfers from 1 side only. Some cabins also have a table and bunk bed. Each cabin has an outside grill and picnic table with extended ends. Bring linens. Among the 379 RV sites, some are waterfront; some have concrete pads and anything from full hookups to only water/elec. Three communal camp kitchens have grills, sinks and picnic tables. The 11 tent sites have no hookups and are separate from RV sites. Three ADA bathhouses have raised toilets and roll-in showers with hand-held sprayers; only the main bathhouse does not have a roll-under sink. On the bayou is a fixed fishing dock and boat ramp. Pool; laundry; game room; camp store; playground on sand & grass (5400 95 St N; N off Tyrone Blvd/Bay Pines Blvd; 727-392-2233; 800-562-7714)

■ **CONDOS**

Carol Ann Condo Hotel, on the Gulf, has 1BR and 2BR ADA condos to sleep 4 to 6. Units have a queen and/or twin beds (22" high/open frames), full kitchens, queen sofa beds in the living rooms, laundries and bathrooms with roll-under sinks and roll-in showers with hand-held sprayers. Pool; fitness room; game room; 4-night minimum. (11360 Gulf Blvd, Treasure Island; 727-367-1991; 866-367-1991)

■ **MOTELS**

Best Western, on Boca Ciega Bay, has 4 ADA rooms, each with a queen bed (21" high/platform), refrigerator, micro-

wave and coffeepot. Bathrooms have raised toilets; room 101 has a roll-in shower, others have tubs; seats are available. Rent poles and fish off a dock on the Bay. Pool; laundry; full restaurant. $$-$$$ (11125 Gulf Blvd, Treasure Island; 727-360-6971)

Don Cesar Beach Resort is a magnificent, turn-of-the-century pink palace towering over the Gulf of Mexico. Each of the 4 ADA rooms have a full bed (24" high/open frame) and bathroom with a raised toilet and roll-under sink; 2 rooms have roll-in showers with hand-held sprayers; 2 have tubs; all have seats. Walkway to narrow beach; pool; lounge; full restaurants; 2 spas; tennis courts; exercise room; retail shops; children's programs. $$-$$$ (3400 Gulf Blvd, St Pete Bch; 727-360-1881; 800-282-1116)

Hilton, in downtown, has 14 ADA 1BR suites, each with a king bed (platform), coffeepot and some with a sofa bed in the living room. Bathrooms have roll-under sinks; 8 have roll-in showers; others have tubs. Lounge; full restaurant. $$$ (333 1 St S; 727-894-5000)

Holiday Inn, on the Gulf, has 2 ADA rooms, each with a full bed (open frame) and coffeepot and each connects to a standard room with 2 full beds. Room 111 has a roll-in shower; room 107 has a tub/shower; both have hand-held sprayers; shower seats and toilet extenders are available. You can roll up to the edge of the beach; stairs lead to the sand. Pool; laundry; lounge; entertainment; full restaurant. $$-$$$ (15208 Gulf Blvd, Madeira Bch; 727-392-2275; 800-360-6658)

Holiday Inn Sunspree Resort, on Tampa Bay, has 4 ADA rooms each with a king bed (open frame), refrigerator, coffeepot and bathroom with a raised toilet, roll-under sink and roll-in shower with a hand-held sprayer and seat. Dock on the bay; pool; lounge; full restaurant; tennis; playground. $$-$$$ (6800 Sunshine Skyway Ln; 727-867-1151)

Renaissance Vinoy Resort, on the

downtown waterfront, has the stately grandeur of the 1920's when it first opened for the rich and famous. The 7 ADA rooms have either a king or 2 queen beds (24" high/open frames), coffeepots and refrigerators. Bathrooms have raised toilets, roll-under sinks and roll-in showers with hand-held sprayers and seats. Pool; laundry; lounge; entertainment; full restaurant; health club; 1 whirlpool with handrail; tennis; golf; croquet. $$$ (501 5 Ave NE; 727-894-1000)

Tradewinds Island Grand is an upscale 18-acre resort on the Gulf with 8 ADA 1BR suites. Each of six suites has a queen bed (22.5" high/open frame) and bathroom with a hand-held sprayer in the tub. Rooms 5215 (beachside) and 1501 each have a king bed and bathroom with a roll-in shower and hand-held sprayer. All units have full sofa beds in the living rooms, kitchenettes and shower seats. Enjoy palm-shaded courtyards with gondola on private waterways and a pool deck on the beach. Poolside bar; laundry; lounge; entertainment; full restaurants; tennis. $$$ (5500 Gulf Blvd, St Pete Bch; 727-562-1212; 800-237-0707)

Tradewinds Sandpiper, overlooking the Gulf, has 3 ADA 1BR suites, each with a queen bed (22.5" high/open frame), full sofa bed in the living room, kitchenette and bathroom with a roll-in shower with a hand-held sprayer and seat. Poolside bar; laundry; lounge; entertainment; full restaurant. $$$ (6000 Gulf Blvd, St Pete Bch; 727-556-1212; 800-237-0707)

Tradewinds Sirata, with 12 acres on the Gulf, has 11 ADA units, both standard rooms and 1BR suites. The 6 suites each have a king bed (22.5" high/open frame), queen sofa bed in the living room and kitchenette. Each room has a full bed (22.5" high/open frame), wet bar, refrigerator and coffeepot. Suite 1849 and rooms 2115, 2117, 4336, 4341 and 4341 have roll-in showers; others have tubs; many with hand-held sprayers and some with seats. Pool; laundry; lounge; entertainment; full restaurant. $$$ (5000 Gulf Blvd, St Pete Bch; 727-562-1212; 800-237-0707)

TAMPA
Apollo Beach, Brandon, Lithia, Oldsmar, Riverview, Ruskin, Seffner, Sun City Center, Thonotosassa, Wimauma, Ybor City

Tampa is home to a wonderful aquarium, distinguished performing arts center, great science museum, professional sports teams and Busch Garden's African theme park. Ybor City, just E of downtown, was once a renowned cigar-manufacturing center and is now a lively spot for tourists and the late-night crowd. But don't miss the rich array of WC sports and, just outside of town, outdoorsy activities.

Tourist Info
Tampa/Hillsborough Visitors Bureau: 111 E Madison St, Suite 1010, 33601-0519; 813-223-1111; 800-826-8358
Visitor Information Guide: 800-448-2672
Centro Ybor Visitor Center: 1600 E 8 Ave, Suite B 104, 33605; 813-241-8838
Web Sites: www.gotampa.com; www.tampabay.com; www. thecentroybor.com; www.ybor.org

Transportation
HART has some buses with lifts or ramps, and through Hart Plus, has vans with lifts

for those can't use buses. Hart services all of Tampa and goes to sites in Brandon, Plant City, Ruskin and Wimauma; call if your destination is a remote area. You must be certified for Hart Plus; visitors certified at home can use Hart Plus for up to 30 days. Wkdy 5am-10pm; wknd 6am-9pm (813-254-4278)

Streetcars, with ramps and lockdowns, run 2.5 mi from the downtown Convention Center through the Channelside area to Ybor City, stopping at attractions along the way. (813-254-4278)

Limo provides airport transportation in a lift-equipped van on 24-hr notice. (727-572-1111; 800-282-6817)

Taxi vans, with ramps, service the airport and around town. Both companies charge taxi rates 24 hrs a day. United Cab (813-253-2424) asks for 2-hr notice; Yellow Cab (813-229-1888/253-8871) asks for 1-hr notice.

WC Resources

Scooter Link sells, rents and repairs scooters and manual and power WCs. Pickup and delivery is included. (8602 Temple Terrace Hwy; 813-984-9400; 888-822-6228)

Self Reliance: Center for Independent Living is a clearinghouse for community services and activities for disabled persons and has an equipment loan closet. (11215 N Nebraska Ave, Suite B-3; 813-975-6560)

ACTIVITIES

■ ARCHERY

Arrowhead Archery instructor Bill Eady teaches archery to physically disabled folks using lightweight bows that even quads can shoot. All gear is loaned to beginners. Classes are held at Arrowhead's indoor range by appointment. (10818 US 92 E, Seffner; 813-621-4279; home 813-622-6434)

■ ATTRACTIONS

See Busch Gardens page 104

Florida Aquarium tells the Florida Water Story, tracing a drop of rain through numerous ecosystems, such as acquifers and wetlands, to the sea. Exhibits also explore water issues around the world. WC guests can take the elevator up then roll down a gentle spiral through successive watery habitats. The Touch Pool has a ramp so you can lean down to pet rays, squid and sharks. Call for special events. Cafe; snack shop; gift shop; CRr in lower lobby; Rr. $. 9:30-5 (701 Channelside Dr; 813-273-4000)

Lowry Park Zoo is one of the country's best mid-size, animal-friendly zoos with more than 1500 animals in natural settings. The park includes a Primate World, Manatee and Aquatic Center, Hands-On Discovery Center as well as a petting zoo, bird and reptile shows. At Stingray Bay, pet 5 species of rays, some up to 5' long. The 4.5-acre Wallaroo Station features Australian animals, from cockatoos to wallabies. The Kangaroo Walkabout is a hard-packed dirt and gravel path where you can pet and feed kangaroos. Muster Ride has a 100-lb limit for the electric cart ride in a field of Australian sheep and cattle. Staff can help lift kids and adults up for a Pony Trek. The only inaccessible feature at the zoo is a raised platform in the aviary. Next door is Lowry Park, a city park with ADA picnic tables. ECV & WC rentals; snack bars; gift shop; Rr. $. 9:30-5 (1101 W Sligh Ave; I-275 exit 48, go W; 813-935-8552)

Tampa Electric's Manatee Viewing Center has a ramped platform past which manatees swim in the winter to enjoy the warm water discharged by the power plant. The Environmental Education Center has films and exhibits on manatees and electrical generation. A 900' boardwalk/nature trail runs along a tidal flat. Docents offer interpretive information. Picnic tables; gift shop; vending machines; Rr. Usually Sep-Apr 10-5 (Big Bend Power Station, Apollo Bch; I-75 exit 246, W for 2.5 mi on CR 672 to Dickman Rd, turn N; 813-228-4289)

■ BIKE TRAILS

Parks: Alderman's, Hillsborough River, Wilderness

Bayshore Blvd has a wide, 6-mi side-walk, separated from the roadway, along Hillsborough Bay past lovely homes. (E end of Gandy Blvd to Davis Island bridge)

Friendship Trail is the old Gandy Bridge, once used by vehicles to cross Tampa Bay between Tampa and St Pete. The 2.5-mi lighted span has a steep hump roughly midway that offers a rigorous climb and potentially dangerous descent. You can also fish (24 hrs) from a lighted catwalk that runs along the bridge. See Handcycles. Bait shop nearby; Rr port-o-let. Dawn-dusk (Gandy Blvd)

Suncoast Trail is a paved, 12' wide bike and pedestrian path through a land-scaped corridor along the Suncoast Parkway/SR 589. Ultimately the trail will run 42 mi N, from Lutz Lake Fern Rd in NW Hillsborough County to the Hernando/Citrus County line; currently 21 mi are complete, from the future Ridge Rd exit (W of Port Richey in Pasco County) N to SR 50 (W of Brooksville). You can access the trail from all county and state roads inter-secting the parkway; parking and Rr are at the trailhead just S of SR 50, W side of the parkway. Along the trail are in-terpretive and rest areas. Call Suncoast Parkway 813-558-1117. Dawn-dusk

■ BILLIARDS/POOL

Planet 9-Ball is a large facility with pool tables, a game room, a full restaurant, bar, entertainment and Rr. WC tourna-ments are held quarterly. See Ken Miller to borrow or purchase adaptive equipment. Mon-Thu 3-3; Fri-Sun noon-3 (11236 W Hillsborough Ave; 813-818-7665)

■ BOAT RAMPS

Fishing Piers: Picnic Island. Parks: EG Simmons, Edward Medard, Wilderness

Courtney Campbell Causeway has a ramp and floating dock on Upper Tampa Bay. (N side of Cswy)

Gandy Boat Ramp is lighted and has a floating dock on Tampa Bay. Bait shop nearby. 24 hrs (SE side of the Gandy Bridge)

Lowry Park has a boat ramp and float-ing dock on the Hillsborough River. ADA picnic tables; Rr by office (7525 North Blvd; I-275 exit 48, go W on Sligh Ave, then N; 813-931-2121)

■ BOAT TOURS

DolphinQuest is a 1 1/2-hr tour of Tampa Bay's wildlife, moderated by Florida Aquarium staff. Crew can help you board the 49-person catamaran by gangway. Because of narrow access in back and into the AC cabin, WC passen-gers are located on the uncovered front deck. If dolphins don't come close, bin-oculars are available. The boat passes by the Alafia River Banks Bird Sanctu-ary, maintained by the Audubon Soci-ety and home to about 20 bird species. Shop & Rr in Aquarium. Wkdy 2pm; wknd 10:30, 1, 3 & 5 (701 Channelside Dr; behind Florida Aquarium; 813-273-4000 x4201)

Rodbenders offers 3 1/2-hr ecotours of Tampa Bay's mangrove islands, estuar-ies and bayous. From the floating dock you can roll aboard the pontoon boat that carries up to 10. (5200 W Tyson Ave; from Gandy Blvd, S on Westshore Blvd 6 blocks, then W; 813-902-8849)

Starlite Princess Riverboat is an authen-tic paddlewheeler offering cruises along the Tampa waterfront or across Tampa Bay to the St Pete Pier. Board by ramp to the accessible 1st level; there's a lip to the dining room. Dinner cruises run 7-10; Dixieland Jazz cruises run Sun 1-3:30; lunch/sightseeing cruises run 2-3 hrs, times vary (651 Channelside Dr; be-hind Florida Aquarium; 813-595-1212; 800-722-6645)

StarShip Dining Yacht offers elegant, 2

1/2-hr luncheon and dinner cruises in Tampa's Channel District with a live band. If needed, stewards can help you board by ramp; then take the elevator to any of the 3 decks on the 181' yacht. Valet parking; Rr. 11:45 & 7:30; sometimes 5:30 & 9:15pm also (603 Channelside Dr; next to Shops at Channelside, E of Ice Palace; 813-223-7999; 877-744-7999)

■ BOCCE

Misc: Hillsborough County

■ BOWLING

Misc: Hillsborough County

AMF has bowling ball ramps, bumpers, glow-in-the-dark bowling, a game room, full snack bar, bar and Rr. Sun-Thu 9-mdnt; Fri-Sat –3am (10400 N Florida Ave; 813-932-6161)

Regal Lanes has bowling ball ramps, glow-in-the-dark bowling, a game room, cafe, bar and Rr. 9am-closing (4847 N Armenia; 813-877-7418)

■ CANOEING

Parks: Hillsborough River, Little Manatee, Wilderness

Canoe Escape offers canoe rentals and guided (private or group) 2-hr trips through the 16,000-acre Hillsborough River State Park. Staff has Adaptive Paddlers Certification, is experienced with disabled paddlers and can lift you into the canoe. Staff can also lift you into the shuttle van. Or, you can drive your vehicle to the launch and staff can drive it to the take-out. Guided group trips depart on Wed at 11:30am. Wkdy 9-5; wknd 8-5 (9335 E Fowler Ave, Thonotosassa; 813-986-2067)

Canoe Outpost rents canoes for the 28 mi of trails on the shallow Little Manatee River. Staff is experienced with disabled paddlers and, with advance notice, can carry you down the steps to the canoe launch. Staff can shuttle you from the take-out in Little Manatee Park or you can wait for someone in your party to shuttle. (18001 US 301 S, Wimauma; 813-634-2228)

■ CASINOS

Seminole Indian Casino offers 24 hrs of high stakes bingo, poker and gaming machines. The non-smoking bingo room upstairs is not accessible. Be forewarned: the few non-smoking bingo tables downstairs are hardly smoke-free. (5223 N Orient Rd; I-4 exit 6; 813-621-1302)

■ DANCE INSTRUCTION

Asher Dance Eclectic offers instructions on dance techniques for folks using WCs or assisted-walking devices. Stage productions engage able-bodied and physically disabled dancers. No dance or acting experience is necessary to audition but you must be able to attend months of rehearsals. (Elizabeth Edelson 813-786-6291)

■ FISHING CHARTERS

Angling Adventures is a group of guides offering half/full-day inshore, offshore and flats fishing. The type of fishing you choose and the number of anglers determines which boat is used. With advance notice, crew can help lift you in your WC aboard any of the boats from an accessible dock. (Capt John Sackett; 941-920-4891)

Capt Blackmore can accommodate 2 WC and 2 able-bodied anglers on his 22' center console boat for inshore and near-shore trips using light tackle. If you like, spend some time sightseeing. The capt can help lift you aboard in your WC and can choose an accessible dock. (813-831-8987)

Light Tackle Fishing offers half/full-day light tackle spinning or flyfishing charters on inshore saltwater and offshore trips. For inshore fishing in the upper Tampa Bay, you can board the 18'-25' flats boats by ramp from a floating dock; the deck is roomy enough for 1 WC and 2 able-bodied anglers. For offshore fishing, crew can lift you aboard the 25'-40' boats in your WC. This group also offers charters in St Pete and Tarpon Springs. (Public launch at E end of Gandy Bridge; 813-855-0430)

Rodbenders offers 4- to 8-hr fishing trips using light tackle, heavy tackle or fly rods aboard inshore, offshore or pontoon boats. You can roll aboard the pontoon boat from the floating dock; crew can lift you aboard the other boats in your WC. (5200 W Tyson Ave; from Gandy Blvd, S on Westshore Blvd 6 blocks, then W; 813-223-7754; 800-872-9880)

■ **FISHING PIERS**
Bike Trails: Friendship. Parks: Al Lopez, EG Simmons, Edward Medard, Wilderness

Ballast Point Pier is a lighted, wood, 960' pier on Hillsborough Bay. Picnic tables; bait/ snack shop (Wed-Mon dawn-dusk); ADA playground; Rr. 24 hrs (5300 Interbay Blvd; S end of Bayshore Blvd)

DeSoto Park has a 300' pier with a paved surface on McKay Bay. Picnic tables; grills; Rr. Dawn-dusk (2615 E Corrinne St; from SR 60, S on 22 St S, then E)

Picnic Island Park is a 125-acre city beach with a 200' lighted, concrete fishing pier and boat ramp on Old Tampa Bay. ADA picnic shelters; Rr. 24 hrs (7404 Picnic Island Rd; from S Westshore Blvd, W on Commerce St)

RE Olds Park, a 15-acre park with a lighted shoreline, has a 400', unlighted wood pier on the upper Tampa Bay. Playground; picnic shelter; Rr. Dawn-11pm (107 Shore Dr, Oldsmar; S of SR 580 & S of St Petersburg Dr)

■ **FITNESS TRAILS**
Misc: Hillsborough County

■ **HORSEBACK RIDING**
Bakas Horses for the Handicapped is a county-sponsored, NARHA recreational program for riders, age 4 through adult, novice through advanced. The 30-min sessions run over 6 wks and are held in a covered arena, outdoor ring or on a trail. Mount from a mounting block with a ramp or hydraulic lift. If you need extra support, volunteers can walk at your side or sit behind you on horseback. Use western or English saddles; adaptive gear is available. If riding doesn't appeal, drive a horse-drawn cart with a lift. An application

and physician's release is required to add you to the 3-4-month waiting list. There is no charge but you or a family member must volunteer. Tue-Sat (11510 Whisper Lake Trail; from Gunn Hwy, W on S Mobley Rd, S into Ed Radice Park, follow signs; 813-264-3890)

■ **MISC**
Hillsborough County Parks and Recreation's Therapeutic Section sponsors a wide range of sports training and competition, events, leisure activities and summer camps for kids and adults with special needs. Sporting opportunities for folks in WCs include track and field, basketball, adapted bowling, bocce and more. The Therapeutic Section is housed at the All People's Life Center, a fully accessible recreation center with a paved fitness trail, ADA playground and greenhouse. The county intends to build an indoor track and field house that will include convertible courts (for tennis, walleyball and basketball) in the center of the track and a weight room. Other activities include Teen Night out, scouting and field trips. Call for schedule. See WC Events. (6015 E Sligh Ave; 2.5 mi E of 56 St/SR 583, 1.5 mi W of US 301; 813-744-5978/903-2248)

■ **MUSEUMS**
Centro Ybor is the building with an 8' cigar on top, displays on Ybor's turn-of-the-century immigrant community, information on the cigar industry and an 8-min film on local history. Self-guided, audio tours are available. Rr. Mon-Sat 10-6; Sun 12-5 (1600 E 8 Ave, Suite B104, Ybor City; 813-241-8838)

Children's Museum of Tampa is a hands-on museum for kids, age 2-12, with indoor, participatory exhibits and an outdoor, miniature Kid City. Inside exhibits have some narrow hallways to negotiate. Rr. $. Wkdy 9-5:30; Sat 10-5:30; Sun 12-5:30 (7550 North Blvd; I-275 exit 48, go W on Sligh Ave, then N; 813-935-8441)

Henry Plant Museum, along with the University of Tampa, is in the former

Tampa Bay Hotel, a luxurious Victorian palace built in 1891. The museum's Moorish domes and minarets give western Tampa a distinctive skyline. The museum features original hotel furnishings and other treasures of the gilded age, along with a series of special events. Ramps in front & back; some parking in front; parking garage 2 blks away at North Blvd & B St N; gift shop; Rr. $D. Tue-Sat 10-4; Sun 12-4 (401 W Kennedy Blvd; W of Ashley Dr; 813-254-1891)

Museum of Science & Industry, or MOSI, is a huge scientific playground with hands-on learning at all turns. Roll among butterflies, take a simulated flight on the Challenger, run experiments from Mission Control, trek through the universe in the planetarium and sit through a hurricane. A .5-mi nature trail, with a plastic surface, takes you through natural wetlands, a gopher tortoise habitat and native fauna and flora. Call for IMAX film schedule, workshops and special events. Snack bar; gift shop; Rr; ask staff to use CRr in employee area. $. Hrs vary (4801 E Fowler Ave; E of I-275; 813-987-6100)

Tampa Bay History Center features exhibits, traveling displays and workshops on geographic, historic and multicultural influences that shaped the region. The library contains a good genealogy section. Rr. $D. Tue-Sat 10-5 (Tampa Convention Center Annex, 225 S Franklin St; 813-228-0097)

Tampa Museum of Art features a nationally renowned permanent collection of classical antiquities, plus traveling exhibitions of photography, contemporary art and sculpture. One gallery features the state's emerging artists. Rr. $. Mon-Sat 10-5; Sun 1-5 (600 N Ashley Dr; 813-274-8130)

Ybor City State Museum, housed in the old Ferlita Bakery, captures the immigrant's experience of Ybor City in days gone by. The WC entrance from the street is on the W side of the building; if the side gate is not open, send someone to the ranger at the front entrance. La Casita is a renovated, cigar worker's home, ramped in back; gardens have paved paths. Enjoy a 1-hr historic walking tour every Sat 10:30. Rr. $. 9-5 (1818 9 Ave, Ybor City; 813-247-6323)

■ **PARKS**

Al Lopez Park is a 105-acre city park with a 1-mi, paved nature trail around the 8.4-acre N lake and an 80' x 20' dock from which you can catch bass, catfish or bluegill. Try out the 1.5-mi paved jogging trail. ADA playground; ADA picnic tables; Rr. 5am-dusk (4810 N Himes Ave; 813-931-2121)

Alafia River State Park is being transformed from a phosphate mine into a lovely, 6800-acre park with rolling hills, freshwater ponds and the river that runs through it. You can fish from flat, open areas at the ponds or in the river from a bridge (at Thatcher Rd) that has little traffic. Talk with a ranger about which horse or bike trails might be accessible in your case. Soon paved paths will lead from HC parking to lakefront, ADA picnic shelters with large fireplaces. Plans also include canoe rentals and an accessible launch. See Campgrounds. ADA playground on mulch; Rr. $D. 8-dusk (SR 39, Lithia; 3.5 mi S of Lithia Pinecrest Rd/CR 640, 10 mi SE of Tampa; 813-672-5132)

Alderman's Ford Park is a 1141-acre county park dense with moss-draped oaks along the Alafia River. A visitor center has environmental displays on the local ecology. The paved, 2-mi hike/bike trail has 3 moderately steep bridges as it goes over the river and through the woods. The park has a canoe launch on the W side of CR 39, but the riverbanks are so steep that WC access is very tough. There is an ADA picnic shelter and grills just beyond HC parking in the Main Park area. ADA playground; Rr. $D. 8-dusk (E side of CR 39, Lithia; just N of Lithia Pinecrest Rd; 813-757-3801)

Edward Medard Park is a 1284-acre

county park with a 600-acre, freshwater reservoir filled with bream, perch and largemouth bass. A 700' boardwalk runs along the shore and has cutouts for WC anglers. Or, try the ramped 10' x 20' Burnt Stump dock near one of 4 fish feeders in the lake. The boat ramp has a ramped, floating dock; no wake is allowed. Across roughly 100' of grass is a white sand beach and another 60'-70' to the swim area with lifeguards. Share the 3-mi, hard-packed shell trail with the occasional horse, through lovely, wooded areas and across 2 bridges over creeks. See Campgrounds. Playgrounds on sand, 1 ADA; ADA picnic shelters; Rr. $D. 6am-closing varies (5726 Panther Loop, Plant City; take SR 60 6 mi E of Brandon, S 1 mi on Turkey Creek Rd; 813-757-3802)

EG Simmons Park is a 258-acre county park on the E shore of Tampa Bay. Fish from piers or from the banks of several inlets on Tampa Bay. HC parking is a fair distance from the soft sand beach; ask at the entrance to drive your vehicle onto the beach where WC riders can get out on the sand; your vehicle must be returned to the parking lot. The boat ramp onto the Bay has ramped, floating docks. See Campgrounds. Lifeguards in summer & winter wknd; ADA picnic shelters; grills; ADA phones; Rr. 8-dusk (2401 19 Ave NW, Ruskin; 1 mi E of US 41, then W; 813-671-7655)

Hillsborough River State Park has over 3000 acres of history, nature and accessible fun. The trail to the reconstructed Fort Foster, built originally in the Seminole Wars, is fairly arduous and the van, in which rangers take visitors, does not have a lift; with advance notice, rangers can escort your vehicle to the fort. You can easily access the fort's grassy ground level, but may need help on the ramps into some buildings. Call for the schedule of guided fort tours Dec-Mar; reenactments, called *Rendez-Vous*, occur each Feb. The 2.2-mi, paved, loop park road is popular for cy-

cling and the site of a WC Derby each Dec; see WC Events. The park rents canoes and staff can help you in and out. Take the trail by the picnic shelter down to the flat canoe launch. The river is so placid here that you can paddle back to the put-in. The riverbanks are mostly quite steep; ask rangers if you can fish along the campground seawall (generally for campers only). A huge, spring-fed swimming pool, open Mar-Dec, is ramped for WC access. Diverse programs range from ranger talks and Tai Chi classes to films and special dinners. See Campgrounds. ADA picnic shelters; amphitheater; snack bar & gift shop by pool; Rr. $. 8-dusk (15402 US 301 N, Thonotosassa; 12 mi N of Tampa; 813-987-6771)

Little Manatee River State Park encompasses over 2000 acres on a beautiful 4.5-mi stretch of the river with some fine bass fishing. The only WC-accessible spots on the riverbanks are closed to the general public; with advance permission, rangers can open the gates for you. You can cycle on the quiet park roads, but the 6.5-mi hiking trail is too rough for most WC riders. Should you have your own steed, enjoy 10 mi of horseback trails and even overnight stalls. The park rents canoes, but the launch site has 5 steps. With 10-day advance permission, rangers can open the gates to an accessible put-in; or rent at Canoe Outpost (see Canoeing) and staff can carry you down to the put-in. See Campgrounds. ADA picnic shelters; grills; playground on sand; Rr. $. 8-dusk (215 Lightfoot Rd, Wimauma; off US 301, 5 mi S of Sun City Center; 813-671-5005)

Wilderness Parks include 6 county parks occupying 16,000 acres along or near the Hillsborough River. All parks, except Dead River, now have paved paths to ADA picnic shelters and Rr. The crushed-shell paths used elsewhere in these parks can be tough to navigate in standard WCs. Staff is often in the field at some of the parks; if so, call 813-

987-6211 for info. **Dead River** is a very primitive site on the banks of the Hillsborough. The scenic, 2-mi, crushed-shell park road is only open for cycling and walking Mon-Thu. You can fish from a bridge over Dead River where it joins the Hillsborough. The 2-mi dirt trail is hard packed. ADA picnic tables; Rr. 9-5:30 (US 301 & end of Dead River Rd; 5 mi N of John B Sargeant Park; 813-987-6210) **Flatwoods** is a gem of a park for cyclists and hikers with 3700 acres of pine wetlands and cypress trees. The welcome center, .5 mi from the main entrance, has paved parking, air pumps, vending machines, Rr and outside ADA picnic tables. One mile from the main entrance is a 7-mi, paved bike/hike loop, mostly in bright sun with 4 shaded water stations along the way. On the W side of the loop is a paved, 2-mi trail to Bruce B Downs Rd. Each of 3 crushed-shell, interpretive trails runs roughly .5 mi. ADA picnic shelters with grills; Rr. Summer 7am-8pm; winter -6 (14302 Morris Bridge Rd, Thonotosassa; I-75 exit 55, NE on Morris Bridge Rd; 1 mi N of Hillsborough River; 813-987-6211) **John B Sargeant**, at the confluence of the Hillsborough River and Flint Creek, has a short boardwalk through oak and cypress trees to the river where you can fish. Trails are rough and natural. There's a boat ramp with a floating dock on the river for boats with 9.9hp motors or less. Nearby is a sloped, crushed-shell canoe launch; you may prefer to board a canoe from the floating dock or boat ramp. ADA picnic shelters; grills; Rr. $D. Summer 8-7; winter -6 (US 301 & Stacy Rd; 813-987-6208) **Morris Bridge Park** is divided by Morris Bridge Rd. The W side of the park has a .4-mi boardwalk over a beautiful, cypress tree island in the Hillsborough River. You can launch canoes or boats (with 9.9hp motors or less) from a boat ramp but the floating dock has a 6" drop to the lower tier. To access the E side of the park, take the shell path

from HC parking to the left of the boat ramp to a boardwalk under the street bridge. Here you'll find a fishing dock near the ADA picnic shelter with a grill and a gorgeous view of the river. A 1-mi, crushed-shell nature trail follows an old railroad/tram bed. Rr. $D. Summer 7am-8pm; winter -6 (Morris Bridge Rd at the Hillsborough River; I-75 exit 55, NE on Morris Bridge Rd; 813-987-6209) **Trout Creek** has 150' boardwalk from which you can fish and a .5-mi, crushed-shell nature trail SE of the parking lot. The canoe launch is simply a grassy slope that is tough for WCs. ADA picnic shelters have grills and overlook the river. Rr. $D. Summer 7am-8pm; winter -6 (Morris Bridge Rd at the Tampa Bypass Canal; just NE of I-75 exit 55; 813-987-6200) **Veterans Memorial Park** has a ramped museum with rotating exhibits on US military actions. Sidewalks lead to major outdoor monuments; some are on grass. The Bypass Canal has rocky, steep banks that preclude fishing from a WC, but you can enjoy the paved, .7-mi trail. ADA picnic shelters; grills; Rr. $D. 10-5:30 (US 301 at Tampa Bypass Canal; 1 blk S of SR 574; 813-744-5502)

■ PARI-MUTUELS

Tampa Bay Downs has 10 thoroughbred races daily from mid-Dec-Apr, plus simulcasts all year. All seating is on ground level. (11225 Race Track Rd; N of Hillsborough Ave/SR 580, just E of Pinellas County line; 813-855-4401) **Tampa Greyhound Track** features live races Jul-Dec and simulcasts all year from 11:30am. WC seating is on raised areas on the 1st level and, via elevator, the 2nd level. The restaurant and Clubhouse also have raised viewing areas with monitors. Rr. Mon-Sat 6:30; also Mon, Wed, Sat 11:30am (8300 N Nebraska Ave; I-27 exit 49; 813-932-4313)

■ PERFORMING ARTS

Tampa Bay Performing Arts Center is the region's largest performing arts center, with world-class productions in 4 different venues including the 2557-

seat Carol Morsani Hall, the elegant 1034-seat Louise Lykes Ferguson Hall, the 150-seat Shimberg Playhouse and the 300-seat cabaret-style Jaeb Theater. WC seating is available in all price locations in each theater. House Management (727-222-1061) can accommodate most special needs. Dining for some shows; gift shop; Rr (1010 N MacInnes Pl; S of I-75, W of Ashley Dr; 813-229-7827; 800-955-1045)

Tampa Theater is a whimsically restored, 1926 movie palace featuring alternative and classic films, concerts, special events and 1-hr tours twice a month. Enjoy a gourmet snack bar and an organist who performs before every film and tour. WC seating on ground level; street parking; Rr (711 N Franklin St; downtown between Polk St & Zack St; 813-274-8981)

■ **POOLS**
Parks: Hillsborough
Bobby Hicks Pool is a heated, Olympic pool with a portable lift (fixed seat). Call ahead so staff can set up the lift in advance; staff operates the lift but cannot help with transfers. Rr, wide stalls no grab bars. $. Apr-late Nov Mon-Sat hrs vary (4120 W Mango; 813-832-1216)
Copeland Pool is heated and has a zero-depth slope. Rr. $. Apr-late Nov Mon-Sat hrs vary (1101 N 15; 813-975-2734)

■ **QUAD RUGBY**
Tampa Generals is a professional quad rugby team that competes May-Oct. Anyone is welcome to join practices or try out for the team on Tue evenings 6:30-9:30. Call Tampa General's Spinal Cord Injury Center 813-844-4287 or Justin Stark 813-719-6151 (Martin Luther King Gym; Rome Ave, S of Columbus Dr)

■ **SCUBA**
Clearwater: Scuba
Adventures Underwater instructor Dan Harvey is HSA-certified and offers individual, performance-based scuba classes at 2 locations roughly 1 1/2 hrs away. Staff can lift you in and out of the water at both sites. At Plantation

Marina in Crystal River, trips use a roll-aboard pontoon boat or a skiff into which crew can lift you. At Lake Denton, near Avon Park, you dive from the shore. Meet Dan in Tampa then follow him in your vehicle to the training site. After certification, he can coordinate accessible dive trips. Wkdy 10:30-6:30; Sat 10-3 (3418 W Swann Ave; 813-875-2376; 888-627-2822)

■ **SHOPPING**
Boutiques: Old Hyde Park Village includes over 60 shops, from chic to The Gap, outdoor cafes and a movie complex. (1509 W Swann; at Dakota Ave; 813-251-3500)
Entertainment Complexes: Shops at Channelside include dining, a movie complex with a 3-D Imax theater and clubs; cruise ships dock here. Park in Port Authority Garage across the street or use valet parking (615 Channelside Dr; 813-221-0700). Centro Ybor has shopping, dining, a 20-screen stadium seating theater, GameWorks and nightclubs, including a comedy club (1600 8 Ave, Ybor City).
Farmers Market: Centro Ybor fills its courtyard Sat 8-1 with local produce, baked goods and flowers. Valet parking at the N end by Camelot Music; city garage at 15 & 16 Sts (1600 8 Ave, Ybor City). Ybor City hosts Tampa's only open-air market Thu-Sat 6pm-3am (7 Ave & 17 St, Ybor City; 813-231-2720).
Flea Market at Oldsmar is a good spot for sports equipment, bikes, computers, you name it. Wknd 9-5 (Hillsborough Ave & Race Track Rd; 813-855-2587)
Malls: Brandon Town Center (Brandon Blvd & SR 60, Brandon; 813-661-6255); Citrus Park Mall (Veterans Expwy exit 9; 813-926-4644); International Plaza (2223 N Westshore Blvd; 813-342-3790); University Square Mall (2200 E Fowler Ave; 813-971-3465); Westshore Mall (250 Westshore Blvd; 813-971-3465)

■ **SPECTATOR SPORTS**
Arena Football Tampa Bay Storm plays indoor football Apr-Aug. WC seating at

all levels; Rr (Ice Palace, 401 Channelside Dr; 813-301-6600)

Baseball New York Yankees have spring training in Mar and the Florida State League Yankees play Apr-Aug. WC seating on concourse level; Rr (Legends Field, 1 Steinbrenner Dr; off N Dale Mabry Blvd, across from Raymond James Stadium; 813-875-7753)

Football NFL Tampa Bay Buccaneers play Aug-Dec. Elevators (at gates A & C) and ramps go to WC seating around the field on all levels. Power stations are available to recharge ECVs, respirators, etc. HC parking in Lot A (off Dale Mabry Hwy at NW corner of stadium) & Lot C (off Himes Ave at SE corner of stadium); Rr; CRr on main & upper concourses near corner ramps (Raymond James Stadium, 4201 N Dale Mabry Hwy; 813-870-2700; 800-282-0683)

Ice Hockey NHL Tampa Bay Lightning play Aug-Mar. WC seating at all levels; Rr (Ice Palace, 401 Channelside Dr, 813-229-2658)

Soccer MLS Tampa Bay Mutiny plays Mar-Oct. All seating for Mutiny games, including WC seating, is at the lower bowl level. Rr (Raymond James Stadium, 4201 N Dale Mabry Hwy; 813-289-6811)

■ **TENNIS**

USTA offers free clinics and games to WC-tennis players, kids through adults beginning through advanced, each Sat 9-10:30am. Drop-ins are welcome; tennis WCs may be available. Call Tracy Wilkerson 813-672-2573. (Univ of South Florida, 4204 E Fowler Ave; behind Sun Dome stadium)

■ **TOURS**

Customized Tours offers 90-min walking tours through Ybor City. Fri at 11am, historic tours depart from the Centro Ybor Visitor Center (1600 8 Ave). Wed at 6pm, tours on Ybor City's romantic history depart from the King Corona Cigar Shop on 7 Ave (between 15 St & 16 St). $. May-Sep (813-247-6692)

Ghostwalks are 75-min, private, walking tours to Ybor City's historic sites, led by an appropriately garbed guide. You'll learn of 10 individuals who shaped Ybor's history. Leave from the Centro Ybor Visitor Center. $. Thu-Sun (1600 E 8 Ave, Suite B104, Ybor City; 813-242-4660)

Ybor City Brewing Company has hourly 45-min tours and a hospitality tasting room. On the E side of the building is a ramp and an elevator making all 3 floors of this microbrewery accessible. $. Wkdy 11-1 (2205 N 20 St, Ybor City; 813-242-9222)

■ **TRACK & FIELD**

Misc: Hillsborough County

ACCOMMODATIONS

■ **CAMPGROUNDS**

Alafia River State Park currently has 30 RV/tent sites with asphalt pads, grills and plans for water/elec hookups. Request a site with an ADA picnic table and near the ADA bathhouses with roll-under sinks, roll-in showers with fold-down seats and lowered hand controls. See Parks. (SR 39, Lithia; 3.5 mi S of Lithia Pinecrest Rd/CR 640, 10 mi SE of Tampa; 813-672-5132)

EG Simmons Park has 88 sunny RV/tent sites, some waterfront, all on sand or grassy terrain. All sites have fire rings and water; most have elec. Although the campground has a no-reservation policy, ask in advance for a site with an ADA picnic table near the ADA bathhouse with roll-under sinks and roll-in showers. In the day-use area are ADA picnic shelters and grills. See Parks. 1st come, 1st serve (2401 19 Ave NW, Ruskin; 2 mi E of US 41, then W; 813-671-7655)

Edward Medard Park has 40 RV/tent sites on hard-packed terrain with picnic tables, grills and water/elec. Although the campground has a no-reservation policy, ask in advance for a site with an ADA picnic table and near the bathhouse with roll-under sinks and grab bars at the toilet and shower (with a 2" drop at the entrance). ADA bathhouses are planned for completion in 2003. See Parks. (5276 Panther Loop, Plant City; take SR 60 6 mi E of Brandon, S 1 mi on Turkey Creek Rd; 813-757-3802)

Hillsborough River State Park has 108 tent/RV sites on hard-packed terrain. Four ADA sites have water/elec, ADA picnic tables and grills and are close to the ADA bathhouse with roll-under sinks and roll-in showers. See Parks. (15402 US 301 N, Thonotosassa; 12 mi N of Tampa; 813-987-6771; 800-326-3521)

Little Manatee River State Park has 30 RV/tent sites on hard-packed terrain in a dense sand pine scrub. Three ADA sites, with ADA picnic tables, grills and water/elec are near the ADA bathhouse with roll-under sinks and roll-in showers. $/50% discount for disabled campers who live in Florida. See Parks. (215 Lightfoot Rd, Wimauma; off US 301, 5 mi S of Sun City Center; 813-671-5005; 800-326-3521)

■ **MOTELS**

Amerisuites has 5 ADA 1BR suites, each with a full bed (24" high/open frame), queen sofa bed in the living room and kitchenette. Bathrooms have raised toilets, roll-under sinks and roll-in showers with hand-held sprayers and seats. Free brkfst; pool; laundry. $$-$$$ (4811 W Main St; 813-282-1037)

Bahia Beach Island Resort & Marina has an ADA room with a queen bed (open frame), kitchenette and bathroom with a raised toilet, roll-under sink and roll-in shower with a hand-held sprayer and seat. The marina, on the Tampa Bay, has a pier for fishing. Pool; laundry; lounge with entertainment; full restaurant. $$-$$$ (611 Destiny Dr, Ruskin; 813-645-3291; 800-327-2773)

Econo Lodge Midtown has 2 ADA rooms, each with a full bed (platform), coffeepot and bathroom with a raised toilet, roll-under sink and roll-in shower with a hand-held sprayer and seat. Free brkfst; laundry. $-$$ (1020 S Dale Mabry; 813-254-3005; 800-905-8861)

Embassy Suites has 13 ADA 2BR suites, each with a king and 2 full beds (23" high/platforms), a sofa bed in the living room, a microwave, refrigerator and coffeepot. Bathrooms have roll-under sinks; 6 units have roll-in showers; others have tubs; all have hand-held sprayers and seats. Free brkfst; pool; laundry; lounge with entertainment; full restaurant; fitness room. $$$ (3705 Spectrum Blvd; 813-977-7066)

Holiday Inn Express has 4 ADA rooms, each with a king bed (22" high/open frame) and a bathroom with roll-under sink; room 101 has a roll-in shower with hand-held sprayer and seat; others have tubs. Free brkfst. $$-$$$ (3113 College Ave, Ruskin/Sun City Center; 813-641-3437; 877-466-9111)

Homestead Village has 4 ADA 1BR suites with either 2 king or 2 queen beds (platforms), full kitchens and bathrooms with raised toilets and roll-under sinks. Units 115 and 107 have roll-in showers; others have tubs; all have hand-held sprayers and seats. Laundry. $-$$ (330 Grand Regency, Brandon; 813-643-5900)

La Quinta has 3 1BR and 4 2BR suites that meet ADA standards. Each suite has either a king and/or a full bed (22" high/open frame), coffeepot and bathroom with a raised toilet and roll-under sink. Suites 108 and 125 have roll-in showers; others have tubs; most have hand-held sprayers. Some units have refrigerators and microwaves. Free brkfst; pool; laundry. $$-$$$ (310 Grand Regency Blvd, Brandon; 813-643-0574; 800-687-6665)

La Quinta has 7 ADA rooms with either a king or 2 full beds (23" high/open frames) and coffeepots. Bathrooms have roll-under sinks; rooms 122 and 124 have roll-in showers; others have tubs. Free brkfst; pool; laundry. $$ (3701 E Fowler Ave; 813-910-7500; 813-531-5900)

Marriott Waterside has 27 ADA rooms, each with a king bed (24" high/open frames) and a coffeepot. Bathrooms have raised toilets and roll-under sinks; 14 rooms (405-1705) have roll-in showers with hand-held sprayers and seats; others have tubs. This hotel is in the Channelside area and close to the Convention Center and Florida Aquarium. Pool; full restaurant; sports bar; laundry; spa; valet parking. $$$ (700 S Florida Ave; 813-221-4900)

Motel 6 Tampa East has 7 ADA rooms, each with a full bed (21" high/open frame) and bathroom with a raised toilet and roll-under sink. Three units have roll-in showers with hand-held sprayers and seats; others have step-in showers. Pool; laundry. $ (6510 US 301 N; 813-28-0888)

Wingate Inn is near Busch Gardens and has 6 ADA rooms with a king or 2 full beds (open frames), coffeepots and bathrooms with roll-under sinks. Room 119 has a roll-in shower; others have tubs; all have hand-held sprayers and seats. Free brkfst; pool; laundry. $$ (3751 E Fowler Ave; 813-979-2828)

Busch Gardens

This 335-acre theme park has awesome, African animal attractions and fabulous shows that are readily accessible, however virtually all rides require transfers. Busch is also a great spot for shopping, particularly if you are into Africana and safari clothes; you can even get an abbreviated admission for a shopping spree. Or, indulge yourself with hair wraps, temporary tattoos and caricatures. Rr are throughout the park; CRr are located in Nairobi (at Kenya Kanteen), Egypt (by Montu), Timbuktu (at First Aid), Congo (at Bumper Cars) and in the Land of Dragons (by Snack Dragon stand). Restaurants; shops; snack bars; HC parking by entrance. $/WC riders 50% discount. 9:30-6; extended hrs in summer (3000 Busch Blvd; I-275 exit 50, go 2 mi E, then N on 40 St; 813-987-5082; 888-800-5447)

General Tips

Be sure to check the show and animal-feeding schedules on the Park map and plan your day accordingly. During peak season, arrive early and catch the popular rides first or stay late and do those rides after everybody else is exhausted. Even when the Park is very crowded, you can usually get into the animal attractions and shows without huge lines or queues throughout the day. If you have small children, you may want to go directly to the Land of the Dragons. Busch offers sizable discounts for next-day admission to the park. Multi-day, discount passes are also available to nearby Adventure Island (a water park with no ride modifications for WC access) and Sea World in Orlando.

WC Tips

For HC parking and drop-offs, turn W into the Park entrance off 40 St. Busch Gardens' steep grades and Florida's heat and humidity can take a toll on someone riding or pushing a manual WC. The textured pavement achieves an aesthetic but bumpy effect for WC riders. You can rent an ECV (or WC) in Jeepers Creepers, the 4th gift shop from entrance on the right; reserve an ECV at 813-985-1431. Should you have problems with your ECV or WC, ask an employee to contact the WC-repair staff who will come to you and make repairs.

Guest Relations staff at the entrance can give you a Disability Guide (with general information) and advise you on rides that might be more accessible in your particular situation. Staff can help steady but not lift guests transferring from WCs into ride vehicles. Except as noted below, WC guests enter rides through exits and to the boarding areas, where staff can stop or steady ride vehicles as you board. WC guests can take up to 3 companions and enjoy a second, consecutive ride without reboarding.

Tours

Check out 3 tours offered for an additional charge in Moroccan Village just past the entrance to the left in the Expedition Outfitters gift shop. *Serengeti Safari* is a 30-min, guided truck tour of the 65-acre plain with exotic animals on the loose. Board by a ramp that is level with the truck bed where you ride. The truck railing may impede your view, but since most of the animals were born here, they are friendly and may come close for some food and a nuzzle. *Animal Adventure* is a 2-hr, behind-the-scenes, guided walking tour to the zoo where Busch's animals relax when off duty. The 4- to 5-hr *Guided Adventure* combines the behind-the-scenes Animal Adventure and front-of-the-line status at major rides and shows.

ATTRACTIONS

The following are described roughly counterclockwise from the entrance:

■ MOROCCO

Gwazi (~~WC~~, ~~ECV~~) is a 2 1/2-min duel between 2 coasters on wooden tracks that make clickety-clack, twisting flybys at 50mph. From the exit take a long, steep, switchback ramp to the boarding deck that is flush with the entry to the roller coaster cart. You must step through the 10" entry and down 10" to the floor before you can sit and fasten the lap restraint. Or, your companions can lift you over the 20" high side of the car into the seat.

Marrakesh Theater is an open-air casbah with 25-min concerts and portable lawn chairs that allow you to sit where you like.

Sultan's Tent is a walk-by stage with anything from snake charmers to belly dancers.

Alligator pit, across from the Moroccan Palace, as the 1st animal viewing area, is usually very crowded and requires patience to work your way up to the fence so you can see the gators.

Moroccan Palace showcases 36-min, international ice-skating extravaganzas. The WC entrance is on the E (left) side of the building, beside the exit ramp and leads to WC seating just above each of the 2 middle sections (mid-way

and at the rear of the theater).

Skyride (~~WC~~, ~~ECV~~) is a gondola that departs across from the Crown Colony House. Go up the very steep entrance ramp then through the exit gate for another steep roll up to the boarding area. You must step up 10" to the gondola that has a 23" wide doorway and a pole between 2 face-to-face bench seats. You cannot take your WC on the ride, so relax and enjoy the 15-min round trip over the heads of African animals to the Congo area and back. (By the way, the gondolas make a brief touchdown as they turn to the Congo; nobody can disembark here.)

Clydesdale Hamlet is a meticulous, roll-through stable where the proud Anheuser-Busch Clydesdales reside. Next door is the Show Jumping Hall of Fame with photos and mementos of horseback competitions.

Crown Colony House, the only Park restaurant with table service, overlooks free-roaming African animals on the Serengeti Plain. The restaurant is on the upper level and a cafeteria is on the lower level. The brick tower, in front of the building and across from Clydesdale Hamlet, has an elevator to both levels.

■ EGYPT

Tuts Tomb is a roll-through replica of the key chambers in a pharaoh's tomb.

Sifting Sands (~~WC~~, ~~ECV~~) is a curbed sandbox for young children.

Montu (~~WC~~, ~~ECV~~) offers 3 min of twists and loops at 60mph. Enter through the gift shop before and to the right of the huge archway. The ride's bucket seats hang 27" above the boarding dock and have 32" high, fixed armrests and shoulder restraints.

Edge of Africa invites 15-min rolls on a sunny, paved path through 15 acres of wildlife, from meerkats to lions, where the only thing between you and the animals is a moat or glass wall. Watch swimming hippos from above and below the water's surface.

■ NAIROBI

Myombe Reserve is a 10-min, shady roll on a paved, somewhat hilly path past gorillas and chimps in a lush natural habitat. Curiosity Caverns, a cave with glassed-in alcoves of nocturnal creatures, has a steep dip at the entrance and exit.

Train Stations at Nariobi, Congo and Stanleyville have accessible main entrances and the coach in back of each train has a WC lift. Take the 35-min round trip, including a loop past wildebeest, bongo and other unusual animals on the Serengeti Plain or disembark at either of the 2 other stations.

Field Station is the nursery for Busch's babies. You can roll past the windows and small corrals where baby giraffes, marmosets and other creatures are nurtured. Then roll past windows of less cuddly types at the reptile house. As you leave here, check out giant tortoises and elephants along the path.

Rhino Rally (~~WC~~, ~~ECV~~) is an 8-to 10-min ride in a 17-passenger Land Rover over hill and on a raft past buffalo, zebra, oryx and of course, rhinoceros. The WC entrance is to the right of and past the queue, near the exit. A designated Land Rover picks up disabled guests and companions at a separate boarding dock. The vehicle's doors swing out such that you can't get your WC parallel and next to the vehicle for an easy transfer. You must step over a lip to the vehicle and down 6" to the floor. Watch your head; the roof is fairly low. And the space between rows of molded seats is tight. Fasten your seatbelt!

■ TIMBUKTU

Das Festhaus is a cafeteria with generous deli fare, AC, a band and dancers with an international repertoire. Seating is at very long picnic tables where you can remove the 8' benches if you can find a space to put it while you eat.

Sandstorm (~~WC~~, ~~ECV~~) is an octopus ride that requires you to step up 1' onto the vehicle's footrest then pivot and sit back.

Sultans Arcade has few electronic games at WC height and many require transfers into seats.

Kiddy Rides (~~WC~~, ~~ECV~~) include an airplane ride, a disc that revolves at an angle and a carousel with a bench for those who choose not to ride an animal. All are elevated and have no modifications for children in WCs.

Phoenix (~~WC~~, ~~ECV~~) is a large, ship-type, crescent that swings or rocks back and forth higher and higher and finally all the way around as you hang from your shoulder harness. Go through the exit front and center to board by taking a 6" step up and into the narrow row seating.

Scorpion (~~WC~~, ~~ECV~~) is 96-second, roller coaster ride at 50mph. Find the exit around the carousel and through the open-air carnival-style arcade games. The 2-person ride seat is lower than WC height; you must step over the 4" side of the car, then down 12" and through a 10" wide opening before you can sit down.

Dolphin Theater features 25 min of thrilling entertainment by dolphins and sea lions, worth the very steep ramp at the entrances on either side of the stadium. WC seating is at the very top of the stadium.

Warning: the bridge from Timbuktu over the railroad track is very steep.

■ **CONGO**

Train Station See Nariobi.

Ubanga Bumper Cars (W€, E€V) are in an arena with an 8" step down to the driving area. Cars sit lower than WC height and require you to step over the 10" side of the car before you can sit down and fasten the lap bar.

Warning: the bridge past Bumper Cars to Kumba and the Congo River is very steep.

Kumba (W€, E€V) gives a 3-min, 60mph ride through diving spirals and loops. Enter through the exit to the boarding area. You must walk through a 23.5" wide entry gate, step over the 8" high side of the car and sit in a molded seat with a shoulder harness.

Congo River Rapids (WC, E€V) is a 5-min tube ride through turbine-generated whitewater. Avoid the flights of stairs by entering through the exit at the far right of the queue. From the boarding dock, step onto the flat rim of the 12-person tube and down two 7" steps between the seats. The seats are molded with high backs and lap belts. You can lean over to hold onto the circular handrail in the center. Or, for 25 cents, you can simply tease riders with accessible water squirts along the Congo River.

Kiddy Rides (W€, E€V) include a swing, flying glider and teacup, all elevated with no modifications for kids in wheelchairs.

Python (W€, E€V) is a 2-min roller coaster ride making twirls and corkscrews at 40mph. Enter through the extremely steep and narrow exit ramp. To board the 2-person car that is below WC height, you must step down 21" through a 17" wide opening, or you must be lifted over the car's 14" high side. Fasten the lap restraint!

Claw Island is home to several beautiful Bengal tigers that sometimes entertain the crowds by swimming or wrestling with each other. Check the feeding schedule on the back of your Park map.

■ **STANLEYVILLE**

Tidal Wave (W€, E€V) is a grand log-flume ride that has a short, ramped, WC entrance to the left of the exit. To board, you must step over the 8" high side of the vehicle and down 23" to the floor or 9" to the 5-person bench seat with a lap restraint. You can get as wet as the Tidal Wave riders by simply parking at the viewing area beside the ride's final splash, close to the WC entrance.

Stanley Falls (W€, E€V) is another log flume, but more mild than the Tidal Wave. The WC entrance is next to the exit with a short ramp to boarding. You must step over the 19" high side of the log, then down 23" to straddle a vertical bench seat for 2 or 3 riders.

Stanleyville Theater features 30-min shows of juggling, tumbling and extraordinary athletic artistry. New international touring groups generally come in every few months. The ramped entrances on either side of the open-air, roofed theater lead to WC and companion seating on the top deck behind stadium seating.

Train Station See Nariobi. On either side of the Stanleyville station reside featured animals – sometimes warthogs and emus, sometimes orangutans and anteaters.

Warning: As you leave Stanleyville, two very steep ramps spiral into the Land of the Dragons. Between the ramps is Lory Landing, an aviary with incredibly colorful birds. The screen door entrance opens outward; the exit opens inward.

■ **LAND OF THE DRAGONS**

This kid's play area is enchanting with a ball crawl, a splash area of squirts, fountains and slides and a rambling, 2-story Dragon's Nest with netting and slides galore. Kiddy rides include cars on a track, flying dragons and a mini-ferris wheel of cracked dragon's eggs. But with all this wonderful creativity, only *Dumpheries' Dream*, a small, ramped section with a slide and some low-key games, is universally designed.

Captain Kangaroo's Theater is an open-air stage with live entertainment for children. A ramp leads to WC seating in front.

Living Dragons is a walk-by display of unusual reptiles, including monitors and Komoda dragons.

■ **BIRD GARDENS**
You know you've entered Bird Gardens when you come across hundreds of flamingos at leisure in a lagoon.

Jack Hanna's Animal Adventures is sometimes the place to meet (and photograph) TV's wildlife star and some of his interesting animal guests. Check at the entrance to see if Jack Hanna is filming at the Park on the day of your visit.

Bird Shows run 30 min in a covered, open-air theater with WC seating on an elevated area along the side behind a few rows of stadium seating.

Hospitality House Stage features oldie-sing-along bands for 20 min while you enjoy free beer (2-beer maximum!) and/or lunch at a table on the patio.

TARPON SPRINGS

Tarpon Springs is a wonderful pita-pocket of Greek flare as well as fun on the water, from boat tours and rentals to fishing and kayaking. The 34-mi Pinellas Trail starts in Tarpon.

Tourist Info
Tarpon Springs Chamber: 11 E Orange St, 34689; 727-937-6109
Web sites: www.tarponsprings.com

Transportation
See Clearwater.

ACTIVITIES

■ **ATTRACTIONS**
Coral Sea Aquarium has a simulated coral reef with tropical fish in a 120,000-gal tank. Watch moray eels eat dinner or peek at creatures in the tidal pool. $. 10-5; Sun 12-5 (850 Dodecanese Blvd; 727-938-5378)
St Nicholas Greek Orthodox Cathedral is a replica of the New Byzantine St Sophia's in Constantinople. The interior of sculptured Grecian marble has elaborate icons and stained glass. $D. Wkdy 9-5 (36 N Pinellas Ave; 727-937-3540)
Sponge Docks along with shops, taverns, Greek cafes, the Spongerama and Coral Sea Aquarium line the street along the Anclote River. (Dodecanese Blvd; W of Alt US 19)
Spongeorama includes a museum and film on sponge diving history. 10-5; Sun 12-5 (510 Dodecanese Blvd; 727-943-9509)

■ **BEACHES**
Parks: Fred Howard
Sunset Beach is a peninsula on the Gulf with access from HC parking to a paved picnic shelter on the city beach. For small boats or canoes, you can use a gently sloped, hard-packed boat ramp (no dock). Grills; Rr. Dawn-dusk (1800 Gulf Rd; from Alt US 19, go W on MLK Dr then S on Wittcomb Blvd)

■ **BIKE TRAILS**
Pinellas Trail runs 34 mi from Tarpon Springs S to St Pete along an old railroad route parallel to Alt US 19. The best WC access point in Tarpon Springs with hassle-free parking is in the city lot behind Winn-Dixie on Lemon St, just W of the Trail.

See St Pete: Bike Trails

■ BOAT RAMPS

Parks: Anderson

Craig Park has a gently sloped boat ramp (no dock) on the Craig Park Bayou that opens to the Anclote River and the Gulf. Rr. Dawn-dusk (6 Craig Park; off Tarpon Ave/CR 582, W of Alt US 19)

Tarpon Springs City Marina has fixed docks and a portable lift (sling seat) to board or disembark WC riders on private boats. The marina rents day and overnight slips on the Anclote River. Call the day before for staff to set up the lift and help with transfers. Rr. 8:30-5 (100 Dodecanese Blvd; next to Pappas' Restaurant; 727-937-9165)

■ BOAT RENTALS

CNR Watersports rents pontoon boats (25" entry) for 4, 6, or 8 hrs for up to 10 people along the Anclote River and out to the Gulf. Boarding from the fixed dock is easier during for higher tides; call beforehand. Bait shop at marina (Landings Marina, 21 Oscar Hill Rd; 727-934-5960) This operator also rents boats for use on Lake Tarpon. With advance notice, staff can take the boat to Anderson Park's accessible docks. Bait shop nearby (40081 US 19 N; 727-937-3933)

■ BOAT TOURS

Island Wind Tours offer 1- and 4-hr sightseeing cruises. Roll aboard the 1st deck of the 60' catamaran. Full bar; snack bar; Rr. 10-5 (600 Dodecanese Blvd; 727-934-0606)

Sun Line Cruises offer 75-min ecotours with a naturalist guide on a 45' catamaran along the Anclote River to the Gulf. Roll aboard by ramp from the fixed dock and sit in the sun or the shade of a bimini top. You may see dolphins and will certainly see plenty of birds in the bayous. Tie-downs available; snacks & beer onboard; Rr, near dock. Oct-May 11:30, 1, 2:30 & 4 (776 Dodecanese Blvd; 727-944-4468)

■ CANOEING/ KAYAKING

Clearwater: Kayaking. Beaches: Sunset

Anclote Kayak rents kayaks and offers guided trips. Rentals of tandem sit-on kayaks run hourly, half/full day. With advance notice, staff may be able to transport the kayaks to a local site of your choice and pick them up at an agreed-on time. Explain your abilities and interests, and staff can suggest accessible sites. Guided trips depend on the season. In winter, you can take 3-hr manatee-watching trips, in glass-bottom, sit-in solo kayaks, along the Homosassa or Anclote River and bayous. In autumn, 5-hr trips take an accessible catamaran to Anclote Key, then tour the island refuge by kayak. Staff can help lift you into the kayak. Rr, near dock (776 Dodecanese Blvd; 727-937-9840)

■ FISHING CHARTERS

Florida Fishing Adventures caters to WC anglers who like light tackle or flyfishing. Choose a half/full-day trip on a pontoon boat for bass on Lake Tarpon or on a flats boat on the Gulf. Capt Zamba can roll you in your WC aboard the flats boat. Both sites have floating docks and boats have tie-downs. Sodas included; cooler provided. Oct-Apr (727-938-8186)

Light Tackle Fishing is experienced with WC anglers and offers Gulf flats trips from Tarpon Springs. See St Pete: Fishing Charters (813-249-5224; 800-972-1930)

Van Horn Charters offers bass fishing on Lake Tarpon, flats fishing in Tampa Bay and tarpon fishing in Boca Grande. Choose from a 19' flats boat or a 23' bay boat; flyfishing and spin casting is available. The capt is experienced with disabled anglers and will get help to board you in your WC. Guarantee: catch fish or no charge! (727-938-8577; 800-757-8577)

■ FISHING-PARTY BOATS

Dolphin Deep-Sea Fishing offers 8-hr trips on the Gulf. If the tide is too low to board by ramp, crew can lift you aboard in your WC and help you over the 4" lip to the cabin. 8-4 (W end of

Sponge Docks, by Dolphin Gift Shop; 727-937-8257)
Miss Milwaukee offers 8-hr trips on the Gulf. Crew can help you board in your WC and over the 4" lip to the cabin. 8-4 (Sponge Docks; 727-937-5678)

■ **FISHING PIERS**
Highland Park has a hard-packed trail to a 640' pier on Lake Tarpon. Picnic tables; Rr. Dawn-dusk (1513 Lake Tarpon Ave/CR 582; E of Keystone Rd)

■ **HANDCYCLES**
St Pete: Handcycles

■ **PARKS**
Anderson Park is a 128-acre county park on Lake Tarpon. HC parking, ADA picnic tables and Rr are at shelters 1, 4, 5, 8 & 9. A 1200' hard-packed nature trail and a 100' boardwalk wind along Lake Tarpon. The most accessible fishing is on either side of the boat ramp and behind shelter 3, although some may need a push on the grass. Boat ramp & floating docks; Rr. 7-dusk (US 19; .5 mi S of Lake Tarpon Ave; 727-943-4085)
*Fred Howard Park is both a park and beach. A paved, 2-mi loop trail leads from parking by the entrance around the shady, meandering park area, past ADA picnic shelters, grills and a paved bridge near shelter 6 where you can fish. A 1-mi causeway, with parking on very broad shoulders that slope steeply to the shore, goes to a very bright, sandy beach. The park plans to obtain a beach WC. Outdoor showers; Rr. 7-dusk (1700 Dusk Dr; from US Alt 19, W on

Spring Blvd, then follow signs Riverside Dr; 727-943-4081)
North Anclote River Nature Park is a new 77-acre city park with almost 1 mi of crushed shell trails that will become hard-packed but currently may require all-terrain WCs or hearty companions. If you can negotiate the trails, you can get to the canoe launch on the level riverbanks or a platform for some fishing. By 2003, ADA picnic shelters; Rr. 7:30-dusk (550 Old Dixie Hwy/CR 429; E off Alt US 19)

■ **PERFORMING ARTS**
Frog Prince Puppetry Theater presents excellent puppet shows and various puppetry classes. With advance notice, seating can be arranged for WCs. Rr (210 S Pinellas Ave; 727-784-6392)
Tarpon Springs Cultural Center offers rotating exhibits, films and other entertainment. WC parking & entry in rear; Rr. Mon-Sat 9-4 (101 S Pinellas Ave; 727-942-5605)
Tarpon Springs Performing Arts Center offers a range of entertainment from chamber music to family-oriented performances. WC seating in front or back; Rr (324 E Pine St; 727-938-3711)

■ **SHOPPING**
Downtown has the lively atmosphere of a Hellenic marketplace with traditional arts and crafts, cotton and gauze fashions, Greek pastries and foods and lots of natural sponges. The main drag, Dodecanese Blvd, has curb cuts and ramps to shops.

ACCOMMODATIONS

■ **B&Bs**
Spring Bayou Inn, after you get up the 2 steps into the home, has the WC-friendly Orchid Room with a 35" entry, queen bed (23" high/open frame) and private bath with a 27" door, roll-under sink and tub. Enjoy your gourmet breakfast in your room or the dining room. Relax on the roomy wraparound porch. Restaurants and antique shops are nearby. $$-$$$ (32 W Tarpon Ave; at

Pinellas Ave; 727-938-9333)

■ **MOTELS**
Holiday Inn has 3 ADA rooms, each with 2 full beds (22" high/platforms) and a bathroom with a raised toilet, roll-under sink and roll-in shower with a hand-held sprayer and seat. Pool; full restaurant. $$ (38724 US 19 N; 727-934-5781; 800-465-4329)
Tarpon Shores Inn has 2 ADA rooms, each with 2 full beds (open frames)

and, at an extra charge, a microwave and refrigerator. Bathrooms have raised toilets, roll-under sinks and tubs.

Pool; laundry; restaurants nearby. $-$$ (40346 US 19N; 727-938-2483; 800-633-3802)

Sail Away...
To an adaptive sailing class.
See Index page 413.

Shoot!
Check out Hunting
See page 13 and Index page 413.

Horseback riding isn't just for horsin' around —
it can also be therapeutic.
See page 13 and Index page 413.

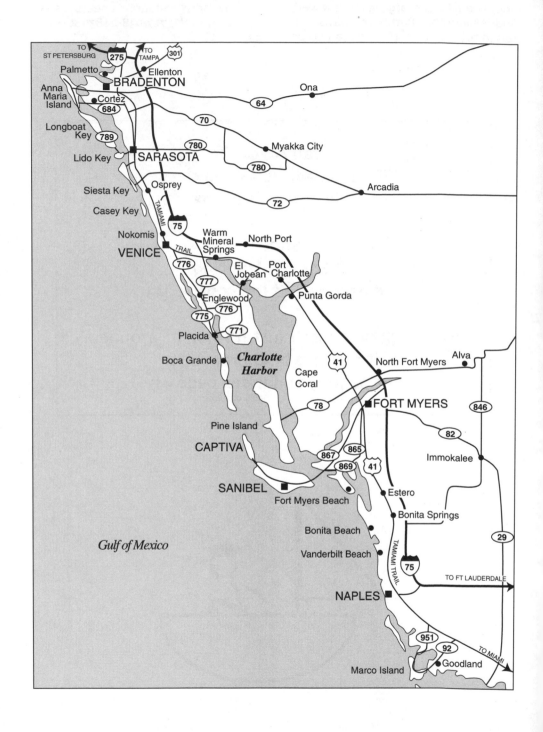

Southwest Gulf Coast

Bradenton
Anna Maria, Bradenton Beach, Cortez, Ellenton, Holmes Beach,
Myakka City, Ona, Palmetto

Bradenton offers good variety: historic sites, car races, dancing horses and baseball-playing Pirates. For a quiet getaway, try Anna Maria Island with beach wheelchairs, fine fishing and friendly folk.

Tourist Info
Anna Maria Island Chamber: 5337 Gulf Dr/SR 789, Holmes Bch, 34217; 941-778-1541; 800-462-6283
Bradenton Visitors Bureau: 1 Haben Blvd, Palmetto, 34221; 941-729-9177; 800-822-2017
Manatee Chamber: 222 10 St W, Box 321, 34206; 941-748-3411
Tourist Info Center: 5030 Hwy 301 N, Ellenton; I-75 exit 224 W; 941-729-7040
Gulf Islands Visitors Guide: 800-462-6283
Web sites: www.amichamber.org; www.flagulfislands.com

Transportation
MCAT or Manatee County Area Transit buses all have lifts and service the entire county between 6am-7pm Mon-Sat. (941-749-7116)
Handi-bus Para Transit offers door-to-door service in a lift-equipped van anywhere in Manatee County. If you are over 60, apply over the phone 2-4pm; if you are under 60, you must have a letter from your doctor explaining why you cannot use the county's fixed-route bus system. Reservations must be made 2 working days in advance. Wkdy 8am-2pm (941-747-1739)

Manatee Trolleys are free, open-air shuttle buses with WC lifts. They service Anna Maria Island every 20 min from 6am-10:30pm. Ask drivers for connections to MCAT. (941-749-7116)

ACTIVITIES

■ ATTRACTIONS

Gamble Plantation State Historic Site is an antebellum mansion built by Major Gamble in the 1840's on his 3500-acre sugar plantation. The visitor center with exhibits and the mansion's 1st floor are accessible. Guided 1-hr tours are at 9:30, 10:30 and hourly from 1-4. ADA picnic table; Rr. $. Thu-Mon 9:30-4 (3708 Patten Ave, Ellenton; 941-723-4536)

Lippizzan Stallions, the world famous dancing horses, perform here in winter. Staff can help you over the grass to the stands. $D. Jan-Mar Thu-Fri 3; Sat 10 (Ottomar Herrmann Training Grounds, SR 70 & Singletary Rd, Myakka City; 941-322-1501)

Manatee Village Historical Park has brick paths connecting an 1887 church, 1903 store, barn, smokehouse, cane mill, 1908 schoolhouse and a 1912 farmhouse. All buildings, except the courthouse, are accessible. Gift shop; picnic tables; Rr. Wkdy 9-4:30; Sep-Jun also Sun 1:30-4:30 (604 15 St E; 1 mi E of US 41 on SR 64; 941-749-7165)

Solomon's Castle, the home and studio of internationally known sculptor, Howard Solomon, contains galleries of his work, numerous stained glass windows and a restaurant (The Boat in the Moat, *literally*). Rr. $. Oct-Jun Tue-Sun 11-4 (Solomon Rd, Ona; from SR 64, S on CR 665; 863-494-6077)

■ BEACHES

Coquina Beach, sometimes called Bradenton Beach, is a 1-mi county beach fringed with tall Australian pines. At the N end is a paved picnic area with ADA tables. In the middle of the beach is a snack bar with Rr and outdoor showers. Lifeguards (winter 10-5; summer 10-7); chair & umbrella concession. Dawn-dusk (1200 Gulf Dr/SR 789; S end of Anna Maria Island)

Cortez Beach is a city beach that extends N from Coquina Beach, with no facilities. Dawn-dusk (Gulf Dr/SR 789, Bradenton Bch; between 5 St & 13 St)

+Manatee Beach, sometimes called Public or Holmes Beach, loans beach WCs that can go in the water (1 has fixed arms, 2 have swing-away arms; 1 has an attachable umbrella). Send a friend over sand to the lifeguard stand (winter 10-5; summer 10-7); the guard will bring it to you at the beachside cafe (6am-8:30pm) that has tables on a large outdoor deck. In the center of the beach is a ramped, 150' ADA concrete fishing pier. Outdoor showers; chair & umbrella concession; Rr. Dawn-10pm (4000 Gulf Dr N/SR 789, Holmes Bch; at W end of Manatee Ave/SR 64; 941-742-5925)

■ BOAT RAMPS

Parks: Lake Manatee

Coquina Beach Bayside has a boat ramp and fixed dock on the Intracoastal at Longboat Pass. 24 hrs (2603 Gulf Dr/SR 789, Bradenton Bch)

Kingfish Boat Ramp is on the Intracoastal with 3 fixed docks. To use the floating dock you must negotiate 2 steps and, at low tide, a steep ramp. Nearby streetlights; dirt/soft sand parking; picnic tables. 24 hrs (3020 Manatee Ave W/SR 64, Holmes Bch; N side of 2nd bridge from mainland to Anna Maria Island)

■ BOAT RENTALS

Bradenton Beach Marina rents pontoon boats (30" entry), runabouts and bow riders for half/full days on the Intracoastal. From a floating dock you can roll aboard the pontoon boats that hold 12; staff can lift you from your WC aboard the other boats and into seats. Restaurant; bait shop across bridge in

Cortez; Rr. 8-5 (402 Church Ave, Bradenton Bch; 941-778-2288)

Catchers Marina rents 24' pontoon boats for up to 14 passengers and skiffs 15'-24' for Tampa Bay by the half/full day or by the week. Generally staff can push you aboard the front of the pontoon boat in your WC; if tides are high staff can ramp it or lift you aboard as with the skiffs. Bait/snack shop; CRr. 6:30am-dusk (5501 Marina Dr, Holmes Bch; 941-778-1977)

Ultimate Powersports rents pontoon boats (24" entry) for a minimum of 1 hr on the bay and Manatee River. From the fixed dock, staff can lift you aboard in your WC. Bait shop nearby. Hrs vary (9915 Manatee Ave/SR 64; 941-761-7433)

■ **BOAT TOURS**

Neva-Miss is a 31' boat for up to 6 on customized, private sightseeing tours. Crew can lift you aboard in your WC. (Cortez Fishing Center, 12507 Cortez Rd, Cortez; 941-792-5835)

Seafood Shack Paddleboat is 110', Mississippi-style stern wheeler that offers 90-min or 3-hr cruises on Sarasota Bay. Trips to the Skyway Bridge have live entertainment and a cocktail bar. Included is a discount at the Seafood Shack restaurant. Call for schedule. Rr in restaurant at dock (4110 127 St W, Cortez; 941-794-5048)

■ **CAMPS**

Foundation for Dreams provides camp experiences for children age 6-18 with special needs. Summer camp can be overnight or days only; weekend and family camps are offered the rest of the year. Certain sessions are specifically for children with physical disabilities. The pristine 160-acre property lies on the Manatee River and includes all accessible structures from dining hall and nature lodge to activity pavilions and a ramped swimming pool. Two beach WCs (fixed arms) are available. Residential campers stay in ADA cabins with bathrooms that have raised toilets, roll-under sinks and roll-in show-

ers. Activities are designed to promote independence, self-esteem and fun. The staff/camper ratio is 1 to 2; if more intensive care is necessary, personal caregivers must attend. For information and an application, call Jodi Franke. (2620 Manatee Ave W, #D, Bradenton, 34205; 941-748-8809; FoundForDreams@aol.com)

■ **CANOEING/KAYAKING**

Ray's Canoe Hideaway rents canoes by the half/full day and solo/tandem sit-on kayaks by the hour for use on the Upper Manatee River. Staff can lift you into either craft from a boat ramp and can arrange for guided tours. The river is slow and you can paddle back to the put-in. 8am-dusk (1247 Hagel Park Rd, Palmetto; I-75 exit 220, 8 mi E; 941-747-3909)

■ **FISHING CHARTERS**

Angling Adventures is a group of guides offering half/full-day inshore, offshore and flats fishing. The type of fishing you choose and the number of anglers determines which boat is used. With advance notice, crew can help lift you in your WC aboard any of the boats from an accessible dock. (Capt John Sackett 941-920-4891)

Capt White offers half/full-day, backcountry trips on a 24' Carolina Skiff for up to 4 anglers. He offers light tackle and flyfishing from Tampa Bay to Boca Grande as well as fly casting and tying lessons. Crew can meet you at an accessible dock and lift you aboard in your WC. (941-756-9258)

Catchers Marina can arrange half/full-day, inshore and offshore guided trips for WC anglers. The marina has fixed docks. Contact the capt directly to discuss any special needs. Bait shop, snacks & CRr at marina (5501 Marina Dr, Holmes Bch; 941-778-1977)

Cortez Cat Charter customizes deep-sea trips on a 30' boat (with a canvas awning) for up to 9 anglers. From the floating dock, crew can lift you aboard in your WC for the 3-hr to full-day trip. (Cortez Fishing Center, 12507 Cortez

Rd, Cortez; 941-795-6969)

Kattina Charters offers half/full-day, offshore trips for up to 6 anglers aboard a 32' boat. From the fixed dock, crew can lift you aboard in your WC and secure it with tie-downs. Rr at dock (Key Royal Marina, 630 Dundee St, Holmes Bch; 941-778-2727; 941-737-5206)

Neva-Miss is a 31' boat that takes up to 6 WC anglers on offshore or deep-sea trips, 4 hrs to all night. Capt Morrison has experience with WC anglers; crew can lift you aboard in your WC. (Cortez Fishing Center, 12507 Cortez Rd W, Cortez; 941-795-6969)

■ **FISHING-PARTY BOATS**

Cortez Cat offers 4- and 6-hr, deep-sea trips on a 38' pontoon boat for 10 anglers. Normally you can roll aboard from the floating dock, in low tide crew can help lower you in your WC. (Cortez Fishing Center, 12507 Cortez Rd W, Cortez; 941-795-6969)

■ **FISHING PIERS**

Beaches: Manatee

Anna Maria City Pier is a 710' lighted wood pier on Tampa Bay. This older facility plans to renovate to ADA standards. Some of the pier's planks are uneven with gaps that make it tough for WCs and the pier has only toe rails, no waist-high railing. The parking lot is hard-packed shell with some sandy spots. At the end of the pier is a bait shop (7am-11pm), an Oyster Bar that will cook your catch (11am-9pm) and Rr, not ADA. 24 hrs (50 Bay Blvd, Anna Maria; 941-708-6130)

Bridge Street Pier is a 350' lighted wood pier on the bay. Bait shop & cafe (7am-9pm); CRr. $. 24 hrs (200 Bridge St, Bradenton Bch; 941-779-1706)

Green Bridge Pier is a 2200' lighted concrete pier, once a vehicular bridge over the Manatee River. Bait/snack shop; ADA picnic shelter; Rr. 24 hrs (101 8 Ave W, Palmetto; N side of river)

Rod & Reel Pier is a 350' lighted wood pier on Tampa Bay. The upstairs restaurant is not accessible but you can order from the menu and have your meal served downstairs in the accessible cafe. Bait shop; Rr, not ADA. $. 8am-10pm (875 N Shore Dr, Anna Maria; 941-778-1885)

Skyway Fishing Piers are the remains of either end of the old Skyway Bridge that was damaged by a barge in 1980. The North Skyway Pier extends .5 mi and the South Pier 2.5 mi into the mouth of Tampa Bay. Both piers are lighted, have bait shops with rentals, snacks and Rr. $. 24 hrs (for the S Pier, take the last exit off I-275 N before crossing the Skyway Bridge to St Pete; 941-729-0117)

■ **MUSEUMS**

South Florida Museum houses Stone Age relics, Civil War memorabilia and pioneer artifacts. You'll find old-time doctor and dentist offices and a pharmacy. The Bishop Planetarium has star shows and laser light shows daily in the afternoon and Fri-Sat 9pm and 10:30pm. Enjoy live astronomy presentations Fri-Sat 7pm. The observatory that houses the large telescope is not accessible. Snooty, the 50-yr old manatee can be observed both above and below the water in the Parker Aquarium and is fed Tue-Sun at 12:30, 2 and 3:30. Gift shop; CRr. $. Hrs vary (201 10 St W; 941-746-4131)

■ **PARKS**

DeSoto National Memorial commemorates Hernando DeSoto's 1539 landing and expedition. The visitor center has a film and artifacts. Dec-Apr costumed settlers demonstrate their 16th century way of life; call for schedule. The short, hard-packed nature trail has some sandy areas. WC loaner; Rr in center. 9-5 (75 St NW; 5 mi W of downtown; 941-792-0458)

Lake Manatee State Park occupies 556 acres along a 3-mi stretch on the S shore of the 2400-acre Lake Manatee. Fish from the floating docks by the boat ramp; only boats with less than 20hp motors are allowed. The grassy, gently sloping beach at the swim area is tough to navigate and the nature trails

are mostly sand. See Campgrounds.
ADA picnic shelter; playground on
sand; Rr. $. 8-dusk (20007 SR 64; 15 mi
E of town, 9 mi E of I-75; 941-741-3028)

■ **PERFORMING ARTS**

Island Players, a community theater
group, performs Oct-May. WC seating
on sides in rear; Rr. Tue-Sat 8pm; Sun 2
(10009 Gulf Dr, Anna Maria; at Pine
Ave; 941-778-6878)

Manatee Players/Riverfront Theater is a
community theater group performing
Sep-May. When you arrive send a
friend to the box office so the accessible
side door can be opened. WC seating in
aisles; Rr. Call for schedule. (102 Old
Main St; 941-748-5875/0111)

■ **POOLS**

GT Bray Park has a heated 50-meter
pool and a portable WC lift (fixed seat)
into which lifeguards can help you
transfer. A small splash park starts at
zero-depth with ground squirts and a
mushroom shower. Call about lap times
and classes. This 140-acre park also has
a roller hockey rink, ball fields and an
off-leash dog park. $. Wkdy 11-5; Sat
noon-4; extended in summer (5502 33
Ave Dr W; enter park from 59 St W or
51 St W; 941-742-5932)

■ **SHOPPING**

Flea Markets: Midway Flea Market is
the largest in the area with paved walkways under cover. Fri-Sun 8-4 (10816
US 41; N of Palmetto; 941-723-6000).
Red Barn Flea Market has 700 booths
under cover. Wed, Fri-Sun 8-4 (1707 1
St E; 941-747-3794)

Malls: DeSoto Square Mall (US 41 &
Cortez Rd); Prime Outlet Shops (I-75 &
US 301, Ellenton; 941-723-1150)

■ **SNORKELING**

Cortez Cat customizes sightseeing/snor-
keling trips. Ask for the 38' boat that
you can usually roll aboard from the
floating dock. If tides are extreme, crew
can lift you aboard in your WC as well
as in and out of the water for snorkeling. (Cortez Fishing Center, 12507
Cortez Rd W, Cortez; 941-795-6969)

■ **SPECTATOR SPORTS**

Auto Racing DeSoto Memorial
Dragstrip is home of the IHRA Snowbird Nationals. On request, parking attendants will direct you to parking
spots up close with about 50' of grass to
the entrance ramp. WC seating is on a
platform at the starting line. The snack
bar is not accessible. Schedule varies
(SR 64 E; 941-748-1320). DeSoto Speedway has stock car racing on a high-
banked oval track, plus special events
and figure eights. WC seating in front
row; Rr. Feb-Nov Sat 7pm (SR 64; 8 mi
E of I-75; 941-748-3171)

Baseball Pittsburgh Pirates hold work-
outs Mar-Apr from 10-1:30. The Pittsburgh Gulf Coast Rookie Leagues play
Jun-Oct. WC seating behind home
plate, next to dugouts, & over outfield;
Rr (McKechnie Field, 1611 9 St W; 941-
747-3031)

■ **WAVERUNNERS**

Ultimate Powersports rents 1- to 3-per-
son waverunners by the hour for use on
Palma Sola Bay. Staff can lift you from
the fixed dock onto the waverunner.
Staff can sometimes lead private,
guided tours to nearby islands. Rr next
door at restaurant (9915B Manatee
Ave/SR 64; 941-761-7433)

ACCOMMODATIONS

■ **CAMPGROUNDS**

Lake Manatee State Park has 60 tent/
RV sites on crushed shell with water/
elec and dense shrubs between sites; 4
have ADA picnic table and grills. Sites 2
and 32 are closest to and have paved
paths to ADA bathhouses with roll-under sinks and roll-in showers. See Parks.
Discount for disabled campers (20007
SR 64; 9 mi W of I-75; 941-741-3028;
800-326-3521)

■ **B&Bs**

Harrington House B&B is a 1925 Victorian beachfront home with a ramped

entrance and a ground floor, WC-friendly room with a king bed (platform), refrigerator and microwave. Doorways in the room are 30"; the bathroom has a tub and step-in shower. A full gourmet breakfast is served in the dining room. The pool and a covered patio overlook the beach. $$$ (5626 Gulf Dr, Holmes Bch; 941-778-5444)

■ CONDOS

Amanda Villa is next to Manatee Beach with a beach WC and fishing pier; see Beaches. A large ADA 1BR unit has a king bed (open frame), queen sofa bed in the living room, full kitchen, dining room and bathroom with a tub. Rentals can be for the night, week or longer. (102 39 St, Holmes Bch; 941-778-4170; 800-436-3648)

Coconuts Beach Resort has 2 WC-friendly 1BR Gulf front condos (# 106 and 107), each with 2 full beds (open frames), a full kitchen and living room with a sofa bed. Standard bathrooms have 30" doorways and grab bars. Pool; laundry (100 73 St, Holmes Bch; 941-778-2277; 800-331-2508)

Island West has WC-friendly 1BR and 2BR apartments with a queen bed in each bedroom. One 1BR unit has 2 twin beds. All have full kitchens, large standard bathrooms and living rooms with sofa beds. A portable ramp is available for the step at each entry. Pool area (3605 Gulf Dr, Holmes Bch; 941-778-6569)

■ MOTELS

Bridgewalk is in downtown Bradenton Beach and 1 block from the beach. It has 2 spacious ADA 1-room suites. Room 505 has a king bed (25" high/open frame), a king Murphy bed (21" high/platform) and kitchenette. Room 503 has a king Murphy bed, a full kitchen (25" entry) love seat and chair. Both units have screened porches and large bathrooms with roll-under sinks, a tub and step-in shower. A portable ramp is available for the 3" step at the entries. Two-story 2BR townhouses are

also available but you must take an outside elevator to access the bedrooms. These units have full kitchens, queen sofa beds in the living/dining rooms and ground floor 1/2 baths. Upstairs are 2 bedrooms each with a king bed and bathroom, however currently the built-in bed blocks the bathroom door from opening fully. The motel plans to make changes. Pool; full restaurant; spa; laundry; retail shops. $$$ (100 Bridge St, Bradenton Bch; E off Gulf Dr; 941-779-2545; 866-779-2545)

Comfort Inn has 5 ADA rooms, each with a king bed (22" high/platform), refrigerator and on request, a microwave. Bathrooms have raised toilets and roll-under sinks; room 121 has a roll-in shower with a hand-held sprayer and seat; others have tubs. Free brkfst; pool; laundry. $$-$$$ (580 66 St Court E; 941-747-7500)

Econo Lodge is located on the beach and has 1 ADA room (# 306) with 2 full beds (24" high/platforms), a refrigerator and microwave. The bathroom has a roll-under sink and roll-in shower with a hand-held sprayer. 2 heated pools; covered patio with grills & tables. $$$ (2502 Gulf Dr, Bradenton Bch; 941-778-6671)

Holiday Inn Riverfront, overlooking the Manatee River, has 3 ADA rooms each with a king bed. Bathrooms have raised toilets, roll-under sinks and tubs. You can fish off the seawall. Heated pool; hot tub; fitness room; full restaurant; gift shop. $$$ (100 Riverfront Dr W; 941-747-3727)

Holiday Inn Express has 3 ADA rooms, each with a king bed (21" high/open frame), full sofa bed and coffeepot. Bathrooms have raised toilets and roll-under sinks; room 129 has a roll-in shower with a hand-held sprayer and seat; others have tubs. Each connects to a standard room if desired. Free brkfst; pool; laundry. $$-$$$ (648 67 St Cir E; 940-747-7500)

Motel 6 has 5 ADA rooms, each with a queen or full bed (platform) and bathroom with a raised toilet, roll-under sink and roll-in shower with a hand-held sprayer. Pool; laundry. $ (660 67 St Cir E; 941-747-6005)

FORT MYERS
Alva, Bokeelia, Cape Coral, Fort Myers Beach, Immokalee, Matlacha, North Fort Myers

This pretty historic city along the Caloosahatchee River is called the City of Palms for the 1800 palms planted by its most famous resident, Thomas Edison. You can rent beach wheelchairs for the beaches here or take a somewhat accessible ferry to the pristine island of Cayo Costa where you can borrow one. The Gulf, river and bays offer a range of boating, fishing, parasailing and scuba. One boat makes daily trips to Key West and back. Many accessible pools hold aquacise classes. On rainy days, try the Edison home or various museums. There's even an accessible dinner train waiting at the station! SR 865 piggy-backs several roads through Ft Myers, including Six Mile Cypress Parkway and San Carlos Blvd as it winds to Estero Island where it becomes CR 865 or Estero Boulevard.

Tourist Info
Lee Island Coast Visitors Bureau: 2180 W 1 St, 33901; 239-338-3500; 800-237-6444. Call 800-533-4753 for an *Access Ability Guide* and a *Nature Guide*.
Pine Island Chamber: 3640 Pine Island Rd, Matlacha, 33993; 239-283-0888
Web sites: www.leeislandcoast.com; www.cityftmyers.com; www.capecoralchamber.com; www.pineislandchamber.org; www.cityftmyers.com

Transportation
Boat Tours: Fast Cats
Lee-Tran buses have lifts and service all of Lee County Mon-Sat 5am-9:30pm with limited service on Sun. (239-275-8726)
Lee County has a door-to-door, para-transit service for medical, employment and grocery needs. (239-656-6444)
Beach Trolleys with lifts run along Ft Myers Beach daily 7am-9:30pm. (239-275-8726)

WC Resources
Advanced Home Medical Equipment rents beach WCs (fixed arms) with 1-wk notice , manual WCs and scooters by the day, week and month. Delivers (3462 Fowler St; 239-278-0060)
DME Shoppe rents beach WCs (removable arms) by the week and manual WCs and scooters by the day. Repairs; delivers (11990 S Cleveland Ave; 239-936-7070)
Fun Rentals rents beach WCs (fixed arms). Delivers (1901 SR 865, Ft Myers Bch; 239-463-8844)
Scooters Plus rents beach WCs (removable arms) with 1-wk notice, manual WCs and scooters by the day, week and month. Delivers (3083 Cleveland Ave; 239-337-1773)
Center for Independent Living has a loan closet and provides referral and support services. (3626 Evans Ave; 239-277-1447)

ACTIVITIES

■ ATTRACTIONS

Burrough's Home is a Georgian Revival home, built and furnished as in 1901, when 2 older sisters lived there; the sisters or their impersonators, now lead tours (call for schedule). Only the 1st floor of the 3-story house is accessible. HC parking in back driveway; Rr. $. Wkdy 10-4 (2501 1 St; at Fowler; 239-332-6125)

Calusa Nature Center & Planetarium is a 105-acre spot to learn about wildlife in the area. A hard-packed shell trail and boardwalk pass an aviary with mostly injured birds and a bobcat home. The center has displays on SW Florida's natural history and related issues from water scarcity to manatees. The daily animal shows allow you to get close to the likes of alligators, snakes and turtles. The planetarium features a range of shows from the traditional stellar projection on the domed ceiling and astronomy slide shows to laser shows with music. A .5-mi hard-packed, crushed-shell trail loops through a pine forest and cypress swamp. Call for the schedule that includes guided walks along a boardwalk, speakers and off-site treks. See Bike Trails. WC loaners; vending machine; ADA picnic tables & shelter; gift shop; Rr. $. Mon-Sat 9-5; Sun 11-5 (3450 Ortiz Ave; just W of I-75, N off SR 884; 239-275-3435)

ECHO is a farm dedicated to solving world hunger. Mulched paths lead through a simulated rain forest and semi-arid conditions, where ECHO is experimenting with crops for third-world regions. Throughout you'll find gardens on rooftops, old tires and other surprising spots. Free 90-min tours cover over 5 acres of mulched ground on Tue, Fri and Sat at 10; if you can transfer, reserve a golf cart in advance for the tour. (17391 Durrance Rd, N Ft Myers; E of I-75, N off Bayshore Rd/SR 78; 239-543-3246)

Edison/Ford Estates were the winter homes of these 2 industrialist buddies and the largest Banyan tree in Florida. The ticket office has steps but, if you can't send someone, staff will come to you. The grounds and botanical gardens are accessible via paved paths. Both houses are ramped and accessible except for small steps to some rooms. Thomas Edison's 1866 home is where he spent vacations working on inventions such as the phonograph, motion picture camera and incandescent light bulb. You exit Henry Ford's modest 1920 home by backtracking through the house, which, if crowded, can be difficult in a WC. The garage houses 3 of Ford's tin lizzies. Admission is only by 1-hr guided tours (starting every 15 min) that end in a museum with many of the duo's inventions. Snack bar; picnic tables; gift shop; Rr. $. Mon-Sat 9-4; Sun 12-4 (2350 McGregor Blvd; just S of MLK Blvd; 239-334-7419)

■ BEACHES

See WC Resources for beach WC rentals.

Bowditch Pointe Park includes 17 acres at the N tip of Estero Island with beachfront along both the Gulf and Estero Bay. A mulched path leads to the wide sandy beach and ADA picnic shelters on cement. Another path that meanders through a wooded area down to the beach is natural and rough. Metered parking; outdoor showers; ADA picnic tables; grills; Rr. 7-dusk (50 SR 865, Ft Myers Bch; 2.5 mi W of US 41; 239-432-2000)

Cape Coral Yacht Club Beach is on the Caloosahatchee River with a ramp onto the sand. Picnic tables; snack bar; Rr (5819 Driftwood Pkwy, Cape Coral)

*Cayo Costa State Park is a pristine 7-mi island that you can reach by private boat or a somewhat accessible ferry; see Boat Tours: Tropic Star. The boat slips at the island have fixed docks. The ranger office by the docks can loan you a beach WC (removable arms) to enjoy the 5 mi of hard-packed shell trails through mangrove and pines or the 7-mi long soft sand beach. If you know when you are arriving, call ahead so a ranger can meet you at the dock with the beach WC. Friends and possibly the ranger can lift you in the WC onto the low trailer or tram that goes to the beach. Otherwise, take the 1-mi hard-packed shell road to the beach. This island offers awesome birding and shelling. It has no electricity but once a day, rangers sell ice made by generator. See Cabins. ADA picnic shelters at beach; outdoor showers by Rr at beach. $. 8am-dusk (just S of Gasparilla Island; due W of Pine Island; 941-964-0375)

Lynn Hall Memorial Park, in the touristy Times Square area and next to the Ft Myers Beach Pier (see Fishing Piers), has a dune crossover onto the 600' soft sand beach. Metered parking; bait shop 8am-9pm (239-765-9700); ADA picnic shelters; grills; ADA playground; restaurants in Times Sq; Rr 24 hrs (950 SR 865, Ft Myers Bch; 239-463-1116)

■ BIKE TRAILS
North Colonial Linear Park is a 7' wide asphalt bike trail that runs almost 3 mi from Metro Pkwy through woods and along a canal to the Calusa Nature Center on Ortiz Ave. The Metro Pkwy trailhead has a few parking spots. The Caloosa Nature Center (see Attractions) has parking, water fountains, Rr and a 100' fishing pier on a pond. Fishing is also popular along the Metro Canal (despite the *No fishing* signs). Along the trail are picnic tables.

Six-Mile Cypress Parkway has a paved multi-use trail that runs roughly 8 mi from MLK Blvd/SR 82 to Daniels Blvd. This flat, mostly sunny trail has no facilities and is separated from the parkway by a grassy median. The trail crosses the parkway at a lighted intersection. You can access the trail from the Caloosa Nature Center with parking, water fountains and Rr.

■ BOAT RAMPS
Beaches: Lovers Key. Parks: Centennial

■ BOAT RENTALS
Fish Tale Marina rents a 19' Grady White for the Gulf and a 19' pontoon boat (23" entry) for the back bays. Both boats hold 8 people and rent for half/full days. Staff can lift you aboard either boat in your WC from the floating dock. Bait shop; Rr. 8-5 (7225 SR 865, Ft Myers Bch; 239-463-3600)

Mid-Island Beach Marina rents pontoon boats (24" entry) for up to 10 on Estero Bay for a half/full day. Staff can lift you aboard in your WC from the floating dock. Bait shop; Rr. 8-5 (4765 SR 865, Ft Myers Bch; 239-765-4371)

■ BOAT TOURS
Adventures in Paradise are yours to choose aboard a 40' catamaran with a large deck and wide gate. On daily trips 12:30-3, you can examine sea life dragged up by net. Dolphin watches run 3:30-5:30 and shelling/snorkeling trips 9-3. Or, choose a romantic sunset cruise along the bay. Usually you can roll aboard; crew can help as needed. Crew also can help lift you in and out of the water for snorkeling. Reservations needed. 7-6 (Port Sanibel Marina, 14341 Port Comfort Rd; 1 mi E of Sanibel toll gate; 239-472-8443/437-1660)

Calusa Coast Outfitters offers ecotours on Estero Bay with a naturalist who describes the history and ecology of estuaries and helps you sight dolphins and birds. Roll aboard the pontoon boat from the floating dock. Hrs vary (Fish Tale Marina, 7225 SR 865, Ft Myers Bch; 239-332-0709)

Fast Cats Ferry Service offers a 3-hr (1-way) trip from N Ft Myers to Key West on a 150-passenger vessel. Staff can help you over the lip into the cabin and lift you into the airline-type seats in the 1st class area where deli foods are served. The VIP area (for adults only) is a full restaurant and bar with couch seating. You can return on the same day if you like. Call for schedule and to check if WC tie-downs are available yet. Each passenger is allowed 1 carry-on and 1 medium suitcase. Rr (City Pier,

1300 Hendry St; 239-332-7777)
JC Sightseeing Boat Cruises offers different cruises aboard a 3-deck paddlewheeler with an accessible 1st deck. Narrated cruises include buffet lunch, dinner, weekend dinner/dance or Sunday brunch on the Gulf, river or Intracoastal. A 1-day Lake Okeechobee cruise departs from Clewiston; if you cannot board the motor coach that takes passengers to the dock, you can follow in your own vehicle. Late Oct-mid-Apr 10-3 or 7:30-10:30pm (Ft Myers Yacht Basin, 2313 Edwards Dr; 239-334-7474)

Tropic Star offers ferry service to the beautiful Cayo Costa State Park as well as full-day cruises. The boat is not readily accessible. The Tropic Star has a 26" entry through which crew can help lift you aboard (in your WC or onto a bench seat) from the fixed dock and down the 2 steps inside the boat. If tides are low, crew can also help lift you down 2 steps from the dock to the boat. Call for the ferry schedule and reservations. The narrated nature cruises make stops where the crew can help lift you out of the boat to disembark. The first stop is at Cabbage Key for lunch where you can transfer into a golf cart or crew can help roll you up the soft hill to the restaurant that you can enter through the kitchen to avoid the 5 steps at the entrance. Then spend 2 hrs at Cayo Costa State Park with a tram to the beach and a beach WC; see Beaches. Usually 8:30-5 (Knight's Landing, 16499 Porto Bello St, Bokeelia; from Stringfellow Rd/CR 767 in Bokeelia, W on Barrancas Ave, then N on Porto Bello; at the N tip of Pine Island; 239-283-0015)

■ **CAMPS**
Lee County offers weekly summer day camp for school-aged children and young adults with physical and cognitive disabilities. Activities include arts and crafts, games, swimming and sports. An assessment must be completed prior to participation. (Gulf Coast Center Gym, 5820 Buckingham Rd; 239-461-7423)

■ **CANOEING/KAYAKING**
Beaches: Lovers Key. Parks: Caloosahatchee, Lakes, Manatee
Tropic Star rents canoes and solo/tandem sit-on/sit-in kayaks on Jug Creek and Pine Island Sound where you can paddle back to the put-in. Guided trips are available for beginning to expert paddlers. You can roll across the hard-packed sand close to the water's edge where, with advance notice, staff can lift you from a boat ramp into your craft. Rentals and trips range from 2 hrs to all day. 8:30-5 (Knight's Landing, 16499 Porto Bello St, Bokeelia; from Stringfellow Rd/CR 767 in Bokeelia, W on Barrancas Ave, then N on Porto Bello; at the N tip of Pine Island; 239-283-0015)

■ **CASINOS**
Seminole Indian Casino has nightly entertainment, a restaurant and an assortment of games: bingo, low-stakes poker, 7-card stud, Texas Hold-em and video slots. Rr. 24 hrs (506 S 1 St, Immokalee; I-75 exit 138, take SR 82 E to SR 29 then S to CR 846; 239-658-1313; 800-218-0007)

■ **DINNER THEATERS**
Broadway Palm Dinner Theater offers a variety of Broadway musicals and comedies. Ramped access to the tiered theater makes all seating accessible. Tickets available with or without buffet. Rr. Tue-Sun (1380 Colonial Blvd; 239-278-4422)

Seminole Gulf Railway features a 3 1/2-hr train ride and 5-course dinner as you solve a murder mystery. Two train cars are ramped. Rr. Wed-Sat 6pm; Sun 5pm (Metro Pkwy & Colonial Blvd; 239-275-8487; 800-736-4853)

■ **FISHING CHARTERS**
Backcountry Charters offers 5- and 8-hr trips with light tackle or fly rods in the mangroves and grass flats. Jun-Sep, for the best fishing and to beat the heat, Capt Hobby prefers night fishing for snook and tarpon anywhere from 2am-

5:30am. He will recommend an accessible dock, can remove the boat's front seat and can help lift you onto his 18' flats boat in your WC. (239-433-1077)

Getaway Deep-Sea Fishing offers half/full-day private or split charters on a variety of boats for 6 or more. Crew can lift you aboard in your WC. Some boats have AC cabins roomy enough for a WC and crew can help you over the lips. (18400 SR 865, Ft Myers Bch; 239-466-3600)

Miss Renee Charters offers both private and split charters for deep-sea fishing in the Gulf on a 40' or 42' boat for 6-14 anglers. Private charters are half/full day; split charters are full day only. Crew can lift you aboard in your WC. (Getaway Marina, 18400 SR 865, Ft Myers Bch; 239-267-6884)

Native Charters offers half-day, and in winter also full-day, offshore or inshore fishing trips on a 24' Morgan boat for 3 anglers. With advance notice, Capt Harvey can get help to lift you aboard in your WC. The Lazy Flamingo restaurant at the marina will cook your catch for you. Rr (Four Winds Marina, 16501 Stringfellow Rd/SR 767, Bokeelia; at the N tip of Pine Island; 239-283-7796)

■ **FISHING-PARTY BOATS**

Adventures in Paradise uses a deck boat for daily backwater fishing trips with light tackle on the Sanibel Grass Flats. The boat has a large deck and a wide gate so usually you can roll aboard. 9-noon (Port Sanibel Marina, 14341 Port Comfort Rd; 1 mi E of the Sanibel toll gate; 239-472-8443; 239-437-1660)

Getaway Deep-Sea Fishing uses a 100' fishing yacht and, with advance notice, crew can lift you aboard in your WC. Brkfst/lunch sold onboard. 8-5 & 9-3 (18400 SR 865, Ft Myers Bch; 239-466-3600)

Island Lady goes deep-sea fishing on the Gulf with up to 40 anglers. Crew can help lift you in your WC through the gate to board. AC cabin; BYO drinks & food. 8-4 (702 Fishermans Wharf, Ft Myers Bch; off SR 865 at Sky Bridge; 239-482-2005)

■ **FISHING PIERS**

Beaches: Lovers Key. Parks: Centennial, Lakes, Manatee, Six Mile

Bokeelia Seaport Pier is a 150' wood fishing pier on Charlotte Harbor. WC anglers can use the pier up to the 1st gate for free; $ to go out further. 7:30am-dusk Bait shop; restaurant next door; Rr (8421 Main St, Bokeelia; at the N tip of Pine Island)

Cape Coral Yacht Club Municipal Pier is a 400' lighted wood pier on the Caloosahatchee River. Bait/snack shop; Rr. 24 hrs (5819 Driftwood Pkwy, Cape Coral)

Ft Myers Beach Pier is a 600' lighted concrete pier with a depth of 10' on the Gulf and next to the Lynn Hall Memorial Park. Bait shop; CRr in park. 24 hrs (950 SR 865, Ft Myers Bch)

■ **HORSEBACK RIDING**

Special Equestrians Horses & Handicapped are members of the NARHA and offer classes for disabled riders, beginners and beyond. You can use special saddles and equipment, including a platform for mounting paraplegics on horseback. You must be pre-approved; call for an application and medical forms. The cost is surprisingly inexpensive. Rr. Schedule varies (Bayshore Stables, 17840 Palm Creek Dr; 239-731-1212)

■ **MISC**

Lee County Parks would like to hear from you if you use a WC or adaptive equipment are interested in playing golf, archery or other sports. (239-461-7422/461-7423) For basketball call Dana Lamb 239-277-1447.

Riverside Community Center, sitting on 4 acres along the Caloosahatchee River, hosts various functions, from classes for adults and kids to open rehearsals of Fred's Big Band. The SW Florida Symphony also performs here in the fall. A paved nature trail leads 467' to a small lighthouse on an island in the river where you can fish from the banks. ADA playground; ADA picnic tables; Rr.

Dawn-dusk (3061 E Riverside Dr; 239-461-3788)

■ **MUSEUMS**

Children's Science Center has hands-on scientific fun in a small house with a ramped entrance; staff will gladly move things to make more room for WC guests. Play with a Van de Graaff generator that makes your hair stand on end, cuddle a python and conquer the brain teasers. Rr. ⚡. Wkdy 9:30-4:30; wknd 12-5 (2915 NE Pine Island Rd, Cape Coral; 239-997-0012)

Ft Myers Historical Museum is a restored railroad depot housing artifacts of the area, from the Calusas and Spanish conquistadors to a recent resident who developed Alka Seltzer. The longest private railroad car is also here. Rr. ⚡. Tue-Sat 9-4 (2300 Peck St; 239-332-5955)

Imaginarium is an interactive children's museum, aquarium and science center with over 60 hands-on exhibits. See iguanas, tortoises and alligators. Examine a living reef and an outdoor lagoon with native and exotic fish. Gift shop; Rr. ⚡. Tue-Sat 10-5; Sun 12-5 (2000 Cranford Ave; off MLK Blvd; 239-337-3332)

Museum of the Islands houses many artifacts from the Calusa and Seminole tribes, a potpourri of antique items and historic pictures. Rr. ⚡. Hrs vary (5728 Sesame Dr, Bokeelia; W off Stringfellow Rd/CR767 on Pine Island; 239-283-1525)

■ **PARASAILING**

Rebel Water Sports is experienced with paraplegic parasailors. Staff can wheel you to the edge of the water, lift you from your WC into the water and wade with you to the boat anchored close to shore. Staff then hoists you on the platform at the stern and into a boat seat. After that, parasailing is easy! Advance notice; calm days only. 10-5 (1010 SR 865, Ft Myers Bch; 239-463-3351)

Ranalli Parasailing is experienced with disabled parasailors and can arrange to meet you at an accessible dock. Crew

can lift you aboard in your WC or into a boat seat and then onto the deck for takeoff. Call Patrick Ranalli 239-565-5700.

■ **PARKS**

Beaches: Lovers Key

Caloosahatchee Park, a 768-acre natural refuge, has a 630' hard-packed shell trail to an overlook on the Caloosahatchee River. Other trails are narrow and rough. The park rents solo sit-on and tandem sit-in kayaks by the hour. With advance notice you can drive down a rough road to the launch or staff can shuttle you in a golf cart. Staff can usually help you transfer into your kayak. Occasionally the park offers 6-hr guided kayak trips. Some 1-hr guided hikes on Sat at 9 are accessible. Call for the schedule of classes and special events. See Campgrounds. Fishing pier to be constructed; ADA picnic tables; Rr. ⚡ (18500 CR 78, Alva; I-75 exit 141, E on SR 78, N on SR 31, then E; 3 mi W of Alva; 239-693-2690)

Centennial Park includes 10 acres of city parkland along the Caloosahatchee River with sidewalks throughout. The .5-mi Riverwalk runs past the park and the next door Yacht Basin to the Edison Bridge on BR US 41; another 765' concrete trail skirts the mangroves. A lighted cement fishing pier extends 300' over the water. The boat ramp (239-332-6898), toward the private Yacht Basin next door, has a floating dock. Call for the schedule of events and concerts held here. You can purchase fresh flowers and produce every Thu morning at a Farmers Market. ADA picnic table; ADA playground; Rr. 6:30am-10:30pm (2000 W 1 St; 239-332-6638)

Lakes Park has a 2.5-mi paved trail through the 279 acres of fun. Fish from a wood deck on a large freshwater lake. Kids, supervised by an adult, can borrow a rod and tackle by calling 941-432-2000 beforehand. At the end of parking lot 3, enjoy a fragrance garden with exotic and native plants, elevated for your nose's pleasure! The Train Village (941-267-1905) has a locomotive, coal car and gift shop; the miniature train is inaccessible. The Lakeside Grill has a private marina (wkdy 10-4, wknd 9-5; 239-432-2017) that rents flat-bottom and conventional canoes by the hour. You may only board from the dock, but, if available, staff can help lift you into a canoe. The marina also has a fishing deck on the lake. Across grass is a beach and swim area, open with lifeguards Memorial-Labor Day. Near the beach is a climbing wall and accessible water playground. Call for the schedule of interpretive programs, low-impact fitness classes, fishing classes for kids and campfire programs in the amphitheater. Metered parking; ADA picnic tables; 2 playgrounds; roll-in showers in locker room; CRr. $. Winter 8-6; summer -8 (7330 Gladiolus Dr; between S Cleveland Ave & Metro Pkwy; 239-432-2034)

Manatee Park has a ramped platform with viewing areas and informational kiosks where, during winter, you can see manatees drawn to the warm water discharged by a nearby power plant. Nov-Mar 9-4, volunteer naturalists are on site to talk with you about manatees and other wildlife. A boardwalk winds through forest to a fishing deck and pier on the Orange River. Nov-Mar 9-3, you can rent solo/tandem sit-in kayaks by the hour. Staff cannot lift you down the grassy slope to the launch nor into a kayak. The river is so mellow you paddle back to the launch. Paved walks pass through a butterfly garden and a native plant habitat. Call for the schedule of guided nature walks, kayak trips and workshops in the amphitheater. Metered parking; visitor center & gift shop 9-4; ADA picnic shelters; Rr. $. Apr-Sep 8-8; Oct-Mar 8-5 (SR 80, N Ft Myers; 1.5 mi E of I-75; 239-432-2038; manatee info 239-694-3537)

Six Mile Cypress Slough Preserve has a 1-mi elevated boardwalk through 2200 acres of wetland with observation decks and a fishing dock on a freshwater lake. Self-guiding trail maps are available. Call for the schedule of guided walks and amphitheater presentations. ADA picnic tables; Rr. 8-dusk (7751 Penzance Crossing; 239-432-2042/482-0488)

■ **PERFORMING ARTS**
County parks host a number of free outdoor concerts; call 941-461-7400 for schedule.
Parks: Riverside
Ft Myers Theater Conspiracy is a community group performing plays from classics to the cutting edge. Removable seating; Rr. Aug-Jun (10091 McGregor Blvd; 239-936-3239)
Barbara Mann Performing Arts Center has Broadway productions and nationally renowned entertainers all year. WC seating on side of orchestra section; Rr (8099 College Pkwy; 239-489-3033; box office 239-481-4849)

■ **POOLS**
The following pools are heated and have lifts (fixed seats). Lifeguards can help with transfers but cannot lift. All pools offer either an adaptive swim program for kids and families or Arthritis Foundation Aquacise classes. Rr. $. Hrs vary: **Aquatic Center** with a water basketball unit (Sam Fleishman Sports Complex, 1750 Matthew Dr; 239-931-7020); **Lehigh Acres Community Pool** (1400 W 5 St, Lehigh Acres; 239-369-8277); **N Fort Myers Pool** (5170 Orange Grove Blvd, N Ft Myers; 239-656-7763); **Pine Island Pool** (5675 Sesame Dr, Bokeelia; 239-283-2220); **San Carlos Community Pool** (8208 Sanibel Blvd; 239-267-6002)
Cape Coral Yacht Club has a ramped Jr Olympic pool and an aquatic chair for loan. Rr. $. Hrs vary (5819 Driftwood Pkwy, Cape Coral; 239-542-3903)

■ **SCUBA**
Aqua Diving School is run by a physical therapist with experience certifying disabled divers with good upper body strength. Private and group sessions for certification are performance based and

move at your pace. Review the video and manual on your own beforehand. Instruction includes 3 evening classes, 2-3 evening pool sessions at the Aquatic Center (see Pools), 2 open water dives at a beach or lake in the area and 2 at West Palm Beach. Discuss any special needs with Tom Ricketts so he can arrange extra help if needed. (1914 Boy Scout Dr; 239-277-0123)

■ SHOPPING
Flea Markets include the Ortiz Flea Market Fri-Sun 6-4 (1501 Ortiz Ave; 239-694-5019) and Fleamasters Fri-Sun 8-4 (SR 82; 1 mi W of I-75; 239-334-7001).
Malls: Bell Tower Mall (US 41 S at Daniels Rd); Edison Mall (4125 Cleveland Ave); Metro Mall with outlets and specialty shops (2855 Colonial Blvd); Royal Palm Square (1400 Colonial Blvd); Tanger Factory Stores (20350 Summerline Rd; 239-454-1616)
Speciality Shops: Shell Factory has the largest shell collection outside of the ocean and 17 acres of gift items from around the world. (2787 N US 41, N Ft Myers; 239-995-2141)

■ SPECTATOR SPORTS
Baseball Boston Red Sox and the Minnesota Twins both start spring training mid-Feb and play exhibition games Mar-Apr. The Red Sox play at City of Palm Park (2001 Edison Ave; 239-334-

4700; 877-733-7699). Both the Twins and the Fort Myers Miracle (a minor league team that plays Apr-Aug) compete at Lee County Sports Complex. (Daniels Rd & Six Mile Cypress Pkwy; 239-768-4210; Twins 239-768-4200; 800-338-9467) Both stadiums have WC seating on the 1st level and Rr.
Ice Hockey Florida Everblades plays Nov-Apr. WC seating on ground floor & upper level; Rr (Teco Arena, 11000 Everblades Pkwy; 239-948-7825)

■ TENNIS
USTA WC-Tennis clinics are held on Sat 11:15-1 for beginning through advanced players, all ages. Call Steve Martin 239-945-4850. (Rutenberg Park, 6500 S Pointe Blvd)

■ TOURS
Sun Harvest Citrus offers hourly 30-min tours of a packinghouse where you learn the history of the citrus industry and see how citrus is cleaned, sized and packaged. Rr. Nov-Apr 11-3 (14810 Metro Pkwy S; 239-768-2686; 800-743-1480)
Matlacha is a village on Pine Island along the Matlacha Pass that features Art Night Oct-Apr on the 2nd Fri. Six galleries, with mostly local work, have live music and wine and stay open until you've finished dinner at one of the local eateries.

ACCOMMODATIONS

■ B&Bs
Li-Inn Sleeps B&B is in a 1912 Florida home 2 blocks from the Caloosahatchee River. The ADA Shawn Room has 2 twin beds (25" high/open frames) and a private bath with a raised toilet, rollunder sink and step-in shower with a hand-held sprayer and seat. A full breakfast is served in the dining room. $-$$ (2135 McGregor Blvd; 239-332-2651)
Bayview B&B, on the Matlacha Pass, has a WC-friendly, ground floor guestroom with a queen bed and a day bed (open frames) and a standard pri-

vate bathroom. Enjoy a large continental breakfast. A paved path leads to a 90' dock where you can fish or watch birds and manatees. $$ (12251 Shoreview Dr, Matlacha; 239-283-7510)
■ CABINS/ CAMPGROUNDS
Caloosahatchee Park has a primitive tent camp area including a site with an ADA picnic table, grill and ADA fire ring. The site is close to the ADA bathhouse with a raised toilet, roll-under sink and roll-in shower. See Parks. (18500 N River Rd/CR78, Alva; I-75 exit 141, E on SR 78, N on SR 31, then E; 3 mi

W of Alva; 239-693-2690)

*Cayo Costa State Park has a tram to take you the 1 mi from the boat dock to 12 rustic, 1-room cabins on the Gulf side of this gloriously undeveloped island. The ADA cabin is ramped and has bunk beds to sleep 6 and an ADA picnic table. Just outside on sand is another ADA picnic table and grill. Cross the hard-packed shell road to the Rr with potable water and cold outdoor showers. The island has no electricity so bring lanterns and a cooler with plenty of ice; once a day, rangers sell ice made by generator. See Beaches for information on the tram and beach WC; see Boat Tours: Tropic Star for information on the ferry. (just S of Gasparilla Island; due W of Pine Island; 941-964-0375)

Red Coconut RV Resort is on the Gulf and has 200 RV sites with full hookups, cement pads and picnic tables. Some are in the shade of tall Australian pines; others are across the street from the beach. The bathhouse has raised toilets, roll-under sinks and roll-in showers. A walkway leads to the beach. Laundry; entertainment; full restaurant; camp store; library (3001 SR 865, Ft Myers Bch; 2 mi E of San Carlos Blvd; 239-463-7200; 888-262-6226)

■ **CONDOS**

Abaco Beach Villas has a WC-friendly ground floor 1BR unit overlooking Estero Bay. The unit has a king bed (22" high/open frame), living room with a queen sofa bed, a full kitchen and patio grill. The standard bathroom has grab bars and a step-in shower. Across the lawn is a fishing dock on the Matanzas Pass and next door is Bowditch Park; see Beaches. Registration is on the 3rd floor; either send someone upstairs or call ahead so staff can meet you in the parking lot. (131 CR 865, Ft Myers Bch; 239-463-2611)

Bay to Beach Resort has a WC-friendly 1BR condo with a queen bed and a 2BR condo with a queen and 2 twin beds (all beds on open frames). All units have full kitchens, washer/dryers and

screened balconies on the Gulf. Standard bathrooms are large. Neither the pool area nor the beach is accessible. Parking is beneath the building and accessible by elevator. (740 CR 865, Ft Myers Bch; 239-463-5846; 800-670-4554)

Grandview has 3 small 1BR ADA units each with a king bed, full kitchen and queen sofa bed in the living room. Bathrooms have roll-under sinks; unit 205 has a roll-in shower with a hand-held sprayer and seat; others have tubs. Ramp to beach; heated pool; rental boats; canoes; kayaks; sailboats; jet boats; nature cruises; fishing; laundry (8701 CR 865, Ft Myers Bch; 239-765-4422; 800-956-8377)

Gull Wing Beach Resort is on the beach and has 4 ADA units, 2- and 3BR. Each condo has a king and 2 queen beds (25" high/open frames), a full kitchen and living room with a sofa bed. Bathrooms have raised toilets and roll-under sinks; 2 rooms have roll-in showers with hand-held sprayers and seats; others have tubs. Heated pool; hot tub; tennis; exercise room; social program; paved walkway to the beach (6620 CR 865, Ft Myers Bch; 239-765-4300)

Lovers Key Beach Club & Resort is on the beach and has 5 ADA 2BR condos each with a king and queen bed (24" high/open frames), a full kitchen and queen sofa bed in the living room. Bathrooms have roll-under sinks and roll-in showers with hand-held sprayers and seats. Pool; full restaurant overlooking the bay (8771 CR 865, Ft Myers Bch; 239-765-1040; 877-798-4879)0

■ **COTTAGES**

Matlacha Cottage is a roomy ADA 2BR/2BA cottage with a fishing dock on the Matlacha Pass. The cottage has 36" wide doorways, a queen and 2 twin beds, a full kitchen, dining area and living room with a full sofa bed. One bathroom has a raised toilet, raised sink and roll-in shower; the other is standard with a step-in shower. This privately owned unit is available by the week in winter; other minimums apply in off-season. (12190 Shoreview Rd, Matlacha; 239-334-8199)

■ MOTELS

Best Western Airport has 6 ADA rooms each with a king or 2 full beds (platforms), refrigerator and microwave. Bathrooms have roll-under sinks and roll-in showers with hand-held sprayers and seats. Free brkfst; pool; laundry. $-$$$ (8955 Daniels Pkwy; 239-561-7000)

Casa Loma is on a canal off the Caloosahatchee River and has 3 ADA efficiencies, each with a queen bed (open frame) and full kitchen. Bathrooms have raised toilets and roll-under sinks; room 118 has a roll-in shower with a hand-held sprayer and seat; others have a tub or step-in shower. Pool; laundry. $-$$ (3608 Del Prado Blvd, Cape Coral; 239-549-6000)

Casa Playa Hotel is on the beach with 4 ADA rooms, each with a king or 2 full beds (24" high) and a kitchenette. Bathrooms have raised toilets, roll-under sinks and tubs with seats. Pool; laundry. $$-$$$ (510 CR 865, Ft Myers Bch; 239-765-0510)

Comfort Suites has 3 ADA 1-room suites each with a king bed (20" high/platform), sofa bed, refrigerator, microwave and coffeepot. Bathrooms have raised toilets, roll-under sinks and tubs with hand-held sprayers and seats. Free brkfst; pool; bar. $$-$$$ (13651 Indian Paint Ln; 239-768-0005)

Diamondhead All Suite Beach Resort is on the beach and has 8 ADA 1BR suites each with a king bed (24" high; open frame), a full kitchenette and a queen sofa bed in the living room. Bathrooms have roll-under sinks; rooms 211 and 311 have roll-in showers with hand-held sprayers; others have tubs. Heated pool; hot tub; laundry; bar; entertainment; full restaurant; poolside bar & grill; weight room; activity program; parasailing; jet ski rentals; boardwalk to beach. $$-$$$ (2000 CR 865, Ft Myers Bch; 239-765-7654)

Hampton Inn Airport has 4 ADA rooms each with a king bed (24" high/platform) and bathroom with a raised toilet, roll-under sink and roll-in shower with a hand-held sprayer and seat. Free brkfst; pool. $$-$$$ (9241 Market Place Rd; 239-768-2525)

Homewood Suites has 6 ADA suites each with a queen bed (open frame), full kitchen and full sofa bed in the living room. Bathrooms have roll-under sinks; rooms 110 and 140 have roll-in showers with hand-held sprayers and seats; others have a tub or step-in shower. Free brkfst; pool; laundry; Mon-Thu free happy hr. $$$ (5255 Big Pine Way; 239-275-6000)

Motel 6 has 5 ADA rooms each with a queen bed (platform) and bathroom with a raised toilet, roll-under sink and roll-in shower with a seat. $ (3350 Marinatown Ln; 239-656-5544)

*Outrigger Beach Resort room 105 is an ADA efficiency on the beach with 2 full beds, a full kitchen and bathroom with a roll-under sink and step-in shower. Ask at the front desk to borrow a beach WC (fixed arms). Heated pool; tiki bar; ramped sundeck; children's program; bike rentals; gift shop; laundry; full restaurant. $$$ (6200 CR 865, Ft Myers Bch; 239-463-3131; 800-749-3131)

Sleep Inn Airport has 3 ADA rooms each with a queen bed (platform) and bathroom with a raised toilet, roll-under sink and roll-in shower with a hand-held sprayer and seat. Free brkfst; free happy hr; heated pool. $$-$$$ (13651 B Indian Paint Ln; 239-561-1117)

Wellesley Inn has 8 ADA rooms each with a king bed (platform). Bathrooms have raised toilets and roll-under sinks; room 107 and 113 have roll-in showers with hand-held sprayers and seats; others have tubs. Free brkfst & paper; heated pool; laundry. $-$$$ (4400 Ford St; 239-278-3949)

NAPLES

Bonita Beach, Bonita Springs, Estero, Goodland, Marco Island, Vanderbilt Beach

Naples is chic and sophisticated but on the edge of an uncivilized, uniquely Floridian wilderness. Boat tours range from elegant luncheon cruises to swamp tours.
The city has an impressive arts agenda, endless boutiques and swishy hotels as well
as excellent fishing. You can borrow beach wheelchairs at most of the splendid
beaches along the Gulf. Briggs Nature Center, off the main route to Marco Island,
offers a stunning array of eco-adventures on the beaches and in the bays. US 41 is
also called the Tamiami Trail.

Tourist Info

Bonita Springs Chamber: 25071 Chamber of Commerce Dr, Bonita Springs, 34133;
239-992-2943; 800-226-2943
Marco Island Chamber: 1102 N Collier Blvd, Marco Island, 34145; 239-394-3061;
800-788-6272
Naples Visitor Information Center: 895 5 Ave S, 34102; 239-262-2113; 800-605-7878
Web sites: www.bonitaspringschamber.com; www.marcoisland.com; www.naples-
florida.com; www.naplesnet.com/naples/naples.htm

Transportation

Boat Tours: Key West
Collier County buses have lifts. Call beforehand and the driver will be watching to
assist you. Mon-Sat 6am-7pm (239-596-7777)

ACTIVITIES

■ **ATTRACTIONS**
Caribbean Gardens is a 52-acre zoological preserve where you can learn about
and interact with exotic animals. Near
the entrance, sidewalks lead to 2 animal
shows. Safari Canyon is a 30-min show
with video monitors and large cats in a
canyon-type setting. Scales and Tales is
a 30-min show where you may be able
to touch live lemurs, kinkajous, small
felines and juvenile large cats. The
natural mulch and crushed shell trails
through the rest of the park can get
soft with rains. The Meet the Keeper
series schedules a trainer for 15 min
chats in front of different exhibits. At
Alligator Bay you can pet a baby alligator during a 15-min talk. You must be
able to walk a short distance to board
the pontoon boat for the 1/2-hr cruise
around islands of primates. No designated WC seating at shows; picnic
tables; Subway or BYO snacks; gift

shop; WC rental; CRr. $/free in WC.
9:30-5:30 (1590 Goodlette-Frank Rd;
239-262-5409)
Everglades Wonder Gardens is home to
panthers, crocodiles, flamingos and
more. At the entrance, ask staff to unlock the nearby WC entrance. You can
watch an alligator dine, otters perform
and tour an eclectic natural history museum. Take a 1-hr guided tour available
throughout the day. Gift shop; snack
bar; Rr not ADA. $. 9-5 (27180 Old US
41, Bonita Springs; 239-992-2591)
■ **BEACHES**
*Barefoot Beach Preserve is on a 342-
acre barrier island. At the 1st parking lot
take the N boardwalk to the ranger station where you can borrow a beach WC
(fixed arms). Here you'll also find a
snack bar, ADA picnic tables on a covered wood deck and Rr. The 1700'
boardwalk goes through native coastal
dunes where you can see wading birds,

bald eagles and osprey. An outdoor learning center features rotating environmental displays. Use the 3rd parking lot for canoe rentals. Rangers can help you over the hard-packed sand to the launch and help lift you into a canoe for paddling the back bays. On request, rangers may be able to guide a walk. Call for the schedule of ranger programs including walks and canoe trips. Umbrella & chair rentals 8-5; outdoor showers; Rr. $. 8am-dusk (505 Lely Bch Blvd, Bonita Bch; just S of Bonita Bch Rd; 239-591-8596)

Bonita Beach is a 4-mi beach with a boardwalk from the 1st parking lot to the beach. HC parking is in a raised area that's great for catching sunsets. ADA picnic table; grills; outdoor showers; umbrella/chair rentals; Rr. 8-dusk (SR 865; 2.5 mi W of US 41; 239-495-5811)

*Clam Pass Park has a .5-mi boardwalk through a mangrove swamp, over a tidal bay and mud flats to a beautiful 3200' beach, rated as one of the top 20 in the USA. You can fish from the boardwalk or watch wading birds as they fish. Borrow a beach WC (fixed arms) at the concession stand. Snack bar; umbrella/chair rentals; picnic tables at concession; outdoor showers; Rr. $. 8am-dusk (475 Seagate Dr; W on Pine Ridge Rd off US 41; 239-591-8596)

*Delnor-Wiggins Pass State Park is the N tip of a narrow barrier island with a causeway from the mainland. While mangrove covers most of the island, the beautiful 1-mi beach is the main draw. Stop at the ranger station as you enter the park to reserve a beach WC (removable arms); you can pick it up behind the concession stand. Area 1 has a boardwalk to a beach overlook with a ramp to the sand, a lifeguard and ADA picnic tables on sand. The boat ramp between Area 1 and 2 has a fixed dock on the bay. Area 5 has an ADA picnic shelter. Call for the schedule of rangers programs. Snack bar; umbrella/chair rentals; outdoor showers; Rr. $. 8-dusk (11100 Gulf Shore Dr N, Vanderbilt Bch;

from US 41 W on CR 846; 239-597-6196; concession stand 239-594-3400)

*Lovers Key/Carl E Johnson State Park has a gorgeous beach on the Gulf as well as frontage on Estero Bay. Ask to borrow a beach WC (removable arms) at the entrance. A ranger can bring it to you at the N beach where you take a brick bridge from parking onto the soft sand or, at the S beach where you can take a ramped tram to the beach. Australian pines shade ADA picnic tables and grills on sand, but you can also find ADA tables on grassy, hard-packed areas. Four bridges offer accessible saltwater fishing on the back bays and canal. On the bridge to the N beach, the park plans to build a large deck with ADA picnic tables that overlook the beach. Across from the entrance is a boat ramp with a floating dock on Estero Bay. The gift shop (239-765-880) by the main parking lot rents canoes and solo/tandem sit-in kayaks by the hour or day; the launch onto the bay is hard-packed with a gentle slope where staff can help lift you into your craft. The 2.6-mi Black Island Trail is quite accessible with a few sandy spots. It goes through mangrove and maritime hammock passing a butterfly garden, freshwater ponds and decks where you can see a variety of birds and possibly manatees. Another 1-mi paved trail has a canopy of palms and sea grapes and leads to 3 wildlife overlooks. Lifeguards; outdoor showers; Rr. $. 8-dusk (8700 CR 865; just N of Bonita Bch; 239-463-4588)

*Tigertail Public Beach has a boardwalk down to the beach and a beach WC (fixed arms) that you can borrow at the pavilion. Briggs Nature Center naturalists lead 2 eco-adventures here; see Parks. Snack bar; umbrella/chair rentals; outdoor showers; Rr. $. 8-dusk (490 Hernando Dr, Marco Island)

■ **BOAT RAMPS**
Beaches: Delnor-Wiggins, Lovers Key

Calusa Island Marina has a ramp on the Gulf of Mexico and nearby, in front of the ship store, a floating dock. Bait/snack shop; fuel. $. Hrs vary (300 Goodland Dr W, Goodland; 239-394-3668)

Caxambas Park has a ramp with floating docks on Caxambas Pass that leads to the Gulf. You can also fish from the docks. Picnic tables; bait shop; Rr. $ (909 S Collier Ct, Marco Island; 239-642-0004)

Cocohatchee River Marina has a ramp and fixed dock on Vanderbilt Bay from which you can access the Gulf. Staff can help you down the 4 steps to the dock where you can also fish. Bait shop; picnic tables; Rr. $. 7-6 (13535 Vanderbilt Dr/SR 901, Vanderbilt Bch; 239-566-2611)

Sugden Park has a boat ramp, floating dock and two 50' fishing piers on the 60-acre freshwater Lake Avalon. A 1-mi paved trail goes through a wooded area around the lake. Call for the schedule of ranger programs. ADA picnic tables; Rr. 8-dusk (4284 Avalon Dr; E on Lakewood Dr off US 41; 239-793-4414)

■ **BOAT RENTALS**

Cedar Bay Marina rents a 12-person pontoon boat (23" entry), deck boats, cabin cruisers and bow riders for half/full days. If available, staff can lift you aboard in your WC or into a boat seat from the ramped fixed dock. Bait/snack shop. 7-7 (705 E Elkham Cir, Marco Island; 239-642-6717)

Cocohatchee River Marina rents pontoon boats for 8-12 people (30" entry) for Vanderbilt Bay or Wiggins Pass for half/full days. Staff can help you down the 4 steps to the dock where you can also fish. Bait shop; picnic tables; Rr. $. 7-6 (13535 Vanderbilt Dr/SR 901, Vanderbilt Bch; 239-566-2611)

Fish Finder rents pontoon boats (30" entry) for half/full days on Vanderbilt Bay and the backwaters. With advance notice, staff can help you down the steps to the dock and aboard. Bait shop. 7-6 (179 S Bay Dr, Vanderbilt Bch; 239-597-2063)

Marco River Marina rents 8- and 10-person pontoon boats (26.5" entry) for half/full days on the Intracoastal. From the floating dock you can roll aboard by ramp. Bait/snack shop. 7-7 (951 Bald Eagle Dr, Marco Island; 239-394-2502)

Port-O-Call Marina rents a 22' deck boat for touring from Naples Bay to Marco Island for half/full day. Crew can help lift you in your WC from the floating dock and over the boat railing. 8-5 (550 Port-O-Call Way; 239-774-0331)

Port of the Islands Marina rents pontoon boats (31" opening) for up to 8 people on the 10,000 Islands. Usually you can roll aboard from the floating dock; staff can help if needed. Weekday rentals are for half day or longer and on weekends, only for full days. Bait shop. Hrs vary (25,000 US 41; 239-642-3133)

Wiggins Pass Marina rents 8- and 10-person pontoon boats (25" or 26" entry) for half/full days exploring the backwaters from Vanderbilt Bay to Ft Myers Beach. If you can't roll through the gate from the floating dock, staff can lift you over the railing in your WC. Bait shop. 8-4:30 (13635 Vanderbilt Dr, Vanderbilt Bch; 239-597-3549)

■ **BOAT TOURS**

Parks: Briggs, Collier-Seminole

Capt Ed invites you to design a private tour aboard his 34' pontoon boat. Perhaps you'd like to sightsee in residential canals, or take a nature or sunset cruise. Roll aboard from the floating dock. (27598 Marina Point Dr SE, Bonita Bch; 239-566-6510)

Double Sunshine offers 90-min narrated cruises of Naples Bay and the 10,000 Islands focusing on the history and wildlife. Roll aboard. 10-4 (Maritime Marketplace, US 41 at SR 85; 239-263-4949)

Estero Bay Boat Tours makes 2-hr sightseeing and sunset trips on a 38' pontoon boat in search of dolphin, manatee and other wildlife. Learn about the Calusa Indians and the many shell mounds on Estero Bay. Shelling trips stop at inaccessible islands. Roll aboard; if tides are extreme, crew can help. 8-5 (5231 Mamie St, Bonita Springs; 239-992-2200)

Key West Shuttle takes passengers aboard a 130' Supercruiser for a day of shopping and sightseeing in Key West. The ship can accommodate folks in manual not power WCs. Depart at 9am, take the 4-hr ride and spend 5 hrs in Key West then depart at 6pm for the return. With prior arrangements, you can return at a later date. Remember, trips can be cancelled due to high seas. Crew can help you over the lip into the main deck's cabin where you can enjoy breakfast or for an extra charge, drinks and sandwiches. The 2nd deck, with entertainment, is inaccessible. To avoid disappointment, call to discuss any special needs with Eric Crawford before making reservations. Nov-May 15 (951 Bald Eagle Dr, Marco Island; off SR 951; 239-732-7744; 888-539-2628)

Naples Princess is a luxurious ramped cruise ship offering a variety of tours, from 90-min afternoons sightseeing to 2-hr dinner cruises on Naples Bay. CRr. Hrs vary (550 Port O Call Way; 239-649-2275)

Nautilus Boat Tours takes 90-min nature and sunset trips aboard a 78' catamaran or a 40' pontoon boat along Vanderbilt Lagoon and the Gulf. Or try a 4-hr cruise to lunch at the Fish House Restaurant on Bonita Beach. Learn about the wildlife and history of the area and view beautiful homes along the Intracoastal. With advance notice, crew can carry you in your WC down 4 steps to the dock; from here you can roll aboard by ramp. Hrs vary (179 S Bay Dr, Vanderbilt Bch; W off of Vanderbilt Dr; 239-597-4408)

Port of the Islands Marina offers 2-hr narrated cruises to learn about the history and ecology of the Everglades and 10,000 Islands. Be aware: you're in a manatee sanctuary. Roll aboard the Island Princess, a large pontoon boat; if tides are extreme, crew can help. (25,000 US 41; 239-642-3133)

Sea Excursions makes 2-hr trips on a power catamaran for sightseeing, dolphin watching and a bit of shelling at an inaccessible island. Or take a sailing catamaran for a morning dolphin watch or sunset cruise; neither make stops. With prior notice, staff can lift you aboard in your WC. 9-9 (Cedar Bay Marina, 705 E Elkham Cir, Marco Island; 239-642-6400)

Sunshine Tours invites you for 2-hr daytime, sunset or dinner cruises aboard a ramped 65' yacht with an accessible main deck. See wildlife including manatees and dolphins and the high life as you pass some multi-million dollar homes. Hrs vary (Marco River Marina, 951 Bald Eagle Dr, Marco Island; 239-642-5415)

■ **CANOEING/KAYAKING**
Beaches: Barefoot, Lovers Key. Parks: Briggs, Collier-Seminole, Koreshan

Canoe Estero River rents canoes and solo/tandem sit-in and sit-on kayaks for this serene river where you paddle back to the launch. The banks have a slight grade but staff can carry you down and into your craft. At the shop, you can rent fishing gear and bait for the trip. (20991 S US 41, Estero; 239-992-4050)

■ **FISHING CHARTERS**
Capt Dave Eimers fishes the bays and channels in the 10,000 Islands National Wildlife Refuge. He is experienced with WC anglers and his 18' Maverick flats skiff gives a smooth, dry ride. Charters run half/full-day for 2 anglers. Roll aboard from the floating dock. (Calusa Island Marina, 300 Goodland Dr W, Goodland; 239-353-4828)

Capt Ed offers half-day backwater trips on Estero Bay aboard a pontoon boat for up to 6 anglers. Roll aboard from the floating dock. (Bonita Bay Marina, 27598 Marina Point Dr SE, Bonita Bch; 239-566-6510)

Fish Finder can take you backwater fishing on a pontoon boat (30" entry) for half/full-day trips. Crew is experienced with disabled anglers and can carry you down the 2 steps to the dock but needs advance notice. 7-5 (179 S

Bay Dr, Vanderbilt Bch; 239-597-2063)

Fish Trap Marina offers half/full-day fishing in Estero Bay on a pontoon boat for up to 6. If you are not a die-hard angler, you can get some sightseeing in as well. Usually you can roll aboard; in low tide, with advance notice, staff can help lower you in your WC. (4794 Bonita Bch Rd, Bonita Bch; 239-992-6055)

Peg Leg Charters offers half/full-day offshore trips and back bay trips in the 10,000 Islands. Capt Kennedy has cut the back transom from his 31' boat and installed a door for WC access. You can usually roll aboard from the floating dock. (Barge Marina, 3200 SR 92, Marco Island; 239-250-0625; cell 239-642-4333)

Port-O-Call Marina offers deep-sea half/full-day charters on a 39' catamaran. Crew can lift you aboard in your WC from the floating dock. 8-5 (550 Port-O-Call Way; 239-774-0331)

Port of the Island Marina will arrange half/full-day charters in the 10,000 Islands with capts experienced with disabled anglers. Marina staff can help lift you aboard in your WC from the floating dock. Hrs vary (25,000 US 41; 239-642-3133)

Sunshine Charters offers private or split offshore and backwater trips for half/full days on a variety of vessels. Crew is experienced with WC anglers and can lift you aboard in your WC from the floating dock. 7-7 (Marco River Marina, 951 Bald Eagle Dr, Marco Island; 239-642-5415)

■ **FISHING-PARTY BOATS**
Sunshine Tours makes 3-hr trips in the inland bays of the 10,000 Islands on a pontoon boat with up to 8 anglers. Usually you can roll aboard from the floating dock; if not, crew is experienced with WC anglers and can help as needed. Schedule depends on tides. 7-7 (Marco River Marina, 951 Bald Eagle Dr, Marco Island; 239-642-5415)

■ **FISHING PIERS**
Boat Ramps: Sugden
Naples Fishing Pier is a 1000' lighted

wood pier on the Gulf. Bait/snack bar during daytime; Rr. 24 hrs (Gulf Shore Blvd; at 12 Ave S; 239-213-3062)

■ **FITNESS TRAILS**
Boat Ramps: Sugden. Pools: Golden Gate

■ **HORSE BACK RIDING**
Equestrian Challenge, a member of NARHA, offers therapeutic classes for disabled riders, adults and children. You can use adaptive equipment, including a mounting block, and side walkers, if needed. Call Mindy Cowan for application and medical forms. (Pine Ridge Subdivision, Center St & Goodlette-Frank Rd; 239-591-4665)

■ **MISC**
Collier County offers programs for kids with special needs including a summer camp weekdays 8-2, grades K-8, with games, field trips, arts and crafts and therapeutic activites. Kids Night Out is a program for the whole family. Call Lynn Clarke 239-353-0404.

Marco Movie Theater offers dining, with beer and wine available, while you watch a current flick. WC seating is limited so call ahead to reserve a spot. Film & meal priced separately; Rr. Matinees & evening shows (Mission Plaza, 599 S Collier Blvd, Marco Island; 239-642-1111)

■ **MUSEUMS**
Collier County Historical Museum traces the area's history from the Calusa Indians onward. Brick paths take you to a recreated Seminole Village, a native plant garden, orchid house and steam logging locomotive. Rr. Wkdy 9-5 (3301 US 41; 239-774-8476)

Teddy Bear Museum displays 3000 bears along with teddy bear art and memorabilia. Rr. $. Wed-Sat 10-5; Sun 1-5 (2511 Pine Ridge Rd; just W of CR 31; 239-598-2711)

■ **PARASAILING**
Marco Ski & Water Sports is experienced with disabled parasailors. Staff can pull your WC over the sand to the shore then carry you out to the boat and set you on the back deck. The boat seat has a low back so you may want a

companion for additional support and balance. Staff helps you don the harness onboard. Call Ron Hagarman so he can arrange extra staff and time. (behind Mariott Hotel, 400 S Collier Blvd, Marco Island; 239-394-6589)

■ PARI-MUTUELS

Naples/Ft Myers Greyhound Track features live racing, simulcasting and a poker room (opens 1-hr before live races) all year. Take an elevator to the grandstand or clubhouse where all tables have good views of the track. Rr. Call for matinee and evening schedules. (10601 Bonita Bch Rd, Bonita Bch; 239-992-2411)

■ PARKS

Briggs Nature Center, in the Rookery Bay National Estuarine Research Reserve, is a naturalist's treasure. An elevated .5-mi boardwalk passes through 5 different ecosystems and a mulch trail leads to a butterfly garden. The Interpretive Center has hands-on exhibits and large aquariums of native occupants. Call for the schedule and make reservations for the Center's *learning adventures* when staff leads on- and off-site eco-experiences throughout the year. Dec-Apr, the Center offers 2-hr guided trips on a pontoon boat through Rookery Bay. Meet at the center for the 1.5-mi convoy to the dock but be aware the ramp may be steep depending on the tides. The morning trip to the estuary and the evening birding trip are both accessible. Afternoon shelling trips go to inaccessible beaches. At Tigertail Beach, where you can reserve a beach WC beforehand (see Beaches), naturalists lead a 1-hr walk Jan-Apr weekdays at 8:30am. Tigertail is also the spot for night seining when naturalists drag a net along the surf to collect nocturnal sea creatures. After examining the catch, the creatures are returned to the water. You can also reserve a sunset canoe trip to mangrove islets off Marco Island (canoes provided). At the Center, just prior to the trip naturalists present a slide show on

the birds you'll encounter. Then you convoy to the put-in where trip leaders can help lift you into the canoe. It's a good trip for novice paddlers. Picnic tables; Rr. $. Mon-Sat 9-4:30 (401 Shell Island Rd; from US 41, S on SR 951 for 2.5 mi then W on dirt road; 239-775-8569)

Collier-Seminole State Park celebrates this 6400-acre swamp as a slice of the unique and terribly fragile Everglades. To avoid being eaten alive by mosquitoes, visit Nov-Apr! The 1-mi Royal Palm Hammock Nature Trail is a boardwalk leading through mangrove to an observation deck overlooking a salt marsh. Although the top deck is inaccessible, you can get above the tree line for a good view. Anglers should try the boat docks on the brackish Blackwater River. Take a 1-hr, ranger-led tour along the river on a roll-aboard pontoon boat; in extreme low tide staff can lower you aboard in your WC (Oct-Aug 9-4; 239-642-8898). The tour describes the animals, plants and early settlers of the Everglades. The park rents canoes to explore a 13.6-mi marked loop on the river. Staff can help lift you in and out of the canoe from the gently sloped and firm-packed riverbank. Sun at noon Oct-Apr, with 1-wk advance reservations, rangers lead a 3-hr canoe trip. Check out the historic walking dredge that was used to build the Tamiami Trail in the 1920's. A small visitor center resembling an Army blockhouse has wildlife displays. See Campgrounds. Camp store; picnic tables; campfires on winter wknds; Rr. $. 8-dusk (20,200 US 41; 17 mi S of Naples; 239-394-3397)

Corkscrew Swamp Sanctuary is what this region looked like before the Army Corps of Engineers arrived. The National Audubon Society maintains this 11,000-acre ecosystem of 500-yr old trees and various endangered species. Start in the visitor center with a 15-min continuous video on the swamp. In winter you can take advantage of educational programs as well as food service. A mostly shady 2.25-mi elevated boardwalk loops through a primeval cathedral of cypress forest and marshland and is punctuated with interpretive displays, benches and decks in scenic areas. Chances are you'll see alligators along the way. You can take a shortcut at Lettuce Lakes that cuts back to the visitor center. ADA picnic tables; nature store; Rr. ֆ. Oct-Mar 7-5:30; Apr-Sep 7-7:30 (375 Sanctuary Rd; 16 mi E of I-75 on CR 846; 239-348-9151)

Koreshan State Historic Site is the remains of a Utopian communal group that practiced equal rights for women and the Golden Rule – in 1894! Tours are offered Sat-Sun at 1 along hard-packed shell paths. Of the 12 remaining buildings, 2 are accessible: the Art Hall and the founder's home with an historic video. You can also find a few fishing spots along the Estero River or rent a canoe for a paddle. The launch is a boat ramp where you can roll close to the water; with advance notice staff can help lift you into a canoe. See Campgrounds. ADA picnic tables; Rr, in Art Hall. ֆ. Historic site 8-5; park 8-dusk (3850 Corkscrew Rd, Estero; 239-992-0311)

Naples Nature Center has a Museum of Natural History with interactive displays where you can learn about the Everglades and its inhabitants and a Marine Conservation Station where you can view live sea turtles and other marine animals. Docents are available at the various exhibits to answer questions. In the Wildlife Rehabilitation Center, watch native wildlife being nursed back to health. Buildings are connected by boardwalks. Borrow a beach WC (removable arms) for the two 1/2-mi mulch trails. One goes through an arboretum and connects to a short boardwalk through a mangrove swamp; the other loops through a hardwood hammock. Presentations and guided walks are daily in season and by request in summer; call for schedule. Snack bar in season; picnic shelters; na-

ture store; Rr. ֆ. Mon-Sat 9-4:30 (1450 Merrihue Dr; at 14 Ave N off Goodlette-Frank Rd; 239-262-0304)

Vineyards Community Park has an accessible water playground and a .5-mi paved walking trail. Picnic tables; ADA playground; ball fields; tennis; basketball; racquetball; Rr. 8am-10pm (6231 Arbor Blvd; 239-353-9669)

■ **PERFORMING ARTS**

Actors Repertory Theater is a professional company staging dramas and comedies Nov-Apr. Call for schedule, location and access. (239-513-8600)

Marco Players is a community theater group offering lighthearted dramas, comedy and musicals. Arrive a bit early so staff can remove a seat in front at the end of a row so you can sit there in a WC. Rr (Town Center Mall, N Collier Blvd, Marco Island; 239-642-7270)

Naples Players is a community group performing Broadway musicals, dramas and comedies. WC seating is on the aisles, 1st row in the upper section. A small experimental theater features more avant-garde performances. Oct-Aug (Sugden Community Theatre, 701 5 Ave S; 239-263-7990)

Philharmonic Center for the Arts is home to the Naples Philharmonic Orchestra and the Miami City Ballet. World-class touring dance, music and theater groups perform here also. Call for the schedule of docent-led tours in the art gallery. WC seating on main floor, in box seats & guest circle; museum shop; Rr (5833 Pelican Bay Blvd; 239-597-1900)

■ **POOLS**

Bonita Springs Pool has a 25' pool with a ramp. Rr. ֆ. Hrs vary (10151 W Terry St, Bonita Springs; 239-947-1948)

Golden Gate has a heated pool with a lift (fixed seat); lifeguards can help with transfers but cannot lift. Adaptive aquatics; water slides (inaccessible). The park also has a 1-mi paved fitness trail; ADA picnic tables; ball fields; tennis; basketball; racquetball; shuffleboard; remote-control car track; snack bar. 10-7 (3300 Santa Barbara Blvd; pool 239-353-7128; park 239-353-0404) **Immokalee Sports Complex** has a heated pool with a lift (fixed seat). Lifeguards can help with transfers but not lift. Showers; picnic tables; Rr. Jun-Aug Mon-Sat 10-7, Sun -5; Sep-May Mon-Sat 12-7, Sun -5 (505 Escambia St, Immokalee; 239-657-1951)

■ SAILING

SHARE offers a basic course in recreational sailing for folks age 8 and older with all levels of disabilities, even quads. Staff can help you transfer into the lift (sling seat) and lower you aboard the 2-person or 1-person boat operated by joy stick. Call Dan Davison 239-417-0146. (Sailing Center, 1101 9 St S)

■ SHOOTING RANGES

Port of the Islands Gun Club has a paved trap and skeet range. To reach the pistol range you must go over grass and sand. You can rent guns, buy ammunition and take instructions from a world champion pro. Snack bar. Hrs vary (12425 Union Rd; off US 41; 239-642-8999)

■ SHOPPING

Boutiques: Third Street South and Fifth Avenue South, both in the historic district of Old Naples, have numerous shops, galleries, restaurants and outdoor cafes (239-649-6707). Old Marine Marketplace, or Tin City, houses 40 waterfront shops and eateries restored to the pioneer era (US 41 & SR 85; 239-262-4200). Village on Venetian Bay has boutiques, restaurants and galleries in a Mediterranean setting (4200 Gulf Shore Blvd N; 239-262-4200).

Galleries on Marco Island include the Art League of Marco Island, where you'll also find classes and lectures (1010 Winterberry Dr; 239-394-4221) and Mangroves Wildlife Gallery in the Town Center Mall.

Malls: Coastland Center Mall (1900 US 41); Coral Isle Factory Shops (7222 SR 951; 239-775-8083); Miromar Outlet Mall (I-75 exit 123, Estero; 239-948-3766); Mission Plaza (599 S Collier Blvd, Marco Island; at Winterberry Dr); Town Center Mall (N Collier Blvd, Marco Island; just E of Bald Eagle Dr); Waterside Shops (US 41 & Seagate Dr)

ACCOMMODATIONS

■ CAMPGROUNDS

Collier-Seminole State Park has 130 RV/tent sites on hard-packed gravel, grass or dirt. Sites 22-24 and 93-96 with ADA picnic tables, raised grills and water/elec are close to the ADA bathhouse with raised toilets, roll-under sinks and roll-in showers. The road in the main camp area is paved. Between the heat, humidity and mosquitoes, summers can be miserable but in the winter, the park offers plenty of fun; see Parks. (20,200 US 42; 17 mi S of Naples; 239-394-3397) **Koreshan State Historic Site** has 60 RV/tent sites with water/elec, plenty of shade and dense foliage between them. Sites 7 and 8 have ADA picnic tables, raised fire pits and grills. Hard-packed paths lead to the ADA bathhouse with roll-under sinks and roll-in showers

with hand-held sprayers and seats. See Parks. Pool; laundry; playground (US 41 at Corkscrew Rd, Estero; 239-992-0311)

■ CONDOS

Marco Bay Resort has WC-friendly 1BR condos with 2 full beds and 2BR condos with a king and 2 twins. All units have kitchens, sofa beds in the living rooms and large standard bathrooms. Some units have balconies overlooking the bay. Elevator; pool; tennis. $$$ (1001 N Barfield Dr, Marco Island; 239-394-8881; 800-228-0661)

■ INNS

Inn at Pelican Bay has a bit of European charm overlooking a small lake. Each of the 5 ADA rooms has a king or 2 full beds (22" high/open frames) and, on request a refrigerator and bathroom with a raised toilet. Room 105 has a roll-in shower with a hand-held sprayer and seat; others have tubs or step-in showers. Fluffy robes, triple sheeting and French-milled soap are some of the extra comforts. Free brkfst can be served in your room; pool; hot tub; exercise room; happy hr. $$-$$$ (800 Vanderbilt Beach Rd, Vanderbilt Bch; 239-597-8777; 800-597-8770)

Trianon Bonita Bay Hotel has lusciously landscaped grounds with outside sitting areas on a small lake. Each of the 5 spacious ADA rooms has 2 full beds (open frames), a coffeepot and bathroom with a raised toilet, roll-under sink and roll-in shower with a hand-held sprayer and seat. Free brkfst; heated pool; bar. $$-$$$ (3401 Bay Commons Dr, Bonita Springs; 239-948-4400; 800-859-3939)

■ **MOTELS**

Baymont Inn & Suites has 7 ADA rooms each with a full bed (23" high/platform) and a coffeepot. Bathrooms have raised toilets and roll-under sinks; rooms 125, 225 and 325 have roll-in showers with hand-held sprayers and seats; others have tubs. Free brkfst; pool; laundry; free paper. $-$$ (185 Bedzel Cir; 239-352-8400)

Clarion Inn has 4 ADA rooms each with 2 full beds (24" high/open frames), a refrigerator, microwave and coffeepot. Bathrooms have roll-under sinks and roll-in showers with hand-held sprayers and seats. Pool; restaurant for brkfst & lnch. $-$$ (4055 US 41; 239-649-5500; 800-895-8858)

Days Inn has 1 ADA room with a full bed (open frame) and bathroom with a raised toilet, roll-under sink and roll-in shower. Pool; laundry. $-$$$ (28090 Quails Nest Ln, Bonita Springs; 239-947-3366)

Doubletree Guest Suites, along the Cocohatchee River, has 7 ADA 1BR suites, each with a king or 2 full beds (open frames), a full sofa bed in the living room, refrigerator and coffeepot. Bathrooms have roll-under sinks; rooms 130, 210 and 330 have roll-in showers with hand-held sprayers and

seats; others have step-in showers or tubs. Pool; spa; exercise room; bar; full restaurant. $$$ (12200 US 41; 239-593-8733)

Edgewater Beach Hotel, on the Gulf, has 3 spacious, 1BR ADA suites each with a queen bed (30" high/open frame), a full sofa bed in the living room and a kitchen with refrigerator, microwave, coffeepot, utensils and plates. Bathrooms have raised toilets and roll-under sinks; rooms 106 and 206 have roll-in showers with hand-held sprayers and seats; room 309 has a tub. Pool; bar; entertainment; full restaurant; game room; boat rental. $$$ (1901 Gulf Shore Blvd N; 239-403-2000; 800-821-0196)

Hampton Inn is 2 mi from Bonita Beach and has 5 ADA rooms each with a king bed (open frame). Bathrooms have raised toilets and roll-under sinks; room 137 has a roll-in shower; others have tubs. Free brkfst; pool. $$ (27900 Crown Lake Blvd, Bonita Springs; 239-947-9393)

La Playa Beach Resort has 9 ADA rooms each with a king or 2 full beds (open frames). Bathrooms have toilet extenders on request and roll-under sinks; rooms 240 and 402 have roll-in showers with hand-held sprayers and seats; others have tubs. You can take a ramp to the hotel beach on the Gulf. 2 heated pools; gift shop; laundry; boat dock; kayaks; parasailing; waverunners; recreation program; fitness center; spa; bike rentals; bar; wknd entertainment; full restaurant. $$$ (9891 Gulf Shore Dr; 239-597-6278; 800-237-6883)

Lemon Tree Inn, in Old Naples, is a small Key West-style hotel with 2 ADA rooms each with a queen bed (open frame), kitchenette and private patio. Bathrooms have raised toilets, roll-under sinks and tubs. Free brkfst; heated pool. $-$$$ (250 9 St S; 239-262-1414; 888-800-5366)

Marco Island Hilton Beach Resort has 2 ADA rooms with a king or 2 full beds (open frames). Bathrooms have raised toilets, roll-under sinks and roll-in showers with hand-held sprayers and seats. The hotel beach is ramped to the sand. Heated pool; sauna, hot tub & exercise room; recreation programs; windsurfing; water skiing; charter fishing; parasailing; kayaks; waverunners; game room; gift shop; free happy hr; full restaurants; bar; entertainment. $$$ (560 S Collier Blvd, Marco Island; 239-394-5000)

Marriott Courtyard has 4 ADA rooms each with a king or 2 full beds (open frames). Room 124 has a roll-in shower; others have tubs. Pool; laundry; bar; restaurant for brkfst. $$-$$$ (3250 US 41 N; 239-434-8700)

Marriott Resort & Golf Club, on the Gulf with a tropical decor, has 22 ADA rooms each with a king or 2 full beds (open frames). An ADA 2BR suite also has a living room. Bathrooms have raised toilets and roll-under sinks; 7 rooms have roll-in showers with hand-held sprayers and seats; others have tubs. Pool; laundry; bar; entertainment; full restaurant; walkway to beach; boat rentals; 5 restaurants. $$$ (400 S Collier Blvd, Marco Island; 239-394-2511; 800-438-4373)

Port of the Islands Resort has 2 ADA rooms each with 2 full beds and a kitchenette with a 2-burner stove, microwave and refrigerator. You can rent cooking utensils but bring your own plates and utensils. See Boat Rentals, Boat Tours and Fishing Charters. Pool; skeet & trap; full restaurants; bar; tennis; pool. $$-$$$ (25,000 US 41; 239-394-3101)

Radisson Suite Beach Resort has a walkway to its Gulf front beach and 12 ADA 1BR suites. Each has a king or 2 queen beds (23" high/platforms), a living room with a queen sofa bed and a full kitchen. Bathrooms have raised toilets and roll-under sinks; rooms 219-220 and 222-224 have roll-in showers with seats; others have tubs. Pool; laundry; bar; entertainment; full restaurant; children's program; tennis; fitness center. $$-$$$ (600 S Collier Blvd, Marco Island; 239-394-4100; 800-992-0651)

The Registry is on the Gulf and has 1 ADA room with a king bed (open frame) coffeepot and on request, a refrigerator and microwave. The bathroom has a raised toilet and roll-in shower with a hand-held sprayer and seat. Pool; bar; entertainment; full restaurant. $$$ (475 Seagate Dr; 239-597-3232; 800-247-9810)

Sanibel/Captiva Islands

Descriptions of Sanibel and Captiva Islands justly wax poetic. The 2-mile by 12-mile Sanibel Island connects to its exclusive and much smaller neighbor, Captiva Island. Exquisite tropical resorts, environmental adventures and accessible fun on the water are plentiful. You can also rent an adaptive tandem bike for the miles of bike trails and quiet roads on CR 869 or Summerlin Road leads to the Sanibel Causeway. San-Cap Rd refers to Sanibel-Captiva Road, the main drag on both islands; on Captiva, the road goes under a canopy of thick foliage.

Tourist Info
Sanibel-Captiva Chamber: 1159 Causeway Rd, Sanibel 33957; 941-472-1080
Web sites: www.sanibel-online.com; www.sanibelisland.com; www.captiva.com; www.sanibelcaptiva.org; www.sanibel-captiva.org

WC Resources

Billy's Rentals rents a beach WC (swing-away arms) and a 2-person adaptive bicycle to which you attach your WC in front and an able-bodied friend can pedal from behind. The company will deliver if your rental is for more than 1 day. (1470 Periwinkle Way; 941-472-5248)

FISH or Friends In Service Here is a volunteer organization that loans equipment such as WCs, walkers and canes and provides other support services. (941-472-0404)

Island Rentals rents and delivers beach WCs (fixed arms), manual WCs and other adaptive items by the week or longer. 8:30-5:30 (941-472-9789)

ACTIVITIES

■ ATTRACTIONS

CROW, Clinic for the Rehabilitation of Wildlife, cares for injured, sick or orphaned native wildlife that you can view from a hard-packed sand path on guided tours weekdays at 11 and Sun at 1. Rr. $ (3883 San-Cap Rd, Sanibel; across from Darling Refuge; 941-472-3644)

■ BEACHES

Bowman's Beach is the longest and most secluded of the public beaches here. A boardwalk leads to the sugar sand with great shelling. Picnic tables; Sanibel; S off San-Cap Rd)

Gulfside Park is great spot for a quiet picnic under Australian pines. A boardwalk leads through the sea grasses to a narrow beach along the Gulf. Picnic tables; Rr (S end of Algiers Ln, Sanibel; off Casa Ybel Rd)

Lighthouse Beach wraps around the SW tip of Sanibel Island. A boardwalk leads to the popular Gulf side beach with plenty of shells. The historic lighthouse here is closed but the nearby 100', T-shaped wood pier on the San Carlos Bay, is a bright spot for snook, red fish and other prize catches. Picnic tables; restaurants nearby; Rr (E end of Periwinkle Way,Sanibel)

Tarpon Bay Road Beach has a boardwalk to the beach. Rr (Tarpon Bay Rd, Sanibel; at West Gulf Dr)

Turner Beach has a natural graded path to the beach and is a great place to watch sunsets over the Gulf. (17200 Captiva Dr, Captiva; S tip of the island)

■ BIKE TRAILS

See WC Resources for an adaptive tandem bicycle.

Sanibel has some 20 mi of paved bike paths or very wide sidewalks, some of which have grassy medians separating riders from the roadway. Captiva, on the other hand, has very narrow roads with dense vegetation that preclude biking.

■ BOAT RENTALS

Jensen's Twin Palm Marina rents pontoon boats (23" entry) for 10 people on the back bays and outer islands for half/full days. Staff can help lift you in your WC from the floating dock and over the boat railing. 7-6 (15107 Captiva Rd, Captiva; 941-472-5800)

Seawave Boat Rentals offers half/full-day rentals on 20' or 23' center consoles and 20' bow riders for the Gulf or bays. With advanced notice, staff can lift you aboard in your WC or into a boat seat. Bait shop; Rr nearby. 8-5 (Bayside Marina, South Seas Plantation, 5400 Plantation Rd, Captiva; 941-472-7540)

■ BOAT TOURS

Captiva Cruises offers a natural history and wildlife cruise with a guide from the Conservation Foundation from 4-5pm and a 1-hr sunset cruise with live entertainment. Roll aboard by ramp. Cash bar & snacks onboard; Rr. 8-5 (South Seas Plantation, 5400 Plantation Rd, Captiva; 941-472-5300)

■ CANOEING/KAYAKING

Tarpon Bay Canoe Outpost, located in the Ding Darling Refuge, rents canoes and tandem sit-in kayaks and also offers 2-hr guided trips. Try a private early morning tour for up to 4 people, a daily group tour with a naturalist at 10:30am or a Rookery Islands sunset tour for some great birding. If you choose, you can ride in a kayak or canoe with the trip leader. The launch is in a protected bayou where you can drive close to the water and staff can lift you into your craft. 9-5; summer 9-4 (Darling Refuge, 1 Wildlife Dr; off San-Cap Rd, Sanibel; 941-472-8900)

■ **FISHING CHARTERS**

Bayside Marina can refer you to several capts experienced with disabled anglers. Staff can help lift you aboard in your WC or onto a boat seat. Talk with Dave O'Conner, the dockmaster, who will make reservations for you. 8-5:30 (South Seas Plantation, 5400 Plantation Rd, Captiva; 941-472-7611; 800-237-6000x3447)

Makin' Waves offers flats and offshore charters; 2-hr minimum. Crew can lift you in your WC aboard either boat. If you like, you can borrow the capt's beach WC (fixed arms) for the trip. 8-5 (Bayside Marina, South Seas Plantation, 5400 Plantation Rd, Captiva; 941-395-7696)

'Tween Waters Inn Marina offers half/full-day charters on a 25' center console in the back bays. Staff can lift you aboard in your WC. 7-5:30 (15951 Captiva Dr, Captiva; 941-472-5161; 800-223-5865)

■ **FISHING PIERS**

Beaches: Lighthouse

■ **MUSEUMS**

Bailey-Matthews Shell Museum has over 3000 shell specimens, many in dioramas of their habitats. Enjoy interactive exhibits and playing the *shell game*. Take the elevator to the museum. CRr. $. Tue-Sun 10-4 (3075 San-Cap Rd; 1 mi W of Tarpon Bay & Palm Ridge, Sanibel; 941-395-2233)

Sanibel Historical Village is a flashback to days when island folks traveled by ferry to buy supplies. The museum, in the old Rutland House, displays memo-

rabilia from the early 1900's. Boardwalks connect the general store, Miss Charlotta's Tea Room and the Burnap Cottage all of which are ramped. $D. Mid-Oct-Aug Wed-Sat 10-4 (950 Dunlop Rd, Sanibel; 941-472-4648)

■ **PARKS**

Ding Darling National Wildlife Refuge is a 6000-acre sanctuary for hundreds of species some threatened or endangered. The visitor center houses wildlife exhibits, shows and an orientation film. Try to come at low tide when birds are feeding and explore along an 800' boardwalk with interpretive signs. You can drive a scenic 5-mi wildlife trail in your car or join a naturalist on a ramped tram that runs twice a day. The Tarpon Bay Recreation Area has a viewing deck with a spotting scope. Call for the schedule of guided walks Jan-Apr and see Canoeing. Rr, in visitor center. $. 9-5; summer 9-4 (1 Wildlife Dr; off San-Cap Rd, Sanibel; 941-472-1100)

Sanibel-Captiva Conservation Foundation maintains nearly 1000 acres along the freshwater Sanibel River and educates the public on preserving the islands' natural resources. The ramped nature center has a variety of wildlife exhibits, a marine-life touch tank, gift shop and bookstore. You can also peek into a butterfly house. Four miles of nature trails are wide, hard-packed dirt, but not routinely maintained; a .5-mi boardwalk takes you down to the river. Call for a schedule of guided tours. Gravel parking; Rr. 8:30-4; summer 8:30-3 (3333 San-Cap Rd, Sanibel; 941-472-2329)

■ **PERFORMING ARTS**

Olde Schoolhouse Theater is an 1896 schoolhouse that now hosts professional performances. This 90-seat theater is ramped and has WC seating in the rear. Nov-Aug (1905 Periwinkle Way, Sanibel; 941-472-6862)

J Howard Wood Theatre is a 180-seat theater with a variety of comedy, musical and dramatic performances by professionals. WC seating on aisles in rear;

Rr. Jun-Aug; Nov-Apr (2200 Periwinkle Way, Sanibel; 941-472-0006)

■ **SHOPPING**

Browsing is an art form on these islands. Sanibel's Periwinkle Way, W of the causeway, is lined with delightful shops, galleries and restaurants that spill over onto Palm Ridge Rd. Also head for Tarpon Bay Rd and Old Town Sanibel at Lighthouse Point. On Captiva, check out Chadwick's Square.

ACCOMMODATIONS

■ **CONDOS**

Sanibel Arms West rents 2 privately owned ADA 2BR/2BA condos each with a king and 2 twin beds (open frames), a full kitchen and living/dining room with a sofa bed. Unit E-4 is on the beach and has a roll-under sink and a roll-in shower with a hand-held sprayer in one bathroom. This unit is available by the week Apr-Dec; WC-friendly units are available all year. You must get down 3 steps to the boat ramp and fixed dock here. Screened heated pool; ramps to beach; boat rentals; laundry. (827 E Gulf Dr, Sanibel; 941-472-1138; 800-950-1138; office of owner, Rob Tortorelle, 716-247-3030)

⁺Sundial Beach Resort is a beach resort with WC-friendly 1-room efficiencies and 1BR and 2BR condos with full kitchens and living rooms. All have standard bathrooms and screened balconies; some units have washer/dryers. Staff is happy to help with special needs from shopping to renting beach WCs. On the grounds, enjoy an Ecological Center with exhibits, touch tanks, an aquarium, and a hermit crab petting zoo. Elevators to all floors; heated pool with bar & grill; hot tub; fitness room; tennis; bike, kayak and boogie board rentals; full restaurant; children's program; groceries; boutiques (1451 Middle Gulf Dr, Sanibel; 941-472-4151; 800-965-7772)

■ **INNS**

Song of the Sea is a 30-room Mediterranean-style resort with an ADA room (#4100) that has a king bed (open frame; can be split into twins), a refrigerator, microwave and coffeepot. The bathroom has a raised toilet, roll-under sink and roll-in shower with a hand-held sprayer. A portable ramp is available on request to get up the small step at the entry. Partake your continental breakfast on the garden terrace. Heated pool; hot tub; shuffleboard; bike & kayak rentals. $$$ (863 E Gulf Dr, Sanibel; 941-472-2220; 800-965-7772)

Seaside Inn is a modern beachfront retreat with Old Florida ambience. WC-friendly rooms 109 and 110 each have a garden view, ramped entrances, 2 queen beds (open frames), an eat-in area and a wet bar with a refrigerator, microwave and coffeepot. Bathrooms have wide doorways, raised toilets, roll-under sinks and tubs with hand-held sprayers. Breakfast is delivered to your room. Heated pool; free videos; shuffleboard; library; bike loaners; grills; picnic tables. $$$ (541 E Gulf Dr, Sanibel; 941-472-1400; 800-965-7772)

■ **MOTELS**

Holiday Inn is on the beach and has 4 ground floor ADA rooms each with a queen or 2 full beds (open frames). Bathrooms have raised toilets and roll-under sinks; room 147 has a roll-in shower with a hand-held sprayer and seat; others have tubs. Heated pool with bar & grill; tennis; ping pong; bike rentals; gift shop; laundry; restaurant for brkfst & dinner; bar. $$$ (1231 Middle Gulf Dr, Sanibel; 941-472-4123)

Sanibel Inn, on the Gulf, is nestled on 8 acres of vegetation with paved paths through butterfly and topiary gardens. A lift accesses 2 ADA rooms, each with a king bed (open frame), refrigerator, microwave and coffeepot. Bathrooms have raised toilets and roll-under sinks; room 3213 has a roll-in shower with a hand-held sprayer and seat; the other has a tub. Pool with bar & grill; hot tub; adult & kids' programs; boat, canoe and kayak rentals; tennis; restaurant for brkfst & dinner. $$$ (937 E Gulf Dr, Sanibel; 941-481-3636; 800-965-7772)

*South Seas Plantation is a fabulous resort at the far end of the island with ramped trolleys that take you around the exquisite 330-acre property. The Harborside Hotel has 4 ADA rooms, each with a king or 2 queen beds (open frames), a refrigerator and coffeepot. Bathrooms have roll-under sinks and roll-in showers with hand-held sprayers and seats; toilet extenders are available on request. The resort also offers a variety of WC-friendly units, from homes and condos to efficiencies and motel rooms. Bathrooms are standard but on request, grab bars and raised toilet seats can be installed. The main pool has a lift (fixed seat) and the resort loans 2 beach WCs (with or without fixed arms) for beaches on the bay or Gulf. 18 heated pools; sauna; hot tub; marina with boat rentals, charters, sailing instruction and water sports; recreation, social & nature programs; playground; exercise classes; golf; tennis; bike rentals; game room; gift shop; laundry; beauty salon; 4 restaurants. $$$ (5400 Plantation Rd, Captiva; 941-472-5111; 800-554-5454)

'Tween Waters Inn is a charming old resort sitting 'tween the Gulf and the bay with 5 ADA units. The Queen suite has 2 queen beds, a living room with a sofa bed, a screened balcony, full kitchen with lowered counters (but no oven) and a roll-in shower with seat. The King suite has a king bed, a Murphy bed in the living room and a refrigerator, microwave and tub. Two 1-room efficiencies each have a king bed, kitchenette with a stove and refrigerator, and a step-in shower with seat. A motel room has 2 queen beds and a step-in shower with a seat. Cooking & eating utensils provided; pool with tiki & snack bar; tennis; fitness center; marina with boat rentals & charters; shuffle-board; bike rentals; laundry; full restaurant. $$$ (15951 Captiva Rd, Captiva; 941-472-5161; 800-223-5865)

SARASOTA
Longboat Key, Osprey, Siesta Key

Sarasota, in the heart of Florida's Cultural Coast, has an extensive arts calendar as well as upscale shopping, fine gardens, adaptive golf and, in the winter, polo. You also might come here for two of the state's finest beaches with beach wheelchairs, an accessible sailing program and two wonderful state parks. Lodging options include accessible condos, a private home and a resort with adaptive golf carts, beach wheelchairs and a pool with a lift. City Island is on Lido Key. US 41 is also called the Tamiami Trail.

Tourist Info
Sarasota Visitors Center: 655 N US 41, 34236; 941-957-1877; 800-522-9799; and 5947 Clark Center Ave, Albritton Grove Market; 800-800-3906
Siesta Key Chamber: 5100 Ocean Blvd, Unit B, Siesta Key, 34242; 941-349-3800
Longboat Key Chamber: 5360 Gulf of Mexico Dr/SR 789, Suite 107, Longboat Key, 34228; 941-383-2466; 800-462-6283
Web sites: www.sarasotafl.org; www.flagulfislands.com

Transportation

SCAT buses all have lifts and tie-downs and service the entire county Mon-Sat 6am-7pm. (941-316-1234)

SCAT Plus provides door-to-door, lift-equipped van service to those who cannot use public buses. You must complete an application in advance. Call if you are visiting and are approved at home. Minimum 2-day advance reservations. (941-926-0135)

Trolleys with lifts and tie-downs run every 20 min downtown along Main St and from downtown to Lido Beach. (941-316-1234)

WC Resources

Center for Independent Living provides referral and support services, including a loan closet where you can borrow manual WCs, lifts and other equipment. (1945 Northgate Blvd; 941-351-9545; 800-299-0297)

ACTIVITIES

■ ARCHERY

Sarasota County Archers is a club that invites the public to participate in shoots (with *friendly* competition) the 3rd Sat of each month. Members receive keys that permit them to shoot on their own; short-term visitors may get fees waived to shoot on their own as well. Facilities include a paved indoor range, a hard-packed outdoor range and a field course, although you must traverse narrow bridges to reach some positions. Call William Clark 941-351-3011 afternoons. The 96-acre park also has ball fields and a fenced-in Paw Park where dogs can run off leash. Vending machine; cooler for drinks; hard-packed parking (17 Street Park, 4570 17 St)

■ ATTRACTIONS

Circus Sarasota is an extraordinary 1 1/2-hr, 1-ring circus with international acrobatic performers, clowns and talented domestic animals. WC seating (with 1 companion) is right at the ring. The 4-wk season occurs in Jan or Feb. CRr. $. Tue-Fri 7pm; wknd matinee & evening performances (Tuttle St; 1 blk S of Ringling off Fruitville Rd; 941-355-9335)

Historic Spanish Point is a 30-acre prehistoric to historic site on Little Sarasota Bay with hard-packed shell paths throughout. Look through an archeological window in a shell mound with artifacts from 4000 yrs ago. Roll through several restored structures from the late 1800's, including a pioneer homestead, citrus packing house and the remains of formal gardens from 1910. Only the chapel, with 4 steps, is inaccessible. With reservations, you can transfer into a 7-person golf cart for a tour of each building. Or, enjoy 2-hr walking tours with a docent (schedule varies by season). The visitor center, in the Old Osprey Schoolhouse, has 8- to 20-min videos, rotating exhibits and a gift shop. Jan-mid-Apr living history performances take place on Sun afternoons. Picnic tables under trees; CRr in White Cottage. $. 9-5; Sun noon-5 (337 N US 41, Osprey; 941-966-5214)

Marie Selby Botanical Gardens has 8.5 acres of lush gardens with many unusual specimens of orchids, bromeliads and carnivorous plants. A paved path and boardwalk wind through a waterfall garden, mangrove swamp and butterfly garden. A learning center offers hands-on activities and horticultural classes. Box lunches for sale 11-3; Rr. $. 10-5 (811 S Palm Ave; 941-366-5731)

Mote Aquarium is an outstanding research center with shark, whale, manatee and sea turtle exhibits. Pet live stingray and other sea creatures in 2 touch tanks. *Shark Attack* is a 12-min interactive film. Guides describe current research projects as you tour the displays. Educational programs; cafe; gift shop; Rr. $. 10-5 (1600 SR 789, City Island; just

S of Longboat Key; 941-388-4441; 800-691-6683)

Pelican Man's Bird Sanctuary rescues, rehabilitates and releases injured birds. Take the boardwalk past the caged homes of more than 200 permanently injured birds. Gift shop; vending machines; Rr. $D. 10-5 (1708 SR 789; 941-388-4444)

Sarasota Classic Car Museum features antique and classic vehicles from the past 100 yrs, mechanical music machines and antique arcade games. Demonstrations of the music machines occur hourly and guided tours of the car museum start every 30 min. Roll through an outside butterfly garden. WC loaner; picnic tables; snacks bar; gift shop; Rr. $. 9-6 (5500 N US 41; 941-355-6228)

Sarasota Jungle Gardens has paved trails winding through a 10-acre tropical jungle inhabited by flamingos, swans, leopards, otters, wallabies and monkeys. Check out the daily reptile and bird shows, birds of prey exhibit and a shell museum. WC rental; restaurant; gift shop; Rr. $. 9-5 (3701 Bayshore Rd; 941-355-1112)

■ **BASEBALL**

Challenger Baseball is a little league team for kids in WCs on a specially designed field. Visitors or drop-ins are welcome. Rr (Twin Lakes Park, 6700 Clark Rd; 941-924-0209)

■ **BEACHES**

The following beaches have free parking, accessible dune crossovers with decks and pavilions with Rr. Beaches are open 6am-midnight; where lifeguards are indicated, they are on duty 10-4:45, summer 10-6:45. Where indicated by asterisk (*), you can borrow beach WCs (fixed arms) from 10-5 beside lifeguard headquarters. Because of frequent use, you are asked to use the beach WC only to get to a spot on the beach; an able-bodied companion should then return the WC to lifeguard headquarters. If lifeguards are nearby, they are happy to help with transfers.

For information, call 941-346-3310. The following are arranged from north to south:

*****Lido Beach** is 15 acres with a 3100' stretch of popular frontage on the Gulf. The pool here is indefinitely closed due to storm damage. Lifeguards; snack bar; swing set on sand; outdoor showers; gift shop; Rr (400 Ben Franklin Dr, Lido Key; .25 mi W of St Armands Cir)

*****Siesta Beach** boasts the finest, whitest sand in the world along its 2400' shore. A fitness trail with 20 exercise stations is on wood chips. Lifeguards; snack bar; main picnic shelter with concession stand is ADA, other shelters on sand; playground on sand; tennis; ball fields; outdoor showers; Rr (948 Beach Rd, Siesta Key; 3 mi N of Stickney Pt Rd)

Turtle Beach, with a boardwalk to the beach, is popular for surf fishing. Boat ramps and ramped fixed docks (lighted except during turtle season) are on the Blind Pass Lagoon that connects to Little Sarasota Bay. ADA picnic shelters across grass; grills; playground on sand; Rr (Midnight Pass Rd, Siesta Key; S end of Siesta Key)

■ **BIKE TRAILS**

Longboat Key has a paved bike path that runs past resorts and homes almost the entire 10 mi of the island. The path is comfortably separated from Gulf of Mexico Dr by a grassy median.

■ **BOAT RAMPS**

Beaches: Turtle

Centennial Park has a boat ramp and fixed dock on Sarasota Bay. Rr port-a-let. 6am-mdnt (1059 N US 41; at 11 St)

Ken Thompson Park on City Island has a lighted boat ramp and fixed dock on Sarasota Bay. Bait/snack shop; Rr. 6am-mdnt (1700 SR 789, Lido Key)

■ **BOAT RENTALS**

Cannons Marina rents 22' and 25' deck boats for half/full days or long term for use on the Sarasota Bay. The gates are too narrow for WCs but, with advance notice, staff can lift you aboard in your WC. The shop is not accessible. 8-6 (6040 Gulf of Mexico Dr, Longboat

Key; 941-383-1311)

Club Nautico rents a pontoon boat (31" entry) for up to 10 people for use on the Intracoastal. You can also rent 20' bow riders and 22' center console boats for the Gulf. With advance notice, staff can arrange for extra help to lift you aboard in your WC. 9-5 (Marina Jack, US 41 & Ringling Blvd; 941-951-0550)

Mr CB's rents deck boats (23" entry) and pontoon boats (36" entry) for up to 8 for use on the bay. Staff can help you board the boat of your choice. Bait shop. 7-6 (1249 Stickney Point Rd, Siesta Key; 941-349-4400)

Osprey Marina rents a pontoon boat (26" entry) for up to 13 for use on the bay and Intracoastal. The dock is ramped and staff can lift you aboard in your WC. Bait shop; CRr. 8-5 (480 Blackburn Point Rd, Osprey; 941-966-5657)

■ **BOAT TOURS**
Parks: Myakka River

Bay Lady offers sightseeing tours on a 40' catamaran along the Intracoastal heading S to Venice or N to Stickney Point. Usually you can roll aboard; in extreme tides, crew can help. (Osprey Marina Center, 480 Blackburn Point Rd, Osprey; 941-485-6366)

LeBarge Tropical Cruises features 2-hr sightseeing and dolphin cruises during the day and a sunset cruise with live music. The barge's 1st floor, including cabin, snack bar and outside deck, is accessible. Hrs vary (Marina Jack, US 41 & Ringling Blvd; 941-366-6116)

Sarasota Bay Explorers, of the Mote Aquarium, offer 2-hr educational cruises on Sarasota and Roberts Bays. With a drag net, mates pull up and describe aquatic creatures that you can examine up close. Crew can lift you in your WC aboard the 40' canopied pontoon boat. Tours stop at a sandy, inaccessible island for about 10 min; you remain on the boat. Rr. 9-5 (Mote Aquarium, 1600 SR 789, City Island; just S of Longboat Key; 941-388-4200)

■ **BOWLING**
AMF Gulfgate has bowling ball ramps.

Game room; snack bar; lounge; Rr. 9am-11pm; wknd -1am (7221 US 41; 941-921-4447)

■ **CAMPS**
Sarasota County offers a camp program for kids, age 3-21 with a range of special needs, both after school and during school vacations. Long-term visitors are welcome to participate in this recreational program of sports, arts and crafts, riding therapy and special events. Call Nancy Raney 941-412-0402.

■ **CANOEING**
Parks: Oscar Scherer

■ **DINNER THEATERS**
Golden Apple Dinner Theatre presents musicals along with a buffet. WC seating is on the 3rd tier of the theater. The buffet is not accessible but a server will gladly fill your plate. Rr. Tue-Sun 6; Sat also noon (25 N Pineapple Ave; 941-366-5454)

■ **FISHING CHARTERS**
Angling Adventures is a group of guides offering half/full-day inshore, offshore and flats fishing. The type of fishing you choose determines the boat and the number of anglers you can bring. With advance notice, crew can arrange an accessible dock and help to lift you aboard in your WC. (Capt John Sackett 941-920-4891)

Big Catch offers 4- to 8-hr deep-sea fishing trips on a custom 39' sports fisherman. Crew can lift you aboard in your WC. (Marina Jack, US 41 & Ringling Blvd; 941-366-3373)

■ **FISHING-PARTY BOATS**
Flying Fish Fleet goes out for 4- to 8-hr deep-sea fishing trips on large party boats in the Gulf. If you can't roll aboard, crew can lift you aboard in your WC. The cabin where food is sold has a lip at the door. (Marina Jack, US 41 & Ringling Blvd; 941-366-3373)

■ **FISHING PIERS**
Parks: Myakka, Oscar Scherer

New Pass Piers are 3 small wood docks for fishing on the Sarasota Bay. Bait/snack shop (941-388-3050); parking on crushed shell; Rr. Dawn-dusk (Ken Thompson Park, SR 789, City Island; 941-316-1172)

Osprey Fishing Pier extends 300' on Little Sarasota Bay. Limited parking. 24 hrs (W end of Main St, Osprey)

Tony Saprito Pier is a 500' lighted concrete pier on Sarasota Bay. Bait shop across street at Hart's Landing; Rr. 6am-10pm (Causeway Park, 420 SR 780; 941-955-0011)

■ GOLF

Foxfire Golf Club is a public course with an adaptive golf cart for its 27 holes where you can drive into sand traps and on the greens. Every Wed at 3 the pros offer a clinic that includes using the cart. Snack cart; Rr on courses. (7200 Proctor Rd; 941-921-7757)

■ MISC

Healthsouth Rehabilitation Center sponsors a variety of sports clinics for folks in WCs including water sports, adaptive golf, rugby, basketball and more. Call Scott Wienmaster 941-921-8790.

■ MUSEUMS

Crosley Museum is a 1929 mansion on the Sarasota Bay that is open for free guided 45-min tours by appt. The gracious 3-story home is not furnished. A paved walk leads to the ramped N entrance and an elevator. Oct-May Wed (1 Seagate Dr; .5 N of University Pkwy & US 41; 941-722-3244x221)

G Wiz is a science center in a glass pyramid where you can dig for fossils, play a laser harp, dissect radios and clocks, or play in a computer center. Rr. $. Tue-Sat 10-5; Sun 1-5 (1001 Blvd of the Arts; 941-906-1851)

John & Mable Ringling Museum of Art shares a 66-acre complex on Sarasota Bay with other attractions. The museum houses a vast collection of international works of the past 5 centuries, from Old Master paintings to decorative arts and a bronze cast of Michelangelo's David. Among the Banyan trees, flower gardens and statuary is Ca d'Zan, the Ringlings' 30-room palatial residence (with an elevator) that is open for 30-min guided tours. The Circus Museum has a rich variety of circus memorabilia from ostentatious costumes to hand-carved wagons. The Asolo Theater, originally built in 1728 as part of Queen Catherine's castle near Venice, Italy, was dismantled piece by piece and reassembled here in 1958; unfortunately this baroque theater is closed indefinitely. You may want to drive between buildings because some paths are mulch and difficult to navigate. Gift shop; restaurant; Rr. $. 10-5:30 (5401 Bay Shore Rd; 941-359-5700)

Longboat Key Center for the Arts has 3 galleries, one with regularly changing work of regional artists. Art classes; gift shop; Rr in studio bldg across green. Sep-May wkdy 9-4 & wknd 1-4; summer Mon-Thu 9-4 (6860 Longboat Key Dr S, Longboat Key; 941-383-2345)

Museum of Asian Art exhibits 2000 yrs of art from China, Thailand, Cambodia, Nepal and Burma. Lecture series Nov-Apr; gift shop; Rr. $. Wed-Fri 11-5 (Arts & Antique Center, 640 S Washington Blvd; 941-954-7117)

■ PARASAILING

Siesta Parasail is experienced with both quad- and para-parasailors. Extra staff can help lift you from your WC onto a cushion on the boat floor; someone sits behind you for support. Staff double harnesses you and lifts you onto the staging area for takeoff. The automatic winch system controls the speed of landing and keeps it relatively gentle. Allow about 4 hrs for the trip and speak to Dee Dee Northern about any special needs. 8-4 (1265 Old Stickney Point Rd, Siesta Key; 941-349-1900)

■ PARI-MUTUELS

Sarasota Kennel Club has live greyhound racing Nov-Apr and year round simulcasts of greyhound, thoroughbred and harness racing (Mon-Sat). WC seating is on the lower level of the grandstand. Or, take an elevator up to the Miss Whirl Room where you can dine as you watch races through huge windowed walls or on tabletop monitors. Rr. Call for schedule (5400 Old Bradenton Rd; across from Sarasota-Bradenton Airport, 5 mi W of I-75; 941-355-7744.)

■ PARKS

Crowley Museum & Nature Center is a pioneer history area within a 190-acre nature preserve. The pioneer area, near the entrance, has hard-packed terrain and parking with some sandy spots. The museum houses old-time tools, collectibles, period furniture and items from a general store. Accessible pioneer structures include a blacksmith shop, sugarcane mill and the Tatum cracker house. Call for the irregularly scheduled tours or use the park booklet for a self-guided tour. A short hard-packed trail with a few sandy stretches leads to a .5-mi boardwalk through a marsh to an observation tower with an accessible lower level. Other trails are fairly rough and not maintained but work for all-terrain WCs. Picnic tables; 2 steps to gift/snack shop; composting Rr in pioneer area; CRr at learning center. $. Nov-Apr Tue-Sun, May-Oct Thu-Sun 10-4 (16405 Myakka Rd; 11 mi E of I-75; 941-322-1000)

Myakka River State Park encompasses 45 square mi of wetlands, prairies, hammocks and pinelands, 2 large lake and a *Florida Wild and Scenic* river. But be aware, with rains the terrain gets soggy and in droughts the water levels can get so low that access to boats and fishing from the banks can be problematic. For a real bird's eye view, able-bodied visitors can climb 35' of stairs to the 85' long Canopy Walk suspended in the treetops. The Outpost (941-923-1120) is a camp store and snack bar that rents bikes (for park roads), canoes and solo/tandem sit-in kayaks. The launch is hard-packed shell and you can roll to the water's edge where friends can lift you into your craft. From the boat basin you paddle to the river or open lake and return to the launch. Nearby is a paved boat ramp with no dock. The size

of boat motor is not limited, but the park is a no-wake zone where trolling motors work best in the weeds. A private operator (941-365-0100 for recorded info) offers 2 tours for a fee. Reportedly the world's largest airboat makes a 1-hr narrated tour of the Upper Myakka Lake year round, weather permitting (at 10, 11:30 and 1; also 2:30 in winter). When water levels are high you can board the airboat by ramp; when water levels are low you must negotiate 1-3 steps down to the boat. The park posts a notice at the entrance when the tour is inaccessible by WC. Dec-May a land tram goes out for 1-hr narrated rides into the backcountry (at 1 and 2:30); staff can set up a portable ramp for you to board. A hard-packed trail leads to an ADA fishing pier on the Upper Lake behind the Lake Picnic area. Other accessible fishing spots include the 2 bridges and the riverbanks at Clay Gully, Fishermen's area and near the log pavilion. Rangers lead nature walks every Sat; call ahead so they can plan for an accessible trail. The hard-packed .6-mi Boylston nature trail is usually quite accessible. The dirt service roads can also take you into the wilds except in rainy seasons or droughts when they become too sandy. Only Paul Bunyan-types should try the 39-mi, 4' wide trail with palmetto roots, hog rooting and ankle- to knee-deep water. The visitor center has interactive wildlife displays and videos. Call for the schedule of campfire programs and beginner birding walks. See Campgrounds. ADA picnic tables in all areas; Rr. $. 8-dusk (13202 SR 72; 9 mi E of I-75; 941-361-6511)

***Oscar Scherer State Park** has plenty for WC nature lovers on its 1384 acres, including salt- and freshwater fishing. At the South Creek Picnic Area, the lime-stone-surfaced Lester Finley Trail loops .5 mi through scrubby flatwoods with audio-boxes to describe the habitat, including a butterfly area. The trail leads to a 50' ADA pier for fishing the brackish South Creek. Near the pier, the park rents canoes and on Wed rangers lead 1-hr canoe trips. The launch has a small low dock on which you can sit while friends stand in the shallow water and lift you into a canoe. With advance notice, park staff may be able to help. The creek is so mellow that you can paddle back to the put-in. A nature center has ecology displays and videos and also loans an all-terrain WC (swing-away arms) for the 15 mi of natural trails (trail maps are available) or the nearby Lake Osprey beach. You can take the WC by ramp onto the soft sand beach and into the freshwater lake. You can also use the WC or, with permission, drive your vehicle to the far side of the lake with level open areas for fishing from the banks. Winter-spring rangers offer guided walks and campfire programs; call for schedule. See Campgrounds. Rr. $. 8-dusk (1843 S US 41, Osprey; 6 mi S of Sarasota; 941-483-5956)

Phillippi Estate Park is a 60-acre wooded nature park with an historic plantation house where community groups hold anything from environmental meetings to classes on watercolors. Guided tours of the accessible 1st floor are available on request. The park road is popular with cyclists and a hard-surfaced, 1-mi nature trail with interpretive signage through mangrove and hammock is planned. The 70-person picnic gazebo has an ADA picnic table and HC parking. 8-7, later for special events (5500 S US 41; N of SR 72; 941-316-1309)

Twin Lakes Park is a 123-acre sports complex with some great family picnic spots. The E picnic area has ADA picnic shelters and grills along a lovely lake where you can fish from the fairly level, open grassy shores. A scenic .5-mi trail around the lake has a hard-packed lane beside a mulched lane. This park is also the site of the Orioles' spring training (see Spectator Sports) and a Challenger Baseball field (see Baseball). Large ADA

playground; tennis; basketball; handball; Rr in E picnic area. Dawn-mdnt (6700 Clark Rd/SR 72; .5 mi E of I-75; 941-316-1194)

■ **PERFORMING ARTS**

Beatrice Friedman Symphony Center is a 500-seat hall where chamber ensembles, the chamber orchestra and soloists perform. WC seating is throughout the ground level. Rr. Oct-Apr (709 N US 41; 941-953-4252)

FSU Center for the Performing Arts has 2 theaters off the same lobby. The 500-seat Mertz Theater is home to the Asolo Theater company and the Sarasota Ballet of Florida. WC seating is in the last row of the orchestra section. The theater is a reconstructed 1903 Scottish opera house and tours are on most Wed-Sat 10-12. The Cook Theater, part of the FSU/Asolo Conservatory for Actor Training, features performances by outstanding graduate students. WC seating 3rd row center; Rr. Oct-Jun (5555 N US 41; 941-351-8000)

Florida Studio Theater is a professional contemporary group that selects new plays, conducts public readings, develops the work and then presents selective premieres. The Mainstage has WC seating in front. Next door the affiliated **Cabaret Club** offers musical reviews and 1-person shows in an intimate Parisian cafe-style theater. WC seating on ground level; street parking; Rr, in Cabaret. Oct-Aug (1241 N Palm Ave; 941-366-9000)

Players of Sarasota is a community theater group specializing in musicals Oct-Apr. WC seating is in front down a very steep ramp. Performing arts classes for kids; Rr (838 N US 41; 941-365-2494)

Sarasota Film Society offers foreign and art films. Enjoy beer, wine, cappuccino and upscale refreshments during the show. WC seating in back; street parking; Rr (Burns Court Cinema, 506 Burns Ln; 941-364-8662)

Sarasota Opera House is the 1926 Mediterranean Revival home to the local professional opera company Feb-Mar and other groups the rest of the year. Theater seats are removed for WC seating along the aisle. Rr (61 N Pineapple Ave; 941-953-7030)

Theater Works is a professional company performing musicals, dramas and comedies Nov-May. Operetta Works also performs here. WC seating in front; street parking (1247 1 St; at Cocoanut-Downtown; 941-952-9170)

Van Wezel Performing Arts Hall was designed by the Frank Lloyd Wright Foundation to look like a giant purple seashell. World-class dance companies, classical and popular musicians and Broadway productions light the stage. WC seating on aisles in sections A & C; Rr (777 N US 41; 941-953-3366)

■ **POOLS**

Arlington Park has a ramped, heated, 3' deep therapeutic pool where exercise classes are open to folks, including drop-ins, with mobility impairments (weekdays at 7:45am; Mon, Wed and Fri at 6pm). Independent use of the pool can be arranged. In winter the pool is covered with a dome. The other pool at this complex is not accessible. The park (dawn-11pm) also has a .7-mi paved nature trail around a pond, with some slight inclines, through woods and open areas. ADA picnic tables under shade or on concrete; playground, part ADA; tennis; basketball; CRr with roll-in shower at pool; Rr. $/pool. Wkdy 10:30-7:30; Sat 12-5 (2650 Waldemere St; just S of Bahia Vista, E of US 41; 941-316-1346/316-1172)

■ **QUAD RUGBY**

Sarasota Riptide practice is open to both able-bodied and WC players Sep-Mar. For the schedule and locations of practices and games, call Ed Hooper 941-924-1804.

■ **SAILING**

Sailing Alternatives offers a range of sailing opportunities to people with disabilities, from classes for beginners and experts to training for competition. Sailors need only minimal hand motion, not the ability to grasp. Sailors use a hydraulic lift to board a single person boat that won't capsize or sink even in severe weather. Call Serge Jorgensen 941-377-4986. See St Pete: Sailing. (Sarasota Sailing Squadron, Ken Thompson Park, SR 789, City Island)

■ **SHOPPING**

Antiques/Galleries: Palm Ave and Main St is an historic area filled with art galleries, antiques stores and fine shops. Towles Court is a colorful artist colony of 16 studios (2 blks S of Main St, just W of US 301). Art Center Sarasota is accessible except for the lower tier in back (707 N US 41; between 6 St & 10 St; 941-365-2032).

Boutiques: Sarasota Quay offers specialty shops, restaurants and nightclubs on the water (US 41 & Fruitville Rd). St Armands Circle is an upscale shopping area with boutiques, galleries, fine restaurants and horse drawn carriages (W on SR 780 off of US 41).

Farmers Markets occur in downtown every Sat morning. (Lemon Ave at Main St)

Malls: Sarasota Square Mall (8201 S US 41); the upscale Southgate Plaza (US 41 at Bee Ridge Rd; 941-955-0900); Town & Country Shopping Center (3535 Fruitville Rd)

Specialty Shops include Artisans' World Market Place with the work of international disadvantaged artisans. (104 S Pineapple Ave; 941-365-5994)

■ **SPECTATOR SPORTS**

Baseball Cincinnati Reds have spring training Mar-Apr. WC seating at all levels; Rr (Ed Smith Sports Complex, 2700 12 St; at Tuttle Ave; 941-954-4101x5200) Baltimore Orioles' minor league plays at the Twin Lakes Park fields Jun-Sep (6700 Clark Rd; 941-923-1996)

Polo Sarasota Polo Club hosts polo matches Dec-Apr on Sun at 1. You must go over grass to get to the viewing area. Your companions can bring their own chairs and picnic at the N end of the field or sit in the grandstand midfield. Gates open at noon (8201

Polo Club Ln; University Pkwy 3.5 mi E of I-75, then N on Lorraine Rd; 941-907-0000)

Water Skiing The Sarasota Ski-a-Rees present free water ski shows each Sun, late Jan-Mar. Call the Sarasota Visitors Bureau 941-957-1877. (SR 789, City Island; near Mote Aquarium)

■ **TOURS**

Friday Walks occur monthly at 6pm at 3 locations: 1st Fri, the Palm Ave Arts Alliance (941-365-7414); 3rd Fri, Towles Court Artist Colony (941-362-0960); and 4th Fri, St Armands Cir (941-388-1554).

ACCOMMODATIONS

■ **CABINS/CAMPGROUNDS**

Myakka River State Park has a rustic 1-room ADA cabin with 2 full beds (open frames/26.5" high), a full kitchen (with 30" high countertops), a fireplace, full sofa bed, porch and just outside, a grill and ADA picnic table on hard-packed dirt. The bathroom has a raised toilet, a tub and roll-under sink. Linens are provided. The Big Flats campground area has tent/RV sites with water/elec, ADA picnic tables (on request), grills and fire rings. The ADA bathhouse has raised toilets, roll-under sinks and roll-in showers with hand-held sprayers and seats. Make reservations far in advance but remember that rains can make the terrain difficult; see Parks. Playground (13202 SR 72; 9 mi E of I-75; 941-361-6511)

*****Oscar Scherer State Park** has 104 tent/RV sites with water/elec, fire pits or grills and some with ADA picnic tables. The ADA bathhouses have roll-under sinks and roll-in showers with hand-held sprayers and seats. The campground terrain is flat and fairly hard-packed dirt. The park loans an all-terrain WC for the trails and lakeside beach; see Parks. (1843 S US 41, Osprey; 6 mi S of Sarasota; 941-483-5956; 800-326-3521)

■ **CONDOS**

Crescent View Beach Club is on the Gulf and has WC-friendly 1BR and 2BR units each with a king or queen and/or 2 twin beds. Each condo comes with a full kitchen, full sofa bed in the living room, washer/dryer and standard bathroom. You can roll from parking onto the

beach. Garden-view units are inaccessible. Elevators from parking to all floors; heated pool; hot tub; grills (6512 Midnight Pass, Siesta Key; 941-349-2000; 800-344-7171)

Sand Cay Beach Resort has an ADA ground floor 2BR/2BA condo (#120) with an ocean view. The master bedroom has a queen bed; the 2nd bedroom, with 30" wide doorways, has 2 twin beds; all beds are on open frames. One bathroom has a wide door, raised toilet, roll-under sink and roll-in shower with a hand-held sprayer; the standard bathroom has a tub/shower. The unit has a queen sofa bed in the living room, full kitchen and washer/dryer. You can roll from the patio over lawn to a sidewalk onto the beach. Rentals are by the week or month only. Pool; shuffleboard; tennis; picnic area with grills (4725 Gulf of Mexico Dr/SR 789, Longboat Key; 941-383-5044; 800-843-4459)

Timberwoods Vacation Villas offer WC-friendly 2BR/2BA units in a park-like setting. Each villa has a queen bed (open frame) in both bedrooms, standard bathrooms, a full kitchen, living room/dining room, washer/dryer and screened porch. The garage has an automatic opener and a step into the kitchen. Heated pool; hot tub; putting green; tennis; basketball; shuffleboard; volleyball; picnic area with grills; library; game room (7964 Timberwood Cir; 941-923-4966)

■ **HOUSES**

Cedarhouse is a WC-friendly, 2BR/2BA, private house on the beach with ramped front and back doors and a full kitchen. The master bedroom has a king bed (24" high/open frame), the 2nd bedroom has 2 twin beds and the living room has a queen sofa bed. The master bathroom has grab bars and a fixed seat in the step-in shower; the standard bathroom has a tub. Rentals are weekly or monthly, generally May-Nov. Linens included; washer/dryer; near to shopping plaza with groceries & restaurants (3025 Gulf of Mexico Dr/SR 789, Longboat Key; 4 mi S of St Armands Cir; Owner Nancy Najer 518-494-2012; najer@superior.net; www.Najer-Realty.com)

■ **MOTELS**

American Hotel & Suites has 3 ADA rooms and a 1BR and a 2BR suite that are ADA. Units offer a choice of a king or 2 queen beds (platforms) and all have roll-in showers. Each suite has a queen sofa bed, refrigerator, microwave and coffeepot. Free brkfst; heated pool; hot tub; fitness room; laundry. $$-$$$ (5931 Fruitville Rd; 941-342-8778; 800-716-3924)

Comfort Inn has 3 ADA rooms, each with a king or 2 queen beds (platforms). Bathrooms have raised toilets and roll-under sinks; room 126 has a roll-in shower with a hand-held sprayer and seat; others have step-in showers or tubs. Free brkfst & paper; pool; laundry. $$-$$$ (5778 Clark Rd; 941-921-7750)

Hampton Inn has 7 ADA rooms with a king or 2 queen beds (open frames). Bathrooms have raised toilets and roll-under sinks; rooms 105 and 109 have roll-in showers with hand-held sprayers and seats; others have tubs. Free brkfst; heated pool; hot tub; laundry. $$-$$$ (5995 Cattleridge Rd; 941-371-1900; 800-720-9005)

Holiday Inn is across from the Gulf and has 5 ADA rooms with a king or 2 queen beds (open frames). Bathrooms have raised toilets and roll-under sinks; room 609 has a roll-in shower with a hand-held sprayer and seat; others have tubs. Heated pool & pool bar; gift shop; laundry; exercise room; lounge; entertainment; full restaurant with roof top dining. $$-$$$ (233 Ben Franklin Dr, Lido Bch; 941-388-5555; 800-892-9174)

Holiday Inn Express has 4 ADA rooms with a full bed (25" high/open frame), coffeepot and, on request, a refrigerator. Bathrooms have raised toilets and roll-under sinks; room 104 has a roll-in shower with a hand-held sprayer and seat; others have tubs. Free brkfst; heated pool; exercise room; laundry. $$-$$$ (6600 US 41 S, Siesta Key; 941-924-4900)

Hyatt has 11 ADA rooms each with a king or 2 full beds (open frames). Bathrooms have raised toilets and roll-under sinks; rooms 214 and 218 have roll-in showers with hand-held sprayers and seats; others have tubs. Heated pool; hot tub; pool tables; gift shop; massage; boat dock; charter fishing; lounge; entertainment; full restaurant. $$$ (1000 Blvd of the Arts; 941-953-1234)

*Longboat Key Club is a lovely 400-acre resort on the Gulf with adaptive golf carts at 2 PGA championship courses, beach WCs (swing-away arms), a pool with a lift (sling seat) and a whirlpool with a lift (fixed seat). While none of the privately owned units are currently ADA, you can request WC-friendly 1BR and 2BR suites that have large bathrooms with grab bars and shower seats for the tub/showers. When making reservations, you can request toilet extenders and other adaptive equipment. Each suite has a king bed (open frame) in the master bedroom, a queen sofa bed in the living room, full kitchen, washer/dryer and a view of the beach, lagoon or golf course. The 2BR suites have 2 twin beds in the 2nd bedroom. Locker rooms in the Islandside Clubhouse have roll-in showers. Full restaurants; children's programs; fitness center. $$$ (301 Gulf of Mexico Dr/SR 789, Longboat Key; 1.5 mi N of St Armands

Cir; 941-383-8821; 800-237-8821)
Wellesley Inn is close to St Armands Cir and has 6 ADA rooms with a king or 2 full beds. Bathrooms have raised toilets and roll-under sinks; rooms 101 and 102 have roll-in showers with seats; others have tubs. Free brkfst; pool. $$-$$$ (1803 US 41; 941-366-5128)

VENICE

Arcadia, Boca Grande, El Jobean, Englewood, Nokomis, North Port, Placida, Port Charlotte, Punta Gorda, Warm Mineral Springs

Certainly this is the place to hit the beach. Most have beach wheelchairs and most are quite lovely. Venice beaches are famous for sharks' teeth, but don't worry, the source of all those teeth is an ancient shark burial ground offshore. In fact, there's plenty to get you onto or into the waters here as well: boating, canoeing, fishing and even an 87-degree spring. For a quiet getaway or world-renowned tarpon fishing, take the two-mile toll way to Boca Grande.

Tourist Info

Venice Chamber: 257 US 41 N, Venice 34285-1908; 941-488-2236
Englewood Chamber: 601 S Indiana Ave, Englewood, 34223; 941-474-5511
Charlotte County Chamber: 2702 US 41, Port Charlotte, 33952; 941-627-2222; 888-478-7352
North Port Chamber: 12705 S US 41, North Port, 34287; 941-426-8744; 888-426-8744
Boca Grande Chamber: 5800 Gasparilla Rd, Boca Grande, 33921; 941-964-0568
Web sites: www.venice-fla.com; www.englewood-fla.com; www.pureflorida.com; www.charlotte-florida.com; www.bocagrandechamber.com; www.bocabeacon.com

Transportation

See Sarasota for Venice and north Englewood.
Dial-a-Ride provides curb-to-curb service in lift-equipped vans anywhere in Port Charlotte, Punta Gorda and south Englewood. Call well in advance for pick up. (941-575-4000)

ACTIVITIES

■ **ARCHERY**
Le Katch Ka Archers is a club that invites the public to monthly shoots (usually the 2nd Sun) and offers a seasonal membership for visitors that includes a key so you can shoot on your own Tue-Sun 9-5. The range is hard-packed ground with paved walkways. Call Eric Cook 941-493-0025. Unpaved parking; Rr (Knight Trail Park, 3445 Rustic Rd, Nokomis; from Laurel Rd E of I-75, N on Knights Trail Rd, then W;

941-488-3223)
■ **ATTRACTIONS**
Octagon Wildlife Sanctuary provides a 6-acre refuge for injured or unwanted wild and exotic animals, including lions and tigers and bears . . . and cougars. You can view the animals from the hard-packed dirt and grass paths. Sometimes staff can lead tours. $D. Tue-Sun 10-4 (41160 Horseshoe Rd, Punta Gorda; 941-543-1130)
Peace River Wildlife Center rehabili-

tates wildlife for release and offers self-guided tours along hard-packed shell and gravel paths through aviaries of injured birds. Sometimes staff can lead tours. Gift shop; Rr in park. $D. Wed-Mon 11-3 (Ponce De Leon Park, 3400 W Marion Ave, Punta Gorda; 941-637-3830)

■ **BEACHES** (from north to south) The following 5 beaches have free parking, accessible dune crossovers with decks and pavilions with Rr. Beaches are open 6am-midnight; where lifeguards are indicated, they are on duty 10-4:45, summer 10-6:45. Where indicated by asterisk (*), you can borrow beach WCs (fixed arms) from 10-5 beside lifeguard headquarters. Because of frequent use, you are asked to use the beach WC only to get to a spot on the beach; an able-bodied companion should return the WC to lifeguard headquarters. If lifeguards are nearby, they are happy to help with transfers. For information, call 941-346-3310.

*Nokomis Beach includes 22 acres, 1700' on the Gulf and 3200' along the Intracoastal. A boardwalk, with observation decks, runs the length of the beach. The boat ramp and fixed dock are on the Intracoastal. Lifeguards; ADA picnic shelters; outdoor showers; Rr (109 Casey Key Rd, Nokomis; go W on Albee Rd, then S on Casey Key)

*North Jetty Beach is the Gulf coast's spot for surfers. You can also watch boats enter the Gulf through the Venice Inlet. The paved tops of the jetties offer some good fishing. Lifeguards; bait/snack shop; ADA picnic shelter across hard-packed shell terrain; outdoor showers; Rr (S tip of Casey Key, Nokomis)

*Venice Beach, close to downtown, offers 875' of Gulf frontage from where divers swim out to a reef just offshore. Lifeguards; snack bar with accessible tables on deck; outdoor showers; Rr (W end of Venice Ave; 1 mi W of BR US 41)

Caspersen Beach is the place to find sharks' teeth along its grayish 9150'

Gulf beach. An 1100' boardwalk, with an ADA picnic table on one of the decks, winds through fresh- and saltwater marshes, but the nature trail is soft sand. Next door is the Venice Fishing Pier; see Fishing Piers. Outdoor showers; Rr (4100 Harbor Dr S; take Venice Ave W then S on Harbor Dr; S of Venice Airport)

*Manasota Beach's 1394' Gulf frontage is famous for shelling. Across the road from the beach is a 620', partially lighted, fixed dock with boat slips that offers a pleasant stroll and good fishing in the lagoon. Lifeguards; ADA picnic shelter; outdoor showers; Rr beachside (W end of Manasota Beach Rd)

*Englewood Beach or Chadwick Park is a 12-acre stretch on the Gulf where you can borrow a beach WC (swing-away arms) to get to a spot on the beach; an able-bodied friend must return the WC to the pavilion. A 900' boardwalk with covered overlooks runs the length of the beach. Across the street are restaurants and tourist shops. Metered parking; picnic shelters; grills; ADA playground, partially on sand; Rr. 6am-9pm (2100 N Beach Rd, Englewood; S off SR 775; 941-473-1018)

*Port Charlotte Beach Park packs a range of fun into its 15 acres along Charlotte Harbor. A heated pool is open year round and has a lift (fixed seat); lifeguards can help with transfers. The locker room has Rr and step-in showers with a bench. Call 941-627-1628 for the schedule of aquacise classes and pool hours (usually 10-4). At the pool from 8-5, you can borrow a beach WC (swing-away arms) to get to a spot on the beach; an able-bodied friend must return the WC to the pool. A boardwalk leads to the beach. A lighted 600' ADA pier offers fishing 24 hrs (bait/snack shop 9-5; 941-766-9393). Two boat ramps with fixed docks are not lighted but are open 24 hrs. Metered parking; no lifeguards at bch; picnic shelters; grills; ADA playground on sand; outdoor showers; tennis; Rr. 6am-9pm

(4500 Harbor Blvd, Port Charlotte; S off US 41)

+Gasparilla Island State Park is at the S end of the island at the 1890 Boca Grande Lighthouse that still functions. With an HC permit you can drive to the lighthouse and take a boardwalk to a museum on the 2nd floor, with an elevator to a gift shop and exhibits on local history, shells and fish. (Wed-Sun 10-4; Feb-Apr Tue-Sun 10-4; Aug closed; 941-964-0060) The porch off the museum and the nearby picnic area are great spots to watch boats going through the pass to the Gulf. Ask at the park office to borrow a beach WC (fixed arms); with advance notice, a ranger can help you transfer. Sandspur Beach at the N end of the park has a paved path to an unguarded swim area where the currents aren't as powerful as on the other beaches here. ADA picnic table on concrete pad in Lighthouse picnic area; Rr. $. 8-dusk (CR 775; 7 mi S of Boca Grande Cswy toll bridge; 941-964-0375)

■ **BIKE TRAILS**

Boca Grande Bike Path is a 6.5-mi asphalt path running the length of the island, separated from main roads by a grassy median. If you can transfer into a golf cart, you can rent one by the hour, day or long-term at Island Bike 'n Beach (333 Park Ave; 941-964-0711), Millers Marina (222 Harbor Dr; 941-964-2232) and Dolphin Cove (421 Park Ave; 941-964-0109).

Cape Haze Pioneer Trail is a paved multi-use path along an old railroad bed parallel to CR 771. Currently the level trail starts at SR 776 in Charlotte Beach and runs 5.5 mi SW past Harness Rd; by 2005 it will run a total of 9 mi to the town of Placida on the Gasparilla Sound. Picnic shelters and Rr at 3 trailheads along the way; the mid-way trailhead, N of Rotunda Blvd E, has a water fountain.

■ **BOAT RAMPS**

Beaches: Nokomis

El Jobean Park, across from the VFW Park, has a boat ramp and fixed dock on the Myakka River. Hard-packed shell parking; picnic table; grills; Rr in park. 24 hrs (4333 Kerrigan Cir, El Jobean)

Hathaway Park has an ADA boat ramp and floating dock on the freshwater Shell Creek that feeds into the Peace River. Picnic shelter; Rr. 24 hrs (35461 Washington Loop Rd, Punta Gorda; off US 17; 941-627-1628)

Higel Park has a boat ramp and fixed dock on Dona Bay. ADA picnic shelter; Rr. 6am-mdnt (1330 Tarpon Center Dr)

Indian Mound Park has lighted boat ramps with fixed docks on Lemon Bay. This spot is popular with wind surfers. You can take a short mulch trail over a ceremonial mound. ADA picnic shelter; Rr. 6am-mdnt (210 Winson Ave, Englewood; from SR 776 go W on Dearborn St; 941-474-8919)

Marina Boat Ramp Park has a deep-water boat ramp and ramped fixed dock on the Intracoastal. The park plans to light the ramp. Rr port-a-let. 6am-mdnt (215 E Venice Ave)

Marina Park has a lighted boat ramp and floating dock on a canal to the Myakka River. 6am-mdnt (7030 Chancellor Blvd, North Port)

Placida Park has 2 boat ramps and fixed docks on the Placida Harbor, near the Gasparilla Pass to the Gulf. Lighted parking; Rr port-a-let. 24 hrs (E side of Boca Grande Cswy, Placida)

Springlake Park has a boat ramp and fixed docks on Akerman Waterway that leads to Charlotte Harbor. Port-a-let, not ramped. (Edgewater Dr & Lakeview Rd, Port Charlotte)

■ **BOAT RENTALS**

Beach Place rents Carolina Skiffs and pontoon boats (32" entry) for up to 10 people on Lemon Bay. Staff can help you over the 2 steps to the dock. If tides prevent you from rolling aboard, staff can lift onto either boat in your WC. 9-5; Sep-Oct wknd only (1863 Gulf Blvd, Englewood; 941-474-1022)

Capt Russ Boat Rental rents several types of boats, from 15' Boston Whalers to 23' Sea Craft with center consoles for half/full days in the Gulf or Gasparilla Sound. With advance notice, crew can help lift you from your WC into a boat seat. Bait shop. 8-5 (Whidden's Marina, 1 St & Harbor Dr, Boca Grande; 941-964-0708)

Holidaze Boat Rental rents pontoon boats (27"-36"entries) that can carry from 8-20 people in the Charlotte Harbor and Peace River. Crew can help you down the step to the fixed dock and can help lift you aboard in your WC. Rentals range from 2 hrs to long term and include Bimini tops. Captain available for hire. Restaurants & Rr at marina; bait shop nearby. 8-5; extended hrs by reservation (Fishermen's Village, 1200 W Retta Esplande, Punta Gorda; I-75 exit 164, 3 mi W on US 17; 941-505-8888)

Holidaze Boat Rental rents pontoon boats (27" entry) for up to 14 people on Lemon Bay. Crew can help lift you aboard in your WC from the fixed dock. Rentals range from 2 hrs to long term and include Bimini tops. Captain available for hire. Bait shop. 8-5; extended hrs by reservation (Rocky Creek Marina, 1990 Placida Rd, Englewood; off SR 776; 941-473-8520)

Snook Haven Retreat rents a pontoon boat (28" entry) for up to 10 on the Myakka River by the hour or day. In extreme low tides, staff can ramp the boat or otherwise help you board. 8am-9pm (5000 E Venice Ave; 941-485-7221)

SunSplash Boat Rentals have 17' to 20' center consoles for half/full days on the Gulf or bays. Staff can help lift you onto a boat seat. Bait shop; Rr at marina. 8-4:30 (Uncle Henry's Marina, 5800 Gasparilla Rd, Boca Grande; 941-964-1333)

VIP Boat Club rents pontoon boats (24" entry) for up to 12 and a pontoon boat (22" entry) for 5 for the Intracoastal. Staff can help you over the step to the dock and help lift you in your WC aboard over the boat railing. (1990 Placida Rd, Englewood; 941-473-8520)

■ **BOAT TOURS**

Capt Scott invites you for a private expedition exploring the coastal islands aboard his 34' sport fishing boat. Capt can help lift you aboard in your WC. See Useppa Island where Calusa Indians lived, catch dusk from the bayou or lunch at Cabbage Key Restaurant, built in 1938. If you call the restaurant (941-283-2278) ahead of time, staff can transport you in a golf cart uphill to the restaurant. You can eat outside or enter through the kitchen to avoid the 5 steps at the entrance. (Pink Docks, E end of 5 Ave, Boca Grande; 941-964-2333)

Grande Tours offers a range of group tours Dec-May and customizes private tours all year on roll-aboard catamarans. Try a 90-min ecotour of Charlotte Harbor Aquatic Preserve or a dolphin tour with a hydrophone so you can eavesdrop on dolphins and other underwater creatures. Or, hunt for pirate treasure on a hard-packed, deserted island. Rr at dock. 8:30-4 (12575 Placida Rd, Placida; 941-697-8825)

King Fisher Cruise Lines offers a rich variety of tours from 1 hr to all day. Crew can help you down 2 steps to the fixed tour dock. The Island Star is the most readily accessible tour boat in the fleet because you can board and disembark by ramp. Choose an ecotour of the Peace River led by a naturalist, a sunset trip in Charlotte Harbor or one featuring live folk music. Some tours stop at different sites. One goes to the beautiful Cayo Costa State Park (only accessible by boat; see Ft Myers: Beaches) where you can borrow a beach WC and take a tram to the beach with ADA picnic tables and Rr. Another cruise stops at Salty's in Burnt Store Marina, where a steep ramp leads to the restaurant. Or, visit Cabbage Key, the former home of Mary Roberts Reinhart, where if you call 941-283-2278 ahead of time, staff can transport you in a golf cart uphill to the restaurant. You can eat outside or enter through the kitchen to avoid the 5 steps at the entrance. Restaurants & Rr at marina. Schedule varies (Fishermen's Village, 1200 W Retta Esplanade, Punta Gorda; I-75 exit 164, 3 mi W on US 17; 941-639-0969)

Nav-A-Gator Tours offers 2-hr ecotours along the Peace River on a roll-aboard 44-person pontoon boat. You may see gators, manatees and nesting birds while you learn the history of the area. Some trips include lunch. Hrs vary (9700 SW Riverview Cr, Arcadia; I-75 exit 167, 3 mi NE on CR 769, E at billboard; 941-627-3474; 800-308-7506)

■ **BOWLING**

AMF Venice Lanes will ramp lanes for WC bowlers at any time. A WC league plays on Thu afternoons in winter. Bumpers available; game room; snack bar; lounge; Rr. Wkdy 9am-closing varies; Fri-Sat 9am-mdnt (1100 US 41 Bypass S; 941-484-0666)

■ **CAMPS**

Sarasota: Camps

■ **CANOEING/KAYAKING**

Canoe Outpost has experience with WC paddlers and offers trips down the serene Peace River through towering cypress trees with mossy beards. Paddle 10 mi on half-day trips or 16 mi on full-day trips in canoes or solo sit-on or tandem sit-in kayaks. The put-in for the 10-mi trip is a paved boat ramp; the 16-mi trip leaves from a sloped sandy riverbank. At both sites, staff can get you in your WC to the water's edge and help lift you into your craft. At the take-out, staff can carry you up the tiered stairway to your WC. You can drive to the launch and staff can shuttle your vehicle (and WC) to the take out. Or, leave your vehicle at the take-out and staff can carry you in your WC onto the shuttle bus that has room for WCs. Wkdy 8-4:30; wknd 8-6 (2816 NW CR661, Arcadia; I-75 exit 170, 3 mi E on SR 769; 863-494-1215; 800-268-0083)

Grande Tours rents solo/tandem sit-in/ sit-on kayaks and guides 2 1/2-hr to full-day ecotours of the Charlotte Harbor Aquatic Preserve. Staff can lift you from your WC into the kayak. Rr. 8:30-4 (12575 Placida Rd, Placida; 941-697-8825)

Snook Haven Retreat rents canoes by the hour for the Myakka River where you paddle back to the launch. Normally you can roll to the water's edge where staff can help lift you into a canoe; in extreme low tides, staff can help carry you to the water's edge. When you make reservations, check the tides and explain any special needs. 8am-9pm (5000 E Venice Ave; 941-485-7221)

■ **DINNER THEATER**

Golden Apple Dinner Theater offers a buffet in a restaurant followed by the live performance in a theater. You can buy tickets for the show without dinner. WC seating in front row on aisles; Rr. Oct-May Tue-Sat evenings & some matinees (Holiday Inn, 455 US 41 N Bypass; 941-484-7711)

■ **FISHING CHARTERS**

Capt Mark Sutherlin offers half/full-day trips either offshore or on the flats. The offshore boat has a large deck with plenty of shade for 6 anglers. The flats boat can hold up to 3. Capt can help you over the 2 steps to the dock. Depending on tides, he may be able to roll your WC onto either boat, otherwise crew can help lift you aboard in your WC. (941-484-3483)

Capt Scott offers half/full-day trips on the bayou for bottom fishing, trout spin casting or mackerel trolling for up to 6 anglers. Capt Scott can help lift you aboard his 34' sport fishing boat in your WC. (The Pink Docks, E end of 5 Ave, Boca Grande; 941-964-2333)

Gaona Sportfishing Charters has a 50' boat with a 16' wide back deck for up to 6 anglers. Crew can lift you aboard in your WC or into a fighting chair with straps. Offshore trips run half/full day with light to heavy tackle. (505 US 41 N; 941-488-2311)

Grande Tours specializes in family fishing trips on a 30' or 40' pontoon boat in Gasparilla Sound, Charlotte Harbor or elsewhere depending on your interests. This operator specializes in helping kids with their first fish and sends them home with a photo. Roll aboard from the floating dock. Rr. 8:30-4 (12575 Placida Rd, Placida; 941-697-8825)

King Fisher Charters offers full-day deep-sea fishing on a 35' boat or half/full-day flats fishing on a 19' or 24' boat. Boats can handle up to 6 anglers. The 35' boat has a step into the cabin; the 24' boat offers some shade under a Bimini top. Capt Allen and crew can help you down 2 steps to the floating dock and lift you from your WC and back into your WC onboard. Fly rods on request; bring your cooler with food & beverages; restaurants & Rr at marina. 8-4; 8-noon or 1-5 (FIshermen's VIllage, 1200 W Retta Esplanade, Punta Gorda; I-75 exit 164, 3 mi W on US 17; 941-639-0969)

Let's Go Fishing with Capt Van Hubbard for a 4- to 7-hr fishing trip in-shore and backcountry on a 23' Dorado for up to 6 anglers. He can help lift you aboard in your WC or onto a swivel seat, without a footrest. (Stumps Pass Marina, 3060 Placida Rd, Englewood; 941-697-6944)

■ **FISHING PIERS**

Beaches: Manasota, North Jetty, Port Charlotte

Anger Pier, also called the Tom Adams Bridge pier and Englewood pier, is a 200' lighted wood pier on Lemon Bay. Bait shop nearby; Rr. 24 hrs (Beach Rd at the Tom Adams Bridge, Englewood)

Bayshore Fishing Pier is 621' ADA pier over Charlotte Harbor. Picnic shelter; Rr port-o-let. 24 hrs (22967 Bayshore Rd, Port Charlotte)

Coral Creek Fishing Pier is a 251' pier over a creek leading to Lemon Bay. 24 hrs (Placida Rd, Placida)

Gasparilla Pier N is a 665' pier over Gasparilla Sound and across the street from Coral Creek Pier. Limited hard-shell parking. 24 hrs (SR 775, Placida)

Gasparilla Pier S is a 410' pier over Gasparilla Sound. Hard-packed shell parking. 24 hrs (SR 775; W side of Cswy to Boca Grande)

Harbor Heights Park has 2 boat ramps, fixed docks and boat slips on the Peace River. Picnic shelter; grills; ADA playground on sand; lighted tennis; basketball; shuffleboard; Rr. 24 hrs (3350 San Marino Dr, Punta Gorda)

Lashley Park Municipal Pier is a 525' lighted concrete pier on Charlotte Harbor. Rr. 24 hrs (1 Nesbit St, Punta Gorda)

Venice Pier is a lighted 750' wood pier on the Gulf with Sharky's Restaurant. The pier is on the contiguous beaches of Brohard (with a dog park/beach), Casperson and Service Club. Bait/snack shop 6-9; Rr. $/during day. 24 hrs (1600 Harbor Dr S; S of Venice by airport; 941-488-1456)

■ **MISC**

Charlotte County Memorial Auditorium is a civic center where you'll find everything from a Broadway series and top name entertainers to Big Band dances, antique shows and community garage sales. All seating is accessible by ramps and in some cases, lifts. Rr (75 Taylor St, Punta Gorda; just E of Collier Bridge into Punta Gorda; 941-639-5833; 941-639-1976; 800-329-9988)

Warm Mineral Springs is a spring-fed lake of 87-degree water. You can borrow a WC here to take just into the water; if available, staff can help with transfers. The grassy area down to the lake and the lake itself are naturally graded such that you can comfortably roll in. A paved ramp is also available. Masseuses offer relaxing, even therapeutic massages by appointment. Call for the schedule of wellness classes and other special events. Cafe; roll-in showers; Rr. $. 9-5 (12200 San Servando Ave, North Port; from US 41, N on Ortiz Blvd to end; 941-426-1692)

■ **MUSEUMS**

Florida Adventure Museum has rotating exhibits on Florida history and natural science themes and permanent collections on local history and Florida's military heritage. To ease getting to the entrance, don't go to the museum's street address; instead park in the SW corner of the parking lot for the Charlotte County Memorial Auditorium. $. 10-5; Sat 10-3 (260 W Retta Esplanade, Punta Gorda; 941-639-3777)

■ PARKS

Carlton Reserve Park is a 40-acre wooded parcel sitting on the gloriously undeveloped 20,000-acre Carlton Reserve. The only facilities are at the park entrance, including Rr, ADA picnic tables in individual sites and a large ADA picnic shelter. Trails start here with interpretive signage on almost 1 mi of pavers and hard-packed shell then become natural where you probably want an all-terrain WC. To access the rugged trails beyond, you must get a backcountry permit from the staff. The reserve usually floods during the summer, attracting more bugs than people. Ranger-led tours in winter. Dawn-dusk (1800 Mabry Carlton Pkwy; I-75 exit 193, N on Jacaranda Blvd, E on Border Rd for 2.5 mi, then N .5 mi; 941-486-2547)

Charlotte Harbor Environmental Center sits on the 3000-acre Charlotte Harbor Aquatic Buffer Preserve. Boardwalks lead to the visitor center with rotating ecological exhibits, a nature shop, the Discovery Museum where you'll find biodiverse species *in their stuffed phase* and, open by appointment, the Florida Bat Center (941-637-6990). The self-guided 1-mi Eagle Point Trail is mulched and the 2-mi Pine Flatwoods Trail is a bit rough. Nov-Apr free guided walks (wkdy 10 & 1:30; Sat 10); picnic tables; Rr. $D. Hrs vary (10941 Burnt Store Rd, Punta Gorda; 1 mi S of US 41; 941-575-5435)

Kidspace is a large ADA playground with a tot area on a rubberized surface and just off a sidewalk from parking. Picnic tables; grills; water fountain; Rr by ball field (Maracaibo Park, Acocado

St & Maracaibo St)

Lemon Bay Park is 196 acres of mangrove forest, pine flats, scrub and wetlands where you can see birds of the shore and forest, including bald eagles. All trails have interpretive signage; some are quite sandy or rough. The paved section of Bayside Trail leads through a butterfly garden, past a day lily garden to a deck overlooking Lemon Bay. Eagle Trail branches into other trails with a 2-mi stretch of hard-packed shell through mangrove estuaries. The environmental center has ecology displays. Call for schedule of guided walks and wildlife talks, mostly during winter. ADA picnic table; Rr. 9-dusk; summer hrs vary (570 Bay Park Blvd, Englewood; from Old Englewood Rd, W on Ohio Ave, S on Curtis, then W on Brengle; 941-474-3065/2092)

Shamrock Park is an 82-acre scrub oak habitat with a 1-mi paved nature/bike trail through pine flatwoods and coastal shrub where you can see gopher tortoises and scrub jays. The visitor center has ecological displays. Call for schedule of guided walks, mostly during winter. ADA picnic tables; playground on sand; tennis; basketball; Rr. Dawn-dusk (3900 Shamrock Dr; off SR 41; 941-486-2706)

■ PERFORMING ARTS

Lemon Bay Playhouse is a community theater performing mostly comedies. WC seating in front row on left; Rr. Sep-Jul (96 W Dearborn St, Englewood; 941-475-6756)

Port Charlotte Cultural Center is a 5-acre complex with a 418-seat theater offering concerts, shows and more. The Charlotte Players, a community theater group, as well as other performing groups present plays, musicals and concerts here. WC seating on side aisles; Rr (2280 Aaron St, Port Charlotte; 941-625-4175)

Royal Palm Players offer community theater Nov-May. WC seating in aisles or rear with folding chairs for companions; Rr. (Boca Grande Community

Center, 1 St & Park Ave, Boca Grande; 941-964-2670)

Venice Little Theater is an active community theater with 2 venues. The 432-seat Mainstage showcases musicals, dramas, concerts and children's shows. WC seating is available by ramp to a platform just left of the stage or by elevator to the balcony in front at either side. Also, several theater seats on the aisles and in the last row have swing-away arms for easy transfers. Stage II has 90 seats and features smaller, sometimes non-conformist productions. With advance notice, theater seats can be removed for WC seating up front. Rr. Tue-Sat 8pm; Sun 2pm (140 W Tampa Ave; on Venice Island; 941-488-1115)

Venice Symphony performs at the Church of the Nazarene mid-Dec-Apr. WC seating in aisles at end of pews; Rr (1535 E Venice Ave; 941-488-1010)

■ **POOLS**
Beaches: Port Charlotte

Dallas White Park is the location of the North Port Aquatic Center with a heated 25-meter pool with a lift (fixed seat). Staff can help with transfers. From 11-noon the pool is open only to disabled persons of all ages and seniors. Lap time is 7:30-9am; exercise classes occur Tue, Wed and Fri 10-11am. The park also has picnic tables, a playground with an ADA section, ball fields and tennis. WC loaner to get to pool; roll-in showers in locker rooms. $. Tue-Fri 10:30-7:30, Sat 12-5 (5925 Greenwood Ave, North Port; from US 41, N on North Port Blvd, then E, behind police station; 941-423-2065)

■ **SHOOTING RANGES**
Babcock-Webb Wildlife Management Area has a ramped shooting range with a 150' pistol and a 600' rifle range. Dawn-dusk (29200 Tucker Grade, Punta Gorda; I-75 exit 158, then E; 941-575-5768)

Knight Trail Park has a pistol and rifle range with paved positions at 7, 25, 50 and 100 yds. Ramps allow you to retrieve your targets. (Tue-Sun 9-4:30; 941-486-2350) The Sarasota Trap, Skeet & Clays Club invites the public, novice to experienced marksmen, to shoot and enter club competitions and leagues. Courses are hard-packed terrain. (Summer Wed 9-9, Fri 9-1, wknd 9-4; winter also Thus 9-1; 941-488-3223) Pro shop; unpaved parking; picnic tables in park; Rr. (3445 Rustic Rd, Nokomis; from Laurel Rd E of I-75, N on Knights Trail Rd, then W)

■ **SHOPPING**
Boutiques & more: Historic downtown Venice, with its vintage 1920's buildings along Venice, Tampa and Miami Avenues, offers plenty of neat little stores, antique shops, galleries and restaurants. In Punta Gorda, check out Fishermen's Village, along the Peace River, with fun shops, restaurants and a marina (1200 W Retta Esplanade, Punta Gorda; 941-639-8721; 800-639-0020). Boca Grande is rife with art galleries, unique shops and fun touristy stores; try the historic Railroad Depot and Railroad Plaza, both in downtown; Millers Marina (222 Harbor Dr; 941-964-2232); and Courtyard Plaza at the N end of the island.

Flea Markets: Dome Flea market has dozens of stalls under shelter and paved walkways but the parking lot is dirt and gravel. Oct-Aug wknd 9-4 (SR 775 W of US 41; 941-493-6773)

Galleries: Venice Art Center (390 S Nokomis Ave; 941-485-7136); Englewood Art Center (350 S Mc Call Rd, Englewood; 941-474-5548)

Malls: Port Charlotte Town Center (US 41 & SR 776, Punta Gorda; I-75 exit 179; 941-624-4447)

ACCOMMODATIONS

■ CONDOS

Beach Retreat on Casey Key lies between the Gulf and Intracoastal and has WC-friendly ground floor units each with a great view, full kitchen and 1 small step at the entry. Choose from a 1-room efficiency with a kitchen and sitting area, a 1BR unit with a living room/kitchen or a 2 BR unit with a separate living room and kitchen. The condos have a king, queen or 2 twin beds. Some standard bathrooms have a tub and large shower; others have small showers. The courtyard has grills and picnic tables. Small step to pool area; stairs to fishing & boat docks; laundry (105 Casey Key Rd, Nokomis; 941-485-8771; 866-232-2480)

Emerald Palms Resort, on Lemon Bay, has WC-friendly 1BR and 2BR apartments and a portable wood ramp for the 4" step at the front door. Bed sizes vary but all are on open frames. Standard bathrooms have tub/showers; ask for unit with a wide bathroom door. Fishing pier; boat slips; laundry; carports; tables with umbrellas; grills (540 S McCall Rd, Englewood; 941-475-0100)

Marina Inn, on the gated resort of Burnt Store Marina, has 2 WC-friendly 1BR condos. Units 127 and 223 each have a king bed, full kitchen, sofa bed in the living room and a screened porch. Standard bathrooms have grab bars and tubs. You can fish from the docks on Charlotte Harbor. Heated pool; sauna; golf; tennis; bike rentals; gift shop; laundry; boat rentals & fishing charters at marina (3160 Matecumbe Key Rd, Punta Gorda; 941-575-4488)

Palm Manor Resort has WC-friendly 2BR units on the ground floor, each with a queen and 2 twin beds (21" high/open frames), a sofa bed in the living room, full kitchen and washer/dryer. Bathrooms have 28" wide doorways, tubs, step-in showers and on request, grab bars. The resort is 2 mi from the beach. Heated pool; shuffleboard; tennis (1531 Placida Rd, Englewood; 941-474-3700; 800-848-8141)

Quarterdeck Resort Condominiums has WC-friendly, ground floor 1BR/1BA and 2BR/2BA condos on the beach with full kitchens and living rooms with sofa beds; bed sizes vary. Bathrooms are standard; staff can remove the bathroom door if needed. The 1BR bathrooms have tubs; the 2BR units have tubs and large step-in showers. Three steps lead to the beach. Heated pool; laundry; social programs (1275 Tarpon Center Dr; across from Venice Yacht Club; 941-488-0449; 800-845-0251)

Westons Resort has WC-friendly units from studio efficiencies to 2BR condos in high rises on the Gulf or bay. Units have various bed sizes, full kitchens, standard bathrooms and linens. Condos in the 2 newer buildings have wider bathroom doors. Two night minimum; fishing dock on bay; tennis; grills; laundry (985 Gulf Blvd, Englewood; 941-474-3431)

■ INNS

Gasparilla Inn is a stately WC-friendly place originally built in 1912. Large rooms each have a full or 2 twin beds (that can be adjoined for a king). Large standard bathrooms have grab bars in either tubs or step-in showers. Dec-Apr the charge includes 3 daily meals in the various eateries on site; Apr-Jun breakfast and dinner are included. At the beach club, 2 blocks away, are 2 heated pools, sauna, massage & exercise room, a restaurant and a huge patio that overlooks the beach. Golf; tennis; billiards. $$$. Mid-Dec to Jun (500 Palm Ave; 941-964-2201)

■ MOTELS

Best Western Ambassador Suites has 4 spacious ADA suites, each with a king or 2 queen beds (24" high/open frames), a refrigerator, microwave, coffeepot and sofa bed. Bathrooms have raised toilets, roll-under sinks and roll-in showers with hand-held sprayers and seats. Free brkfst; heated pool; exercise room; laundry. $$-$$$ (400 Commercial Ct; 941-480-9898; 800-822-4853)

Best Western Sandbar Beach Resort has 1 ADA room with a queen bed (platform), refrigerator, microwave and coffeepot. The bathroom has a roll-under sink and roll-in shower with a hand-held sprayer and seat. Free brkfst & paper; heated pool; shuffleboard; laundry. $$$ (811 Esplanade N; 941-488-2251; 800-822-4853)

Holiday Inn has 3 ADA rooms. Rooms 182 and 187 each have a king bed (open frame) and roll-in shower; the other has a king bed (platform) and tub. The Golden Apple Dinner Theater is on the premises. Heated pool; hot tub; exercise room; shuffleboard; bar; full restaurant. $$-$$$ (455 US 41 N Bypass; 941-485-5411)

Holiday Inn, on the Charlotte Harbor, has 5 ADA rooms and an ADA 1BR suite, each with a king bed (platform) and coffeepot. The suite has a full sofa bed and full kitchenette (with a cook top but no oven). Bathrooms have raised toilets, roll-under sinks and roll-in showers with hand-held sprayers and seats. Pool; dock for fishing; boat slips; exercise room; lounge; entertainment; full restaurant. $$-$$$ (33 US 41, Punta Gorda; 941-639-2167; 877-639-9399)

Holiday Inn Express has 3 ADA rooms, each with a king bed. Bathrooms have roll-under sinks; one room has a roll-in shower with a hand-held sprayer; others have tubs. Free brkfst; pool. $$-$$$ (24440 Sandhill Blvd, Punta Gorda; 941-764-0056)

Motel 6 has 3 ADA rooms, each with a king bed and bathroom with a raised toilet, roll-under sink and roll-in shower with a hand-held sprayer and seat. Pool. $ (9300 Knights Dr, Punta Gorda; I-75 exit 161; 941-639-9585)

Motel 6 has 5 ADA rooms, each with a queen bed (open frame) and a bathroom with a raised toilet, roll-under sink and roll-in shower with a hand-held sprayer and seat. Pool. $ (281 US 41 N Bypass; 941-485-8255)

Nokomis Motor Inn has 2 ADA rooms, each with a queen bed (23" high/open frame) and bathroom with a roll-in shower with a hand-held sprayer. Free brkfst. $-$$ (119 N US 41, Nokomis; 941-488-1155; 800-329-1156)

Uncle Henry's Marina Resort has 1 ADA room with a full and a twin bed (open frames) and a private balcony on the parking lot. The bathroom has a raised toilet, roll-under sink and a tub. The marina has boat rentals and fishing charters; see both. Boat ramp with fixed docks; pool; laundry; restaurant for brkfst & lnch. $$$ (5800 Gasparilla Rd, Boca Grande; 941-964-2300)

DON'T BE DISAPPOINTED, CALL FIRST!

Owners change, staff change, conditions change, hours change, even addresses change!

Please call beforehand.
Make sure the business can still accommodate you.

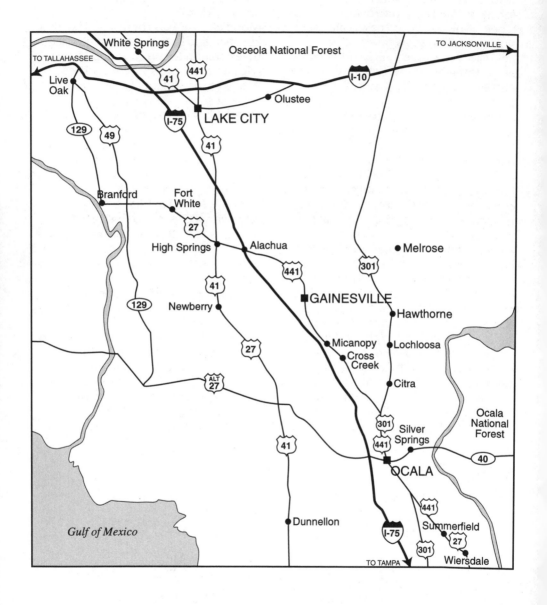

GAINESVILLE
Cross Creek, Fort White, Hawthorne, High Springs, Lochloosa, Melrose, Micanopy, Newberry

Gainesville is the proud home of the Florida Gator, a species bred only at the University of Florida. This small city has the diversity you might expect in a major college town, including a teaching zoo open for tours, fine museums and a competitive equestrian center. The extraordinary array of accessible sports includes fencing, tennis, basketball and a camp specifically for disabled folks to try out a variety of sports. The range of outdoors fun is wide as well – from a Florida-style prairie and a sinkhole to historic sites and a botanical garden. Check out the Santa Fe River by canoe or tube. Three B&Bs offer accessible lodging.

Tourist Info
Alachua County Visitors Bureau: 30 E University Ave, 32601; 352-374-5231
Web sites: www.visitgainesville.net; www.highsprings.com

Transportation
Regional Transit has a lift-equipped bus on each route Mon-Sat. Call for a schedule. (352-334-2605)
Para-Transit offers curb-to-curb service to areas not covered by the city's bus routes. To qualify you must complete an application and be approved. (352-378-7474)

WC Resources
Center for Independent Living of North Central Florida provides many services to people with disabilities including WC rentals, information on access to local events and travel training for the public bus system. (720 NW 23 Ave; 352-378-7474)

ACTIVITIES

■ **ATTRACTIONS**
Kanapaha Botanical Gardens features 1.5 mi of paved paths through 62 acres of beautiful ornamental gardens of butterflies, hummingbirds, bamboo, rocks, water lilies, ferns and more. You can also see demonstrations of water reclamation. WC loaners; picnic areas; gift shop; plant nursery; Rr. $. Fri-Wed hrs vary (4625 SW 63 Blvd; W of I-75

off SR 24; 352-372-4981)

Marjorie Kinnan Rawlings Historic Park is a 19th century cracker house and natural area where Rawlings penned *The Yearling*. The East Grove Trail through a wooded area is short, flat and hard-packed with a few sandy areas. Staff can set up a portable ramp so you can join a tour through the 8-room house. Because of the age of the structure, heavy WCs cannot access the house. Oct-Jul guided tours occur Thu-Sun at 10, 11 and hourly 1-4; tours are limited to 10 visitors so you may need to wait. Picnic area; unpaved parking; Rr. $/tours (CR 325 at Cross Creek; 21 mi SE of Gainesville; 352-466-9273)

Santa Fe Community College Teaching Zoo offers 45-min guided tours over mulch paths to view animals, including endangered species, from around the world. This free 14-acre zoo is a classroom for students of zoo management. Rr. Wkdy by appointment; wknd 9-2 (3000 NW 83 St; I-75 exit 390; 352-395-5604)

■ **BASKETBALL**

Gator Wheels is an NWBA team; practices are open to women, men and teens. Competitive matches occur Oct-Mar. Able-bodied players are welcome but must play from a WC. Contact Dug Jones 352-395-5269. WC loaners. Practice times vary (Santa Fe Community College, 3000 NW 83 St)

■ **BIKE TRAILS**

Gainesville-Hawthorne State Trail is a paved 17-mi trail through open fields and some shady, wooded areas in the Paynes Prairie State Preserve and Lochloosa Wildlife Management Area. Access points include the Boulware Springs Trailhead (3300 SE 15 St, Gainesville), just W of Hawthorne (at CR 2082 & SE 200 Dr) and the Hawthorne Trailhead (300 SW 2 Ave, Hawthorne). About 2.5 mi from the Boulware Trailhead, is a .5-mi stretch of long gradual hills; the rest of the trail is fairly flat. The water fountain

and Rr at Boulware Springs are on hard-packed dirt. At the 1-mi marker from Boulware Springs, is a dirt path, and in Rochelle (at CR 234 & CR 2082) a paved path to Rr. See Parks. 8am-dusk (352-466-3397)

■ **BOAT RAMPS**

Fishing Piers: Lochloosa, Newnans.
Parks: Poe Springs

Holden Pond has a boat ramp and floating dock for some fine fishing on several connected lakes. Picnic table; grill (9725 Holden Park Rd, Hawthorne; S on US 301, turn E)

Santa Fe Lake Park has a boat ramp and floating dock on a 5300-acre lake. Bait shop in town; playground; ADA picnic shelter; Rr (24500 NE SR 26, Melrose)

■ **CAMPS**

Gator Sport Exploration Camp is a 2-day session, usually in Jul, for kids and adults with physical disabilities, especially those with spinal cord injuries. Here's a chance to try out sports such as tennis, basketball, golf, fencing, quad rugby, racing, weight lifting and swimming. University of Florida's Dept of Occupational Therapy sponsors this camp where competitive athletes with disabilities demonstrate and instruct. Evening social and recreational activities are planned; accommodations are not included. Call Dr Carolyn Hanson 352-846-1023.

■ **CANOEING/TUBING**

Parks: Poe Springs

Ginnie Springs Outdoors rents canoes, tubes and wet suits for the Santa Fe River. Staff can lift you from your WC down carpeted steps and into a canoe or tube. Canoeists paddle back to the put-in; tubists float 2 mi (about 1 hr) to the take-out. With prior notice staff can take your car to the take-out or can help lift you from the water into a golf cart and take you to your car. Fri-Sun 8-10; Mon-Thu 8-7 (7300 NE CR 340; 7 mi W of High Springs; 386-454-2183)

Santa Fe Canoe Outpost offers 3- to

15-mi trips, usually 2 to 5 hrs long, down the Santa Fe River past many beautiful springs and parks where you can stop and disembark. On request, staff can meet you with your WC at a stop along the way. At the launch, staff can lift you into a canoe and either drive your vehicle to the take-out or lift you into the shuttle van to return to the launch. Once a month, the operator leads a full moon trip. Wkdy 9-6; wknd 8-6 (US 441; N of High Springs at the Santa Fe River Bridge; 386-454-2050)

■ FENCING

The Fencing Academy has experience teaching WC folks to fence in group and private lessons. Call Brian Harper 352-373-4816.

■ FISHING PIERS

Parks: Poe Springs

Blue Springs, a private facility, has a short boardwalk that ends over the Santa Fe River where you can fish. The parking lot, outside the park, is not paved but visitors can unload at entrance and traverse a hard-packed area to the ramped boardwalk. A ramped dock leads to a swim area in the springs. Picnic tables; Rr in bathhouse. $. 9-7 (7450 NE 60 St, High Springs; off CR 340; 386-454-1369)

Lake Johnson, a fairly remote 52-acre lake, has a 60' L-shaped pier. Picnic shelters; Rr. Dawn-dusk (Hawthorne Park, Hawthorne; E end of CR 2082 on E side of US 301)

Lochloosa Park is a tiny county park on the E shore of the 6000-acre lake reportedly filled with bass. The 60' pier has a roof at the end. The boat ramp has a floating dock. Bait shop 1 mi N on US 301; picnic tables; water fountain & Rr up a hard-packed incline (rk, 16204 SE 207 St, Lochloosa; from US 301, W on 162 Ave, proceed to end)

Newnans Lake, a 5700-acre lake just E of Gainesville, has a 10-acre county park on its SW shore. A 200' pier is at the end of a long, hard-packed area along a canal. The boat ramp has a floating dock. Bait shop at entrance; picnic shelters; playground; Rr (Earl P Powers Park, 5910 SE SR 20)

■ MISC FUN

Thelma Boltin Senior Center offers craft classes, community service projects, cards, bingo and socials. Call for calendar. Rr. Wkdy 8-5 (516 NE 2 Ave; 352-334-2189)

■ MUSEUMS

Florida Museum of Natural History features a range of exhibits on the geologic events that resulted in Florida. Roll through an inside forest and cave, replicating the Marianna Caverns in the Florida panhandle. Examine Native American artifacts found in the area. Rr. Mon-Sat 10-5; Sun 1-5 (UF Campus, Powell Hall, SW 34 St & Hull Rd; 352-846-2000)

Fred Bear Museum is a tribute to Fred Bear's 50-yr efforts to promote bow hunting and wildlife management. View a video on his travels and his collection of trophy animals, weapons and art from around the world. Elevator to museum on 2nd floor; unusual gift shop; WC loaner; Rr. $. 10-6 (Fred Bear Rd; W of I-75, off Archer Rd; 352-376-2411)

Micanopy Historical Museum has exhibits of photographs and memorabilia from the *old days*. Ramped entrance on N side; bookstore; Rr. $. 1-4 (607 Cholokka Blvd at Bay St, Micanopy; 352-466-3200)

Samuel P Harn Museum of Art houses art from around the world. One-hr guided tours occur Wed 12:30 and weekends at 2. WC loaner; Rr. Tue-Fri 11-5; Sat 10-5; Sun 1-5 (UF Campus, SW 34 St & Hull Rd; 352-392-9826)

■ PARKS

ADA Playgrounds are located at Kiwanis Park (NW 8 St & 8 Pl), Martin Luther King Center (1028 NE 14 St; 352-334-2304) and Northeast Community Center (1700 NE 8 Ave; 352-334-2185).

Bivens Arm Nature Park is a 57-acre city park at the edge of Paynes Prairie.

A 1200' boardwalk and 2 observation decks are on a marsh that draws a rich variety of birds and other wildlife. From the end of the boardwalk, a natural trail with some sandy areas leads onto the prairie for 1 mi. A sidewalk leads to the boardwalk, picnic area and Rr. 9-5 (3650 S Main St; 352-334-2231)

Devil's Millhopper State Geological Site covers 63 acres around a 120' deep sinkhole that formed when the roof of an ancient underground cavern collapsed. Shark teeth and other fossils found here have yielded much insight to the state's natural history. A .5-mi natural trail goes around the top edge and has an overlook. The visitor center has exhibits and a video. ADA picnic tables; CRr. $. 9-5; summer wknd - dusk (4732 CR 232; 352-955-2008/386-462-7905)

Dudley Farm Historic State Park complex sits on 17 acres where staff, in period dress, work the farm as in the early 1900's and demonstrate various crafts. A ramped tram takes you from parking to the farm where dirt walks are compact and coated for WC riders. The farmhouse has an elevator to the porch where you can enter the first floor. Gift shop; ADA picnic tables; grills; Rr. Wed-Sun 9-5 (18506 W Newberry Rd, Newberry; 352-472-1142)

Ginnie Springs Outdoors is a private 200-acre property along the Santa Fe River that includes 7 natural springs. Fish for bass and bream along the level, hard-packed banks of the river. The 5 mi of trails are mostly sand and limerock. A boardwalk leads from parking to a series of decks around the springs; if your friends can get you down the carpeted steps, you can swim or snorkel in the crystal clear, 72-degree spring. The park offers open water scuba lessons for which staff can lift you out of your WC and down the steps. You can become certified in 5 days, or if you are already certified,

you can take instructions on cavern and cave diving. ADA picnic tables; grills; gift shop; deli Fri-Sun; Rr. $ Fri-Sun 8-10; Mon-Thu 8-7 (7300 NE CR 340; 7 mi W of High Springs; 386-454-2183)

Morningside Nature Center is a 278-acre city sanctuary for the small remaining longleaf pine ecosystem that once covered Florida's uplands. Seven miles of connected trails are wide, level and hard-packed with some sand and tree roots. A short boardwalk leads through a cypress dome. The visitor center has a small exhibit of native reptiles and amphibians. A hard-packed but rutted path leads to a 10-acre Living History Farm. With permission, WC visitors can drive to and around the Farm where most of the buildings are from the 1800's; the old school house is now a ramped gift shop. Only the cabin has steps. Most Saturdays (when there is a small admission fee to the Farm), costumed staff tend crops and chores, such as making syrup and spinning wool, a la 1900. Shady picnic tables; grills; Rr. 9-5 (3540 E University Ave; 352-334-2170)

O'Leno State Park, with 6400 acres along the Santa Fe River, has 13 mi of trails that are mostly hard packed with some sandy areas and tree roots. See Cabins/Campgrounds. ADA swing in playground; Rr. $. Dawn-dusk (US 441, 6 mi N of High Springs; 386-454-1853)

Paynes Prairie State Preserve is a 21,000-acre wet prairie, home to gators, bison, wild horses and a variety of birds. A sidewalk leads from parking to a visitor center that has a video and museum on the history and ecology of this unexpected terrain. To get a sense of the expanse from the east, take a bumpy paved path to an observation tower, ramped to the first level. For a mirror view from the west, drive 4.5 mi N of the main entrance on US 441 where a 100' boardwalk leads to an observation deck. By the main entrance, a boardwalk offers some good fishing on Lake Wauberg. Nearby are sidewalks to an ADA picnic shelter and a playground on mulch. Trails are mostly hard-packed dirt with some sandy spots and tree roots; call for the schedule of ranger-led walks. See Bike Trails and Campgrounds. Rr. $. 8-dusk (100 Savannah Blvd; off US 441, 1 mi N of Micanopy; 352-466-3397)

Poe Springs Park is a 202-acre county park of rolling fields and woodlands along the springs and the Santa Fe River. A 600' boardwalk leads to the springs with several steps into the water for swimming. Along the river you'll find a T-shaped fishing dock and boat ramp with a floating dock. The park rents canoes and playaks (small sit-on kayaks for kids) that you can launch from the boat ramp; call ahead, staff may be available to help with transfers. ADA picnic shelters; Rr. Dawn-dusk (2880 NW 182 Ave; off CR 340, 3 mi W of High Springs; 386-454-1992)

Ring Park is a 19-acre city retreat with a rich diversity of plants and wildlife along the Glenn Springs Run and Hogtown Creek. Park at the Elks Lodge, close to the picnic area where a mulched trail leads through a wildflower garden. The garden has a pond, waterfall and interpretive signage. Naturalists lead walks and workshops, by appointment and for a fee. Rr. 7-6; May-Oct -8 (1801 NW 23 Blvd; 352-334-2170)

■ **PERFORMING ARTS**

Center for the Performing Arts offers Broadway shows, opera, dance, and pop, jazz, classical and country music. WC seating is in the aisles at the side of the orchestra and mezzanine sections and in the rear of the theater. Rr. Oct-Apr; smaller performances in summer (UF Campus, 315 Hull Rd; 352-392-2787)

High Springs Community Theater pre-sents 4 shows a year, including light comedy, musicals and children's shows. WC seating along aisles; Rr (NW 1 Ave & 1 St, High Springs; 386-454-3525)

Hippodrome State Theatre is a former 1801 post office and courthouse that features contemporary plays with national professional casts. WC seating is front and center in this 3/4-round theater. An elevator takes you to the cinema series and local art gallery on the 2nd floor. Free parking garage 1 blk N on 2 Ave; CRr (25 SE 2 Pl; 352-375-4477)

■ **POOLS**

Northeast Pool is a ramped pool. Staff can take you down the ramp and remove (and return) your WC once you're in the water. Adult lap times; locker room with roll-in shower and Rr. Apr-Oct hrs vary (1100 NE 14 St; 352-334-2191)

McPherson Pool (1717 SE 15 St; 352-334-2190) & **Westside Pool** (1001 NW 31 Dr; 352-334-2187) have portable ramps. Staff can set up the ramp, take you into the water and remove (and return) your WC. Call for adult lap times. Apr-Sep hrs vary

■ **SCUBA**

Parks: Ginnie Springs

■ **SHOPPING**

Boutiques: High Springs and Micanopy have tree-lined downtowns with antiquing, boutiques and restaurants.

Farmers & Flea Markets: Waldo Farmers & Flea Market has covered areas with sidewalks, hard-packed outside areas and unpaved parking. Wknd 7:30-4 (US 301; 1 mi N of Waldo; 352-468-2255). The covered Alachua County Farmers Market has fresh produce, flowers and plants. Sat 8:30-1; Thu 8:30-noon (US 441 & NW 34 St; 352-392-1845)

Malls: Oaks Mall (6419 Newberry Rd; I-75 exit 387; 352-331-4411); Paddock Mall (College Rd; .3 mi E of I-75; 352-237-1221)

■ SPECTATOR SPORTS

Canterbury Equestrian Center is a 160-acre horse facility featuring a variety of shows. The indoor arena is ramped; WC seating is on either side on concrete and with advance notice, staff can set up companion seating in movable chairs. Outdoor competition rings are over grass. Call for schedule. Limited paved parking; at big events, ask attendants to direct you up front; Rr (23100 NW SR 26, Newberry; 352-472-6758)

Gainesville Raceway offers car and motorcycle drag racing. Stands are not covered. WC & companion seating in front of grandstand at starting line & designated mid-track sections; Rr. Call for schedule; most Wed & Sat nights (11211 N CR 225; N on SR 24; 352-377-0046)

■ TENNIS

Johnny Johnston, a local WC athlete, gives private lessons and clinics under the auspices of USTA. (352-331-4060)

ACCOMMODATIONS

■ B&B/INNS

Emerald Inn B&B is a 1-story WC-friendly home that sits on 2 grassy acres overlooking Lake Victoria where you can fish from a dock. After the small step at the entrance, you can roll into two guestrooms, each with a queen bed (27" high/open frame). Private bathrooms have roll-under sinks and different doorway widths; the Ruby room has a 28" entry and a tub; the Diamond room has a 29" entry and a step-in shower. Staff can remove the bathroom door if you need more space. Your full gourmet breakfast is served in a very large Florida room with a fireplace, indoor garden, fountain and views of the lake. You can also use a microwave and small refrigerator in the kitchen. A rollaway bed is available. $$-$$$ (27751 Lake Jem Rd; 352-383-2777; 800-366-9387)

Herlong Mansion B&B is an imposing southern colonial brick home with an ADA guestroom, called Amber's Suite. It has a queen bed (29" high/open frame), a private porch, fireplace and bathroom with a roll-under sink, roll-in shower (with a seat) and a Jacuzzi for 2 (15" off the floor) with a grab bar. The building is ramped in back, near the entrance to Amber's Suite. Breakfast, along the line of blueberry waffles, is served in a gracious dining room with floor-to-ceiling windows

overlooking the 2.5 acres of shady oaks and lovely gardens. Laundry; antique stores nearby. $$$ (402 NE Cholokka Blvd, Micanopy; I-75 exit 374, .5 mi E on CR 329, then N; 352-466-3322; 800-437-5664)

Rustic Inn B&B has 10-acre grounds that were formerly part of a ranch. An ADA guestroom has a queen bed (open frame), full sofa bed, microwave, coffeepot and refrigerator filled with juice and soda. The bathroom has a raised toilet, roll-under sink and tub/shower. Every evening a breakfast basket of fresh fruit and muffins is delivered to your room. (3105 S Main St, High Springs; 386-454-1223)

■ CABINS/CAMPGROUNDS

O'Leno State Park rents two ADA 2BR cabins Sep-Apr that you can reserve 1 yr in advance. One has 4 bunk beds; the other has 4 bunk beds and 2 twin beds. Both bathrooms have raised toilets, roll-under sinks and roll-in showers. You can park next to the ramped cabins that both have a grill and ADA picnic table on the hard-packed terrain. See Parks. (US 441; 6 mi N of High Springs; 386-454-1853)

Paynes Prairie State Preserve has 35 RV and 15 tent sites all with water/elec, picnic tables, fire pits, and sidewalks to an ADA bathhouse. Tent sites 19 and 20 have ADA picnic tables; if you call in advance, staff can move an

ADA table to an RV site for you. RV sites are on hard limestone; tent sites are on a natural surface. The bath-house has raised toilets, roll-under sinks and step-in showers with seats. See Parks and Bike Trails. (100 Savan-nah Blvd; off US 441, 1 mi N of Micanopy, 10 mi S of Gainesville; 352-466-3397)

■ MOTELS

Baymont Inn & Suites has 6 ADA rooms each with 1 full bed (24" high/open frame). Bathrooms have roll-un-der sinks; rooms 105 and 205 have roll-in showers; others have tubs. Free brkfst; lounge. $$ (3905 SW 43 St; 352-376-0004)

Best Inn has 5 ADA rooms each with a king bed (24" high/platform). Bath-rooms have raised toilets, roll-under sinks, showers and seats; rooms 108 and 111 have roll-in showers. Free brkfst; pool. $$ (3455 SW Williston Rd; 352-378-2405)

Best Western Gateway Grand has 8 ADA rooms each with a king bed (23" high/platform) and a bathroom with a raised toilet, roll-under sink and roll-in shower with a hand-held sprayer and seat. Free brkfst; full restaurant; pool, laundry; lounge. $$ (4200 NW 97 Blvd; 352-331-3336)

Courtyard by Marriott has 5 ADA rooms each with a king or 2 full beds (platforms). Bathrooms have roll-un-der sinks; rooms 103 and 131 have roll-in showers with hand-held sprayers and seats; others have tubs. Restau-rant for brkfst; pool; laundry; lounge. $$-$$$ (3700 SW 42 St; 352-335-9100)

Red Roof Inn has 7 ADA rooms with a king or 2 full beds (21" high/open frames). Bathrooms have raised toi-lets and roll-under sinks; rooms 115 and 117 have roll-in showers with hand-held sprayers and seats; others have tubs. Pool. $-$$ (3500 SW 42 St; 352-336-3311)

University Centre Hotel has 6 ADA rooms each with a king bed (26" high/platform), sofa bed and bathroom with a raised toilet, roll-under sink and tub with a seat. Full restaurant; laundry; lounge; hair salon; onsite rental cars. $$ (1535 SW Archer Rd; at US 441; 352-371-3333; 800-824-5637)

LAKE CITY
Branford, Live Oak, Olustee, Osceola National Forest, White Springs

Even the highways offer a sense of the verdant beauty in this area. But the parks, rivers and bike trails invite a more intimate view. The Stephen Foster State Folk Cultural Center, way down upon the Suwannee River, will have you humming. Or, perhaps you prefer the lure of the hunt. If so, three operations have accessible hunting.

Tourist Info

Columbia County Tourist Information: 601 Hall of Fame Dr, 32055; 386-758-1312)
Lake City Chamber: 106 S Marion St, 32025; 386-752-3690
Florida Tourist Welcome Center: Box 1847, 32056; at US 90 & I-75; 386-758-1312
Nature & Heritage Tourism Center, managed by the State Dept of Recreation and Parks, showcases information on the state's natural, cultural and historical sites. Rr. 8-5 (10499 Spring St, White Springs; 386-397-4461)
Suwannee County Chamber: 601 E Howard St, Live Oak, 32064; 386-362-3071
Suwannee River Valley Region: 601 Hall of Fame Dr NW, 32055; 877-746-4778
Web sites: www.originalflorida.org; www.whitesprings.org; www.suwanneevalley.org

ACTIVITIES

■ ATTRACTIONS

Florida Sports Hall of Fame touts the successes of athletes with any kind of connection to Florida, particularly the state's college football teams. Exhibits and videos cover the sports you find in Florida. Rr. $. Thu-Mon 10-3 (N on Hall of Fame Dr; off US 90, W of I-75; 386-758-1310)

■ BIKE TRAILS

Suwannee River Greenway Trail is a 12-mi, 10' wide paved trail through the floodplain of the Suwannee River. The trail runs from CR 248/US 129 and ends at Ichetucknee River. The only trailhead however is at mid-point in downtown Branford with parking, picnic tables and a water fountain. Other than benches, there are no facilities along the trail. (US 129 & Owens St, Branford; 386-362-3004)

■ BOAT RAMPS

Fishing Piers: Suwannee. Parks: Osceola

Alligator Lake is an 800-acre lake with boat ramps at several locations. At the Alligator Lake Recreation Area on the NE shore, you'll find a canoe launch, ADA picnic shelters and Rr (from US 90, E on Baya Ave, S on CR 133 for 2 mi). On the NW side of the lake is a boat ramp with a fixed dock (US 441; .5 mi S of Baya Ave, E at high school). The S shore has another boat ramp and a fixed dock from which you can fish (US 441; 1.5 mi S of Baya Rd, E by the Dept of Transportation) Dawn-dusk (386-758-0525)

■ BOAT TOURS

Campgrounds: Suwannee

■ BOWLING

Lake City Bowl has bowling ball ramps. Game room; pro shop; snack bar; lounge; Rr. 11-11; Fri-Sat -12 (1995 Branford Hwy; 386-755-2206)

■ CANOEING/TUBING

Ichetucknee Springs State Park has a crystal clear river winding through at 1 mph. Near both park entrances, you can rent canoes, inner tubes and, for those who want their bottoms dry, floating islands. Staff can help with transfers and runs a free WC-accessible tram shuttle during the summer. With advance notice, staff can shuttle WC-canoeists/tubists year round and deliver your WC to the take-out you select. The tram shuttles drivers back to the various launches and shuttles parties from take-out points to parking lots. The most northern put-in is 900' below the Ichetucknee Headspring (open only Memorial Day-Labor Day); park in Canoe Launch Parking, take an unpaved road to an ADA ramp to the waterline, transfer from your WC and negotiate a small step, then transfer into your canoe/tube. The second launch, Midpoint, is 1.5 mi downstream and is very steep. Another .5 mi downstream is the first take-out (or launch, if you prefer a 1-mi trip) at Dampiers Landing, where you can disembark (or load) at a floating dock or a nearby flat limestone area. From the dock, a boardwalk and sidewalk go to the parking lot, snack bar and Rr. The final point in the park is 1 mi further downstream at South Take-Out where you disembark at a fixed dock. Here you transfer into your WC and take a steep ramp with handrails up to parking. With prior notice, park staff can help. On weekends and holidays, arrive before 10am because tubing is limited on various stretches. See Parks. Lockers. $. 8-dusk (4 mi N of Fort White, off CR 238 & SR 47; 386-497-4690)

Suwannee Canoe Outpost rents canoes for trips from 2-13 mi or 1-6 hrs along the milder sections of the Suwannee River. Guided trips can also be arranged. Staff is experienced with disabled paddlers and can choose a launch site that best suits your needs. But be aware, sites are very steep. With advance notice staff can lift you into the shuttle van and into and out of the canoe. Or, you may prefer to drive your vehicle to the put-in and ask staff to shuttle it back to the shop. You take out at the outpost, on the grounds of the Spirit of the Suwannee Music Park, where your WC will be waiting. See Performing Arts and Campgrounds. Feb-Dec Thu-Tue 9-3 (3076 95 Dr, Live Oak; off US 129, 5 mi N of I-10 & 5 mi W of I-75; 386-364-4991; 800-428-4147)

■ **FISHING PIERS**
Boat Ramps: Alligator Lake. Parks: Ichetucknee Springs, Osceola
Suwannee Lake is a 63-acre man-made lake fringed by cypress trees and abundant with largemouth bass. Catch them from two 150' piers, one designed for WC anglers. Or, launch your boat from the ramp (with no dock). Rr port-o-let. Dawn-dusk (8000 91 Rd, Live Oak; from US 90, N on CR 417, just before I-10 follow signs to boat ramp; 386-758-0525)

■ **HUNTING**
Holton Creek Wildlife Management Area is the site for several FWC Mobility-Impaired Hunts for deer, wild hogs, gray squirrel and rabbit usually in late Sep, mid-Oct, late Oct and early Nov. Mobility-Impaired Hunts for turkey are usually held in late Mar and mid-Apr. The FWC randomly selects 40 applicants for the general gun hunts and 10 for the spring turkey hunts. As of 2003, an able-bodied companion can hunt with a disabled hunter. To apply, see Hunting p 13. ATVs are prohibited here. See Campgrounds for accommodations near this remote site. (from CR 751, S on Adams Grade; S of SR 6, NW of Live Oak; 386-758-0531)
Oaks Plantation invites you to hunt - with or without a guide – and practice on a clays course. For doves, you can drive to the field to hunt. Quail hunts are accessible only if you can get into a jeep and sit on a tractor-type seat with no back or armrests; you can

hunt from the jeep. Hunt for deer by shotgun only; you can drive to the blind if you have a vehicle with a high wheelbase. Guides must accompany you while turkey hunting and you must use a shotgun. By appointment, you can use the 1.5-mi sporting clays course; you can drive over grass to the different stations. Call in advance and staff will try to accommodate your interests and any special needs; meals can be catered on request. Rr, not ADA (from US 441/41, W on CR 240 for 2 mi, S on CR 131 for 2 mi; 386-454-7466; 800-437-4441)
Suwannee River Ranch offers guided hunting year round for deer, wild boar and exotic game on 350 wooded acres. You can hunt from your vehicle or drive to one of the blinds; one has a hydraulic lift and others are on the ground. Guides will customize your hunt according to your interests and any special needs. All hunts are guaranteed. Rr, not ADA (US 27 & CR 349, Branford; 386-935-0012)

■ **MUSEUMS**
Columbia County Historical Museum is a former residence built in the 1870's and decorated with period furnishings. The front porch is ramped. Exhibits cover local history but the specialty is Civil War items. The 2nd floor is accessible only by stairs. Street parking; CRr. $D. Wed, Fri-Sat 2-5 (105 S Hernando St; 386-755-9096)

■ **PARKS**
Ichetucknee Springs State Park has 2241 acres of sandhill, hammock, floodplain and a series of springs where the main draw is canoeing or tubing (see Canoeing). The Headspring, by the park's North Entrance, has a steep stone ramp to the waterline for swimming in the 72-degree spring water. Except when the spring is too crowded with swimmers, you can fish off the stone bulwark for bass. The 3 trails are dirt and tree roots can be a challenge. Trestle Point Trail, by the canoe launch, is .75 mi

with an accessible observation deck over the river. From there, the 1.25-mi Pine Ridge Trail goes over sandhills where you encounter some sandy spots. The park may soon connect these trails to the .5-mi trail from the Midpoint tube launch to Dampiers Landing where a sidewalk leads to parking. Snack bar; ADA picnic tables; Rr. ⚥. 8-dusk (4 mi N of Fort White, off CR 238 & SR 47; 386-497-2511)

Nice Wander Trail, in the Osceola National Forest, is a favorite of birders and part of the Florida National Scenic Trail that will ultimately run 1300 mi from Florida's panhandle to the Everglades. Nice Wander trail loops 1.8 mi on hard-packed natural terrain through a glorious long-leaf pine and palmetto hammock. All-terrain WCs or ECVs may work best for the few 10'-20' sandy stretches. You can take short cuts across the loop for a 1-mi or 1.3-mi trek. The trailhead is at Olustee Battlefield, site of Florida's largest Civil War battle, with a small museum, water fountains, picnic tables and unpaved parking (with plans for pavement). (US 90, 2 mi E of Olustee)

Osceola National Forest is 200,000 acres of forest and swamps, mostly inaccessible. The visitor center, located in an old railroad depot, has exhibits about the railroad, timber and turpentine industries, a gift shop and Rr. (US 90, 14 mi E of Lake City; 386-752-2577). *Olustee Beach* is a day-use area on the S side of 1760-acre freshwater Ocean Pond (from the visitor center, N on CR 231 for .5 mi, E on FR 785 for .5 mi). Over grass is the beach and swim area. Take the interpretive boardwalk through a shady pine and cypress canopy to the lake where signs explain the history of a sawmill that operated here in the early 1900's. You'll also find a 40' ADA fishing pier and a boat ramp with a fixed dock. See Campgrounds. ADA picnic tables; grills; bathhouse; Rr. ⚥. Dawn-dusk

Stephen Foster State Folk Culture Center is an antebellum-style mansion surrounded by 247 acres of huge pines and moss-draped oaks way down upon the Suwannee River. The museum (9-5) has a 15-min video on Foster's life and animated dioramas that feature his songs such as *Oh! Susanna*. One-hr walking tours of the museum and grounds start at 9, 11, 1 and 3. The 200' carillon tower presents daily concerts. A ramp leads down to a gazebo overlooking the river. If the water level is high, you can fish near the gazebo, but otherwise the banks are too steep to get close to the water. The quiet roads here are popular for biking and, if you borrow the park's ECV, you can enjoy 6 mi of nature trails. Call 386-397-1920 for the schedule of demonstrations by craftsmen in stained glass, syrup making and more. Special events and crafts classes occur throughout the year. See Campgrounds. ECV & WC loaners; gift shop with local crafts; ADA picnic tables; Rr. ⚥. 8-dusk (US 41N, White Springs; I-75 exit 439, 3 mi E; 386-397-4331)

Suwannee River State Park is 1800 wooded acres that offer mostly views for the WC bound. From the ranger station, go across grass to a short boardwalk over earthworks, built by Rebel soldiers during the Civil War. Further along the grass another short boardwalk leads to a lovely vista where the Suwannee and Withlacoochee Rivers join. The park trails have some steep areas and are quite rough with some tree roots and sandy stretches. The banks of the river are as high as 35' precluding any fishing from a WC. Canoeing is popular here, but the slope to the launch at the boat ramp (no dock) is very steep. See Canoeing: Suwannee Canoe Outpost whose staff can help you to the ramp and aboard a canoe. ADA picnic shelter & grill by ranger station; playground on grass; Rr. ⚥. 8-dusk (20185 CR 132, 13 mi W of Live Oak; off US

90, 5 mi N of I-10; 386-362-2746)

■ **PERFORMING ARTS**

Alphonso Levy Performing Arts Center brings music, theater and dance attractions here Dec-Apr. WC seating on sides in rear; Rr (Lake City Community College, Student Way; off Rt 19; 386-752-1822)

The Spirit of Suwannee Music Park has an amphitheater (WC seating at top) and a music hall (with movable seating) that host events such as clogging and concerts from gospel, rock and folk to country, bluegrass and blues. Other events include Hot Air Balloon Festivals, giant garage sales and a Renaissance Festival. The Suwannee River Jam, held each spring and fall, features many well-known country recording artists. See Campgrounds. Rr (3076 95 Dr, Live Oak; off US 129, 5 mi

N of I-10 & 5 mi W of I-75; 386-364-1683)

■ **POOLS**

Billy Jerengin Pool has a lift (fixed seat) that is open only in summer. Bathhouse; Rr, not ADA. Hrs vary (1300 Walker St, Live Oak)

Columbia Aquatic Complex has a heated pool that is ramped into the water. Bathhouse; Rr. Feb-Nov hrs vary (602 W St John St; 386-755-8195)

■ **SHOOTING RANGES**

Hunting: Oak Plantation

■ **SHOPPING**

Antiques and collectibles can be found in shops along Marion St in Lake City and along Howard St in Live Oak. Also, Webb's Antique Mall has over 200 dealers on 50,000 sq ft. (Rt 3; US 441 & I-17; 386-758-5564)

ACCOMMODATIONS

■ **CABINS/CAMPGROUNDS**

Ocean Pond Campground is under tall pines on the NE shore of the 1760-acre pond in the Osceola National Forest. Of the 68 RV/tent sites with concrete pads, 2 have ADA picnic tables and raised ground grills; one has water/elec, the other water only. Paved roads lead to the ADA bathhouse with roll-under sinks and roll-in showers. Dense foliage lends campsites some privacy. A sidewalk goes down to a beach on the pond, but a better place to swim is a few miles away at Olustee Beach on the S shore; see Parks: Osceola. No reservations (from US 90 in Olustee, N on CR 250A for 4 mi; 386-752-2577)

The Spirit of the Suwannee Campground always has music in the air under its huge oaks drooping with Spanish moss. This 600-acre camping resort has 1 ADA cabin, campsites and plenty of recreation as well as impromptu jam sessions and a schedule of big-name entertainment; see Performing Arts. Cabin H is a ramped 1BR

unit with a full bed, full kitchen and sofa bed in the living room; linens are included. The bathroom has a raised toilet, roll-under sink and roll-in shower. Campsites include 250 RV sites with full hookups, picnic tables, some on paved pads and some with grills. The 750 tent sites, with picnic tables and some with water/elec and grills, are in primitive areas or along paved roads. ADA bathhouses in the Lake and Loop areas have raised toilets, roll-under sinks and roll-in showers. If the river isn't too low, crew can lift you from your WC into a boat seat aboard a paddlewheel boat for a 1-hr tour on the Suwannee. You can fish from a dock on Rees Lake. The boat ramp on the river has no dock. See Canoeing. Guided horseback trail rides; horseshoes; evening activities; bike rentals; putt-putt golf; playground on grass; pool; golf cart rental; country store; restaurant with Southern fare; wknd craft village (3076 95 Dr, Live Oak; off US 129, 5 mi N of I-10 & 5 mi W of I-75; 386-364-1683)

Stephen Foster State Folk Culture Center has 45 RV/tent sites on a hard-packed surface in an exquisite flat wooded area near the Suwannee River. ADA sites have water/elec, ADA picnic tables and fire rings. Sites 1-3, 16 and 29-32 are close to the bathhouse with a large stall and a raised toilet, roll-under sink and roll-in shower. See Attractions. (US 41N, White Springs; I-75 exit 439, 3 mi E; 386-397-4331)

Suwannee River State Park Campground is on level, hard-packed terrain under a thick forest of slash pines with 30 RV/tent sites that have water/elec, grills, fire rings and some ADA picnic tables. The park has plans to renovate the bathhouse to ADA standards, including roll-under sinks and roll-in showers. See Parks. (20185 CR 132, 13 mi W of Live Oak; off US 90, 5 mi N of I-10; 386-362-2746)

■ **MOTELS**

Comfort Inn has 3 ADA rooms each with a king bed (25" high/platform) and bathroom with a raised toilet, roll-under sink and step-in shower with a seat or a tub. Free brkfst; pool; laundry; tennis. $$ (4515 US 90 W; 386-755-1344)

Country Inn & Suites has 3 ADA rooms and 1 ADA suite, each with a king bed (24" high/platform), refrigerator, microwave and coffeepot. Bathrooms have roll-under sinks. The suite, #104, has a queen sofa bed and a roll-in shower with hand-held sprayer and seat; other rooms have tubs. Free brkfst; pool; laundry. $$ (1608 FL Gateway Blvd; 386-754-5944)

Holiday Inn has 4 ADA rooms each with a king bed (23" high/platform) and coffeepot. Bathrooms have raised toilets and roll-under sinks; room 156 has a roll-in shower with a hand-held sprayer and seat; others have step-in showers or tubs. Full restaurant; pool; laundry. $$ (4590 US 90 W; 386-752-3901)

Jameson Inn has 4 ADA rooms and a 2-room suite each with a king or 2 full beds (platforms). The suite has a full sofa bed, refrigerator, microwave and coffeepot. Bathrooms have raised toilets and showers with hand-held sprayers and seats; room 110 has a roll-in shower. Free brkfst; pool. $$ (1393 Commerce Blvd; 386-758-8440)

Mictrotel Inn has 4 ADA rooms each with a queen bed (platform); 2 rooms have refrigerators. Bathrooms have roll-under sinks and roll-in showers with hand-held sprayers and seats. Free brkfst; laundry. $-$$ (1395 Commerce Center Blvd; 386-755-6300)

OCALA

Citra, Dunnellon, Ocala National Forest, Silver Springs, Summerfield, Weirsdale

The Ocala region is best known for its rolling green pastures studded with championship horses. You can tour many of the horse farms that have bred some of the country's most renowned equines; Jan-May is a great time to visit because many foals are born then. You can also get in the saddle yourself at 3 local stables. Other outdoors activities await you in the vast Ocala National Forest and the area's springs, lakes and rivers.

Tourist Info

Ocala/Marion County Chamber: 110 Silver Springs Blvd, 34470; 352-629-8051
Dunnellon Area Chamber: 20500 W Pennsylvania Ave, Dunnellon, 34432; 352-489-2320

Web sites: www.ocala.cc.com; http://onf.net

Transportation

Sun Tran buses on all routes have lifts. (352-401-6999)
Marion Transit can transport folks in WCs, who cannot use the bus service, to medical appointments and shopping. Call for the schedule for your area and, if you cannot transfer, ask for a lift-equipped van. Wkdy (352-622-2450)

ACTIVITIES

■ ATTRACTIONS
Don Garlits Museum of Drag Racing
traces the history of the sport through a collection of Big Daddy Garlits' cars and memorabilia. For an extra fee, you can visit the antique car museum. Gift shop; Rr. $. 9-5 (13700 SW 16 Ave; 352-245-8661)
Silver Springs is a 350-acre nature park where the famous glass-bottom boats and 2 other boat rides are inaccessible. Staff cannot help with transfers, but with some mobility and friends, you may be able to negotiate the 2 steps into the boats. Animal shows and exhibits include panthers, bears and gator feedings. A boardwalk leads through gator lagoon and sidewalks lead through the botanical gardens. The small petting zoo is on hard-packed dirt. Special events include live concerts with Nashville's biggest names. WC & ECV rentals; gift shop; snack bar; Rr. $/WC riders free. 10-5 (5656 E Silver Springs Blvd, Silver Springs; 352-236-2121)

■ BIKE TRAIL
Marshall Swamp Trail is a 5-mi paved, slightly rolling trail through forest and flatlands, which connects a series of looped trails. The following trailheads have ADA picnic shelters, water fountains, parking and Rr: Base Line Rd (SR 35 & CR 464), Marshal Swamp (8300 SE CR 314) and Banyan Rd. (352-236-7111)

■ BOAT RAMPS
Moorehead Park has a ramp and floating dock on the 2800-acre Lake Kerr. ADA picnic table; Rr. Dawn-dusk (Ocala Nat'l Forest, NE 203 Rd; off FR 88 between CR 314 & CR 316; 352-236-7111)
Moss Bluff Park has a ramp, floating dock and a 50' ADA T-shaped fishing pier on the Ocklawaha River. ADA picnic shelter; Rr. Dawn-dusk (CR 464 & SE 96 St; 352-236-7111)
South Lake Dorr is 1800 acres and has a ramp and floating dock. (Ocala Nat'l Forest, CR 8776; off SR 19, just S of main entrance to the lake)

■ BOAT RENTALS
Angler's Resort rents pontoon and 14' flat-bottom fishing boats for the Withlacoochee and Rainbow Rivers. The pontoon boats (30" entry) can carry up to 12 people; the flats boats have 6hp motors and live wells. Staff can help you down the hill to the dock and, with advance notice, will help lift you into the swivel seat on a 14' boat. 2-hr minimum; bait shop (12189 S Williams St, Dunnellon; 352-489-2397)
Salt Springs Run Marina rents pontoon boats (31" entry) for 8-12 adults for half/full days; staff can help you board. The 4.5-mi run leads to the 46,000-acre Lake George. Fixed dock; snack bar; bait shop nearby; Rr along a gravel path. Dusk-dawn (25711 NE 134 Pl, Salt Springs, Ocala Nat'l Forest; 352-685-2255)

■ BOAT TOURS
Fishing Charters: Capt Tom's
Florida Water Safari makes all-day narrated trips to Silver Springs. You will go through the Moss Buff Lock that lowers the boat 22' on the Oklawaha River. Wildlife is plentiful. Ask for the accessible 14-person pontoon boat and either order lunch in

advance or bring your own. Rr stops along the way. 9-4:30 (Nelson Fish Camp, SR 42; 5 mi E of Weirsdale; 352-360-8130; 407-298-8011)

■ **BOWLING**

Galaxy Lanes have ramped lanes and bowling ball ramps. Snack bar; Rr. 9am-11pm (1818 SW 17 St; 352-732-0300)

Galaxy Lanes East has ramped lanes and bowling ball ramps. Snack bar; game room; pool table; Rr. 9am-11pm (3225 SE Maricamp Rd; 352-694-1111)

■ **CANOEING/KAYAKING/TUBING**

Alexander Springs Area, of the Ocala National Forest, rents canoes for the slow-moving creek where you can paddle back to the put-in from wherever you choose or take the full 7-mi trip (4-5 hrs) downstream to a take-out near FR 552. Staff can help with transfers into canoes and into the shuttle van at the take-out; or a companion can shuttle back to the launch and return with your WC and vehicle. Picnic tables; Rr (SR 445, Ocala Nat'l Forest; 5 mi N of SR 19; 352-669-3522)

Dragon Fly Water Sports rents tubes, canoes, inflatable boats and a variety of kayaks for the mellow Rainbow River. You can drive your vehicle to the put-in and then, with advance notice, staff will drive it to the take-out but staff cannot help with transfers. Bring drinks and snacks packed in thermoses and non-disposable plastics, as no disposable items are allowed on the river. Depending on your paddling and dawdling, the trip takes about 4 hrs. Reservations. May-Sep 9-5; Oct-Apr hrs vary (CR 484, Dunnellon; I-75 exit 341, W roughly 22 mi; 352-489-3046; 800-919-9579)

Florida Pack & Paddle offers guided, customized, 2-hr to full-day canoe trips on various lakes and rivers, including those in the Ocala National Forest. If you choose a river trip, staff can shuttle your car to the take-out. Staff can determine the best sites to accommodate different levels of abil-

ity and can help with transfers. (352-669-0008; 800-297-8811)

Juniper Springs Run rents canoes for the 7-mi trip (4-5 hrs) through pristine forest to Juniper Wayside Park (Rr Port-o-let). A sidewalk leads to two 8" high, broad steps to the launch. The take-out is specially designed for WC paddlers to transfer out of the canoe and take a tiered ramp with a railing up to the parking lot. Concession staff can help with transfers and can lift you into the shuttle van at the take-out; or a companion can shuttle back to the launch and return with your WC and vehicle. Bring drinks and food in reusable containers. Reservations (SR 40; 22 mi E of Silver Springs, Ocala Nat'l Forest; 352-625-3147)

KP Hole is a 4.3-acre county park with tube and canoe rentals, a snack bar, ADA picnic tables, outdoor shower and paved paths. The launch is a ramp on the Rainbow River. If you cannot transfer into the shuttle, you can paddle upstream and float back to the put-in. Bring drinks and snacks in thermoses and non-disposable plastics, as no disposable items are allowed on the river. Rr. 8am-closing varies (9335 SW 190 Avenue Rd, Dunnellon; I-75 exit 341, W on CR 484 for 23 mi, N on US 41 for 2.5 mi, then E; 352-489-3055)

■ **FISHING CHARTERS**

Angler's Resort can set you up with a guide for the Withlacoochee River, the state's top river for largemouth bass. Staff can help you down the hill to the dock and, with advance notice, help lift you into the seat of a 21' bass boat. (12189 S Williams St, Dunnellon; 352-489-2397)

Capt Tom's Custom Charters offers 3-, 4 1/2- and 8-hr guided trips on the Ocklawaha and Silver Rivers. Along with or instead of fishing, you can take a nature tour on the pontoon boat. Roll aboard from a ramp on the fixed dock. (Ray Wayside Park, SR 40; 3 mi E of Silver Spring; 352-546-4823)

■ **FISHING PIERS**
Boat Ramps: Moss Bluff Park

Fore Lake is a remote 20-acre lake where you can take a rough, grassy path 40' from a clay parking lot to a 60' L-shaped pier. (CR 314; N of SR 40, Ocala Nat'l Forest)

Grasshopper Lake has a 30' T-shaped pier over its 300 watery acres. A 30' rough, grassy path leads from the clay parking lot to the pier. (SR 19; N of SR 445 A, Ocala Nat'l Forest)

Lake Eaton is 200 acres in size. A sidewalk goes from a clay parking lot to a 100'pier. (FR 96A, Ocala Nat'l Forest; from SR 40, N 5 mi on CR 314A then E on FR 96 and N on FR 96A)

Orange Lake has a 40' T-shaped ADA pier. A sidewalk leads to the pier from paved HC parking spots in an otherwise sandy lot. 7am-9pm (Heagy-Burry Park, Orange Lake; E off US 441 onto NW 191 Pl, proceed to end)

Rodman Recreation Area, just N of the Ocala National Forest, has a 30' T-shaped pier on the Oklawaha River side of the Rodman Dam. Picnic tables; Rr port-a-let. (Kirkpatrick Rd; from SR 19, W on SR 310 2 mi to pier; 904-972-1654)

■ **HORSEBACK RIDING**
Exceptional Equestrians at Ride Right, member of the NARHA, offers long-term hippotherapy, therapeutic and recreational riding for folks with a range of disabilities. Staff must evaluate riders. The mounting deck is ramped and staff can lift you into a special saddle. By appointment, one-time riders are welcome. (14776 N Magnolia Ave, Citra; 352-595-1927)

Marion Therapeutic Riding, member of the NARHA, offers pleasure riding and lessons. Staff must evaluate riders; a doctor's permission may be necessary. Ramps are used to board horses. Or, you may prefer a horse-drawn carriage, also boarded by ramp; your WC is locked down and an able-bodied driver accompanies you. (SW 17 St; behind the Hillcrest School; 352-624-4240)

Young's Paso Finos gives lessons and trail rides and can accommodate riders with certain mobility impairments. Staff can lift you onto the horse and can ride behind you on the horse to give extra support and stability. These horses are very smooth-gaited. Make arrangements with Betty. (8075 NW SR 326; 352-867-5305)

■ **MISC FUN**
Senior Center offers bingo, cards, shuffleboard, woodcarving and more. Call for a schedule. Rr. Wkdy 9-5 (830 NE 8 Ave; 352-629-8545)

Therapeutic Recreation sponsors activities, mostly for kids with special needs, such as T-ball, horseback riding and exercise classes. Special events include Fishing Derbies. Call for a schedule and locations. (352-401-3916)

■ **MUSEUMS**
Appleton Museum of Art houses antiquities, paintings, sculptures, furniture and decorative arts. Docent-led tours are offered Tue-Fri at 1:15. Gift shop; Rr. $. Tue-Sat 10-4:30; Sun 1-5 (4333 NE Silver Springs Blvd; 352-236-7100)

■ **PARI-MUTUELS**
Jai Alai features live jai alai Sep-Nov and simulcasts all year. WC seating on lower & top levels; restaurant; Rr. Wed-Mon hrs vary (4601 NW CR 318, Orange Lake; 352-591-2345)

■ **PARKS**
Ocala National Forest has 383,000 acres of semi-tropical forest with lakes, rivers, trails and campgrounds. Public roads connect the dispersed recreation areas described below. The Florida National Scenic Trail winds 67 mi over rolling terrain past day-use and camp facilities. The 24" wide trail gets sandy during dry seasons (winter-spring); it is maintained but, particularly in the 7-mi Juniper Prairie Wilderness stretch, you may encounter logs; ask rangers about potential barriers on different stretches. You pay *user fees* to get into specific day use

and camping areas; Golden Access/ Age discounts apply. If you plan on spending much time here, or visiting different areas within the Forest, consider buying the map at the Ocklawaha Visitor Center (CR 315 at SR 40; 352-236-0288). Day use areas are generally open 8-8. *Alexander Springs Area* has sidewalks from parking to a snack bar and Rr. Take the bumpy sidewalk to a beach around a natural pool with lifeguards during the summer. On the other side of the beach a boardwalk leads .5 mi along the spring with 2 overlooks where you can fish. The Timucuan Trail includes a .5-mi boardwalk with good birding in the mornings Oct-May. The 22-mi Paisley Woods Bike Trail has long stretches of deep sand. Ranger talks occur at an amphitheater on summer evenings. See Canoeing and Campgrounds. (SR 445; 6 mi NE of SR 19; 352-669-3522) *The Pittman Visitors Center* has steps. (7 mi S of Alexander Springs on SR 19; 352-669-7495) *Juniper Springs Area* has 1.5 mi of hiking trails and a 1-mi interpretive trail along Juniper Creek that is wide and hard-packed sand; both have some tree roots. Ranger talks occur on summer weekends at a ramped mill house. Picnic shelters & grills near a swimming pool; snack bar; small store; Rr. See Canoeing. (SR 40; 22 mi E of Silver Springs; 352-625-3147) *Ocklawaha Visitor Center*, at the W entrance, has a bookstore, small wildlife display and Rr. (CR 315 at SR 40; 352-236-0288) *Salt Springs Area* has a visitors center with a pioneer life display and Rr. A sidewalk leads from parking to a snack bar, ADA picnic table, grill and a small beach at the spring with lifeguards in the summer. A sidewalk spans the spring run to a nearby marina where you can fish off grassy banks or rent pontoon boats for freshwater fishing. See Boat Rentals and Campgrounds. (SR 19; just N of SR 314; 352-685-3070)

Rainbow Springs State Park was a tourist attraction from the 1930's to 1970's and is still popular for its exquisite azalea gardens (in bloom late Feb-Mar), 3 waterfalls and a spring all in a breathtakingly beautiful setting. After a 1-mi drive into the grounds, you park and take a 500' sidewalk up to the entrance. The park has mostly paved and some brick paths, but it is very hilly so bring either an ECV or a hearty friend. The picnic area is on a sloped, grassy bowl overlooking the spring; at the top are ADA shelters and grills. Ask at the entrance so staff can unlock a gate for you to drive closer to the shelters. Down a steep sidewalk to the springhead is a dock with a ladder where swimmers and snorkelers jump 6' into the water; you can also get out of the water at a level spot around the corner from the dock. The park rents canoes and solo/tandem sit-in kayaks for the Rainbow River. You can roll to the water's edge at the launch site and with advance notice, staff may be able to help you board. The river is mild enough that you can paddle back to the put-in. The campground is 6 mi N from the dayuse area; see Campgrounds. Rr. $. 8am-dusk (19158 SW 81 Place Rd, Dunnellon; off US 41, 3 mi N of Dunnellon; 352-489-8503)

Silver River State Park, between the attraction at Silver Springs and the Ocala National Forest, is a 5000-acre mix of forest and marsh with a 4-mi stretch along the fast-moving Silver River and a 3-mi stretch along the Oklawaha River. This is a beautiful spot for canoeing, but you must bring your own canoe and carry it a .5 mi from parking along the Silver River Trail to the level sandy launch. Call ahead and rangers may be able to help you transfer for a 2.5-mi downstream trip to Wayside Park off SR 40 (take the canal to the left just before the Silver River feeds into the Oklawaha). The hard-packed Silver River Trail runs about 1 mi along the river. The 3-mi

Sinkhole Trail has soft sand in many areas. On weekends from 9-5, you can visit the Marion County Schools' museum (9-5), with displays of the local history and ecosystems, and Cracker Village. The Village is on grass with some sandy areas and some accessible buildings. Cracker Days occur in Nov when costumed staff demonstrates life in Florida's pioneer days. See Campgrounds. ADA picnic shelter near museum; Rr. $. 8-dusk (1425 NE SR 35; 1 mi S of SR 40; 352-236-7148)

■ **PERFORMING ARTS**

Central Florida Symphony performs classical and pop concerts in the community college's Fine Arts Auditorium. WC seating is across the front and in the aisles. Use the parking lot beyond the guard station to get closest to the WC entrance on the side of the building. Rr. Oct-Apr (3001 SW College Rd; 352- 687-3696)

Ocala Civic Theater is a community group that performs musicals and classics. WC seating in rear; Rr. Sep-May (4337 E Silver Springs Blvd; 352-236-2851)

■ **SHOOTING RANGES**

Ocala National Forest has an unstaffed range for rifles, pistols and shotguns. A sidewalk leads to the shooting shed but you must traverse grass to attach your targets. Thu-Tues dawn-dusk (FR 88, Ocala Nat'l Forest; turn N off SR 40)

■ **SHOPPING**

Antiques: Ocala, Dunnellon and McIntosh have historic downtowns with plenty of antique and collectibles.

Flea Markets: Flea Market of Marion has over 1000 booths with both new and old merchandise. The terrain is flat; roads are paved; parking is on grass, with drop-off areas by entrances. Auctions are held every other Sun at 2:30. Restaurants; Rr. Wknd 8-4 (12888 S US 441; 3 mi S of Belleview; 352-245-6766)

■ **SPECTATOR SPORTS**

Auto Racing Ocala Speedway races primarily late model, modified 4-cylinder bombers, hobby and pure stock cars. The stands are ramped; WC seating is on the straightaway. Snack bar; Rr-port-a-let. Mar-Oct Sat 6:30 (9050 NW Gainesville Rd; 352-622-9400)

■ **TOURS**

Double Diamond Horse Farm allows you to drive through the grounds; call beforehand because the office is inaccessible. Wkdy 1-4 (899 SW 85 Ave; 352-237-3834)

Emergency-One conducts 75-min guided tours of the fire truck factory. Be aware, tours are strenuous and can be very noisy and hot as you proceed almost 2 mi in and out of buildings. You may also need to circumvent obstacles on the floor, such as air hoses. Children under 6 are not allowed on the full tour but can take an abbreviated tour that includes sitting in a fire truck and testing its lights and sirens. $. Wkdy 8:30, 11 & 1 (1601 SW 37 Ave; 352-237-1122)

Fiddle Leaf Horse Farm is open for guests on most Mon evenings to watch drill team practice. Call ahead. 6:30-8:00 (17401 SE CR 475, Summerfield; 352-245-4715)

Marion County Horse Farms offers 2-hr guided tours. Depending on the time of year, you may attend a thoroughbred auction, visit a farm or a training facility specializing in racehorses. You can follow the tour in your own car to the different facilities. When making reservations, let Lorna Hagmeyer know your abilities so she can determine the tour to best accommodate you. Tours depart weekdays from the Ocala Breeder/ Sales Co. $ (1701 SW 60; 352-351-5524)

Ocala Breeder/Sales Co welcomes the public to watch horses training around the track. 6am-10am (1701 SW 60; 352-237-2154)

Ocala Stud Farm, from Sep-Jun, allows you to watch early morning horse training sessions 7-10:30 or early afternoon horse swimming lessons 2-

3:30. (SW 27 Ave; 352-237-2171)
Young's Paso Finos offers 30-min to 1-hr guided tours through paved horse barns. By appointment. $. Mon-Sat 8-3 (8075 NW SR 326; 352-237-2154)

ACCOMMODATIONS

■ **B&B/INNS**

Heritage Country Inn is a 1-story B&B with old-fashion charm. Six WC-friendly rooms offer a choice of king, queen or 2 full beds (24" high/open frames) and fireplaces (for winter use!). Private bathrooms have tubs or roll-in showers with hand-held spray-ers and seats. Each room has a Jacuzzi with grab bars into which you may be able to transfer from a 6" wide ledge, 22" off the floor. The beautifully land-scaped, 1-acre grounds include a large gazebo for socializing in the center courtyard. Full 3-course breakfasts are served in the dining room; with ad-vance notice, special dietary needs can be accommodated. $$ (14343 W SR 40; 352-489-0023; 888-240-2233)

Shamrock Thistle & Crown is an 1887 B&B with a large, newly renovated, ADA guestroom in a Victorian cottage and a room in the ramped main house that may work for guests with some mobility. The ADA unit has vaulted ceil-ings, a fireplace, king bed (35" high/open frame), sofa bed, refrigerator and coffeepot. The private bathroom has a raised toilet, roll-under sink and step-in shower with a seat. Outside on the deck is a Jacuzzi with a grab bar that has a 6" wide ledge and is 1' off the floor. The ground floor room in the main house has a 28" entry, a queen bed (32" high/open frame) and a bathroom with a 22" wide door, grab bars, raised toilet and a tub. Full breakfast is served in the din-ing room or can be delivered to your room. The large porches are ramped and delightful spots to enjoy the peace-ful 3-acre grounds. $$-$$$ (12971 SE CR 42, Weirsdale; 3 mi E of US 27; 352-821-1887; 800-425-2763)

■ **CABINS/CAMPGROUNDS**

Angler's Resort, on the Withlacoochee River, has a WC-friendly efficiency with 2BRs; one bedroom has a queen bed, the other has 2 twin beds. The unit has a full kitchen, sofa bed in the living room and bathroom with wide doors and a ramp into the shower. Roll down a hill in back to a dock where you can fish, rent a fishing boat or board a charter with a local guide. See Boat Rentals. (12189 S Williams St; 352-489-2397)

Ocala National Forest has, in addition to the campgrounds described below, numerous primitive camp areas to which you can drive and where the terrain is flat and cleared. Contact any of the 3 visitors centers listed under Parks. *Alexander Springs* campsite #49 in Loop C has an ADA picnic table, raised fire pit and nearby ADA bathhouse with raised toilets, roll-un-der sinks and roll-in showers. See Parks and Canoeing. Amphitheater (E on SR 445 off SR 19, Ocala Nat'l For-est; 352-669-3522) *Lake Dorr* has an ADA 2BR cabin on the lake with a boat ramp and fixed dock that can be used for fishing. The cabin has a queen and 2 bunks along with 2 full sofa beds, a full kitchen and bathroom with a roll-under sink and roll-in shower. Bring your fishing pole and linens. (SR 19, Ocala Nat'l Forest; N of Altoona; 352-669-3153) *Salt Springs* has 162 tent/RV sites on paved or grassy terrain, 106 with full hookups and all with ADA tables and grills. The bathhouse has roll-under sinks and roll-in showers. Sites 11, 12, 18, 19, 44, 45, 55 and 56 and primitive site #128 have short grassy paths to the bath-house. (SR 19, Ocala Nat'l Forest; just N of SR 314; 352-685-2048)

Rainbow Springs State Park camp-ground is 6 mi from the very beautiful day-use area. The campsites by the Rainbow River are heavily wooded; campsites in the field have no shade. The terrain is hard packed, sidewalks are plentiful and roads are hard-packed, crushed limestone. All 105 RV/tent sites have water/elec, picnic tables and fire rings; 40 also have sewer hookups. Sites #10, 14, 37, 43, 81 and 82 have partial concrete pads and are close to both the picnic area along the river (with HC parking and ADA picnic tables) and to the ADA bathhouse with roll-in showers. During severe droughts the park issues a burn ban during which you must use your own gas grill. Campers can fish off the fixed dock and use the unpaved canoe launch. Long-term winter campers organize various social activities. See Parks. Pool; laundry; camp store (18185 SW 94 St, Dunnellon; off SW 180 Avenue St, 2 mi N of CR 484; 352-489-5201)

Silver River State Park has 59 RV/tent sites on level limerock all with water/elec, ADA picnic tables, grills and fire pits. During severe droughts the park issues a burn ban during which you must use your own gas grill. As a camper, you receive a key to the unisex ADA bathhouse with a raised toilet, roll-under sink and roll-in shower with a seat. Sites 10, 12, 13, 40-42 are closest to the bathhouse. The loop roads in the campground are paved. See Parks. (1425 NE 58 Ave; 352-236-7148)

■ **MOTELS**

Courtyard by Marriott has 2 ADA rooms with a king or 2 full beds (24"/open frames), a queen sofa bed, microwave (on request) and coffeepot.

Bathrooms have raised toilets, roll-under sinks, step-in showers with hand-held sprayers and seats. Pool; laundry; marina; lounge; full restaurant. $$ (3712 SW 38 Ave; 352-237-8000)

Fairfield has 5 ADA rooms with a king or 2 full beds (21"/platforms). Bathrooms have roll-under sinks; room 102 has a roll-in shower with a hand-held sprayer and seat; others have tubs. Free brkfst; pool; laundry. $-$$ (4101 SW 38 Ct; 352-861-8400)

Hilton is located on 14 wooded acres and has 4 ADA rooms each with a king bed (open frame), coffeepot and on request, a refrigerator and microwave. Bathrooms have raised toilets, roll-under sinks and tubs with hand-held sprayers and seats. Pool; lounge; full restaurant. $$-$$$ (3600 SW 36 Ave; 352-854-1400)

Holiday Inn has an ADA room with a king bed (24" high/open frame) and a bathroom with a raised toilet, roll-under sink and tub with a hand-held sprayer and seat. Full restaurant; pool. $$ (5751 E Silver Springs Blvd/E Hwy 40, Silver Springs; 352-236-2575)

Holiday Inn Express has 3 ADA rooms each with a king bed (22" high/platform) and bathroom with a raised toilet, roll-under sink and roll-in shower with a hand-held sprayer and seat. Free brkfst; pool; laundry. $$ (1212 S Pine Ave; 352-629-7300)

La Quinta Inn has 7 ADA rooms with a king or 2 full beds (24" high/open frames), refrigerators and microwaves. Bathrooms have raised toilets, roll-under sinks, tubs or roll-in showers with hand-held sprayers and seats. Free brkfst; pool. $$ (3530 SW 36 Ave; 352-861-1137)

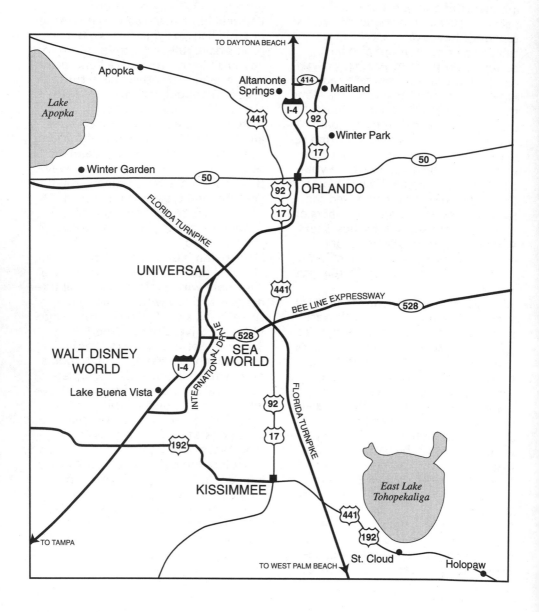

ORLANDO

KISSIMMEE
Lake Buena Vista, St Cloud

Since 1971 when the Mouse moved into the neighborhood, Kissimmee has grown beyond citrus and snowbirds into an entertainment mecca in its own right. Modest to extravagant hotels, phantasmagoric dinner shows and exciting tourist attractions line the two main thoroughfares here. US 192 (Irlo Bronson Memorial Highway) links Kissimmee to Walt Disney World. I-4 links Kissimmee to downtown Orlando, 15 miles NE. Not far from the mouse's shadows, you can also find plenty of cabins, camping and outdoors fun on beautiful, even remote lakes.

Tourist Info
Kissimmee/St Cloud Visitors Bureau: 1925 US 192, 34742; 407-847-5000; 800-327-9159/831-1844
Web sites: www.floridakiss.com

Transportation
See Orlando.

ACTIVITIES

■ **ATTRACTIONS**
Forever Florida is a 4500-acre private preserve that includes a working cattle ranch and pristine prairies and hammocks. Elevated swamp buggies offer 90-min tours (at 10 and 1) and 2 1/2-hr tours during which you are likely to see turkeys, eagles and sandhill cranes; call ahead to reserve the buggy with a WC lift. Picnic shelter; gift shop; restaurant. Mon-Thu 8-5; Fri-Sun -9 (US 441/SR 15; 7.5 mi S of Holopaw; 407-957-9794; 888-957-9794)

Jungleland has 300 hundred exotic animals in this 7-acre wildlife park and petting zoo. Daily shows feature gators, large cats and birds. The .5-mi path around the zoo is hard-packed sand.

WC loaners; CRr. $. 9-6 (4580 W US 192; 407-396-1012)

Medieval Life is a 12-cottage village from the Dark Ages where costumed artisans use methods, materials and tools of the period. Check out the dungeon and torture chamber. Most paths are paved but some are cobblestone or hard-packed dirt. Visit the village only or try the dinner show (see Dinner Theater) that includes entry to the village. Rr. $. 4-8pm (4510 W US 192; 407-396-1518; 800-229-8300)

Reptile World Serpentarium is actually a producer of snake venom for biomedical research but the public is welcome to learn about the program and reptiles in general. Inside a ramped building is a 200' display where some 60 species are housed. Paved paths lead to outside colonies of iguanas, gators and turtles. In a covered amphitheater, staff explains and demonstrates various aspect of the venomous snake program at noon and 3; WC seating is up front by glass panels that protect the audience. Gift shop. $. Oct- Aug Tue-Sun 9-5:30 (5705 E US 192, St Cloud; 407-892-6905)

Splendid China transports you 10,000 mi to China at a fraction of the cost of airfare. Experience 5000 yrs of Chinese culture through 60 fabulous, hand-carved miniature reproductions of its most historic landmarks, including the Great Wall and the Forbidden City. After a film on the construction of the exhibits, roll along paved, level paths to each exhibit. You can see all but 2 exhibits if you can transfer into a golf cart for a 1-hr tour; extra charge. Shows feature a variety of music and dance, including a spectacular evening (6-7:30pm) acrobatic show at the Golden Peacock Theater (that you can attend without paying park admission). A cafeteria and fine restaurant offer cuisine from different regions within China and can be entered without paying park admission. Rr. $. 9:30am-closing varies (3000 Splendid China Blvd; I-4 exit 64B; 407-396-7111; 800-244-6226)

Warbird Adventures, next to the Flying Tigers Warbird Air Museum (see Museums), is where you can fly a T-6 Fighter-Trainer from WWII. Inside the hangar, staff lifts you (200-lb limit) into the pilot's seat in the front cockpit. Your instructor handles take off and landing from the rear cockpit and you do the rest of the flying, including, if you choose, aerobatic loops and rolls. If you can't grasp the control stick, you can simply enjoy an exciting flight. Choose from different flights and options, including a still photo and an in-flight video. Rr at Museum (233 N Hoagland Blvd; off US 192; 407-870-7366; 800-386-1593)

World of Orchids has an indoor rain forest full of orchids, other lush vegetation, waterfalls, unusual birds and goldfish ponds. The entrance to the building has a slight slope but the paths inside are flat and paved. Look for colorful Indonesian squirrels; get gardening tips from horticulturists. The .5-acre grounds have an elevated 900' boardwalk through wetlands. Rr. Tue-Sun 9:30-4:30; closed last 2 wks in Jul (2501 Old Lake Wilson Rd; I-4 exit 25B, 2 mi W on US 192; 407-396-1887)

■ **BIKING**
Parks: Lakefront. Campgrounds: Merry 'D' Sanctuary

■ **BOAT RAMPS**
Parks: Lakefront

Alligator Lake, 3400 acres in itself, leads into a chain of 5 other lakes that range from fairly developed to fairly remote. A public boat ramp, #C33, is next to a floating dock. (CR 534/Hickory Tree Rd; off US 192, 5 mi SE of St Cloud; 352-732-1230)

Lake Jackson has a ramp with a floating dock in a very remote area. $ (Three Lakes Wildlife Management Area; 13.5 mi S of Holopaw on 441, E on Canoe Creek Rd to 2nd entrance; 352-732-1225)

Southport Park has a boat ramp, floating dock and fishing docks on W Lake Toho's S shore. Grass/dirt parking; bait/

snack shop (2001 Southport Rd; E of SR 231, 20 mi S of Kissimmee; 407-933-5822)

■ **BOAT RENTALS**

Airboat Rentals rents airboats, canoes and electric boats by the hour to catch sight of gators, otters and waterfowl. On the airboat take a 3-mi round trip through Cypress Swamp; on an electric boat or canoe, enjoy Shingle Creek. Roll onto the dock; staff can lift you from your WC into either boat. To board the canoe, roll down a steep sandy incline to the water's edge and staff can lift you aboard. The airboat bench seats 4 adults; only the driver's seat has back support but if you don't mind a limited view, you can sit on the floor with cushions for support. The electric boat, a conventional boat with a small trolling motor, has 6-person bench seats with backs. CRr (4266 W US 192; .5 mi E of Medieval Times; 407-847-3672)

■ **BOAT TOURS**

Aquatic Wonders offers 2-hr narrated tours for 6 on a 30' pontoon boat through the 22,000-acre Lake Tohopekeliga. During the day, try an Eagle Watch or a history tour. Summer evenings seek gators and winter evenings enjoy StarLight Wonders. There's also a 3-hr ecology tour when you help test water samples and explore the catch from a drag net. With reservations, you can roll aboard from the Kissimmee Marina next to the tour dock. Rr at marina. Schedule varies (Big Toho Marina, 101 Lakeshore Blvd; 407-846-2814)

Boggy Creek Airboat Rides makes 1/2-hr trips during the day and, by reservation, 1-hr trips at night on airboats at 2 wilderness locations. Trips from East Lake Fish Camp tour Boggy Creek and East Lake Toho; staff can lift you in your WC down 3 steps to a floating dock, then into a bench seat with a back. Trips from Southport Park tour West Lake Toho where you can roll over grass and up the ramped floating dock where staff lifts you into a bench

seat with a back. 9-5:30 (East Lake Fish Camp, 3702 Big Bass Rd; S off Boggy Creek Rd after Hwy 436; 407-344-9550. Southport Park, 2001 Southport Rd; I-4 exit 25A, E 3 mi to Poinciana Blvd, S for 19 mi; 407-933-4337)

■ **CANOEING**

Boat Rentals: Airboat

■ **DINNER THEATERS**

Arabian Nights is an equestrian show featuring the Royal Lipizzaner Stallions and their equine friends along with a prime rib feast. WC seating is on the ground floor at each corner of the arena. Rr. Doors open for a cash bar and a singer 90 min before show time; show times vary from 7:30-8:30pm (6225 US 192; 407-239-9223; 800-553-6116)

Capone's Dinner Show presents Broadway-style dance, comedy and suspense while you enjoy an all-you-can-eat buffet of mostly Italian fare. WC seating on ground floor; Rr. 7:30pm (4740 US 192; 407-397-2378; 800-220-8428)

Medieval Times regales you with knights, jousts, sword fights and of course, damsels not-so-distressed, while you feast on BBQ ribs and chicken. WC accessible tables are located at the end of the oval arena. Come 1 hr before the show to tour Medieval Life (see Attractions above). Rr. 1 or more shows nightly, usually 8 or 8:30 (4510 US 192; 407-239-0214; 800-229-8300)

■ **FISHING CHARTERS**

A #1 Bass Guide Service has half/full-day or night charters on fully rigged bass boats at a variety of lakes within a 60-mi radius. With advance notice, Capt Pete can get help to lift you from your WC onto a boat seat. The capt can meet you at your hotel or an accessible dock near where fish are running. (352-394-3660; 800-707-5463)

Aquatic Wonders offers half/full day charters on beautiful Lake Tohopekaliga for bass, blue gill and speckled perch. Roll aboard the 30' pontoon boat from the Kissimmee Park Marina next door to the Aquatic Wonders dock. See Boat Tours. Portable commode onboard (Big Toho Marina, 101 Lakeshore Blvd; 407-846-2814)

■ **FISHING PIERS**
Parks: Lakefront. Boat Ramps: Southport

■ **HUNTING**
Three Lakes Wildlife Management Area is the site for an FWC Mobility-Impaired Hunt, usually in early Nov, for wild hogs, deer and small game. FWC notifies the 150 applicants randomly selected for this hunt. To apply, see Hunting p 13. Vehicles, including ATVs, are allowed off road during the MI Hunt. (13 1/2 mi S of Holopaw on US 441, E on Canoe Creek Rd; 352-732-1225)

■ **MUSEUMS**
Flying Tigers Warbird Restoration Museum is a working museum where WWII vintage planes are restored. On a 1-hr guided tour through a hangar and PX, you can watch mechanics work on planes and you can browse exhibits of WW II memorabilia and armament. Try flying a T-6/SNJ at Warbird Adventures; see Attractions. Find vintage items, from authentic armament and uniforms to traditional souvenirs, at the gift shop. Sign up for a weeklong class on restoration of vintage aircraft. Picnic tables under tiki huts; Rr. $. 9-5:30; Sun 9-5 (Kissimmee Arprt, 231 N Hoagland Blvd; off US 192; 407-933-1942)

■ **PARKS**
Lakefront Park stretches along the N shore of the 22,000-acre Lake Tohopekeliga. The Toho Marina has boat ramps and fixed docks. The 100' T-shaped Brinson Fishing Pier, equipped with fish-attracters, is lighted and open 24 hrs. A shaded playground has an ADA swing. A paved trail, with ADA water fountains along the lakefront, winds from the boat basin almost 5 mi through residential areas to St Cloud. Special events, from fishing tournaments to outdoor concerts, occur frequently; call 407-933-8368. Bait shop nearby; ADA picnic shelter; Rr. Dawn-

dusk (100 Lake Shore Blvd; 407-847-2388; marina 407-846-2124)

Osceola Schools Environmental Study Center has an 1800' raised boardwalk through a cypress swamp with abundant wildlife and osprey nests. The visitor center has displays of local wildlife, including panthers and black bears. CRr. Sat 10-5; Sun 12-5 (4300 Poinciana Blvd; 407-870-0551)

■ **PERFORMING ARTS**
Osceola Center for the Arts is home to a community troupe that presents mostly Broadway musicals and comedies. Visiting groups also perform here. Ramps are at either side of the main entrance; WC seating is in the rear of this small theater. Sep-Jul (2411 E US 192; 407-846-6257)

■ **SHOPPING**
Antiques: St Cloud has a 10-block historic district along New York Ave with plenty of antique stores.
Boutiques: Old Town is like stepping onto Main St in the 50's with curb cuts added! Enjoy 70+ shops, restaurants and, for the able-bodied, amusement rides. Sat night classic cars cruise the brick streets. (5770 W US 192; 407-396-4888; 800-843-4202)
Farmers & Flea Markets: Downtown Farmers Market occurs every Thu morning (7-2) in the Kissimmee Civic Center parking lot. Rr (407-846-2488). Osceola Flea Market has 900 booths of antiques, collectibles and new merchandise. Most are under cover on concrete; a garage sale is on grass. WC rentals; restaurant; Rr. Fri-Sun 8-5 (2801 E US 192; 407-846-2811)
Malls: Lake Buena Vista Factory Stores (SR 535/Apopka Vineland Rd at Poinciana Blvd)
Specialty: Shell World is the next best thing to the beach. (4727 W US 192; 407-396-9000)

■ **SPECTATOR SPORTS**
Baseball Houston Astros have spring training in Mar at the Osceola County Stadium. Ramps lead to WC seating (not covered) behind the box seats by

1st and 3rd. Rr. $. Schedule varies (1000 Bill Beck Blvd; I- 4 exit 65; 407-933-5500)

Rodeo, on Fri nights from Jan-Nov, features calf roping, bareback riding, steer wrestling, team roping, barrel racing and bull riding. The arena is outdoors; seating is covered. WC seating is ramped to a raised platform for a good view from the center. Rr. $. 8-10pm (Kissimmee Sports Arena, 958 S Hoagland Blvd; 407-933-0020)

■ **TOURS**

Attractions: Forever Florida

Green Meadows Farm offers tours of this 40-acre working farm where you can try chores such as milking a cow. Navigate hard-packed sand and grass to see, feed or pet more than 200 farm animals. Staff can help lift you from your WC onto a tractor-pulled hayride, and, onto a bench seat in a miniature train for a short tour. ADA picnic shelters; Rr. $. 9:30-4 (1368 S Poinciana Blvd; 407-846-0770)

■ **WATER PARKS**

Water Mania has accessible grounds but the only accessible attraction is the wave pool. Roll down the paved slope into the pool; your WC must be removed, but you can rent a single or double inner tube for use in the pool. Shaded picnic areas; Rr. $/free for WC riders. Hrs vary (6073 US 192; 407-396-2626)

ACCOMMODATIONS

■ **CABINS/CAMPGROUNDS**

East Lake Fish Camp has 24 WC-friendly 1BR cabins and 263 shady campsites on the 12,000-acre East Lake Tohopekaliga, renowned for its bass, crappie and shellcrackers. Cabins have flat entrances, wide doors, 2 full beds (open frames) and large standard bathrooms. Cabins include linens, AC, maid service, microwave, refrigerator, cable TV, table and chairs. The RV/tent sites have full hookups, paved roads, picnic tables and no cooking/fire facilities. RV sites have concrete pads. Bathhouses are standard and have small lips at the entries. Cast a line on a shaded dock; use the floating docks for a rental boat; or launch your own on the boat ramp. Airboat tours are also available here; see Boat Tours. The camp can arrange for fishing guides experienced with disabled anglers and can help lift you aboard from your WC. Pool; laundry; full restaurant (3702 Big Bass Rd; from Boggy Creek Rd, turn S; 407-348-2040)

Merry 'D' Sanctuary is a lovely, wooded 54-acre campground with 121 RV/tent sites with full hookups and picnic tables. The main bathhouse has roll-under sinks and roll-in showers. A .5-mi paved road winds by all sites. Because trails are mostly sand, you may choose to drive to 2 stocked ponds where you can fish from flat, grassy banks. A 7-mi bike trail runs past the campground. Laundry; craft classes; 3 mi to WDW (4261 Pleasant Hill Rd/CR 531; 7 mi S of US 17-92; 407-870-0719; 800-208-3434)

Secret Lake RV Resort has a 1BR cabin and 675 campsites on 100 somewhat hilly acres with a 30' lighted fishing pier over a 4-acre lake and a heated pool with a zero-depth entry. The WC-friendly cabin has a queen bed (open frame), full sofa bed in the living room, full kitchen and a standard half bath; linens are included. Tent sites are WC-friendly with water/elec; RV sites also have cement pads and sewer hookups; all sites have picnic tables; and grills are near the picnic shelter. The ADA bathhouse has raised toilets, roll-under sinks and roll-in showers with hand-held sprayers and seats. Camp store; laundry; lounge; entertainment; activities from bingo to billiards; playground; restaurants nearby; 5 mi from WDW (8550 W US 192; 407-396-6101; 800-400-9304)

Tropical Palms Resort has an ADA cottage and 575 campsites on 60 acres of wooded property. The 1BR cottage has a queen bed (platform), sofa bed and full kitchen with lowered counters; the large ADA bathroom has a raised toilet, a shower with a seat and hand-held sprayer. Many RV/tent sites have cement pads, picnic tables and full hookups. The ADA bathhouse is near registration. Paved paths connect all buildings. The fishing pond has grassy, flat banks and a ramped deck. Take the paved path into nearby Old Town (see Shopping above). WC-accessible shuttles take you to local attractions for a fee; reserve 24 hrs in advance. Pool; camp store; outdoor cafe; 3 mi to WDW (2650 Holiday Trail; 407-396-4595; 800-647-2567)

■ CONDOS

Deluxe Florida Villas has very spacious 3BR condos at the Villas at Somerset. The condos are on the ground floor and have standard bathrooms (2777 Poinciana Blvd, Suite 128; 407-396-2744; 800-949-2744)

Medical Travel rents a 3BR/2BA ADA villa in Somerset Resort, 4 mi from WDW. The unit has a full kitchen, queen sofa bed in the living room, a queen bed in the master bedroom and 2 twin beds in the other bedroom. The master bath has a raised toilet, roll-under sink and roll-in shower; the standard 2nd bathroom has a tub. Medical Travel can also arrange for a minivan with a lift and medical needs such as oxygen and dialysis. Heated pools; sauna; hot tub; game room; exercise room; tennis (2734 N Poinciana Blvd, #59; 561-361-9384; 800-778-7953)

Royal Oaks has 3 ADA 3BR/2BA villas that can sleep up to 9. The master bedroom has a king or queen bed (21"-24" high/open frames); the living room has a queen sofa bed; units have full kitchens. One bathroom in each unit has a roll-under sink and roll-in shower with a hand-held sprayer. Pool; laundry (5075 W US 192; Magical Memories Mgmt 407-390-8200; 800-736-0402)

Westgate Vacation Villas has 4 ADA 2BR condos each with a king and 2 full beds and full kitchens; some units have sofa beds in the living rooms. Master bathrooms have raised toilets, roll-under sinks and roll-in showers with hand-held sprayers and seats; second bathrooms have tubs. Pool; grocery store; fitness room; tennis; basketball (2770 Old Lake Wreson Rd; off US 192 W; 407-239-0510; 888-808-7410)

■ MOTELS

Best Western Eastgate has 12 ADA rooms each with a king bed (platform) and bathroom with a raised toilet and roll-under sink. Pool; restaurant for brkfst & dnr; WC-accessible shuttle to local attractions for a fee. $-$$ (5565 W US 192; 407-396-0707; 800-223-5361)

Comfort Suites Maingate has 6 ADA 1-room suites each with a king or 2 queen beds (open frames), kitchenette and full sofa bed. Bathrooms have raised toilets and roll-under sinks; 2 units have roll-in showers with hand-held sprayers and seats. Free brkfst; pool; cabana bar; game room; laundry; full restaurant; free WC-accessible shuttles to local attractions with 24-hr advance reservations. $-$$ (7888 W US 192; next to Splendid China; 407-390-9888; 888-390-9888)

Comfort Suites Maingate East has 8 ADA 1-room suites each with a king or 2 queen beds (25" high/open frames, a full sofa bed, refrigerator, microwave and coffeepot. Bathrooms have raised toilets and roll-under sinks; 2 rooms have roll-in showers; others have tubs; all have hand-held sprayers and seats. Free brkfst; pool; laundry; free WC-accessible shuttles to local attractions with 24-hr advance reservations. $$ (2775 Florida Plaza Blvd; 407-397-7848; 888-784-8379)

Days Inn Eastgate has 5 ADA rooms each with 2 full beds (open frames) and a bathroom with a raised toilet, roll-under sink and roll-in shower with a hand-held sprayer and seat. Pool; laundry;

restaurant for brkfst. $-$$ (5245 W US 192; 407-396-7700; 800-423-3864)

Days Inn Maingate W has 8 ADA rooms each with a king bed (open frames), refrigerator and bathroom with a raised toilet, roll-under sink. Four units have roll-in showers with hand-held sprayers and seats; others have tubs. Each connects to standard rooms with 2 full beds. Pool; game room; laundry; restaurant for brkfst & dnr; kids under 12 stay/eat free; reserve free scheduled WC-accessible shuttle to local attractions 24 hrs in advance. $-$$ (7980 W US 192; 407-997-1000; 800-327-9173)

Homewood Suites has 6 ADA 1-room suites each with a king bed (open frames), full kitchen and bathroom with a raised toilet, roll-under sink and roll-in shower with a hand-held sprayer and seat. Free brkfst; pool; laundry; WC-accessible shuttles to local attractions. $$$ (3100 Parkway Blvd; 407-396-2229; 800-255-4543)

Howard Johnson has 6 ADA rooms, each with 2 full beds (open frames), a coffeepot and, on request, a refrigerator and microwave. Bathrooms have roll-under sinks; 2 rooms have roll-in showers with seats; others have tubs. Pool; laundry; lounge; restaurant for brkfst & dnr. $ (2323 E US 192; 407-846-4900; 800-521-4656)

Hyatt Orlando has 19 ADA rooms with a king or 2 full beds (open frames) and, on request, refrigerators. Bathrooms have raised toilets, roll-under sinks, hand-held sprayers, roll-in showers and seats. Pool; full restaurant; lounge; WC-accessible shuttle to local attractions for a fee. $$-$$$ (6375 W US 192; 407-396-1234; 800-233-1234)

Palms Tempus Resort has 5 ADA suites with a king, queen or 2 full beds (open frames), queen sofa bed in the living room and full kitchen. Bathrooms have raised toilets, roll-under sinks and roll-in showers with hand-held sprayers and seats. Pool; kids activities; tennis. $$-$$$ (7900 Palms Pkwy; 407-226-9501)

Ramada Inn Maingate has 4 ADA rooms with 2 full beds (platforms) and bathrooms with raised toilets, roll-under sinks and roll-in showers with hand-held sprayers. Pool; restaurant for brkfst & dnr; free WC-accessible shuttle to WDW. $-$$ (2950 Reedy Creek Blvd; 407-396-4466; 800-365-6935)

Ramada Plaza Hotel & Inn/Gateway has 13 ADA rooms, with 2 queen beds (platforms), a refrigerator, microwave (in some) and coffeepot. Bathrooms have raised toilets; 6 have roll-in showers, others have tubs or step-in showers; some have hand-held sprayers and seats. Pool; laundry; lounge; entertainment; restaurant for brkfst & dnr. $$ (7470 W US 192; 407-396-4400; 800-327-9170)

Sheraton Inn Lakeside has 18 ADA rooms each with a king or 2 full beds (platforms), refrigerator and bathroom with a raised toilet, roll-under sink, roll-in shower with a seat. Pool; laundry; lounge; full restaurant; free WC-accessible shuttles to local attractions with 24-hr advance reservations. $$ (7769 W US 192; 407-396-2222; 800-848-0801)

Wynfield Inn Main Gate has 7 ADA rooms with a king bed or 2 full beds (24" high/platforms). Bathrooms have 18" high toilets; 3 rooms have roll-in showers, others have step-in showers, all with seats. Pool; laundry; special alarms; WC-accessible shuttle to attractions. $-$$ (5335 US 192; 407-396-2121)

ORLANDO
Altamonte Springs, Apopka, Maitland, Winter Garden, Winter Park

Orlando, one of the world's hottest destination points, is 15 miles northeast of Walt Disney World (WDW). The main thoroughfare is I-4 with International Drive (or I-Dr), running roughly parallel from the WDW area north to the southern city limits. Both are jam-packed with attractions, shopping areas and hotels. But the Orlando area offers more than glitzy attractions. It boasts an impressive cultural agenda, professional sports, fine fishing on its many small lakes and a fabulous Science Center. As for unusual opportunities for WC riders, try tennis lessons, hot air ballooning or even water skiing!

Tourist Info
Orlando/Orange County Visitor Center: 8723 I-Dr, Box 690355, 32869-9902; 407-363-5872; 800-554-1529
Web sites: www.go2orlando.com; www.in.visitseminole.com

Transportation
Commercial Wheelchair Van Co runs lift-equipped service in and around Kissimmee, Orlando and Sanford. Advanced reservations are required. (407-568-4512)
I-Ride Trolleys, with lifts and lock-downs, run along a 14-mi stretch of I-Dr from 7am-mdnt, every 15 min. Exact change is required and kids under 13 ride free. (407-354-5656)
LYNX public buses all have lifts and tie-downs and service Orlando, Kissimmee, the airport, Apopka and other towns in Orange, Seminole and Osceola Counties. Exact change is required. Riders with disabilities can obtain a LYNX ID card to get a discount; riders over 65 get a discount. Call for schedule and routing. (407-841-8240)
Mears Transportation Group runs lift-equipped service between hotels, attractions and the airport, with 24-hr advance reservations. (407-839-1570; 800-223-3868)
World Transportation runs lift-equipped service between hotels, area attractions and/or to (but not from) the airport. Call for the schedule; reservations must be made by 5pm the day before. You can also call here for accessible taxi service. (407-826-9999; 800-781-8999)

WC Resources
Center for Independent Living provides information and some equipment for loan. (720 N Denning Dr, Winter Park; 407-623-1070)
Care Medical Equipment offers rental and free delivery of manual and power WCs and ECVs. (407-856-2273; 800-741-2282)
Walker Medical offers rental and free delivery of manual and power WCs and ECVs. (407-331-9500; 888-726-6837)

ACTIVITIES

■ ATTRACTIONS
Audubon Center for Birds of Prey rehabilitates up to 22 species of threatened birds, such as eagles, falcons and owls. Paved paths take you to cages of injured birds and a butterfly garden. ADA picnic table; Rr. $. Tue-Sun 10-4 (1101 Audubon Way, Maitland; 407-644-0190)
Back to Nature Wildlife Refuge takes in annually some 2000 non-domestic animals that have been abandoned, in-

jured, raised in captivity or born with defects. The goals of this all-volunteer refuge are to rescue, raise, rehabilitate and release. Sidewalks lead to cages. Rr nearby. $D. 9-4 (18515 E Colonial Dr; 407-568-5138)

Gatorland features 110 acres of gators and crocs as well as more cuddly guys such as goats and a bear. You can hand-feed emus, lorikeets and deer. Paved paths or boardwalks lead through most of the park; a few paths are hard-packed shell that can be problematic when wet. The 2000' Swamp Walk boardwalk winds through a cypress swamp to an observation tower, ramped to the second story, which overlooks a 10-acre alligator breeding marsh. The 10-min, miniature train has a ramp for WCs and goes through un-explored areas in the park. There are entertaining educational shows with WC viewing areas. Chow down on gator ribs or nuggets in the restaurant. Gift shop; ADA picnic tables; Rr. $. 9am-6; summer -7pm (14501 S Orange Blossom Trail; 407-855-5496; 800-393-5297)

Guinness World Records Experience has an 8-min introductory film inviting you to break world records in a variety of venues; WC seating is to the side or in front of bench seating. Then head into Computer Gateway where you are quizzed by computers or onto the Playground where several games, from Whack-a-Ball to basketball shoots, are accessible. Roll through a motion tunnel to try to break records set in a weightless state and then into Guinness Town where you are quizzed some more and can watch videos of world records being set. In the Simulator, watch a 6-min Imax-style film from a stationary viewing area. Or, take an elevator up to where you can transfer into bucket seats that move in place to give you the thrill of riding the world's fastest roller coaster and bob sled; the seats have footrests and headrests as well as seat belts. Gift shop; Rr. $. 10-10;

summer hrs vary (8445 I-Dr; at The Mercardo; 407-345-9255)

Holy Land Experience is a 15-acre *biblical museum* or scaled re-creation of sacred Christian sites in Israel from 1450BCE to 66CE. The park's mission is unabashedly evangelical. Paved paths lead through all attractions around a landscaped lagoon. Enter through the 1st century Jerusalem Street Market with themed gift shops. The Wilderness Tabernacle showcases a 20-min multimedia/enactment of the ancient sacrificial system; WC seating is beside the bleachers in front, just left of center. The Temple on Mount Moriah features a 20-min film shot in Israel taking you from the Garden of Eden to a second coming; WC seating is at either end of bench seats. A costumed narrator talks you through the 45' long model of ancient Jerusalem, set low for easy viewing. The cafe offers American and Middle Eastern cuisine. Special events, from concerts to lectures, occur Fri and Sat evenings. WC rentals; Rr. $. Hrs vary (4655 Vineland Rd; I-4 exit 78, 5 mi SW of Orlando; 866-872-4659)

Master of Magic Show regales you for 90 min with 19 grand illusions. Seating is on the ground floor at small tables. For an extra charge you can enjoy drinks, chips, even hot dogs. Rr. Wed-Sun 6:30 & 9pm (8815 I-Dr; 1 mi S of Sand Lake Rd; 407-352-3456)

Orlando Science Center is a huge interactive fun/learning environment for kids and adults. In the 10 themed exhibition halls you can take a trip through the human body, experience the relationship between electricity and magnetism, conduct physics experiments, create a world from your own imagination, discover the science involved with movie-making and tour the solar system. Enter the Dr Phillips CineDome on the 3rd floor for breath-taking films and planetarium shows on the 8-story dome; WC seating is on the top row. The Darden Adventure Theater features live science-themed musical comedies, science demos or animal shows; WC seating is in the 1st row. The facility is almost completely WC accessible with some exceptions: KidsTown, a creative play area for those under 48", has some inaccessible activities and the bridge over Physics Park is inaccessible. The Crosby Observatory, housing Florida's largest public refractor telescope, offers astronomic views on Fri and Sat evenings. Although WC riders cannot get up the spiral staircase to peer through the main telescope, you can see the live video feed in the Discovery Labs and you can peer through smaller telescopes on the observation deck. Call for special events and show schedules. HC Parking is on the ground floor of the garage where you take an elevator to the 3rd level then use the bridge over the street to enter the Science Center. Cafe for lunch/snacks; gift shop; Rr. $. Tue-Thu 9-5; Fri-Sat 9-9; Sun noon-5 (Loch Haven Park, 777 E Princeton St; I-4 exit 85, .5 mi E; 407-514-2000; 888-672-4386)

Ripley's Believe It or Not! has some 200 unbelievable oddities to look at, from a Rolls-Royce built of matchsticks to a torture chamber. The Tilted Room with angled floors and walls is not accessible. WC loaner; gift shop; Rr. $. 9am-1am (8201 I-Dr; 407-345-8010)

Titanic - Ship of Dreams is a permanent ground-floor exhibit with 17 rooms of artifacts from the ill-fated ship. Costumed passengers provide 1-hr guided tours; then you can spend some time with interactive displays. Rr in mall. $. 10-8; tours every 30 min (8445 I-Dr; at the Mercado; 407-248-1166)

WonderWorks is an upside-down building where science merges with virtual reality. Over 100 hands-on activities range from reaction timer games and a pitching tunnel to the world's largest (and accessible) laser tag arena. The virtual reality games afford unique experiences, such as swimming with sharks, being a virtual drummer and even protecting the universe from aliens. Some of the experiences, such as rock climbing and the simulated roller coaster, are inaccessible. While you can't roll into the earthquake simulator, you may transfer onto a seat for the 5.3 experience. And, you can roll over the small step into the Hurricane Hole. HC parking in Pointe Orlando garage next door; pizzeria; gift shop; Rr. $. 9am-mdnt (9067 I-Dr; 407-352-0411)

■ **BASKETBALL**

Orlando Magic Wheels (men) and **Orlando Ice** (women) games run Oct-Mar. Join them during practice or if you'd like to learn, sign up for the free summer program for men, women and children age 8 and up. For information, call Mary Davis at 407-654-4315. (Valencia Community College, West Campus, 1800 S Kirkman Rd; 407-855-9989)

■ **BIKE TRAILS**

Parks: Turkey Lake

Cady Way Trail runs 3.5 mi along a former railway corridor linking the lovely Ward Park (W of SR 436, Winter Park) to the Fashion Square Mall (3201 E Colonial Dr, Orlando). The trail is flat terrain, mostly asphalt with a .5-mi stretch of boardwalk; ADA water fountains and shelters are along the way. It winds from the park (with parking, ADA picnic tables and Rr) through a shady residential area and then a more urban area close to the mall. In the near future, the trail will run an additional 2.7 mi from Ward Park across SR 436 through the Goldenrod area to connect with the Cross Seminole Trail (see Sanford) for over 30 mi of continuous trail. (407-246-2775)

Lake Fran Trail is a 2-mi, off-road asphalt trail connecting Poppy Park (Lescot Ln & Poppy Ave) and the Dr Smith Recreation Center (1723 Bruton Blvd; 407-291-7308). Along the way are water fountains, shade trees, picnic pavilions, and on the shores of Lake Fran, wildlife, including a pair of American Bald Eagles.

Little Econ Greenway is a popular 4-mi paved trail from the county's Blanchard

Park W to SR 50, just E of Goldenrod Rd; someday this trail will link to the Cady Way Trail. The terrain is fairly flat passing a butterfly garden and lily pond; there are 2 boardwalks over the river and a canal and a few street crossings. The park has ADA picnic tables and shelters, fishing from a bridge over the Little Econ River, tennis and Rr. Parking at both trailheads; trail has Rr (Blanchard Park, 2451 Dean Rd; .75 mi N of Colonial Dr; 407-249-4586)

West Orange Trail is a 19-mi asphalt trail through beautiful countryside from County Line Station (at SR 50 & 438) through downtown Winter Garden to Apopka (at 6 St & Forest Dr). The 5-mi stretch from the County Line to Winter Garden is level and midway is a butterfly garden. Hills between Winter Garden and Apopka are gradual but very long. Each station has an ADA picnic shelter. Rr & ADA water fountains along the trail (Office: 9-5; 455 E Plant St, Winter Garden; 407-654-5144)

■ **BOAT RAMPS**
Parks: Moss Park; Lake Lawne
Butler Chain of Lakes, a 4700-acre chain of 9 lakes, has a ramp and floating dock in RD Keene Park on Lake Isleworth. Rr; picnic tables. $. Dawn-dusk (10900 Chase Rd, Windermere; 7 mi NW of I-4 on CR 535; 407-876-6696)
Clear Lake, a 339-acre lake, has a ramp, floating dock and fishing pier in George Barker Park. Rr; ADA picnic table. 6am-11pm (Tampa Ave & Gore St)

■ **BOAT RENTALS**
Parks: Turkey Lake

■ **BOAT TOURS**
Scenic Boat Tour offers a 1-hr narrated tour of the lakes and canals of Winter Park. With advance notice, staff carries you in your WC down 14 steps to the dock to board the pontoon boat. And, yes, staff has taken many WCs down those steps. Hourly 10-4 (312 E Morse Blvd, Winter Park; 407-644-4056)

■ **BOWLING**
AMF Lanes have 2 ramped lanes and bowling ball ramps. Rr. 9-mdnt (280

Douglas Ave, Altamonte Springs; 407-862-2500)
World Bowling Center's has ramped lanes and bowling ball ramps. Rr. Hrs vary (7540 Canada Ave; 407-352-2695)

■ **CANOEING**
Parks: Wekiwa

■ **DINNER THEATERS**
See Theme Parks pg 202
Aloha! Luau Dinner Show at SeaWorld is a 2-hr South Seas barbecue during a Polynesian musical revue and flashy Somoan fire dance. WC seating is throughout. You may enter the park 30 mins before the dinner show without paying park admission. Advance reservations; Rr. 6:30 & 8:45 (7007 SeaWorld Dr; I-4 exit 71 or 72; 407-351-3600; 800-327-2424)
Enzian Theater & Cafe is where you watch American or foreign independent films and classics while you sit at a table enjoying light food, beer and wine. WC seating extends across the 3rd tier where you enter. Rr. Matinees on wknds; shows nightly (1300 S Orlando Ave, Maitland; show times 407-629-0054; 407-629-1088)
Mark Two stages professional full-scale Broadway shows after a 2-hr buffet and open bar. Tables are for parties of 2 or 4 and all are accessible. Reservations; Rr. Matinee buffet Wed, Thu & Sat 11:30; Wed-Sat 6pm; Sun 4:30 (3376 Edgewater Dr; I-4 exit 86 W; 407-843-6275; 800-726-6275)
Pirate's Dinner Adventure serves a swashbuckling meal with all the beer, wine or soda you can guzzle while you are dazzled by an action-packed show of music and daring stunts. WC seating is in the first row of the arena. Rr. Hrs vary (6400 Carrier Dr; E off I-Dr; 407-248-0590; 800-866-2469)
Sleuths Mystery Dinner Theater is your chance to play Sherlock Holmes as the audience tries to solve a comedy/murder mystery. Parties with WC riders are seated in front. Reservations; Rr. Wkdy 7:30; wknd 6, 7:30 & 9 (7508 Republic Dr; E on Carrier Dr off I-Dr; 407-363-

1985; 800-393-1985)

■ **DISC GOLF**

Parks: Lake Lawne, Turkey Lake

■ **FISHING CHARTERS**

A #1 Bass Guide Service has half/full-day or night charters on fully rigged bass boats at a variety of lakes within a 60-mi radius. With advance notice, Capt Pete can get help to lift you from your WC into a boat seat. The capt can meet you at your hotel or an accessible dock. He can also arrange saltwater trips from Port Canaveral. (352-394-3660; 800-707-5463/533-4746)

Bass Challenger offers half/full-day bass fishing on a 19' Ranger with the terms *No bass, No pay!* With your companion, the capt helps lift you into a boat seat. You can board the boat from a floating dock at Keene Park, where they usually launch. Rr at park (407-273-8045; 800-241-5314)

Fishing Connection offers half/full-day trips for 2 anglers on a 22' flats boat in fresh or saltwater. Staff lifts you onto a bench seat, with a back but no armrests. Explain any special needs so Capt Phil chooses a spot that best suits you. (407-469-2279; 800-583-2278)

Pro Bass Guide Service offers half/full-day freshwater trips on a bass boat for 2 anglers. Fish either from your WC or a boat seat. Explain your needs and Capt Paul, who is experienced with disabled anglers, can get help in boarding. (407-877-9676; 800-771-9676)

■ **FISHING PIERS**

Parks: Lake Lawne, Turkey Lake, Downey. Bike Trails: Little Econ Greenway

■ **HELICOPTER TOURS**

Air Florida Helicopters offers 5-min to 1-hr narrated tours of Orlando or as far as the Kennedy Space Center. Roll up to the copter and staff, experienced with disabled passengers, can lift you 4.5' into a seat with a shoulder strap. Rr. 9:30-dusk (8990 I-Dr; 407-354-1400/466-3570)

■ **HOT AIR BALLOONING**

Orange Blossom Balloons has a basket large enough for 4 passengers, including a WC rider. At 6am, you meet at the Days Inn (US 192, W of Disney Maingate) for a briefing and follow the van (or you may transfer into it) to the launch site. The location depends on the weather. Staff helps lift you aboard in your WC; you can either transfer onto the seat or remain in your WC that gets strapped down. The 1-hr flight goes roughly 2000' over Florida countryside and Orlando attractions. If you can't transfer into the van, a companion must follow the chase vehicle to the landing site. After a champagne toast at landing, staff joins you for a full breakfast buffet back at the Days Inn. The whole experience takes 3-4 hrs. (407-239-7677)

■ **MUSEUMS**

Cornell Fine Arts Museum, at Rollins College, houses one of Florida's oldest and largest collections of paintings, prints and photos. Exhibits rotate. A security guard must unlock the WC access door. Rr. Tue-Fri 10-5; wknd 1-5 (1000 Holt Ave, Winter Park; 407-646-2526)

Holocaust Memorial Resource & Education Center has a 1-room museum/memorial with multimedia displays and an exhibit/film hall where exhibits rotate and films are scheduled. There's also an extensive research and lending library. Rr & Cr. $D. Mon-Thu 9-4; Fri 9-1; Sun 1-4. (851 N Maitland Ave, Maitland; 407-628-0555)

Maitland Art Center started as a 1930's home studio for the artist/architect Andre Smith who used Mayan and Aztec details in the 23 buildings and 6-acre grounds. Smooth brick walks wind through hidden courtyards and connect the gallery of contemporary American art, an open-air chapel and an excellent gift shop. Call for a schedule of lectures, demonstrations and classes. Rr. $D. Wkdy 9-4:30; wknd 12-4:30. (231 W Packwood Ave, Maitland; 407-539-2181)

Morse Museum has a vast collection of

Tiffany leaded glass, American paintings and decorative arts. Rr. $. Tue-Sat 9:30-4; Sun 1-4 (445 N Park Ave, Winter Park; 407-645-5311)

History Center offers an audiovisual and interactive look at the people and events that have shaped Central Florida from the Conquistadors and cracker cowmen to astronauts and mouse-eared tourists. In a meticulously restored 1927 courthouse, the downtown Center has elevators to all 5 floors, including a research library (with historic photos and postcards). You'll find many delights including the Orientation Theater, designed like a front porch with rockers, the fabulous dome decorated with Central Florida icons, a restored 1920's courtroom with reenactments and the Historium selling vintage souvenirs. The 2-acre Heritage Square in front has paved paths and postage sculpture. HC parking on Washington Ave behind Center; Rr. $. Mon-Sat 10-5; Sun noon-5 (65 E Central Blvd; near Magnolia; 407-836-8500)

Polasek Galleries includes 3 galleries and a 3-acre garden with many of this Czech-American sculptor's finest stone and wood pieces. Polasek used a WC so the grounds and museum are readily accessible. Paved paths lead down to Lake Osceola. Rr. $. Sep-Jun Tue-Sat 10-4; Sun 1-4 (633 Osceola Ave, Winter Park; 407-647-6294)

Orlando Museum of Art has permanent collections of art from Africa, America and the ancient Americas as well as temporary exhibits. The Discovery Centers and Gallery Activity Bags are geared to help guests learn more and think about the exhibits in new ways. Visiting artists also conduct workshops and lectures. Gift Shop; Rr. $. Tue-Sat 10-5; Sun noon-5 (Loch Haven Park, 2416 N Mills Ave; 407-896-4231)

■ **PARI-MUTUELS**
Orlando Jai-Alai offers betting on live jai alai and simulcast horse racing. WC seating is in the front box seats and by elevator on the restaurant's top level.

Rr. WC guests free. Thu-Sat 7:30; Mon-Sat noon; Sun 1pm (6405 S US 17-92, Fern Park; 20 min N of Orlando off I-4; 407-331-9191)

■ **PARKS**
Downey Park is a 47-acre park with a fishing pier and a hard-packed canoe launch on Lake Downey. You must traverse 30'-50' on a gently sloping soft sand beach to the swim area. In 2003 a splash park should be completed. ADA playground; ball fields; fitness area on sand; ADA picnic shelters; Rr. 8-6 (10107 Flowers Ave; at E SR 50 & Dean Rd; 407-249-6195)

Lake Eola Park, in downtown Orlando, is a delightful family affair with a 1-mi paved path around a lake and fountain illuminated at night. The amphitheater, with WC seating throughout, presents Shakespeare in the Park (Apr-May), Family Comedy Night (2nd Tue each month at 7:30pm), free family movies (Aug) and concerts. Call for a schedule. The Swan pedal-boats are inaccessible. Street parking; ADA picnic tables; Rr. Cafe Mon-Thu 10-8; wknd 10-9. Park 7-mdnt (Rosalind Ave & Washington St; 407-246-2827)

Lake Lawne, a 156-acre lake has a paved ramp, floating dock and 50' fishing pier in the county's 124-acre Barnett Park. There are ball fields, tennis, an 18-hole disc golf or Frisbee course and a paved path around the park's perimeter. ADA picnic tables; grills; playground on sand; Rr. 8-6; summer-7; softball nights -9ish (4801 W Colonial Dr; next to Central FL Fairgrounds; 407-836-6246)

Leu Gardens, once the estate of a citrus magnate, has 3 mi of paved paths through 50 acres of colorful annuals and century-old live oaks overlooking Lake Rowena. The gazebo in the south woods is accessible. The largest camellia garden in the south blooms Nov-Mar. The formal rose garden is the largest in the state. The 1st floor of the restored 1880's home is accessible and guided tours occur 10-3:30. Gift shop; Rr. $. 9-5 (1920 N Forest Ave; 407-246-2620)

Moss Park is a remote, 2.5 square mi park, just E of Orlando. This low-lying property can make WC access difficult: The hard-packed shell paths can be problematic when wet. And the 2 paved boat ramps have fixed docks that can be too high for WCs during droughts. But the shallow lakes offer good fishing and can accommodate canoes, pontoon boats and other boats up to 17'. The beach has about 70' of soft sand leading to the swim area. During dry winters, try the 3 mi of natural trails under majestic oaks and through freshwater marshes. See Campgrounds. ADA playground; lifeguards in summer; Rr. (12901 Moss Park Rd; 4 mi SE of SR 15; E of Orlando Arprt; 407-273-2327)

Turkey Lake Park is a 300-acre city park with lots of outdoors fun. An All Children's Playground and Five Senses Walk are specifically designed for folks with disabilities. A 3-mi paved bike trail, with ADA water fountains along the way, meanders throughout the wooded park. You can pet barnyard animals at Cracker Farm where the barn is ramped but the yard is soft dirt. Fish from the 200' lighted fishing pier or rent a bass boat, with a trolling motor; staff cannot help you board from the floating docks. The grassy terrain on the disc golf course is fairly rough and the 7 mi of nature trails have spots with tree roots and hills. See Campgrounds. ADA picnic tables; grills; shelter #4 is ramped; Rr; 1 mi from Universal. Oct-Mar 7:30-5; Apr-Sep -7 (3401 S Hiawassee Rd; S off SR 408; 407-299-5581)

Wekiwa Springs State Park has almost 8000 acres of varied scenery from river and swamp to high sandy ridges. This popular park has a boardwalk from parking around the high rim of the spring that pumps 42 million gal of freshwater daily into the 15-mi river. The 6- and 13-mi trails are narrow, with sand and tree roots in stretches. However, another boardwalk runs through a swamp into some woods and to the dry sandhills; along the way you're likely to see wildlife, including limpkins and eagles. Many flights of stairs go down a grassy bowl to the swim area at the springhead. The canoe launch is not easy to reach either. From the concession stand where rentals are handled (wkdy 9:30-5, wknd 8:30-5; 407-880-4110), another boardwalk winds down to a sidewalk beside the spring. From here you take a bridge across the spring and roll along a hard-packed stretch (where environmental webbing can impede your passage) to the launch, which is a small level sandy riverbank. The pathway is narrow and often crowded with canoes being portaged; staff cannot help with transfers. The Wekiwa River is slow moving and paddlers return to the put-in. See Campgrounds. ADA picnic tables & ADA shelters; Rr. $. 8am-dusk (1800 Wekiwa Cir, Apopka; from SR 436, E on Wekiwa Springs Rd for 3 mi; 407-884-2008)

■ **PERFORMING ARTS**

Annie Russell Theater stages Rollins College student dance and theater productions in a Mediterranean-style theater. WC seating is front and center behind the orchestra pit or in the box seats. Sep-May (1000 Holt Ave, Winter Park; 407-646-2145)

Bob Carr Performing Arts Center features dance, classical music and theater, including big Broadway performances. WC seating is on the orchestra/ground level and in the rear, accessible by elevator. CRr (401 W Livingston St; 407-849-2577) You can contact the following for particular schedules at the Arts Center: Festival of Orchestras (Nov-Mar; 407-896-2451); Orlando Opera Company (Nov, Feb & Mar; 407-426-1717); Orlando Philharmonic Orchestra (407- 896-6700); Southern Ballet Theater (Sep-May; 407-426-1733) and the Pace Theatrical Broadway Theater (Sep-May; 407-423-9999).

UCF Civic Theater presents shows for children and adults in several venues with WC seating in front. Advise the box office so accommodations can be made beforehand. Shows range from Broadway productions and family classics to avant-garde works. Rr (Loch Haven Park, 1001 E Princeton St; between US 17-92 & I-4. And at UCF campus in Oviedo area; 407-896-7365)

Orlando Arena, right downtown, hosts many big-name entertainers. Take a ramp or elevator to the mid-level WC seating on the concourse. Rr (W Amelia St; 407-849-2020)

■ POOLS

College Park has a heated pool for lap swimming with a lift (fixed seat). Staff can help with transfers. CRr; roll-in showers with bench seats (2411 Elizabeth Ave; 407- 246-2649)

Dover Shores has a heated pool for lap swimming with a lift (fixed seat). Staff can help with transfers. Outdoor showers; roll-in showers in community center next door; Rr (1400 Gaston Foster Rd; 407- 246-2649)

Engelwood Neighborhood Center has a heated pool with a lift (fixed seat). Staff can help with transfers. Roll-in showers with bench seats; Rr. Apr-Sep (6123 LaCosta Dr; 407- 246-2649)

Ft Gatlin Park has a heated pool; ask the lifeguard to set up the lift (fixed seat). Rr (2009 Lake Margaret Dr; S of Michigan St between Ferncreek & Bumby; 407-858-3290)

Northwest Community Center has a heated L-shaped pool with a zero-depth ramp so you can roll directly into the pool. Roll-in showers with bench seats; Rr. Apr-Sep (3955 Country Club Dr; 407-521-6231)

Westmonte Park has a therapeutic heated pool with a ramp, a lift (fixed seat), exercise rails and a whirlpool section. Staff cannot help with transfers. Call for information and the required physician's consent form. Roll-in showers; Rr. Wkdy 8-8 (624 Bills Ln, Altamonte Springs; from SR 436, N on Spring Oaks Blvd; 407-571-8740)

YMCA Aquatic Center has a 4' deep, indoor pool heated to 88 degrees that has a lift (fixed seat). Staff can help with transfers. Membership is not required. Roll-in showers; Rr. Wkdy 6am-9pm; Sat 8-5; Sun noon-4 (8422 I-Dr; 407-363-1911)

■ SHOOTING RANGES

Shooting Gallery has double-wide, 50' long pistol caliber ranges and rents handguns, shot guns and other weapons. Lane barriers are removable should they interfere with WC shooters' views. Sodas; CRr. 10-8 (2911 W 39 St; 1 blk S of I-4; 407-428-6225)

■ SHOPPING

Antiques: Check out downtown Orlando on Orange Ave between Princeton St and New Hampshire St.

Boutiques: The Mercado is a Mediterranean-style plaza with attractions, boutiques, ethnic shops and dining (8445 I-Dr). Pointe Orlando has over 60 stores, including Armani's and FAO Schwarz, a 21-movie theater, restaurants and clubs (9101 I-Dr; across from Convention Center; 407-248-2838). Winter Park has boutiques, galleries and eateries along the charming, oak-lined Park Ave.

Malls: Florida Mall (8001 S Orange Blossom Trail; 407-851-6255); Altamonte Mall (SR 436 at I-4, exit 92; 407-830-4400); Orlando Fashion Square (3201 E Colonial Dr; 407-896-1131). Beltz Factory Outlet World (5401 W Oakridge Rd; 407-352-9611) and Beltz Designer Outlet Center (5296 I-Dr; 407-352-3632) are an enormous stretch of complexes with over 170 factory outlet stores, from Saks Fifth to Reebok.

■ SPECTATOR SPORTS

See Theme Parks pg 231.

Arena Football Orlando Predators play Apr-Aug in the Orlando Arena. Take a ramp or elevator to the mid-level WC seating on the concourse. Rr. Fri &/or Sat pm (Orlando Arena, 600 W Amelia St; 407-648-4444)

Basketball NBA Orlando Magic plays Oct-May and the WMBA Orlando Miracles play Jun-Aug. Take a ramp or elevator to the mid-level WC seating on the concourse. Rr (Orlando Arena, 600 W Amelia St; 407-896-2442)

■ TUBING

Kelly Park is a 245-acre county park with a short boardwalk along Rock Springs. Outside the park, along Rock Springs Rd, are places to rent tubes. Companions must get you down 4-5 steps to the water's edge where you can launch into deep water. Enjoy the 15- to 25-min float to the end of the run where you can get out by a wooden ramp or roll into the 3' deep water to swim. See Campgrounds. ADA picnic tables; Rr. $. Winter 8-6; summer 9-7 (400 E Kelly Park Rd, Apopka; off CR 435, N of US 441; 407-889-4179)

■ WATER SKIING

Wakeboard Orlando offers sit-ski instruction with David Briscoe, a former US Disabled Team coach, who has taught disabled and able-bodied skiers since 1991. Lessons are on Lake Ivanhoe. Advise him if you need help with transfers so that extra staff can be arranged. (1413 Orange Ave; 407-894-5012)

ACCOMMODATIONS

■ B&Bs

Meadow Marsh B&B, an exquisite Victorian home circa 1877, has a WC-friendly, ground-floor room with an antique brass full bed (28" high/open frame) and a very small standard bathroom with a 31"-wide doorway. A long asphalt drive leads through the beautiful 12-acre grounds and to the ramped entrance to the home. A 3-course breakfast is served in a glassed porch; desserts and beverages are available at no charge at any time. Orlando area attractions are 20-30 min away. $$ (940 Tildenville School Rd; 407-656-2064; 888-656-2064)

Veranda B&B is a lovely 1920's building surrounded by lush landscape and set in the historic Thornton Park district with restaurants nearby. The WC-friendly room, The Erte, has a 4-poster queen bed (36" high/platform with a 3-stair step up to the bed), a kitchenette and roomy bathroom with grab bars, a roll-under sink and roll-in shower with a seat. The ramped room entrance is from one of several outside courtyards. Other similar ground-floor rooms have standard baths. Continental breakfast is served in the ramped Magnolia Build-. ing. Pool. $$$ (115 N Summerlin Ave; 407-849-0321; 800-420-6822)

■ CABINS/CAMPGROUNDS

Kelly Park has 21 shady RV/tent sites with full hookups and 3 tent sites with no hookups. All have ADA picnic tables on concrete pads, grills and hard-packed paths to an ADA bathhouse with 3" lips into large showers. See Parks. (400 E Kelly Park Rd, Apopka; off SR 435; 407-889-4179)

Moss Park has 2 ADA RV/tent sites with concrete pads, water/elec, ADA picnic tables, grills, fire rings and paved paths to the ADA bathhouse. The bathhouse has raised toilets, roll-under sinks and roll-in showers. Primitive campsites are also available. See Parks. (12901 Moss Park Rd; 4 mi SE of SR 15/Narcoossee Rd; E of Orlando Aport; 407-273-2327)

Turkey Lake Park has 5 rustic cabins, each sleeps 10 in bunk beds. Two ADA cabins are ramped and have paths to the nearby ADA bathhouse with raised toilets, roll-under sinks and roll-in showers. Of the 32 RV sites, several have ADA picnic tables, 11 have full hookups and all have asphalt pads. Tents can be pitched on an open field. Turkey Lake offers plenty of recreational activities for the family and is 1 mi from Universal; see Parks. Pool; laundry; ADA playground (3401 S Hiawassee Rd; S off SR 408; 1 mi from Universal; 407-299 5581)

Wekiwa Springs State Park has 60 RV/tent sites. Two sites (#30 and 60) have ADA picnic tables, grills and ADA fire pits; they are right off the main road and have a sidewalk to an ADA bathhouse with a roll-in shower. See Parks. Reservations (1800 Wekiwa Cir, Apopka; from SR 436, E on Wekiwa Springs Rd for 3 mi; 407-884-2008)

■ CONDOS

Oasis Lakes Resort has 2 WC-friendly 2BR/2BA units each with a king bed and either a queen or 2 twin beds (platforms) and a queen sofa bed. One bathroom has a roll-under sink and a roll-in shower; the other has a tub/shower. Pool; tennis courts; playground; exercise room; basketball; laundry (12400 S I-Dr; 407-905-4100)

Westgate Lakes has 14 ADA 2BR condos that sleep 8, each with a king and 2 full beds (21" high/platforms), a queen sofa bed in the living room, full kitchens, washer/dryers, 52" TVs and screened porches. Master bathrooms have raised toilets, roll-under sinks, Jacuzzi tubs and roll-in showers with hand-held sprayers and seats; second bathrooms have tubs. A pier/walkway extends over a lake to a gazebo on a small island. Pool; full restaurant; deli; maid service (extra fee); tennis; basketball; kayak rentals; shuffleboard; playground. (10,000 Turkey Lake Rd; 2 mi W of Sand Lake Rd; 407-345-0000; 800-925-9999)

■ HOUSES

Private house, built for a paraplegic and overlooking a golf course, has 3BR/2BA to sleep 6 comfortably. This lakeside home is available by the week and has a full kitchen, lowered closets, laundry and double garage. Rental includes membership to 2 nearby country clubs, tennis and golf. The master bedroom has a king bed; the other bedrooms each have 2 twin beds; all beds are on platforms. Bathrooms have raised toilets and roll-under sinks; the master bathroom has a lift to get into the tub while the other has a step-in shower, both with hand-held sprayers and seats. The house is 15 min from Orlando International Airport and 20 min from WDW. (Sue Fisher, 5 Park Ln, Broughton Park, Salford, UK; 0161-792-3029)

■ MOTELS

Amerisuites/Airport has 7 ADA 1-room suites each with a king or queen bed (24" high/open frame), a sofa bed and kitchenette. Bathrooms have roll-under sinks; 2 units have roll-in showers with hand-held sprayers and seats; others have tubs. Free brkfst; pool; laundry; accessible shuttle to local attractions for a fee. $$-$$$ (7500 Augusta National Dr; 407-240-3939)

Amerisuites/Convention Center has 8 ADA 1-room suites, each with a king bed (22" high/open frame), a full sofa bed and kitchenette. Bathrooms have raised toilets and roll-under sinks; 2 units have roll-in showers with handheld sprayers and seats; others have tubs. Free brkfst; pool; laundry; fitness room. $$-$$$ (8741 I-Dr; 407-370-4720; 800-787-0353)

Best Western Mt Vernon Inn has 2 ADA rooms, each with a king bed (open frame) and refrigerator. Bathrooms have roll-under sinks, roll-in showers with hand-held sprayers and seats. Pool; lounge; restaurant for lnch & dnr; entertainment. $$ (110 S Orlando Ave, Winter Park; I-4 exit 87 E 3/4 mi, N on US17-92; 407-647-1166; 800-992-3379)

Candlewood Suites has 6 ADA studios and 2 ADA 1BR suites. Each has a queen bed (24" high/open frame) and full kitchen. Bathrooms have roll-under sinks, hand-held sprayers and seats; 4 units have roll-in showers; others have tubs. Suites also have a queen sofa bed. Laundry; fitness room. $$ (644 Raymond Ave, Altamonte Springs; off Central Pkwy; 407-767-5757)

Caribe Royale Resort Suites has 12 ADA 1BR suites each with a king bed, sofa bed and kitchenette. Bathrooms have roll-under sinks and roll-in showers with seats. Free breakfast; pool; laundry; lounge; full restaurant; WC-accessible shuttles (with reservations) to area attractions. $$$ (14,300 I-Dr; 407-

238-8000; 800-823-8300)

Crosby's Motor Inn has 11 WC-friendly rooms, some with full kitchenettes and 1 or 2 queen beds (21" high/platforms). Standard bathrooms have 30" doorways, raised toilet seats and tubs with seats; grab bars are available. Pool; laundry. $-$$ (1440 W US 441, Apopka; 407-886-3220; 800-821-6685)

Crown Plaza Resort Orlando has 2 ADA 1BR suites each with a king bed (open frame), sofa bed and full kitchen. Bathrooms have roll-under sinks and roll-in showers with hand-held sprayers. Pool; laundry; lounge; entertainment; full restaurant. $$$ (12,000 I-Dr; 407-239-1222)

DoubleTree Castle Hotel has 11 ADA rooms with 2 queen beds (platforms), sofa beds, coffeepots, refrigerators and, in some, microwaves. A junior suite has a king bed, microwave and sofa bed. Bathrooms have raised toilets and roll-under sinks; 3 have roll-in showers with hand-held sprayers and seats; others have tubs. Pool; laundry; lounge; entertainment; full restaurant; free accessible shuttles to local attractions with reservations. $$-$$$ (8629 I-Dr; 407-345-1511; 800-952-2785)

Embassy Suites/I-Dr has 2 ADA 1BR suites each with a king bed (platform), sofa bed in the living room and kitchenette. Bathrooms have roll-in showers with seats. Free brkfst; pool; laundry; lounge; full restaurant. $$$ (8978 I-Dr; 407-352-1400; 800-433-7275)

Embassy Suites/Orlando N has 3 ADA suites with a king (open frame), sofa bed in the living room and kitchenette. Bathrooms have raised toilets, roll-under sinks and roll-in showers with seats. Free brkfst; laundry; lounge; full restaurant; WC-accessible shuttles to attractions at a fee. $$$ (225 E Altamonte Dr, Altamonte Springs; 407-834-2400)

Extended Stay America has 7 ADA rooms each with a queen bed (open frame) and kitchenette. Bathrooms have raised toilets and roll-under sinks; 2 have roll-in showers; others have tubs; all have hand-held sprayers and seats. Laundry. $-$$$ (6451 Westwood Blvd; 407-352-3454)

Hampton Inn has 3 ADA rooms each with a queen or 2 full beds (platforms), a refrigerator and coffeepot. Bathrooms have raised toilets, roll-under sinks and roll-in showers with hand-held sprayers and seats. Free brkfst; pool; laundry. $$ (151 N Douglas Ave, Altamonte Springs; 407-869-9000)

Four Points Sheraton Orlando/downtown has 7 ADA rooms, each with a queen bed (platform) and a bathroom with a raised toilet, roll-under sink, roll-in shower and hand-held sprayer. One ADA room connects to a standard room with 2 full beds. Pool; lounge; full restaurant. $$ (151 E Washington St; 407-841-3220)

Holiday Inn Express has 3 ADA rooms each with 2 full beds (open frames) and coffeepots. Bathrooms have roll-under sinks and tubs with hand-held sprayers and seats. Free brkfst; pool; laundry. $$ (8750 E Colonial Dr; 407-282-3900)

Holiday Inn Select/Airport has 7 ADA rooms each with a king or 2 full beds (platforms), a sofa bed and refrigerator. Bathrooms have raised toilets. Rooms 110, 116, 127 have roll-in showers; others have tubs; all with hand-held sprayers and seats. Pool; laundry; lounge; full restaurant; WC-accessible shuttles to attractions at a fee. $-$$ (5750 T G Lee Blvd; 407-851-6400)

Holiday Inn Select/at UCF has 2 ADA rooms, each with a full bed (23 " high/open frame), wide doors and a coffeepot. Bathrooms have raised toilets, roll-under sinks and tubs. Pool; full restaurant. $$ (12125 High Tech Ave; 407-275-9000)

Homewood Suites has 7 ADA 1BR and 3 ADA 2BR suites with a king and/or 2 full beds (22" high/platforms) and full kitchens. Bathrooms have raised toilets and roll-under sinks; rooms 122, 128 and 130 have roll-in showers with hand-held sprayers and seats; others have tubs. Free brkfst; pool; laundry; 24-hr convenience shop; WC-accessible shuttles to local attractions by reservation. $$$ (8745 I-Dr; 407-248-2232)

La Quinta/Airport W has 6 ADA rooms with a king bed (open frame). Bathrooms have raised toilets and roll-under sinks; rooms 139 and 145 have roll-in showers with hand-held sprayers and seats; others have tubs. Free brkfst; pool; laundry; full restaurant. $-$$ (7931 Datewyler Dr; 407-857-9215)

Motel 6 has 3 ADA rooms each with a queen bed (21.5" high/open frame). Bathrooms have roll-under sinks and roll-in showers with seats and hand-held sprayers. Pool; laundry. $ (5300 Adason Rd; 407-647-1444)

Peabody Orlando has 23 luxurious ADA rooms each with a king or 2 full beds (open frames). One room has a roll-in shower; others have tubs. Additional features vary by room, from lowered AC controls and peepholes to hand-held sprayers and roll-under sinks. The stately Peabody is known for its pet duck family that waddles twice a day from the elevator through lobby and into the fountain at the center of the hotel. Pool; laundry; full restaurant; lounge; entertainment; WC-accessible shuttles to attractions for a fee. $$$ (9801 I-Dr; 407-352-4000; 800-732-2639)

Radisson Barcelo Hotel has 2 ADA and 15 WC-friendly rooms, each with 2 queen beds (open frames), wide doors, a refrigerator and, for an additional charge, a microwave. The 2 ADA bathrooms have raised toilets and roll-in showers with seats; other bathrooms have tubs; all have hand-held sprayers. Pool; lounge; full restaurant; free WC-accessible shuttles to attractions. $$ (8444 I-Dr; 407-345-0505)

Renaissance Orlando Hotel/Airport has 2 ADA and 4-WC friendly rooms with a king or 2 queen beds (open frames). Two units have roll-in showers and roll-under sinks; others have raised toilets and tubs with seats. Pool; lounge; full restaurant. $$-$$$ (5445 Forbes Pl; 407-240-1000)

Studio Plus, close to Universal, has 4 ADA studios each with a queen bed (open frame) and lowered kitchenette features. Bathrooms have raised toilets; 2 have roll-in showers; 2 have tubs; and all have hand-held sprayers and seats;. Pool; laundry. $-$$ (5610 Vineland Rd; 407-370-4428)

Universal Portofino Bay Hotel is the luxurious recreation of the stunning Italian seaside village imported to the lagoon at Universal Studios and Islands of Adventure. In addition to free accessible ferry service to the parks, hotel guests can use Express lanes on all rides and attractions; see Theme Parks: Universal. With 22 ADA rooms, including several that connect to standard motel rooms, you have a choice of a king or 2 queen beds. Bathrooms have roll-under sinks; 8 have roll-in showers with seats; others have tubs. Pool; social programs; playground; game room; free happy hour; full restaurant. $$$ (5601 Universal Blvd; 407-503-1000)

Wellesley Inn has 5 ADA rooms each with a queen bed (22" high/platforms), refrigerator, microwave and coffeepot. Bathrooms have roll-under sinks and roll-in showers with hand-held sprayers and seats. Free brkfst; pool; laundry. $$ (5635 Windhover Dr; 407-370-5100)

Check out Walt Disney World's non-park activities. See page 229.

THEME PARKS

For Splendid China see Kissimmee and for the Holy Land Experience see Orlando.

Tips on Theme Parks

The theme parks in Central Florida are so enormous, so diverse and can get so crowded that you really need a plan of attack. If limited on time, plan a minimum of 1 day per park. If you have time, or simply prefer an easier pace, think about spending morning and later in the day in the theme parks and taking respites during the hotter, more crowded afternoons at your hotel or attractions in town. Explore multi-day and multi-park ticket packages: Some can save beaucoup bucks, while others aren't worth the commitment!

Holidays and summer are the most crowded, and most parks open earlier and close later. Be sure to check operating hours during your visit. Regardless of when you visit the parks, go armed with crowd-coping strategies. Arrive early. Parking opens an hour before the parks. When you enter a park, check the day's schedule of shows, parades and special events and plan your day. Look for notices, or ask Guest Services if any major attractions are closed that particular day. If you want to attend major shows on busy days, arrive at least 20-30 mins before show time, particularly if you want companion seating. After standard seating fills up, those companion seats are taken. Or, do the nearby popular rides while most visitors are attending the major show in that area. You have to be flexible to take advantage of Disney's and Universal's system of offering designated times for the most popular rides. Otherwise, do the popular attractions first thing in the morning (but check the park schedule because some rides open later) or in the evening when others are exhausted and head home. Since most people start off to their right, you might start off to your left. Alternate between inside attractions where you're in air conditioning and outdoor attractions or those with long queues or lines of visitors. Think about using peak hours (late mornings and afternoons) for shopping, shows or exhibits. You might also bring or buy portable munchies and eat your meals on line.

Roads to the theme parks are well marked with directions, but traffic can get heavy at times. Many hotels in the area provide shuttle service to the parks, either free or for a charge. Check Accommodations in Kissimmee, Orlando and WDW for those with WC-accessible shuttles.

WC Tips on Theme Parks

Universal and SeaWorld offer discounts on admission for folks with disabilities. Each of the parks has a brochure or guide for guests with disabilities that you should pick up as you enter the park. You can ask the park to send you one in advance (generally, it takes 6 weeks or more by mail), or you can get the information online (each web site is indicated below). Quite honestly, you have more detailed information in this book with descriptions of each ride/attraction, boarding procedures and any required transfers as well as location of WC entrances and seating in shows. But be sure to pick up the guide at Guest Services when you arrive at a park because it is compact to carry and most current.

All parks offer WC and ECV rentals and replacement/repair options. Throughout the parks, staff cannot lift guests making transfers but can push WCs onto accessible rides, help steady you or the ride vehicle as you transfer and retrieve a WC after a ride. ECVs are helpful in a theme park for covering the distance and getting up some very steep ramps and hills. A disadvantage is that even some WC-accessible attractions are not open to ECVs; in some cases you must leave the ECV outside as you wind through the inside queue. However, the parks have standard WCs at such attractions that you can use at that particular ride or attraction. If you anticipate getting out of your WC or ECV, tie a balloon or ribbon to the armrest to ease finding it in the midst of many others and to reduce chances of it disappearing. ADA restrooms (Rr), drinking fountains and pay phones are located throughout the parks; Companion restroom (CRr) locations are specified below for each park.

Be sure to read the warning signs by rides that are turbulent, high speed or otherwise stressful to people with heart, back and neck problems. Particularly with the simulator rides, you may not realize how very rough they can be. Rides times are listed in the descriptions below because some rides are simply too short to warrant heroic transfers into ride vehicles. If you do expect to take such rides but have a problem with upper body balance or strength, bring along a seat belt (see Boating pg 11) that you can use as a shoulder restraint by belting yourself diagonally across your chest to the ride vehicle. Emergency evacuations on rides may require walking, climbing stairs or a patient wait until you can be assisted.

You'll find that separate WC entrances to attractions do not always mean short waits. Where you find long queues in the hot sun, you may want to wait in a shady spot while your companions wait on line; then meet them at the entrance.

Using this Book

Descriptions below of each attraction in the parks follow a roughly clock-wise order from the main entrance.

(ECV): Guests in electric convenience vehicles or scooters must walk or transfer into a ride vehicle or a standard WC to enter the attraction or take the ride. Unless otherwise indicated, WCs are available for use at these attractions and you must leave your ECV outside the attraction or building.

(WC, ECV): the ride or attraction is NOT accessible to either ECV or WC riders; in these cases, transfers are described.

SeaWorld

Anheuser-Busch has two separate parks in Orlando that celebrate marine life. Discovery Cove blends and redefines the concepts of water park and nature experience. A few blocks away, SeaWorld is a more traditional theme park with rides and shows. Admission to SeaWorld does not include Discovery Cove, but admission to the pricier Discovery Cove entitles you to a 7-day pass at SeaWorld. If you also plan to visit Universal's parks or Busch Gardens in Tampa, explore Flex Tickets.

Discovery Cove

Discovery Cove ensures an extraordinary day at the beach. You can swim with dolphins, wade with rays, snorkel among exotic fish and converse with gorgeous birds – all in over 30 perfect acres of tropical beach, lush landscaping and coral reefs. This aquatic Camelot has water temperatures from 75 to 85 degrees. Your admission includes a freshly prepared, 3-course gourmet lunch; sunscreen; snorkel gear; and use of a wet suit, lifejacket and towels. You even get free food to feed the fish and birds. Lower admission is charged for guests who do not swim with dolphins. Be aware you must have reservations to enter the park and your reservations hold rain or shine. If you are going to swim with dolphins, you are told the general time when making reservations so you know how early to arrive. Discovery Cove is open 9-5:30, but you can enter as early as 8 to start the preliminaries. (6000 Discovery Cove Way; I-4 exit 71 or 72, next to SeaWorld; 877-434-7268; www.discoverycove.com)

Begin your day having a photo taken for your ID card that you can use to charge anything extra. If you have opted for a dolphin swim, the card indicates the precise time. Staff gives a 5-min orientation on the facilities and geographic layout. At your leisure, pick up the snorkel gear you want along the paved path to the beach. And now, other than your appointment for the dolphin encounter, you have the day to loll on the beach and explore the Cove. Sometime between 11 and 4, you lunch at the al fresco Laguna Grill at lawn tables on the deck, or bring your meal down to the beach where umbrellas, chaises and tables are waiting for you. Meantime, you can gnosh at the two snack bars or even enjoy beer or cocktails at your own expense.

General Tips
Crowds are not an issue because no more than 1000 visitors are admitted each day. The staff is knowledgeable and readily available to answer any questions about the permanent inhabitants at the Cove. Bathhouses offer amenities such as towels, hair dryers and even plastic bags for your wet clothes.

WC Tips
Discovery Cove is readily accessible. Follow signs to valet parking, complimentary for vehicles with HC permits. With advance reservations you can borrow a beach WC (removable arms) at the entrance in the Reception Building. Paved paths run between and through most of the beaches and all other areas so you can get around the rather compact property without a beach WC. But because of the sand and all the fun in the water here, the beach WC can certainly make your day easier. All lagoons and waterways are ramped; with the beach WC you can roll down the

gradual ramp into 3' of water where you can ease yourself from the WC and into the water. Remember, you can borrow life vests, if you like. Staff cannot lift you, but will happily steady you as you transfer. All restrooms include CRr. In addition to the amenities described above, the ADA bathhouses have raised toilets, roll-under sinks, roll-in showers and roll-in changing rooms.

ATTRACTIONS

■ AVIARY
More than 250 people-friendly birds, from all over the world, call this aviary home. Hold up a cup of food and colorful birds will perch on your arms or head. The foliage is so profuse that you hardly realize you are in a screened aviary.

■ TROPICAL RIVER
This 3300' long, freshwater river flows through the aviary, under some footbridges and around an island. While you'll see no fish, you can enjoy snorkeling the 2'-8' depths over various artifacts planted on the sand bottom.

■ CORAL REEF
Here's a different snorkel experience. This saltwater reef features a shipwreck and some 10,000 tropical fish from all over the world in 2'-12' depths. Don't worry, the shark and barracuda are behind glass.

■ RAY LAGOON
Are you a fan of the Rays? Come wade or snorkel in the 3' deep tidal pool with 36 rays (debarbed, thank you very much) that you can pet and feed. You can remain in a beach WC if you prefer.

■ DOLPHIN LAGOON
The dolphin encounter is the highlight of Discovery Cove. At your designated time you meet at your assigned cabana by Dolphin Lagoon for a 15-min session on dolphin behavior. You are assigned to one of 3 coves for your 30-min swim session with 5-7 other guests, 2 trainers and one playful bottlenose dolphin. You can stay in a beach WC in 3' of water on a very wide ledge that ultimately drops to 10'. Trainers train you to give commands to your dolphin and you can take a turn holding fins with your dolphin for a glide through the water. Or you can swim in the deeper water where the dolphins cavort. Afterward you select and probably buy prints or a video of your encounter with the dolphin.

SeaWorld

This 200-acre park is dedicated to teaching us about marine creatures through a good mix of outstanding shows, often interactive watery wildlife habitats and thrills. In summer and on holidays, a 20-min laser, fountain and fireworks show over the central lake closes the park. The Aloha! Luau Dinner Show may be a good way to wind up your visit to SeaWorld; see Orlando: Dinner Theater pg 193. Make advance reservations at the Maps & Info Center or call SeaWorld. The park is open generally 9-6 or 7, later on holidays and in summer. (7007 SeaWorld Dr; I-4 exit 71 or 72; 407-351-3600; 800-327-2424; www.seaworld.com)

General Tips
See Tips on Theme Parks pg 202. SeaWorld opens in phases: parking opens at 8:45am, the ticket area at 8:45, shows in the N side of the park start at 9 and shows in the S side or Shamu's side, start at 10. Believe the park warnings, indoor theaters close the doors promptly at show time. If you choose to sit in the Splash Zones at water shows where the saltwater can range from 55-72 degrees, you may want to

bring extra clothes. Two restaurants, Dine With Shamu and Sharks Underwater Grill, offer table service. Gift shops throughout the park can deliver any purchases to Shamu's Emporium near the exit for you to pick up as you leave the park.

WC Tips
At the parking entrance, ask for directions to HC parking. One-day park admission is discounted 50% for a guest with a disability and one companion. Get a *Guest Safety and Accessibility Guide* at Guest Relations outside the park entrance or inside the park at Guest Services or the Maps & Info. Most attractions are in readily accessible theaters or stadiums (all with designated WC seating), but the slopes at the entrances can be taxing. Three thrill rides require transfers from WCs and ECVs; the kids' play area is largely inaccessible. ECVs can be helpful for the distances and steep ramps; the only additional transfer is to ride the Sky Tower. Just inside the entrance at the Children's Store, you can rent ECVs and WCs. To rent ECVs, guests from age 16-17 must have adult companions. The park map uses red arrows to denote the most WC-friendly entrance into attractions. If you sit in the Soak Zone, you might want to bring or buy a poncho because the saltwater can corrode equipment such as ECVs. CRr are located at the main entrance next to Exit Gifts, across from the Polar Parlor Ice Cream Shop in Village Square, at the Friends of the Wild Gift Shop and at Terrors of the Deep. Most restaurants offer cafeteria-style service but on request can serve you.

Tours
Reasonably priced 1-hr guided tours occur throughout the day; one is a general behind-the-scenes tour and others focus on particular animal habitats. A 6-hr behind-the-scenes tour includes front-of-the-line status on rides, reserved seating at shows and private animal encounters. The Trainer for a Day program is for those over 13 who want to work with and learn from staff. Check at the Guided Tour Center to the left of Guest Services for the schedule and reservations. Or, call 407-363-2398/800-406-2244 in advance.

ATTRACTIONS

The following are described roughly counterclockwise from the entrance, using the main theater to identify the area:

■ **ATLANTIS BAYSIDE STADIUM**
Water Ski Show has traditionally occurred in front of a covered amphitheater where a steep ramp takes you to WC seating in the last row above the bleachers. Currently this show is closed indefinitely.

■ **SHAMU STADIUM AREA**
Wild Arctic includes a simulated thrill ride, great wildlife viewing and an educational experience, all in the frozen Arctic. To board the 4 1/2-min ride simulating a turbulent jet helicopter flight, you must walk a short distance to a theater-type seat with armrests and a lap belt. A stationary alternative for those without mobility shares the ride audio and visuals. Next, visit the indoor tanks of gray beluga whales, polar bears and walruses where you can chat with SeaWorld research staff. After seeing the animals on the water's surface, go down a series of ramps to watch them underwater. Next are the interactive computer exhibits. As you enter the gift shop, look to the right for the Observation Bay where you can see the technology behind the simulated chopper.

Shamu Stadium's stage is a 7 million-gal tank where 7 Orcas, or killer whales, put on a spectacular 25-min acrobatic show. The evening show is under lights with rock music. A steep ramp takes you to WC seating roughly midway from the tank; if you don't want to get wet, sit to the far right or left in the WC area. Or ask staff to seat you in the Soak Zone up front.

Underwater Viewing are glass walls on tanks beside Shamu Stadium where you have a wonderful underwater view of Orcas doing their own thing. Videos and time-lapse photography enhance your appreciation.

Shamu's Happy Harbor is a 3-acre outdoor play area. The remote-control boats and cars are the only accessible features here. The tube slides, moon walk and spectacular 4 stories of nets, ropes and tunnels involve climbing. Be aware, it's very easy to lose track of your children in this hurly-burly tumult of fun!

Shamu Splash Attack is an accessible water play area for kids. You must pay an additional charge.

Games is an outdoor carnival-type arcade with skeeball, pinball and more.

■ **NAUTILUS THEATER AREA**

Anheuser-Busch Hospitality Center offers cafeteria-style food, free beer and the Busch Beer School where you can take a 30-min lesson on brewing and enjoy a beer tasting (*if* you are 21 or over).

Clydesdale Hamlet is a walk-through stable where you can meet the Anheuser-Busch equine symbols.

Nautilus Theater currently features Cirque de la Mer, a 35-min dazzling show of athleticism, comedy and special effects. WC seating is in the rear of the theater.

■ **SEA LION & OTTER STADIUM AREA**

Terrors of the Deep has a moving walkway within a 60' series of glass tunnels through a 660,000-gal tank where poisonous fish, eels, barracuda and 6 species of sharks prowl. You must have a companion to help you transition onto and off the conveyor belts.

Sea Lion & Otter Stadium features a 25-min comedy routine by Clyde, a talented sea lion, Seamore, a pesky otter and a humongous anonymous walrus. Arrive early to avoid becoming victim to the pre-show entertainer! You have 3 choices for WC seating. The middle ramp is very steep but takes you to the top of the stadium under shade. A ramp left of the entrance is less steep and takes you midway from the tank. Or, you can enter at the ground level on either side of the stadium and sit up front where WC guests sit in front of companions; you may get splashed depending on how frisky the performers are that day.

Pacific Point Preserve is a roll-through 2.5-acre stretch of northern Pacific coast, with sea lions and harbor and fur seals. Enjoy their over- and underwater antics.

Penguin Encounter is the artificially refrigerated Antarctic home to penguins, diving murres and puffins. Underwater viewing areas enable you to watch stuffy penguins transform into graceful swimmers. You can take a 120' moving walkway through the exhibit; WC guests are required to have a companion to help transition onto and off the conveyor belt. Or, you can take the high road, a fixed walkway elevated above the moving one. Toward the exit are interactive exhibits and videos.

■ **KEY WEST**

Kraken (~~WC~~, ~~ECV~~) is a mythological creature from below and also Orlando's highest roller coaster making 7 rollovers at 65mph. WC guests enter through the exit left of the entrance. At the boarding dock, you can roll next to the ride vehicle for a parallel transfer over the 32" high armrest into a seat with shoulder restraints. Your feet dangle and swing in air for the 4-min experience. For a minimal fee you can store any items in the lockers to the right of the entrance.

Journey to Atlantis (~~WC~~, ~~ECV~~) is a 6-min roller coaster/water ride through darkness, with sharp turns, high speeds and sudden drops and stops; riders and any belongings can get soaked. You must be lifted or be able to walk to the edge of the boat and step down into a low seat with a lap bar. For a minimal fee you can store any items in the lockers to the right of the entrance.

Manatees: The Last Generation? suggests an answer to this poignant question. Enter the theater for a 4-min film on the threats to this gentle mammal. Then proceed to an underwater viewing area to see the 3.5-acre lagoon where manatees happily munch their veggies. Touch-screen monitors provide more information.

Alligator Habitat is a roll-by place to learn the difference between crocs and gators.

Dolphin Cove invites you to feed and pet dolphins *if* you can reach over the 30" high wall that surrounds the lagoon. Check the posted feeding times when you can purchase fish to feed the dolphins, but arrive early because supplies are limited.

Stingray Lagoon has a 30" high wall to lean over to pet velvety stingrays.

Key West Dolphin Stadium presents bottle-nosed dolphins and false killer whales in a 20-min spectacle of leaps, jumps and flips. The easiest access is through the ground floor entrances at either side of the stadium; WC seating is up front at the side of the pool – outside the Splash Zone. The very steep ramps in front of the stadium take you to WC seating at the top, behind the bench seating.

■ **SEAWORLD THEATER AREA**

Turtle Point is home to injured sea turtles on the endangered species list.

Tide Pool has a 2' high, 18" wide wall to lean over and dip your hand into the shallow water to bring up a gentle sea creature. Staff is there to answer questions. Getting up close through crowds of excited children can require patience.

SeaWorld Theater presents Pets Ahoy, with dogs, cats, even rats, mostly from animal shelters, performing tricks and skits for 25 min. WC seating is along the front row.

Paddle Boats (~~WC~~, ~~ECV~~) are rented by the 1/2 hr and require a transfer from a WC onto a boat shaped like a flamingo; one rider must be able to use the foot pedals.

Sky Tower (~~ECV~~) has a glass-enclosed, circular platform that rotates slowly while rising 400' for a 6-min panoramic view at an additional charge. To avoid the turnstile, go to the far left of the main entrance and proceed to the ticket booth. Each trip can accommodate 2 WC riders. ECV riders can borrow a manual WC at the ride entrance. This ride will be closed until the summer of 2003.

Golden Seahorse gift shop has tanks lining the room and a unique aquarium that you view through the glass floor and glass ceiling.

Dolphin Nursery, a play tank for baby dolphins, is difficult to see from a WC because of the 40" high fence around the lagoon with a 30" high wall.

Tropical Reef faces the lighthouse at the entrance and sits behind a crowd of pink flamingoes. It is dimly lighted and full of aquariums with tropical fish from around the world.

UNIVERSAL

The Universal complex includes two theme parks, Islands of Adventure and Universal Studios, CityWalk for dining, shopping and music and three onsite resort hotels (see Orlando: Accommodations pg 198). Both theme parks are open 9am-6 or 7pm during most of the year and 8am-10 or 11pm during holidays and summers. (1000 Universal Studios Plaza; I-4 exit 75A; 407-363-8000; www.universalstudios.orlando.com)

General Tips
See Tips on Theme Parks page 202. The two parking garages are connected by a rotunda where you can take a long moving walkway to CityWalk from where you can enter both parks. Valet parking is available; you can also drop off passengers at the rotunda before parking. As a guest at one of the onsite hotels, you can take a roll-aboard ferry to CityWalk. **Universal Express** is a system to minimize long waits at the most popular attractions. Near each Express attraction is a kiosk or Distribution Center where you insert your park ticket and receive an Express pass with a time span when you can enter that particular attraction through the Express lane. The pass also indicates when you can use Universal Express for *another* Express attraction. As a guest at one of the onsite hotels, show your room key to use the Express lanes without stopping at the Distribution Centers. Hotel guests also can enter the park one hour early. The most popular rides have singles lines, as at ski resorts, where individuals can move up to take scattered empty seats in ride vehicles. Pricey 4- to 8-hr guided VIP Tours give you front-of-the-line priority on attractions for up to 15 guests; advanced reservations are a must (407-363-8295).

WC Tips
Guests with disabilities can receive a 15% discount on admission to both Universal parks – at the discretion of the staff at the front gate. If the disability is not obvious, you may want to bring some documentation of your condition. Be aware, you must *ask* for the discount. Both Universal are unique in that WC riders can enjoy several motion rides without having to transfer. On these rides, staff very carefully secures your WC in place with tie-downs. Companions can sit next to you on all accessible rides and help stabilize you, if needed. After your ride, staff asks if you and your party would like a second turn, even when the attraction is crowded. If you're not accustomed to thrill rides, the second time may be more fun because you know you survived the first one. WC and ECV rentals are in the parking garage rotunda and inside both parks. You must be 18 to rent an ECV. At Universal, you can reserve ECVs; do so at least 24 hrs beforehand at 407-224-6350.

CityWalk
The walkway from the parking garage leads into CityWalk. From here you turn left for Islands of Adventure or right for Universal Studios. CityWalk has no entry fee, but you can certainly find ways to spend money. This 30-acre area has several casual and a few fine restaurants open for lunch and dinner, from Pastamore to Emeril's (where you want advance reservations). Shops feature everything from cigars and women's clothing to toys and funky things that glow in the dark. Vendor carts offer hair wraps, caricatures and temporary tattoos. A water play area teases

you with squirts from the ground beneath your feet. And at night there's plenty of live music for dancing or just listening: jazz, Margaritaville-style, reggae and hard rock. Concerts feature top names and special events are endless. For the easily bored, try the 18-screen movie theater. CRr are located in every restaurant and outside the Latin Quarter, Nascar Cafe and the guest service area. CityWalk is open 11am-2am.

ISLANDS OF ADVENTURE

This 110-acre park is purely for fun. Most attractions are rides, with absolutely no pretense of having a message. The Five *islands* around a lagoon each have extravagant architecture, shows and rides geared to a different theme.

General Tips
See Tips on the Theme Parks pg 202. Use Universal Express; see Tips on Universal pg 209. Here, most people seem to start to the left and move in a clockwise direction to the Marvel Super Hero Island where the most popular thrill rides are located. If you start to the right, you'll find yourself in Seuss Landing where most of the kiddie rides and the 3 WC-accessible motion rides are located. Continuing counterclockwise you certainly may avoid crowds for a good while, however, you might feel like a salmon swimming upstream as the day goes on. Wait times for all the park's most popular rides are posted on each island. Several of the rides have varying minimum heights. If you have children with you, avoid disappointment by sizing them up against the measuring wall at the park entrance so they know before time which rides they cannot take.

WC Tips
Compared to Universal Studios that opened in 1990 and is unusually accessible, Islands of Adventure, open in 1999, is disappointing in terms of access. Of 17 major rides or shows, guests can remain in WCs for 7 or in ECVs for 4. The 3 WC-accessible motion rides are actually for kids, but certainly can be fun for adults as well. Almost all queues are readily accessible so you can get close to the ride vehicle for transfers. Disabled guests may bring 7 companions to attractions with separate WC entrances. You can rent WCs and ECVs at Stroller Rentals just inside the entrance. CRr are in Health Services by the entrance and on Lost Continent.

ATTRACTIONS

■ **MARVEL SUPER HERO ISLAND**
Incredible Hulk (WC, ECV) is an incredible 2-min roller coaster that starts off at super sonic speeds and twists and doesn't quit. To transfer, board a 26" high bucket seat with an over-the-head shoulder restraint that straps to a hump between your legs to keep you neatly in place. Exit on the boarding side where your WC has been stored and take the elevator down to exit through a gift shop.

Storm Force Acceleatron (WC, ECV) is a whirling 2-min spin in a 4-passenger, futuristic, cup-like vehicle. Take a small step up to the 24" wide entry onto a circular bench seat with no restraints. Hang onto the wheel in the center to keep yourself steady and to control your speed.
Dr Doom's Fearfall (WC, ECV) is a 150' high, faster-than-freefall, 3-min experience. WC riders enter through the Arcade to the left of the ride entrance for

the elevator. Staff then shows you and 3 others to a boarding area where elevator-type doors finally open to reveal 4 bucket seats 24" off the ground. The over-the-head shoulder restraints that connect to a hump between your legs feel quite comforting as you swoosh up, then are sucked back down to the starting point where your WC is waiting. Take the elevator back down to the Arcade/gift shop.

Spider Man (WC, ECV) is a truly harrowing 6-min, 3-D ride through an eye-popping battle of good and evil in a cityscape. Be prepared for plenty of lurching and changes in direction. Take the regular queue to transfer into a 12-passenger vehicle through a low 13" wide entry onto a bench seat for 4 with a lap bar. You literally feel the heat and the wet as your vehicle is slung up, down, spun around and jerked fast forward and back amongst colorful villains. Staff moves your WC to the exit side that ramps into - you guessed it! - a gift shop.

Meet the Heroes as you leave this island, and snap photos with the obliging heroes in wonderfully corny poses!

■ **TOON LAGOON**
Several times a day, Popeye, his pals and other cartoon favorites, dance and regale you in the streets.

Pandemonium Shows are special events in a covered amphitheater where WC riders can enter by ramp from either side to WC seating midway in the theater. And, if the occasion calls for it, you can take ramps on either side to get onto the stage.

Me Ship, The Olive is a 3-level play area with an elevator but few accessible activities. Bouncy nets, crawling spots, slides and a funky piano are fine, but the view over the lagoon of the islands to come is enough to make most kids to hyperventilate.

Popeye's Bilge-Rat Barges (WC, ECV) are round 12-person rafts where you should be prepared to get wet on the 7-min swirling careen down the *white-*

water river. Folks can pay to squirt you from the bridge. The regular queue takes you to a flat, revolving boarding area where, through an 18" wide entry, you take 2 steps down inside the raft to a bucket seat with high backs, no armrests and seatbelts.

Ripsaw Falls (WC, ECV) is where Dudley Do-Right's 6-min log flume can get you VERY wet, especially on the plunge at the end! The regular queue takes you up to a 4-person log, 1' high, where you must step over and down, then straddle a narrow bench in the center. Two positions in each log have seat belts and a third rider can sit in front.

■ **JURASSIC PARK**
Camp Jurassic is sizable interactive play area with a moderate slope through very dark caves (with lighted minerals along the way) to the upper levels with dinosaur nets and slides. Take the tunnel to the left of the Camp entrance to get to Pteranodon Flyers.

Pteranodon Flyers (WC, ECV) is an 80-second glide for young kids (and parents, if desired) over Camp Jurassic. The flyers are fixed seats at the end of thin metal struts at the front and back of the seat. A child must be lifted from a WC into the front of the seat then staff secures a seat belt and lap bar.

Jurassic River Adventure (WC, ECV) is another flume ride that starts off as gentle tour through dinosaur habitats until the carnivores eliminate the security system. The waterway floods causing a rocky 6-min ride and a steep drop as dinosaurs lunge out to get you. The regular queue takes you to a 6-row vehicle where you must step up 1' then down 1' to a 4-person bench seat with a lap bar. The bench back is only shoulder height and the main incline is steep. No matter what people say, you get wet even in the back rows!

Triceratops Discovery Trail is a walk/roll-through tour guided by animatronic trainers who introduce you to a 24' long, 10' tall animatronic

Triceratops. Trainers explain the care and feeding of this sensitive dinosaur whom you get to pet.

Discovery Center has a cafe and shop on the upper level and an interactive, fun, semi-educational center below. You can enter on either level and an elevator takes you between floors. Features include touch boxes, dinosaur egg incubators and computer quizzes on dinosaurs. You can manipulate a scanner along a rock wall of fossils; when focused, it creates an image of the whole creature and provides information.

■ THE LOST CONTINENT

Flying Unicorn (W̶C̶, E̶C̶V̶) is a kid's (not kiddie) roller coaster that soars for 1-min through an enchanted forest. The last passenger car has a side that swings open for easier transfers onto the 9" high bench seat. You disembark on the same side then roll across the very last car with a platform to the exit.

Dueling Dragons (W̶C̶, E̶C̶V̶) is a 2-min dual roller coaster ride where you choose to ride the Ice or the Fire Dragon that take almost intertwined paths at incredible speeds. Regardless of your choice, you spend a good amount of time upside down. The regular queue is through very dark winding caves to the boarding area where you must transfer into a 28" high bucket seat with over-the-head shoulder restraints that strap to a hump between your legs. Staff moves your WC to the disembarking area.

Eighth Voyage of Sinbad is a 20-min dramatic tale of Sinbad and a beautiful but entirely competent princess who together overcome an evil, gaudily dressed witch. The stunts, pace and flash are enough to engage even a cynic. The easier entrance is on either side of the amphitheater, up a steep but short slope to WC and companion seating at the top, rear row. Or, at the extreme sides of the theater, take the longer and only somewhat gentler slope down to the front row where the view is not as good.

Mystic Fountain is a smart-mouthed, talking fountain in front of Sinbad's theater that teases, spits at and delights even the teens in the crowd.

Poseidon's Fury is a 20-min show in which a good-hearted, not brave-hearted anthropologist's assistant takes you through a series of supposedly under-the-sea theaters to witness the god of the sea recapture his trident and power over an evil force. The passages and theaters are very dark; able-bodied guests inadvertently use the WC lane and may block the view from a WC. The special effects are stunning, maybe too intense for little ones, but you leave thinking that the technology has not quite yet arrived.

■ SEUSS LANDING

This, the most accessible island, is an area for kids - and adults who are kids at heart. Check out the photo ops to be pictured, for a charge, in a Seuss cartoon you can take home.

Caro-Seuss-el (E̶C̶V̶) is surely what Dr Seuss would have designed for a merry-go-round. Staff directs WC riders through the exit to a ramp hidden under the carousel. Staff pulls it out and sets it up to ramp into a purple sleigh where the side swings away so a WC rider and a companion can easily enter. Staff clamps the WC lock-downs, closes the side and around you go - up and down along with the other Seuss creatures for 2 min.

Circus McGurkus is a chance to help the Cat in the Hat, Thing 1 and Thing 2 get rambunctious as you lunch in this Big Tent a la Seuss. Check the park guide for show times.

One Fish, Two Fish (E̶C̶V̶) is your chance to fly a fish to calypso music within a circle of spitting fountains. Staff directs WC riders through the exit to a fish with a swing-away side then slides out the compartment and out comes a ramp for you and a friend to board. Position your WC in a groove on the floor, buckle the lap belt and staff slides the compartment back into the fish. With a lever, you control how high you fly for 2 min.

Cat in the Hat (~~ECV~~) spins and lurches for 5 min through the classic poem of a rainy day while Mother's away. Go to the very back of the gift shop, then turn left before the ride exit where staff asks you to wait until an accessible 5-person vehicle arrives. Staff swings the vehicle side away, a companion can board then you roll aboard pivoting your WC into position for staff to clamp the lock downs and put down the lap bar. You'll spin left then suddenly right and vice versa to see what havoc the Cat, Thing 1 and Thing 2 can bring about.

If I Ran the Zoo is a small interactive play area where all little ones need to be lifted onto most of the Seussian-type creatures.

UNIVERSAL STUDIOS

Universal's advertising slogan is on target: come here to *ride the movies*. Just going from one place to another is literally stepping in and out of famous movie sets. The 444-acre maze of rides, films and movie/TV production lots requires a very full day to experience.

General Tips

See Tips on the Theme Parks pg 202. Use Universal Express; see Tips on Universal pg 209. Do the most popular attractions with no WC entrances (Twister, Earthquake, Jaws and Terminator) first thing in the morning or in the evening. For up-to-the-minute info on line waits, check the Studio Information Boards in front of Studio Stars Restaurant or Mel's Drive In. The International Food Bazaar offers a breakfast buffet with the likes of Barney, the Flintstones and Yogi Bear; for reservations call 407-224-6339. For lunch or dinner with table service, call ahead at the 3 restaurants that accept reservations: Studio Stars (407-363-8769), Lombard's Landing (407-362-9955) and the Hard Rock Cafe (407-351-7625). Interested in watching a live show in production at Nickelodeon Studio? If so, call ahead (407-363-8586) for the schedule. There are no advance reservations. The studio is completely accessible and you should allow a half day.

WC Tips

Universal Studios incorporates information for disabled guests into a global guide for all guests. This theme park is unusually accessible with power-assist buttons on heavy doors, lap tables in gift shops and smoothly paved strips or sidewalks along cobblestone roads. Of 19 major rides and shows, you can enjoy 15 from a WC and 10 from an ECV; at Hanna Barbera, you can experience the ride from a stationary platform. Kongfrontation and Back to the Future have special WC entrances where you can take up to 7 companions. Other queues are reasonably wide for WC passage. WC seating for the closing 20-min Dynamite Nights Stuntacular, an outdoor speedboat stunt show, is behind Richter's Burger. The reserved viewing area is limited so arrive 30 min beforehand and take just 1 companion. WC and ECV rentals are inside the entrance near *It's a Wrap* shop. CRr are at Health Services to the right of the entrance, next to the First Union Bank, and on Canal Street across from Beetlejuice.

ATTRACTIONS

■ **FRONT LOT** is the park entrance with shops, snack bars and most services. The descriptions below are broken into the color coded areas on the Studio Guide map. Within each area the listings roughly follow a clockwise direction.

■ **PRODUCTION CENTRAL**

Alfred Hitchcock: The Art of Making Movies is a 30-min celebration of its masterfully spooky namesake. Inside the lobby, look for the roped-off lane to the right for WC riders and companions to enter the rear of the theaters via a steep slope. First enjoy a film tribute to Hitchcock that includes a 3-D attack by screeching birds. Then move into the Psycho sound stage where the shower scene is recreated with a volunteer from the audience and, not surprisingly, a surprise ending! Finally, enter an area with live demonstrations and interactive devices used in Hitchcock's special effects.

The Funtastic World of Hanna-Barbera starts off with a rollicking 8-min flight-simulator ride (WC, ECV) that requires a transfer up a small step and through an opening into a vehicle and holding onto the bar to stay upright. You sense you are moving at the speed of light, but in reality you are lurching and jolting without covering any distance at all. Or, opt for stationary seating up front in your WC. After the ride, explore the world of animation and sound effects on dated, but still interesting interactive electronics.

Bone Yard has paved paths through an outdoor display of familiar movie props.

■ **NEW YORK**

Twister allows you a safe but sobering taste of a tornado. Once inside the building, WC riders are directed to a lane in front for pre-show movie clips. Then you roll onto a rural set design where a tornado soon hits, sending swirling debris, including an airborne cow, and igniting a very hot fire for those in the front.

Kongfrontation (ECV) is a 5-min aerial tram ride under attack by King Kong. WC riders and up to 7 companions can skip the line outside. At the entrance staff leads you to an elevator to the boarding area on the 2nd floor. WCs can roll aboard the back of trams where the back seats lift up; staff will help you strap in. Or, you can transfer through the tram's broad opening onto a bench seat with back. Regardless, you need to hold on to handle the sudden movements as the angry ape shakes and drops the tram!

The Blues Brothers is a Dan Ackroyd-John Belushi routine performed a few times daily at a raised storefront along Delancey Street, across from Kongfrontation. A WC viewing area is near the stage, but depending on the crowds, you can also see from across the intersection where it's less congested.

■ **SAN FRANCISCO/AMITY**

Enjoy several carnival-type skill games here; all are accessible.

Beetlejuice's Graveyard Revue scares up monsters from the past for a 20-min irreverent song and dance show with wonderful twisted humor. Both entrances are ramped and lead to WC seating on a wide aisle midway across the amphitheater with WC seating.

Earthquake -The Big One (ECV) has a 15-min pre-show where audience volunteers help demonstrate techniques for filming the Big One. Inside the lobby, staff directs you to an entrance for WC riders and companions to be in front of a stand up theater and then to the front far right of the pre-show theater. Next roll aboard the back of an ill-fated subway and staff straps you in. Or, you can transfer through the train's walk-through aisles and onto bench seats with backs. ECVs can get up to the subway. You must hold onto a grab rail and maintain an upright position for the 5-min ride during which you're jarred, lifted and dropped by a 8.3 earthquake.

Jaws (ECV) is a 7-min boat tour that

goes smoothly until Jaws decides to gnosh on your boat; at times you may wish he'd get your corny boat captain. At the end of a snaking queue, wait for an accessible boat where you roll aboard at the back and staff clamps the lock downs. Be prepared to get jolted and wet!

Wild, Wild, Wild West Stunt Show is a 16-min riveting display of stunts and pyrotechnics with great wisecracks. The WC entrance is to the left; WC seating is front and center. The covered amphitheater seats 2,000 so crowds are not usually a problem.

■ **WORLD EXPO**

Men in Black (EEV) ask your help in shooting nasty aliens with a laser gun that keeps your personal score. The queue goes up a fairly steep slope where you should stay to the left so staff can direct you to an elevator down to a WC loading area. Here, staff rolls you onto a platform and secures tie-downs. T, they roll the platform onto an accessible 5-person vehicle. If you don't need to hold onto the lap bar, you can shoot aliens as you spin 360 degrees and lurch your way through an urban landscape.

Back to the Future...The Ride (WC, EEV) is a 5-min flight-simulator ride to beat all. If you can transfer, enter through the exit, right of the entrance. Staff directs you to a chamber for the pre-ride briefing. Then you transfer to a 20" high bucket car seat. The 8-passenger De Lorean has a lap bar to handle the abrupt jerking and extreme roller coaster-type motion. Once airborne, a 7-story Omnimax screen becomes your blur of reality at supersonic speeds (actually, you're moving less than 2' in any direction).

■ **KIDZONE**

Animal Planet Live runs 20 min, featuring live and video animal superstars, from dogs to exotic monkeys and birds. WC entrances to the covered amphitheater are on ground level at both sides; WC seating is front and center.

A Day in the Park with Barney is a 25-min sing-along show where you can actually meet the purple dinosaur and friends after the show. WC riders can go in front of this standup amphitheater with fencing for able-bodied to lean against.

Curious George Goes to Town and so do all the kids in this interactive water play area with water guns, unpredictable squirts and tipping buckets. If you choose to stay dry, follow the painted footsteps into the ball arena in back where you can shoot soft foam balls at the unsuspecting. A ramp in back of the ball arena takes WCs to the upper levels of the water play area and the ball arena.

Woody's Nuthouse Coaster (WC, EEV) is a 1-min, clankety, kiddie roller coaster - not a ride for tots but too tame for older children. You must go up a fairly steep slope to the loading area. A transfer requires going over the side of a 2-person car and onto a bench seat with a back and lap bar.

Fievel's Playland area is spacious and accessible but activities require crawling, climbing and sliding on a 30' spider web and other oversized objects. Rather than climb the stairs, you can take an elevator to the top of a 200' water slide and then transfer to a flat rubber mat.

E T Adventure (EEV) is a 5-min flying bike ride through misty, scented forests, across the face of the moon and onto ET's home planet. The inside queue is fairly tight with sharp turns, but at least you're in a forest with air conditioning. At the boarding area, wait for a 5-person accessible vehicle where WCs roll aboard behind the bikes. Staff clamps the lock downs, but you need to hold on to a lap bar and stay upright during the sudden accelerations and tilting. One companion can ride a bike next to you.

Trolley Character Greets and photo ops take place in front of ET.

■ **HOLLYWOOD**

Horror Make-Up Show is actually rated PG-13! It's an amazing, if gory 25-min demonstration of gimmicks, including computer-generated wizardry, used to create horror movie effects, from decapitations to the transformations in *The Mummy*. Inside the lobby, the WC entrance is to the right and takes you to WC seating in the middle.

Lucy: A Tribute is a chance to browse through Lucille Ball memorabilia and TV clips at your own pace. You've got to try the computerized trivia test on Lucy and Desi.

Terminator 2 sits you in the middle of an awesome 12-min, 3-D, live Battle Across Time. The outside and inside queues are fairly wide but with many hairpin turns. When you finish the inside queue, staff directs WC riders and companions to an entrance for the pre-show that leads you to a wide aisle across the middle of the theater with WC seating.

WALT DISNEY WORLD

Walt Disney World (WDW), covering 46 square miles, is truly a world unto itself. In addition to the four major theme parks, WDW contains a range of resorts, minor theme parks, hoards of restaurants, nightclubs and shops, and an array of activities independent of the parks. If you have time, explore some of the Other WDW Activities (pg 229), from the Richard Petty Driving Experience or golf with an adaptive cart, to fishing or tubing behind a powerboat. (I-4 exits 64B-68, Lake Buena Vista; 407-824-4321; www.disneyworld.com)

General Tips

Debating about staying at WDW or offsite? See WDW Accommodations pg 232. Hours of operation vary at Disney parks; call the phone number listed above and you can punch in dates to find out the hours for each park.

As a WDW resort guest, you can enter 1 1/2 hours early to a designated park each day of the week. Even if you are not staying at a Disney hotel, you can make reservations to have breakfast in a park with a Disney character before the park opens and get a head start. Disney offers a free **FASTPASS** to minimize waiting for the most popular attractions in each park. When you get to a participating attraction, look for the FASTPASS kiosk or Distribution Center, slide in your Disney ticket and you are issued a FASTPASS with a designated ride time for that attraction. When it's your ride time, go in through the FASTPASS entrance. But a string is attached! You can only use FASTPASS for one attraction at a time; your FASTPASS will indicate the time that you can use it for *another* attraction.

Throughout WDW are refreshment kiosks, fast food places and some very fine restaurants. Even many kiosks now offer healthy snacks. For full-service restaurants in the parks, make reservations, called *Priority Seating* at WDW. Especially if you have little ones, consider sharing a meal with Disney characters at various parks and hotels in WDW; see Other WDW Activities: Dining with Characters. If you make reservations for before or after popular mealtimes, you may minimize crowds. You can make reservations up to 60 days in advance by calling 407-939-3463. If you're staying at a Disney resort, the concierge can make your reservations. Or, each park has designated spots for making same-day dining reservations; do so when you first enter a park in the morning.

If you do serious shopping, staff can deliver your packages to the exit for pick up as you leave the park or to your WDW hotel. Or, you can ship packages home from the shop.

WC Tips

Transportation
HC parking lots are near park entrances and require HC permits. These lots get filled on busy days, so if you can walk short distances and transfer into the tram (where you can store your WC), please use regular parking. The Monorail has 2 loops from the Transportation and Ticket Center (TTC): one to Epcot and another to Magic Kingdom, Grand Floridian Resort, Polynesian Resort and Contemporary Resort. Change at the TTC to get between Epcot and the Magic Kingdom. At the Monorail boarding dock, you may need to ask staff to set up a portable ramp so you can roll aboard the particular car with space and a horizontal grab bar for WC riders. WDW has free buses with lifts and tie-downs for standard WCs that run every 15-20 mins between parks, hotels and all other WDW destinations. Some hotels have unusual ferries, such as swan boats, that shuttle to the nearest park; these are not accessible. Many offsite hotels offer accessible shuttle service to park entrances with specified pick up times; see Accommodations in Kissimmee, Orlando and WDW.

WC Rentals
Each park rents standard WCs and, for those over 18, a limited number of ECVs for the day within the park. Disney does not permit reservations for ECVs. The TTC rents WCs, not ECVs. Some of the WDW hotels rent WCs to guests. If your rental disappears or breaks down, Wheelchair Replacement Locations are listed under each park where, with a receipt, you or your companion can pick up a new rental. If you visit another park that day, save your receipt so you won't be charged again.

Inside the Parks
At Guest Relations, outside each park, pick up a *Guidebook for Guests with Disabilities* for that particular park. The trend at WDW is to mainstream WC riders through regular lines and entrances. While perhaps politically correct, the policy means you sometimes confront hairpin turns in queues that snake up to an attraction, and heat can be problematic. Generally, you can take up to 5 companions through WC entrances. Many of the turbulent rides have portable shoulder restraints that can help someone with limited upper body strength. Companion restrooms (CRr) are located at all First Aid stations and specific sites described below under each park.

Tours
Special VIP tours, for up to 10, are available at each park; guides may even push your WC throughout a park. Special seating at shows is included. Tours generally run a minimum of 5 hours at a hefty hourly fee, in addition to park admission. Call 407-560-4033.

More Info
WDW's web site (www.disneyworld.com) has extensive information on the parks, resorts and other recreational activities at WDW. Online, you can make reservations and ask questions of Guest Relations. You can also write or call WDW Guest Relations (Box 10040, Lake Buena Vista, FL 32830; 407-824-4321).

ANIMAL KINGDOM

The most beautiful WDW park is Animal Kingdom, a glorious collaborative effort between Mother Nature and Disney's Imaginaneers. With 500 acres and only a dozen or so major attractions, Animal Kingdom is the largest and most spread out theme park. And, because this park is all about seeing animals in natural habitats, you cover a lot of territory by foot or wheel. The park's layout exacerbates the distance because five areas spoke out via bridges from the central Safari Village. To go from one area to another (except Asia and Africa), you backtrack across a bridge to Safari Village, then cross another bridge. Animal Kingdom deserves a leisurely and more thoughtful pace so you don't miss the wildlife viewing areas, the chance to chat with people of the continents represented here and other delights snuggled into the lush landscape. Because of the natural settings and the shy or nocturnal nature of some animals, a good view of some wildlife may require patience. Animal Kingdom is open 8-7. (I-4 W exit 62D, I-4 E exit 65D; 407-824-4321)

General Tips
See Tips on Theme Parks pg 202. Use FASTPASS; see Tips on WDW pg 216. At the park entrance, beneath the massive waterfall, is a Rainforest Cafe where meals are periodically interrupted by thunderstorms and other natural disturbances. Even with reservations, there's a planned browsing time in the store before seating. You can enter the restaurant without entering the park or from within the park.

WC Tips
Of the 12 major attractions here, 8 are accessible by WC and 7 by ECV. While WC access is good, manual WC riders will find the distance between attractions hefty and the terrain quite hilly in spots. Consider renting an ECV for the day. WC and ECV rentals are at Garden Gate Gifts locatedright of the entrance and at the Outpost in the entrance plaza. If your rental needs to be repaired or replaced, go to Creature Comforts in Safari Village or Mombassa Marketplace in Hambre Village. CRr are in First Aid and in Safari Village across from the Flame Tree Barbecue; Hambre Village's Marketplace; Dinoland's Dinosaur Treasures; and Asia's Jungle Trek.

ATTRACTIONS

■ **OASIS** is a paved path from the entrance to Safari Village through a tropical garden with wildlife viewing areas tucked here and there.

■ **DISCOVERY ISLAND**
The hub of Animal Kingdom contains plenty of shops and eateries with colorful architectural whimsy and street entertainers, from storytellers to crafts folk.

Tree of Life is the park's 14-story high centerpiece, with 325 hand carved animals along its trunk, limbs and roots.

It's Tough to be a Bug! is an 8-min, 3-D flick, at the base of the Tree of Life. The show is clever and wonderfully intense, except perhaps for very young children. WC seating is in the front; ECV seating is in the rear. If you can transfer into a theater seat, you can enjoy some fleeting, but unusual sensory fun.

Discovery Island Trails are meandering paved paths around the Tree of Life and through a dense tropical forest with some exotic wildlife, such as lemurs, tortoises and otters, along the way.

■ **CAMP MINNIE-MICKEY**
Beyond the Campside Circle, site of the Lion King show, are spots to meet Mickey, Minnie and a range of Disney

characters.

Pochahontas & Her Forest Friends, such as Grandmother Willow and some live animals, provide a 10-min show on environmental preservation.

Festival of the Lion King is a 28-min live theater spectacular to thrill all in your group. Look for the misters to cool guests waiting on line. WC seating is on the floor beside companions on the theater's 4 bleachers.

■ **AFRICA**

Harambe is an East African town a la Disney with some eating spots, a shop, outdoor bar and entertainers. Perhaps most delightful is the chance to meet charming Africans who meander in traditional garb and strike up conversations with visitors.

Kilimanjaro Safaris (~~ECV~~) are 18-min expeditions through 110 acres of savannah and other African habitats where you'll see plenty of wildlife as you splash through riverbeds and barely make it across a rickety bridge. After you go through the queue, go to the exit area where you can roll aboard an open-sided lorry for a bouncy all-terrain ride. Only a few lorries are WC accessible and each carries 1 WC at a time. ECV riders can transfer to a Disney WC or walk 20' to a bench seat in the vehicle.

Pangani Forest Exploration Trail is a .5-mi trail largely through wooded areas with African wildlife featured every so often and knowledgeable research staff who chat with you about the animals, their habits and needs for survival. The Research Center, where you'll see anything from hedgehogs to rats, is quite cramped for maneuvering in a WC. Before you go through the aviary, grab the bird guide so you can recognize what you are observing. Exit the aquarium to the right for an overlook on a savanna where exotic animals are grazing. After the gorilla habitat, look carefully for wildlife hidden in the foliage as you take a slightly swinging bridge and a path to the exit.

Wildlife Express is a roll-aboard 6-min train ride to and from the Conservation Station. Take the WC gate right of the train's main boarding area. The Habitat Habit is the long paved path from the train to the Conservation Station, with animal viewing and tips on backyard wildlife along the way.

Conservation Station has interactive and informational videos, as well as exhibits on wildlife. Look through large windows into examining rooms, and see feeding areas where staff cares for the Kingdom's animals. Sometimes staff makes presentations. Outside is Affection Section, a shaded petting zoo on hard-packed sand where standard WCs are allowed. You never know when some Disney character might show up here for a photo op.

■ **ASIA**

Flights of Wonder is an impressive 20-min bird show in an open air theater. Go down the far left aisle for WC seating in the 1st row and ECV seating in the last row.

Kali River Rapids (~~WC~~, ~~ECV~~) features 12-passenger rafts swirling for 6 min down a Disney whitewater river in a rain forest. Take heed from those exiting the ride as to how wet you may get! Remember those ponchos for sale at the gift shop you just passed? The WC boarding dock is tricky to find. Just before the Jungle Trek entrance, turn right and go to the Exit Only sign. You wait here then roll up to a raft that gets a yellow tag so it returns to the same dock where you leave your WC or ECV. You must step up 4" to the top of the raft then down 3 steps through a 20" opening that narrows to 11" before you can sit in the molded seat with a lap belt and no armrests. You can hold onto the circular bar in the center. Or, you park yourself on the bridge and shoot water at the raft riders (as if they need to get wetter!).

Maharajah Jungle Trek is a .5-mi paved path supposedly from a small Asian village through the jungle to the hunting lodge of a maharajah who has declaimed hunting. The set design is wonderful but it's the 5' komodo dragon, the huge Fruit Bats, the Malayan tapir and the half-dozen tigers that you will remember. Borrow a bird guide before you head into the roll-through aviary with 52 species from Asia. You can roll right up to the large windows for great views.

■ DINOLAND

Boneyard (EEV) has a WC entrance ramp to this barely accessible playground and a sandy dig area where, if you can navigate sand and reach down, you can uncover fossils. The upper levels and most play features are not accessible.

Theater in the Wild is a large amphitheater, currently featuring a swinging 30-min live show of Tarzan-type stunts, gymnastics and in-line skaters set to rock music. Once inside the entrance, take the far right ramp to WC seating.

Primeval Whirl (WC, EEV) is a new spin on a roller coaster. The curves, dips and heights aren't as extreme as many coasters, but you and other guests sit in a round vehicle that whirls around on the track. You can roll up to the boarding deck then step up 18" and through a 12" diagonal opening to the seat with a lap belt. Staff can stop the vehicle that normally keeps moving during boarding.

TriceraTop Spin (WC, EEV) gently flies around and around and, depending on the rider, up and down. Move over Dumbo! Roll to your dinosaur, step up 18" and down through a 12" opening to the bench seat with a lap bar.

Dinosaur (WC, EEV) is a 3 1/2-min thrill ride in a time rover under attack by fierce dinosaurs and asteroids. Once inside the attraction, you are directed to the elevator. Once downstairs, go to the exit side of the boarding area where you can roll to the vehicle. Step up 8" through a 12" entry to a bench seat with a lap bar. Prepare to be jolted and rocked; this would be a good ride to use your own shoulder restraint.

EPCOT

The most *entercational* of WDW parks is the 300-acre Experimental Prototype Community of Tomorrow or EPCOT. The 19 major attractions are located in 2 distinct areas: Future World, where corporations celebrate their techno achievements and visions for the future, and the World Showcase (open at 11am), where 11 countries offer up a sampling of their culture, cuisine and souvenirs. Hours vary. (I-4 E exit 67; I-4 W exit 62D; 3 mi S of Magic Kingdom; 407-824-4321)

General Tips
See Tips on Theme Parks pg 202. Use FASTPASS; see Tips on WDW pg 216. From the main entrance, you enter Future World. Trams from hotels in the Epcot Resort Area drop you off at the International Gateway in the World Showcase. IllumiNations, a laser and fireworks display, occurs over the Showcase Lagoon every night before closing; find a spot at least 30 min beforehand along the lagoon where trees won't block your view. You need reservations for lunch or dinner at any of the fine restaurants in the World Showcase. Do so at Guest Relations (E of Spaceship Earth), at the kiosk with WDW-DINE phones (near Germany in the World Showcase) or at the restaurants when they open at 11am. See Living Seas below for two special in-water programs. Several behind-the-scenes tours (2-5 hours long) can be reserved 3 weeks ahead (407-939-8687).

WC Tips

Of 19 major attractions or rides, only 2 are inaccessible by WC and one more requires a transfer from an ECV. Four attractions include several activities, one of which requires a transfer; you can bypass that activity and enjoy the accessible ones. WC and ECV rentals and replacements are in the Gift Shop left of Spaceship Earth; WC rentals and replacements are at the International Gateway near the French pavilion; and WC replacements are in Germany. CRr in Future World are at First Aid in the Odyssey Center, by Spaceship Earth, at East Block across from Test Track and at West Block across from the Land. CRr in the World Showcase are by Canada, Morocco and Germany.

ATTRACTIONS

■ FUTURE WORLD

Spaceship Earth (W̶C̶, E̶C̶V̶) is a 15-min time-ride from the days of cave-persons to the future. WCs enter through the exit to the boarding ramp. Staff can stop the ride for you to transfer through an 18" opening on the side of the cart-type vehicle. The slow moving ride goes up then down a steep incline; you travel backwards going down.

Universe of Energy (E̶C̶V̶) is a 45-min high-tech, entertaining crash course on energy via a theater-ride. From dank swamps with life-size dinosaurs to the 3-screen spectacle on today's energy concerns, you are transported on a traveling theater. After the first presentation, take the regular exit but go right of the carpeted ramp (where able-bodied guests go) until staff can lower a small ramp for you to roll aboard. Lock your wheels! Because WC seating is limited to 6 per show, you can bring only 3 companions on this ride.

Wonders of Life is one of the great *educataining* wonders of WDW! But, unfortunately you must go up an arduous ramp to the entrance of building and then down another steep ramp inside to the activities. Staff directs you to WC seating for the various theater presentations: The *Anacomical Theater* is a fun 10-min improv comedy show on health. *Cranium Command* is a delightful 15-min flick capturing the anatomical orchestration of a 12-year old male body on a typical day. *The Making of Me* is a 15-min film on the facts of life

with a gentle, humorous and tasteful touch. *Goofy about Health* is a 10-min film on healthy life styles. *Body Wars* (W̶C̶, E̶C̶V̶) is a 5-min simulated thrill ride through the body's bloodstream that requires a transfer. With only 24" of space beside the seat, most WC riders cannot get parallel to transfer over the 23" high armrest and down into the theater seat. Extra shoulder restraints are available. ECVs must be left at the beginning of the queue for Body Wars; WCs can fit through the queue.

Test Track (W̶C̶, E̶C̶V̶) is a 5-min experience more hair-raising than cruising with a teen driver! After the briefing, you must transfer into a 6-passenger vehicle in which you go through tests performed on automobiles, from braking and skidding, to sharp turns and careening along a steeply banked loop. You can scope out the transfer in privacy on a stationary ride vehicle before actually trying the ride. You must make a parallel transfer over the 20" side of the vehicle and down 10" into a car seat (staff will bring a seat cushion if you ask). To bypass the ride and enter the Test Track exhibits and store, go through the FASTPASS Distribution Center, right of the attraction entrance. ECVs must be left at the entrance; staff can bring you a standard WC to get to the ride and check out the exhibits.

Innoventions offers interactive exhibits on tech to come and the latest video games. At *Innovations West,* a 15-min presentation gives you a peek of what the future has in store. At *Innovations East,* take a 15-min tour through a house of the future.

Living Seas starts with a 7-min film on the beauty of our planet's oceans. Then take a souped up elevator, hyped as a *hydrolator,* down to educational exhibits. From there, you can take stairs or a standard elevator to the upper level to see the huge 6 million-gal aquarium, with more than 65 species of marine life. Two special in-water programs in the Living Seas require advance reservations (407-939-8687) and must pay a charge that goes to the Disney Wildlife Conservation Fund; you do not pay park admission. In both programs, staff meets you at Guest Relations and escorts you to the attraction. Both take 8 guests at a time, start with classroom sessions and include all equipment. The 3-hr *Dolphin InDepth Program,* offered once each weekday, is a chance for adults over age 15 to get up close to a dolphin (407-560-6141). At the top of the aquarium, you go down a ramp and stand or sit in waist-high water while staff brings a dolphin to you. Staff can help guests without mobility transfer into a Disney WC and provide a weight belt to keep them seated while in the water. The 3-hr *Dive Quest,* offered twice each weekday, is restricted to certified divers (guests age 10-14 must be accompanied by a parent) who scuba dive in the aquarium along with an HSA-certified Disney dive master (407-560-6360). As in the dolphin program, divers can enter the water in a Disney WC.

The Land serves up over 6 acres of agricultural fun. But you must take the very long and steep ramp to the entrance. When first inside, you should get a FASTPASS for the boat ride. Take the elevator left of the Garden Grill Restaurant to the lower leve, and go to the FASTPASS lane where staff can get your designated time for you. While you wait, explore the exhibits or eat. *Food Rocks* is a 13-min hip nutritional

concert performed by the likes of Chubby Cheddar. The popular food court downstairs offers plenty of greens and fruits that will tempt even the kids. Upstairs is the *Circle of Life,* a 20-min film where the Lion King and his friends teach the fragility of our environment. For the 15-min boat ride, *Living with the Land,* (ECV) you can roll aboard the platform boat and travel through 4 diverse habitats, including an experimental greenhouse. If you want a more in-depth look, reserve a 60-min *Behind the Seeds Tour* (ECV) across from the boat ride entrance.

Imagination includes 3 blockbuster activities. Pick up your nerdy 3-D glasses to enjoy the snazzy 18-min film, *Honey, I Shrunk the Audience.* Use the regular entrance; the 8 WC spots are in the back row where only 1 companion can sit with you. *Journey into Your Imagination* is an 8-min, red carpet, behind-the-scenes look at an imagination scanner on a roll-aboard vehicle. Take the elevator to access *Image Works,* a thoroughly delightful interactive play area that will tap your creativity.

■ **WORLD SHOWCASE**
The World Showcase, with pavilions representing 11 countries, rings a 40-acre lagoon. Happily, the 1.3-mi path is flat and easily navigable because the Promenade buses are inaccessible. You can cross the lagoon on a boat to and from Future World, Morocco and Germany. While each pavilion is accessible, some have inside attractions that are not. All have cultural exhibits, plenty of shops and sell ethnic fast food; and all but America and Canada have full restaurants where you'll want reservations. Many also offer live entertainment or demonstrations during the day outside in their accessible plazas. The following offer a ride or film:

Mexico invites you up a fairly steep ramp (right of the main entrance) into a Mayan pyramid for an art exhibit, shops and a ride (ECV). Go through the gift shop for a pleasant 8-min boat ride through the diversity of Mexican geography and culture. Enter at the ride's narrow exit (left of the gift shop) where you can roll aboard between 2 seats.

Norway features a Viking ship, the Malestrom (~~WC~~, ~~ECV~~), for a rough but fascinating 15-min ride through mythic and real Norwegian landscapes, including down a waterfall backward. You must leave a WC/ECV at the dock, then walk 10' through handrails and step down into the boat. Staff will bring your WC/ECV to the exit area. Or, by-pass the ride and enjoy a short flick on Norway's scenic wonders.

China shows a 19-min panoramic of its people and places on a 360-degree screen in a sensational Chinese temple.

There are no seats and the screen is high enough that the standing audience should not block your view. **American Adventure** is housed in a WDW-version of Liberty Hall where you can take an elevator to a theater for a spirited 30-min musical review of American history. Outside, on the Lagoon, is the American Garden Theater where you can catch periodic patriotic concerts and shows.

France presents an 18-min film, *Impressions de France*; enter the theater through the left door.

Canada shows a 17-min Circle Vision film; enter the seatless theater by the path to the right of the building (past the restaurant).

MAGIC KINGDOM

With 107 acres, Magic Kingdom is the smallest and, with 34 attractions and rides, the most jam-packed of the Disney parks. Magic Kingdom opened in 1971 and is the heart of WDW, but access is disappointing unless you can transfer easily from a WC or ECV. With so much exquisite imagination and detail portrayed here, only a wicked stepmother would not recommend it. However, if you are not traveling with small children, you may want to devote your time to the more accessible parks. Nightly, just before closing, Tinkerbell starts off a classic in fireworks above Cinderella's castle. During holidays and summer, Tink is the close to a fabulous 30-min night parade. Hours vary. (I-4 W exit 62D; I-4 E exit 67; 407-824-4321)

General Tips

See Tips on Theme Parks pg 202. Use FASTPASS; see Tips on WDW pg 216. Five restaurants offer table service; make reservations at City Hall as you enter the park or at the restaurant itself. For a walloping 45-min show and a buffet of cold sandwiches and salads, try the Diamond Horseshoe Saloon Revue (arrive at least 15 mins before show times listed in the Guide map).

WC Tips

Of 34 rides and shows, 18 are accessible by WC and 12 by ECV. HC parking gets filled on busy days, so if you can transfer into the tram (where you can store your WC), please use regular parking. From HC parking you must go up and down a steep hill to the Ticket and Transportation Center (TTC) where you buy your ticket for the Kingdom. Trams from regular parking and shuttle buses drop you off at the TTC. From here, you have 2 choices for entering the park. The Monorail circles the lagoon in front of Magic Kingdom. When you arrive at the Monorail station in the kingdom, you must descend a fairly steep 100' ramp. At the end of the day, that ramp becomes VERY steep up to the Monorail boarding area. A slightly slower way to and from the park is the roll-aboard ferry that crosses the lagoon. You might want to enter by Monorail and exit by ferry. You can rent standard WCs at the TTC; inside the park entrance to the right you can rent both WCs and ECVs. WC replacements are at Tinker Bell's Treasure, Frontier Trading Post and Mickey's Star Traders. CRr are in First Aid next to the Crystal Palace off Main Street, on the lower level of Cinderella's Royal Table, at Splash Mountain, Mickey's Toontown Fair, Ursa's Major Minor Mart and TTC East Gate.

ATTRACTIONS

■ MAIN ST USA
Here are many shops and the Main St Cinema (with continuous footage of vintage Disney cartoons). The horse drawn trolley, carriage and other transportation anachronisms (WC, ECV) require a transfer up and into a seat for a 3-min ride in Town Square (WCs can be folded and carried in all vehicles, except the jitneys). Stop in the Barbershop for, in addition to some great harmony, a real haircut; the barbers only dress - not shave - as in the 1800's.

City Hall, where Guest Relations is located, has a ramp to the right, near the Rr.

WDW Railroad (ECV) has boarding from ground level at Toontown Fair; see Toontown.

■ ADVENTURELAND
Swiss Family Robinson Treehouse (WC, ECV) is a clever spiral of 128 steps and rope bridges through 600 branches in a multi-level tree condo.

Shrunken Ned's Junior Jungle Boats are miniature African Queens you can *remotely* control.

Magic Carpets of Aladdin (ECV) make 2-min rides around and, at your control by lever, up and down. You can roll aboard your special magic carpet.

Tiki Birds is a delightful 9-min comedy show run by 4 animatronic parrots and a chorus of 250 feathered friends. Enter the pre-show presentation right of the turnstiles. The air-conditioned Polynesian longhouse, where the show occurs, has a WC aisle with a fine view of the birds mostly perched on the ceiling.

Jungle Cruise (WC, ECV) is a 10-min outdoor boat ride along famous rivers with a speed-talking, wise-cracking guide and animatronic animals at most turns. WCs and ECVs can roll through the exit to the boarding dock and up to the boat where you must step over the 12" side and onto the bench seat around the deck of the boat. You then step down to the deck and sit back for the ride.

Pirates of the Caribbean (WC, ECV) is a 10-min inside boat ride through a pirate attack and plunder that includes a short roller-coaster-type drop down a waterfall. After you have gone through the queue, staff admits WCs past the turnstiles to the boarding dock. You must step over the 13" boat side onto a bench seat with a back and a lap bar. Your WC must be loaded onto the boat because you disembark at another dock where you'll find Rr before a fairly steep moving walkway up to the exit.

■ FRONTIERLAND
WDW Railroad (ECV) has boarding from ground level at Toontown Fair; see Toontown.

Splash Mountain (WC, ECV) is an 11-min wet and wild ride in a hollow log through splashing turns and a thrilling plunge down a 5-story flume into a briar patch. After the queue, staff directs you to the exit side of the boarding dock where you leave a WC or ECV. To board, you step over the 2' high side of the log and sit on a bench seat with narrow leg room and a lap belt.

Big Thunder Mountain RR (WC, ECV) is a 4-min runaway mine train that, by roller coaster standards, is relatively tame but still has some quick turns and fast drops. Enter through the exit at the far right of entrance; stay along the wall to the loading area where you step up 18" to the floor of the train car and sit in a bench seat with a lap bar.

Tom Sawyer's Island (WC, ECV) is a .6-mi natural play area along what Mark Twain might have designed; but only mobile kids can partake the stairs to the play fort, the bridges, hills and caves. WC (not ECV) riders can take the short raft trip if they can get up the 10" from the dock to the raft and wait at the island's dock while able-bodied friends do the exploring.

Country Bear Jamboree is an 18-min show of joking and singing bears. The WC entrance is to the left; WC seating is on the side.

Shootin' Arcade is a chance to try your skill with a 54-caliber buffalo rifle with an electronic beam. The ramp at the left leads to 2 guns at WC height.

■ LIBERTY SQUARE

Diamond Horseshoe Saloon is where dance-hall gals and cowboys regale you for 45 min while you snack or lunch on sandwiches and salads. A ramp is on right by the Hat Shop; with advanced reservations you can sit at a table up front.

Hall of the Presidents opens with a roll call of over 42 lifelike presidential figures and ends with a 24-min film on the Constitution. Enter right of the turnstiles.

Liberty Belle Riverboat is a steam-driven paddlewheeler that takes you for a 20-min ride around Tom Sawyer's Island. Enter through the exit ramp on the extreme left or right of the landing, then roll onto the dock and aboard. Best views are from the railing toward the front.

Haunted Mansion (WC, ECV) offers a slow, spooky 8-min ride through an eerie old mansion inhabited by ghosts and ghouls. WC and ECV riders should go through the FASTPASS lane where staff will direct you to the boarding dock by the exit. Vehicle #2 has a cut-away side for a lateral transfer onto the bench seat with a lap belt. Or, you can step up

10" into the vehicle. Staff can stop the vehicle while you board.

■ FANTASYLAND

It's a Small World (ECV) offers an 11-min slow boat ride through the dang cutest animated international dolls singing the dang cutest tune that will stay with you for the dang rest of the day. Enter through the exit at the far left of the entrance, then take the very steep ramp down to the unloading dock where you are going downstream through the folks heading up to the exit. ECVs must be left at the dock and WCs can roll aboard one of the accessible boats.

Peter Pan's Flight (WC, ECV) requires a transfer into a magic flying ship for a spectacular 2-min trip to Never Land. The WC entrance is to the left. It would take some fairy dust to be able to transfer from a moving walkway and step up 10" into a moving ship and onto the bench seat with a lap bar.

Mickey's Philharmagic is the upcoming musical show just as this book is going to print.

Cinderella's Surprise Celebration is a 30-min stage show with 25 of Disney's favorite characters. The open-air show occurs on the Forecourt Stage (with no seating) in front of the landmark castle. After the show, meet Cinderella and her co-stars.

Cinderella's Carrousel (WC, ECV) requires a transfer to one of the 90 exquisite ponies or stationary chariots on a raised revolving platform. Go to the right of the entrance. Parents can remain by their children on steed.

Ariel's Grotto is a dry lagoon where you can meet the Little Mermaid.

Fantasyland Character Festival, a popular hang out for Pluto, Goofy and friends, is near Ariel's Grotto.

Dumbo (WC, ECV) is one of the most popular rides at the park! A WC entrance is next to regular entrance. The elephant takes small children who can step or be lifted up 12" through a 10" opening to a bench seat. For 2 min riders can determine how high or how many ups and downs Dumbo makes.

Snow White's Scary Adventure (~~WC~~, ~~ECV~~) is a surprisingly rough 3-min ride with quick turns past the evil queen to a happily ever after ending. The WC entrance is at the far right of the queue, next to the exit. Leave your WC or ECV at the boarding dock, then step up 12" through a 10" opening in the vehicle and sit on a bench seat with a lap bar.

Fairytale Garden is an outdoor area where Belle, the Beauty, sometimes reads stories.

Winnie the Pooh (~~ECV~~) has some WC-accessible Hunny Pots to take you to meet Pooh, Eeyore, Tigger and the rest of the Hundred Acre Wood gang. ECVs can't negotiate the tight turns on the queue, but WC riders can roll to the boarding dock and aboard with 1 companion.

Mad Tea Party (~~WC~~, ~~ECV~~) takes place in an elevated teacup for a 2-min twirl that will test even those with good balance. Wait at the exit, right of booth, and staff will lead you in your WC or ECV to a cup. You step 10" up onto the saucer, then up 2' and through an 18" opening into the cup.

■ **MICKEY'S TOONTOWN FAIR**
This largely accessible area is geared for little ones who want to meet and tour the homes of Mickey and his pals.

Barnstormer (~~WC~~, ~~ECV~~) at Goofy's Wiseacres Farm is a 1-min kiddie coaster where WCs and ECVs go through the exit to the boarding dock then step over the car's 18" high side and down into a bench seat with a lap bar.

WDW Railroad (~~ECV~~) is a steam-powered train, with open cars, that circles the entire Kingdom in 21 min. Only at the Toontown Station can you roll aboard from the ground floor. The other stations, at Main Street Station, directly in front of the park entrance, and at Frontierland, have steep 3-tiered ramps to and from boarding. ECV riders must park on the boarding deck and

may want to take the round trip ride to easily return for the ECV. For the better view, keep the park to your right.

■ **TOMORROWLAND**
Speedway (~~WC~~, ~~ECV~~) offers the roar and the grease of a real Grand Prix and the laughs of amateur hour. If you can transfer into the low racecar, you can ride as a passenger. If you're also 52" tall and can handle a gas pedal, brake pedal and steering wheel, you can drive. The wait is long; the race 5 min. After you wait on queue, staff will direct you to a flat boarding area where you roll to the racecar, step over the 23" side of the car and down 10" to the seat, then slide your legs under the dashboard.

Space Mountain (~~WC~~, ~~ECV~~) is an exciting 3-min roller coaster ride in the dark. After the queue, roll through the WC entrance to the boarding area where you must step up 12" over the side of the car and down onto the seat with a lap belt. Staff brings your WC to the disembarking deck where you roll onto a moving belt that goes up and then down a steep hill to the exit. Check your brakes first!

AstroOrbiter (~~WC~~, ~~ECV~~) is a 2-min elevated kiddie ride around space that requires a transfer into a sort of space shuttle. Use the regular entrance where WCs can pull up next to the vehicle that is 32" off the ground and has a bench seat with a lap bar.

Transit Authority (~~WC~~, ~~ECV~~) is a 10-min elevated ride around Tomorrowland that requires you to walk onto a steep moving ramp up to a moving turntable to board a moving vehicle. If this is mass transit in the future, we're in trouble!

Carousel of Progress is a revolving stage that for 21 min traces technological progress during the 20th century. WC and ECV seating is in the rear on a slight incline.

Galaxy Palace Theater is an outdoor venue for live entertainment, with WC seating up front.

Buzz Lightyear's Space Ranger Spin

(ECV) is where you help fight off the evil Emperor Zurg for 5 min by shooting infrared lasers. Two of the space vehicles have ramps that drop to the boarding dock.

Timekeeper is a 20-min, high tech, time-traveling movie in the round. There are no seats in the theater, but staff can advise you on the best viewing spots.

ExtraTERRORestial Alien Encounter (ECV) is a 20-min multimedia, multi-sensory multi-thriller show in total darkness. It is so intense that although no motion is involved, audience members are confined by head and shoulder restraints (with built-in sensory devices, that is). The entrance doors to the left have a more gradual ramp to WC seating (with 1 companion) in the back row. Those nasty aliens may breathe down your neck and spray you with chilly liquids.

MGM Studios

Disney-MGM is a movie theme park as well as a functioning TV and movie production studio. People old enough to be familiar with TV and flicks from *the old days* will probably enjoy it the most. With 154 acres and 18 sizable attractions, MGM can readily be experienced in a day. Oh, but what a fun day! WC access is very good at MGM and distances are not overwhelming, although you do have to backtrack on some streets. Hours vary. I-4 W exit 62D; I-4 E exit 67; 407-824-4321)

General Tips
See Tips on Theme Parks pg 202. Use FASTPASS; see Tips on WDW pg 216. Some say Fantasmic!, the nighttime laser/fireworks show with special water effects, is the best in WDW; see description below. Be aware, on crowded days, the Fantasmic! amphitheater can fill up as early as 90 min before show time. MGM offers some unusual shopping, from movie costumes and Hollywood memorabilia to magic tricks and animating kits. In the entrance plaza ask at the Production Info Window how to get into any shows being taped that day. At Guest Relations (just beyond the entrance, at Hollywood and Sunset), you can make reservations for any of the 5 full-service restaurants, from the Brown Derby to a Sci-Fi drive-in.

WC Tips
Of 18 rides and shows, only 3 rides are WC inaccessible; ECV riders need to transfer at 2 additional rides. Rental WCs and ECVs are in Oscar's Super Service to the right of the entrance. If your rental needs repair or replacement, go to Tattooine Traders (at Star Wars). CRr are in First Aid, adjacent to Guest Relations right of the entrance, and on Sunset Blvd just before the Tower of Terror.

ATTRACTIONS

■ **HOLLYWOOD BLVD**
Tinseltown's main street takes you into the park amidst obvious starlets who happily sign autographs. Try on a movie costume so you can become the cover feature of a major magazine. Sorcerer's Hat is right smack at the end of Hollywood Blvd. Underneath are interactive stations with historic trivia on Disney. The hat makes a great navigational tool for your day because it is roughly in the center of the park.

Great Movie Ride (ECV) takes place in a replica of Grauman's Chinese Theater, behind the Sorcerer's Hat. Ride for 22 min through great movie moments from Gene Kelly's Singin' in the Rain and Bogey's farewell to Bergman, down the Yellow Brick Road, to a hug between Rhett and Scarlett. Enjoy movie clips while on queue. Once inside, keep to the left side of the ramp to roll onto the 12th row of any vehicle.

■ **ECHO LAKE**

Sounds Dangerous starring Drew Carey, in the ABC Sound Studio, is a 12-min movie with headphones for the binaural audio effects. Take the ramp to the left of the entrance for WC seating.

Indiana Jones Epic Stunt Spectacular is a 30-min, truly action-packed live demonstration of lollapalooza stunts in a 2,220-seat amphitheater. WC seating is in the rear. Or, before waiting on queue, let staff know you'd like to sit in front so you can be escorted to the one of the 4 WC spots in front.

Star Tours (ECV, WC) is a thrilling 5-min flight simulator ride on which you accidentally detour through an intense intergalactic war. Once inside, stay left; there's only 24" of space beside the theater seat where you must transfer over the 23" high armrest into a seat with a seat belt. The ride makes sudden jolts and jars; additional shoulder restraints are available.

■ **NEW YORK STREET**

Jim Henson's Muppet Vision 3D, including a pre-show, is a 25-min revue of Muppets, music and special sensory effects. Once inside, staff directs you past the turnstiles where you stay to the right for WC seating in the rear.

Honey, I Shrunk the Kids is a minimally accessible playground amidst giant toadstools and other huge vegetation. A WC gate is right of the turnstiles. The larger than life perspective is fun but most of the play features and the upper levels are inaccessible. The walkway's bumpy surface, narrow passageways and the frenetic traffic of kids-at-play present a severe challenge for WC and ECV riders.

Backlot Theater presents 35-min live stage versions of current Disney animated films. Arrive 20 mins before the show. You have 2 choices for WC seating: one area is level with the entrance, behind the first section of seats; or, take a ramp down to the 1st row in this open-air theater.

■ **MICKEY AVE**

Studios Backlot Tour includes a 35-min tram ride through buildings where costumes are sewn, sets built and lighting tested. Your tram then goes outdoors past 2-dimensional movie sets, a large prop yard and on to Catastrophe Canyon where you experience an earthquake, explosion and flood . . . all at once! If you can transfer, a foldable WC can be stored on the tram for the ride. Or, take a WC-accessible tram, lock your wheels and be prepared for the heat, wet and careening motion at the Canyon. The American Film Institute Showcase is the final scene with memorabilia from the big and little screens and a shop of classy souvenirs like palm-buzzers.

Who Wants to be a Millionaire? is a recreation of the popular TV show in which the audience participates - albeit without a million dollar prize. You can take a lift to the top deck behind arena seating or, use WC seating beside the theater seats on a glass floor at stage level. Disney ECVs are too heavy to sit on the glass floor but you can transfer into a standard WC and staff will return the ECV after the show.

Walt Disney Theater presents the 25-min film, *One Man's Dream,* that tells the story of Walt's life, the birth of the mouse and his visions for the Disney empire. WC seating is in the rear.

Magic of Disney Animation has roll-through exhibits of an animated cartoon as it moves from concept to production.

Voyage of the Little Mermaid is a 17-min live stage show incorporating movie clips, puppetry and special effects. WC seating is in the rear.

Playhouse Disney features 20-min stage shows for tots with the likes of

Pooh and the Bear in the Big Blue House. WC seating is behind the carpeted floor where most of the audience sits.

■ **SUNSET BLVD**

Theater of the Stars, a Hollywood Bowl replica, presents a popular 25-min stage version of Beauty and the Beast. A ramp on the left of the entrance takes you to WC seating in the rear.

Rock'n'Roller Coaster (W̶C̶, E̶C̶V̶) is an extreme 3-min roller coaster ride to the tunes of Aerosmith where you loop upside down and almost inside out! Each roller coaster has one seat with a swing away door for transferring from a WC. You can pull alongside and transfer down into the seat below floor level. You have 30 seconds to complete the transfer.

Twilight Zone Tower of Terror (W̶C̶, E̶C̶V̶) is aptly named. It's a deserted 13-floor haunted hotel where you enter a creaky elevator for a 130' free fall. This 3-min ride requires a short walk to board a seat with a lap belt.

Fantasmic! is an awesome laser light show in which the sorcerer's apprentice fights off the most infamous Disney villains. Take the long incline right of the Tower of Terror to the amphitheater that, on crowded days, can fill up 90 mins before show time. You might want to grab a portable dinner on Sunset Blvd and eat in your seat before the show. Most WC seating is in the rear. Or, if you are willing to risk getting wet, ask staff to take you down in front.

Additional **WDW** Activities

■ **AUTO RACING**

Richard Petty Driving Experience is a chance to take 3 laps around a 1-mi NASCAR track at speeds up to 145 mph! Staff can lift you from your WC down through the stock car's window; the only weight or size limit is that you fit in that window. To drive you must be able to handle the steering wheel, clutch and foot pedals; after a classroom session, your instructor drives a car in front of you. Or, you can simply take the ride of your life as a passenger. Reservations advised. Snack bar; gift shop; Rr. Feb-Sep driving classes start at 8 & 2; ride-alongs run 9-5 (3450 N World Dr, Lake Buena Vista; stay left through the parking lot at Magic Kingdom; 407-939-0130; 800-237-3889)

■ **BOAT RENTALS**

Sammy Duvall's Water Sports Center has a driver/instructor who can take your party out for 1 hr on an 18' powerboat for tubing, water skiing and wakeboarding on Bay Lake near the Magic Kingdom. The marina has a floating dock where you can roll aboard.

From there, with 1-day advance reservations, staff can lift you from your WC into a seat. The driver can help your friends lift you from the seat to the platform in back and into the water for tubing. These are 2-person tubes that you can lay across or sit inside. No swimming or fishing is allowed. (behind the Contemporary Resort; 407-939-0754)

Resorts, including Beach Club, Caribbean Beach, Contemporary, Port Orleans, Polynesian, Wilderness Lodge, Yacht Club, Fort Wilderness and Old Key West as well as Downtown Disney, have marinas with floating docks or floating gangways. Staff cannot help with any transfers. You can rent roll-aboard pontoon boats (30" entries) for up to 6, canoes, rowboats, pedal boats, water mice (boats for 2 with 9hp motors) and canopy boats (basically dinghies for 6) by the half hour. No swimming or fishing is allowed, but you can tour either Bay Lake or Lake Buena Vista and its 3-mi canal, depending on which resort you choose. (407-939-7529)

■ DINING WITH CHARACTERS

Make reservations 60 days beforehand (407-939-3463).

Artist Point Restaurant offers an all-you-can-eat breakfast with Winnie the Pooh, Tigger and Eeyore. 5:30-11am (Wilderness Lodge, 901 Timberline Dr)

Cape May Cafe serves breakfast with Chip n' Dale, Admiral Goofy and Pluto. 7:30-11am (Beach & Yacht Club Resort, 1800 Epcot Resorts Blvd)

Chef Mickey's serves breakfast and dinner buffets with the chef and his friends. 7:30-11:30am; 5-9:30pm (Contemporary Resort, 4600 N World Dr)

Cinderella's Royal Table is an all-you-can-eat breakfast buffet in Cinderella's Castle with Disney characters and Cinderella as the guest of honor. This is THE most popular breakfast in town; book 60 days ahead at 7am EST! 8-10am (Castle, Magic Kingdom)

Donald's Pre-historic Breakfastosaurus Buffet is where you'll find Donald, Mickey, Goofy and Pluto. 7-10am (Dinoland, Animal Kingdom)

Garden Grill is a slowly revolving *tretaurant* (be wary, those of you with motion sickness!) overlooking a desert, prairie and the Great Plains. Disney's gang is there. 8:30am-8pm (The Land, Epcot)

Polynesian Breakfast may tempt Mickey and friends to show up in grass skirts. 7:30-11am (Polynesian Resort, Seven Seas Dr; by Magic Kingdom)

1900 Park Fare offers a buffet breakfast with Mary Poppins (7-11am) and a dinner buffet with a variety of villains (5:15-9pm). (Grand Floridian, Floridian Way; by Magic Kingdom)

■ DINNER THEATER

Make advance reservations by calling 407-939-3463.

Hoop-Dee-Doo Musical Revue is a chance to sing, stomp and laugh your way through a 90-min corny show and barbecue. WC- accessible tables on the first floor; enter by a ramp on the side of the building. If you're not staying at Fort Wilderness, park in the outer lot and take an accessible bus to the Pioneer Hall for the show. (Pioneer Hall, 3520 N Fort Wilderness Trail)

Polynesian Luau Dinner Show is an authentic grass-skirted dance show and luau held outdoors at 5:15 and 8pm Tue-Sat. Arrive early for pre-show fun. (Polynesian Resort, 1600 Seven Seas Dr; near Magic Kingdom)

■ FISHING CHARTERS

Resorts, including Beach Club, Caribbean Beach, Contemporary, Port Orleans, Polynesian, Wilderness Lodge, Yacht Club, Fort Wilderness and Old Key West as well as Downtown Disney, have marinas with floating docks or floating gangways. Staff cannot help with transfers. Various fishing trips are offered at these marinas, from serious 2-, 3- and 4-hr excursions to kids' trips and old-fashioned cane pole fishing. All are catch-and-release and all include gear and bait. Depending on which resort you select, fish either the Bay Lake or Lake Buena Vista and its 3-mi canal; both have been stocked. Minimum 24-hr advance reservations during summer and holidays (407-939-7529)

■ GOLF

WDW has an adaptive golf cart that, with 24 hr advance notice, can be used on any of 5 18-hole PGA Tour level golf courses as well as a challenging 9-hole course. You can ride the cart on the greens but not through the deep bunkers. Staff cannot help with transfers. Rr at each club house; beverage carts sell sandwiches (407-939-7529)

■ NIGHTSPOTS

BoardWalk is a Disney-style Atlantic City with no gambling but a variety of waterfront shops, dining and nightspots. Choices range from the ESPN Club where even the bathrooms have sports running on TVs to the Atlantic Dance's swing bands and Jellyrolls (where you sing along with dueling pianos). $ only at Atlantic Dance & Jelly Rolls (W of Epcot; off Epcot Resort Blvd; 407-939-3492)

Pleasure Island is just what a grown-up Pinocchio might imagine: 8 theme nightclubs, each with its own style of music from old time rock 'n' roll to jazz and a comedy club. Performances are often held at the outside main stage. While all is accessible, you must contend with a hilly walkway and at night, often immense crowds. Guests under 18 must be accompanied by adults; in the Mannequins Dance Palace and BET SoundStage you must be 21 or older. After 7pm $. Shops 11am-mdnt; clubs 7pm-2am (Downtown Disney)

Disney West Side has the House of Blues. (Downtown Disney)

Laughing Kookaburra Good Time Bar offers great music, dining, dancing and an every night special. Free valet parking. Tue-Sat 5pm-2am; entertainment 9pm (Wyndham Palace Resort & Spa, 1900 Buena Vista Dr; across from Downtown Disney; 407-827-3722)

■ **PARASAILING**

Sammy Duvall's Water Sports Center offers 10-min solo/tandem parasailing at 450' or 600' over Bay Lake. From a floating dock you can roll aboard the back of the 18' powerboat. From there, staff can lift you into a seat and then onto the platform for take-off. Solo flyers must be 100-325lbs. Kids under 14 must be accompanied by a paying adult. (back of Contemporary Resort; by Magic Kingdom; 407-939-9754)

■ **SHOPPING**

Disney provides for shopaholics throughout WDW - in the parks, many restaurants and even at Cirque du Soleil. For serious sprees, check out the Marketplace in Downtown Disney where you'll also find several fabulous restaurants for lunch and dinner.

■ **SHOWS**

Cirque du Soleil is an astounding 90-min performance of extreme choreographed gymnastics. Take the elevator to WC seating behind the 1st section, about midway from the stage. Rr. Mon, Thu-Sat 6 & 9pm; Sun 3 & 6pm (Downtown Disney; off of

Buena Vista Dr; 407-939-7719)

■ **SPECTATOR SPORTS**

Wide World of Sports/World International Sports is a complex of stadiums and fields that hosts more than 100 tournaments and events in more than 40 sports, amateur and professional. From basketball, gymnastics and inline hockey to tennis, cricket and martial arts, the state-of-the-art venue is here. All facilities offer a wide range of WC seating and Rr. The All Star Cafe serves lunch and dinner. (Victory Dr; I-4 exit 64B; 407-363-6600)

Baseball The Atlanta Braves hold spring training here in Mar and the Orlando Rays, Class AA of the Tampa Bay Devil Rays, play here Apr-Sep. See Wide World of Sports.

Basketball The Harlem Globetrotters train here periodically throughout the year. See Wide World of Sports.

■ **VIDEO ARCADE**

DisneyQuest, in Disney's West Side, is a 5-story interactive adventure pushing, the old video arcade into the electronic age. The building, including 2 restaurants and a gift shop, is accessible, however many of the traditional arcade games and virtual extravaganza are not. The accessible highlights include a pinball machine (where you are the ball getting blitzed around a huge screen in front of WC-height controls), a creative area where even non-artistes can create funky masterpieces and the chance to record your own CD. Unfortunately, other virtual reality experiences are virtually inaccessible, requiring tough transfers to a motorcycle-type vehicle, a raft or a capsule for a self-designed roller coaster ride. 10:30am-midnight (Downtown Disney; off Buena Vista Dr; 407-824-4500)

■ **WATER PARKS**

Typhoon Lagoon is minimally accessible but it is the most accessible of the 3 water parks in WDW. Remember, staff cannot help with transfers. You can borrow waterproof WCs (fixed arms) at the entrance and enter the surf pool where waves bob comfortably during odd hours. During even hours, surf is up (for 10 min, then off for 10 min) and the 4' waves are extremely strong; you can find protection in the coves off the lagoon. You can also roll up the spill deck at Shark Reef, where you need to manage a 3 1/2' drop into (and out of) the water to snorkel among tropical fish, including some sharks (equipment included). At Castaway Creek, you must negotiate 4 steps to transfer into a tube for a 1/2-hr float through rain forests, caves and *broken pipes* as you circumvent the park. The slides and rafting/tubing rides have steps, often many flights of stairs, to the boarding areas. Snack bars/restaurants; Rr; CRr. Summer 9-7; winter 10-5 alternate days with Blizzard Beach; closed Oct-Dec (off Buena Vista Dr; W of Downtown Disney; 407-560-4027)

ACCOMMODATIONS

■ WDW

Within WDW, you'll find a huge array of accessible lodging, from luxurious resorts and villas to modest hotels and camping. If your plan is to visit only Disney attractions, the convenience of staying at WDW and not having to use your own vehicle is a definite plus. The traffic near the parks can get fearsome, especially during the summer and holidays. You'll find it quite easy to get around WDW by accessible and frequent buses. If you make reservations far enough in advance (several months for peak season!), you should find rooms starting in the $$ category. Disney owns some but not all onsite accommodations.

We do not describe individual Disney facilities here (except for Fort Wilderness Campground) because of the ease in finding a wide range of accessible lodging through WDW's Resort Special Reservations at 407-939-7807. If you stay in a Disney facility, you receive some special perks: each day of the week you can enter a designated park 90 mins before opening; you can charge meals and purchases to your room; and you're guaranteed entrance even when a park has reached capacity.

Here are some choices to ponder before you call for Disney accommodations. If you're most interested in a particular park, ask about facilities closest to that park. Most of the hotels have themes and special features. For example, the Polynesian Resort not only looks like Fiji, it has a beach, a pool with caves and boat rentals for the Seven Seas Lagoon. The newest hotel is the resplendent 1300-room Animal Kingdom Lodge where you can watch African animals right off your balcony. Even the least expensive Disney hotels, the All-Star Sports and All-Star Music Resorts carry out themes in whimsical architecture and cuisine.

Many hotels offer childcare, even elaborate dinner shows for kids and dormitories for those late adult-only nights. And, various Disney characters routinely frequent several hotel restaurants. Disney facilities offer a range of choices, from basic hotel rooms to villas with full kitchens and championship golf course privileges (an adaptive cart is available). Ask which Disney hotels offer special features, from roll-in showers and lower-level kitchen appliances to lower beds and portable commodes.

For information on non-Disney hotels in WDW (although they call themselves *official* WDW hotels) and off WDW grounds in Lake Buena Vista, see below. Two of the non-Disney hotels, the Swan and the Dolphin, offer the same perks as Disney hotels. Dolphin (407-934-4000; 800-227-1500); Swan

(407-934-3000; 800-248-7926).

■ **B&Bs**

PerriHouse B&B Inn has 2 charming ADA Bird House Cottages nestled on 16 secluded acres of woodlands and grassy fields. Each 1BR cottage has a 4-poster king bed (platform), see-through fireplace and whirlpool for 2. Bathrooms have raised toilets, roll-under sinks and roll-in showers with seats. Continental breakfast buffet; laundry; mini-kitchenette; WC-accessible shuttles to attractions. $$$ (10417 Centurion Ct, Lake Buena Vista; I-4 exit 68, N on 535, at 2nd light E on SR 535 for 3 mi; 407-876-4830; 800-780-4830)

■ **CONDOS**

Vistana Resort has 17 ADA and 32 WC-friendly 1BR and 2BR condos. Each unit has a king bed (open frame) in the master bedroom and queen sofa bed in the living room. The 1BR units have kitchenettes; the 2BR units have full kitchens and either 2 twins or 2 full beds in the 2nd bedrooms. ADA units have bathrooms with raised toilets and roll-in showers; WC-friendly units have tubs; some bathrooms have hand-held sprayers and seats. Pool; laundry; full restaurant; entertainment; miniature golf course; free accessible shuttles to area attractions. $$$ (8800 Vistana Centre Dr; 407-239-3100)

■ **MOTELS**

Buena Vista Suites has 14 ADA 1BR suites, each with a king bed (platform), sofa bed in the living room, kitchenette and bathroom with a roll-under sink, hand-held sprayer and seat; rooms 122, 124 and 224 have roll-in showers. Free brkfst; pool; laundry; lounge; restaurant for breakfast & lunch; free WC-accessible shuttles to WDW. $$$ (14450 I-Dr; 407-239-8588; 800-537-7737)

Country Inn has 2 ADA rooms each, with a king or 2 queen beds (platforms), a refrigerator, microwave and coffeepot. Bathrooms have raised toilets, roll-under sinks and roll-in showers with hand-held sprayers and shower sears. Free brkfst; laundry; fitness room. $$ (12191 S Apopka Vineland Rd; 407-239-1115; 877-737-8546)

Homewood Suites have 6 ADA 1BR suites, each with a king or 2 queen beds (23" high/platforms), full sofa bed and full kitchen. Bathrooms have raised toilets and roll-under sinks; rooms 131 and 132 have roll-in showers with hand held-sprayers and seats; others have tubs. Free brkfst; pool; laundry. $$-$$$ (8200 Palm Pkwy; 407-465-8200; 800-370-9894)

Summerfield Suites have 8 ADA suites. The 1BR suites have a king bed; the 2BR suites have a king and 2 full beds (all 22" high/open frames). All have full sofa beds in the living room and full kitchens. Bathrooms have roll-under sinks and roll-in showers with hand-held sprayers. Free brkfst; pool; laundry. $$$ (8751 Suiteside Dr; 407-238-0777; 800-334-0890)

**Did you know that:
...Epcot's Living Seas has two in-water programs?
See page 222.**

**...there's a discount for disabled guests at SeaWorld and both Universal parks?
See WC Tips on pages 206 and 209.**

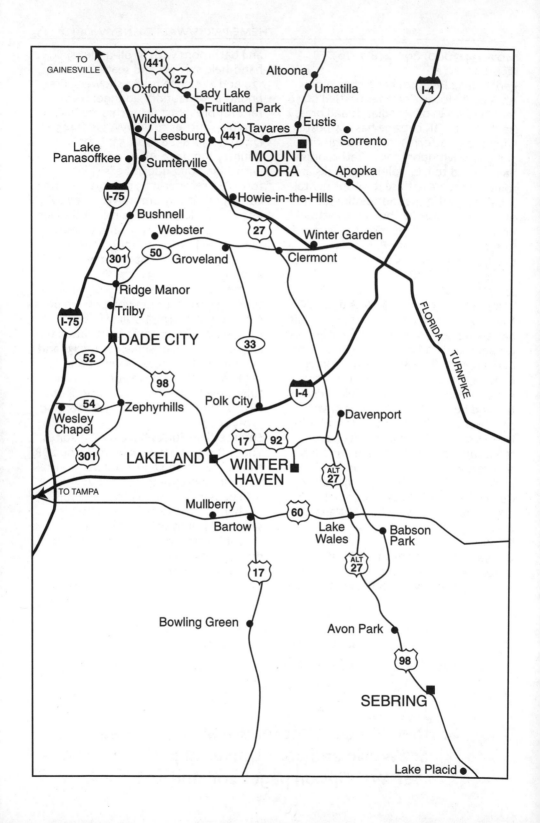

CENTRAL

DADE CITY
Bushnell, Lake Panasoffkee, Oxford, Ridge Manor, Sumterville, Trilby, Webster, Wesley Chapel, Wildwood, Zephyrhills

Enjoy Dade City's charming, historic downtown, the Withlacoochee River Park and a 46-mile bike trail that starts in north Pasco County. Anglers can enjoy the Withlacoochee River and local lakes while land lovers can spend Mondays at one of the country's largest flea markets or any day at Dade Battlefield.

Tourist Info
Chamber: 14112 8 St, Dade City 33525; 352-567-3769
Sumter County Chamber: 225 S US 301, Sumterville, 33513; 352-793-3099

ACTIVITIES

■ **BIKE TRAILS**
Parks: Millennium
Withlacoochee State Trail is a paved, fairly flat, rails-to-trails path running N 46 mi from Trilby to just S of Dunnellon. The trail follows the Withlacoochee River and goes through the Withlacoochee State Forest (where hunting seasons occur Oct-Apr; call for schedule and wear fluorescent orange at those times). The only steep grade on the trail is the bridge over SR 50 at Ridge Manor. Access points, with parking, Rr and water, include: Lake Townsen Park (.5 mi W of trail; CR 476; just E of CR 39 & Nobleton), Silver Lake Park (1 mi E of trail; from SR 50, N 3.5 mi on Croom Rital Rd; 352-754-6896) and Ridge Manor Trailhead (at US 98/SR 50, just E of I-75). The southern terminus is the Trilby Trailhead, near the Post Office off CR 575 with HC parking. Order the Trail Guide with a mile-by-mile history, recreational sites and businesses through Rails-to-Trails of the Withlacoochee. (Box 807, Inverness, 34451; 352-726-2251)
■ **BOAT RAMPS**
Lake Deaton Park is a 10-acre county

park with a lighted boat ramp and fixed dock (dawn-10pm) on the 778-acre lake. By 2003, a 150' fishing pier and ADA picnic tables should be available. Dawn-dusk (5300 CR 115, Wildwood)

Lake Miona Park is a 5-acre county park with a lighted boat ramp and fixed dock (dawn-10pm) on the 418-acre lake. By 2003, a 225' dock with a fishing area, ADA picnic tables and Rr should be available. Dawn-dusk (1051 CR 115, Oxford; off CR 472)

Lake Okahumpka Park is a 108-acre county park with a boat ramp and fixed dock (dawn-10pm) on the 670-acre lake. By 2003, a paved 1-mi nature trail, fishing pier, ADA picnic tables and Rr should be available. Dawn-dusk (6085 E SR 44, Wildwood)

■ **BOAT RENTALS**
Idlewild Lodge rents a 20' pontoon boat (31" entry) for a day of fishing on Lake Panasoffkee. With low rainfall, water levels can be problematic, so call a week ahead; if necessary, staff can often arrange a rental at another marina with an accessible dock. Bait shop (4110 CR 400, Lake Panasoffkee; CR 470, 5.5 mi W of I-75, then N 1 mi; 352-793-7057)

■ **FISHING PIERS**
Parks: Withlacoochee. Boat Ramps

■ **FITNESS TRAILS**
Kenny Dickson is a 20-acre city sports complex with a 1-mi fitness trail on hard-packed clay. ADA picnic shelters; ball fields; tennis; racquetball; Rr (824 W Noble Ave, Bushnell)

■ **MUSEUMS**
Pioneer Florida Museum has restored structures from Florida's pioneering days including a railroad depot, schoolhouse and church, all connected by paved paths. The buildings house priceless antiques, farm tools, household utensils, carriages, buggies, a fire engine and a steam locomotive. In the main building there is a collection of dolls depicting Florida's governors' wives in their inaugural gowns. Only

the logging buildings and shoe shop are inaccessible. Rr, in barn. $. Tue-Sun 1-5 (Pioneer Museum Rd; E of US 301, 1 mi N of Dade City; 352-567-0262)

■ **PARKS**
Dade Battlefield Historic State Park is where the 2nd Seminole War began. Get an overview of the battle at the visitor center (9-5), then navigate hard-packed grass to check out the battlefields, a short historic trail and a 1-mi nature trail. Call for the schedule of the annual 2-day Seminole War reenactment in late Dec or early Jan; the annual WWII commemorative is the 1st Sat in Aug. ADA picnic tables on grass; Rr. $. 8-dusk (Battlefield Dr, Bushnell; off CR 476, 1.5 mi E of I-75; 352-793-4781)

Millennium Park is a 117-acre city sports and nature complex that will be under development through 2011. A community center, ball fields, basketball courts, tennis, ADA picnic tables and trails are planned for the early years. A .5-mi paved walking trail and a 4- to 5-mi bike trail will wind through this lovely shady park. (Huey St, Wildwood; 1.5 mi E of US 301)

Sam Harris Park is a city sports park with an ADA playground. By 2003, a .5-mi paved trail will lead to downtown. ADA picnic tables; ball fields (SE Central Ave, Webster; just E of downtown)

Withlacoochee River Park is a 408-acre county park with 12 mi of packed-mulch nature trails and an observation tower with a steep ramp to the 1st level looks over the tree line. You can fish in the Withlacoochee River from a very wide dock with benches but no railing or lip. Each Mother's Day, Powwows are held at the park's Indian village of teepees, a lean-to and roundhouse. With advance permission, drive most of the way to the village. The marked interpretive trail is mostly boardwalk or hard packed with one hill where you may need help. Primitive campsites have no facilities; with advance notice, you may drive near your site. ADA picnic shelters; grills; playground; Rr. 7am-dusk (12449 Withlacoochee Blvd)

■ **POOLS**

Hercules Aquatic Center has a Jr Olympic pool with a lift (sling seat). Lifeguards cannot help you transfer but will lower you into the pool. ADA picnic table; locker room with roll-in shower. Summer noon-7pm; Sep wknds only (38110 SR 54, Zephyrhills; at US 301; 813-782-8215)

■ **SHOPPING**

Antiques & Boutiques abound in historic downtown Dade City.

Wester Flea Market has 40 acres and 1500 vendors selling antiques, new and used merchandise and fresh produce. Hard-packed grounds & parking; restaurant & snack bars; Rr. Mon 6:30-2 (SR 471 at CR 478, Webster; 352-793-2021)

ACCOMMODATIONS

■ **CABINS/CAMPGROUNDS**

Idlewild Lodge, at the remote N end of Lake Panasoffkee, rents 1 and 2BR cabins, each with a living room and full kitchenette. Cabin entrances have 3" lips; large standard bathrooms have roll-under sinks. Choose a king or 2 full beds; linens, not towels, are included. RV sites have concrete pads, full hookups and picnic tables. Bathhouses have grab bars, roll-under sinks and roll-in showers (ladies get a hand-held sprayer). Enjoy a dock for fishing; see Boat Rentals. Pool; small laundry (4110 CR 400, Lake Panasoffkee; I-75 exit 321, W 5.5 mi to CR 400, then N 1 mi; 352-793-7057)

Withlacoochee State Forest-Croom Tract is minimally accessible because of sandy soil and soft dirt roads. However, the Silver Lake area has campsites with elec, close to a bathhouse with roll-in showers. There are some level, open areas to fish along the Withlacoochee River. Hours depend on hunting season and staffing. (from US 301 in Bushnell, go W on CR 50, then N on Rital-Croom Rd; 352-754-6777)

■ **MOTELS**

Best Western has 2 ADA rooms, each with a king or 2 queen beds (22" high/open frames), refrigerators and bathrooms with toilet extenders, roll-under sinks and roll-in showers with hand-held sprayers and seats. Free brkfst. $-$$ (57434 Gall Blvd/US 301, Zephyrhills; 813-782-5527)

Best Western Guest House has 24 ground-floor rooms, with 1 or 2 full beds (open frames). The bathroom door is narrow, but you can access the sink in the vanity area. Free brkfst; pool; restaurant nearby. $-$$ (2224 W CR 48, Bushnell; 352-793-5010)

Budget Suites has a WC-friendly suite with wide doors, 2 full beds (platforms), a full sofa bed in the living room and a kitchen (no plates or pots). The standard bathroom has a grab bar at the tub. Pool; restaurants nearby. $ (343 E SR 44, Wildwood; I-75 exit 329; 352-748-8883)

Days Inn has an ADA room with 2 full beds (open frames) and a bathroom with a grab bar and tub/shower. Free brkfst; pool; laundry. $-$$ (551 E SR 44, Wildwood; I-75 exit 329; 352-748-7766)

Hampton Inn has 2 ADA rooms, each with 1 full bed (platform) and a bathroom with a roll-under sink and roll-in shower with hand-held sprayer and seat. Free brkfst; pool; nearby restaurants. $$ (301 Cortez Rd, Ridge Manor; I-75 exit 301; 16 mi N of Dade City; 352-796-1000)

Sleep Inn has 4 ADA rooms, each with a queen bed (platform) and a bathroom with raised toilet, roll-under sink and roll-in shower with hand-held sprayer and seat. Free brkfst; pool; laundry. $-$$ (5703 Oakley Blvd, Wesley Chapel; 813-973-1665)

Super 8 has a WC-friendly room with wide doors, 2 full beds (open frames) and a bathroom with a raised toilet and grab bar at the tub. $ (344 E SR 44,

Wildwood; I-75 exit 329; 352-748-3783)

LAKELAND
Bartow, Mulberry, Polk City

Lakeland's burgeoning cultural calendar and beautiful lakes attract both residents and visitors alike. Check out the remote Tenoroc Fish Management Area for some uniquely accessible fishing.

Tourist Info
Chamber: 35 Lake Morton Dr, 33801; 863-688-8551
Polk County Visitors Information: 863-298-7565
Web site: www.sunsational.org

Transportation
Citrus Connection serves Lakeland, Bartow, Winter Haven and much of western Polk County; most buses have lifts. (863-688-7433)

ACTIVITIES

■ ATTRACTIONS
Fantasy of Flight starts with *immersion experiences,* or interactive, multi-media displays that bring aviation history to life. Then check out 20 vintage aircraft and a flight simulator. Two 45-min tours enter restricted areas: at 1:15, a Back Lot Tour explores an extensive collection of aircraft; at 3, a Restoration Tour takes you where aircraft is being restored. From 2:30-3, watch vintage aircraft in flight. Art Deco restaurant 8-4pm; loaner WCs; gift shop; Rr. $. 9-5 (1400 Broadway Blvd SE, Polk City; I-4 exit 44; 863-984-3500)

Frank Lloyd Wright Architecture is best seen at the campus of Florida Southern College. Self-guided tours should start at the visitor center (wkdy 10-4; Sat 10-2; Sun 2-4) where you can examine the architect's drawings, photos and correspondence. Parking at corner of Johnson & McDonnell Sts (111 Lake Hollingsworth Dr; 863-680-4597)

■ BOAT RAMPS
Tenoroc Fish Management Area has 14 lakes, 8 with boat ramps and no docks, and 3 (Lakes 2, 3 & Picnic Lake) with boat ramps and floating docks. See Fishing Piers. $/free with FL Disabled Fishing Licenses or Management Area Stamps. Fri-Mon 6-5:30 (3829 Tenoroc Mine Rd; I-4 exit 38, S on SR 33 1 mi, S on SR 659 1 mi, then E; 863-499-2422)

■ BOWLING
AMF Bowling Center has 2 ramped lanes and a bowling ball ramp. Game room; snack bar; Rr. Sun-Thu 9-11; Fri-Sat –2am (4111 S Florida Ave; 863-646-5791)

■ FISHING CHARTERS
Lake Wales: Fishing

■ FISHING PIERS
Tenoroc Fish Management Area, a 6400-acre former phosphate mine site, has 14 lakes, 7 to 250 acres in size. Each has its own regulations and angler quotas. The 17-acre Derby Lake facilities are designed and reserved for physically challenged anglers and 1 companion each (with a state fishing license). The lake has 3 fishing platforms, a 200' pier, a ramped ADA picnic shelter and Rr. $/free for those with FL Disabled Fishing License or Management Area Stamps. Fri-Mon 6-5:30 (3829 Tenoroc Mine Rd;

I-4 exit 38, S on SR 33 1 mi, S on SR 659 1 mi, then E; 863-499-2422)

■ **KAYAKING**

Search 4 Adventure gives lessons and guides trips on the W coast in either solo sit-in or tandem sit-on kayaks; must have upper body control. The instructor/guide, Jimmy Long, has taken the course in adaptive paddling and has a wilderness medical license. He can arrange for staff to help with transfers and for the staff physical therapist to be available. Classes can be given in the Gandy Pool, which has a lift. Call for schedule. (863-425-2822)

■ **MISC**

Lake Morton Senior Center has a range of guest speakers, classes, card games, daily 1-mi walks on a paved path around the lake and more. Rr. Wkdy 9-3:30 (90 Lake Morton Dr; 863-687-2988)

■ **MUSEUMS**

Explorations V is an interactive museum for kids, 2-12 yrs old, where they learn to be smart shoppers, pilot the space shuttle and report news at a miniature TV station. Call about rotating exhibits and workshops. Rr. $. Hrs vary (125 S Kentucky Ave; 863-687-3869)

International Sport Aviation Museum displays aircraft including ultra-lights, home-built and experimental aircraft, warbirds and a collection of 1930's vintage planes. The flight simulator is inaccessible. Each Apr the museum sponsors the popular Sun 'n' Fun Fly-In. Rr. Mon-Sat 10-4; Sun 12-4 (4175 Medulla Rd; 863-644-0741)

Mulberry Phosphate Museum has an extensive collection of fossils that were recovered locally during phosphate mining, including a unique 10 million-yr old Baleen whale and a 5 million-yr old Dugong skeleton. A 15-min film describes the phosphate industry. Rr. Tue-Sat 10-4:30 (SR 37, Mulberry; 1 block S of SR 60; 863-425-2823)

Polk County Historical Museum, housed in a 1908 courthouse, tells the region's history from prehistoric, Semi-nole and pioneer times. Other displays chronicle the area's natural history as well as the cattle, citrus and phosphate industries. Ramp on E side of bldg; Rr. $D. Tue-Fri 9-5; Sat 9-3 (100 E Main St, Bartow; 863-534-4386)

Polk Museum of Art features Pre-Columbian, contemporary American, European decorative and Asian art as well as rotating exhibits and an outdoor sculpture garden. Call for the schedule of lunchtime lectures, classes for kids and adults, docent-led tours and weekend films. Rr. Mon-Sat 10-5; Sun 1-5 (800 E Palmetto St; 863-688-7743)

Water Ski Hall of Fame houses a large collection of photos, displays, equipment and a video on the history and stars of water skiing. $D. Wkdy 10-5 (1251 Holy Cow Rd, Polk City; I-4 exit 44; 863-324-2472)

■ **PERFORMING ARTS**

Lakeland Center has an arena that holds sporting events and big-name entertainment. The Youkey Theater hosts Broadway shows and musical performances, including classical and pops concerts by the Imperial Symphony Orchestra. The arena's WC seating is on all levels; the theater's WC seating is midway on the sides and in the center rear of the orchestra section. For the arena and exhibition hall, park at the W entrance; for the theater, use the E lot. Rr (700 W Lemon St; 863-834-8111)

Pied Piper Players are local actors performing musicals, dramas, comedies or children's shows in Oct, Dec, Mar, Apr and Jul. WC seating in rear; parking behind theater; entrances in front & on side; Rr (Lake Mirror Theater, 121 S Lake Ave; 863-603-7529)

Polk Theater, once a vaudeville theater, now features nationally known performers Nov-Mar or independent and foreign films on weekends. WC seating is in the aisle on a slight incline near the front and on a level area at the rear. Park in neighboring business parking lots; CRr (121 S Florida Ave; 863-682-8227)

■ POOLS
Gandy Pool has a zero-depth ramp and a submersible WC you can borrow to enter the heated pool. Call for the lap and open swim schedule. Rr. May-Oct daily; Nov-Apr wkdy hrs vary (401 Imperial Blvd; 863-648-3157)

■ SCUBA
Deep Six Divers offer dive lessons, certification and trips. The 5-wk classes meet Mon and Wed or Tue and Thu 6:30-10:30pm at the Gandy Pool; see Pools. Open water dives are at a local lake where you can drive to the water's edge, then staff can help you from your WC and into deeper water. Dives can also be arranged at Atlantis Dive Center (in Key Largo) over a weekend when HSA-certified staff is available. Call John Appelboom 863-688-0830.

■ SHOOTING RANGES
Tenoroc Shooting Facility has air rifle, 100-yd rifle, 15- and 50-yd pistol ranges, sporting clays and an elevated archery facility with an elevated shooting platform. Rr. Thu-Mon 8-5 (3755 Tenoroc Mine Rd; I-4 exit 38, S on SR 33 1 mi, S on SR 659 1 mi, then E; 863-666-2500)

■ SHOPPING
Antiques are found in historic downtown Lakeland (near Kentucky Ave & Pine St).
Malls: Lakeland Square Mall (US 98 & I-4)

■ SPECTATOR SPORTS
Baseball Detroit Tigers hold spring training in Mar and the Class A Lakeland Tigers play Apr-Sep. The stadium is being renovated and WC seating may be expanded; currently it is behind home plate, with folding chairs for companions. Rr (Joker Marchant Stadium, 2301 Lakekand Hills Blvd/SR 33; 863-688-7911)

ACCOMMODATIONS

■ MOTELS
AmeriSuites has 2 ADA suites, each with a king bed (open frame), sofa bed, refrigerator, microwave and coffeepot. Bathrooms have raised toilets, roll-under sinks and roll-in showers. Free brkfst; pool; laundry. $$ (525 W Orange St; 863-413-1122)

Baymont Inn has 8 ADA rooms, each with a full bed (platform). Bathrooms have raised toilets and roll-under sinks; rooms 123 and 223 have roll-in showers with hand-held sprayers and seats; others have tubs. Free brkfst; pool. $-$$ (4315 Lakeland Park Dr; 863-815-0606)

Hampton Inn has 4 ADA rooms, each with a queen bed (24" high/open frame). Bathrooms have raised toilets and roll-under sinks; room 119 has a roll-in shower with a seat; others have tubs. Free brkfst; pool. $$ (4420 N Socrum Loop Rd; 863-816-2525)

LaQuinta Inn has 4 ADA rooms with a king or 2 full beds (23" high/platforms) and an ADA suite with a king bed, sofa bed in the living room, coffeepot, refrigerator and microwave. Bathrooms have raised toilets and roll-under sinks; room 121 has a roll-in shower and hand-held sprayer; others have tubs. Free brkfst; pool; laundry. $$ (1024 Crevasse St; 863-859-2866)

Terrace Hotel, a luxury hotel built in 1924 and restored in 1998, has 4 ADA rooms and an ADA 1BR suite, each with a king or 2 queen beds (open frames) and a coffeepot; the suite has a sofa bed in the living room. Bathrooms have raised toilets, roll-under sinks and step-in showers with seats; room 20 has a roll-in shower. Lounge; full restaurant. $$$ (329 E Main St; 863-688-0800; 888-644-8400)

MOUNT DORA
Altoona, Clermont, Eustis, Fruitland Park, Groveland, Howey-in-the Hills, Lady Lake, Leesburg, Sorrento , Tavares, Umatilla

Mt Dora is reminiscent of New England with hills, huge shady oaks, fine antique stores and northern architecture. The unspoiled beauty of 1400 lakes, filled with bass and crappies, is one of the main draws to this area.

Tourist Info
Chamber: 341 N Alexander St, Mount Dora 32757; 352-383-2165; 800-798-1071
Chamber: 691 W Montrose St, Clermont 32712; 352-394-4191
Web sites: www.mt-dora.com; www.lakecountyfl.com; www.clermont-fl.com

Transportation
Lake County Transit has lift-equipped vehicles for door-to-door service throughout the county at the same charge as public bus. Call 352-360-6618 the day before by 2pm.

ACTIVITIES

■ ATTRACTIONS
Citrus Tower is a 226' observation platform, with an elevator, where you can see miles in all directions. The gift shop sells and ships citrus. Restaurant; Rr. $. Mon-Sat 9-6; Sun 11-5 (141 N US 27, Clermont; 352-394-4061)

House of Presidents is a museum of wax figures and memorabilia of all US presidents. A doll-size White House has such details as ticking clocks and pens on desktops. Gift shop. $. 9-5 (123 US 27 N, Clermont; 352-394-2836)

Uncle Donald's Farm offers 1-hr tours, including a chance to milk a goat and feed baby animals. A Florida panther, hawks and owls reside here too. You can board the hayride by ramp. Paths are grass or wood chips. ADA picnic tables; CRr. Tue-Sat 10-4; Sun varies (2713 Griffin Ave, Lady Lake; 352-753-2882)

■ BIKE TRAILS
Parks: Lake Louisa, Waterfront
General James A Van Fleet State Trail is a 20-mi, paved trail through the half million-acre Green Swamp, with pine flatlands, wiregrass savannahs, wetlands and cypress ponds. Take a trail map and water because you are out in the wilds. Access points are in Mabel (off SR 50) and on Green Pond Rd (off SR 33, 10 mi N of Polk City). Both trailheads have Rr, ADA water fountains and ADA picnic shelters. (Map & info: 352-394-2280)

West Orange Trail is a 19-mi asphalt trail through beautiful countryside from County Line Station (at SR 50 and US 438) through downtown Winter Garden to Apopka (at 6 St and Forest Dr). The 5-mi stretch between County Line and Winter Garden Trail Stations is mostly level and mid-way is an accessible butterfly garden. The hills between Winter Garden and Apopka are gradual, but long. Each station has an ADA picnic shelter. Rr & ADA water fountains along the trail (Office 9-5; 455 E Plant St, Winter Garden; 407-654-5144)

■ BOAT RAMPS
Parks: Hickory Point. Campgrounds: Fisherman's Cove
Herlong Park has a boat ramp and floating dock on the 9000-acre Lake Griffin. 24 hrs (US 441 between Lake & Canal Sts; 352-728-9885)
Palatlakaha River has a boat ramp and floating dock in a remote area where

Water Boy was filmed. This ramp is the only access to the Clermont Chain of Lakes. (Hull Rd, Clermont; from US 27, S of SR 50, turn W on Hook St, S on Lakeshore Dr, E on Hull; 352-343-9761)

■ BOAT RENTALS
Accommodations: Mission Inn
Fun Boats rents 7- and 10-person pontoon boats (32" entry) and speedboats by the hour or for the day on Lake Dora. If you choose, staff can drive and lift you aboard in your WC from a floating dock. Dawn-dusk (Lakeside Inn, 100 N Alexander St; 352-735-2669)

Palm Gardens Rentals has a 9-person pontoon boat (30" entry) to rent on Lakes Eustis and Harris, 2-hr minimum. Because the water level varies, you may need help boarding from the fixed dock; if so, call in advance. Bait shop; restaurant. 9-5 (Palm Gardens Cottages, 11801 US 441, Tavares; 352-343-2024)

■ BOAT TOURS
Capt Charlie's Cruises offers 1 1/2-hr nature tours on the Dora Canal. Request the accessible *Miss Dora.* Hrs vary (Gator Inland Marina, 1505 US 441, Tavares; 352-343-0200)

Heritage Lake Tours offers 1 1/2-hr wildlife tours on a pontoon boat along the Dora Canal and Dead River. Call to check the water level for WC boarding. Rr at marina. Mon-Sat 11 & 2 (Palm Gardens, 11801 US 441, Tavares; 352-343-4337)

Rusty Anchor features 3-hr luncheon cruises (11:30) on Lakes Eustis and Dora and 1-hr sunset cruises on Lakes Dora and Beauclair. On the luncheon cruise, you stop at a restaurant (lunch not included in price). Call in advance to check water levels and to schedule a pick up at the accessible dock in Gilbert Park. (400 W 4 Ave; 352-383-3933)

Yesteryear Boat Cruises offers 3 different trips on a 58' riverboat; the 1st deck is accessible. Try the 1 1/2-hr sightseeing or 3-hr dinner cruise along the Dead River and Lake Harris or a 2-hr lunch cruise on Lake Eustis. CRr. Mon-Sat 9-6 (12423 US 441, Tavares; 352-343-7047)

■ CAMPS
Boggy Creek Gang is a camp designed, equipped and staffed for children, age 7-16, with chronic or life-threatening illnesses. Founders include Paul Newman and Gen Norman Schwarzkopf. Choose week-long summer camps or family retreat weekends; each session is specifically geared for kids with a particular medical condition, such as spina bifida, epilepsy, cancer and more. Activities include boating, fishing, horseback riding, swimming, archery and art. Staff can help anyone in a WC to participate in every activity possible. The Boggy Creek Gang is funded by donations; campers pay no fees. Call for information and an application. (30500 Brantley Branch Rd, Eustis; 352-483-4200)

Camp Challenge is sponsored by Easter Seals for folks with physical disabilities who want to experience the outdoors and good ole fashioned camp fun. Summer sessions run 12 days for either children (from age 5), teens, young adults or adults that include fishing, swimming, arts and crafts, archery, a rifle range, nature trails, a petting zoo, campfires, hayrides through the woods and much more. ADA dorm-type cabins have AC and roll-in showers. The pool is ramped and submersible rolling chairs are used to enter the pool. Call for information year round. (31600 Camp Challenge Rd, Sorrento; 352-383-4711)

■ CANOEING/TUBING
Parks: Lake Griffin

■ FISHING CHARTERS
Palm Gardens Fishing Service offers half/full-day trips on a 24' pontoon boat adapted for up to 3 WCs. Fish the Harris Chain of Lakes. You can reserve a capt, who is also an RN and can tend to medical needs. Rr. 9-5 (Palm Garden Cottages, 11801 US 441, Tavares; 352-343-2024)

■ FISHING PIERS
Parks: Downtown Mt Dora, Hickory Point, Lake Louisa, Palatlakaha, Waterfront

Eustis Lake Walk is a 3000' sidewalk along the lovely Lake Eustis with some covered areas where you can fish. If you are coming by boat, you can disembark on the floating docks (no boat ramp). 24 hrs (601 N Shore Dr, Eustis)

Singletary Park has a 100' pier on Little Lake Harris. Picnic tables. Dawn-dusk (US 27; 1 mi S of Leesburg; 352-728-9885)

Herlong Park has a 40' lighted pier on Lake Griffin. (US 441; between Lake & Canal Sts, Leesburg; 352-728-9885)

■ **GLIDING**

Seminole-Lake Gliderport offers a chance to soar as high as 1 mi in a glider. Staff can lift you from your WC (weight limit 240 lbs) and 3' into the semi-reclining padded seat in the glider cockpit. The pilot/instructor sits behind you. A tow plane takes you up to the elevation you select; the height determines the charge and length of your trip, from 25 to 45 min. You can use the control stick to make turns. To learn to fly here, you must be able to use your feet to control the rudders. The National Senior Glider Championships are held here each Mar. Call for schedule. CRr (4024 Soaring Ln, Clermont; SR 33 & SR 561; 352-394-5450)

■ **HANG GLIDING**

Quest-Air Hang Gliding School is the spot for a thrilling ride or lessons in hang gliding. Staff can lift you from your WC and lay you prone in a harness, which is then suspended from the hang glider. The instructor is suspended beneath you. An ultralight tows you up 2500', the glider is released and you glide for 15-20 min over glorious rolling countryside. Mornings and evenings are usually the best flight times. For a ride, hand dexterity isn't needed. For lessons, you must be able to grip the control bar; anticipate 20 lessons before you're ready to solo. CRr (6548 Groveland Airport Rd, Groveland; E of Clermont off SR 50; 352-429-0213)

■ **HOT AIR BALOONING**

Rise and Float Balloon Tours can carry up to 2 WCs and 6 companions in a balloon adorned with pink flamingos! Staff can lift you from your WC, board the WC and then lift you back into it. A champagne toast follows the 1-hr trip. Launch sites are generally near Howie-in-the-Hills. Lift-off just after sunrise (407-352-8191)

■ **MISC**

Senior Center has crafts, cards and bingo weekly. Call for schedule. For lunch, sign up the day before. Rr. 8:00-5:00 (1211 Penn St, Leesburg; 352-326-3644)

■ **MUSEUMS**

Mt Dora Center for the Arts features rotating exhibits of Florida artists. $D. Wkdy 10-4; Sat 10-2 (138 E 5 Ave; 352-383-0880)

■ **PARKS**

Downtown Mt Dora has several lovely, small parks. These 3 are connected: Gilbert Park has a playground with ADA equipment, a picnic area and Rr. Palm Island Park has a short boardwalk around Lake Dora. Grantham Point has a sidewalk out to a lighthouse and 4 fishing docks. Dawn-dusk (S Tremain St & Liberty Ave; 352-735-7183)

Hickory Point Park is a 68-acre county park on the shores of the 14,000-acre Little Lake Harris. Enjoy the lighted 250' ADA fishing pier and boat ramps with fixed and floating docks. A .5-mi boardwalk loops through the woods. A 2-story picnic shelter, with an elevator, is available for rent. ADA picnic tables; ADA playground; CRr. 24 hrs (27341 SR 19, Tavares; 352-343-3777)

Lake Griffin State Park is a lovely 460-acre park, half of it wetlands, on the shore of the 9000-acre Lake Griffin (with more gators than University of Florida). Near the ranger station is a 300-year old, live oak tree, one of the largest in the state. A 300' cement dock offers fishing on a freshwater canal. A .5-mi, hard-packed trail goes through an oak hammock. You can rent canoes by the hour. Staff can help WC paddlers transfer from the slightly sloped, grassy launch area into a canoe; on return send someone in to the ranger station. See Campgrounds. ADA picnic tables; playground; Rr. $. 8-dusk (3089 US 441/27, Fruitland Park; 2 mi N of Leesburg; 352-360-6760)

Lake Louisa State Park includes over 4000 acres on the shores of Lakes Louisa and Dixie. The quiet park roads offer some 5 mi for biking. One road leads to a boardwalk that takes you to an ADA bathhouse (with roll-in showers), beach and swim area on Lake Louisa. The other road leads to a paved path to an ADA fishing dock on Dixie Lake. A campground with ADA bathhouses and furnished ADA cabins should be completed by 2004. ADA picnic table; CRr on Dixie Lake. $. 8-dusk (US 27; 5 mi S of Clermont; 352-394-3969)

Palatlakaha Park is a city sports and nature park with a 605' boardwalk winding through a wooded wildlife area along Lake Palatlakaha to a small fishing pier. Picnic area; Rr. Dawn-dusk (1250 12 St, Clermont; 352-394-6763)

Waterfront Park, 2 blocks from downtown on Lake Minneola, has 2 fishing piers (one 600' long), a picnic area, concession stand and 3.5-mi paved trail along the lake. Across a grassy area is a beach and a sidewalk to a swimming pier, that, depending on the water level, can be 1'-6' above the water. Dawn-dusk (938 Lake Minneola Dr, Clermont; 352-394-6763)

■ **PERFORMING ARTS**

Bay Street Players, a local theater group, performs musicals, classics and a children's production Oct-Jul in the State Theater. WC seating on aisles in rear of theater; street parking; Rr (109 Bay St, Eustis; 352-357-7777)

Melon Patch Players perform Sep-May. WC seating in front on left; Rr (311 N 13 St, Leesburg; 352-787-3013)

Mt Dora Community Building is home of 2 concert series: A Pop Organ Series

features international artists performing one Sun each month Jan-Apr (352-383-6975). A Winter Concert Series features visiting orchestras and bands Jan-Mar (352-735-0411). WC seating in rear of theater; Rr (520 Baker St)

Mt Dora Theater Company offers a variety of shows Sep-Jun by performers from throughout the state. WC seating in rear of theater; Rr (Ice House Theater, 1100 N Unser St; 352-383-4616)

The Villages Organ Series is held one Sat each month Jan-Apr. WC seating at ends of pews; Rr (Church on the Square, Main Street, Lady Lake; reservations: 352-383-6975)

■ **POOLS**

Aquatic Center has a heated pool with a lift (fixed seat); lifeguards can help with transfers. Rr. Days/hrs vary (250 Ferran Park Dr, Eustis; 352-357-3264)

Lincoln Ave Pool is heated and, if you call beforehand, staff can set up the portable lift (sling seat), help you transfer and lower you into the water. Rr; locker room with roll-in shower. Hrs vary (Lincoln & Unser Sts; 352-735-7173)

■ **SHOPPING**

Antiques: Mt Dora has antique shops, galleries, boutiques and fine restaurants in downtown.

Umatilla Antique & Flea Market is a large, indoor, AC facility. Rr. Aug-Jun Thu-Sat 9-4 (811 N SR 19, Umatilla; 5 mi N of Eustis; 352-669-3202)

■ **TOURS**

Lakeridge Winery is a working vineyard with self-guided tours, wine sampling and frequent events, from car shows and jazz concerts to craft shows and grape stomping. You need to be able to climb stairs to get an overview of the production facilities, however, on the 1st floor is a video of the winemaking process. You can roll through part of the arbors. Gift shop; Rr. Mon-Sat 10-5:30; Sun 11-5:00 (19239 US 27, Clermont; 352-394-8627; 800-768-9463)

ACCOMMODATIONS

■ B&B/INNS
Darst Victorian Manor is a lovely house, just outside downtown, with the charm of the Victorian era and the convenience of ADA construction. The ADA Priscilla Room is on the 1st floor with its own entrance from the driveway as well as an interior entrance. The room has a full bed (28" high/open frame) and the private bath has a raised toilet, roll-under sink and roll-in shower. A hearty breakfast is served in the dining room. $$$ (495 Old Hwy 441; 352-383-4050; 888-533-2778)

Lakeside Inn, circa 1883, is a downtown Mt Dora landmark with a WC-friendly room in the ramped Carriage House. The room has 2 twin beds (open frames) and a small standard bathroom. The main building, with a lovely restaurant and lively lounge, has a ramp in the back. A very wide pier over Lake Dora is a great spot for socializing or fishing. See Boat Rentals. $$$ (100 Alexander St; 352-383-4101)

Lakeside Landing, in downtown Mt Dora, has a charming ADA 1BR suite with a queen bed (25" high/open frame), sitting room, full kitchen and private entrance. The bathroom has a raised toilet, roll-under sink and roll-in shower with a hand-held sprayer and seat. Check-in & free brkfst at the Lakeside Inn, 100 Alexander St. $$$ (644 N Donnelly St; 352-383-4101)

■ CABINS/CAMPGROUNDS
Parks: Lake Louisa
Fisherman's Cove, with 40 acres on Lake Harris, has a small motel and 336 RV sites. The WC-friendly room #3 has a king bed (platform) and a large bathroom with grab bars, a roll-under sink and roll-in shower. RV sites have full hookups, picnic tables and a bathhouse with a step at the door and a step-in shower. You can fish off the docks at the onsite marina with a boat ramp and fixed docks. Shuffleboard; pool; social program Nov-Apr; 9-hole, par-3 golf course. $ (29115 Eichelberger Rd, Tavares; 352-343-1233; 800-254-9993)

Lake Griffin State Park has 40 RV/tent sites with ADA picnic tables and access to a gently sloped boardwalk to an ADA bathhouse with roll-under sinks and roll-in showers. Sites 31 and 34 have ADA fire pits. The roadway can be a bit bumpy for manual WCs. Reservations 11 mo in advance for winter (3089 US 441/27, Fruitland Park; N of Leesburg; 352-360-6760)

■ MOTELS
Campgrounds: Fisherman's Cove
Holiday Inn Express has 4 ADA rooms, each with a king or 2 full beds (26" high/open frames). Bathrooms have raised toilets and roll-under sinks; rooms 107 and 215 have roll-in showers with hand-held sprayers and seats; others have tubs. Free brkfst; pool; laundry. $$ (1810 S US 27, Clermont; 352-243-7878)

Comfort Inn has 2 ADA suites and 2 ADA rooms. Each 1BR suite has a living room, refrigerator, microwave and king bed (platform); rooms have 2 full beds (platforms). Bathrooms have raised toilets, roll-under sinks and roll-in showers. Free brkfst; laundry; pool. $$ (16630 US 441 W; 352-383-3400)

Mission Inn Golf & Tennis Resort, set on 625 acres of rolling countryside on Lake Harris, offers 4 ADA rooms with 2 full beds (platforms). Bathrooms have roll-under sinks; rooms 516 and 520 have roll-in showers with hand-held sprayers and seats; others have tubs. A boardwalk leads to a marina with a floating dock and pontoon boats (30" entry) for half/full-day rentals. Pool; lounge with entertainment; full restaurant; tennis courts; 36 holes of championship golf. $$$ (10400 CR 48, Howey-In-The-Hills; 352-324-3101; 800-874-9053)

SEBRING
Avon Park, Bowling Green, Lake Placid

This small town is known worldwide for its 12-hour International Grand Prix of endurance each March. Enjoy Highlands Hammock State Park or an ultralight experience!

Tourist Info
Lake Placid Chamber: 18 N Oak St, 33852; 863-465-4331; 800-557-5224
Highland County Visitors Bureau: 309 South Cir, 33870; 863-385-8448; 800-255-1711
Web sites: www.sebring.com; www.lpfla.com

ACTIVITIES

■ **ATTRACTIONS**
Archibold Biological Station is a unique environmental research operation with seminars and educational opportunities for the public. The station also manages the 10,000-acre Buck Island Ranch. Rr. $D. Wkdy 9-5 (Old SR 8, Lake Placid; 863-465-2571)

■ **BOAT RAMPS**
Parks: Bishop

■ **BOWLING**
Royal Palms Bowling Center has ramped lanes and bowling ball ramps. Special Olympics bowling competitions are held here. Game room; pool tables; snack bar; lounge; Rr. Hrs vary (800 US 27 S, Lake Placid; 863-699-0925)

■ **DINNER THEATERS**
Highlands Little Theater offers community performances of Broadway shows. WC seating at table ends on 1st level; parking lot on slight hill; Rr. Fri-Sat dinner shows; Sun dessert matinee; Wed show only (Lakeside Playhouse, Lakeview Dr & W Center St; 863-382-2525)

■ **FISHING PIERS**
Parks: Bishop

■ **HORSEBACK RIDING**
Heartland Horses & Handicapped, sponsored by Kiwanis, offers recreational, 30-min riding lessons for disabled folks with at least some balance. Two sidewalkers accompany each rider. Staff can lift you onto a horse from a mounting block; other adaptive equipment is available. The program is free but pre-approval and a physician's release is needed. Call Sandy Kuhn 863-655-0553. Sat mornings (4-H Arena, George Blvd; off US 27)

■ **MISC**
Sun Room Senior Center has lunch socials Wed and Fri 9-3 and bingo Thu 1-4. Call beforehand with any special needs. (3015 Herring Ave; 863-382-8188)

■ **MUSEUMS**
Children's Museum offers hands-on activities including banking, working a TV station, making music and painting your own face. Special programs are offered throughout the year. Rr. $. Tue-Sat 10-5; Thu -8 (219 N Ridgewood Dr; 863-385-5437)

■ **PARKS**
Bishop Park has a lighted 200' fishing pier over Lake June, where bluegill and crappie test your angling skills. The railing precludes easy WC fishing, except at the end of the pier. The canal also has a fishing dock and boat ramp with a floating dock . Across grass is a playground and beach, both on very soft sand. Picnic tables & grills on grass; Rr (6-5). 6am-10pm (10 Lake June Clubhouse Rd, Lake Placid; .5 mi W of US 27; 863-699-3717)
Highlands Hammock State Park, with over 5000 acres, has a loop road through scenic virgin forest, cypress

swamp and marsh. Some trees are 400 to 1000 yrs old. Nov-May rangers give guided walks but check beforehand because trails vary and may not be accessible. The Cypress Swamp Trail has a short boardwalk ending at an overlook on a creek; the Fern Garden Trail has a 200' boardwalk through a fern marsh and gator habitat. A museum tells the history of the Civilian Conservation Corps in Florida (10-3:30). ADA picnic tables on grass; WC loaner; snack bar Nov-May; Rr. See Campgrounds. $. 8-dusk (5931 Hammock Rd; off CR 634, 3 mi W of US 27; 863-386-6094)

Paynes Creek State Historic Site once contained a trading post and Army fort in the 1850's. The original structures no longer exist but a visitor center explains the history. Use a brochure about the flora along a .5-mi, paved nature trail. You must negotiate grass and dirt to reach the banks of a fine fishing creek that branches from the nearby Peace River. ADA picnic shelters; grills; ADA playground; Rr. $. 8-dusk (888 Lake Branch Rd, Bowling Green; 25 mi W of Sebring; 863-375-4717)

■ **SHOOTING**
Silver Harbor Lodge has a .5-mi sporting clays course through the woods and a target game area. The course is mostly mulched with some sandy surfaces and several of the 13 stations are above WC level. You can drive your vehicle up to the target game area. Reservations; Rr. Tue-Sun hrs vary (1630 Virginia Ave, Lake Placid; from US 27, E on Virginia Ave, then N 5 mi; 863-699-0035)

■ **SHOPPING**
Antiques: Quaint downtown Sebring and the beautifully landscaped Mile Long Mall in nearby Avon Park have specialty and antique shops.
Malls: Lakeshore Mall (901 US 27 N; 863-471-3535)

■ **ULTRALIGHTING**
Rans East can take you on a 15-min to 1-hr ultralight flight above beautiful natural areas. Staff can lift you 2' from your WC into a seat on the plane (250-lb limit). Lessons are available but require use of foot pedals. Your pilot, Jeff Hudson, has been flying ultralights for 25 yrs. He can put floats on the ultralight for landing and taking off on water. (Sebring Airport, 11 Crosley Ln; from US 27, 1.5 mi E on US 98; 863-382-3203)

ACCOMMODATIONS

■ **CAMPGROUNDS**
Highlands Hammock State Park has 112 RV sites (full hookups) and 26 tent sites (water only) with picnic tables and grills. Sites 1-40 are near a hard-packed path to the ADA bathhouse with raised toilets, roll-under sinks and roll-in-showers. You can drive to 16 primitive sites in a pine flatwoods. See Parks. Campfire programs Nov-Apr; camp store (5931 Hammock Rd; off CR 634 W of Sebring; 863-386-6094; 800-326-3521)

■ **MOTELS**
Quality Inn has an ADA room and 2 ADA suites, each with a queen bed (platform). Bathrooms have raised toilets and tubs with hand-held sprayers and seats. Suites have sofa beds in the living room, coffeepots, refrigerators and microwaves. Pool; lounge; entertainment. $$-$$$ (6525 US 27 N; 863-385-4500)

WINTER HAVEN
Babson Park, Lake Wales

In addition to Cypress Gardens, Winter Haven boasts world-class fishing on two chains of lakes. Lake Wales, with one of Florida's higher elevations (at 250' above sea level!), looks out on miles of citrus groves. Bok Tower lures most tourists.

Tourist Info

Chamber: 401 Ave B NW, Winter Haven 33882; 863-293-2138; 800-871-7027
Chamber: 340 W Central Ave, 33859; 863-676-3445
Polk County Visitors Information: 1339 Helena Rd, 33884; 863-298-7565
Web site: www.sunsational.org; www.winterhavenfl.com

Transportation
See Lakeland.

ACTIVITIES

■ ATTRACTIONS
Audubon Center has a nature museum, ramped bird observation area and soft sand trail. To enjoy the various workshops and programs, you must handle a grassy parking lot and dirt path to the center. Sep-May Tue-Sat 10-2 (200 N Crooked Lake Dr, Babson Park; off SR 17; 863-638-1355)

Bok Tower Gardens cover 157 tranquil acres around the historic, 205' bell tower that houses 57 bronze carillon bells. Recitals occur daily at 3 and for special events. The visitor center has an 8-min video and exhibits. You may want to rent an ECV here to navigate the mulched paths through the gardens. A 1-mi, hard-packed but hilly trail has interpretive signs along the way. One-hour tours of the gardens occur twice a day Jan to mid-May. Oct to mid-May, docents lead 1-hr tours (for an additional charge) through the 1930 Pinewood House, a 220-room Mediterranean mansion with an elevator. Tours at 11 and 1:30 are limited to 12 people; the path to the mansion is hilly. Oct-Apr the Gardens are popular with morning bird watchers. ECV rentals; WC loaners; restaurant; gift shop; Rr. $. 8-6 (1151 Tower Blvd; from SR 60 in Lake Wales, N on SR 17, E on Burns Ave; 863-676-1408)

Cypress Gardens is the oldest and, perhaps, most beautiful of Florida's attractions. In addition to botanical gardens and a world famous water ski show on Lake Eloise, enjoy some fine entertainment. If you have a little girl in your party, ask about the 2-hr Jr Belle program in which she can learn about and dress as a Southern belle. Be aware, the 200 acres are hilly with some steep grades. The Bazaar Gift Shop, at the entrance, rents WCs and ECVs. Gift shops; restaurants; Rr in Magnolia Mansion & Banyan Terrace. $. 9:30-closing varies (2641 S Lake Summit Dr; S of CR 540; 863-324-2111; 800-282-2123)
Botanical Gardens include 16 acres of 8000 exquisite plants, trees and flowers from 90 countries. The 2-mi paved paths are hilly and steep in areas. ADA water fountains are midway. *Botanical Boat Cruise* (~~WC, ECV~~) is a 15-min tour along a canal through the Botanical Gardens. Staff can help you get down a step at the dock, then step onto a boat seat and down to the floor to sit in a bench seat. Cruises are continual. *Water Skiing Show* is a 30-min medley of thrills and grace on skis interspersed with comedy, climaxing with the famed 4-level human pyramid. Both ski stadi-

ums are ramped: the North Stadium, at either end and the South, in the center. WC seating is at the rear of both stadiums. Two to 4 shows occur daily. *Paddlewheel Boat* (ECV) makes daily 30-min excursions at an additional charge, and has dinner and Sunday brunch cruises by reservation. Staff can help you over the lip at the entry to the 100' boat. The 1st deck includes the restaurant, dance floor, bar and Rr; the open-air upper deck is inaccessible. Cruises make a 7-mi trip past many birds, maybe alligators and some lovely lakeside homes. *Butterfly Conservatory* is a huge, glass Victorian structure with a stream, waterfall and 1000 free-flying butterflies and exotic waterfowl. *Ice Palace* has a 30-min ice show starring many former Olympic skaters. WC seating is in the rear of this nice cool theater. Several shows occur daily. *Carousel Cove* is a kiddy area of games and rides. While the area is flat, all rides require transfers. *Wacky Water Park* has slides and water play for kids and higher, longer and more daring slides for adults; slides are inaccessible. There are dressing rooms and lockers. *Cypress Junction* is an exhibit of 20 model trains speeding through miniature replicas of US landmarks, from Miami to Mt Rushmore. *Plantation Gardens* has sidewalks along rows of herbs and vegetables with mulched paths to some plants. Staff is available for questions. *Island in the Sky* is an enclosed rotating platform, with WC seating that ascends 153' for a 5-min panorama of Cypress Gardens and surroundings. As you leave this area, enjoy the *Railway Garden,* an expansive floral and waterfall display. *Crossroads Pavilion* presents concerts on weekends, from Big Band to country. WC seating is in the rear of the pavilion; additional seating is in a large grassy area. *FloraDome* is a world of colorful flowers and exotic plants in a setting of ponds, streams, bridges and a waterfall. *Cypress Roots* is a small display of the park's history. *Nature's*

Arena presents a 20-min nature show on either birds of prey or reptiles; WC seating is in front. *Antique Radio Museum* is a small museum of radio history. *Birdwalk Aviary* is a 5000 sq ft, netted home to lorries and lorikeets who are so friendly they land on your shoulder and eat from your hand. The door to the entry chamber is quite heavy to push; a companion or staff may need to help. *Nature's Boardwalk* winds along the lakefront and past habitats occupied by animals from swans to patagonian cavies. It's a great place to catch Florida sunsets. *Nature's Way* is home to small animals that often not seen in large zoos. A short sidewalk takes you close to prairie dogs, cotton-topped tamarins and baby gators.

Spook Hill is where, inexplicably and for free, your car can coast UPhill. (from downtown Lake Wales, go N on Scenic Hwy, E at North Ave, follow signs)

■ **FISHING CHARTERS**
Lake Wales: Fishing Charters
A #1 Bass Guide Service has half/full-day or night charters for 2 anglers on a bass boat at a variety of lakes within a 60-mi radius. With advance notice, Capt Pete can get help to lift you from your WC into a boat seat. He can meet you at your hotel or a dock. (352-394-3660; 800-707-5463)
Capt Tucker offers freshwater fishing from a pontoon boat (30" entry) for half/full-day trips on local lakes. (863-299-1188)
Memory Makin Guides offer half/full-day trips on various central Florida lakes aboard a pontoon boat (30" entry) for up to 6 anglers or a bass boat for 2 anglers. Tell Capt Reno if you need help transferring onto the bass boat. (863-635-6499; 800-749-2278)

■ **FISHING PIERS**
Parks: Lake Kissimmee

■ **MISC**
Senior Center has shuffleboard, bingo, card games and weekly entertainment. Call for a calendar. CRr. Wkdy 9-4 (250

Lake Silver Dr; 863-291-5870)

■ MUSEUMS

Art Center has rotating exhibits and programs that include guest speakers and films. A concert series with classical and popular music runs Nov-Apr. Rr. Mon-Sat 9-4; Sun 1-4 (1099 SR 60 E, Lake Wales; 863-676-8426)

Lake Wales Depot Museum is a restored, 1928 railroad depot with exhibits on local history including the turpentine, railroad, citrus and cattle industries. View a Pullman car, 1926 caboose and 1944 engine. WC parking is in front but someone must notify staff to open the door at the ramp on the right. To enter one exhibit room you must exit the building and go to the back where a lift takes you to the upper level. $D. Wkdy 9-5; Sat 10-4 (325 S US 27A, Lake Wales; 863-678-4209)

■ PARKS

Lake Kissimmee State Park covers 5000 acres of forest teeming with wildlife, from bald eagles to bobcats. Flatwoods Pond has a fishing dock. Learn about Florida's cattle industry, pet a Brahman and meet a *cow hunter* (who shares his tales) at the 1876 Kissimmee Cow Camp (wknd 9:30-4:30). The way to the camp is hard packed but tough to navigate if wet; you can arrange at the ranger station to drive to it. Picnic areas are plentiful. Trails are soft sand. Rr. $. 7-dusk (14248 Camp Mack Rd, Lake Wales; 863-696-1112)

■ PERFORMING ARTS

Museums: Art Center

Lake Wale's Little Theater performs mid-Sep to mid-Jun with each season's opening and closing shows geared to children. WC seating is upfront on the right. Park next to the bldg; Rr (411 N 3 St, Lake Wales; 863-679-8587)

Theatre Winter Haven is a community theater with WC seating in the 1st row on either side. Rr (Chain of Lakes Civic Center, 210 Cypress Garden Blvd; 863-294-7469)

■ SHOPPING

Antiques and collectibles can be found in historic Lake Wales between Central and Park Aves.

Malls: Eagle Ridge Mall also has good birding at the retention pond on the N side Oct-Apr mornings. (3700 US 27 N; 863-676-2300)

■ SKYDIVING

World Skydiving Center can take paraplegics on tandem jumps. After a 30-min, on-the-ground briefing, staff can lift you onto the plane's floor or bench seat. Extra staff assists in the plane with exiting and on the ground with landing. Enjoy 14,000' by free fall for 60 sec and parachute the remaining 5 min over lakes and countryside. The additional staff necessitates a small extra charge. 8-dusk (Lake Wales Airport, 440 Airport Rd; 863-678-1003)

■ SPECTATOR SPORTS

Baseball: The Cleveland Indians hold exhibition games at the Chain of Lakes Stadium in Mar. WC seating is behind the 13th row. Rr (500 Cletus R Allen Dr; 863-293-3900)

ACCOMMODATIONS

■ B&Bs

Chalet Suzanne is a whimsical hodgepodge of an inn with turrets and a multi-star restaurant. Two WC-friendly rooms have a king or 2 full beds (open frames). The Brick Road room has a roll-in shower; the other has a tub. The pool area is not accessible. Staff can help your WC up the steep ramp to the 4-star restaurant. $$$ (3800 Chalet Suzanne Rd; 4 mi N of Lake Wales, off US 27; 863-676-6011; 800-433-6011)1

■ MOTELS

Historic Hillcrest Lodge has WC-friendly rooms and villas on 6 acres on Lake Caloosa. Rooms have a queen or 2 twin beds. Choose a king or 2 twin beds (open frames) in the 1BR villas, each with a full kitchen, living room, dining room and attached garage with a 3" step into the villa. All units have standard bathrooms with grab bars available. A 150' pier offers fishing and the 2nd floor restaurant has a ramp. $ (241 Palm Ave, Babson Park; 863-638-1712)

Holiday Inn has 3 ADA rooms, each with a king bed (24" high/platform) and a bathroom with a raised toilet and roll-in shower with a hand-held sprayer and seat. Pool; full restaurant. $$-$$$ (1150 3 St SW; 863-294-4451)

Lake Roy Beach Inn has 2 WC-friendly suites, each with 2 full beds (open frames or platforms), a full kitchen, sofa bed in the living room, screen porch and bathroom with a step-in shower and hand-held sprayer. This spotless resort sits on Lake Roy, popular for sunsets and water sports, including fishing off a dock, fishing from a boat (see Fishing Charters) and, for able-bodied guests, free paddleboats and water bikes. Free brkfst; boat ramp & cleats on the beach for private boats; pool. $$$ (1823 Cypress Gardens Blvd; 1 mi W of Cypress Gardens; 863-324-6320)

Ranch House Motor Inn has 6 ADA rooms, each with 2 full beds (open frames) and a bathroom with a raised toilet, roll-under sink and step-in shower with a seat. Pool; laundry; full restaurant. $-$$ (1911 Cypress Gardens Blvd; 863-324-5994)

If you can't swim but tend to sink...
Maybe you should think...
about scuba diving!

See page 14 and Index page 413.

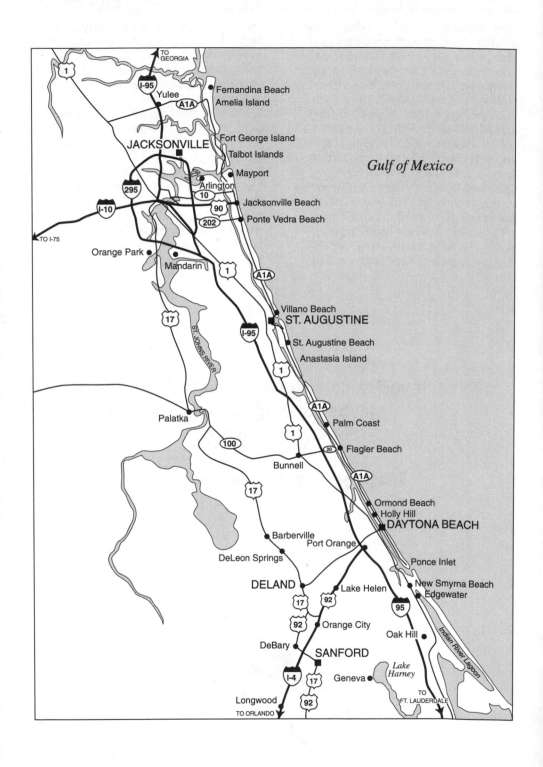

NORTHEAST ATLANTIC COAST

DAYTONA BEACH
Edgewater, Holly Hill, New Smyrna Beach, Oak Hill, Ormand Beach,
Ponce Inlet, Port Orange

The Daytona area is known for more than 20 miles of very wide, hard-packed beaches where you may drive and park on the sand (and borrow beach wheelchairs!). Daytona's love affair with the automobile doesn't end there. In addition to watching auto races, you can get behind the driver's wheel at two racetracks. Hurricanes have battered these shores in recent years but happily have meant reconstruction of piers and dune crossovers to ADA specs. You'll find here a public golf course with an adaptive golf cart and ample saltwater fishing. US 92 is also called International Speedway Boulevard; SR A1A is called Ocean Shore Blvd north of Daytona Beach and Atlantic Ave through Daytona south to the Space Coast.

Tourist Info
Daytona Beach Visitors Bureau: 126 E Orange Ave, 32114; 386-255-0415; 800-854-1234/544-0415
Daytona USA Visitors Center: 1801 W US 92, 32176; 386-253-8669
New Smyrna Beach Visitor Center: 115 Canal St, New Smyrna Bch, 32168; 386-428-2449
Web sites: www.daytonabeach.com; www.newsmyrnabeachonline.com

Transportation
Votran has buses with lifts serving all of Volusia County. (386-761-7700)
Votran Gold offers door-to-door, lift-equipped van service in Volusia County for residents and visitors who cannot use the bus. You must pre-qualify and make 24-hr advance reservations. 6-6 (Applications 386-756-7496 x 230; Reservations 386-322-5100)

ACTIVITIES

■ ATTRACTIONS

The Casements, formerly the winter home of John D Rockefeller, is a museum and event center with an elevator to all 3 floors. Permanent collections include Rockefeller family items, Hungarian cultural artifacts and Boy Scout memorabilia. One room is furnished as it was in 1913 when the Rockefellers moved in. Guided 20-min tours occur on weekdays from 10-2:30 and Saturday 10-11:30. Art shows, concerts and other events are frequently held on the grounds. WC entrance near parking on S side; cafeteria; Rr. $D. Wkdy 9-5; Sat 9-noon (25 Riverside Dr, Ormond Bch; S of E Granada Blvd; 386-676-3216)

Daytona USA is a high tech hands-on attraction where you experience some of the thrills of racing. A 55' screen surrounds you in a 14-min film, *The Daytona 500*. In the STP, exhibit you design and video-test your own racecar, and in the ESPN exhibit, you broadcast the race of your choice; both have special kiosks for WC riders. You can purchase a souvenir video of your race. One exhibit traces the history of racing from 1903. Electronic arcade; souvenir/apparel store; restaurant; WC loaner; Rr. $. 9-7 (1801 W US 92; by International Speedway; 386-947-6800)

■ AUTO RACING

Finish Line Racing School gives wannabe racers a chance to learn and veterans a place to hone their skills. The school can accommodate drivers with mobility impairments. Wheel up to the car by ramp, transfer onto the windowsill and use the grab bar overhead to transfer into the driver's seat with hand controls; staff can help. Take a ride-along session if you just want the experience of riding in a stock car. Half/full-day instructions are for novices; 2- to 3-day programs are for serious racers. Schedule varies (New Smyrna Speedway, 3113 S Ridgewood Ave, New Smyrna Bch; 2 mi S of SR 442; 386-427-8522)

Richard Petty Riding Experience puts you in the front seat of a NASCAR racecar as a professional takes you over 100 mph around the 2.5-mi banked Daytona International Speedway. You can drive if you can handle the steering wheel, clutch and foot pedals. After a 1-hr classroom session, your instructor drives a car in front of you. Staff lifts you from your WC down through the stock car's window; the only weight or size limit is that you fit in that window. Reservations. Days vary 9-4 (Daytona USA, 1801 US 92; by International Speedway; 800-237-3889)

■ BEACHES

Unless otherwise indicated in the individual descriptions, the beaches below share the following arrangements. Beaches have designated approaches (free for vehicles with HC permits) for you to drive and park your vehicle on the wide expanse of hard-packed sand during daylight (restricted during turtle season May-Oct). Below the row of parked cars are lanes of traffic moving up to 10mph. Remember to check for traffic before crossing from your car to the water's edge. An asterisk (*) denotes that you can borrow a beach WC (fixed arms; on request, a fishing pole holder) from 9-5 (extended hrs in summer) at the area's 60' tall, main lifeguard tower that you can reach by boardwalk or sidewalk. Lifeguards can help you transfer into the WC. Paved off-beach parking is available at areas with lifeguard towers and is free to vehicles with HC permits. Beaches are open and lifeguards patrol 24 hrs a day. Traveling from N to S:

***Ormond by-the-Sea**, in a largely residential area, allows no cars on the beach. The beach has no facilities other than the lifeguard tower and Rr. However, Bicentennial Park, across the street, has a boardwalk to a 50' fishing pier on the Halifax River, picnic tables and Rr. Unpaved parking at beach (1665 N SR A1A, N Ormond Bch; N of Granada Bridge; 386-441-1544)

*Ormond Beach's main lifeguard tower is across from the Cardinal Ave approach. Snack trucks & various concessions on beach; snack bar, umbrella/chair rentals, outdoor showers & Rr by lifeguard tower (301 Cardinal Ave, Ormond Bch; S of Granada Bridge; 386-676-4160)

*Daytona Beach's lifeguard tower is across from Main St in a zone where no vehicles are allowed on the beach (from Seabreeze Blvd to International Speedway Blvd). Along the beach are concessions for parasailing and 4-wheelers; surfing is particularly popular at the N end. A flight of stairs leads to the Main St Pier, located here. Restaurants & shops line the beach; snack bar, umbrella/chair rentals, outdoor showers & Rr by lifeguard tower (11 Ocean Ave; 386-239-6484)

Sun Splash Park is a 3-acre county facility, just off the Boardwalk in downtown, where you can cool off in an electronically choreographed water fountain. A boardwalk leads to 2 ADA ramps onto the sand. Outdoor showers; ADA picnic table; shady playground; off-beach parking; Rr. 24 hrs (611 S SR A1A; .25 mi S of International Speedway Blvd)

*Daytona Beach Shores' main lifeguard tower is across from the Dunlawton Ave approach (3425 S SR A1A; 386-756-7491). A smaller lifeguard station (2201 S SR A1A; 386-239-6490), just off the wall at Perry's Ocean Edge Resort (2209 S SR A1A) also loans a beach WC. Hotels, restaurants & shops line the beach; snack bar, umbrella/chair rentals, outdoor showers & Rr by lifeguard tower.

*Lighthouse Point Park is the 52 acres wrapping around the southernmost point of Daytona Beach on the Ponce de Leon Inlet. Because it is a few miles S from where SR A1A juts back to the mainland and because cars are re-stricted to just in front of the light-house, the park offers a relatively quiet beach. Ask at the park entrance to borrow a beach WC that you can pick up at the oceanfront pavilion. Five boardwalks take you through much of the park. A 1000' boardwalk leads through the dunes and onto a jetty that offers great views of the inlet and some good fishing. Serious surfers love this spot. In addition to the lighthouse, several museums share the grounds; see Museums. Lifeguards patrol here in summer and sporadically during the rest of the year. Nearest bait shop at Critter Marina on inlet; ADA picnic shelters; outdoor showers Rr. $. 6am-9pm (5000 S SR A1A, Ponce Inlet; S end of Peninsula Dr; 386-756-7488)

*New Smyrna Beach's main lifeguard tower is at the Flagler Ave/N Cswy approach. Outdoor showers & Rr by lifeguard tower (207.5 Buenos Aires Ave, New Smyrna Bch; 386-424-2345)

27th Avenue Park has an ADA ramp to the beach that allows no vehicles. Outdoor shower; playground; picnic tables; Rr. Dawn-dusk (3701 S SR A1A, New Smyrna Bch; 3.5 mi S of S Cswy)

■ **BOAT RAMPS**

Parks: Cassen, Flagler, Gamble Rodgers, Tomoka

Halifax Harbor Marina has a boat ramp, floating dock and 350' fishing pier on the Halifax River (about 12 mi from the Ponce Inlet that opens to the Atlantic). Picnic tables; Rr. 7-6 (450 Basin St; off Beach St, just S of Silver Bch Bridge; 386-671-3600)

North Causeway Park has boat ramps with floating and fixed docks and a boardwalk to several small, lighted fishing piers on the Indian River. ADA playground; ADA picnic tables; Rr. 24 hrs (New Smyrna Bch; S side of N Cswy, before bridge to beach)

River Breeze Park is a 37-acre park with a boat ramp, fixed dock and a small fishing pier on Mosquito Lagoon. Sep-Apr you can see numerous shorebirds feeding at low tide. ADA picnic tables;

playground on ADA surface; Rr (250 HH Burch Rd, Oak Hill; off US 1; 386-345-5525)

Riverfront Park, on the banks of the Halifax River, has a ramped boardwalk to a boat ramp with a fixed dock and a 300' lighted fishing pier. Playground on an ADA surface; ADA picnic tables; Rr. 5am-11pm (1933 S Palmetto Ave, S Daytona; 386-322-3070)

■ **BOAT RENTALS**

Backwater Marine rents 8-person pontoon boats (30" entry) for half/full days on the Indian River. Roll aboard from the floating dock; staff can help if needed. Bait/snack/marine shop; Rr (248 N Cswy, New Smyrna Bch; 386-426-7976)

■ **BOAT TOURS**

Beach River Cruises offers a variety of trips along the scenic Halifax River. A 4-hr Dock & Dine tour stops for lunch at the Inlet Harbor Restaurant where the crew can help you disembark and reboard. Or, stay onboard for a 3-hr Lighthouse Cruise, a Scenic North Tour or occasionally, themed evening cruises. Usually you can roll aboard; in extreme tides crew can carry you aboard in your WC. Crew can help you over the 6" lip into the cabin and may be able to carry you in your WC upstairs to the observation deck. Reservations; bar/snacks onboard. Tue-Sun (Halifax Harbor Marina, 351 Basin St; off Beach St, just S of Silver Bch Bridge; 386-248-1441)

Sunny Daze/Starry Night Cruises are narrated tours on a pontoon boat along the Halifax River, its creeks and tributaries. Roll aboard by ramp for a 2-hr trip at 10 and 1, or a 1-hr trip at 4 and sunset. (409 Halifax Dr, Port Orange; behind Aunt Catfish's Restaurant; 386-253-1796)

■ **CANOEING/KAYAKING**

Parks: Bulow Plantation, Tomoka

New Smyrna Kayak & Bike rents solo/tandem sit-on kayaks for self-guided or guided half/full days on the tidal Indian River. Lessons are also available. Staff delivers and picks up the kayaks and can help with your transfers. Staff can assist you down the gently sloped bank to the launch. The take-out is in Callalisa Park (.25 mi from the shop) where you either meet staff at a pre-arranged time, call or send someone to the shop when you're done paddling. Rr. Mon-Sat 10-6 (553 3 Ave/S Cswy, New Smyrna Bch; .25 mi E of bridge over Intracoastal; 386-426-8684/423-8123)

■ **CASINOS**

SunCruz Casino offers Vegas-style gaming aboard a 160' ship for 5 hrs during the day or evening. Roll aboard by ramp to the accessible 1st deck with 21 tables (with games from blackjack to roulette), slot machines and a bar. Free hors d'oeuvres, coffee & soda; light food available; entertainment; Rr (4880 Front St, Ponce Inlet; 386-322-9000; 888-675-2921)

■ **DINNER THEATERS**

Teauila's Hawaii features hula, fire dancers and a comedy act with audience participation during an all-you-can-eat luau of pepper steak, sweet and sour chicken, mahi-mahi and more. WC seating is throughout. Rr. Wed-Sun 6:30 (Daytona Bch Resort, 2700 N SR A1A; just S of Riverbeach Dr; 386-255-5411)

■ **DISC GOLF**

Tuscawilla City Park has a Frisbee course on grass and through trees with both paved and hard-packed paths. ADA playground; ADA picnic tables; Rr. Dawn-dusk (1000 Orange Ave; 386-671-8551)

■ **FISHING CHARTERS**

All Star Sport Fishing can take you and 5 able-bodied friends on half/full-day deep-sea trips on a 34' boat. Crew can lift you from the fixed dock aboard in your WC or into a chair. Restaurant & Rr in marina (Adventure Yacht Harbor, 3948 Peninsula Dr; 386-304-0105)

Backcountry Charter Service offers half/full-day backcountry trips on a 19' flats boat for 2 anglers; you can flyfish or spin cast if you like. Capt Kent Gibbens is experienced with WC anglers. He can help your companion, or arrange for someone else to help lower you in your WC aboard the front of the boat. When you make reservations, he can suggest accessible docks closest to where the fish are running. (386-672-8929)

Backwater Marine has a 35' sports fisherman and a 43' Hatteras. Crew can help lift you from the floating dock aboard in your WC or into the fighting chair. Half-day trips (7-11am) troll or bottom fish the reefs just offshore. Full-day trips (6:30am-2:30pm) run further offshore and either troll or bottom fish the rock piles and ledges. On the deepwater trips (6:30-4:30), you deep-drop bait and troll the weed lines and tide rips farther offshore. Gulf Stream trips (6-6) go 45 mi offshore where large fish come to feast. Moonlight bottom fishing trips (6:30pm-2:30am) are offered 5 days before and after a full moon May-Aug. Or, consider inshore trips on Mosquito Lagoon, Indian and/ or Banana River. (The Fishin' Store, 248 N Cswy, New Smyrna Bch; 386-427-4514)

SeaLover Sport Fishing can take up to 6 anglers on 4- to 12-hr bottom fishing or trolling trips up to 60 mi offshore. Roll onto the dock and crew can lift you in your WC aboard the 40' boat. Restaurant & Rr in marina (Sea Lovers Marina, 4884 Front St, Ponce Inlet; 386-761-1750)

Taylor Made offers 4- to 12-hr trips for bottom fishing and sport fishing up to 40 mi offshore. Staff can lift you in your WC aboard the 35' boat that can carry up to 6 anglers. Restaurant & Rr at marina (Sea Lovers Marina, 4884 Front St, Ponce Inlet; 386-788-2654)

■ **FISHING-PARTY BOATS**
Critter Fleet makes half/full-day deep-sea trips on a 90' boat. Depending on tides, you can roll aboard or crew can lift you aboard in your WC and over the 8" lip at the 26" entry to the AC cabin. Snack bar onboard; Rr in marina. Full day 8-4:30; 1/2 day depart 8 & 1 (4950 S Peninsula Dr, Ponce Inlet; 386-767-7676; 800-338-0850)

■ **FISHING PIERS**
Beaches: Lighthouse Point. Boat Ramps. Parks: Ames, Bicentennial, Cassen, Lake Ashby

Buena Vista Park is a 4-acre city park with a boardwalk and lighted 200' fishing pier on the Indian River. ADA picnic tables; ADA playground; bait shop nearby; Rr. Dawn-dusk (S side of N Cswy, New Smyrna Bch; W of bridge to beach)

Central Park II has a boardwalk from which you can fish on a large pond. ADA picnic shelter; Rr. 24 hrs (S Orchard St, Ormond Bch; S of SR 40, W on Hammock Ln)

Colin's Park has a lighted 100' fishing pier on the Halifax River. ADA playground; ADA picnic tables; Rr. Dawn-dusk (201 University Blvd; across from Fire Dept)

Riviera Park has a gazebo over the Halifax River that's a great spot for fishing. Picnic tables. Dawn-dusk (915 S Beach St, Ormond Bch)

Rocco Park is a small neighborhood park with a lighted 200' fishing pier over Turnbull Bay. ADA playground; picnic tables; Rr. Dawn-dusk (Sunset Dr, New Smyrna Bch; just S of South St)

Sanchez Park is a shady city park with a fishing dock and a boat ramp on Strickland Creek. ADA picnic shelter; Rr. Dawn-dusk (N Beach St & Sanchez Ave, Ormond Bch)

Spruce Creek Park has a 200' fishing pier on Strickland Bay. Bait shop nearby; picnic tables; Rr. Dawn-dusk (6250 S Ridgewood Ave, Port Orange; 5 mi E of US 595; 386-322-5133)

Sunglow Fishing Pier is a 1000' lighted pier on the Atlantic. Bait shop; restaurant; CRr. $. Hrs vary (3701 S SR A1A; S of Dunlawton Ave; 386-756-4219)

■ GOLF

Daytona Beach Country Club has 2 adaptive golf carts for use at the 2 public, 18-hole golf courses and the driving range. You can drive the carts on the greens and through sand traps. Lessons are available. Staff cannot generally help with transfers. Call to reserve. A group of WC golfers play Apr-Nov; if you are interested in joining them, call Bud Harden 386-788-8583. Restaurant; Rr. 6:30-6 (600 Wilder Blvd; N of Bellevue Ave, W of MLK Blvd; 386-258-3119)

■ MISC

New Smyrna Beach hosts a monthly get together at the City Gym for residents and visitors with special needs, including physical disabilities. Activities include sports and off-site trips for horseback riding and more. Call for the schedule. Rr; shower with bench & hand-held sprayer (1000 Live Oak St, New Smyrna Bch; 386-424-2175)

Atlantic Center for the Arts is a 69-acre complex where graphic artists, dancers, musicians, writers and others congregate to generate a synergistic creativity. The grounds include performance space, studios, galleries and residences, all connected by boardwalk. Call for the schedule of performances, readings and art shows and a possible tour. (1414 Art Center Ave, New Smyrna Bch; W off US 1; 386-427-6975)

■ MUSEUMS

Parks: Tomoka

Art League of Daytona Beach features state and national artists in monthly shows. Art video library; workshops. Tue-Sat 1-4 (433 S Palmetto Ave; S of Live Oak Ave, N of Loomis Ave; 386-258-3856)

Halifax Historical Museum, an elegant former bank building, features Native American and Spanish artifacts found locally, memorabilia from the early days of racing cars on the beach and a newspaper file dating back to 1883. A video and murals portray the region's history. WC entrance in back by parking; only men's Rr. ⚲. Tue-Sat 10-4 (252 S Beach St; N of Orange Ave; 386-255-6976)

Klassix Auto Museum has a huge collection of racing and automobile memorabilia, including over 40 vintage motorcycles, collector and muscle cars and Corvettes dating back to 1953. Displays chronicle the roll of the auto in American history. Staff can help WC riders up a ramp to the 2nd floor. Gift shop; ice cream parlor; Rr. ⚲. 9-6 (2909 W US 92; just W of I-95; 386-252-3800; 800-881-8975)

Memorial Art Museum has historic exhibits, rotating displays of Florida artists and sidewalks through 4 acres of lovely gardens. Gift shop; Rr. ⚲. Wkdy 10-4; wknd noon-4 (78 E Granada Blvd, Ormond Bch; 386-676-3347)

Museum of Arts & Science is a truly eclectic place. You'll find African, Cuban, French, American and Chinese art, as well as exhibits on Florida history, pirates of the east coast and rotating science/art displays. Don't miss the 13' skeleton of a 130,000 yr-old giant ground sloth. The Root Family Collection of Americana includes Coca-Cola memorabilia, 800 teddy bears and replicas of some of the country's most famous architecture. A video in the auditorium explains exhibits in detail. The Planetarium has shows Tue-Fri at 2; weekends at 1 and 3. The Frischer Sculpture Garden contains work by major contemporary sculptors. The 60-acre grounds also feature the *Window in the Forest* interpretive center where you learn about the coastal hammock habitat. Gift shop; Rr. ⚲. Tue-Fri 9-4; wknd noon-5; 1st Tue of month -8pm (1040 Museum Blvd; from Nova Rd/SR 5A, W on South St, then N; 386-255-0285)

Ponce de Leon Inlet Lighthouse, built in 1887, is still operational and, at 175', is the 2nd tallest lighthouse in the USA. Sidewalks connect various city museums on the grounds. Learn the history of the lighthouse and take a virtual tour in the video theater. The Light-house Museum, once the light keeper's home, has ancient lighthouse artifacts, including a huge Fresnel Lens. The Maritime Museum has a video and nau-tical artifacts, ancient navigational tools and ship models. You can take a ramp to the viewing platform by the tugboat. Explore the Marine Science Center which has interactive displays on the local ecology and a gift shop. See Beaches. Gift shop; Rr. ⚡. 10-4; summers 10-8. (S Peninsula Cr, Ponce Inlet; 386-761-1821)

Southeast Museum of Photography is one of 12 photography museums in the USA, featuring historic and contempo-rary photos. Rr. Wkdy 9:30-4:30; Tue - 7; wknd 12-4; closed part of Jan, May & Sep (Daytona Bch Community College, Bldg 37, 1200 US 92; E of SR 483; 386-254-4475)

■ **PARI-MUTUELS**

Daytona Beach Kennel Club has live greyhound racing all year. An elevator takes you to WC seating on several lev-els. Lunch or dine in the Pavilion Res-taurant by the window or on the top tier with a tabletop monitor. Rr. Mon, Wed, Fri-Sat 7:45pm; Mon, Wed & Sat 1pm (2201 W US 92; next door to the International Speedway; 386-252-6484)

■ **PARKS**

Ames Park is a shady little city park along the Halifax River with a paved path meandering along a garden and ponds. A 40' fishing pier ends in 15' x 15' overlook. Bait shop 4 blocks N in Cassen Park; Rr. Dawn-dusk (173 S Beach St, Ormond Bch; 386-676-3220)

Bicentennial Park is a 40-acre county park with a 200' boardwalk to a 50' fishing pier over the saltwater Halifax River. Over grass you'll also find a fit-ness trail, shuffleboard courts and pic-nic tables. The mulched nature trail is quite hilly. Bait shop nearby; picnic tables; playground; ball fields; tennis; Rr. Dawn-dusk (1800 N SR A1A, Ormond Bch)

Bulow Creek State Park is a 2576-acre

wooded and marsh preserve with a great spot for picnicking. A sidewalk leads from parking to an ADA picnic shelter next to the 900-2000-yr old Fairchild live oak tree. Rr. 8-dusk (3351 Old Dixie Hwy, Ormond Bch; 4.5 mi N of Tomoka State Park; 386-676-4050)

Cassen Park is a 2.5-acre park on the Halifax River, has a very long, lighted 3-sided fishing pier. The pier ends in a lovely pocket park called Bailey River Bridge Gardens where a paved path winds through flower and herb gar-dens. Cassen Park has a boat ramp with a floating dock. ADA picnic table; bait shop; Rr. Dusk-mdnt (22 S Beach St, Ormond Bch; S of Granada Bridge; 386-676-3220)

Lake Ashby Park is a remote 64-acre park with a .5-mi boardwalk located un-der a canopy of trees that leads to a 200' pier over the 800-acre lake. You may want to try the 2-mi mulch nature trail. See Campgrounds. Picnic shelters; Rr. Dawn-dusk (4150 Boy Scout Camp Rd, New Smyrna Bch; off CR 415, 6 mi S of CR 44W; 386-428-4589)

Lenox Playground is supervised and has ADA equipment. Rr. Wkdy 2-5 (825 S Grandview Ave; 386-239-6573)

Riverside Park is an 8-acre park down-town, frequently the site for festivals and concerts. Paved paths lead throughout the park, including to a 900' boardwalk along the Indian River that leads to a lighted 250' fishing pier. ADA playground; bait shop nearby; pic-nic tables; Rr. Dawn-dusk (Riverside Dr, New Smyrna Bch; end of Canal St)

Smyrna Dunes Park is a 250-acre beach park with 2 mi of boardwalks through woods, mangroves and over the dunes, but all entrances to the sand have at least 2 steps. This area is especially good for bird sightings Oct-Apr. A 20' fishing pier extends over the inlet. Picnic shel-ters; large Rr not ADA. ⚡. Dawn-dusk (2995 N Peninsula Dr, New Smyrna Bch; 386-424-2935)

Tomoka State Park covers 2.4 sq mi at the confluence of the Tomoka and

Halifax Rivers, once the site of a Timucuan Indian village. The lush forest and marsh have wide, well maintained and hard-packed nature trails. Fish on the Tomoka River from either the 30' dock at the canoe launch or the 150' dock at the boat ramp. You can rent canoes here and board at the fixed dock or boat ramp. If you need help boarding or disembarking, ask at the entry gate. The pristine river is mildly tidal; you can paddle back to the launch. During spring and summer, you may see manatees in the lagoon area for birthing. The Fred Dana Marsh Museum (9:30-4:30) features the diverse work of the sculptor and architect as well as interesting local cultural, nature and historic exhibits. Reenactments occur periodically. See Campgrounds. ADA picnic shelters; Rr. $. 8-dusk (2099 N Beach St; 3.5 mi N of SR 40 in Ormond Bch, W side of Halifax River; 386-676-4050)

■ **PERFORMING ARTS**
Attractions: Casements
Daytona Playhouse is a community theater that performs a range of plays and musicals. WC seating on sides of front & back rows; ramped entrances at side, by parking, & in front. Sep-Jun (100 Jessamine Blvd; 386-255-2431)
Ocean Center hosts many diverse events including concerts, plays, wrestling and ice-skating. WC seating varies with event. Rr (101 N SR A1A; 386-245-4545)
Ormond Beach Performing Arts Center features children's musicals, community theater, professional concert series and touring theater productions. WC seating in front on aisles; Rr (399 N US 1, Ormond Bch; 386-676-3375)
Peabody Auditorium is home to the Daytona Beach Symphony, Civic Ballet and Concert Showcase as well as host to touring theater groups and entertainers year round. This 2500-seat theater has WC seating in the aisles on the mezzanine or ground floor and in the balcony's front row. Elevator; Rr (600 Auditorium Blvd; 386-258-3169)

Seaside Music Theater is a professional music theater group with a full pit orchestra. Jun-Aug, the groups stages Broadway plays and operetta at the Daytona Beach Community College Theater. WC seating behind middle section; Rr (1200 W US 92, Bldg 8) Oct-Feb includes more serious fare at the Ormond Beach Performing Arts Center. WC seating in front on aisles; Rr (399 N US 1, Ormond Bch; 386-252-6200)

■ **POOLS**
Aqua Park has an indoor therapeutic pool with a lift (fixed seat) and an 18" deep bench along the entire length of the 3.5'-4.5' deep pool. Staff can help with transfers and offers therapy, water aerobics, lap swimming and arthritis classes. Dressing room; Rr. $. Mon-Sat hrs vary (600 Eaton Rd, Edgewater; 386-428-5074)
Campbell Pool has 2 pools, one of which is ramped to its 4' depth. Staff can help you enter the pool. Call about the various aquatic programs. Bathhouse; Rr. Jun-Aug hrs vary (313 School St; 386-258-3106)

■ **SHOOTING RANGES**
Strickland Gun Range has a 7-, 15-, and 25-yd handgun range, and a 50- and 100-yd rifle range. The parking lot is hard-packed clay and you must go over grass to access the ranges. $. Wed-Sun 9-2 (1670 Strickland Range Rd, Holly Hill; 386-274-3811)

■ **SHOPPING**
Boutiques: Daytona Beach Historic District (4 blks along Beach St); Bellair Plaza (Seabreeze Blvd; W of SR A1A); Fountain Square (Granada Blvd in Ormond Bch)
Flea Markets: Daytona Flea Market has over 1000 vendors spread over 40 acres, some covered, others in a mall with AC. WC rentals; Rr. Fri-Sat (US 92 at I-95; 1 mi W of International Speedway; 386-253-3330)
Malls: Volusia Mall (1700 W US 92; 386-253-6783)

■ **SHUFFLEBOARD**
Coronado Shuffleboard Club has 20

lighted courts. Reservations (Flagler St & Pine St, New Smyrna Bch; 386-424-2175)

Mainland Shuffleboard Club has 17 lighted courts and 3 bolina courts. Reservations (Sams Ave & Julia St, New Smyrna Bch; 386-424-2175)

■ **SPECTATOR SPORTS**

Auto/Motorcycle Racing Daytona International Speedway was built in 1959 to replace the beach as the spot for car races. The Speedway hosts events throughout the year but the most popular are the Daytona 500 in Feb and the Pepsi 400 in Jul. Motorcycle races are held in Mar and Oct. The best WC seating is on the front side of the track at the 1st and 4th turns where you can see pit action and the start/finish line. WC seating is also on the backside of the track in the 1st row and in the tower. Ramps to all ground level platforms; elevator to tower; HC parking on grass in front; concession stand; Rr

(1801 W US 92; 386-253-7223)

Baseball The Daytona Cubs, a Chicago Cubs' affiliate, plays Apr-Labor Day at Jackie Robinson Ballpark. Take a ramp to WC seating along the first base line. Rr. (103 E Orange Ave; 386-257-3172)

■ **TENNIS**

USTA Wheelchair-Tennis clinics are available for beginners and advanced players. Call Nancy Olson 386-322-1122. Rr. Wed 6:30-8 (Daytona Beach Community College, 1200 W US92)

■ **TOURS**

Daytona International Speedway offers 30-min narrated tours of the 2.5-mi oval track on a tram that can be ramped for WC access. Learn the history of the speedway and see points of interest along the track such as the pit, victory lane and garage. Schedule varies due to races. Rr. $. 9:30-4 (1801 W US 92; 386-947-6800)

ACCOMMODATIONS

■ **B&B/INNS**

Night Swan B&B has an ADA suite, the Mainsail, on the 1st floor of a cottage overlooking the scenic Intracoastal. The suite has a kitchenette, sitting room with a queen futon and bedroom with a king bed (26" high/open frame). The private bath has a raised toilet, roll-under sink and roll-in shower. You can take a sidewalk from the cottage and by ramp enter the main house for a full breakfast in the dining room, or, on request, breakfast can be delivered to your room. Enjoy the wrap-around porch with a great view of the water and take the sidewalk through historic downtown. You can fish from the B&B's 140' pier (but you must go over a curb) or, a lighted pier at Riverside Park across the street (see Parks). $$-$$$ (512 S Riverside Dr, New Smyrna Bch; at Anderson St; 386-423-4940; 800-465-4261)

Little River Inn, an 1883 riverfront es-

tate, has an ADA guestroom, the Library, with a queen and a twin bed, both on open frames. The private bath has a raised toilet and roll-in shower with a hand-held sprayer and seat. The rear entrance has a brick ramp. You can enjoy gourmet breakfast in the dining room or on the deck. With advance notice, dinner and even picnic lunches can be provided. Guests may use a common refrigerator and microwave. Brick paths take you through 2 acres of lovely gardens and wonderful views of the Indian River Lagoon. $$-$$$ (532 N Riverside Dr, New Smyrna Bch; N of Canal St/Business 44 where it dead ends at the Indian River; 386-424-0100; 888-424-0102)

■ **CAMPGROUNDS**

Lake Ashby Park has 10 primitive tent sites with water. The terrain is level pine mulch, fine for ECVs, but problematic for standard WCs. See Parks. Outdoor cold shower; Rr (4150 Boy Scout

Camp Rd, New Smyrna Bch; CR 415 6 mi S of CR 44W; 386-428-4589)

Tomoka State Park has RV/tent sites on flat, hard-packed terrain with trees in between most sites. Ten sites have ADA picnic tables, grills and water. Sites 22, 43, 64 and 73 are closest to ADA bathhouse with a roll-in shower. See Parks. (2099 N Beach St, Ormond Bch; 3.5 mi N of SR 40, W side of Halifax River; 386-676-4045)

■ **CONDOS**

Grand Seas Resort has 4 ADA units. The studio has a Murphy bed, two 1BR condos each have a king bed, and the 2BR condo has a king and queen bed (platforms). Condos also have queen sofa beds and full kitchens. Bathrooms have raised toilets and roll-under sinks. The 2BR unit (1026) has a roll-in shower; the rest have step-in showers with hand-held sprayers. Pool; laundry; lounge; full restaurant. (2424 N SR A1A; 386-677-7880; 800-982-9386)

Regency, along the Atlantic, has six 1BR ADA condos each with a queen bed (platform), a queen sofa bed in the living room and a full kitchen. Bathrooms have roll-under sinks, raised toilets and roll-in showers with hand-held sprayers and seats. Indoor & outdoor pools; laundry; lounge; entertainment in summer; game room. (400 N SR A1A; 386-255-0251; 800-535-2036)

■ **MOTELS**

Adams Mark has 20 ADA rooms with a choice of 2 king, queen or full beds (23" high/platforms) and all with refrigerators, queen sofa beds and coffeepots. Bathrooms have raised toilets, roll-under sinks and tubs with hand-held sprayers and seats. Room 123 has a roll-in shower. Pool; laundry; lounge; full restaurant. $$$ (100 N SR A1A; 386-254-8200)

Bahama House is on the Atlantic Ocean and has 4 ADA rooms each with 2 full beds (22" high/platforms), a full kitchen and bathroom with a raised toilet and roll-under sink. Room 209 has a roll-in shower; other rooms have tubs or step-

in showers with hand-held sprayers and seats. Free brkfst; pool; laundry; free cocktail hour. $$-$$$ (2001 S SR A1A, Daytona Bch Shores; 386-248-2001; 800-571-2001)

Beachcomber Oceanfront Inn has 2 ADA units including an efficiency with a full kitchen. Both have 2 full beds (20" high/platforms). The standard room has a small refrigerator. Bathrooms have raised toilets, roll-under sinks and roll-in showers with hand-held sprayers and seats. Pool; laundry; lounge; restaurant for brkfst & lunch. $$ (2000 N SR A1A; 386-252-8513; 800-245-3575)

Coral Beach Motel is on the Atlantic and has 4 ADA 1st floor efficiencies with 2 full beds (22" high/platforms) and kitchenettes. Bathrooms have roll-under sinks and tubs. Free brkfst; pool; laundry. (711 S SR A1A, Ormond Bch; 386-677-4712; 800-553-4712)

El Caribe Resort has 6 ADA units, 3 efficiencies and 3 1BR suites. Each has 2 queen beds (22" high/open frames) and a full kitchen. Suites also have queen sofa beds. Bathrooms have raised toilets, roll-under sinks and tubs with hand-held sprayers. Free brkfst; pool; laundry; nearby car ramp to beach. $$-$$$ (2125 S SR A1A; 386-252-1558; 800-445-9889)

Hilton is located on the ocean with beach access and has 8 ADA rooms each with 2 full beds. Bathrooms have raised toilets and roll-under sinks; 7 rooms have roll-in showers with hand-held sprayers and seats; the other has a tub. Pool; laundry; full restaurant; game room; fitness room. $$-$$$ (2637 S SR A1A; 386-767-7350)

Lapponia Motel, along the Indian River Creek, has 1 ADA room with a kitchenette and 2 full beds (open frames). The bathroom has a raised toilet, roll-under sink and roll-in shower with a hand-held sprayer and seat. Pool. $-$$ (1157 N Dixie Hwy, New Smyrna Bch; 386-423-3812; 888-253-8506)

Radisson Resort, an oceanfront hotel, has 8 ADA rooms and 3 ADA 1BR suites each with a king or 2 full beds (30" high/open frames). Suites have kitchenettes. Bathrooms have roll-under sinks and tubs with hand-held sprayers; 3 rooms have roll-in showers. Pool; laundry; lounge; full restaurant; $$-$$$ (640 N SR A1A; 386-239-9800)

Treasure Island Resort, an oceanfront hotel, has 6 ADA rooms each with a full bed (platform), mini-refrigerator and coffeepot. An ADA efficiency has 2 full beds and a full kitchen. Bathrooms have raised toilets, roll-under sinks and tubs or step-in showers with hand-held sprayers and seats. The efficiency, room 124, has a roll-in shower. A ramp to the beach is 1 block away. Pool; lounge; entertainment; full restaurant. $$-$$$ (2025 S SR A1A; 386-255-3368; 800-543-5070)

DeLand
Barberville, DeLeon Springs, Lake Helen, Orange City

Historic downtown DeLand has curb cuts, but be aware, some sidewalks are uncomfortably angled toward the street. Outdoorsy folks can find plenty of fun on local freshwater springs and lakes, many strung together by the eminently fishable St Johns River. How about renting a houseboat for a cruise on the St Johns?. US 92 is also called International Speedway Blvd

Tourist Info
St Johns River Country Visitors Bureau: 101 N Woodland Blvd, 32720; 386-734-0575; 800-749-4350
Web sites: www.stjohnsrivercountry.com; www.delandchamber.org

Transportation
Votran provides WC-accessible bus service in DeLand and throughout Volusia County. Each bus has a lift and the driver will straps down your WC. (386-943-7033)

ACTIVITIES

■ **ATTRACTIONS**
Pioneer Settlement for the Creative Arts preserves Florida's heritage through folk crafts. The main building houses local history displays and demonstrations, such as spinning, weaving and butter churning. Other exhibits about the lifestyle of early settlers are spread out on 10 acres with natural paths that are sandy in spots. If you can transfer, ride an 8-person golf cart to the railroad depot, blacksmith shop, woodworking shop and authentic log cabin. The church and pottery shops have stairs. $. Guided tours wkdy 9-3; Sat 9-1 (1776 Lightfoot Ln, Barberville; 386-749-2959)

Spring Garden Ranch is a training facility for standard bred trotters, pacers and their drivers. You can watch from a patio or trackside restaurant. Rr. Oct-Apr 7-2 (900 Spring Garden Ranch Rd, DeLeon Springs; 386-985-5654)

■ **BOAT RAMPS**
Lake Dias has a ramp and floating dock. Rr (Hwy 11; 4 mi N of SR 40, between Astor & Barberville)
St Johns River has ramps and floating docks at Butler St, Astor (off SR 40) and at Ed Stone Park (2993 W SR 44) which also has an ADA picnic table.

■ **BOAT RENTALS**
Holly Bluff Marina rents pontoon boats for up to 10 people (36" entry) for the

264 NORTHEAST ATLANTIC COAST

St Johns River from half day to weekly. Unless the water level is very high, WCs can roll aboard from the ramped dock. Bait shop nearby; Rr. 8:30-5 (2280 Hontoon Rd; just N of Hontoon State Park; 386-822-9992; 800-237-5105)

Hontoon Landing Resort rents pontoon boats for up to 10 people (36" entry) for the St Johns River for half/full days. Ramp to dock; bait shop; CRr. 8-5 (2317 River Ridge Rd; 386-734-2474; 800-248-2474)

■ **BOAT TOURS**

Manatee Seeker Cruises offer 2-hr narrated nature tours on a pontoon boat along the St Johns River with manatees, otters and birds galore. Floating dock; CRr in the St Johns Cafe at the marina. 10, 12:30 & 3; Jun-Aug closed Sun (Pier 44 Marina, 34526 W SR 44; 352-357-7195; 800-587-7131)

Safari River Tours offers 90-min narrated trips on a 42-passenger boat along the St Johns River to Lake Woodruff National Wildlife Refuge. Oct-Apr is the time for unusual bird sightings. Boats depart from DeLeon Springs Park at 11 and 1:30; they depart from High Banks Tue-Sun at 10 and 2. Board by a portable ramp from either fixed dock. Rr. Hrs vary (DeLeon Springs State Park, 601 Ponce de Leon Blvd, DeLeon Springs; 386-740-0333; and High Banks Marina, 488 W High Banks Rd, DeBary; off US 17-92; 386-668-1002)

St Johns River Cruises offers 2-hr guided wildlife and nature tours. Roll aboard the 50' pontoon boat by ramp; staff can help if needed. CRr. 9-3:30 (Blue Spring State Park, 2100 W French Ave, Orange City; 4255 Peninsula Pt; 386-917-0724)

■ **BOWLING**

Sunshine Lanes can set up a ramp down to the lanes and has bowling ball ramps. CRr. 9am-mdnt (595 US 92; 386-738-5566)

■ **CANOEING**

Parks: DeLeon Springs

■ **FISHING CHARTERS**

Highland Park Fish Camp can hook you up with a guide to fish the St Johns River in a bass boat. Crew can lift you in your WC down the 4 steps to the dock and from your WC aboard into a boat seat. 6-6 (2640 W Highland Park Rd; 386-734-2334; 800-525-3477)

Hontoon Landing Resort can arrange for a guide for fishing on the St Johns River in a bass boat or pontoon boat. With advance notice, crew can help lift you into the seat of a bass boat. CRr (2317 River Ridge Rd; 386-734-2474; 800-248-2474)

■ **FISHING PIERS**

Parks: Blue Spring, DeLeon Springs

■ **MUSEUMS**

African-American Art Museum has a permanent collection of African art and rotating exhibits of local work. Rr. $D. Wed-Sat 10-4 (325 S Clara Ave; 386-736-4004)

Cultural Arts Center, adjacent to the Stetson campus, houses an art museum, theater and a local symphony. Be aware, the front doors are very heavy. Rr. $D. Tue-Sat 10-4; Sun 1-4 (600 N Woodland Blvd; 386-736-7232)

Gillespie Museum of Minerals, at Stetson University, has a world-class collection of gems. The front porch is ramped into the museum. CRr. $D. Tue-Fri 10-4 (Michigan & Amelia Aves; 386-822-7330)

Henry DeLand House, circa 1886, is filled with period furnishings and collectibles. Enter by ramp on the E side of the building. CRr. $D. Ongoing 1-hr guided tours Tue-Sat 12-4 (137 W Michigan Ave; 386-740-6813)

■ **PARKS**

Blue Spring State Park is a great place in the colder months for observing manatees and, in the morning, birds. A boardwalk runs along the clear waters of the spring run where you can easily make out the many manatee who winter here. The boardwalk leads to a fishing pier and a swim dock at the spring. Trails have soft sand and low, wet areas. The park rents canoes for the spring run and the St Johns River. Except when the water is very high, you can roll down a rather bumpy hard-packed slope to the water line to transfer into a canoe. Bring friends because staff cannot always help. Call for the schedule of free nature talks. See Campgrounds below. ADA picnic tables; snack bar; Rr. $. 8-dusk (2100 W French Ave, Orange City; 386-775-3663)

De Leon Springs State Park is another of Florida's Fountains of Youth where a concrete pool now surrounds a natural spring. You can roll down the pool's ramp to a flat area with about 1' of water. Then transfer from your WC to a paved staging area with 3'-4' of water and swim into deeper water should you choose. The children's swim area has 2 very wide, shallow steps. A concession rents canoes, paddleboats and kayaks for the spring run; the launch is a paved boat ramp. If available, staff can help you board. The riverbanks have ample flat areas for fishing. One flat paved 1750' nature trail is a delightful loop through the woods. A 600' boardwalk from parking goes to an old sugar mill, which was converted to a restaurant where you make your own pancakes on a griddle, that is built into your table. Arrive early to avoid lines at the restaurant (wkdy 9-4; wknd 8-4). See Boat Tours. ADA picnic tables in shelters; Rr. $. 8-dusk (601 Ponce De Leon Blvd, De Leon Springs; 386-985-4212; restaurant & boat rentals: 386-985-5644)

Hontoon Island State Park is a 1650-acre island of swamp, savannah and forest between the St Johns and Huntoon Dead Rivers. This great birding spot is accessible by private boat or roll-aboard free ferry (8 to 1 hr before sunset). You can fish from the flat, grassy areas along the riverbanks. Trails are generally hard-packed but rather rough and, at times, muddy. The park rents canoes. You can roll down to the flat area at the water's edge, next to the canoe dock with 2 steps, and transfer with the help of friends. See Campgrounds. ADA picnic tables; Rr; CRr in campground. $. 8-dusk (2309 River Ridge Rd; off SR 44, 6 mi W of DeLand; 386-736-5309)

■ **PERFORMING ARTS**

Cultural Arts Center offers local theater, concerts and children's shows. WC seating is center stage in front. Rr. Sep-May (600 N Woodland Blvd; 386-736-7232)

Shoestring Theater is a community theater. WC seating is on the side in front. Rr. Sep-May (380 S Goodwin, Lake Helen; 386-228-3777)

■ **POOLS**

Parks: De Leon Springs

■ **SKYDIVING**

Skydive DeLand offers skydiving from a twin-turbine aircraft, 13,500' high, for both paras and quads. Call Bob Hallett to discuss your abilities, your weight and phsyical condition so he can determine the safety of a tandem dive. He can modify equipment to suit your particular needs. Jumpers first get a 30-min, on-the-ground briefing. (1600 Flightline Blvd; SE corner of DeLand Municipal Airport, from US 92 take E airport entrance; 386-738-3539)

ACCOMMODATIONS

■ **B&B/INNS**

Clauser's is an early 1900's B&B on a secluded 3-acre tract with 2 ADA guestrooms in the carriage house. Each room has a queen bed (on open frames), a daybed and screen porch.

Bathrooms have step-in showers and roll-under sinks. A full country breakfast is served in the carriage house Pub. The grounds include an accessible gazebo over a hot tub with 3 steps. You must take stairs to the main house. $$-

$$$ (201 E Kicklighter Rd, Lake Helen; 386-228-0310; 800-220-0310)

Howry Manor, built in 1903, has the WC-friendly Suite Scarlet with a living room, full kitchen and a bedroom with a queen bed (open frame). The standard bathroom has a wide door. Howry is close to downtown and has a pool and tearoom open to the public Tue-Fri 11-2. Breakfast is included for overnight stays; breakfast is an additional charge for weeklong stays. $$-$$$ (422 W New York Ave; 386-736-2483)

■ CABINS/CAMPGROUNDS

Blue Spring State Park has an ADA 2BR cabin, with 2 full beds and a bunk, AC/heat, linens and a full kitchen. The standard bathroom has a 30" doorway and grab bars. Roads are paved and the terrain is hard-packed. The 51 RV/tent campsites have full hookups, picnic tables and fire pits or grills. Sites 6, 7 and 8 are closest to the bathhouse with roll-in showers. See Parks. Camp store (2100 W French Ave, Orange City; 386-775-3663)

Hontoon Island State Park has an ADA rustic cabin (#3) with electricity, 3 bunk beds and no kitchen or supplies. A boardwalk leads to an ADA bathhouse with a roll-in shower. Tent camping is also available. Grills are on hard-packed terrain. Once you disembark from the accessible ferry, you can take the short dirt road or transfer into a van to the camp area. See Parks. (2309 River Ridge Rd; off SR 44, 6 mi W of DeLand; 386-736-5309)

■ HOUSEBOATS

Holly Bluff Marina, on the St Johns River, rents a 44' houseboat with a 30" entry that sleeps 8 and a 53' houseboat with a 26" entry that sleeps 10. Unless the water level is very high, WCs can roll aboard from the ramped dock. The front deck, galley and main salon with steering controls and a sofa bed are WC-friendly, but the bedrooms and bathrooms have narrow doors/hall-ways. Houseboats have AC, linens and kitchen supplies. Be aware, docks at most restaurants and gas stations along the river are fixed, so disembarkingby WC can be difficult. (2280 Hontoon Rd; just N of Hontoon State Park; 386-822-9992; 800-237-5105)

Hontoon Landing Resort & Marina rent a 52' houseboat with a 27" entry that sleeps 8 and a 52' and 58' houseboat with 39" entries that sleep 10 as you cruise the St Johns River. The front deck, galley and main salon with steering controls and sofa bed are WC-friendly, but the bedrooms and bathrooms have narrow doors/hallways. Every boat has AC, linens, kitchen supplies, a microwave, gas grill, color TV/VCR, radio, cell phone and carpeting inside and out. The 58' boat also has a water slide, 1.5 baths and a sundeck. (2317 River Ridge Rd; 386-734-2474; 800-248-2474)

■ MOTELS

Comfort Inn has 4 ADA rooms with a king or 2 full beds (24"/platforms). Bathrooms have raised toilets, roll-under sinks; room 115 has a roll-in shower; others have tubs. Free brkfst; pool. $$ (400 E US 92; 386-736-3100)

Holiday Inn has 10 ADA rooms with a king or 2 full beds (platform). Bathrooms have a raised toilet and tub or roll-in shower. Restaurant; lounge, laundry, pool. $-$$$ (350 E US 92; 386-738-5200)

Hontoon Landing Resort & Marina has WC-friendly motel rooms and suites with full kitchens. Bedrooms have queen or full beds (22" high/open frames) and 28" doors. Bathrooms have 24" doors with step-in showers; staff can remove the bathroom door if needed. You can fish from a dock on the St Johns River or use the boat ramp with a fixed dock. See Boat Rentals. Bait shop. $$ (2317 River Ridge Rd; 386-734-2474; 800-248-2474)

Howard Johnson Express has 2 ADA rooms, each with 2 full beds (open frames) and a roll-in shower with a hand-held sprayer. For an extra charge, you can have a microwave oven and refrigerator in your room. Pool; restau-rant for brkfst & dnr; lounge; laundry. $-$$$ (2801 E New York Ave; 386-736-3440)

JACKSONVILLE
Amelia Island (Fernandina Beach), Arlington, Fort George Island, Jacksonville Beach, Mandarin, Mayport, Orange Park, Talbot Islands, Yulee

Jacksonville, with a downtown riverwalk and resurgence of cultural activities, is becoming a sophisticated city well worth a visit. The list of museums, performing arts, historic parks, pools open in summer with lifts and nearby beaches with beach wheelchairs is impressive. The coastal road to Amelia Island is beautiful and full of history. Amelia Island invites you to ADA or WC-friendly B&Bs, condos and a fabulous resort.

Tourist Info
Amelia Island Chamber: 102 Centre St, Fernandina Bch, 32034; 904-277-0717; 800-226-3542
Jacksonville Beaches Visitor Center: 1101 Beach Blvd, Jacksonville Bch, 32250; 904-249-3868
Jacksonville Visitors Bureau: 201 E Adams St, 32202; 904-798-9111. And, 3 Independent Dr; 904-798-9148; 800-733-2668
St Johns County Visitors Bureau: 88 Riberia St, #1400, St Augustine, 32084; 904-829-1711; 800-653-2489
Fun Phone (904-630-7020) is a 24-hr taped message on special events in Jacksonville parks.
Web sites: www.ci.jax.fl.us; www.jaxcvb.com; www.ameliaisland.org; www.ameliaisland.com; www.amelianow.com

Transportation
Jacksonville Transportation Authority has some lift-equipped buses; call 904-630-3100 for a schedule. A lift-equipped van provides door-to-door service throughout the county for those who can't use the bus service. Apply by mail, including a physician's signature. Reserve 24 hrs ahead. Mon-Sat 5am-10:30pm; Sun 6am-8:30pm (904-393-4200)
Automated Skyway Express is an elevated people mover with roll-aboard cars (no tie-downs) in downtown and across the river. Mon-Thu 6:30am-7pm; Fri -10pm; Sat 10-10 (904-633-8503)
Care-A-Van Consolidated Transportation Services provides door-to-door service in a lift-equipped van anywhere in Duval County. Apply by phone; reserve 24 hrs ahead. Wkdy 6-5 (904-261-0700)
Dial-a-Ride provides door-to-door service for seniors and WC riders in Jacksonville Beach, Atlantic Beach and Neptune Beach. 24-hr advance reservation. Tue- Fri 8-3 (904-246-1477)
Dana's Limo has a lift-equipped mini-bus to go anywhere anytime at limo prices, discounted for WC passengers. Reservations (904-744-3333; 800-456-5466)
Gator City Cab has a lift-equipped van. Reservations. (904-355-8294)
St Johns Ferry transports vehicles (and passengers) on SR A1A across the St Johns

River between Mayport and Fort George Island. The 6-min ride reduces the drive time from Jacksonville to Amelia Island by roughly 40 min. 6:30am-10:15pm (904-241-9969)

WC Resources

Directory of Services for People with Disabilities is a free, comprehensive list of local and national organizations and companies with a range of support services. Write Community Services Department, City of Jacksonville, 421 W Church St, 32202 or call 904-630-4940.

Independent Living Resource Center has a loan closet and also provides information on available services and housing. (2709 Art Museum Dr; 904-399-8484; 888-427-4313; loan closet 904-399-5668)

Wheelchairs Plus rents, repairs and delivers manual and power WCs, ECVs and beach WCs (removable arms; umbrellas). (5150-6 Timuquana Rd; 904-779-5603)

ACTIVITIES

■ ATTRACTIONS
Beaks is an 8-acre, non-profit rehab center and sanctuary for injured eagles, owls and other birds. Mulched paths; picnic tables. $D. Tue-Sun 12-4 (12084 Houston Ave, Big Talbot Island; N off Hecksher Dr; 904-251-2473)

Jacksonville Zoo is the 73-acre home to 800 exotic animals. Paved paths lead through the Plains of East Africa and the Rift Valley habitats with great apes and birds. Demonstrations and animal encounters occur on weekends. Board the ramped, open-air train for a 1.3-mi narrated ride. Call for special events. WC & ECV rentals; picnic areas outside zoo; playground; gift shop; restaurant; CRr. $. 9-5 (8605 Zoo Pkwy; 1 mi E of Heckscher Dr; 904-757-4462)

Kingsley Plantation has the oldest antebellum home in the state, once owned by a man who married and later freed one of his slaves. A 2-mi drive passes through a forest canopy to a hard-packed sand parking lot. A sidewalk leads to the barn and ramped house. Rr. 9-5 (11676 Palmetto Ave, Fort George Island; S of Talbot Island; 904-251-3537)

■ BASKETBALL
River City Rollers, a professional WC-basketball team, welcomes anyone to join in practices or cheering at their games. Call Arthur Greene 904-955-4462 for the schedule and locations.

Sep-Apr
■ BEACHES
Parks: Fort Clinch
Amelia Island's beachfront spans 13 mi along the ocean but most dune crossovers have stairs leading to the sand. The following Nassau county beaches offer paved parking and WC friendly access: Burney Beach Park with Rr, roll-in showers and ADA picnic shelters (Burney Rd; off SR A1A at the S end of the island); Peters Point Park with Rr, roll-in showers and ADA picnic shelters (off S Fletcher Rd; S end of island); and Scott Road with no facilities (S end of Amelia Island Pkwy).

*****Hanna Park** is a popular 450-acre beach with 4 boardwalks through wooded dunes and accessible walkovers to a 1.5-mi stretch of soft sand beach. Parking lot 8 has the most WC-friendly beach access. Call to reserve the beach WC (fixed arms; umbrella); check at the entrance gatehouse so staff can meet you with the WC at the beach area of your choice. Surfing is reserved for the N end of the beach. A 65-acre freshwater lake by the campground has a T-shaped fishing pier. Try out the fountains and squirt guns at the large water playground near the lake. Neither the boat rentals, hiking or mountain biking trails are readily accessible. See Campgrounds. ADA picnic shelters;

campfire programs; lifeguards & snack bars in summer; playground; Rr in campground & parking lot #8. ⚲. 8-dusk (500 Wonderwood Dr, Atlantic Bch; off Mayport Rd; 904-249-4700)

+Huguenot Park is a 449-acre remote beach on a small peninsula jutting into the Atlantic. You can drive your car onto the usually firm sand along the calm Ft George Inlet and the ocean-front beach. Ask at the park gatehouse to borrow the beach WC (fixed arms; umbrella). The WC is bulky and stored 2 mi from the beach; if you cannot transport it, ask if staff can bring it to you. Beyond the gatehouse is a ramped gazebo popular for bird watching on Ft George Inlet. Windsurfers use the inlet and surfers use the S-end ocean beach. See Campgrounds. Lifeguards & snack bar in summer; Rr & bait shop in campground; outdoor showers; picnic tables & grills on sand. ⚲. Winter 8-6pm; summer -8pm (10980 Heckscher Dr; 1 mi E of Mayport Ferry; 904-251-3335)

+Jacksonville Beach is a 3.5-mi stretch of soft sand beach with a lifeguard station in the center where you can borrow a beach WC (fixed arms). Take the ramp to the S side of the lifeguard building. Arrive early because parking is limited. Only the following beach accesses are WC friendly: the lifeguard station at SR A1A and Beach Blvd; 1 St and 16 Ave S where the beach is street level; 1 St S and 6 Ave S by the pier; and, 1 St S between 4 and 5 Aves S where there is also an Rr. The 1-mi boardwalk, just N of the lifeguard station, passes restaurants and an amphitheater for outdoor concerts. Beach WC available in summer 10-6; rest of the year, call 904-249-9141.

+Talbot Islands State Parks include acreage, strung along SR A1A, on Amelia, Big Talbot, Little Talbot and Fort George Islands. Able-bodied folks can ride horses on the pristine beaches in Amelia Island State Park (Seahorse Ranch 904-261-4878/491-5166). Big Talbot has a beautiful picnic area (with ADA tables and grills) on the bluffs over Nassau Sound. Little Talbot loans beach WCs (with either removable or no arms; umbrellas) to enjoy the 5.5-mi expanse of white sand. The long accessible dune crossovers are located in the middle and at the S end of the island. ADA picnic tables; outdoor showers; Rr. Stop at the ranger station and staff will meet you with the beach WC. In addition to swimming and surf casting, you can enjoy watching the surfers. The canoe rental launch and boat ramp in the campground have a steep slope at low tide. Staff can help you to the water's edge and into a canoe to explore the trails through a salt marsh. The ranger station has an extensive bird watching guide, but talk with the rangers about hiking trails in these parks; tree roots are problematic on many. Or, get a self-guiding brochure from the rangers and enjoy the 4-mi historic drive on Fort George Island. ADA tables in all picnic areas; lifeguards in summer; campfires & ranger walks on Sat in summer. See Campgrounds. ⚲. 8-dusk (12157 Hecksher Dr; N of the Mayport Ferry; 904-251-2320)

■ **BIKE TRAILS**

Chuck Rogers Park has a paved track around its 13.5 acres of sports fields. ADA picnic shelters; playground; Rr (11950 San Jose Blvd, Mandarin; 904-573-2498)

Jacksonville-Baldwin Rail Trail is a 14.5-mi paved, multi-use trail through rural areas. The W trailhead is at Brandy Branch Rd/CR 121 (just W of Baldwin) and the E trailhead is at Imeson Rd, just W of Jacksonville. The trail is flat and mostly shaded. Park at either trailhead or in Baldwin (behind the Community Center). You may encounter a friendly cow begging for food and catch sight of feral pigs and deer. The county sponsors naturalist-led bike rides along the trail; call 904-573-2498. Port-o-lets at both trailheads. (904-630-5401)

Riverwalk runs on both sides of the downtown stretch of the St Johns

River. The Southbank has a 20' wide cement promenade running 1.5 mi past Friendship Fountain, museums, restaurants and the Lone Sailor Monument where you can picnic (1001 Museum Cr). The Northbank is a 1-mi boardwalk passing Jacksonville Landing with shops, restaurants and street entertainment. (201 E Coastline Dr)

■ **BOAT RAMPS**
Parks: Arlington
Beach Marine has a ramp and floating dock on the Intracoastal. Bait/ship store; restaurant; Rr. $. Dawn-dusk (2327 Beach Blvd, Jacksonville Bch; 904-249-8200)
City of Jacksonville offers the following boat ramps with floating docks. 5am-10pm unless otherwise noted: Mayport Boat Ramp on the St Johns River, Rr (4870 Ocean St; near SR A1A); Intracoastal Waterway, near Beach Marine with Rr (2501 2 Ave; at Beach Blvd); Wayne B Stevens on the Ortega River/St Johns (4555 Ortega Farms Blvd); T K Stokes on the Ribault River/St Johns (2120 Riverview Ave); Arlington on the St Johns River (Arlington Rd); Oak Harbor on the Intracoastal (2428 Seaway St, Mayport); Hood Landing on Julington Creek, open 24 hrs, Rr in Clark's Fish Camp next door (S end of Hood Landing Rd); Dinsmore Boat Landing on Trout River (11101 US 1; at Dunn Rd); Lonnie Wurn on the St Johns River (4131 Ferber Rd); Joe Carlucci Boat Ramp on the Intracoastal/St Johns, Rr (8410 McKenna Dr); and Lighthouse Marine on the Cedar River, Rr (5434 San Juan Ave).
Egans Creek Marina has a ramp and floating dock on the Intracoastal. Bait shop; Rr. $ (1641 N 14 St, Fernandina Bch; 904-277-0503)
Fernandina Harbor Marina has a boat ramp and floating dock on the Amelia River. Bait shop; restaurants nearby. Rr. $ (1 Centre St, Fernandina Bch; 904-261-2870)
Holly Point has a ramp with a floating dock on the Nassau River. ADA picnic shelters; Rr. 24 hrs (End of CR 107 S, Nassauville)
Melton Nelson Memorial Park has a boat ramp and floating dock on the Lofton Creek. ADA picnic tables. 24 hrs (SR A1A, Yulee)
Sisters Creek Marina has a ramp and floating dock on the Nassau Sound. (8203 Heckscher Dr, Big Talbot Island)

■ **BOAT RENTALS**
SR A1A Watersports rents pontoon and deck boats (33" entry) that you can usually roll aboard from the floating dock. Or, rent a 19' dual console; staff can help lift you from your WC into a boat seat. Boats can be used on the Intracoastal by the half/full day. Bait shop; Rr at marina. Wkdy 10-6; wknd 9-7; reservations Dec-Feb (2327 Beach Blvd, Jacksonville Bch; 904-249-6666)
Doc Holiday's rents pontoon boats (36" entry) for use on the 5-mi Doctors Lake or on the St Johns River. Rent for half/full day. Rr (3108 US 17S, Orange Park; 904-215-5363)

■ **BOAT TOURS**
Fishing Charters: Amelia Anchors Away, Backwater Charters
Island Water Sports offers 2-hr private excursions for up to 6. With advance reservations, the capt can help lift you from your WC into a boat seat from a floating dock. Sights include Fort Clinch, Cumberland Island, a shipwreck at Tiger Island, the backwaters of Beach Creek and the set of the film, PiPi Longstocking. (Fernandina Harbor Marina, 1 Centre St, Fernandina Bch; 904-261-1230)
SS Marine Taxi is a 40' pontoon boat servicing the St Johns River in downtown. Two sites have floating docks where you can roll aboard: on the Northbank, Jacksonville Landing (2 Independent Dr) and on the Southbank, Radisson Hotel/Chart House Restaurant (1501 Riverplace Blvd). If you want a quick tour of the riverfront, stay aboard for a 20-min ride. Wkdy 11-

9; wknd -11 (904-733-7782)

■ BOWLING

Beach Bowling Center has bowling ball ramps. Game room; snack bar; lounge; Rr. Tue, Thu & Sat 9am-midnight; other days open at 11am (818 Beach Blvd, Jacksonville Bch; 904-249-5416)

Jax Lanes has bowling ball ramps. Game room; snack bar; lounge; Rr. 24 hrs (8720 Beach Blvd; 904-641-3133)

West Lanes has bowling ball ramps and offers Cosmic bowling on Wed, Fri and Sat. Game room; snack bar; lounge; Rr. 9am-mdnt (6526 Ramona Blvd; 904-781-4422)

■ CANOEING/KAYAKING

Beaches: Talbot Islands

Outdoor Adventures offers customized, guided canoe and solo/tandem sea kayak trips around the region's creeks, rivers and barrier islands. Trips can last anywhere from 3 hrs to a full day. Discuss any needs in advance with the owner, Howard Soloman, so you can select the trip that best suits your interests and abilities and to work out shuttle arrangements. Normally, a 15-passenger van is used for shuttles. He can help you board. Equipment & instruction included; boxed lunches extra. (904-393-9030)

Kayak Adventures has guides experienced in adaptive paddling and offers instructions, customized group or private tours and guided fly/light tackle fishing trips throughout the area. After discussing your interests and abilities, staff can suggest classes and trips, including launch sites. Guides can help lift you into a solo/tandem sit-in kayak or can arrange for extra help. Equipment can be adapted to your needs, even for those who cannot grip. Group lessons usually take place at Guana River State Park on Sun at 9; group tours on tidal waters and estuaries occur on Sat at 9; both last 3 hrs. (Walter Bunso 904-249-6200; 888-333-2480)

■ CASINOS

LaCruise Casino offers 5-hr cruises aboard a 250' ship with over 200 slot machines as well as black jack, poker and crap tables. Roll aboard the ramp to the lower deck with the Las Vegas style casino, cafeteria and Rr. Crew may be able to carry you in your WC to the upper level where there is live entertainment, a dance floor and an outside deck. Sun 1pm; Tue-Thu, Sat 11am; Tue-Sat also 7pm (4738 Ocean St, Mayport; 904-241-7200; 800-752-1778)

■ DINNER THEATERS

Alhambra Dinner Theatre features musicals and comedies following a dinner buffet. WC seating is on the top level; a waitress can serve you from the buffet. Rr. Tue-Sun 6:30; matinees Sat 11:30 & Sun 12:15 (12000 Beach Blvd; 904-641-1212)

■ FISHING CHARTERS

Boat Tours: Hot Ticket Charters.
Canoeing: Kayak Adventures

Amelia Anchors Away Charters has customized a 36' boat so you can roll aboard from the floating dock on a ramp that has been cut into the side of the boat. Or, the capt can help your fishing buddy lift you aboard a 21' flats boat for 4 to fish the backwaters. Inshore, offshore and flats trips are for half/full day. Or, check out private sightseeing and sunset cruises. Rr at dock (Fernandina Harbor Marina, 1 Front St, Fernandina Bch; 904-277-2086)

Backwater Fishing Adventures offers half/full-day inshore fishing with light tackle or fly rods. The capt meets you at a dock near where the fish are running and usually can roll you aboard the flats boat from a floating dock. If you have more than 2 anglers, or if you cannot board the flats boat, he can arrange for a pontoon boat (33" entry). The capt also offers bird watching, sightseeing and photo safaris. (904-821-8245)

Blane Greene Charters fishes the backwaters and rivers in an 18' flats boat for up to 3 anglers for half/full days using light tackle. The capt meets you at a floating dock near where the fish are running and, if needed, helps lift you aboard in your WC. (904-714-2140)

Tradewinds has a fleet of 14 boats and offers half/full-day offshore fishing trips for up to 6 anglers. Crew can lift you aboard in your WC from the floating dock. Choose from sport fishing, bottom fishing or river fishing using light tackle or fly. Restaurant & Rr at marina (Fernandina Harbor Marina, 1 Centre St, Fernandina Bch; 904-261-9486)

■ **FISHING-PARTY BOATS**

Mayport Princess takes you out 25-50 mi for deep-sea fishing. Roll aboard by ramp and crew can lift you in your WC down 2' onto the deck. WC anglers sit in the rear. Crew can help you over the lip into the cabin. For weekdays, make your reservations 10 days ahead; for weekends, 1 month ahead. BYO food & drinks. 7-4 (4378 SR A1A N, Mayport; 904-241-4111)

Tradewinds boats #1 and #2 are set up for WC anglers. You can roll aboard and into the cabin. Half/full-day trips go out 15-20 mi. BYO food & drinks; restaurant & Rr at marina. Summer only, hrs vary (Fernandina Harbor Marina, 1 Centre St, Fernandina Bch; 904-261-9486)

■ **FISHING PIERS**

Beaches: Hanna Park. Parks: Arlington, Bethesda, Crystal Springs Rd, Ft Clinch, Mandarin

Nassau River has a fishing bridge between Big Talbot and Amelia Islands, W of the vehicular bridge. A hard-packed sand trail leads from parking on Big Talbot. Rr port-o-let (SR A1A)

Oceanway Park is a 20-acre park, half of which is a stocked pond with a boardwalk to 2 fishing decks (one is roofed). Picnic tables; Rr in Community Center. Dawn-dusk (12215 Sego Ave W; 904-751-3386)

■ **FITNESS TRAILS**

Parks: Crystal Springs Rd Park

■ **HORSEBACK RIDING**

Hearts, Hands & Hooves offers hippotherapy and therapeutic riding classes. Hippotherapy are 30-min private sessions with a trained healthcare professional, with specific treatment goals. The 1-hr group therapeutic classes are aimed at teaching riding skills. Classes are given at various locations, some of which have mounting blocks and ramps. Staff can help with transfers. Call ahead for an application. (Kim Fowler 904-778-9697)

■ **HUNTING**

Ralph E Simmons Memorial State Forest is owned by the St Johns River Water Management District that hosts a mobility-impaired hunt for deer, gray squirrels, quail and rabbit over 4 days in mid-Oct. This forest is located along the St Mary's River bordering Georgia. You must have Mobility-Impaired Certification; see p 13 on Hunting. Get an application for this hunt in late Jul by calling 386-329-4404. The 30 applicants randomly selected for this hunt are notified by mail. You may bring 1 or 2 able-bodied companions who may not hunt. Vehicles, including ATVs, are allowed during the MI Hunt. Primitive camping with an Rr port-a-let is available, but you must apply for a camping permit to the Division of Forestry, Rte 5, Box 9821, Hilliard, FL 32046; 904-845-3597. (from US 1 in Boulogne, go W on Lake Hampton Rd, then N on Penny Haddock Rd; 386-329-4500)

■ **MUSEUMS**

Alexander Brest Museum houses an extensive collection of ivory, pre-Columbian artifacts and rotating art exhibits. Rr. Wkdy 8:30-4:30 (Jacksonville Univ, 2800 University Blvd N; 904-745-7371)

Cummer Museum of Art & Gardens is a former estate housing 12 galleries of western art and is noted for its Meissen porcelain and classic European and American works. Enjoy an interactive teaching gallery for children and adults. Paved paths lead through spectacular formal gardens on the St Johns River. Rr. $/free Tue 4-9. Tue-Sat 10-5; Tue

&Thu -9pm; Sun noon-5 (829 Riverside Ave; 904-356-6857)

Museum of Modern Art features rotating exhibits in a recently renovated 5-story historic building downtown. Call for schedule of special events and hrs. Rr. $ (333 N Laura St; in historic Heming Plaza; 904-366-6911)

Jacksonville Maritime Museum houses artifacts, paintings and photos from maritime history 1842-1945. The Titanic and Saratoga are some of the model ships on display. Gift shop; CRr. 10-3:30 (1015 Museum Cir; 904-398-9011)

Karpeles Manuscript Library Museum houses historical manuscripts of literature, science, music and politics. Have a companion go in the main entrance so staff can open the side door to the elevator up to the museum. Street parking. Tue-Sat 10-3 (101 W 1 St; 904-356-2992)

La Villa Museum focuses on the area's African-American heritage, including the Civil Rights Movement. Traveling and local art exhibits are on display. Rr. $. Tue-Fri 9-6; Sat 10-2; Sun 2-5 (829 N Davis St; 904-632-5555)

Museum of Southern History presents the lifestyle and culture of antebellum South through displays and artifacts. CRr. $D. Tue-Sat 10-5 (4305 Herschel St; 904-388-3574)

Museum of Science & History has natural history, Native American and physical science displays. Kidspace is an interactive play environment for a child's first encounter with science. Attend one of the live demonstrations with birds, snakes, spiders and an alligator snapping turtle. The planetarium offers 20- to 45-min multimedia shows. Gift shop; Rr. $. Wkdy 10-5; Sat 10-6; Sun 1-6 (1025 Museum Cir; 904-396-7062)

Pablo Historical Park is a step back in time with the restored 1901 Museum House, formerly home to a railroad foreman, with a ramp at the back door. Next door is the ramped Mayport Depot, a railroad museum and gift shop (with a step at the door). A steam locomotive is on display. Docents are available for tours. ADA picnic shelter; street parking; Rr in Visitor Center. $D. Mon-Sat 10-3 (415 Beach Blvd, Jacksonville Bch; 904-246-0093) The Archives are 1 block E and contain displays of the Life Saving Corps. Rr. Thu 10-5 (380 Pablo Ave; 904-241-5657)

■ **PARI-MUTUELS**

Greyhound Racing is available at 2 locations: from May-Sep at Jacksonville Kennel Club (1440 N McCuff Ave, Westside) and from Sep-May at Orange Park Kennel (455 Park Ave, Orange Park). Racing occurs on Mon, Wed-Sat at 7:45pm; matinees are Sun at 1:30, Wed and Sat at 12:30. Both locations have Rr and WC seating in the grandstand and clubhouse; Orange Park also has a restaurant. Simulcast (rotating between dog, thoroughbred and jai lai) is available Wed-Mon 11:30-11:30 at each site during its off-season and year round at St Johns Greyhound Park that also has a snack bar and Rr. (US1 & Racetrack Rd, Bayard; 904-646-0001)

■ **PARKS**

Arlington Lions Club Park is 36-acre nature park with a paved trail (just past the Rr) that loops through woods to a boardwalk along the St Johns River. One low, 15' stretch sometimes gets sandy when the river overflows. You'll also find a boat ramp with floating docks and a 50' lighted wood fishing pier on the river. Occasional nature programs; ADA picnic shelters; grills; Rr. Dawn-dusk (4122 Richard D Gatlin Rd, Arlington; off University Blvd, 2.5 mi N of Jacksonville Univ; 904-573-2498)

Bethesda Park is a 66-acre, barrier-free nature park. A 1400' boardwalk takes you through the woods and along a stocked 20-acre lake. You can fish from the boardwalk (there are some shady spots) or from a 50' ADA pier. By the pier and along the boardwalk there are ADA picnic tables; grills are behind the main lodge. A hall with a kitchen, designed for WC folks, is popular for dances and other group activities and can be rented on weekends. See Cabins. Rr. Dawn-dusk (10790 Key Haven Blvd; off Dunn Ave, 5 mi W of I-95; 904-764-5531)

Crystal Springs Rd Park is a 40-acre nature park with extensive paved paths, including one along a stocked fishing pond. Fish from the path or from a wooden bridge over the lake. A paved exercise course has 12 stations, some usable by WC folks. Playground and nature trails with ADA mulch; ADA picnic shelters; grills; sports fields; tennis; Rr; CRr in community center. Dawn-dusk (9800 Crystal Springs Rd; off Chaffee Rd, 2 mi from I-10; 904-693-4909)

Fort Caroline National Memorial sits in the 46,000-acre Timucuan Preserve and includes a reconstructed fort from the 16th century, where French Huguenots fought the Spanish. The visitor center has a museum, bookstore and 10-min film on the preserve. Nearby is a Rr and ADA picnic shelter. A .25-mi, hard-packed path, with a slight hill, takes you to the replica fort; the 1st level and parade grounds are accessible. Or, a ranger can take you to the fort in a golf cart and help with transfers. Most trails are narrow, hilly and blocked by tree roots. 9-5 (12713 Fort Caroline Rd, Arlington; near Monument Rd; 904-641-7155)

*Fort Clinch State Park includes 1121 acres at the N tip of Amelia Island with a 5-sided fort, which was occupied by both Union and Confederate troops during the Civil War. With help up the 6" rise, you can get from room to room on the ground level. A smooth, steep ramp to the second tier allows a great overlook but the rest of the rampart is crumbling and tough to navigate. Ask the Civil War soldier if he can give you a tour. In front of the fort is a visitor center with a gift shop and historic display. Call to reserve a beach WC (fixed or no arms; umbrella) and pick it up at the ranger station. The easiest access to the soft sand beach is a long boardwalk from the beach overlook (outdoor showers; Rr) on the Atlantic. Nearby is a 2400' cement, lighted fishing pier over the Atlantic. The park has 6 mi of quiet roads for easy wheeling. There's also a .5-mi stretch of service road reserved for inline skaters and bikers. Of the 3 hiking trails, the mulched Dune Trail, behind the River Campground, is the most graded. Willow Pond and Magnolia Trails are hard-packed, but have some tree roots, hills and 4 broad steps to a pond; Magnolia also has a steep slope up to parking. The picnic area at the fort has ADA tables on mulch. See Campgrounds. $. 8-dusk (2601 Atlantic Ave, Fernandina Bch; N tip of Amelia Island; 904-277-7274)

Mandarin Park is a 36-acre county nature park with paved paths, including one to a secluded duck pond. The outdoor nature discovery center with signage is ramped. There's a fishing pier on Julington Creek. Nature programs; ADA picnic shelter; grill; Rr. Dawn-dusk (14780 Mandarin Rd, Mandarin; off Westberry Rd; 904-573-2498)

Ringhaver/Ortega Stream Valley Park includes 600 acres of nature park and sports fields. Just S of the ADA playground is a .5-mi paved nature trail/boardwalk that loops into a hardwood hammock. Nature programs; picnic tables; grills; Rr. Dawn-dusk (5198 118 St; near Ortega Farms Rd, E of Landing Blvd; 904-779-1519)

Treaty Oak Park is a small park with a huge live oak between 500 and 850 yrs old. A raised walkway leads from parking and around the tree. Nature/history programs; picnic tables (1123 Prudential Dr; 2 blks from Southbank Riverwalk)

Tree Hill is a 50-acre, urban wilderness where sidewalks lead to separate gardens of butterflies, hummingbirds and herbs and organic vegetables. Check out the swamp garden! The pyramid-shaped museum (with a ramp to the 2nd floor) has exhibits on energy, natural history and native species. The Sabal Palm Trail is a 500' paved nature trail with interpretive signage. Family nature programs are held the 3rd Sat of each month from 10-12. Gift shop; picnic tables; Rr. $. Mon-Sat 8:30-5 (7152 Lone Star Rd, Arlington; 904-724-4646)

Westside Regional Park is 509 acres of woods with paved paths throughout. A WWI brick road testifies to the area's history. The nature center, with interactive exhibits, and an amphitheater host frequent nature programs. A .5-mi nature trail is paved for 900' then mulched with a few sandy spots; it leads to an inaccessible wildlife watch tower. ADA picnic tables; Rr. Dawn-dusk (7000 Roosevelt Blvd; across from Naval Air Station; 904-573-2498)

■ **PERFORMING ARTS**

Amelia Community Theater features drama, comedy and musicals. With advance notice, a ramp can be set up at the front entrance. WC seating in front; Rr (209 Cedar St, Fernandina Bch; 904-261-6749)

Fernandina Little Theater offers community performances of comedy and drama. WC seating throughout. Ramp on the side of the building; street parking. (1014 Beach St, Fernandina Bch; 904-277-2202)

Florida Theater is a restored 1920's movie palace, where Elvis first performed indoors, and where you can now attend concerts, plays and classic movies. WC seating is in front on the aisle and in the center rear of the theater. Street parking & nearby city lots; Rr. Movies Jul-Aug Sun 2pm (128 E Forsyth St; 904-355-2787)

Ritz Theater hosts a variety of cultural activities, concerts and special events. WC seating is at the ends of the front and last rows. Rr (829 N Davis St; 904-632-5555)

Theater Jacksonville offers community performances of comedy and drama. WC seating is in the front aisle. Street parking; Rr. Sep-May (2032 San Marco Blvd; 904-396-4425)

Times-Union Center has 2 venues. The Jacoby Symphony Hall is home to the Jacksonville Symphony Orchestra, performing Sep-May. WC seating is on the aisles in the front and back of the orchestra section and in the boxes on the mezzanine. The Moran Theater hosts Broadway shows, an artist's series, concerts and operas. WC seating is in the first 2 rows in orchestra and 2 boxes in the loge. Rr (300 Water St; 904-633-6110)

■ **POOLS**

Jacksonville is unique in having 20 city pools with powered lifts (fixed seats) where lifeguards can help with transfers. All pools are open weekdays, early Jun to mid-Aug, and weekends from late Apr to early Jun and mid-Aug to late Sep. Aquarobic and swim classes are offered at many of the pools; for info call 904-745-9630. All pools have outdoor showers and Rr. Andrew Jackson (128 W 30 St; 630-0281); Adolph Wurn (2115 Dean Rd; 724-8218); Baldwin (345 Chestnut St; 266-2478); Charles Clark/Sherwood (8739 Sibbald Rd; 768-6422); Clanzel T Brown (4515 Moncrief Rd; 768-1330); Ed White (1700 Old Middleburg Rd; 783-4958); Englewood (4412 Barnes Rd; 448-6895); Eugene Butler (900 Acorn St; 630-0322); Forrest (5530 Firestone Rd; 573-2485); Highlands (10913 Pine Estates Rd; 751-1533); Lakeshore (2519 Bayview Rd; 387-1772); Lee (1200 S McDuff Ave; 387-6959); Mandarin (4831 Greenland Rd; 292-1541); Terry Parker (7301 Parker School Rd; 723-6144); Paxon (3239 W 5 St; 783-0377); Ribault (5820 Van Gundy St; 766-5319); Sandalwood (2750 John Prom Blvd; 642-5900); Thomas Jefferson (390 N Jackson Ave; 783-2540); Wolfson (7000 Powers Ave; 448-6894); and Woodland Acres (8200 Kona Ave; 724-6169).

■ SHOPPING

Antiques: Worth & Co is a 55,000 sq ft gallery of antiques with everything from furniture to African items, colonial cookware and English silver (1254 Beach Blvd; 904-249-6000). For mostly American heirlooms, try China Cat Antiques (246 4 Ave S, Jacksonville Bch; 904-241-0344). Canterbury House Antiques is another worthwhile stop (1776 Canterbury St; 904-387-1776). Fernandina Bch has a 50-block historic area with antiques, shops and restaurants (Centre St).

Boutiques: Jacksonville Landing is a downtown riverfront marketplace with shops, restaurants and live entertainment (2 Independent Dr; 904-353-1188). Palmetto Walk has several up-scale shops on Amelia Island Plantation (4800 SR A1A).

Malls: Avenues Shopping Mall (10300 Southside Blvd; 904-363-3060); Orange Park Mall (1910 Wells Rd); Regency Square (9501 Arlington Expwy, Arlington; 904-725-1220)

Specialty shops include Mambo's Entertainment's Historic Record Store, specializing in Latino music (5340-1 Timucuana Rd; 904-772-1841)

■ SPECTATOR SPORTS

Arena Football Jacksonville Tom Cats play Apr-Jul in the Veterans Memorial Coliseum with WC seating in all price categories. Rr (1145 E Adams St; 904-358-7825)

Football NFL Jaguars play in Alltel Stadium with WC seating throughout and elevators to all levels. Rr. Aug-Dec (1 Stadium Pl; 904-633-2000)

■ TENNIS

USTA WC-Tennis instruction is available for adults, beginners and advanced, on Mon 5-7:30pm. To register call Carol Anderson 904-384-1999. For information on the children's tennis program, call Janice Smith 850-910-8820/646-3414. (Univ of N FL, 4567 St Johns Bluff Rd S; athletic complex at N end of campus)

■ TOURS

Amelia Island can be toured in your own car with a self-guiding brochure from the Chamber. (102 Centre St, Fernandina Bch; 904-261-3248; 800-226-3542)

Amelia Island Museum of History teaches island history with docents leading onsite tours via maps, photos and artifacts (Mon-Sat 11 & 2). The 1st floor of the former jailhouse has a ramp at the Cedar St entrance; the archaeological display on the 2nd floor is not accessible. The museum also offers a range of walking and driving tours in Fernandina Beach; some require reservations and a minimum of 4 or 10 persons. A guide can accompany you in your vehicle. Depending on the tour, some of the historic sites are accessible. $. Wkdy 10-5; Sat 10-4 (233 S 3 St, Fernandina Bch; 904-261-7378)

Buccaneer Trail is a beautiful, 52-mi scenic route heading S along SR A1A from Amelia Island, past the Talbot Islands State Parks and near the Kingsley Plantation. There are several beaches and other great stopping points on the way to historic St Augustine. (904-798-9111)

Budweiser Brewery allows you to view the brewing and packaging process from a gallery overlooking Brew Hall. Take a self-guided or a 1-hr guided tour (10am-3pm). Adults can enjoy free tastings. Rr. Mon-Sat 9-4:30 (111 Busch Dr; Hwy 95 exit 360, near airport; 904-751-8117)

Sally Corporation is one of the creators of Disney-like animatronic (robotic) characters for high-powered theme parks. Hour tours (only for guests age 5 and older) include the production floor, art and programming areas plus an entertaining animatronics show. Reservations; Rr. Tue & Thu 9-1 (745 W Forsyth St; 904-355-7100)

ACCOMMODATIONS

■ B&B/INNS

Addison House, circa 1876, has a garden house built in 1997 that sits in a court-yard surrounded by gardens and water fountains. The ADA guestroom, The Lily, has a king bed (27" high/open frame) and a private bath with a tub. Take the ramp into the main house where a full breakfast is served in the dining room. This B&B is located 1 block from historic downtown. $$$ (614 Ash St, Fernandina Bch; 904-277-1604; 800-943-1604)

Ash Street Inn has an WC-friendly guestroom, the Magnolia, with a king bed (24" high/open frame) and a private bath with an over-sized tub and hand-held sprayer. A full gourmet breakfast is served on the wrap-around front porch or dining room. $$$ (102 S 7 St, Fernandina Bch; 904-277-4941; 800-277-6660)

Elizabeth Pointe Lodge is an old-Nantucket style 25-room inn with an ADA guestroom (#4) that has a king bed (27" high/open frame) and a bathroom with roll-under sink and step-in shower with a seat. While the beach is inaccessible, you can enjoy the view and homemade lemonade on the large oceanfront deck. Free buffet brkfst; full restaurant. $$$ (98 S Fletcher Ave, Fernandina Bch; 904-277-4851; 800-772-3359)

Hoyt House has WC-friendly guestrooms. The friendliest is the Oliver with wider doorways and a king bed (25" high/open frame). The private bathroom has a 1" rise at the doorway, grab bars, a raised toilet, roll-under sink and Jacuzzi tub with a hand-held sprayer and seat. A complete, hot breakfast is served in an elegant dining room; wine is served in the evenings and appetizers are served on weekends. This 1905 home is ramped and has a huge front porch, patio, gazebo and off-street parking. $$$ (804 Atlantic Ave, Fernandina Bch; 904-277-4300; 800-432-2085)

Williams House, with a Civil War history and an extraordinary opulence, is in the historic district near quaint shops and restaurants. Leonardo DaVinci is an ADA guestroom with a queen bed (open frame). The private bath has a raised toilet, roll-under sink, claw-footed tub and roll-in shower with a hand-held sprayer and seat. Because the 1856 main house next door is inaccessible, gourmet breakfast on heirloom china is served in your room. $$$ (103 S 9 St, Fernandina Bch; at Ash St; 904-277-2328; 800-414-9258)

■ CABINS/CAMPGROUNDS

Bethesda Park has 4 ADA cabins, each with 4 bunk beds, a kitchenette and grill. Bathrooms have roll-under sinks and roll-in showers with hand-held sprayers and seats. The cabins are duplexes that share a screened-in porch with an ADA picnic table. Bring linens. See Parks (10790 Key Haven Blvd; off Dunn Ave, 5 mi W of I-95; 904-764-5531)

*Fort Clinch State Park has 62 RV/tent sites in 2 different areas, all with water/elec, picnic tables and fire pits. The River Camp is wooded and has 2 bathhouses, but the stalls and showers are too small for WCs. The Atlantic Camp is flat, treeless and just over the dunes from the beach. The bathhouse has a standard-size stall with grab bars, a roll-under sink and roll-in shower; sites 2-4 and 14-16 are closest to this bathhouse. Laundry; vending machines. You can borrow a beach WC at this historic beach; see Parks. (2601 Atlantic Ave, Fernandina Bch; 904-277-7274)

*Hanna Park has 293 RV/tent sites (with full hookups) and 15 tent sites nestled in the woods beside a 65-acre freshwater lake and just over the dunes from the ocean. Each of the 3 ADA bathhouses have roll-under sinks and roll-in showers. Beach WC for loan; see Beaches. Campfire programs in amphitheater; laundry; general store; shuffleboard; playgrounds. 10% discount for disabled (500 Wonderwood Dr, Atlantic Bch; off Mayport Rd; 904-249-4700)

*Huguenot Park has 40 RV and 32 tent sites, none with hookups but all close to the beach. Some sites have picnic tables and grills; all are very sandy with no shade. But, you can use the park's beach WC while you stay in the campground. Site 49 is ADA with a cement pad, ADA picnic table, raised fire ring and a paved path to the ADA bathhouse that has raised toilets, roll-under sinks and roll-in showers. See Beaches. Small grocery store; bait shop (10980 Heckscher Dr; 1 mi E of Mayport Ferry; 904-251-3335)

Little Talbot Island State Park has 40 wooded RV/tent sites with water/elec hookups on hard-packed natural terrain. ADA sites 4 and 17 have ADA picnic tables, grills, fire rings, special water faucets and are near a bathhouse that is up a short hill. The 2 bathhouses are standard with plans to upgrade to ADA in 2003. This park loans a beach WC for its fabulous 5.5-mi white sand beach. See Parks. Reservations advised; laundry. (12157 Hecksher Dr; 17 mi NE of Jacksonville; 904-251-2320)

■ CONDOS

Amelia South Condos have WC-friendly 2BR oceanfront condos each with a full kitchen, a king and 2 full beds (open frames), queen sofa bed and bathroom with a 27" wide door, grab bars and tub. Pool; laundry; lounge (3350 S Fletcher Ave, Fernandina Bch; 904-261-7991; 800-543-0664)

Ketch Courtyard has WC-friendly 2BR/2BA and 3BR/3BA condos each with an oceanfront balcony, full kitchen, washer/dryer, queen sofa bed in the living room, a king, queen and 2 twin beds (24" high/open frames). The bathrooms have tubs. Pool; path to the beach (3150 S Fletcher Ave, Fernandina Bch;

904-261-0677)

Summer Beach Resort has 52 WC-friendly 2BR/2BA condos with ocean or pool views, full kitchens and living rooms with a sofa bed. Each master bedroom has a king bed and the 2nd bedroom has a queen or 2 twin beds (on open frames). Some bathrooms have grab bars and hand-held sprayers in the step-in showers. Pool; laundry; championship golf course (5456 First Coast Hwy, Fernandina Bch; 904-277-0905; 800-862-9297)

■ MOTELS

*Amelia Inn, at the Amelia Island Plantation resort, has 7 ADA rooms with balconies and an ocean view. Rooms have a king or queen bed (open frames) and bathrooms with raised toilets, roll-under sinks and roll-in showers with a hand-held sprayer and seat. Three rooms also have a sofa bed. This luxury resort has it all, from championship golf to children's and teen programs. The jogging trails and bike paths are either paved or boardwalks. Borrow the beach WC to enjoy the ramped beach or (with advance reservations) naturalist-led tours on the grounds. A lift-equipped van can take you sightseeing on the island and pick you up at the airport. Fitness center; lounge; restaurants. $$$ (S end of Amelia Island off SR A1A; 904-261-6161; 800-874-6878)

Candlewood Suites has 8 ADA rooms, each with a kitchenette, queen bed (open frame) and bathroom with a raised toilet and roll-under sink. Four rooms have roll-in showers; others have step-in showers with hand-held sprayers and seats. Laundry. $-$$ (4990 Belfort; 904-296-7785)

Club Continental Suites has an ADA room (#201) with a balcony overlooking the St Johns River, a kitchen, 2 queen beds (24" high/open frames) and a bathroom with a raised toilet, roll-under sink and roll-in shower with a hand-held sprayer and seat. Free brkfst; pool; laundry; lounge; full restaurant. $$$ (2143 Astor St, Orange Park; 904-264-

6070; 800-877-6070)

Comfort Inn Oceanfront has 6 ADA rooms, each with a queen bed (open frame) and a bathroom with a raised toilet and roll-under sink. Rooms 218 and 318 have roll-in showers with hand-held sprayers and seats; others have tubs. $$-$$$ (1515 N 1 St, Jacksonville Bch; 904-241-2311; 800-654-8776)

Days Inn Oceanfront has 8 ADA rooms, each with a king or 2 full beds (open frames), a refrigerator and, for an extra fee, a microwave. Bathrooms have roll-under sinks and tubs with hand-held sprayers and seats. Pool; entertainment, restaurant for brkfst & dnr; walkway to the beach. $$-$$$ (1031 S 1 St, Jacksonville Bch; 904-249-7231; 800-321-2037)

Fairfield Inn has 5 ADA units. Room 107 is a 1BR/2BA suite with a king bed (24" high/open frame) and a sofa bed in the living room; both bathrooms have raised toilets and roll-under sinks; one bathroom has a roll-in shower with a hand-held sprayer; the other has a tub. Other ADA rooms have a king or 2 full beds (20" high/open frames). Bathrooms have raised toilets, roll-under sinks and tubs or step-in showers with hand-held sprayers and seats; room 505 has a roll-in shower. Free brkfst. $$ (8052 Baymeadows Cir W; 904-730-0739)

Hampton Inn has 6 ADA rooms, each with a king bed (23" high/open frames) and bathroom with a raised toilet and roll-under sink. Room 113 has a microwave, refrigerator, sofa bed and roll-in shower; room 122 has a roll-in shower; others have tubs with hand-held sprayers and seats. Free brkfst; pool. $$ (1331 Prudential Dr; 904-396-7770)

Holiday Inn Airport has 9 ADA rooms each with a king or 2 full beds (24" high/platforms) and coffeepots. All bathrooms have raised toilets, hand-held sprayers and seats; some have roll-under sinks; rooms 1115, 1135, 3109 and 3111 have roll-in showers; others have tubs. Pool; laundry; lounge; full restau-rant. $$ (14670 Duval Rd; 904-741-4404)

Holiday Inn Express has 7 ADA units. Each of the 3 rooms has a king bed; each of the 4 1BR suites has 2 full beds (22" high/platforms), a kitchenette and full sofa bed. Bathrooms have raised toilets and roll-under sinks; suite 105 has a roll-in shower with hand-held sprayer and seat; others have tubs. Free brkfst; pool; laundry; lounge; fitness room. $$ (4675 Salisbury Rd; 904-332-9500; 888-610-3555)

Holiday Inn Express has 3 ADA rooms, each with a king bed (26" high/platform) and coffeepot; bathrooms have a roll-under sink. Room 125 has a roll-in shower with a hand-held sprayer and seat; others have tubs. Pool. $-$$ (3276 Hwy 17 N, Yulee; 904-225-5114)

Homestead Guest Studios has 6 ADA rooms with kitchenettes, a choice of a king, queen or 2 full beds (on platforms) and bathrooms with raised toilets and roll-under sinks. Rooms 117 and 119 have roll-in showers with hand-held sprayers; others have tubs. Laundry. $ (10020 Skinner Lake Rd; 904-642-9911)

Homestead Village has 6 ADA 1BR suites with kitchens, king or queen beds (22" high/open frames) and bathrooms with roll-under sinks. Two rooms have roll-in showers with hand-held sprayers; others have tubs. Laundry. $ (8300 Western Way; 904-739-1881)

Hospitality Inn has 3 ADA 1BR suites each with a king (21" high/open frame) or queen bed (on platform), a queen sofa bed and kitchenette. Bathrooms have raised toilets, roll-under sinks and tubs with seats. Free brkfst; pool; laundry. $$ (7071 103 St; 904-777-5700; 800-772-8929)

Red Roof Inn has 7 ADA rooms with a king or 2 full beds (21" high/open frames) and bathrooms with raised toilets and roll-under sinks. Rooms 115 (with 2 full beds) and 117 (with a king bed) have roll-in showers with hand-held sprayers; others have tubs. Free brkfst; pool; laundry. $ (6969 Lenoir

Ave E; 904-296-1006)
Wellesley Inn & Suites has 8 ADA 1BR suites each with a queen bed (23" high/platform), queen sofa bed, kitchenette and bathroom with a raised toilet and roll-under sink. Three rooms have roll-in showers with hand-held sprayers; others have step-in showers and seats. Free brkfst; pool; laundry. $$ (8801 Perimeter Park Blvd; 12 mi to beach and 10 mi to downtown; 904-620-9008)

St Augustine

Anastasia Island, Bunnell, Flagler Beach, Palatka, Palm Coast,
Ponte Vedra Beach, St Augustine Beach, Vilano Beach

As the oldest city in the USA, St Augustine is a premiere historical experience. The Old City is closed to vehicles; your best bet for parking is at the visitor center (10 Castillo Dr); be prepared to cope with some cobblestone roads and paths. Beyond sightseeing, there are beach wheelchairs, swimming pools in Palm Coast and fabulous campgrounds, one with a ramped pool. For thrills, try flying vintage airplanes!

Tourist Info
St Johns County Visitors Bureau: 88 Riberia St, 32084; 904-829-1711; 800-653-2489
St Augustine Visitor Center: 10 Castillo Dr, PO Box 210, 32085; 904-825-1000
St Augustine Beach Visitors Bureau: 350 SR A1A/Beach Blvd, St Augustine Bch, 32080; 904-471-1596
Web sites: www.visitoldcity.com; www.oldcity.com; www.staugustinechamber.com

Transportation
Council on Aging has a lift-equipped van to provide transportation for medical appointments and shopping throughout the county. Call at least a day in advance. Applications are not required. Wkdy 7:30-2 (904-823-4800)
Flagler County Transport has lift-equipped vans providing door-to-door service throughout the county for residents and visitors. You need not pre-qualify, but you must make reservations at least 24 hrs in advance. (386-437-7272)

WC Resources
American Home Patient rents and repairs manual and power WCs. Pickup and delivery is available. Wkdy 9-5 (1949 SR A1A S; 904-471-2011)

ACTIVITIES

■ ATTRACTIONS
See Old City.
Alligator Farm offers 20-min shows with gators, reptiles and birds from the rainforest. Wood walkways take you past monkeys, crocs and a petting area. WC loaners; gift shop; snack bar; Rr. $. 9-5 (2 mi S of the Bridge of Lions on SR A1A, Anastasia Island; 904-824-3337)
Castillo de San Marcos National Monument, a Spanish colonial fort built in the late 1600's along the Mantanzas Bay, is the premiere landmark in St Augustine. Sidewalks lead from parking to the fort and around the grassy courtyard, where you can roll into the shot furnace, powder magazine, chapel and the troops' quarters. The 35' ramparts are not accessible. Special events and reenactments occur throughout the year.

Ranger-led tours; Rr. $. 8:45-4:45 (1 S Castillo Dr; 904-829-6506)

Fountain of Youth is reportedly where Ponce de Leon landed in 1513 and built his signature cross of coquina stones. You can drink from the spring believed to be the Fountain of Youth, see the remains of a Timucuan Indian burial ground and enjoy exhibits on Spanish colonization. A planetarium show, every 30 min, reveals the skies as they looked from de Leon's ship. Mulched & paved walkways; snack bar; picnic tables; Rr. $. 9-5 (11 Magnolia Ave; 904-829-3168; 800-356-8222)

Marineland, an attraction built in 1938, is recovering from Hurricane Floyd in 1999 and is being restored to its original glory. Hopefully the renovations will improve access as well. Currently you can watch dolphin training and penguin and sea lion shows as well as their residence. However, the dolphin show at the Top Deck is inaccessible. The Oceanarium is a huge tank where divers hand-feed sea turtles and other marine life. Along the paved paths are small sheltered aquariums and a tidal pool with marine science information. A seashell exhibit is in the gift shop. The dolphin encounter and the scuba/snorkel program are inaccessible. Snack bar; Rr. $/WC visitors free. Wed-Mon 9:30-4:30 (9507 SR A1A; 18 mi S of St Augustine on SR A1A; 904-460-1275)

Museum Theater presents a 52-min film on the settlement of St Augustine that is required viewing for all first-time visitors. WC seating on aisles; Rr. $. On the hr from 9-4 (Visitor Center, 10 Castillo Dr; 904-825-1000)

Ripley's Believe It or Not is the original Ripley's and has the usual eclectic collection of the strange and bizarre. You can now take an elevator to the 2nd and 3rd floors where the exhibits are located. Vending machines; Rr. $. 9-7 (19 San Marco Ave; 904-824-1606)

3D World offers an interesting 30-min experience. The Motion Theater features two 7-min computer generated, 3D films that resemble a simulator ride at a theme park. Wearing nerdy 3D glasses, you can experience the severe jolting and sense of careening movement if you can transfer into a theater seat. Otherwise, you can watch from stationary seat or WC area to the side. The Fountain Theater features a 15-min laser light show with music and choreographed water fountains. Again, if you cannot transfer into a theater seat, use WC seating in the back left. Rr. $. 10-8 (28 San Marco Ave; 904-824-1220; 800-998-4418x5)

World Golf Hall of Fame traces the history of golf from its Scottish origins to today through rotating exhibits and interactive fun. Enjoy memorabilia and footage of golf's greatest players. Try putting with a wood-shafted putter and gutta percha golf ball on an 1880's green or have your swing analyzed to discover which golf pro's swing most resembles your own. Restaurant; gift shop; Rr. $. 10-6 (1 World Golf Pl, World Golf Village; 904-940-4000)

■ **BASEBALL**

Challenger Baseball is a Little League program for kids with various disabilities. Call Ron Brown 904-824-9032.

■ **BEACHES**

*St Johns County Beaches cover a long stretch of hard-packed sand along the Atlantic where you can drive your car. Vehicle access points are along SR A1A at Ocean Trace Rd; St Augustine By the Sea; Matanzas Rd; Mary St; Frank Butler Park E; Crescent Beach; and Ft Matanzas. Or, if you'd rather, park off-beach and take WC accessible dune crossovers at Mickler Landing, Guana River State Park and Crescent Beach. Call to borrow a beach WC (fixed arms); you can pick it up at the county office (901 Pope Rd; S of SR 312 & SR A1A). Motels, restaurants (with Rr) and open-air snack bars line much of the beach. Lifeguards May-Sep. $/vehicles (SR A1A; 904-471-6616)

■ **BIKE TRAILS**

Parks: Anastasia, Guana River, Treaty,

Ravine

SR A1A, for over 20 mi from Ponte Vedra S to Flagler Beach, has a some-times adjacent and sometimes parallel bike trail passing beautiful beaches, residential areas and downtown St Augustine.

■ **BOAT RAMPS**

Parks: Guana, Faver-Dykes, Lighthouse, Trout Creek

Devils Elbow Fish Camp has a ramp and floating dock on the Intracoastal. Bait shop 7-6. $. 24 hrs (7507 SR A1A S; 904-471-0398)

Intracoastal has a boat ramp and a floating dock. ADA picnic table; Rr (Moody Lane, Flagler Bch; off SR 100)

Frank Butler Park W is a 53-acre park with ramps and fixed docks on the Intracoastal. Picnic tables; Rr. 24 hrs (399 Riverside Dr; 2 mi S of St Aug Bch off SR A1A)

Riverdale Park is a small park with a ramp and fixed dock on the St Johns River. ADA picnic tables; playground. 24 hrs (CR 13 S of CR 214)

Vilano Boat Basin has boat ramps and a floating dock on the Matanzas River, near the outlet to the ocean. 24 hrs (May St; W of Vilano Bridge on SR A1A)

■ **BOAT TOURS**

Scenic Cruise offers 75-min narrated trips on Mantanzas Bay to view histori-cal sites and wildlife. With advance no-tice, crew can help you up the steep ramp to the boat's 1st deck. Cash bar. 11, 1, 2:45, 4:30 (Municipal Marina, 111 Avenida Menendez; 904-824-1806; 800-542-8316)

■ **BOAT/KAYAK/WAVERUNNER RENTALS**

Devils Elbow Fish Camp offers half/full day 8-person pontoon boat (29" entry) rentals for use on the Intracoastal and Mantanzas Inlet. Floating dock; bait shop. 7-6 (7507 SR A1A S; 904-471-0398)

Palm Coast Resort Marina has 8-person pontoon boats (30" entry) for use along the Intracoastal; 1-hr minimum. The dock is fixed, but staff can help lift you aboard in your WC or into the driver's seat. Staff can direct you to parking for easy WC access to the dock. Rr in ma-rina. 8-5 (200 Clubhouse Dr, Palm Coast; 386-446-6370)

Ragin Water Sports rents waverunners, kayaks, speedboats and pontoon boats (24" entry) for use in the Matanzas Bay; 1-hr minimum. Ramps lead to the floating docks where crew can lift you in your WC aboard a boat or onto a waverunner or kayak. Summer 10-6; Fall-spring by appt (Conch House Ma-rina Resort, 57 Comares Ave; 904-829-5001)

Watersports rents pontoon boats (33" entry) and solo/tandem sit-on kayaks for use on the Intracoastal; 1-hr mini-mum. You can roll aboard a pontoon boat from the floating dock. Crew can lift you from your WC to a wave runner or a kayak. Mar-Labor Day 6-8; Sep-Feb by appt (250 Vilano Rd; 904-829-0006)

■ **BOWLING**

Anastasia's has ramped lanes. Lounge; snack bar; game room with billiards; Rr. Hrs vary (3245 SR 3; 904-471-3565)

■ **FISHING CHARTERS**

Fishing-Party Boats: Sea Love

Camachee Cove Charters has over 20 boats, from 20'-58', for backwater flyfishing, light tackle and offshore trolling and bottom fishing. Trips range from 4-12 hrs and can go out beyond 35 mi. Take a ramp to a floating dock where crew can lift you aboard in your WC. Rr in marina (107 Yacht Club Dr; 904-825-1971)

Davis Fishing Charters can book char-ters on a variety of boats for flats fish-ing or offshore trips from 2 hrs to all night for up to 6. Offshore trips go out as far as 40 mi for trolling or bottom fishing. You can also combine a 2-hr sightseeing trip with fishing. The capt will meet you at a dock that best suits your needs; crew can lift you aboard in your WC. (904-824-0328)

K-2 offers light tackle flats fishing on a 21' Carolina Skiff for up to 4 anglers. Try a 4- or 6-hr trip. Crew lifts you aboard in your WC from a floating dock. Rr at marina (New Sebastian Harbor Marina, 821 S Ponce de Leon Blvd; US 1 & SR 207; 904-824-9499; 800-608-8195)

■ **FISHING-PARTY BOATS**

K-2 offers 5- and 9-hr deep-sea fishing trips. Crew can lift you aboard in your WC from a floating dock and, should you desire, over the 5" lip to the cabin. The boats have a section where the railing can be lowered for WC anglers. Rr at marina. Half day 7 & 1; full day 7:30 (New Sebastian Harbor Marina, 821 S Ponce de Leon Blvd; US 1 & SR 207; 904-824-9499; 800-608-8195)

Sea Love Charters offers deep-sea trips for 4 or 8 hrs of bottom fishing. Crew can lift you aboard in your WC from a floating dock. This operator also offers half/full-day private sports fishing charters for 4 anglers. 8-5 (Sea Love Marina, 250 Vilano Rd; across New Vilano Bridge; 904-824-3328)

■ **FISHING PIERS/BRIDGES**

Parks: Lighthouse, Treaty

Flagler Beach City Pier is a 750' lighted pier on the Atlantic. Bait shop (dawn-dusk); restaurants nearby; Rr. ∫. Dawn-mdnt (215 S SR A1A, Flagler Bch; 904-439-2200)

Old Shands Bridge is a lighted, wood fishing bridge over the St Johns River. But be aware: there's no HC parking. Close to the pier, you can find level areas to park beside the paved road but further from the bridge, the sides slope steeply to the river. Convenience store on S side of bridge. 24 hrs (SR 16; near CR 13)

St Augustine Beach Fishing Pier is a 600' lighted pier on the Atlantic. Bait shop 6am-10pm; ADA picnic tables on oceanfront porch; vending machines; Rr. ∫/discount for WC anglers/seniors free. 24 hrs (SR A1A, St Augustine Bch; 904-461-0119)

Vilano Fishing Pier is a lighted, cement fishing bridge over the Intracoastal. Bait/snack shop. 24 hrs (Vilano Rd, Vilano Bch; next to the Unisa Bridge)

■ **FLYING**

North American Top-Gun gives you a chance to be Top Gun in a range of experiences in WW II fighter aircraft, from introductory 15-min rides and aerobatics to 3- or 5-hr air-to-air combat training. If you can grasp the control stick, you can be the pilot. Depending on the program you choose, an instructor sits in the front or back cockpit with dual controls. Staff lifts you from your WC onto the wing and then over into the cockpit. All flights require a cockpit briefing; aerobatic and combat courses also require a classroom session. Be prepared to travel up to 200 mph! In the combat mission, a radar targeting system that senses hits has replaced the original M-2 machine guns. You can purchase a video of your ride shot onboard from the wings and cockpit. Call for schedule at this site. (St Augustine Airport, 270 Estrella Ave; 904-823-3505)

■ **MUSEUMS**

Florida Heritage Museum traces local history from the time before European exploration through the Flagler era. Exhibits include historic photos, antique dolls and toys, Confederate items, colonial Spanish weapons, a life-size sunken ship, its treasures and a replica of an Indian village. The Old Jail is also on the grounds and charges separate admission; see Old City below. Rr. ∫. 8:30-5 (167 San Marco Ave; 904-829-3800; 800-397-4071)

Lightner Museum is housed in the 1888 Hotel Alcazar, built by Henry Flagler. An elevator takes you to 3 floors of Victorian and Tiffany art, antique furnishings, costumes and other artifacts from the 19th century. There's an antique mall (closed Mon) and a cafe open Tue-Sat for lunch. Street parking in back; WC loaner; Rr on top floor & in courtyard. ∫/kids under 12 free. 9-5 (City Hall Complex, 75 King St; 904-824-2874)

Museum of Weapons & Early American History features swords, muskets, unusual firearms and shipwreck artifacts dating back to the 18th century. Spanish and English colonial artifacts and Civil War items are also on display. Gift shop. $/discount for seniors. 9:30-5 (81C King St; 904-829-3727)

Oldest Store Museum contains more than 100,000 items from the store's original stock. It also houses an antique steam tractor, a Model T Ford and a Conestoga wagon. $. Mon-Sat 10-4; Sun 12-4 (4 Artillery Ln; 904-829-9729)

Potter's Wax Museum is home to more than 170 life-like famous figures and a 12-min motivational film (WC seating in front). Check out the wax studio where the figures are created. Street parking; gift shop; Rr. 9-5; Fri-Sat -9; summer -9 (17 King St; 904-829-9056; 800-584-4781)

■ **OLD CITY**
The district is made up largely made up of 18th and 19th century coquina buildings, many with steps and some with Rr. The stretch of the Old City along St George St is closed to vehicles. The following sites are accessible:

Cathedral Basicalla is a Catholic church built in 1797. Ramp on W side; 15-min tours at 1 & 3. $D. 9-4:30 (38 Cathedral St; 904-824-2806)

Memorial Presbyterian Church is a Renaissance structure built in 1889 by Henry Flagler as a memorial to his daughter. Ramp on E side; 5-min talks by docents. $D. Mon-Sat 9-4:30; Sun 12-4:30 (36 Sevilla St; at Valencia St; 904-829-6451)

Nombre De Dios is the site of our country's 1st Catholic Mass and mission. These exquisite grounds have paved paths past shrines, chapels and memorials. A 208' cross marks the founding of St Augustine in 1565. The Shrine of Our Lady of LaLeche has 2 steps. Gift shop; Rr. $D. 8-5 (27 Ocean Ave; SR 16 & San Marco Ave; 904-824-2809)

Old Jail, built in 1890, served as the county jail until 1953. Now costumed guides, portraying the sheriff and his wife, take you through the sheriff's quarters, maximum security, women's cell and the gallows in the courtyard. Only the 1st floor is accessible. Continuous 30-min tours; Rr. The Florida Heritage Museum is also on the grounds and charges separate admission. $. 8:30-4:30 (167 San Marco Ave; 904-829-3800; 800-397-4071)

Oldest House dates back to the early 1700s but the site served as home to a Spanish soldier as early as 1565. The entry has a step and only the 1st floor is accessible, but you can view the 2nd floor on video. In the ornamental gardens, with paved paths and plants typical of the Spanish, British and American occupants, is a museum that portrays the 400-yr plus history of the city. Gift shop; continuous 30-min tours; Rr. $. 9-5 (14 St Francis St; 904-824-2872)

Oldest Wooden Schoolhouse, built in the 1750s still holds class, albeit with a teacher and students of wax, dressed in period clothing, discussing the school's history, the barter system and dunce caps. Educational artifacts are on display. $. 9-5; summer 9-6 (14 St George St; 904-824-0192)

Pena-Peck House was originally the Spanish Treasury in the 1740's, then home of the British Lt Governor. Displays include early Spanish artifacts and furnishings from the 18th century. Only the 1st floor is accessible. With reservations, you may lunch in the gardens Mar-Apr on Thu. Guided 30-min tours occur Sun-Fri 12:30-3:30 and Sat 10:30-3:30. Summer: closed Sun. $ (143 St George St; 904-829-5064)

St Photios National Greek Orthodox Shrine contains exhibits and a multimedia presentation on Greek immigrants and the development of the church in the US. The exquisite tiny chapel is ramped and filled with outstanding Byzantine-style frescoes. Gift shop. 9-5 (41 St George St; between Orange St & Cuna St; 904-829-8205)

Spanish Military Hospital reveals the medical practices of the Spanish colony. Costumed staff re-enact daily life of patients and staff for 30-min guided tours. The entrance has a step. ⚡. 10-5 (3 Aviles St; 904-797-5604; 800-597-7177) **Spanish Quarter Village** consists of 1.5 acres with 9 reconstructed Spanish colonial homes and a sand/shell path throughout. Costumed guides demonstrate textiles arts, woodworking, smithing and other activities from the 1740s. Most buildings have a step at the entrance and some doorways are narrow. Take a guided 30-min tour of the de Mesa home (at 10, 12, 2 or 4:30) where only the 1st floor is accessible. Gift shop; Rr. ⚡. Sun-Thu 9-6; Fri-Sat 9-9 (29 St George St; 904-825-6830) **Ximenez-Fatio House,** built in 1798 as a Spanish merchant's home and store, has been restored to its 1821 incarnation as an inn. Only the 1st floor is accessible. Guided 20-min tours run every 30 min. Gift shop. ⚡D. Thu-Mon 11-4; Sun 1-4 (20 Aviles St; 904-829-3575)

■ **PARASAILING**

Watersports offers solo/tandem parasail rides up to 1400' for 10 to 15 min. Staff lifts you in your WC aboard the boat from a floating dock, helps you don the harness and lifts you to the platform for takeoff. Experienced with disabled parasailors, staff promises a gentle landing. Mar-Labor Day 6-8; Sep-Feb by appt (240 Vilano Rd; 904-829-0006)

■ **PARKS**

†Anastasia State Park includes 1722 acres of relatively undeveloped beach and forest along the Atlantic. Ask at the ranger station to borrow the beach WC (no arms). A ranger meets you with the WC at the beach parking lot where you can take a boardwalk out to the 4-mi stretch of broad white sand beach and where you can surf cast. Or, drive to the edge of the Salt Run Lagoon where you're protected from the wind and the sand is hard packed. At the Lagoon, canoes, sit-on kayaks, sailboards and windsurfers are rented daily in summers and weekends in spring and fall (904-460-9111). The launch site is hard-packed and flat; staff can help you transfer. The camp store, with bait, bike rentals and beach chairs, is inaccessible but staff can come outside to serve you. The 1.5-mi nature trail is hilly, narrow, overgrown and on soft sand; the short trail to where the Spanish mined coquina is on rough terrain. The sunny sidewalk along the 1.5-mi road to the beach is great for wheeling. See Campgrounds. ADA picnic shelters; lifeguards in summer; playground on soft sand; vending machines; Rr. ⚡. 8am-dusk (SR A1A at SR 3, St Augustine Bch; 2 mi N of CR 312; 2.5 mi S of Bridge of Lions; 904-461-2033)

Bulow Plantation Ruins State Historic Site is the 152-acre remains of a former cotton, sugar, indigo and rice plantation that was destroyed in the Seminole Indian Wars. A ramp and concrete path lead through the ruins to a small museum. Examine the old sugar mill and an open-air collection of Seminole and plantation relics. You can fish off a gently sloping boat ramp or use the ramp to board and disembark a rental canoe. Staff can help with transfers for the 3- or 6-mi paddle along the mild Bulow Creek. The hiking trails are rough terrain. ⚡. 9-5 (Old Kings Road, Bunnell; I-95 exit 278 E to Old Kings Rd, turn S; 386-517-2084)

Faver-Dykes State Park is a tranquil, 1449-acre preserve on the brackish Pellicer Creek. Call ahead if you'd like to rent a canoe for the 4-mi canoe trail that remains the same as when the Spanish explored this area. The easiest launch is at the rough cement boat ramp. Be aware, if windy, it can be a tough paddle back. An ADA picnic shelter and fishing docks are at the boat ramp. A short nature trail runs along the creek and another through pinelands; both are flat, hard-packed trails with some roots. Call in advance to arrange a ranger-led nature walk. Playground on mulch; Rr. ⚡. Dawn-dusk (US 1; 15 mi S of St Augustine, near I-95; 904-794-0997)

Flagler Beach City Parks include 3 sites connected by a 1-mi boardwalk along a natural marsh and the Intracoastal. At *Moody Boat Ramp*, you find a floating dock beside the lighted boat ramp, ADA picnic tables and a Rr. In *Flagship Park* the boardwalk leads to a T-shaped dock for fishing on the Intracoastal, a large, lighted ADA picnic shelter and Rr. *Wickline Park* has 2 lighted ADA picnic shelters, Rr, library, tennis and basketball. All are open 24 hrs. (Moody Lane; off SR 100; 386-437-7490)

Fort Matanzas is a small, coquina-stone fort, built by the Spanish in 1742. You take a 5-min ferry from the visitor center across the Matanzas River to the island fort. The ferry and the fort itself require visitors to navigate steps (a few at the ferry and 15 at the fort). But you can enjoy the visitor center, with exhibits, an 8-min video and small bookstore. Get a self-guiding brochure to explore the .5-mi boardwalk/nature trail. Rr in parking lot. 9-4:30 (8536 SR A1A S; S end of Anastasia Island; 904-471-0116)

Gamble Rogers Memorial State Park has 144 acres bordered by the Atlantic and Intracoastal. An ADA dune crossover gets you to an overlook and ramp to the edge of the beach. From May-Sep, with luck, you may observe sea turtles nesting or hatching. On the Intracoastal side is a boat ramp with a fixed dock where you might fish. Or, fish off the level bank or the paved walkway around the basin. With 2-wk advance notice, ranger programs can be arranged. See Campgrounds. ADA picnic table with grill & water on cement; Rr. $. 8-dusk (3100 S SR A1A, Flagler Bch; 386-517-2086)

Guana River State Park, the spot where Ponce de Leon may have first landed, has 2400 acres with varied ecosystems, from hardwood hammock to beach. The S parking lot has an accessible dune crossover and ramp down to the grainy sand beach (about 75' from the water). Surfers and surf casters love this beach. For fishing, drive to the dam where the riverbanks are level and grassy and you can picnic at the ADA picnic table. Bring a canoe. Launches are on both sides of the dam where you can paddle into the lake and river. The 9 mi of former service roads are hard-packed, except after rains, and popular for biking. Rr- port-o-lets at the 3 beach parking lots. $. 8-dusk (2690 S Ponte Vedra Blvd, Ponte Vedra Bch; off SR A1A; 904-825-5071)

Haw Creek Preserve is a 400-acre park with a 1-mi boardwalk over wetlands that passes 4 T-shaped docks where you can fish on Haw Creek. Be aware of tides if you launch a boat here because the lighted boat ramp has a fixed dock. Lighted ADA picnic shelter (CR 2007; off CR 305, SW of Bunnell)

Lighthouse Park is a 3-acre park around the 165' candy-striped lighthouse built in 1876 that you can see from 20 mi away. The light keepers' house is now a museum (open 9-6) with exhibits on local history, a 30-min video on light keepers, paintings of lighthouses and a gift shop (904-829-0745) on the 1st floor. Anglers can use the 60' lighted fishing dock or boat ramps and floating dock 24 hrs a day on Salt Run, a large inlet off the Mantanzas River. Restaurant with bait shop; ADA picnic tables on deck; Rr. $/Museum. Dawn-dusk (Red Cox Rd; E off SR A1A at Old Beach Rd; 904-829-8172)

Ravine State Gardens were first carved by the St Johns River and, since 1933, shaped by gardeners who planted azaleas and other exotics that peak Jan-Apr. A 2-mi road winds around and into the two 90' deep ravines. You can pull off the road at several spots to enjoy the spectacular views. After 4pm, the road is closed to vehicles and open only to pedestrians and bikes. Most visitors in WCs take the perimeter road only part way because the slope up from the ravine is quite steep. Gift shop; vending machines; ADA picnic tables; Rr. $. 7:30am-dusk (1600 Twiggs St, Palatka; 386-329-3721)

Treaty Park is a 47-acre park with a 1-mi nature/bike trail that loops through a lovely forest. Roll through the ADA picnic shelter to access a wood fishing dock that crosses a 3-acre lake. Along the banks are several flat hard-packed areas where you can transfer to a canoe (if you bring your own) and enjoy the marked canoe trail. Check out the dog park where pets can run off leash and a skateboard park with a viewing area. Playground on sand; ADA picnic tables; grills; ball fields & courts; snack bar; Rr. 24hrs (1595 Wildwood Dr; 2 mi E of I-95 off SR 207; 904-829-8807)

Trout Creek Park is a secluded 16.5-acre reserve along the St Johns River. Anglers can fish from the long dock at the 2 paved boat ramps on the St Johns or from a dock on Trout Creek. A nature trail loops 1 mi around the park, with several smaller trails branching off; trails are hard-packed shell and well maintained; a bridge goes over the only hilly part. The paved roads here are popular with joggers. An active community center hosts naturalist programs and, for seniors, lunch, bridge and bingo. ADA playground planned; ADA picnic tables; CRr in center; Rr. Wkdy 8-5 (6795 Collier Rd; off SR 13, S of town; 904-284-9488)

Washington Oaks State Gardens lie on either side of SR A1A, between the Atlantic and Matanzas River. On the ocean side, from HC parking is a 300' boardwalk that leads to a scenic overlook with steps down to the beach. On the W side of SR A1A is the interpretive center, a private home built in 1938, which is ramped in back. From here, the .5-mi Mala Compra Nature Trail (generally hard-packed but with some roots) takes you to the picnic area. Paths of compacted sawdust meander through ornamental gardens of roses, citrus, camellias, azaleas and native species. These paths can be problematic for WCs and virtually inaccessible when wet. Depending on available staff, rangers may be able to open a gate so you can drive your vehicle to the salt-water river for fishing off the banks. ADA picnic tables; Rr. $. 8-dusk (6400 N Oceanshore Blvd, Palm Coast; 386-446-6780)

■ **PERFORMING ARTS**

Flagler Auditorium hosts a range of productions by big bands, chamber groups, and orchestras as well as family shows and Broadway musicals by touring companies. WC seating is in the aisles toward the rear. The entrance is ramped from the parking lot. (3265 E Hwy 100, Bunnell; 386-437-7547)

Limelight Theatre is a community theater with a professional attitude offering comedy, drama, original work or musicals. WC seating in aisles in 1st row; CRr. Fri-Sat 8pm; wknd 2pm (1681 US 1; behind K Tires; 904-825-1164)

■ **POOLS**

Belle Terre Swim & Racquet Club has a heated pool, a lift (fixed seat) and an aquatic rehab program. A weight room, massage facilities and aerobic classes are in a ramped portable. Snack bar; locker room with roll-in shower; Rr. 7am-8pm (73 Patricia Dr, Palm Coast; 386-446-7676)

Frieda Zamba Aquatic Complex has a pool and a lift (fixed seat). When not too crowded, staff can help with transfers. Aquatic rehab program; weight & exercise room; snack bar; Rr. Apr-Oct wkdy 12-8; wknd 10-8 (4520 Belle Terre Pkwy, Palm Coast; 10 mi S of St Aug; 386-446-6717)

■ **SHOPPING**

Antiques & Boutiques: Uptown offers individual shops, an antique mall and restaurants (50-100 San Marco Blvd). The historic district is filled with art galleries, quaint shops and restaurants (King St & Cathedral Place).

Flea Markets: St John's Flea Market has paved paths through 25 acres of bargains under a roof. Rr. Wknd 9-5 (SR 207; off I-95; 904-824-4210)

Malls: St Augustine Outlet Center has 95 stores (I-95 exit 318; 904-825-1555). Beltz Factory Outlet World has over 50 stores (I-95 exit 318; 904-826-1311)

■ **SPECTATOR SPORTS**

Auto Racing Florida Speed Park offers 5 divisions of stock car racing. WCs can sit next to the stand. Snack bar; Rr. Feb-Nov Sat 8:15pm (900 Big Oak Rd; off US 1; 904-825-2886)

■ **TOURS**

Ancient City Tours takes you back in time with tales and scenes of romance, murder and ghostly haunts. By appointment, private walking tours trace the plot of the historic novel, *Maria*, by Eugenia Price, or the true story of an unsolved murder in 1974. Take a walking tour of the south historic district with a guide carrying a lantern. Or, try the 90-min water taxi tour along the Intracoastal communing with spirits of the sea. Beverages are served before the tours and guides are dressed in period clothing. 8pm (3 Aviles St; 904-797-5604; 800-597-7177)

St Augustine Transfer Co, in operation since 1877, provides narrated tours in horse-drawn carriages down the streets and alleys of the historic district. On the 2.5-mi journey, you will learn about the architecture and history of the past 400 yrs. A Ghost Ride evening tour reveals true ghost stories, legends and folklore. Call to reserve the carriage that has a lift; it carries 1 WC and 11 companions. $/WC rider free (Avenida Menendez St; next to the stone fort; 904-829-2391)

Tour St Augustine offers a range of 1-hr historic walking tours at 10am that depart from the Casa Monica Hotel (King & Cordova Sts). Ghostly 90-min walking tours leave at 8pm from the N end of St George St, near the Milltop Water Wheel. Reservations (904-825-0087; 888-461-1009)

Whetstone Chocolate Factory offers self-guided tours that start with a 15-min video explaining the delicious process from the cocoa bean harvest to the final decorative touches. Then watch 500 candies a minute be processed and then hand-packed at a slower rate. Gift shop; CRr. Mon-Sat 10:30-5:30 (2 Coke Rd; off SR 312; 904-825-1700)

ACCOMMODATIONS

■ **B&B/INNS**

Augustin Inn, in historic downtown near the waterfront, has an ADA guestroom (#1) with a queen bed (24" high/open frame) and a private bath with a raised toilet, roll-under sink and roll-in shower with a hand-held sprayer and seat. Guests enjoy the front porch, parlor and a full breakfast in the dining room. HC parking beside inn. $$ (29 Cuna St; at St George St; 904-823-9559; 800-248-7846)

Casa de Suenos B&B, a turn-of-the century Mediterranean inn, has an ADA guestroom, the Nieves, with a private entrance and queen-size canopy bed (open frame). The private bath has a raised toilet, roll-under sink and roll-in shower with a hand-held sprayer and seat. A 2-course breakfast is served in the lovely dining room. Off-street parking. $$-$$$ (20 Cordova St; at Saragosa St; 904-824-0887; 800-735-7534)

Centennial House, in the heart of the historic district, has the ADA Main Room, with a queen bed (30" high/open frame). The private bath has a raised toilet, roll-under sink and roll-in shower with hand-held sprayer and seat. Breakfast is served in the dining room. $$$ (26 Cordova St; at Saragosa St; 800-611-2880)

■ **CAMPGROUNDS**

+Anastasia State Park has 139 RV/tent sites under moss-draped oaks; 5 have ADA picnic tables, grills, full hookups and are close to the ADA bathhouse. The bathhouse has raised toilets, roll-under sinks and roll-in showers. While the park has a great oceanfront beach and beach WC (see Parks), the campground is along a lagoon. Laundry. (SR

A1A at SR 3, St Augustine Bch; 2 mi N of CR 312, 2.5 mi S of Bridge of Lions; 904-461-2000)

Faver-Dykes State Park has 30 RV/tent sites with water/elec hookups on hard-packed shell; 2 ADA sites have ADA picnic tables and grills. One has a paved path to the ADA bathhouse with raised toilets, roll-under sinks and roll-in showers. See Parks. (US 1; 15 mi S of St Augustine, near I-95; 904-794-0997)

Gamble Rogers Memorial State Park has 34 tent/RV sites, including an ADA site with an ADA picnic table, grill, water/elec and concrete pad. The nearby bathhouse has roll-under sinks and a roll-in shower. While you can see the beach from the campground, the ADA dune crossover is in the day use area. See Parks. (3100 S SR A1A, Flagler Bch; 3 mi N of Flagler City Pier; 386-517-2086)

North Beach Camp Resort, with its oak and myrtle trees, is located on the Intracoastal and the Atlantic and has 110 RV/tent sites with full hookups, 10 with water/elec only. The 2 WC-friendly bathhouses have raised toilets, roll-under sinks and roll-in showers with hand-held sprayers. Low numbered sites are closest to the bathhouses. The roads, walkways and sites are all gravel. A unique feature here is the large, ramped pool. You can also enjoy a fishing dock, boat ramp and a ramp to the floating dock on the Intracoastal (depending on tides, the ramp may be steep). Game room; playground; group campfires; laundry. (4125 SR A1A; 904-824-1806; 800-542-8316)

■ **MOTELS**

Anastasia Inn has an ADA room with a queen bed (24" high/open frame), refrigerator, microwave and coffeepot. The bath has a roll-under sink and roll-in shower with a hand-held sprayer and seat. Free brkfst; pool. $-$$$ (218 Anastasia Blvd; just E of downtown, over the Bridge of Lions; 904-825-2879; 888-226-6181)

Comfort Suites World Golf Village has 8 1BR suites, each with a full sofa bed, refrigerator, microwave and coffeepot. One unit has 2 queen beds; the others have a king or queen bed (open frames). Bathrooms have raised toilets and roll-under sinks; rooms 104 (with 2 queen beds) and 106 have roll-in showers with hand-held sprayers and seats; the others have tubs. The Village includes 3 golf courses, residences and vacation villas, restaurants and a Mayo Clinic facility. See Attractions: World Golf. Free brkfst; pool; laundry; lounge. $$$ (475 Commerce Lake Dr; I-95 exit 323; 904-940-9500; 877-940-9501)

Hampton Inn has 5 ADA rooms, each with a king bed (27" high/open frame) and coffeepot. Bathrooms have raised toilets, roll-under sinks and roll-in showers with hand-held sprayers and seats. The path to the beach overlook and pier is soft sand. Free brkfst; pool; laundry. $$-$$$ (430 SR A1A , St Augustine Bch; 904-471-4000; 888-889-4904)

La Fiesta Oceanside Inn has an ADA room with a king bed (open frame) and bathroom with a raised toilet, roll-under sink and roll-in shower with a hand-held sprayer. A boardwalk leads to an overlook on the beach, but there is no WC access to the sand. Restaurant for brkfst. $$-$$$ (810 SR A1A, St Augustine Bch; 904-471-2220; 800-852-6390)

Monterey Inn is quaint, with 3 ADA rooms, each with 2 queen beds (open frames). Bathrooms have raised toilets and roll-under sinks; one room has a roll-in shower; others have step-in showers. You must go up steps to the office, restaurant and pool, but this motel is right across the street from the Mantanzas River and Castillo de San Marcos in downtown. $-$$$ (16 Avenida Menendez; 904-824-4482)

Ocean Sands Motor Inn is 4 mi from downtown and has an ADA room (101) with a king bed (open frame), refrigerator, microwave, coffeepot and private patio. The bathroom has a roll-under sink and roll-in shower with hand-held sprayer and seat. Free brkfst. $-$$ (3465 SR A1A N, Vilano Bch; 904-824-1112;

800-609-0888)

Palm Coast Resort has 12 ADA rooms, each with a king or 2 full beds (25" high/open frames) and coffeepots. Bathrooms have raised toilets and tubs with hand-held sprayers and seats. The marina on the premises has a boat ramp, floating docks, boat rentals and bait shop. Pool; lounge; entertainment; full restaurant. $$-$$$ (300 Clubhouse Dr, Palm Coast; 386-445-3000; 800-654-6538)

Quality Inn has 2 ADA rooms, each with a king bed (24" high/platform), coffeepot and bathroom with a raised toilet, roll-under sink and roll-in shower with a hand-held sprayer and seat. Downtown location; full restaurant;

gift shop. $-$$ (2700 Ponce de Leon Blvd; 904-824-2883; 800-223-4153)

Radisson has 6 ADA rooms, each with 2 queen beds (22" high/open frames) and a coffeepot. Bathrooms have roll-under sinks; rooms 122 and 130 have roll-in showers; others have step-in showers with hand-held sprayers and seats. Pool; laundry; lounge; full restaurant. $$-$$$ (4000 US 1 N; 904-824-2821)

Ramada Limited has 2 ADA rooms, each with a king or 2 queen beds (24" high/ platforms). Bathrooms have raised toilets, roll-under sinks and roll-in showers with hand-held sprayers and seats. Free brkfst; pool; laundry. $-$$ (894 SR A1A, St Aug Bch; 904-471-1440)

SANFORD
DeBary, Geneva, Longwood

Sanford, where the St Johns River empties into Lake Monroe, was once a bustling riverboat port amidst celery fields. It's a charming little place with a historic downtown, plenty of natural attractions and 30 min from the glitz of Orlando. Sanford is also the southern terminus of the Auto Train. You'll find outstanding bass fishing in Lake Monroe and rustic cabins in the area.

Tourist Info
Seminole County Visitors Bureau: 105 International Pkwy, Heathrow, 32746; 407-665-2900; 800-800-7832
Web sites: www.visitseminole.com; www.members.aol.com/sanfordfla

Transportation
Lynx provides WC-accessible bus service within Sanford and to the Orlando area. Buses have lifts and tie-downs. (407-628-2897)

WC Resources
Walker Medical rents and delivers WCs and ECVs with reservations. (905 E SR 434, Longwood; 407-331-9500; 888-726-6837)

ACTIVITIES

■ **ATTRACTIONS**
Central Florida's Zoological Park is a 109-acre cypress woodland home to over 230 animals, some of whom you can feed. Boardwalks lead to most exhibits, including a butterfly garden, but

there are some mulched paths. Volunteers offer animal encounters on weekends that describe the zoo's outstanding breeding and conservation programs. Snack bar; gift shop; ADA picnic tables; Rr. $. 9-5 (3755 NW US 17/92;

407-323-4450)

■ **BIKE TRAILS**

Cross Seminole Trail will ultimately run 14 paved mi from Spring Hammock Preserve in Winter Springs to Howell Branch Rd at the Seminole/Orange County line. Currently, it runs 3.7 mi from downtown Oviedo (at SR 434 and SR 426) north to Gardenia Ave in Winter Springs. The Black Hammock Trailhead in Oviedo has gazebos, water fountains for humans and dogs, paved parking and Rr (SR 434; just E of SR 417/Greenway). The natural beauty along this trail has earned incorporation into the Florida National Scenic Trail, a 1300-mi trail from the Panhandle to the Everglades. (407-788-0405)

■ **BOAT RAMPS**

C S Lee Park has a ramp and floating dock on the St Johns River. ADA picnic shelter. Dawn-dusk (SR 46; 15 mi E of US 17/92; 407-788-0405)

Cameron Wight Park has a boat ramp and floating dock on Lake Jessup. ADA picnic shelter. Dawn-dusk (SR 46; 5 mi E of US 17/92; 407-788-0405)

Lake Monroe has a ramp and a floating dock. Dawn-dusk (Monroe Harbour Marina, 531 N Palmetto Ave; 407-321-0000)

Lake Monroe Park has a ramp, floating dock and fishing dock on the St Johns River. Bait shop; concession stand. 7-dusk (975 S US 17/92; 386-668-3825)

■ **BOAT RENTALS**

Skyline Water Sports rents pontoon boats (29" entry) for up to 10 people. You can roll aboard from the ramped floating dock. Call ahead if you need staff to help lift you into a fishing boat. Hrs vary (Monroe Harbour Marina, 531 N Palmetto Ave; 407-321-0000)

■ **BOAT TOURS**

Rivership Romance offers 3- and 4-hr daily lunch and weekend dinner cruises along the St Johns River aboard a 100' 1940's Great Lakes steamer. The boat is ramped to the 1st level. With advance notice, staff removes booth seating and reserves a window-side table for you. On a monitor, you can watch the entertainment on the upper deck or staff can carry you up the steps. CRr (Monroe Harbour Marina, 531 N Palmetto Ave; 407-321-5091; 800-423-7401)

Safari River Tours offers a 2-hr tour on a 24-passanger boat up the St Johns River and the backwaters. Roll aboard on a portable ramp from the fixed dock. Rr at marina. Hrs vary (High Banks Marina, 488 W High Banks Rd, DeBary; off US 1792; 386-668-1002)

St Johns Wildlife Safari offers 1-hr guided trips on Lake Harney in an airboat for 2. Capt Don Davies is experienced with disabled passengers. He grounds the airboat and ramps it, so he can help you roll aboard. He removes the front seat and straps your WC in place. The tour skirts the shorelines looking for wildlife and covers local history and ecology. (105 Jane Creek Dr, Geneva; 321-349-2438)

■ **FISHING PIERS**

Soldier's Creek Park has a boardwalk to a fishing dock on Lake Jesup. ADA picnic shelter; Rr. Dawn-dusk (SR 419; 2 mi E of US 17/92; 407-788-0405)

■ **HUNTING**

Seminole State Forest hosts a FWC Mobility-Impaired Hunt, usually the third week of Oct, for deer and hogs. Sixty applicants are selected from a random drawing. To apply, see Hunting p 13. ATVs are prohibited. (SR 46; 14 mi W of Sanford; 5 mi E of Mt Plymouth; 352-732-1225)

■ **MISC**

Paralyzed Veterans of America sponsors various outings, events and clinics in sports, such as water skiing. Sign up for the bass fishing tournament held every Apr. You can participate in most activities with almost any level of disability. Volunteers are ready to help. Non-Vets can join for $5/yr, which includes a newsletter. (407-328-7041)

■ **MUSEUMS**

Museum of Seminole County History, in a 1926 *Old Folks Home*, displays Native American artifacts, antique farm equipment, early 1890's pictures of the area and exhibits covering the history of the steamship and railroad in Florida. Check out the country store, schoolroom and hospital room from the *old days*. The building is ramped but some rooms are very small. Call ahead for a 30-min tour. $ Tue-Fri 9-12 & 1-4; Sat 1-4 (300 Bush Blvd; 407-321-2489)

Sanford Museum covers the city's history and contains Henry Sanford's art and library collection. Rr. Tue-Fri 11-4; Sat 1-4 (520 E 1 St; 407-302-1000)

■ **PARI-MUTUELS**

Sanford-Orlando Kennel Club offers live greyhound racing and simulcasts year round. WC seating is available anywhere on the 1st level and, with reservations, up an elevator in the 3rd floor Finish Line Dining Room. Rr. Hrs vary (301 Dog Track Rd, Longwood; 407-831-1600)

■ **PARKS**

Big Tree County Park is so-named because it's the 11-acre home to a 138' high, 47' round and 350-yr-old Bald Cypress tree called The Senator. An elevated boardwalk leads through lovely woods to and around the *big* tree. ADA picnic tables; Rr. 8-dusk (Gen'l Hutchinson Pkwy; 1.5 mi W of US 17/92, N of Longwood; 407-788-0405)

Gemini Springs is a beautiful, 210-acre park with plenty to enjoy. Trails include a short, paved loop around the spring, a .5-mi, hard-packed nature trail with interpretive signs and a 1-mi paved bike trail. A shallow swimming area has 5 wide steps (4" high, 18" deep) down to the 72-degree spring waters. Or, you can take a sidewalk to the wooden

floating dock where swimmers can drop into the water and use a ladder to get out. On the bayou is a 120' fishing pier. The county rents canoes and has a floating dock at the launch site; there are no flat areas for boarding from the banks. Call in advance so staff can ensure a canoe and help in boarding. Lake Monroe is an hour's paddle from the launch and you return to the put-in. ADA picnic tables; CRr. $ Dawn-dusk (37 Dirksen Dr, DeBary; 407-668-3810)

Lake Mills Park is a 50-acre county park with a fishing pier over the lake and ADA picnic shelters nearby. The parking lot, most paths and the playground are shell. Rr. 8-dusk (1301 Tropical Ave; 1 mi E of SR 419; 407-788-0405)

Sylvan Lake Park has a 1-mi network of boardwalks through the forests and along the shores of Sylvan Lake. ADA picnic tables; a small dock for fishing; Rr. 8-dusk (845 Markham Rd; 407-322-6567)

■ **PERFORMING ARTS**

Orlando Theater Project offers shows by both professional and student troupes, ranging from classics to off-Broadway. WC seating in front; Rr. Sep-May (Seminole Community College, Fine Arts Bldg G, 100 Weldon Blvd; 407-328-4722 x 3323)

■ **SHOPPING**

Antiques: Sanford's quaint downtown offers numerous antique and gift shops.

Malls: Seminole Town Center (I-4 exit 51; 407-323-2262)

Flea Markets: Flea World has over 1500 dealers of new merchandise. AC bldgs; unpaved parking. Fri-Sun 9-6 (301 US 17/92; 407-330-1792)

ACCOMMODATIONS

■ **B&B/INNS**

Higgins House B&B has a WC-friendly 2BR cottage with a 3" stoop. Each BR has a queen bed (open frame); both bathrooms have 30" wide doors and the living room has a sofa bed. Stairs make

the main house inaccessible. A companion can bring your breakfast to the cottage or you can eat on the patio outside the main house. (420 S Oak Ave; 407-324-9238; 800-584-0014)

■ MOTELS

Holiday Inn Express has 7 ADA rooms with a king or 2 full beds (23" high/plat-forms). Bathrooms have raised toilets, roll-under sinks and showers with hand-held sprayers and seats; rooms 105 and 219 have roll-in showers. Free brkfst. $$ (3401 S Orlando Dr; 407-320-0845)

Springhill Suites by Marriott has 7 ADA 2-room suites, each with a king bed or 2 queens (23" high/open frames), a sofa bed, refrigerator, microwave and cof-feepot. Bathrooms have raised toilets, roll-under sinks, roll-in showers with hand-held sprayers and seats. Free brkfst; laundry; pool. $$ (201 N Towne Rd; 407-995-1000; 888-287-9400)

Remember,
boarding a boat in a WC is often easier from a floating dock that rises and lowers with the tide.

And, bring your own tie-downs and a seat belt for boating or fishing charters.

Be aware,
your weight may exceed
the operator's capacity to help lift you aboard.
See Boating page 11 and Fishing page 12.

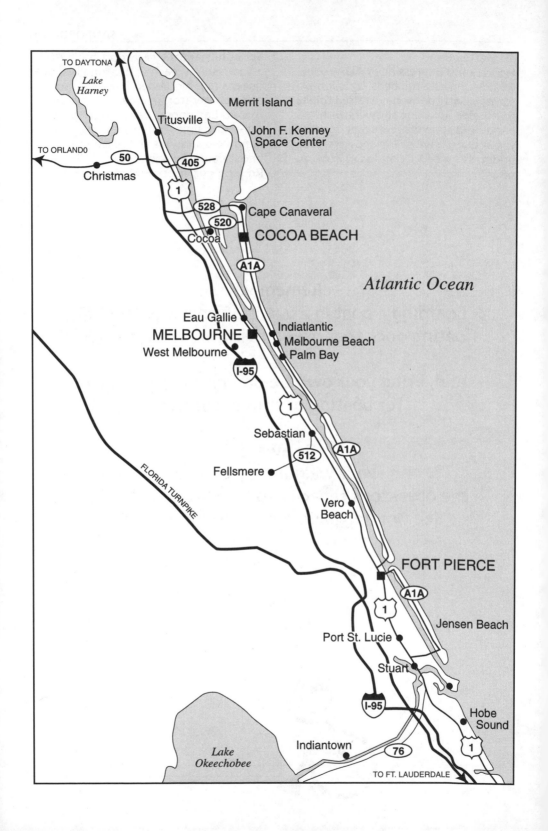

CENTRAL ATLANTIC COAST

COCOA BEACH
Cape Canaveral, Christmas, Cocoa, Merritt Island, Port Canaveral, Titusville

Better than sci-fi movies because it's authentic, the Kennedy Space Center is out of this world! Try to catch a shuttle launch in Titusville from US Hwy 1, in Cocoa Beach or Cape Canaveral from A1A or from the Kennedy Space Center itself. The Canaveral National Seashore and the Merritt Island National Wildlife Refuge are two of the Space Coast's most special treasures; some areas you can explore by car, trail or kayak.

Tourist Info
Brevard County Tourism Council: 2725 St Johns St, Bldg C, Melbourne 32940; 321-633-2110; 800-872-1969
Cocoa Beach Area Chamber: 400 Fortenberry Road, Merritt Island 32952; 321-459-2200
Greater South Brevard Area Chamber: 1005 Strawbridge Ave, Melbourne 32901; 321-724-5400
Titusville Chamber: 2000 S Washington Ave, Titusville 32780; 321-267-3036
Web sites: www.iu.net/cocoabeach/chamber; www.space-coast.com

Transportation
Space Coast Area Transit has buses with lifts that service all cities in Brevard County (Titusville to Palm Bay). With advance reservations and after qualifying by phone, door-to-door service is available if you are not on a fixed route. (321-633-1878)

WC Resources
Space Coast Center for Independent Living has a loan closet. (331 Ramp Rd, Cocoa Bch; 321-784-9008)

ACTIVITIES

■ **ATTRACTIONS**
Ft Christmas Historical Park is 25-acre park with a window on pioneer life in Florida. The museum is a replica of an 1837 wood fort from the 2nd Seminole Indian War. Two blockhouses and a storehouse, displaying early artifacts, are on the ground floor of the fort (Tue-Sat 10-5; Sun 1-). Of 7 restored pioneer homes (Tue-Sat 11-3; Sun 1-3), the

1917 Beehead Ranch house is accessible. With a week's notice, staff can assemble a portable ramp so you can access another of the period homes. A large playground has some accessible activities; although staff must remove a barrier so WCs can enter. The terrain is hard-packed, except after rain. Special events include encampments, demonstrations and country craft festivals. Guided tours daily; ADA picnic table behind visitor center; gift shop; Rr. Winter 8-6; summer 8-8 (Ft Christmas Rd/ CR 420, Christmas; 2 mi N of SR 50; 407-568-4149)

Jungle Adventures is a 20-acre wildlife sanctuary with mostly paved paths. A 700' boardwalk gives you a chance to see a Florida panther, fox, black bear and timber wolves. Monkeys, macaws, bobcats and other wildlife abound here too. Inside the largest man-made alligator, there is a snack bar and gift shop where you can buy food for the wildlife. Watch staff feed gators. At a hands-on wildlife show, where WC seating is in front of the bleachers, you can cuddle snakes and skunks or have your picture taken holding an alligator (with his mouth taped!). The show in the Calusa village demonstrates life in the 1600's. Staff can push you over the steep bridge into the village however the dirt and shell trails can be tough to navigate. For a 15-min cruise through a gator swamp, you can roll onto the dock where staff can help you from your WC, down a step onto the pontoon boat and down a small step into a bench seat with a back. CRr. $. 9:30-5:30 (26205 E Hwy 50, Christmas; 407-568-1354)

Kennedy Space Center (KSC) promises an exciting day in a working NASA facility with general admission that includes the Visitor Complex and a KSC tour on lift-equipped buses. The *Visitor Complex* offers attractions and sometimes, special events; use the schedule to plan your day. Two 40-min IMAX films play in theaters with lifts to WC and companion seating; one film is an inspirational piece on our space program, the other predicts a futuristic lifestyle. An exhibit in the IMAX theater displays incredible images and insights from the Hubble telescope orbiting around earth. The Universe Theater has WC seating throughout for a 20-min show on the search for life elsewhere in the universe. The fully accessible New Millennium Theater features a 30-min multimedia experience looking back and forward in exploration. Outside, under a roof, is the Astronaut Encounter where you can meet men and women who have journeyed into space, ask questions and take pictures. The Complex also has exhibit halls, a playground and 3-acre Rocket Garden planted with history's most famous rockets. Behind the restaurant sits a WC-accessible, life-size replica of the space shuttle and a Launch Status Center with briefings on the next shuttle mission. *KSCTours* run every 15 min and make 3 stops where you can take another bus when you are ready. WC loaners and Rr are at each stop. Each bus has a knowledgeable driver and video monitors that put sights into historical context including the mammoth Vehicle Assembly Building (VAB) and the giant Crawler-Transporter that moves the shuttles to the launch pads. First stop is the LC-39 Observation Gantry with a quick movie on shuttle preparation and lift-off. An elevator takes you to a 60'-high platform where you can see 2 launch pads (about 1 mi away) through telescopes at WC height. Next stop is the Apollo/Saturn V Center where you may choose to have lunch and browse the gift shop after an 8-min film on Apollo 8 and a 10-min film on our visits to the moon; both theaters have WC seating. This site also houses hands-on exhibits, a 363' Apollo/ Saturn V moon rocket and retired NASA employees who answer questions one-on-one. Third stop is the International Space Station Center where you can roll through full-scale replicas of space station modules and view actual components being readied for flight. Two guided tours are offered at an additional charge and both tie into the KSC tour spots. *Cape Canaveral: Then and Now* is a 2-hr bus tour on the early days of space exploration that stops at launch sites for the Mercury, Gemini and Apollo Programs (No Rr at these sites). *NASA Up Close* is a 90-min bus tour into restricted areas, past operations buildings and the huge runway for shuttle landings; stops include an outdoor viewing area near a launch pad and the VAB parking lot for pictures. For information on viewing a launch, call 800-572-4636. WC loaners; gift shop; restaurant/cafeteria; Rr; CRr at Visitor Complex & Apollo/Saturn V Center. $. 9-dusk (SR 405, Cape Canaveral; E of US 1; 321-449-4444/452-2121)

Planetarium is Florida's largest planetarium and public observatory. The International Hall of Space Explorers focuses on the history of manned space programs and the Science Quest Demonstration Hall features hands-on space exhibits. The theater presents virtual reality/multimedia shows at 7pm, a 3-story high IWERKS film at 8pm and laser shows Fri-Sat at 9pm. The rooftop observatory has telescopes set at WC height. The 24" telescope is up 6 steps. Rr. $. Fri & Sat 6:30-10pm (1519 Clearlake Rd, Brevard Community College, Cocoa; 321-634-3732)

US Astronaut Hall of Fame honors those who blazed the trail to the moon. Enjoy the rare video footage, historic artifacts and memorabilia of our pioneers in space. Several experiential opportunities require tough transfers into cramped spacecraft and no restraints under G-Force. US Space Camp is held here. $. 9-5 (6225 Vectorspace Blvd, Titusville; W of KSC; 321-269-6100)

■ **BEACHES**

Parks: Jetty Park

*Canaveral National Seashore includes 24 mi of pristine barrier island N of the Kennedy Space Center and loans beach WCs (fixed arms) at both the N and S ends. Call the visitor center to reserve a beach WC for Apollo Beach at the N end where parking areas 1A and 5 have accessible dune walkovers to the sand. The visitor center has a 15-min orientation video, book store, nature displays and Rr. At Eldora Hammock, just S of the visitor center, a short hard-packed crushed shell path leads to a short fishing pier on the aptly named, Mosquito Lagoon. S of the entrance to Apollo Beach is a 1,000' boardwalk to the lagoon and Turtle Mound, a 35' midden of oyster shells left by the Timicuan Indians between 600 and 1200AD. Go up the steep slope to the mound for a great view. At Playalinda Beach parking areas 8 and Eddy Creek (off SR 406/402 at the S end of the Seashore), boardwalks lead to the beach and Rr. Eddy Creek loans a beach WC (fixed arms) at the entrance station and has a fishing dock on the Mosquito Lagoon. This area is great for birding Sep-Apr. Call for the schedule of ranger programs, some of which are accessible. Memorial-Labor Day lifeguards at Apollo & Playalinda beaches; Rr. $. Winter 6-6; summer -8pm (Visitor Center, A1A; S of New Smyrna Bch and just N of Eldora; 386-428-3384)

Lori Wilson Park is a 32-acre beach and nature park with 6 accessible dune crossovers and a 1000' boardwalk connecting 3 beach pavilions. A 1700' elevated boardwalk meanders through an oak hammock to a nature center where naturalists conduct programs periodically. The park is also a good spot for bird watchers. Picnic tables; lifeguards in summer; Rr. Dawn-dusk (1500 N Atlantic Ave; 3.5 mi S of SR 520; 321-455-1123)

■ **BIKE TRAILS**

Travis Park has a 1-mi paved trail around Clear Lake to the Brevard Museum (see Museums). Picnic tables; Rr in community center open wkdy 3-6, Sat 12-6. Dawn-dusk (2001 Michigan

Ave, Cocoa; 321-633-1871)

■ BOAT RAMPS

Parks: Kiwanis Island, Merritt Island National Wildlife Refuge, Parrish

Barge Canal Fish Camp has a ramp and fixed dock. From here, you can access the Indian River or Atlantic. Or, try out a 100' lighted pier on the canal. Bait shop; food; Rr. $. 7-7 (180 Tingley Dr, Merritt Island; 321-452-0504)

Freddie Patrick Park has a boat ramp with a floating dock on the Atlantic. Picnic tables; Rr (Flounder St & Glen Cheek Dr)

Indian River has a ramp with a floating dock. (451 Marina Rd, Titusville; next to the Titusville Municipal Marina)

James Bourbeau Park has a ramp with a fixed dock on the St Johns River. ADA picnic table; Rr. 24 hrs (8195 SR 520, Cocoa; 321-633-1874)

Kelly Park has a ramp with fixed docks on the Banana River. ADA picnic tables; Rr. 24 hrs (2550 Banana River Dr, Merritt Island; 321-633-1874)

Ports End Park has a boat ramp and floating dock on a channel from where you can access the Intracoastal or Atlantic. Picnic tables; Rr (Ports End Park, Port Canaveral; end of Mullet Dr)

■ BOAT RENTALS

Wave Craze rents 7- and 13-person pontoon boats (28" entry) for the Banana and Indian Rivers. Staff can help you cross the 75' stretch of sand to the dock where you can roll aboard. (1872 E SR 520, Merritt Island; 321-452-0590; 800-829-3314)

■ BOAT TOURS

Midway Air Boats gives 40-min guided trips on the scenic St Johns River looking for alligators and bald eagles. The dock is ramped; with advanced notice, staff can lift you aboard in your WC. Rr. 9-4 (28501 E Hwy 50, Christmas; 321-568-6792)

■ CASINOS

Sterling Casino is a 440' ship with 1000 slots, 50 table games, 5 cocktail lounges and Vegas-style entertainment. All activities are offered on the main deck, but a small elevator can take you to the upper decks. Free deli; massage therapy (!); Rr. Sails 11-4 & 7-mdnt (Terminal 2 B, 180 Jetty Dr, Port Canaveral; 321-784-8558; 800-765-5711)

SunCruz Casino features 4-hr, Vegas-style gaming cruises aboard a 205' 3-decked ship with an elevator to all decks. Enjoy it all, from slots and roulette to a private poker room. Buffet/menu; free coffee/soda; entertainment; Rr on 2nd deck. Call for schedule (Cove at Port Canaveral, 620 Glenn Cheek Dr, Cape Canaveral; E of A1A; 321-799-3511; 800-474-3423)

■ FISHING CHARTERS

Backcountry Charter Service offers half/full-day backcountry trips on a 19' flats boat for 2 anglers into flyfishing or spin casting. Capt Kent Gibbens is experienced with WC anglers. He can help your fishing buddy or arrange for extra help to lower you in your WC into the front of the boat. You'll depart from a dock closest to the fish. (386-672-8929)

Ocean Lady Charters offers trolling, sight fishing, sport fishing, wreck and reef fishing trips 15-30 mi offshore. This 32' sport fisherman can accommodate you and 5 able-bodied anglers for half/full day. Crew can lift you aboard in your WC from a nearby floating dock. Rr at marina (321-452-2564)

Waters Edge Charters fishes the backwaters of Indian Lagoon and Banana River. Try half/full-day flyfishing or spin casting trips in a flats boat for 2 anglers. The capt can help your fishing buddy or arrange for help to lower you in your WC into the front of the boat. Depart from a dock closest to the fish. (321-984-8735)

■ FISHING-PARTY BOATS

Obsession offers all-day and evening deep-sea fishing trips. Crew can lift you aboard the 65' boat, but the galley is not accessible. Food/drinks for sale onboard. 8-5 & 7-11pm (Sunrise Marina, 505 Glen Cheek Dr, Port Canaveral; 321-453-3474; 888-347-4352)

Orlando Princess offers half-day deep-sea trips. Crew can lift you aboard this 70' boat. Lunch, beer/soda included; Rr at dock. 10:30-4:30 (665 Glen Cheek Dr, Port Canaveral; 321-784-6300; 800-481-3474)

■ **FISHING PIERS**

Beaches: Canaveral National Seashore. Boat Ramps: Barge Canal. Parks: Jetty, Kiwanis Island, Merritt Island, Parrish, Space View

Cocoa Beach Pier is an 800' lighted pier on the Atlantic. Bait shop; restaurant with entertainment 6am-dusk; Rr. $. 6am-mdnt (401 Meade Ave; .5 mi N of SR 520 off A1A; 321-783-7549/783-9086)

Indian River has a paved walkway to a 30' sheltered pier. ADA picnic tables; Rr (425 S Tropical Trail, Merritt Island; 321-633-1874)

Intracoastal Waterway Park has a 250' lighted pier and boardwalks along the Indian River. ADA picnic tables; Rr open dusk-dawn. 24 hrs (SR 520 Cswy, Merritt Island; 321-633-1874)

Rotary Riverfront Park is a 6-acre park with a 750' fishing pier on the Indian River. ADA playground; ADA picnic shelters; Rr. Dawn-dusk (4141 S Washington Ave, Titusville; 321-264-5105)

■ **FITNESS TRAILS**

Parks: Kiwanis Island, Space View

■ **HUNTING**

Tosohatchee State Preserve includes over 34,000 acres of wilderness along the St Johns River, inhabited by deer, turkey, fox, bobcat and more. Disabled hunters can hunt from their vehicles or WCs in certain areas, but the preserve has no paved roads. Staff can direct you to the more accessible sites, depending on weather, conditions and the whereabouts of game. Staff asks you to call so a ranger can escort you to scout the sites in advance. Hunting is by special quota permit only. Applications can be found at most sporting goods stores. Instructions to apply for the random drawing and hunting dates are on the application. (Taylor Creek Rd, Christmas; between SR 50 & SR 520, 16 mi W of Titusville; call wkdy 8-noon 407-568-5893)

■ **KAYAKING**

Osprey Outfitters offers half-day guided trips in tandem kayaks on the historic Haulover Canal. The trips in the Merritt Island National Wildlife Refuge go to Rookery Island, where over 3000 birds nest from Mar-Jun. The canal's deep waters are popular with dolphins and shelter manatees during the warm weather months. With advance notice, staff can lift WC kayakers to board and disembark at the flat launch site. Lunch included (132 S Dixie Ave, Titusville; 321-267-3535)

■ **MUSEUMS**

Brevard Museum of History & Natural Science depicts the area's natural and cultural experience from prehistory onward through fossils, artifacts and antiques. Some of the trails through the 22-acre wildlife sanctuary around the museum are paved. WC loaners; gift shop; Rr. $ for museum. Tue-Sat 10-4 (2201 Michigan Ave, Cocoa; 321-632-1830)

■ **PARKS**

Jetty Park is a 35-acre beach and wooded park on the Atlantic, owned by the Canaveral Port Authority. A boardwalk leads from parking along the beach and has a ramp to the sand. The 1500' lighted fishing pier is open 24 hrs and is a good spot to watch NASA's space shuttle launch from 10 mi away. See Campgrounds. Bait shop ~10pm; snack bar; picnic tables; Rr, not ADA. $. 7am-9pm (400 E Jetty Rd, Cape Canaveral; from Port Canaveral's S Cruise Terminal, turn right onto George King Blvd, follow signs; 321-783-2771)

Kiwanis Island Park is an 18-acre athletic park set in a wildlife sanctuary on the Sykes Creek. You can fish off the grassy shoreline or the 200' fishing dock. A hard-packed, 1-mi exercise trail has some accessible equipment. The boat ramp and fixed dock access the Barge Canal and Banana River. Picnic shelters; Rr. Dawn-dusk (951 Kiwanis Island Park Rd, Merritt Island; E of Sykes

Creek Pkwy off SR 520; 321-633-1874)
Merritt Island National Wildlife Refuge
includes 140,000 acres of varied habitat, from marshlands to pine forest and is a great spot for birders Oct-Mar. The visitor center (wkdy 8-4:30, wknd 9-5; Apr-Oct closed Sun) has wildlife exhibits, a 20-min orientation video, gift shop with many nature books and Rr. Behind the center are 2 ADA picnic tables and a .5-mi boardwalk through a hammock and past a pond. A hard-packed trail leads to a fishing dock on a pond, just N of the center. Spring and summer, check out the manatee viewing deck off SR 3, 10.5 mi N of the center at Haulover Canal. On the SW corner of the Haulover Canal is a boat ramp and fixed dock; you access both the Mosquito Lagoon and Indian River. The boat ramp parking lot is hard-packed dirt. The unpaved, one-way Black Point Wildlife Dr (on SR 406, just NE of SR 402) is a 7-mi chance to drive your car by wildlife in salt marsh and open water habitats. Cruickshank Trail, which makes a 5-mi loop from stop #8 on Black Point Dr, is grass and very rough for WCs. Call for the schedule of accessible guided programs Nov-Mar. (SR 402; 4 mi E of Titusville from US1; 321-861-0667)

Orlando Wetlands Park is a 1200-acre, man-made wetlands filled with aquatic plants, fields, forest and wildlife. The 18 mi of hard-packed berm roads can be difficult, when wet, for WCs. In addition to 170 avian species, you may spot otters, deer, bobcat and wild turkey. About 1 mi from the parking lot is an observation platform over the water. Call to arrange a guided tour. Rr. Feb-Sep dawn-dusk (25155 Wheeler Rd, Christmas; from SR 50, N on Ft Christmas Rd/CR 420, E on the unpaved Wheeler Rd; 407-568-1706)

Parrish Park is a 37-acre downtown park popular with windsurfers and jet-skiers. You can park on the gently sloping hard-packed beach to watch or enjoy the shallow water there. Fish from the 100' fishing dock or the boardwalk that runs along both sides of the Indian River. The boat ramp with fixed docks is open 24 hrs. Picnic shelters; snacks, bait shop nearby; Rr. Dawn-dusk (1 Max Brewer Cswy & SR 402, Titusville; 321-264-5105)

Rotary Park-Merritt Island is a 38-acre park with an 1800' boardwalk through an oak hammock and marshlands that is especially good for sighting migratory songbirds Oct-Apr. Playground; picnic tables; Rr. Dawn-dusk (1899 S Courtenay Pkwy, Merritt Island; 321-455-1380)

Space View Park, with a paved path along the Indian River overlooking the Kennedy Space Center, is being developed into a Space Walk of Fame with monuments and descriptions of the milestones in the US space program. This 2.6-acre downtown park has an 85' fishing dock. Across SR 402, Sandpoint Park has a .6-mi paved exercise trail. Bait shop nearby; Rr. Dawn-dusk (8 Broad St, Titusville)

■ **SCUBA**

American Divers International instructor, D J Morris, is HSA-certified and teaches classes for certification here. Group lessons run 2 nights/week for 4 wks. Staff can roll you in your WC to the edge of the pool, help you gear up and lift you into and out of the pool. Open water dives are on the last weekend of classes in West Palm. The dock is easy to access and the crew can lift you aboard the boat in your WC. When it's time to dive, crew can lift you from your WC onto the dive platform, help you gear up and drop you into the water. Call beforehand to discuss any special needs. (691 N Courtenay Pkwy, Merritt Island; 321-453-0600)

■ **SHOPPING**

Boutiques: Cocoa Beach Pier has fun shops, an arcade, ice cream parlor and plenty of restaurants (401 Meade Ave; 321-783-7549). Olde Cocoa Village is a historic district with fine art galleries, restaurants, boutiques, theaters and antique shops in turn-of-the century buildings; not all are accessible (US 1 and SR 520, Cocoa; 321-631-9075).

Flea Markets: Carnival Swap Shop is an indoor flea market mall. Wed-Sun 10-6 (US1, Rockledge; .5 mi S of SR 520; 386-636-4200)

Malls: Merritt Square Mall (777 E Merritt Island Cswy, Merritt island; 321-452-3272); Miracle City Mall (2500 S Washington Ave, Titusville; 321-269-7521); Carnival Mall (940 Rockledge Blvd; 321-636-4200)

Specialty Shops: Ron Jon Surf Shop is the 52,000 sq ft purple and pink castle of a beach store that is advertised on billboards as soon as you enter Florida. 24 hrs (SR A1A & SR 520; 321-799-8888)

ACCOMMODATIONS

■ CAMPGROUNDS

Jetty Park has 117 RV/tent sites on grass or sand with little or no shade, but this park is a great place to watch shuttle launches from the Kennedy Space Center which is 10 mi away. The RV sites have water/elec; all sites have picnic tables and grills. The 2 bathhouses have roll-in showers. See Parks. Laundry; camp store (400 E Jetty Rd, Cape Canaveral; from Port Canaveral's S Cruise Terminal, right on George King Blvd, follow signs; 321-783-2771)

■ CONDOS

Private WC-friendly Condo is on the ground floor with 3BR/2BA and a slider to a patio on the beach. One BR has a queen, the others each have 2 full beds (30" high/open frames). The condo has a full kitchen and standard doors. One bathroom has a roll-in shower and hand-held sprayer; the other has a tub. The Cocoa Beach Pier is down the street. Laundry; 1-wk minimum. $$-$$$ (Richard Arms Apts, 515 Hayes Ave, # 10; Vicki Goldberg 407-737-1743; www.Holiday-Rentals.com; jbgoldie333@hotmail.com)

■ MOTELS

Best Western Cocoa Inn has 1 ADA room with 2 full beds (platforms), a microwave and refrigerator. The bathroom has a step-in shower. Pool; lounge; entertainment. $ (4225 W King St, Cocoa; 321-632-1065)

Best Western Space Shuttle Inn has 2 ADA rooms, each with a king bed (21" high/open frame), lowered clothing rack, electronic door lock and bathroom with a raised toilet and tub with a hand-held sprayer and seat. One room is *Evergreen* for the allergen-sensitive. This hotel has a dock on its own lake stocked with bass and bluegill. Accessible shuttles to area attractions & airport for a fee; free brkfst; pool; lounge; restaurant for dinner. $$ (3455 Cheney Hwy, Titusville; 321-269-9100; 800-523-7654)

Hampton Inn has 6 ADA rooms, each with a king bed (platform), full sofa bed, coffeepot, microwave and refrigerator. Bathrooms have raised toilets, roll-under sinks and roll-in showers with seats. Pool; laundry; free brkfst. $$-$$$ (3425 N Atlantic Ave; 321-799-4099)

Hilton Oceanfront has 6 ADA rooms and 2 ADA 1BR suites with a king or 2 full beds (24" high/open frames). Suites have living rooms; all have coffeepots. Bathrooms have roll-under sinks; rooms 130, 313 and 355 have roll-in showers with hand-held sprayers and seats; others have tubs. Pool; laundry; full restaurant. $$-$$$ (1550 N Atlantic Ave; 321-799-0003; 800-526-2609)

Radisson Resort at the Port has 7 ADA units, 4 motel rooms and 3 1BR suites, with king beds (23" high/open frames) and bathrooms with raised toilets, roll-under sinks and tubs with hand-held sprayers and seats. The rooms have single sofa beds; the suites have queen sofa beds. Free WC-accessible transportation to local beaches, shops and restaurants. Pool; laundry; lounge; full restaurant. $$-$$$ (8701 Astronaut Blvd,

Cape Canaveral; 321-784-0000)
Studio Plus has 5 ADA rooms with a queen bed (open frame) and kitchen-ette with a refrigerator, microwave, coffeepot and dishes. Bathrooms have a raised toilet; room 111 has a roll-in shower with a hand-held sprayer and seat; others have tubs. Pool, laundry. $$ (1701 Evans Rd; 321-733-6050)

FORT PIERCE

Fellsmere, Hobe Sound, Indiantown, Jensen Beach,
Port St Lucie, Sebastian, Stuart, Vero Beach

The Treasure Coast around Ft Pierce is a string of sleepy beach towns that protect their fragile dunes with crossovers, which are not all accessible. Three beaches and one park loan beach wheelchairs. You can use a lift at Rivergate Park's boat ramp and at two public pools. Rainy days are great excuses to visit the diverse museums that features everything from treasure hunting and Navy Seals to baseball memo-rabilia and fine art. If you're into shooting, check out the state-of-the art, accessible range in Sebastian. B&Bs and campgrounds offer ADA accommodations, and one resort has a beach wheelchair and accessible pool. In this area, the Indian River and the Intracoastal are synonymous. SR A1A is also called Ocean Drive.

Tourist Info
Indian River County Chamber: 1216 21 St S, Vero Bch, 32960; 772-567-3491
St Lucie Chamber: 2200 Virginia Ave, 34982; 772-595-9999; 800-344-8443
Sebastian River Chamber: 700 Main St, Sebastian, 32958; 772-589-5969
Stuart/Martin County Chamber: 1650 S Kanner Hwy, Stuart, 34994; 772-287-1088
Web sites: www.indian-river.fl.us/playing; www.vero-beach.fl.us/chamber; www.visitstluciefla.com; www.indianriverchamber.com

Transportation
Community Coach public buses have lifts and offer free service throughout Vero Beach. Door-to-door service to medical appointments and shopping is available for those who cannot use the bus. Reservations are accepted 45 days in advance; prior-ity is given for medical appointments. Pre-qualify by phone. Wkdy 7:30-5 (772-569-0903)
Community Transit has lift-equipped buses that provide door-to-door service throughout St Lucie County for residents and visitors. Call the day before by 2pm for reservations. Wkdy 7-6 (772-464-7433/879-1287)

WC Resources
Home Health Equipment Services rents beach WCs by the day or week. Free deliv-ery (911 NE Jensen Beach Blvd, Jensen Bch; 772-334-4200

ACTIVITIES

■ **ATTRACTIONS**
Energy Encounter offers interactive displays and exhibits on energy, elec-tricity and nuclear power. Check out the computer games, a transparent nuclear reactor model and an energy treasure hunt. The 1-mi boardwalk/na-ture trail is inaccessible. Rr. Sun-Fri 10-4 (6501 S SR A1A, Jensen Bch; 772-468-4111; 877-375-4386)

Florida Oceanographic Coastal Center offers a fun ecological experience for the whole family. The ramped center has a myriad of displays from touch tanks and aquariums (one with tiny jawfish that burrow in an aquatic *ant farm*) to computer games that simulate deep-sea dives and a collection of items washed up from foreign lands. Outside, 40 acres contain a 10,000-gal aquarium of stingrays (debarbed for petting), trails that feature interactive marine life games and a Native American encampment. Stingray feedings are Mon-Sat 10:30 and 2:30 and Sun 1:30; each is followed by a guided tour along a 1.5-mi nature trail that includes boardwalk and some mulched stretches. Call about special programs, such as seining, snorkeling and an ecotour by boat; some are accessible. Gift shop; Rr. $. Mon-Sat 10-5; Sun 12-4 (890 NE SR A1A, Stuart; 772-225-0505)

Heathcote Botanical Gardens has 3.5 acres of different types of gardens including subtropical flowers and foliage, Japanese bonsai and an herb garden. A sidewalk circles through the gardens. Gift shop; Rr. $. Tue-Sat 9-5; Nov-Apr also Sun 1-5 (210 Savannah Rd; 772-464-4672)

Indian River Community College Planetarium schedules 45-min shows on the skies, stars and constellations for specific weekends. Rr. $. Fri-Sat 7 & 8; Sun 2 & 3 (3209 Virginia Ave; W off US 1; 772-462-4750 from 11-3)

Manatee Center, just downstream from Fort Pierce Utilities' power plant, has a ramped walkway along Moore's Creek where, especially during colder months, you can see manatees enjoying the warm waters emitted by the power plant. The Center is staffed by knowledgeable volunteers and has environmental exhibits, including an under-the-docks tank of native fish, a video and interactive computer. Gift shop; Rr. Oct-Jun Tue-Sat 10-5; Sun 1-4 (480 Indian River Dr; 772-466-1600x3333)

McKee Botanical Garden is a lush, tropical Florida hammock with sidewalks past native and exotic tropical plants. Gift shop; Rr. Tue-Sat 10-5; Sun 12-5 (350 US 1, Vero Bch; 772-794-0701)

■ BEACHES

Some beaches in this area experience severe erosion and rebuilding within short periods of time; a ramp may get you right to sand one day and, next month, have a 1' drop.

Hotels: Disney Vero Beach

Bathtub Reef Park is a 1300' county beach with a shallow, offshore reef popular with snorkelers. From HC parking a ramp leads to a wide deck and gazebo with interpretive signage, ADA picnic tables and a great view of the beach. Across the street is Riverwalk, a boardwalk through mangrove, leading to a 100' T-shaped fishing pier over the Intracoastal. Outdoor showers; Rr. Dawn-dusk (S end of Hutchinson Island, S of SR A1A into Stuart, N of St Lucie Inlet)

Bob Graham Beach is an undeveloped, 2000' county beach with a dune crossover from HC parking to the soft sand. Outdoor showers; Rr. Dawn-dusk (SR A1A, Jensen Bch; just S of Sea Turtle Bch)

*Fort Pierce Inlet State Park has 340 acres of ocean beach, dunes and coastal hammock. Ask at the entry gate and rangers can deliver the beach WC (removable arms) to you at beach parking. Three boardwalks from parking are ramped to the sand. Ask for directions to Dynamite Point, a slip of sand where, with the beach WC, you can fish in the inlet. Lifeguards in summer; ADA picnic shelters; ADA playground; Rr. $. 8-dusk (905 Shorewinds Dr; off SR A1A, 4 mi E of Fort Pierce; 772-468-3985)

Humiston Park has a short boardwalk from parking to the beach. This little city park is in the heart of a shopping and restaurant district. Picnic shelters & grills on grass behind dunes; outdoor showers; Rr. 9-5 (SR A1A, Vero Bch; 1 mi S of Beachland Blvd; 772-231-5790)

Jaycee Park/Ft Pierce includes 17 acres

between the Intracoastal and ocean. A dune crossover leads from parking to the sand and shaded overlooks on the beach. Sidewalks lead to picnic shelters; boat ramp with fixed docks; Rr. Dawn-dusk (S SR A1A & Malaleuca Dr)

Jaycee Park/Vero Beach is an 8-acre city beach with a short boardwalk along the dunes to 3 adjacent shelters with some shade and great views. Access the boardwalk in the middle or on the S end. A ramp leads to the sand and a breakfast/lunch cafe with outdoor seating. Picnic shelters & grills on grass behind dunes; playground on sand; outdoor showers; lifeguards; Rr. 9-5 (SR A1A; 1.5 mi N of Beachland Blvd; 772-231-0578)

Pepper Park is a 52-acre county park with a dune crossover from HC parking to the 2000' beachfront. Along the Intracoastal are 6 short fishing docks. A museum on the Navy's special units is located here; see Museums. Picnic shelters; grills; lifeguards; Rr. Dawn-dusk (3300-3400 N SR A1A; 1 mi N of Fort Pierce Inlet State Park)

*Sea Turtle Beach loans a beach WC (fixed arms; detachable footrest; umbrella, drink and fishing pole holders) at the concession stand. The snack bar/restaurant, with ocean views from tables inside and outdoors, is open for breakfast and lunch. Lifeguards 9-5; picnic tables at concession & on sand; outdoor showers; Rr (4191 NE SR A1A, Jensen Bch; 772- 225-0703)

*South Beach Park advises that you call ahead to borrow the beach WC (fixed arms; umbrella). City staff can meet you in parking with the beach WC, or you can send someone to the lifeguard tower on the sand. The center boardwalk by the lifeguard tower leads to a dune crossover. A short, dirt nature trail identifies native plants. Picnic shelters & grills on grass behind dunes; outdoor showers; lifeguards; Rr. 9-5 (E end of Causeway/17 St Bridge; E of SR A1A; 772-231-4700)

Stuart Beach is a 2000' stretch of county oceanfront. From HC parking, a dune crossover leads to a gazebo overlooking the beach and then ramps to the soft sand. A ramped, 250' boardwalk runs parallel to the beach under Australian pines. The Elliott Museum is on the grounds; see Museums. ADA picnic shelters; lifeguards 9-5; snack bar; outdoor showers; Rr. Dawn-dusk (MacArthur Blvd, Stuart; off SR A1A)

Treasure Shores is paradise for surfers. A boardwalk ramps to the sand and a .75-mi, hard-packed trail leads to a playground and picnic area on cement. Outdoor shower; lifeguards; Rr. 9-5 (SR A1A; 3 mi N of Wabasso Bridge/CR 510; 772-589-6441)

■ BIKE TRAILS
Parks: Jonathan Dickinson

■ BOAT RAMPS
Beaches: Jaycee Park/Ft Pierce, Jensen Bch Causeway. Fishing Piers: Jensen Bch, Main St, South Causeway. Parks: Blue Cypress, Oak Hammock, Rivergate, Savannas, Sandsprit, Wimbrow

MacWilliam's boat ramp has a fixed dock on the Indian River. Fish cleaning tables; ADA picnic tables; Rr. Dawn-10pm (Indian River Dr, Vero Bch; E end of Merrill Barber Bridge on SR 60)

Round Island West has a boat ramp, fixed dock, hard-packed canoe launch and a short boardwalk where you can fish along the Indian River. ADA picnic tables; fish cleaning tables; Rr. Dawn-dusk (SR A1A; at the St Lucie County line)

Stuart Causeway has a boat ramp and fixed docks on the Intracoastal. Picnic shelters; Rr. 24 hrs (SR A1A; between Stuart & Hutchinson Island)

Wabasso Bridge boat ramp has fixed docks on the Indian River. You can fish along the flat grassy banks or just watch the many windsurfers. ADA picnic shelters; grills; Rr. Dawn-dusk (CR 510, Wabasso)

■ BOAT RENTALS
Parks: Blue Cypress

Sebastian Watercraft Rentals rents

pontoon boats (32" entry) for up to 10 people on the Indian River. Rentals are for half/full day or from 3-5pm. Bait shop nearby; Rr in restaurant at marina. 9-5 (Capt Hiram's Marina, 1606 Indian River Dr, Sebastian; 772-589-5560)

■ BOAT TOURS

Middleton's Fish Camp offers 2-hr ecotours on the pristine Blue Cypress Lake (see Parks) in the midst of a state wilderness area. Roll aboard the pontoon boat from the floating dock. Bait/snack shop; picnic tables on grass; Rr. 6-6; summer Wed-Mon (18 mi W of I-95, Vero Bch; from SR 60, at sign to Blue Cypress, N on dirt road for 5 mi; 772-778-0150; 800-258-5002)

River Queen Cruises offers a variety of cruises, from 1 1/2 to 3 hrs, on a roll-aboard pontoon boat. Try the Manatee or Dolphin Watch, a Jungle Cruise along the south fork of the Sebastian River or the sunset Pelican Island Cruise past thousands of birds. Snacks & drinks; Rr onboard. Schedule varies (Capt Hiram's Marina, 1606 Indian River Dr, Sebastian; 321-589-6161; 888-755-6161)

■ BOWLING

Fort Pierce Bowl has ramped lanes and bowling ball ramps. Snack bar; game room; bar; Rr. Wkdy 8:30am-mdnt; wknd -3am (2500 US 1 N; 772-464-3343)

Port St Lucie Lanes has a bowling ball ramp. Snack bar; game room; bar; Rr. Wkdy 9am-11pm; wknd -1am (6759 S US 1, Port St Lucie; 772-461-5390)

Vero Bowl has bowling ball ramps. Snack bar; game room; Rr. Hrs vary (Lauria's Plaza, 929 14 Ln, Vero Bch; 772-770-0993)

■ CANOEING/KAYAKING

Parks: MacDonald, Savannas

Adventure Kayaking Tours leads 3-hr to full-day trips along the Indian River where dolphins and manatees are common sights. All trips include instruction, lunch and a canoe or solo/tandem sit-in or sit-on kayak. Staff can lift you aboard from your WC and then pull your boat into the water. Hrs vary (3435 Aviation Blvd, Vero Bch; 772-567-0522)

■ FISHING CHARTERS

Cabins: River Palm

A #1 Bass Guide Service offers half/full-day or night charters on bass boats. The capt can pick you up at your hotel or meet you at a fishing spot that best fits your needs. One of his favorites is the remote lake at Fishes Stick Marsh, a wildlife management area close to Fellsmere, where you can roll onto the floating dock next to the boat ramp. With advance notice, the capt can get help to lift you from your WC into the bass boat seat. (352-394-3660; 800-707-5463)

Pattern Setter Charters offers half/full-day flats trips on the Indian River Lagoon and Sebastian Inlet for 2 anglers. Capt can help your companion or arrange for extra help to lift you aboard the 18' flats boat from the fixed dock. (Capt Hiram's Marina, 1606 Indian River Dr, Sebastian; 772-589-0008)

Surf Rider Charters offers night and half/full-day sports fishing trips on a 34' sports fisherman for up to 6 anglers. You can also book fishing trips in the Bahamas. Capt Rick and his mate can lift you aboard in your WC. (Capt Hiram's Marina, 1606 Indian River Dr, Sebastian; 321-728-0503)

■ FISHING-PARTY BOATS

Angler's Obsession goes out on half/full-day deep-sea trips. Crew can carry you in your WC down the 3 steps to board the boat and over the lip at the cabin entrance. BYO cooler, food & drinks. Sat-Thu 8-5; Fri 7:30am-12:30pm (1653 Indian River Dr, Sebastian; 772-388-0011)

■ FISHING PIERS

Beaches: Pepper. Parks: Jack Island, Jonathon Dickinson, Riverside, MacDonald, Sandsprit

Jensen Beach Causeway has a stretch of land with a lighted, wood, 100' fishing pier and boat ramps with fixed docks on the Intracoastal. Bait shop nearby on SR 707; ADA picnic shelters; playground on sand; Rr. 24 hrs (SR 732; between Jensen Bch & Hutchinson Island)

Little Jim's Fishing Bridge crosses the Intracoastal. Bait shop/snacks; Rr. 24 hrs (601 N Beach Cswy; 772-468-2503)

Main Street Boat Dock has a lighted, wood, 360' fishing pier on the Indian River and a boat ramp with a fixed dock. 24 hrs (Indian River Dr, Sebastian)

Royal Palm Pointe has a lighted, wood fishing deck and an accessible water play fountain where you can cool off. Rr (Royal Palm Blvd, Vero Bch; off Vero Isles Dr, before the bridge over the Indian River)

South Causeway Park is the county's 16-acre island in the Intracoastal with a lighted, 1200' fishing pier along the Banty Saunders Bridge and a boat ramp with fixed docks. The St Lucie County Historical Museum is located here (see Museums). Picnic shelters; grills; Rr. 24 hrs (South Causeway Park, end of Seaway Dr; beside Beach Bridge, S of Fort Pierce Inlet)

■ **FITNESS TRAILS**
Parks: MacDonald

■ **HORSEBACK RIDING**
Special Equestrians of the Treasure Coast, an NARHA member offers therapeutic riding for folks age 4 and up. A hippotherapy program with a physical therapist takes place Wed 5-7; a therapeutic riding program occurs Sat 9-12. Both 6-wk programs have 3 volunteers with each rider during 1/2-hr sessions. Staff transfers you onto the horse from a ramped mounting block; adaptive equipment is available. Those who cannot ride, can enjoy the horse and buggy program. The buggy is ramped and has lock-downs for WCs. You must apply and have a physician's release. Rr porta-let (6450 45 St, Vero Bch; 772-562-7603)

■ **HUNTING**
Dupuis Wildlife & Environmental Area hosts a 3-day FWC Mobility-Impaired Hunt generally in mid-Nov for deer and wild hogs. The 25 applicants randomly selected for this hunt receive notice by mail of the mandatory orientation session held a few weeks before the hunt. To apply, see Hunting p 13. Vehicles, including ATVs, are allowed off road during the MI Hunt. You can try primitive camping (with Rr only) in this area. (SR 76; W of SR 710 at Indiantown; 772-924-1939)

■ **MUSEUMS**
Backus Gallery features works of Florida landscapist AE Bean Backus, beside the works of local professional and student artists. Rr. Tue-Sat 10-4; Sun 12-4 (500 N Indian River Dr; 772-465-0630)

Center for the Arts houses a variety of works from paintings to sculptures. Gift shop; Rr. $D. Mon-Sat 10-4:30; Sun 1- (3001 Riverside Park Dr, Vero Bch; 772-231-0707)

Elliott Museum has an eclectic collection of local historical artifacts, baseball memorabilia, classic cars, motorcycles, bikes and an old time apothecary shop. Ramped entrance; WC loaners; Rr. $. 10-4 (825 NE SR A1A, Stuart; 772-225-1961)

House of Refuge commemorates the series of safe houses for sailors who wrecked along the dangerous shoals on this coast. Enter the boathouse through the gate beside the entry steps. Here you learn the colorful history from murals and a lively docent. Then take the ramp up to the elevated house for a self-guided tour. Gift shop; Rr. $. 10-4 (301 SE MacArthur Blvd; 1.2 mi S of SR A1A; 772-225-1875)

McLarty Treasure Museum memorializes a Spanish galleon that wrecked here in 1715 carrying gold and silver from South America. The museum displays artifacts from the wreck, salvage materials and a 25-min video on the shipwreck and the salvage business. Roll onto the outside deck to watch salvagers at work just offshore. Gift shop. $. 10-4:30 (13180 N SR A1A, Sebastian; 772-589-2147)

Mel Fischer Treasure Museum houses treasures from Spanish shipwrecks and has a 25-min video of his treasure hunts. Gift shop; Rr. $. Mon-Sat 10-5; Sun 12- (1322 US 1; 772-589-9875)

St Lucie County Historical Museum displays Spanish shipwreck treasures, artifacts from the 1837 Old Ft Pierce and Seminole relics. The restored 1919 American LaFrance fire engine and 1907 gardener's home are inaccessible. The memorial garden has sidewalks. Picnic tables; gift shop; Rr. $. Tue-Sat 10-4; Sun 12- (South Causeway Park, 414 S SR A1A; 772-462-1795)

UDT-Seal Museum depicts the history of the US Navy's Underwater Demolition Teams, SEALS (Sea, Air Land Teams), Naval Combat Demolition Units, Scouts and Raiders through photographs and artifacts. The collection features weapons, equipment and suits used by these teams. A 30-min video details the training process. Sidewalks go past small landing craft, a helicopter and Apollo training modules. Rr. $. Hrs vary (Pepper Park, 3300 N SR A1A; 772-595-5845)

■ PARI-MUTUELS

Fort Pierce Jai Alai has live action games Jan-Apr and daily simulcasts all year (at 11:15am). WC seating is in front. Snack bars; Rr. Wed & Sat noon & 7; Fri 7; Sun 1 (1750 S Kings Hwy; 772-464-7500; 800-524-2524)

■ PARKS

Blue Cypress Lake Park is a remote 5-acre park in the midst of a wilderness area with a 7-mi lake full of largemouth bass. Rent a pontoon boat for up to 8 people for 4 or 8 hrs. You can roll aboard from the floating dock. You can also hire a capt. Or, bring your own boat and use the boat ramp. When water levels are down during droughts, only small boats can access the lake. See Cabins. Bait/snack shop; picnic tables on grass; Rr. 6-6; summer Wed-Mon (18 mi W of I-95, Vero Bch; from SR 60, at sign to Blue Cypress go N on dirt road for 5 mi; 772-778-0150)

Environmental Learning Center occupies the 51-acre Wabasso Island in the Indian River Lagoon and offers guided walks, workshops and off-island ecological excursions. Boardwalks and hard-packed nature trails go through native habitats including mangrove and hammocks. Gift shop; Rr. $D. Tue-Fri 10-4; Sat 9-12; Sun 1-4 (255 Live Oak Dr, Vero Bch; 772-589-5050)

Hobe Sound National Wildlife Refuge has a nature center with an exhibit area, including live baby gators. Call for accessible environmental programs, workshops and hikes. Gift shop; Rr. Wkdy 9-3 (13640 SE US 1; 2 mi S of SR 708; 772-546-2067)

Jack Island State Preserve, a 631-acre mangrove island, is for the birder or angler willing to rough it. It's hard to find, has no facilities and limited access. But birds (especially in winter) and fish both love the spot. Park by the 150' cement footbridge over the Indian River where you can fish; be aware, the edge of the bridge has no lip and cables rather than handrails. The trails are dirt roads with frequent soft stretches, but you can see birds from the footbridge. (SR A1A; 1 mi N of Fort Pierce Inlet State Park; 772-468-3985)

Jonathan Dickinson State Park covers 11,500 acres of pine forest, swamp and mangrove. Near the entrance is Hobe Mountain, which at a whopping 86', is the highest peak in S Florida. The observation tower on top is inaccessible, but call in advance to take a service road up the back of the mountain to a small deck with a great view of the forest. A paved bike trail runs about 2 mi through various habitats in sun and shade. The 4 hiking trails here are pretty tough for WCs; talk with rangers about which trails or portions might work for you. On the lower, salty reaches of the Loxahatchee River is a boat ramp and fixed dock where you can fish. Steep stairs lead to canoe rentals and boat tours. Call for schedule of ranger programs. See Campgrounds.

ADA picnic shelters; camp store; playground on mulch; Rr. $. 8-dusk (16450 SE US 1, Hobe Sound; 12 mi S of Stuart; 772-546-2771)

MacDonald/Wimbrow are adjoining parks with 77 acres along the scenic Sebastian River. MacDonald Park, to the N, has a 300' ADA boardwalk that leads to an observation deck where you can fish. Wimbrow Park, to the S, has a boat ramp and fixed dock about 2' above the non-tidal river. Canoeists enjoy the 2-mi paddle to the Indian River Lagoon. For fishing, roll across the flat grassy point by the boat ramp. The 1-mi wooded nature trail, with a gentle slope, is sandy in spots. See Campgrounds. Fitness trail; playground on sand; Rr. Dawn-dusk (CR 510, Roseland; 2 mi S of US 1; 772-589-0087)

Mary Brogan Park has a large, universal playground with an ADA surface and plenty of play features for WC kids. An aggressive skate park has many observation spots, and a .5-mi paved path is popular for running and biking. ADA picnic shelters; Rr. Dawn-dusk (Willoughby Blvd; off Salerno & Indian Sts)

Oak Hammock is the city's beautiful, 49-acre, forested park along the C24 Canal. Under the cool oak canopy, you can enjoy ADA picnic shelters and grills. Two 30' docks (each 12' wide) offer fishing and roofed sections. A boat ramp and floating docks are available. Some 2.5 mi of nature trail are level and hard-packed. Vending machine; Rr. 7am-dusk (1982 SW Villanova Rd, Port St Lucie; from Port St Lucie Blvd, go S on California Blvd, follow signs)

Rivergate Park includes some 22 acres along the North Fork of the St Lucie River, which will someday have a 1-mi boardwalk to downtown. The Veterans Memorial, where services are held periodically in an open-air meeting area, is now a 3-min stroll along a wide sidewalk from the primary park area. The park has 3 lighted boat ramps with fixed docks where, from 7-4, you can use a lift (sling seat) to board your boat. A 1200' boardwalk (lighted until 11pm) goes through a wetland and over the water where you can fish or simply relax in one of the shelters. ADA picnic shelters; grills; horseshoe area; CRr. 24 hrs (2200 SE Midport Rd, Port St Lucie; from Port St Lucie Blvd, go N on Midport)

Riverside Park is a city sports park with fishing from a lighted footbridge to a small island in the Indian River. The park is home to the Riverside Theatre, Center for the Arts (see Performing Arts) and art festivals. The 1-mi jogging trail and fitness path are gravel and sand. You can enjoy ADA picnic shelters with water/elec and grills under majestic live oaks. Boat ramp & floating dock; bait shop nearby; small playground; tennis; racquetball; Rr. Dawn-10pm (Riverside Dr, Vero Bch; off Mockingbird Dr)

St Lucie Inlet State Preserve is a hidden jewel of a spot with a 2.5-mi undeveloped beach that you can only reach by private boat on the Intracoastal. Moor at the fixed dock (from which you can also fish) or at the floating dock by the boat ramp. While the park has plans to make improvements, currently the ramp between the floating dock and main dock can be problematic. There is a 10" step where the ramp hinges to the floating dock; furthermore, the ramp can be very steep at low tide. Once you get onto the main dock, a 3300' boardwalk takes you through a mangrove and hammock habitat to miles of sandy beach. Or, if you can transfer, an 8-passenger golf cart can take you to the beach Fri-Sun. Picnic tables; grills; Rr at dock. $. Dawn-dusk (In Port Salerno on the Intracoastal; N end of Jupiter Island, .66-mi S of the St Lucie Inlet; 772-744-7603)

Sandsprit Park, a 40-acre county park along the Intracoastal, has sidewalks from parking to all points in the park. Fish from a 1200' boardwalk, the seawall or a 100' pier. Boat ramps with floating dock; ADA picnic shelters; fish cleaning table; bait shop; playground; Rr. Dawn-dusk (3443 SE St Lucie Blvd, Stuart)

Savannas Recreation Area, a 550-acre wilderness wetland within the city, is undergoing major upgrades. Coquina shell roads run throughout much of the park. Fish for bass from the flat, grassy banks of the main canal behind the campsites. Rent canoes by the hour to enjoy miles of placid canoe trails through marsh, lagoons and creeks. Launch from the boat ramp only for canoes or small boats (with trolling motors at most); call in advance if you need staff to help you transfer. See Campgrounds. ADA picnic tables; vending machines; Rr (1400 E Midway Rd/ SR 712; E off US 1; 772-464-7855)

Savannas State Preserve stretches 10 mi from Ft Pierce to Jensen Beach with savanna-like freshwater marsh and pine forest. The new education center (Wed-Sun 9-5; 772-398-2779) has displays, videos and plans for programs beyond the current volunteer-guided walks and canoe trips offered in cooler months. You can borrow a beach WC (removable arms; drink holder) to enjoy the 8 mi of unimproved trails that can get sandy in dry seasons and soft in wet seasons. Bring your canoe. A ramp leads to the canoe launch and a platform where you can fish in the freshwater marsh. ADA picnic shelter; Rr & CRr in center. 8-dusk (2541 Walton Rd, Pt St Lucie; 2 mi E of US 1; 772-340-7530)

■ **PERFORMING ARTS**

Mesa Park features concerts by professional entertainers, exhibitions and sporting events. The location of WC seating depends on the show. Rr (CR 512, Fellsmere; 1 mi W of I-95; 772-571-2012; 877-637-2849)

Pineapple Playhouse, a community theater, offers musicals, comedies and dramas. WC seating in aisles near front; grass parking lot. Rr. Sep-May (629 Weatherbee Rd; 772-465-0366)

Port St Lucie Community Center hosts concerts and other productions. WC seating throughout; Rr (2195 SE Airoso Blvd, Port St Lucie; 772-878-2277)

Riverside Theatre is a professional theater hosting musicals, dramas and children's plays. A celebrity series and the Vero Beach Concert Association performances are also featured at this venue. WC seating is on an elevated platform in the rear of the theater. Rr. Oct-May (3250 Riverside Park Dr, Vero Bch; 772-231-6990; 800-445-6745)

St Lucie County Civic Center hosts opera, concerts, circus performances and even dog shows. With advance notice, staff can remove any of the chairs for WC seating. Rr (Virginia Ave & 25 St, Port St Lucie; 772-462-1530)

Vero Beach Community Theater uses local talent in musicals, comedies and dramas. WC seating is on the aisles in the 1st, middle and last rows. Rr. Sep-Jun (2020 San Juan Ave; 772-562-8300)

■ **POOLS**

Indian River Community College has a heated pool and lift (fixed seat) that staff can set up with advance notice. Lifeguards can help with transfers. Lap lanes; locker room with Rr & roll-in shower. Wkdy 12-2; wknd 12-5 (29 St; behind Planetarium at SE corner of Fort Pierce campus; 772-462-4706)

Leisure Square Community Center has a heated pool and lift (fixed seat); lifeguards can help with transfers. Aquacise class for seniors Mon, Wed, Fri 9-10am; locker room with roll-in showers; lap swimming. $. Hrs vary (3705 16 St, Vero Bch; 772-770-6500)

■ **SHOOTING RANGES**

Indian River County Public Shooting Range offers state-of-the-art and fully ADA ranges. Choose your venue: archery, pistol and rifle ranges up to 600', skeet, air pistol and rifle with elevated shooting platforms and accessible lanes to check your targets. Classes, clubs and special events are offered. Vending machines; Rr. $. Wed-Fri 11:30-7:30; wknd 9-5 (10455 102 Ter, Sebastian; I-95 exit

156, E .5 mi, N on 102 Ter; 772-581-4944)

■ SHOPPING

Boutiques: Fort Pierce offers an array of shopping and dining in its lovely historical section (N 2 St & Indian River Dr; 772-466-3880). St Lucie West Shoppes has fun shops and, on the 3rd Fri, monthly sidewalk festivals with live entertainment and crafts 5:30-9pm (St Lucie Blvd, Port St Lucie). Check out the boutiques and galleries along Ocean Dr in Vero Bch near the Portales de Vero Shopping Arcade (2855 Ocean Dr, Vero Bch).

Farmers Markets occur in Fort Pierce mid-Oct to Apr on Sat 8-12 (Ave A & Melody Ln; downtown riverfront) and in Port St Lucie Oct-May on Sat 7-12 (Port St Lucie Community Center, 2195 SE Airoso Blvd; 772-878-2277).

Malls: Indian River Mall (SR 60 & 66 Ave, Vero Bch; 772-770-9404); Manufactures Outlet Mall (Okeechobee Rd; between FL Tpke & I-95; 772-465-7007); Orange Blossom Mall (4300 Okeechobee Blvd; 772-466-5100); the upscale Treasure Coast Square (US 1 at Jensen Bch Blvd, Jensen Bch); and Prime Outlets (SR 60 at I-95, Vero Bch; 772-770-6171; 800-866-5900)

Specialty Shops: Mrs Peter's advertises smoked fish, smoked turkey, "smoked everything but mermaids!" (1500 SR 707, Jensen Bch; 772-334-2184)

■ SKYDIVING

Skydive Sebastian has experience with paraplegic skydivers who want to jump out of a plane at 13,500'. Start with a 30-min briefing on the ground, then enjoy the 15-min plane ride, 1-min free fall and 5 min of actual parachuting over the coast near Sebastian Inlet. Crew can adapt equipment to meet your needs and lift you 3' into the plane (235-lb limit). Skydivers are strapped to the instructor. Summer Wed-Mon 9-dusk; winter 8-dusk (400 W Airport Dr, Sebastian; 772-388-5672; 800-399-5867)

■ SPECTATOR SPORTS

Baseball The Los Angeles Dodgers play exhibition games Mar-Apr and the Vero Beach Dodgers play Apr-Sep. Ramps lead to WC seating, behind companion seating. Rr (Holman Stadium, 4001 26 St, Vero Bch; 772-569-6858) New York Mets have spring training and exhibition games in Mar. The St Lucie Mets play Apr-Sep. Ramps lead to WC seating near home plate. (Thomas J White Stadium, 525 NW Peacock Blvd, Port St Lucie; 772-871-2100)

■ TENNIS

Lawnwood Tennis Complex offers WC-tennis instructions and clinics, by appointment. Call Woody Newson. (1302 Virginia Ave; 772-462-1525)

■ TOURS

Barley Barber Swamp Tour, sponsored by Florida Power & Light, runs 3 hrs and starts with a 30-min video at the Seminole Country Inn. Then, in your own vehicle, follow the inaccessible tour bus for the 7-mi ride to a pristine cypress swamp where a guide leads you on a 1.25-mi ramped boardwalk. Reservations; Rr at Inn. Nov-Mar 8:30 & 1:30 (Seminole Country Inn, 15885 SW SR 710, Indiantown; 772-597-3777; 800-257-9267)

ACCOMMODATIONS

■ B&B/INNS

Casa d'Este B&B, across from the river, has 2 ADA guestrooms, each with a queen bed (open frame), microwave, refrigerator and coffeepot. Private bathrooms have raised toilets, roll-under sinks and roll-in showers with hand-held sprayers. From the porch, watch the sun rise and then enjoy a generous breakfast. The home is near a beach with an accessible dune crossover and observation deck. Pool. $$-$$$ (4030 Indian River Dr/SR A1A, Jensen Bch; 772-225-2729)

Davis House Inn is in the Riverfront District, close to plenty of restaurants. The ADA suite has a king bed (24" high/open frame), full futon and kitchenette with refrigerator, microwave and coffeepot. The bathroom has a raised toilet, roll-under sink and roll-in shower. Enjoy a large sundeck and the nearby Main St Fishing Dock (see Fishing Piers). Laundry. $$ (607 Davis St, Sebastian; off Indian River Dr, 1.3 mi N of US 1; 772-589-4114)

Mellon Patch Inn has a WC-friendly guestroom with a king bed (24" high/open frame). The private bath has a 30" wide doorway, grab bars and tub with a hand-held sprayer and seat. A dock in the backyard offers fishing in the Indian River; across the street is Pepper Park with an accessible dune crossover (see Beaches). A full breakfast is served in the dining room. Catch the sun rising from the ocean across the street or toast the setting sun from the patio in back. $$-$$$ (3601 N SR A1A; 772-4651-5231; 800-656-7824)

■ CABINS/CAMPGROUNDS
Jonathan Dickinson State Park has a 1BR ADA cabin and ADA campsites. The *cabin* is actually a ramped, modular unit with a full bed (open frame) and queen sofa bed in the living room. It has a full kitchenette and bathroom with a roll-under sink and roll-in shower with a hand-held sprayer. Bring linens. Outside, on level hard-packed grass is an ADA picnic table and fire ring. The sunny River Campground has 2 ADA sites with water, ADA picnic tables, fire rings and sidewalks from the edge of the site to an ADA bathhouse. In the more shady Pine Grove Campground, 2 ADA sites have water/elec, ADA picnic tables and fire rings; site 34 has a sidewalk directly to the ADA bathhouse; site 35 has some grass before reaching the path. Bathhouses have raised toilets, roll-under sinks and roll-in showers with lowered controls and benches. Sandy trails lead to an amphitheater where campfire pro-

grams are held each Sat night. See Parks. Camp store; ranger programs (16450 SE /US 1, Hobe Sound; 12 mi S of Stuart; cabin 772-746-1466; campgrounds 772-546-2771)

MacDonald Park has 30 primitive campsites on soft sand terrain. Site 2 has an ADA picnic table, fire pit and onsite parking. You can drive on the dirt road to the bathhouse with a step at the entrance and an ADA stall with a raised toilet, roll-under sink and roll-in shower with a hand-held sprayer. If you can handle the sand, this is a great spot to get away from it all; see Parks. No reservations (CR 510, Roseland; 2 mi S of US 1; 772-589-0087)

Middleton's Fish Camp, on the exquisite Blue Cypress Lake (see Parks), has 3 ramped cabins with full kitchens, 2 twin beds (open frames) and AC. The front and back doors are 32" wide; in back is a deck with a roll-under table and grill. The large bathroom has a 30" wide doorway, roll-under sink and roll-in hot shower. You can dock your own boat out back, rent a pontoon boat and take an ecotour (see Boat Tours). Linens included (18 mi W of I-95, Vero Bch; from SR 60, at sign to Blue Cypress go N on dirt road for 5 mi; 772-778-0150; 800-258-5002)

River Palm Cottages & Fish Camp, along the Indian River, has an ADA 1BR cottage (#7) with a full kitchen; it sleeps 4 with a queen bed (24" high/open frame) and 2 twin beds in the living room. The bathroom has a raised toilet, roll-under sink and roll-in shower with hand-held sprayer and seat. Guests can use the boat ramp with a fixed dock or staff can arrange inshore charters on a pontoon boat at a neighboring marina. Bait shop nearby. $$$ (2325 NE Indian River Dr, Jensen Bch; 772-334-0401; 800-305-0511)

Savannas Park, a marshy wilderness within city limits, has 45 tent/RV sites: 15 for tents only, 15 with water/elec and 15 with full hookups. All sites have flat, grassy terrain and grills; staff can deliver ADA picnic tables to your site. The sites with water/elec are on the very fishable canal and currently have the easiest access to the bathhouse. Reserve sites close to the ADA bathhouse with raised toilets, roll-under sinks and roll-in showers with hand-held sprayers and seats. The Atlantic beaches are 9 miles to the east. Canoeing is popular here; see Parks. (1400 E Midway Rd/SR 712; E off US 1; 772-464-7855)

■ CONDOS

Sheraton PGA Vacation Resort has 3 ADA 2BR condos on the ground floor with full kitchens and private patios. The master bedroom has a king bed (open frame), the 2nd bedroom has 2 full beds and the living room has a queen sofa bed. Bathrooms have raised toilets and roll-in showers with seats. Pool; laundry. $$$ (8700 Champions Way, Port St Lucie; 772-460-5700; 866-207-8598)

■ MOTELS

*Disney's Vero Beach Resort has several ADA units: 5 rooms, 3 1BR villas that sleep 4 and 3 2BR villas that sleep 8. Each room has a king or 2 queen beds (18" high/open frames), a small refrigerator, microwave, coffeepot and wet bar. Bedrooms in the suites have a king or 2 queen beds. Each suite also has a full kitchen, laundry, queen sofa bed in the living room and a private porch. Bathrooms have raised toilets, roll-under sinks and roll-in showers with hand-

held sprayers and seats. A huge back porch and boardwalk overlook the beach. Borrow the beach WC (fixed arms) and take a ramp to the beach. The pool is ramped for WC entry. Kids' programs, including onsite excursions; fitness center with sauna & massage; gift shop; laundry; bar; full restaurants. $$-$$$ (9250 Island Grove Ter, Vero Bch; 772-234-2000; reservations 800-359-8000)

Holiday Inn Oceanside has 8 ADA rooms, each with a king bed (24" high/open frame) and coffeepot. Bathrooms have raised toilets and roll-under sinks; rooms 118 and 159 have roll-in showers with seats; other rooms have tubs or step-in showers. There are stairs to the beach. Pool; laundry; bar; entertainment; full restaurant. $$-$$$ (3793 NE SR A1A, Jensen Bch; 772-225-3000; 800-992-4747)

Key West Inn has 9 ADA rooms and 3 ADA 1BR suites, each with a king or 2 queen beds (24" high/open frames or platforms) and coffeepots. Suites have sofa beds in the living room and kitchenettes; some rooms have a refrigerator and microwave. Bathrooms have roll-under sinks; room 111 has a roll-in shower with a hand-held sprayer and seat; others have tubs. Free brkfst; pool; laundry; bar; entertainment; full restaurant; dock along the Indian River. $$-$$$ (1580 US 1, Sebastian; 772-388-8588; 800-833-0555)

MELBOURNE

Eau Gallie, Indialantic, Melbourne Beach, Palm Bay, West Melbourne

With 33 miles of quiet, pristine white sand beaches, Melbourne is a sunbather's heaven. Add its proximity to the Kennedy Space Center and Orlando, and you've found a neat low-key spot for a family vacation. Sebastian Inlet State Park is a particularly tempting spot with a beach wheelchair for 3 miles of splendid beach, an accessible boat tour, canoe and kayak rentals and ADA cabins.

Tourist Info

Brevard County Tourism Council: 2725 St Johns St, Bldg C, Melbourne 32940; 321-633-2110

Melbourne-Palm Bay Visitors Bureau: 1005 E Strawbridge Ave, 32901; 321-724-5400; 800-771-9922)
Web sites: www.melpb-chamber.org; www.brevardparks.com

Transportation
Space Coast Area Transit has buses with lifts that service all cities in Brevard County (Titusville to Palm Bay). Door-to-door service is available if you are not on a fixed route; after qualifying by phone, you can make reservations. (321-633-1878)

ACTIVITIES

■ **ATTRACTIONS**
Brevard Zoo's inhabitants include 460 animals representing 119 species from around the world featured in settings of original Florida, Latin America, Australia and Asia. A new African section will enable you to hand feed giraffes and take boat rides around a White Rhino habitat. Shaded boardwalks take visitors past the exhibits and through the bird aviary. A 12-min train ride tours Lemur Island to view 4 different species of primates from Indonesia; the front car of the train has been adapted for WCs. The petting zoo is on crushed shell and dirt. Call about kayak eco-tours with adaptive equipment. WC rental; gift shop; snack bar; playground on mulch Rr. $. 10-5 (8225 N Wickham Rd; 321-254-9453)

■ **BEACHES**
Canova Beach Park is a 12-acre beach with an accessible dune cross-over (just N of the bathhouse) that takes you onto the sand and close to the ocean. Be wary, the water has submerged rocks. In a small grassy area is a covered picnic table on cement and a grill. Across the street are restaurants and shops. Outdoor showers; Rr. Dawn-dusk (3299 A1A, Indian Harbour Bch; at Gallie Blvd; 321-779-4047)
Paradise Beach Park has an accessible dune cross-over by HC parking that takes you onto the sand and close to the water where you need to watch out for submerged rocks. The North, South and Main areas each have an ADA picnic shelter and grill. Lifeguards in summers; outdoor showers; Rr. Dawn-dusk

(2301 N A1A; 1.5 mi S of Eau Gallie Blvd; 321-779-4047)
*Sebastian Inlet State Park's 800 acres includes 3 mi of ocean beach popular with surfers. Call ahead to reserve then ask at the entry station for the beach WC (removable arms) that rangers can deliver to the beach of your choice. The beach by the jetty on the S side of park may be best because the sand is harder packed and a boardwalk leads quite far down the beach. In fact, high tides come close to the end of this boardwalk. About 50' offshore are reefs good for snorkelers and scuba divers, but the currents around the inlet are treacherous. The paved N jetty reportedly has some fine fishing. On the S side of the park is the Inlet Marina (open 7-5; 321-724-5424; 800-952-1126) with a boat ramp, fixed docks and a small floating dock on the Indian River Lagoon that opens to the inlet and ocean. The marina rents rowboats, canoes and sit-on kayaks. High tides make it easier for staff to lower you from the dock to board; call ahead to find out the best times. From the marina, rangers lead 2-hr tours on a roll-aboard pontoon boat along the Sebastian Inlet and around Pelican Island, a bird refuge. Learn about the diverse ecosystem and local history. Dolphins, stingrays and birds usually accompany the tour. The Sebastian Fishing Museum (10-4; 561-388-2750), dedicated to the local fishing industry, houses a replica of a fish house and dock, old photos of the Indian River and a gift shop. A bike trail starts in the park and continues N 14 mi

along A1A to Melbourne Beach. Rangers also lead turtle walks on summer nights. Call for the schedule of ranger activities. See Campgrounds. Outdoor showers; snack bar; ADA picnic shelters; Rr. $. 24 hrs (9700 S A1A, Melbourne Bch; at the Brevard-Indian River County line; 321-984-4852)

BIKE TRAILS
A1A has a 14-mi paved bike path from Melbourne Beach S to Sebastian Inlet State Park further along the coast in Indian River County. The path is separated from A1A by a grassy medium and passes relatively undeveloped beachfront with stretches of shops and restaurants along the way.

BOAT RAMPS
Parks: Lake Washington, Long Point

BOAT TOURS
Beaches: Sebastian Inlet

BOWLING
Brunswick Brevard Bowl has ramped lanes and a bowling ball ramp. Lounge; snack bar; game room; billiards; Rr. 9am-mdnt (4851 S Dairy Rd; 321-723-7400)

FISHING CHARTERS
Water's Edge Fishing Charters goes freshwater bass fishing on the river and saltwater flats fishing at Mosquito Lagoon, Indian River, Banana River and the Sebastian Inlet. Choose a half/full-day trip in a flats boat for 2 anglers. The capt can help your companion lower you, in your WC, into the front of the boat. Fly and spin casting are available. (321-984-8735)

FISHING PIERS
Parks: Lake Washington, Long Point, Palm Bay
Indian River has a 140' fishing pier and a boardwalk along the river. ADA picnic tables; Rr (Rotary Park, US 1 & Suntree Blvd; 321-633-1874)
Melbourne Beach Fishing Pier is an 800' lighted wood pier on the Indian River. 24 hrs. (W end of Ocean Ave)

HUNTING
Osceola Outfitters is experienced with disabled hunters and can adapt equipment to meet your needs. Hunt for wild hog, turkey, alligator or white-tailed deer. Single or multi-day packages are available with or without lodging. The WC friendly lodge has twin beds. (6210 Kempfer Rd; off US 192; 407-957-3593)

■ MISC
Special Spotlight Theatre has group dance classes and private lessons for folks with all levels of physical disabilities. Rr (Henegar Center, 625 New Haven; 321-951-2420)

■ MUSEUMS
Beaches: Sebastian Inlet
Museum of Art & Science includes 2 buildings across the street from each other. The art museum houses works by international and regional artists and offers workshops and demonstrations. The science museum has interactive science exhibits and a learning center geared to families. Neither building is accessible from the parking lot; park on Highland Ave where the WC entrances are located. Each has a gift shop and Rr. $. Tue-Sat 10-5; Sun 1-5 (1463 Highland Ave; art 321-242-0737; science 321-254-7782)

■ PARI-MUTUELS
Melbourne Greyhound Park has live racing Nov-Apr and year-round simulcasts. The clubhouse restaurant has WC seating on the top level. Rr (1100 N Wickham Rd; 321-259-9800)

■ PARKS
Erna Nixon Park is a 54-acre preserve with a .5-mi hard-packed nature trail that includes an elevated boardwalk. Periodic events include Moonlight Strolls, with telescopes and live music, and traditional craft festivals. Ranger tours occur on weekends at 2. ADA picnic shelter; Rr. 9-5 (1200 Evans Rd; off Nasa Blvd, SW of Melbourne Airport; 321-952-4525)
Lake Washington Park, a secluded 26-acre wooded park, lines the very fishable, 4-mi long Lake Washington that connects, at high levels, to the St Johns River. Anglers like the 150' wood ADA

fishing pier and the boat ramp with a floating dock. Birders like the mornings. ADA picnic shelters; playground; Rr; CRr. Dawn-dusk (6000 Lake Washington Rd; from I-95, exit S onto Wickham Rd, then W; 321-952-4650)

Long Point Park is an 85-acre, man-made island in the Indian River that you can reach by car. A paved path leads to the edge of a sandy beach with a 30' gentle slope into to a swimming pond, about 6' deep. Another pond is reserved strictly for the wildlife. You can fish from the lighted, 35' wood pier over the river. Campsites offer fishing from the flat grassy banks along the river. Call for the schedule of ranger and birding programs. See Campgrounds. Lifeguards in summer; boat ramp with fixed dock; ADA picnic shelters; grills; playground; Rr. $ 5am-10pm (700 Long Point Rd; off A1A, 1.5 mi N of Sebastian Inlet; 321-952-4532)

Palm Bay Regional Park is being developed into a 200-acre sports and nature park. Currently, you can fish on 2 lakes where bream and bass are caught; a 20' dock extends over one lake. A 4-mi paved bike path leads from the park E through residential areas along Malabar Rd to Minton Rd. ADA picnic table on concrete at concession; playground on mulch; Rr. 7am-dusk (1951 Malabar Rd NW, Palm Bay; 6 mi W of I-95; 321-952-6373)

Rodes Park is an 18-acre sports park with a swim lake. Go over a short expanse of grass to the flat edge of the swim area that gradually slopes into 6' of water. ADA picnic tables; lifeguards in summer; vending machine; Rr. Dawn-dusk (3000 Minton Rd, West Melbourne; 3 mi S of SR 192; 321-952-6344)

Turkey Creek Sanctuary has a 1.25-mi elevated boardwalk through 113 acres of pine scrub and wet hammock. Migratory birds love mornings here from Oct-Nov and Mar-May. The nature center exhibits include a manatee skeleton and a 7 1/2' gator. Call about the 2-hr guided nature tours on weekends. Picnic tables; gift shop; Rr. 7am-dusk (1518 Port Malabar Blvd SE, Palm Bay; 321-952-3433)

■ **PERFORMING ARTS**

Henegar Center for the Arts is a refurbished former public school where concerts and various events take place in the proscenium-style theater and in various smaller rooms. WC seating is at the ends of row G. Elevator; Rr (625 E New Haven Ave; 321-723-8698)

King Center for the Performing Arts is a professional theater featuring Broadway plays, symphony, ballet, jazz and celebrity artists. WC entrance on the W side; WC seating in back; Rr (3865 Wickham Rd; 321-242-2219)

Melbourne Civic Theatre is a community theater offering musicals, dramas and comedies. WC seating in front on sides; Rr (Metro-West Shopping Center, US 192 & Wickham Rd; 321-723-1668)

■ **SHOPPING**

Antiques can be found in downtown Melbourne (along E New Haven Ave) and in the historic district of Eau Gallie by SR 518.

Flea Market: Super Flea & Farmers Market has over 900 booths of new and used merchandise. Fri-Sun 8-4 (I-95 exit 183 at Eau Gallie Blvd; 321-242-9124)

Malls: Melbourne Square Mall (1700 W New Haven Ave; 321-727-8062)

■ **SPECTATOR SPORTS**

Baseball The Florida Marlins hold spring training Mar-Apr (321-633-9200) and the Brevard County Manatees play Apr-Sep in the Space Coast Stadium. Take the elevator up to WC seating on the concourse level. Rr (5800 Stadium Pkwy; 321-633-4487)

ACCOMMODATIONS

■ **CABINS/CAMPGROUNDS**

Long Point Park, a popular campground, has 113 campsites along the Indian River and another 57 in the interior of the park. The 15 RV-only sites have full hookups; the remaining sites are for RV or tents. Waterfront sites have fire rings and all sites are on flat, grassy terrain with ADA picnic tables on request. ADA bathhouses have raised toilets and roll-under sinks; one bathhouse has hot water and a roll-in shower. In addition to fishing from the riverfront campsites, enjoy the fishing pier; see Parks. (700 Long Point Rd; off A1A, 1.5 mi N of Sebastian Inlet; 321-952-4532)

*Sebastian Inlet State Park has 51 RV/tent sites and will soon have 10 cabins on the lagoon side of this wonderful oceanfront park. Two campsites have water/elec, paved pads, ADA picnic tables, grills and great views of the inlet. The ADA bathhouse has raised toilets, roll-under sinks and roll-in showers. The ADA cabins will have kitchens and private baths and will be furnished and fully supplied. The park loans a beach WC for its 3-mi beach; see Beaches. Laundry (9700 S A1A, Melbourne Bch; on Brevard-Indian River County line; 561-589-9659)

■ **COTTAGES**

Oceanfront Cottages are 4 lovely cottages on a boardwalk overlooking the Atlantic and a spot popular with sea turtles. The WC-friendly 1BR unit has a full sofa bed in the living room, a full kitchen, queen bed (platform) and private patio with an ocean view. The bathroom door is 32" wide. Pool; laundry; restaurants & shops nearby. $$-$$$ (612 Wavecrest Ave, Indialantic; 321-725-8474; 800-785-8080)

■ **HOUSES**

Mango House is a WC-friendly 3BR/2BA house 2 blocks from the ocean and even closer to the Indian River. The home rents by the week and has a step up to the front door and a step down to the private pool and Jacuzzi area. One bedroom has a king, another has a queen and the third has 2 twin beds (all on open frames). Doorways are 32" and the bathrooms have step-in showers. Full kitchen; restaurants & shops nearby. $$$ (415 6 Ave, Melbourne Bch; 321-725-8474; 800-785-8080)

■ **MOTELS**

Courtyard by Marriott has 7 ADA rooms with a king or 2 full beds (24" high/platforms), a full sofa bed and coffeepot. Bathrooms have roll-under sinks; rooms 141 and 143 have roll-in showers; others have tubs with hand-held sprayers and seats. Pool; laundry; lounge; brkfst cafe; fitness room. $$-$$$ (2101 W New Haven Ave; 321-724-6400)

Hampton Inn has 3 ADA rooms, each with a queen bed (20" high/platform), coffeepot and on request, a refrigerator and microwave. Bathrooms have roll-under sinks and roll-in showers with hand-held sprayers and seats. Free brkfst; pool; laundry. $-$$ (194 Kike Rd; 321-956-6200)

Hilton Melbourne Airport has 8 ADA rooms with a king or 2 full beds (open frames) and coffeepots. Bathrooms have raised toilets and roll-under sinks; room A has a roll-in shower; others have tubs with hand-held sprayers and seats. Pool; laundry; lounge; entertainment; full restaurant. $$-$$$ (200 Rialto Pl; 321-768-0200; 800-437-8010)

Jameson Inn has 4 ADA rooms with a king or 2 full beds (24" high/platforms). Bathrooms have raised toilets and roll-under sinks; room 123 has a roll-in shower with a hand-held sprayer and seat; others have tubs. Free brkfst; pool. $$ (890 Palm Bay Rd, Palm Bay; 321-725-2950)

Wheelchair riders can't jump...
but they can play basketball.
See Index page 412 to find a team near you.

What are bowling ball ramps?
Adaptive devices so paras and quads can bowl.
See Bowling page 11 and Index page 412.

Crank-cycling is not for cranks!
You use a handcycle — a type of bike
you pedal with your hands and arms.
See Handcycling page 13 and Index page 413.

Golf? You bet!
An adaptive golf cart may work for you.
See page 12 and Index page 413.

If you are looking for love....
try tennis!
See page 15 and Index page 414.

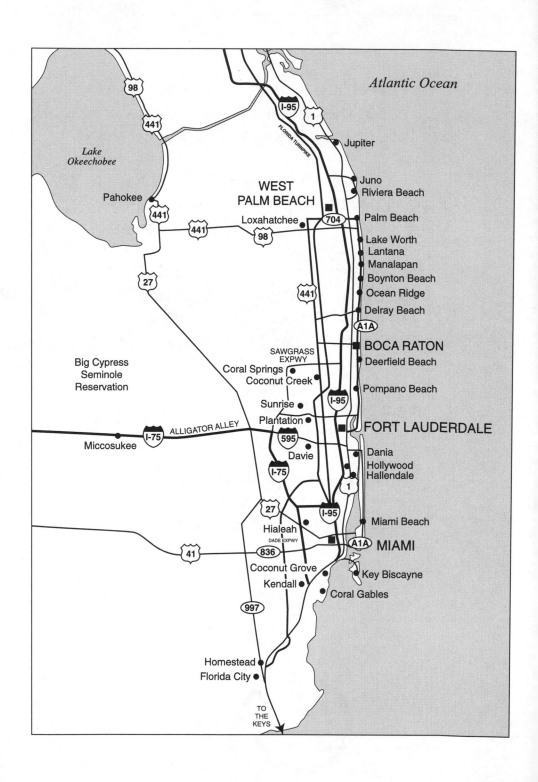

SOUTHEAST ATLANTIC COAST

BOCA RATON
Boynton Beach, Delray Beach, Lantana, Manalapan, Ocean Ridge

Boca has grown into a manicured community with a highbrow gentility that includes polo and an impressive cultural agenda. A public golf course rents an adaptive golf cart, five beaches loan beach wheelchairs and the county loans a
handcycle for several lovely bike trails. Boca also hosts an internationally recog-
nized, wheelchair-tennis tournament; wheelchair-tennis clinics are available too.
Just west of town, the open wildness of the Loxahatchee Refuge calls with canoeing, air boating and fishing. A unique find is Coconut Cove water park with a lift.
SR A1A is also known as Ocean Boulevard; US 1 is also known as Federal Highway.

Tourist Info
See West Palm Beach.
Boca Raton Chamber: 1800 N Dixie Hwy, 33432; 561-395-4433
Web sites: www.boca.com

Transportation
See West Palm Beach.

ACTIVITIES

■ ATTRACTIONS
Morikami Park celebrates Japanese
culture on 207 acres of tranquil pine
forests with Japanese gardens, waterfalls, ponds and a rare bonsai collection. Nearly 1 mi of paved paths lead
through the grounds and to shaded
ADA picnic shelters with grills. One
museum is modeled after a Japanese
residence and features an exhibit on
the Yamato Colony, a group of Japanese farmers who, in the early 1900's,
tried to settle in Boca. Another museum features Japanese arts, crafts
and artifacts as well as a teahouse
with demonstrations of the Japanese
tea ceremony and a theater for lectures and performing arts. Cafe for
Asian lunches; Japanese crafts classes;
gift shop; Rr. $. Park dawn-dusk; muse-
ums Tue-Sun 10-5 (4000 Morikami

Park Rd, Delray Bch; off Jog Rd, just N of Clint Moore Rd; 561-495-0233) **Sandoway House Nature Center** provides hands-on environmental education through labs, touch tanks, nature displays and a range of field trips and workshops. The 1936 former beach home has a ramp and elevator. Sidewalks lead to a coral reef exhibit and gardens. Rr. $D. Tue-Thu, Sat 10-4:30; Fri & Sun 12-4:30 (142 S SR A1A, Delray Bch; 2 blks S of Atlantic Ave/SR 806; 561-274-7263)

■ BEACHES

***Atlantic Dunes Park**, nestled in an elevated wooded area, loans a beach WC (fixed arms) at the lifeguard tower on the sand. A hard-packed, 300' nature trail winds through the dunes, where you may see fox and other wildlife. Lifeguards 9-5; picnic shelter on sand; outdoor showers; cabana & umbrella rentals; Rr. Dawn-dusk (SR A1A, Delray Bch; 1.5 mi S of the Municipal Bch, 1 blk N of Linton Blvd; 561-243-7352)

***Delray Municipal Beach** has 1.5 mi of oceanfront beach. At the N end, a boardwalk leads from HC parking to an elevated shelter and observation platform over the beach. You can borrow a beach WC (fixed arms) at the lifeguard tower on sand, next to the shelter. Sara Gleason Park, directly across SR A1A, has Rr and outdoor showers. Lifeguards 9-5; cabana & umbrella rentals; outdoor cafes nearby. Dawn-dusk (Atlantic Ave/SR 806 & SR A1A, Delray Bch; 561-243-7352)

Lantana Municipal Beach, fringed with tall sea grapes along the dunes, has 2 sidewalks from parking (one in the center, the other toward the S end of the beach) both ramped to a 750' shoreline. At high tide, the beach can shrink to a 20' expanse; at low tide, you may encounter some rocks. Lifeguards; restaurant; gift shop; picnic tables; outdoor showers & Rr at S end of beach. $/parking. Dawn-dusk (Ocean Ave & SR A1A, Lantana; next to Ritz Carlton; 561-540-5731)

***Oceanfront Park** has a 1000' boardwalk past lifeguard headquarters where you can borrow a beach WC (fixed arms; umbrella). Dune crossovers lead from parking and ramp to the sand. After storms, this beach can be narrow and deeply sloped. Lifeguards 9-5; ADA picnic shelters; snack bar; ADA playground; outdoor showers; Rr. $/parking. Dawn-11pm (SR A1A, Ocean Ridge; 1 blk N of Ocean Ave)

Red Reef Park is the city's 1-mi oceanfront beach. From parking, across from the gatehouse, a boardwalk winds through sea grapes and palmettos along the dunes to a shelter overlooking the beach and ramps to the sand. At the N end of the park, sidewalks lead to a playground on sand. Across SR A1A is the Gumbo-Limbo Nature Center; see Parks. A 1-mi path of pavers leads to N South Beach. Lifeguards; ADA picnic tables; grills; outdoor showers; Rr. $/parking. 8am-10pm (1400 N SR A1A; lifeguards 561-393-7820; rangers 393-7815)

South Beach is a pristine beach, largely hidden from the road, with ramps to the sand at the S and N ends. At the N end (at Palmetto Park Rd) is a shelter overlooking a natural reef just offshore. A 1-mi path of pavers leads S to Red Reef Park. Lifeguards; outdoor showers; Rr at the shelter & tower 4. $/parking. 8-dusk (400 N SR A1A; lifeguards 561-393-7820; rangers 393-7815)

***South Inlet Park** is an 11-acre county beach that loans a beach WC (no arms; drink & umbrella holders). A friend can ask at the lifeguard tower on the sand and lifeguards will bring the beach WC to you. A dune crossover leads from parking and ramps to the sand. You can fish from the jetty. Lifeguards 9-5; ADA picnic tables; grills; outdoor showers; Rr. $/parking. Dawn-dusk (1298 S SR A1A; directly S of Boca Inlet, 1 mi S of Palmetto Park Rd)

***Spanish River Park** is a forested 93-acre

park with a .5-mi ocean beach. Along the Intracoastal are secluded, shady ADA picnic areas with grills and parking. Some open flat areas protrude from the woods where you can fish from the rocky seawall. Three tunnels go under SR A1A to the beach. Ask at the entrance to borrow a beach WC (fixed or removable arms); lifeguards can bring it to you at HC parking by the N tunnel. A 2-mi hike/bike path on mulch winds through the park and is popular with birders. Playground on sand; lifeguards 9-5; outdoor showers; Rr. $/parking. 8-dusk (3001 N SR A1A; S of NE Spanish River Blvd; lifeguards 561-393-7820; rangers 393-7815)

■ BIKE TRAILS
Beaches: Spanish River. Parks: Loxahatchee, South County. West Palm Beach: Handcycles

El Rio Trail goes 2.5 mi along El Rio Canal between Glades Rd/SR 808 and Spanish River Blvd. Park on the 3500 block of NW 5 Ave.

Patch Reef Trail runs 3.5 mi along the E-3 Canal between Glades Rd/SR 808 and Yamato Rd. Park at Patch Reef Park (2000 Yamato Rd); in the NW corner near the playground is water and Rr.

■ BOAT RAMPS
Fishing Piers: Boat Club, Pioneer Canal. Parks: Lake Ida

Silver Palm Park has a boat ramp and fixed dock on the Intracoastal, N of the Boca Raton Inlet. For a permit, call 561-998-4400. ADA picnic tables; Rr. 24 hrs (600 E Palmetto Park Rd)

■ BOAT TOURS
Loxahatchee Everglades Airboat Tours offers 1-hr guided tours through 12 mi of the Everglades. Call to discuss boarding from the sandbagged shoreline. Water levels must be high enough for the crew to lift you (200-lb limit) from your WC and aboard into a wide bench seat with a back. Companions can sit on either side of you for support. Hard-packed parking; snack bar; Rr port-o-let. 9:30-4 (15490 Loxahatchee Rd; 5 mi W of US 441; 561-482-8026; 800-683-5873)

■ CANOEING/KAYAKING
Parks: James Rutherford

Dare 2 Adventure rents canoes and solo/tandem sit-on kayaks by the hour or long term, for use in the S end of the Loxahatchee Refuge or the contiguous Everglades Management Area. Or, take 2- to 8-mi guided trips. The terrain is flat and open; the waterways are lined with cattails and in full sun. The launch site near this portable operation has a gentle 6' slope to the water's edge; staff can help lift you aboard. Outdoor gear for rent (W end of Loxahatchee Rd; 7 mi NW of US 441; 561-302-0531)

Loxahatchee Canoeing rents canoes and solo/tandem sit-on kayaks for half days on canoe trails in the N section of the Loxahatchee National Wildlife Refuge. Nov-Apr, the company offers 2-hr guided trips. The launch site near this portable operation has gently sloped, hard-packed banks. Call to ensure that staff can help lift you aboard. Rr in nearby refuge (US 441; between SR 804 & Atlantic Ave/SR 806; 561-733-0192)

■ DINNER THEATERS
Lots of Laughs is where you help solve a murder during a Jewish-Italian wedding feast with your choice of prime rib, salmon or chicken. WC seating throughout; Rr. Nov-May Fri-Sat 7; Sun varies (Flamingo Room, 2410 N US 1, Delray Bch; 561-863-7723; 800-675-7723)

Musicana Dinner Theatre invites you to 2 hrs of gourmet dining and dancing before a Broadway musical review. WC seating on main floor; Rr. Tue-Sat 6; Wed & Sat 12; Sun 4 (2200 NW 2 Ave; 561-361-9704; 800-498-9160)

■ FISHING PIERS
Beaches: South Inlet, Spanish River. Parks: Lake Ida, Loxahatchee, Veterans

Boat Club Park has a lighted 150' boardwalk with fishing piers along the Intracoastal. Two boat ramps have floating docks. ADA picnic shelters; grills; playground; Rr. Dawn-dusk (2100 N US 1, Boynton Bch; S of Gateway Blvd)

Ocean Inlet Park has an ocean jetty (accessible on the N side; open 24 hrs) and a seawall in a marina on the Intracoastal from which you can fish. While there's no ramp to the beach, you can access an overlook on the 600' oceanfront beach. Snack bar; ADA picnic shelters; outdoor showers; Rr. Dawn-dusk (6990 N SR A1A, Ocean Ridge)

Palmetto Greens Linear Park has 2 very high, 15' fishing piers and a 2000' sidewalk along the C-16 canal. ADA picnic shelters; Rr. Dawn-dusk (S side of C-16 canal, between Seacrest Blvd & Railroad Ave, Boynton Bch)

Pioneer Canal Park has a 22' ADA pier and boat ramps (no dock) on the C-16 canal. Tennis; basketball; playground; picnic tables; Rr. Dawn-dusk (End of NW 13 Ave & NW 8 St, Boynton Bch)

■ **FITNESS TRAILS**

Parks: South County

Caloosa Park is a 65-acre county park with a 1.25-mi WC-fitness course with 20 stations. Ball fields; tennis; ADA picnic tables; grills; Rr (1300 SW 35 Ave, Boynton Bch; E of Congress Ave)

■ **GOLF**

West Palm Beach: Golf

Southwinds Golf Course has an adaptive golf cart (reserve 4 days ahead) for its 18-hole public course. You cannot ride the cart on the greens or sand traps. Before using the cart, you must be trained or assessed by the pro. Staff can help with transfers. Non-peak hours are advised. Beverage carts carry sandwiches; driving range; putting green; Rr at clubhouse & on course (19557 Lyons Rd; 561-483-1305)

■ **HANDCYLCES**

West Palm Beach: Handcycles

■ **MISC FUN**

Boynton Beach Senior Center offers a range of activities, from WC-exercise classes and movies to craft classes and parties. Rr. Wkdy 9-5 (1201 S US 1, Boynton Bch)

■ **MUSEUMS**

Boca Raton Museum of Art has an extensive permanent collection, traveling exhibits, an interactive children's gallery and outdoor sculpture garden. Special events include lectures, concerts and films. The affiliated Art Academy (801 Palmetto Park Rd) offers art classes throughout the year. Gift shop; snack cart; Rr. $/Wed evening free. Tue-Sat 10-5; Wed & Fri -9; Sun 12-5 (Mizner Park, 501 Plaza Real; 561-392-2500)

Children's Museum is an old, wood-frame, cracker house that features memorabilia from Victorian and Florida's pioneer days. All exhibits, including the antique toys, are hands-on for kids. Ramp in back; gift shop; CRr. $. Tue-Sat 12-4 (498 Crawford Blvd; 561-368-6875)

Cornell Museum, housed in a 1913 schoolhouse, showcases touring exhibits of regionally or internationally known artists and a collection of military miniatures. Rr. $. Tue-Sat 11-4; Nov-Apr Sun 1-4 (Old School Square, 51 N Swinton Ave, Delray Bch; at Atlantic Ave/SR 806; 561-243-3183)

International Museum of Cartoon Art houses over 160,000 works, including comic strips and books, editorial cartoons, animations, caricatures, illustrations, greeting cards and the original cels and sketches for Road Runner, Bugs Bunny, Donald Duck and Goofy. Create and animate your own cartoon. Family Day, with activities geared toward children, occurs one Sat each month; 45-min lectures on cartooning occur weekly. Cafe; gift shop; street parking; Rr. $. Tue-Sat 10-6; Sun 12-6 (Mizner Park, 201 Plaza Real; 561-391-2200)

Science Explorium teaches physical science concepts to families through interactive, permanent and changing exhibits and demonstrations. Outside is a mostly accessible, 3-story Science Playground that demonstrates scientific principles through activities and a tot lot for kids under 5. Both have rubberized surfaces and ramps. The water play feature is fun and refreshing. Call for schedule of workshops. ADA picnic shelters; Rr. Wkdy 9-6; wknd 10-5 (Sugar Sand Park Community Center, 300 S Military Trail; 561-347-3913)

■ PARKS

Dog Park is a 2-acre, fenced area where pets can run off leash. ADA picnic shelters; doggie bag dispensers. 9-dusk (Broken S Blvd at T-Rex site, just S of Yamato Rd)

Gumbo-Limbo Nature Center sits on the city's 67 acres of hardwood hammock, mangrove and beach. The center has nature exhibits and touch tanks. Outside, a ramped boardwalk takes you past saltwater aquariums and a mulch trail goes through a butterfly garden and woods. Call for schedule of ranger walks, talks and programs. ADA picnic tables; gift shop; Rr. $D. Mon-Sat 9-4; Sun 12-4 (1801 N SR A1A; across from N end of Red Reef Park; 561-338-1473)

James Rutherford Park has 45 acres of forest, mangrove and man-made canals where you can rent a canoe by the hour for the 3 mi of shaded canoe trails. At the launch site is a gently sloped, wide, wood ramp. Canoes are only rented at high tide because the canals are shallow; call 561-393-7845 for times. A 1.5-mi boardwalk roughly parallels the canoe trail. Picnic shelters; grills; playground on sand; Rr. 8-dusk (600 NE 24 St; behind 5 Ave Shops; 561-393-7815)

Kids Kingdom is a huge universal playground with low hand rails, ADA mulch and transfer stations. Rr. Dawn-dusk (200 E Ocean Ave, Boynton Bch; NE side of the 1913 Schoolhouse Museum)

Lake Ida Park (West) is a 189-acre county facility at the S end of a large lake with boat ramps, a fixed dock, and a 50' and a 105' fishing pier. Dog park; ADA playground; ADA picnic shelters; Rr (2929 Lake Ida Rd, Delray Bch; just E of I-95)

Loxahatchee National Wildlife Refuge preserves almost 150,000 acres of northern Everglades for wildlife, including the human species. The refuge has 2 entrances and a 57-mi perimeter canal.

At the Headquarters Entrance, the visitor center (days & hrs vary) offers nature exhibits, an auditorium (with workshops) and guided walks that focus on butterflies, birds, reptiles, or other wildlife. These walks take place along the 1-mi, mostly hard-packed levees or the short, looped, Cypress Swamp boardwalk. One of the levees has a 5' ADA observation deck from which you can get a sense of the varied habitats in the refuge. Boat ramps (no docks) offer access to the canal and you can fish off the gently sloped banks or the ADA fishing platform. A bike trail on a hard-packed levee runs 12 mi (1-way) with no shade and no facilities. See Canoeing. From the Hillsboro Entrance, you'll find boat ramps (no docks), fishing off the canal's gently sloped banks and information kiosks. Rr at visitor center. $. 6am-dusk (Hdqtr Entrance on US 441; 2mi S of Boynton Bch Blvd. Hillsboro Entrance on SR 827; off US 441, 12 mi S of Hdqtr Entrance; 561-734-8303)

Mangrove Nature Park is the city's 12-acre preserve along the Intracoastal with a 1.5-mi boardwalk and an observation deck with interpretive signage. Rr. Dawn-dusk (E end of 3 St, Boynton Bch)

South County Regional Park is an 856-acre sports center with some nature to enjoy. In addition to lighted ball fields, tennis and basketball courts, you can use a fitness trail on mulch and the Coconut Cove Water Park (see Water Parks). Check out the remote-control car track and airplane field. A 2-mi flat and sunny bike path winds through the park and along a lake. The Daggerwing Nature Center (Tue-Fri 1-4:30, Sat 9-4:30) sits in a wet forest with a 2000' boardwalk through butterfly gardens and past bat houses. The center offers workshops and guided walks. One playground is on an ADA surface; others are on sand. ADA picnic shelters; Rr. Dawn-dusk (11200 Park Access Rd; off Cain Blvd, between Yamato Rd & Glades Rd/ SR 808; 561-488-9953)

Veterans Park is 8 shady acres in downtown along the Intracoastal. Sidewalks lead throughout the park, including to the gazebo where concerts take place, and to the Intracoastal where you can fish from the seawall. The Rec Center offers classes in art and bridge as well as lawn bowling and shuffleboard; the patio has ADA picnic tables. Playground on mulch; Rr. Dawn-dusk (802 E Atlantic Ave/SR 806, Delray Bch; 561-243-7351)

■ **PERFORMING ARTS**

Caldwell Theater productions include premieres of new works, current Broadway and off-Broadway hits, revivals and musicals. WC seating on aisles in 1st row; Rr. Nov-May (Levitz Plaza, 7873 US 1; 561-241-7432)

Crest Theater offers Mon evening Broadway Cabarets with top NY performers and, on weekends, world-class professional theater, music and dance. The theater is a restored 1925 schoolhouse with WC seating in the aisles and in the rear (only 10 rows from the stage). Rr. Nov-Apr (Old School Square, 51 N Swinton Ave, Delray Bch; at Atlantic Ave/SR 806; 561-243-7922)

Delray Beach Playhouse is home to a community group that performs musicals, comedies and dramas. WC seating in front on aisles; Rr. Oct-Jul (950 NW Lakeshore Dr, Delray Bch; 561-272-1281)

Florida Stage is a professional group performing works by contemporary American playwrights. WC seating in center on aisles; Rr. Oct-Aug (262 S SR A1A, Manalapan; 561-585-3433; 800-514-3837)

■ **POOLS**

Water Parks: Coconut Cove

Aqua Crest Pool is a heated, 50-meter pool with a lift (fixed seat). Lifeguards can help with transfers. Aquacise classes; lap lanes; wading pool; roll-in showers in locker rooms; vending machines; Rr. $. Hrs vary (2503 Seacrest Blvd, Delray Bch; off Woolbright Rd; 561-278-7104)

Meadows Park Pool is a heated, 75' pool with a lift (fixed seat). Lifeguards can help with transfers. Lap lanes; fitness classes; roll-in showers in locker rooms; Rr. $. Hrs vary (1300 NW 8 St; behind school; 561-393-7851)

Pompey Park has a heated, 75' pool with a lift (fixed seat). Lifeguards can help with transfers. Call for open swim hours. Roll-in showers in locker rooms; Rr. $. 9-4:30 (1102 NW 2 Ave, Delray Bch; 561-243-7356)

Swim & Racquet Center has a heated/chilled, 75' city pool with a lift (fixed seat). Lifeguards cannot lift you but can operate the lift. Lap lanes; fitness classes; locker room (21618 St Andrews Blvd; 561-391-2072)

■ **SCUBA**

Bob Sheridan, who is HSA-certified, offers private lessons for dive certification in the Boca area. He can come to your place for the class work, arrange for pool sessions at a local public pool with a lift and schedule open dives through a local shop. (954-788-3483; 800-374-3792)

■ **SHOPPING**

Antiques: Delray Beach's historic downtown has antiques, galleries, outdoor cafes and the Ocean City Lumber Company complex of fine shops, dining and nightlife. (Atlantic Ave/SR 806; between NE 2 & Pineapple Grove Way; 561-276-2323)

Boutiques: Mizner Park is filled with shops of whimsy, galleries and restaurants (407 Plaza Real; 2 blks N of Palmetto Park Rd; 561-362-0606). Royal Palm Plaza offers some unique shops Mon-Sat (US 1; between Palmetto Park Rd & Camino Real).

Malls: Boynton Beach Mall (801 N Congress Ave, Boynton Bch; 561-736-7902); Plaza del Mar Shopping Center (S SR A1A & Ocean Ave, Manalapan); Town Center (6000 Glades Rd/SR 808; 561-368-6000)

Specialty Shops: Greenmarket features local produce, baked goods and plants. Oct-Apr Sat 8-1 (Royal Palm Plaza, SE 1 Ave)

■ SPECTATOR SPORTS
Polo: Royal Palm Polo Sport Club usually hosts 2 matches each Sun Jan-Apr. The major game is played at 3pm in a stadium with a steep ramp to WC seating; up another short ramp is a bar and Rr. For the 1pm game, you can park and watch from the side of the field. Sun brunch; snack bar; gift shop; parking on grass; Rr, in restaurant. $ (18000 Jog Rd; just N of Clint Moore Rd; 561-994-1876)

■ TENNIS
USTA sponsors WC-tennis clinics every Tue evening. Call ahead to borrow a sports WC and confirm the schedule. Call Bruce Karr 561-655-4930. Roll-in showers; Rr. Novice 5:30-6:30; advanced 6:30-8 (Patch Reef Park, 2000 NW 51 St; W of Military Trail; Tennis Center 561-997-0881)

■ TOURS
Historical Society offers brochures and a map with historical information on many buildings throughout the city that you can use for a self-guided driving tour. The back door is ramped. Tue-Fri 10-4 (71 N US 1; 561-395-6766)

■ WATER PARKS
Coconut Cove is a 5-acre water park that has a lift (fixed seat) to board an inner tube for a float down the 1000' Lazy River; staff can help with transfers. The water playground, with water guns and fountains, slopes gently from zero to an 18" depth. From this playground you can also access lap lanes during non-peak hours. The 4-story water slides have many steps. Snack bar with shaded picnic tables on deck; large umbrellas; inside roll-in showers; Rr $. Spring & fall wknd 10-5; summer 9:30-6 (South County Regional Park, 11200 Park Access Rd; off Cain Blvd, between Yamato Rd & Glades Rd/SR 80; 561-274-1140)

ACCOMMODATIONS

■ MOTELS
Hampton Inn has 9 ADA rooms, each with a king or 2 full beds (open frames), a refrigerator and coffeepot. One unit also has a sofa bed in a living room and a microwave. Bathrooms have raised toilets and roll-under sinks. Rooms 101, 106 and 122 have roll-in showers with hand-held sprayers and seats; others have tubs. Free brkfst; pool. $$-$$$ (1455 Yamato Rd; 561-988-0200)

Holiday Inn has 3 ADA rooms, each with a king bed (27" high/open frame), a refrigerator and coffeepot. Pool; full restaurant. $$-$$$ (8144 Glades Rd/SR 808; 561-482-7070)

Homestead Studio Suites has 3 ADA suites, each with a king or queen bed (open frame) and kitchenette. Bathrooms have roll-under sinks; room 108 has a roll-in shower with a hand-held sprayer and seat; others have tubs. Laundry. $-$$ (501 NW 77 St; 561-994-2599)

Radisson Bridge Resort has 5 ADA rooms, each with a king or 2 queen beds (open frames) and a coffeepot. Rooms 109 and 209 have roll-in showers; others have step-in showers. The beach is 1 block away. Pool; bar; entertainment; full restaurant. $$$ (999 E Camino Real; 561-368-9500)

Seagate Hotel has 4 ADA units: 3 1BR suites (#147, 159 & 160) and a 2BR suite (#148) with king beds (open frames), sofa beds and full kitchens. Bathrooms have raised toilets, roll-under sinks and roll-in showers with hand-held sprayers and seats; the 2BR unit also has a tub. Free brkfst; pool; bar; restaurant. $$-$$$ (400 S SR A1A, Delray Bch; 561-276-2421)

Towneplace Suites has 8 1BR and 2BR ADA suites, with 1 queen bed in each bedroom (open frame), a queen sofa bed and full kitchen. Bathrooms have roll-under sinks; room 101 has a roll-in shower with a seat; others have tubs. Pool; laundry. $$-$$$ (5110 NW 8 Ave; 561-994-7232)

FORT LAUDERDALE

Coconut Creek, Coral Springs, Dania, Davie, Deerfield Beach, Hallandale, Hollywood, Lauderdale-by-the-Sea, Miccosukee, Oakland Park, Plantation, Pembroke Pines, Pompano Beach, Sunrise, Tamarac

Once notorious for spring break, Ft Lauderdale has become a sophisticated family vacation spot with a plethora of accessible fun. Most beaches loan beach wheelchairs and 12 public pools have lifts. In the midst of urban growth, Broward County has a wonderful park system, from woodsy nature preserves to aquatic play lands, a few with beach wheelchairs. Explore the waterways via water taxi, tour boat or snorkel and scuba trips. Explore the city by trolley or on numerous bike trails. Not far from town are several entrees to the culture of the Seminole Indians who own a huge reservation inland. Check out the stables that host horseback riding for folks with physical challenges. Two motels in town offer all-terrain wheelchairs for the beach and pools with lifts. And, you can rent a lift-equipped RV! SR A1A is also known as Seabreeze Boulevard and Ocean Drive.

Tourist Info

Visitor Bureau: 1850 Eller Dr, #303, 33316; 954-765-4466; 800-227-8669/356-1662
Hotlines: Events 954-357-5700; Parks & Rec: 954-761-5363; Cultural Affairs: 954-357-5700/800-249-2787
Web sites: www.sunny.org; www.greatlocations.com; www.fortlauderdalebeach.com

Transportation

Tours: Lolly the Trolley
Broward County Transportation Authority has lift-equipped buses throughout the county. 5:30am-11pm (954-357-8400)
Broward County Para-Transit has curb-to-curb service throughout the county for those unable to use public buses. You must pre-qualify (if you have qualified elsewhere, just show your verification) and make 24-hr advance reservations. Wkdy 6:30am-12:30am; Sat -10pm; Sun -8pm (954-357-6794)
Super Shuttle is a lift-equipped van that runs from the Miami Airport, Port Everglades or the Port of Miami to any location in Dade, Broward or Monroe Counties. Reserve 5 days in advance. (305-871-2000; 954-764-1700)
Tri-Rail Commuter Trains, all equipped for WCs, run along the coast from the Miami Airport to West Palm Beach. With 48-hr advance notice, staff can arrange for accessible courtesy buses from some stops to your destination. 5am-11pm; wknd hrs limited (305-836-0986; 800-874-7240)
Water Taxi services the waterways of Ft Lauderdale and has an accessible boat called the Mega Taxi. From the dock at 651 SR A1A, you can get to particular destinations (marinas, waterfront accommodations or restaurants) or simply cruise the waterways. Depending on tides, you may be able to roll aboard, but staff can lift your WC on and off the boat as needed. 10am-wee hrs (954-467-6677)
Yellow Cab has lift-equipped vans. 24-hr advance reservations (954-565-2800)

WC Resources

Shopping: Flea Markets: Swap Shop
Center for Independent Living can provide helpful information and referrals and also loans WCs and adaptive equipment. (8857 W McNab Rd, Tamarac; 954-722-

6400; 888-722-6400)

Mobility Express rents and repairs electric scooters, and manual and electric WCs. (411 W Hallandale Bch Blvd, Hallandale; 954-457-7433; 888-788-7433)

ACTIVITIES

■ ATTRACTIONS

Billie Swamp Safari is a tourist-tinted window into the Seminole Tribe. An *authentic* village has a cafe with traditional Seminole fare, a souvenir shop, reptile show, petting zoo and cages of predatory birds and Florida panthers. Try the rollicking, narrated, swamp-buggy tour into Seminole lands where you may spot deer, water buffalo, bison, wild hogs, eagles and alligators. Staff can help you up a ramp to the elevated safari vehicle with room for a WC with good brakes. The Cypress Dome Boardwalk runs 1 mi in a U-shape where you can view otters and other wildlife; you may drive to and park near the boardwalk behind the chickee huts. The airboat rides are inaccessible. Call for schedule of activities. Rr. $/rides. 9-6 (Big Cypress Seminole Reservation; from I-75 Miccosukee exit 254, 20 mi W of the toll booth on Alligator Alley/I-75, go N 22 mi on CR 833 to W Boundary Rd; 863-983-6101; 800-949-6101)

Buehler Planetarium features a variety of shows including some for children. After evening shows, you can stargaze through telescopes from your WC. Weekday programs are generally for schools, but if space permits, the public is welcome. Call for schedule, usually Wed, Fri-Sun. Rr. $ (Broward County College Campus, 3501 SW Davie Rd, Davie; 1 mi S of I-595; 954-475-6680)

Butterfly World has sidewalks through 3 acres of screened aviary gardens and a tropical rainforest with thousands of fluttering butterflies. Some gardens are also home to hummingbirds, lorikeets and extraordinary plants. The Laboratory displays butterflies in each life stage and the Insectarium has a collection of truly incredible bugs. At the Garden Center learn how to attract butterflies to your own garden. Seminars on the 2nd Sat by reservation; WC rentals; gift & garden shops; outdoor cafe; Rr. $. Mon-Sat 9-5; Sun 1-5 (Tradewinds Park, 3600 W Sample Rd/SR 834, Coconut Creek; just W of SR 91; 954-977-4400)

Flamingo Gardens includes 60 acres of gardens that showcase rare, exotic and native plants and wildlife of the Everglades. Attractions range from a xeriscaped garden and an otter habitat to an orchid display and a huge aviary with wading birds. Wildlife Encounter shows, at 12:30, 1:30 and 2:30, feature native wildlife, such as birds of prey and reptiles. Paved paths, with some tree roots, run throughout the park. You must transfer onto a bench seat about WC height to enjoy the 30-min, narrated tram rides. Loaner WCs; gift & garden shops; snack bar; Rr. $. 9:30-5:30; Jun-Sep closed Mon (3750 Flamingo Rd, Davie; 2.5 mi S of I-595; 954-473-2955)

Native Village is 2-acre wildlife park with plenty of alligators, Florida panthers, bobcats and more. Paved paths or boardwalks take you through most of the park; staff can help you on the few gravel paths. Tour a replica of a traditional Seminole village. Enjoy gator shows, gator wrestling, petting baby gators (with taped mouths!) and educational shows with venomous snakes. Gift shop of Seminole arts & crafts; vending machines. $. 10-5 Tue-Sun (3551 N US 441, Hollywood; 954-961-4519)

Sawgrass Park is a private, 17.5-acre, former fish camp with ongoing tours through a replica of an 18th century Seminole village along hard-packed dirt paths. Check out the gator and birds of prey shows. From a floating dock, staff can help you (in your WC or from your

WC) aboard an airboat for a 30-min narrated tour on the ecology and history of the Everglades. Private 1-hr tours (for up to 6 passengers) use an airboat that requires some mobility to get from your WC onto the bench seat. Be aware, no seatbelts are available. Staff can also help lift you into the johnboats that are rented for fishing along the Everglades. Bait shop; fishing licenses; gift shop; snack bar; picnic tables. $. 9-5 (5400 US 27 N; 2 mi N of I-75; 954-389-0202; 800-457-0788)

Stranahan House, built in 1901, was owned by Ft Lauderdale's founding family. This restored home is ramped on the W side to the 1st floor and can be viewed on hourly, 45-min tours. $. Wed-Sat 10-3; Sun 1-3 (335 SE 6 Ave; 954-524-4736)

■ BASEBALL

Challenger Baseball League is a countywide Little League for kids (age 5-18) with disabilities. Rules are changed to accommodate players. Drop-ins are welcome. Games Mar-Jun Sun afternoon (Call Debbie Hibshman 954-345-9329)

■ BEACHES

Parks: CB Smith, John Lloyd, Snyder, TY, Quiet Waters. Motels: Sheraton Yankee Clipper/Yankee Trader

*Deerfield Beach offers good shelling and loans a beach WC (fixed arms) at lifeguard tower #3 (behind Howard Johnson's) from 9-5. A sidewalk leads from parking to just behind the tower. Lifeguards can help you transfer and push you to your desired spot on the beach. See Fishing Piers. Concession stands; rental umbrellas; Rr. 24 hrs (Hillsboro Blvd/SR 810 & SE 21 Ave, Deerfield Bch; 954-480-4412)

*Ft Lauderdale Beach is 3 mi long and, from 10-4, loans a beach WC (removable arms) at lifeguard stand #2 out on the sand (near the parking lot at Sebastian St). Just S, at Castillo St, is a ramp to the beach and outdoor showers. (SR A1A; 954-828-4595)

*Hollywood has a 5-mi beach along the Atlantic. The Michigan St lifeguard station (1 block S of the municipal band shell) loans beach WCs (fixed arms; umbrellas) from 9-5. Snack bar; Rr. At Garfield St (and Surf Rd), a ramp leads from parking past the midpoint of the beach where you'll find ADA picnic tables. See Bike Trails: Broadwalk. Restaurant; Rr. Winter 9-5; summer -6 (SR A1A; 954-921-3460)

*Pompano Beach extends 3 mi and loans beach WCs (fixed arms; umbrellas; trays) at the main lifeguard station from 9-4:30. This city beach has a huge swim area on the Atlantic, with lifeguards 9-4:45. A sidewalk leads from parking onto the beach halfway to the water's edge. See Fishing Piers. ADA playground; outdoor showers; ADA picnic shelters; grills; snack bar; restaurant; beach shops; Rr. Dawn-dusk (10 N Pompano Bch Blvd/SR A1A, Pompano Bch; 954-786-4005)

■ BIKE TRAILS

Parks: CB Smith, Markham, Snyder, Tradewinds, Tree Tops, TY

Broadwalk is a 2.5-mi, 27' wide, paved walkway, along Hollywood Beach. Heading N, Broadwalk passes residential areas, shops, restaurants and ends at N Beach Park; see Parks. (Georgia St-Simms St, Hollywood)

Pompano Bike Trail is a flat, 4.5-mi paved path around a small airport (Pompano Airpark) and golf course. This popular, well-maintained trail has little shade, but there is a water fountain behind the fire station on SW 10 St. (Park at the Pompano Bch Golf Course, 1101 N US 1 or in Fashion Square Mall, Copans Rd & US 1, Pompano Bch)

Riverwalk is a 1-mi (and growing!) promenade along the New River in downtown linking attractions, shops, restaurants and nightspots. Along the way are fun novelties, such as *whisper dishes* that amplify sounds from 25' away. Call for the schedule of special events. (SW 7 Ave-SW 2 Ave; 954-468-1541)

■ BOAT RAMPS

Parks: John Lloyd, Markham, West Lake

Everglades Holiday Park, a private park in the Everglades Conservation Area, has a boat ramp and floating dock on a 25-mi canal to the Miami Canal (another 10 mi long). WC folks can use the service road (not open to the public) to the general store with bait shop, deli, gift shop, picnic tables and Rr. $. 9-5 (21940 Griffith Rd; 954-434-8111; 800-226-2244)

■ **BOAT RENTALS**
Attractions: Sawgrass Park
Club Nautico at Bahia Mar rents a 20' bow rider and a 24' center console for half/full days. Staff can help lift you aboard in your WC from the floating dock. (801 SR A1A; 954-779-3866)
Club Nautico at Cove Marina rents a 20' bow rider, 21' and 25' center consoles and a 23' cuddy cabin for half/full days. Staff can usually help lift you aboard in your WC from the fixed dock; call beforehand because often only 1 person is onsite and, at low tide, the drop can be as much as 3'. (1755 SE 3 Ct, Deerfield Bch; 954-421-4628)
Club Nautico at Pier 66 rents ski boats, bow riders, center consoles and speedboats, 19'-33', for half/full days. Staff can help lift you aboard in your WC from the floating dock. (2301 SE 17 St; 954-523-0033)
Pompano Boat Rental rents deck boats (24" entry) for up to 12 people on the Intracoastal. Staff can help lift you aboard in your WC from the floating dock. 1-hr minimum; bait shop; restaurants; Rr. 9-5:30 (101 N Riverside Dr, Pompano Bch; 954-943-7260)

■ **BOAT TOURS**
Transportation: Water Taxi. Attractions: Sawgrass. Parks: West Lake
Carrie B Sightseeing Tours are 90-min narrated tours on a 130' riverboat along the New River and Intracoastal. Staff is happy to help you roll aboard by gangway to the 1st level where you can sit inside the AC cabin or outside on the front deck. While learning Ft Lauderdale's history, check out the yachts and mansions of the rich and famous along Millionaires' Row and the cruise ships docked in Port Everglades. Snack bar. 11, 1 & 3 (Las Olas Blvd & SE 5 Ave; 954-768-9920)
Glass-Bottom Boat Tours spend 2 hrs gliding over spectacular coral reefs. Snorkelers also take this trip and you can watch them hand-feed colorful tropical fish through the glass bottom. Roll aboard the 60' boat from the floating dock onto the dive platform where staff can help you up a step onto the boat deck. Rr onboard. Tue-Sat 9:30am; Sun 2pm (515 SR A1A; 954-467-6030; 800-776-3483)
Jungle Queen Riverboat offers an entertaining, 3-hr sightseeing and a 4-hr dinner cruise along the New River. Roll aboard the 1st deck. The nightly dinner cruise stops at a private island (with sidewalks and ADA picnic tables) for a comedy show and BBQ ribs and shrimp. On the return trip, enjoy a sing-a-long. A full-day Miami Bayside Cruise allows you to get off to browse Bayside's shops, choose your restaurants and see the homes along Millionaires' Row. Rr onboard & at private island. Sightseeing cruise 10 & 2; dinner cruise 7pm (Bahia Mar Basin, 801 SR A1A; 954-462-5596)

■ **BOWLING**
Don Carter's Lanes hosts a league, sponsored by the Paralyzed Veterans, with teams of WC and able-bodied bowlers. Call George Snyder, of the National WC Bowling Association, at 954-491-2886. Bowling ball ramps; game room; billiards; restaurant; Rr. Thu 2:45 (8501 N University Dr, Tamarac; 954-722-2700)
Sawgrass Lanes has ramped lanes and bowling ball ramps. Dynamites Bowling runs Feb-May, Sat 3-5, for kids age 6-18 with mental and physical disabilities; call Christine Bowen 954-236-0654. Billiard room; game room; snack bar; nursery; Rr. Hrs vary (1391 NW 136 Ave, Sunrise; 954-846-8088)

■ **CANOEING/KAYAKING**
Parks: John Lloyd, Markham, Quiet

Waters, Snyder, Tradewinds, Tree Tops, West Lake

■ **CASINOS**

Hollywood Seminole Gaming offers bingo (11:15-10:45), video pull-down machines and 48 tables of poker. Rr. 24 hrs (4150 N SR 7/US 441, Hollywood; 954-961-3220; 800-323-5452)

Sun Cruz Casino features 4-hr cruises with Las Vegas-style gaming aboard a 165' ship. The boarding ramp is somewhat steep but staff can help and an elevator goes to all 3 decks. Enjoy live entertainment, a buffet and a la carte menu, free cocktails and appetizers. Valet parking for disabled; Rr. Wkdy 11am; wknd noon; daily 7:30pm (6024 N SR A1A, Hollywood; 954-929-3880; 800-474-3423)

■ **DINNER THEATER**

Mai-Kai offers a South Seas show and dinner of Asian and/or American fare. Certain rooms offer dinner only; if seats are available, you can buy tickets for the show without dinner. The building, with thatched roof and tiki torches, is ramped with WC seating throughout. CRr. Dinner & show times vary (3599 N US 1; 954-563-3272)

■ **DISC GOLF**

Parks: Tradewinds

■ **FISHING CHARTERS**

Capt Doug Lillard specializes in backcountry fishing with a fly rod or light tackle in Biscayne Bay, the Everglades or local freshwater lakes. He can help you board the 18' flats boat at a dock that best suits your needs. Night tarpon trips and day trips for 2 run half/full day. (954-894-9865)

Fishing Headquarters has a 50' boat for half/full-day offshore trips with room for 1 WC and 5 able-bodied anglers. Staff can pair you up with another party to share costs. Crew can lift you aboard in your WC from the fixed dock. (301 SR A1A; 954-527-3460)

Reel Blues can take up to 6 anglers on a 46' boat for half/full days, 5 mi offshore, to troll for sport fish. With advance notice, extra staff can lift you

aboard in your WC from the floating dock. (Bahia Mar Marina, 801 SR A1A S; 954-523-6607)

■ **FISHING-PARTY BOATS**

Fishing Headquarters offers 4-hr, drift trips over reefs 1 mi out. Because of the tides, usually crew must lift you aboard onto a boat seat and then back into your WC. Coolers & ice available; BYO food/drinks. 8:30am, 1:30pm & 7:30pm (301 SR A1A; 954-527-3460)

Helen S Drift Fishing offers 4 1/2-hr drift trips over reefs 1.5 mi offshore. You can roll aboard in your WC. The boat can handle only 3 WC anglers per trip. Reserve at least a day ahead. Lip to AC cabin; cooler & ice available; soda sold onboard; restaurants & Rr at marina. 8am, 1pm & 7pm (Sand Harbor Marina, 101 N Riverside Dr, Pompano Bch; 954-941-3209)

Sea Legs III offers 4 1/2-hr drift trips over reefs 1 mi out. Crew can lift you aboard in your WC. Beer & soda sold onboard; snacks sold at dock, except Mon; gravel parking lot. 8, 1:30 & 7pm (Sea Legs Marina, 5400 N SR A1A, Hollywood; 954-923-2109)

■ **FISHING PIERS**

Parks: CB Smith, Hollywood North Beach, John Lloyd, Tree Tops, TY, West Lake

Anglin's Fishing Pier is a lighted, 900' wood pier on the Atlantic. Restaurant (7-4); bait shop. $/WC free. 24 hrs (4334 E Tradewinds Ave, Lauderdale-by-the-Sea; 954-491-9403)

Dania Pier is a lighted 920' pier on the ocean with a wood walkway. Snack bar; bait shop; CRr. $. 24 hrs (300 N Beach Rd, Dania; 954-927-0640)

Deerfield Fishing Pier is a lighted, 700' cement pier on the ocean. Restaurant (7-4); bait shop; Rr. $. 24 hrs (200 NE 21 Ave, Deerfield Bch; 954-426-9206)

Fisherman's Wharf is a lighted, 1080' cement pier on the ocean. Restaurant; bait shop; Rr. $. 24 hrs (222 Pompano Beach Blvd, Pompano Bch; 954-943-1488)

■ **FITNESS TRAILS**

Parks: Plantation Heritage

Veterans Park is a 5-acre city park with a WC-exercise course with stations. ADA picnic table. Dawn-dusk (1776 Lauderdale W Dr, Plantation)

■ **HORSEBACK RIDING**

Children's Therapy Services offers hippotherapy for disabled kids (up to age 18) with a prescription. A therapist teaches the 30-min classes that include stretching, balance and focus. Staff lifts riders onto the horses. Call Kathleen Cullen 954-341-0090 x43. Rr. Fri 2-6; Sat 8-12 (Sheridan Oaks North Stables, 5775 SW 130 Ave, Davie; 954-680-5844. Mill Pond Farms, Vinkemulder Rd, Coconut Creek; 954-973-1482)

Horses for the Handicapped of South Florida offers 10-wk riding sessions Sep-May for novice and experienced riders with disabilities. You must complete an application to be added to the waiting list. A summer camp is also offered. Rr (Tradewinds Park, 3600 Sample Rd/SR 834, Coconut Creek; 954-974-2007)

Kiwanis Horses & Handicapped offers a recreational and therapeutic riding program for disabled persons over age 4. Two assistants work with each rider and help with boarding from a mounting ramp. Prior to entering the program, you must fill out an application, have a medical release and be evaluated by staff. Call Patti (wkdy) 954-792-4205. Sep-May Sat 8-1 (Myrland Stables, 5550 SW 73 Ave, Davie; 954-454-9933)

Murray-Paris Rehabilitative Services has 6-wk hippotherapy programs Sep-May for kids (age 5-18). Staff lifts riders onto the horses and walks beside them as a therapist leads the 30-min sessions; special equipment is available. You must have a prescription and complete an application; there may be a waiting list. Call 954-476-4554. Rr. Classes Wed-Thu 3-7 (Appy Pines Stables, 5790 Melaleuca Rd; 954-680-8069)

■ **MUSEUMS**

Ah-Tah-Thi-Ki Museum celebrates the cultural past of the Seminole Tribe, who never surrendered to the US government. A 5-screen orientation theater shows a 17-min film and a folklore theater shows 5-min, animated, Seminole legends. Displays portray Indian life in the 1800's and user-friendly computers offer detailed information. A 1-mi boardwalk leads through a 60-acre cypress dome, past ceremonial grounds, to a village (with grass paths) and an outdoor amphitheater where story-telling occurs. Gift shop; Rr. $. Tue-Sun 9-5 (Big Cypress Seminole Reservation; from I-75 Miccosukee exit 254, 20 mi W of the Alligator Alley/I-75 toll booth, go N 17 mi on CR 833 to West Boundary Rd; 863-902-1113)

Art & Culture Center features rotating exhibits, an art reference library, outdoor sculpture garden and art classes. Classical and jazz concerts are held some weekends. Gift shop; Rr. $. Tue-Sat 10-4; Sun 1-4 (1650 Harrison St, Hollywood; 954-921-3274)

Bonnet House is a 1920, 35-acre, beachfront estate, formerly the winter home of artists Frederic and Evelyn Bartlett. The home is open for 1-hr guided tours of the Bartletts' own work, their collections and the exquisite decorative detailing throughout. Only the ground floor is open to the public. To enjoy a self-guided tour through the spectacular grounds, you must navigate paths of mulch, crushed shell or natural and somewhat uneven terrain. The long driveway to the house is crushed shell. You can be dropped off at the house but your car must be parked in the lot at the entrance. Or, at the gift shop by the entrance, transfer to a golf cart and staff can take you to the house and/or on a tour of the grounds. Check out the range of lecture and music series, garden walks with horticulturists and art classes. Gravel parking lot; Rr. $. Wed-Fri 10-2; wknd 12-3 (900 N Birch Rd; 2 blks S of E Sunrise Blvd/SR 838; 954-563-5393)

Ft Lauderdale Historical Society Museum, located in an old downtown hotel where only the ground floor is accessible, covers the city's history through artifacts, photographs, furnishings and a model of old Ft Lauderdale. There's also an exhibit on movie production. Gift shop; Rr. $. Tue-Fri & Sun 12-5; Sat 10-5 (231 SW 2 Ave; 2 blks E of Museum of Discovery & Science; 954-463-4431)

IGFA Fishing Hall of Fame & Museum is an enormous facility celebrating fishing. Seven interactive galleries have displays, from mounts of world-record sport fish to antique, historic and current equipment. You can find the perfect place to hook a trophy catch via interactive computer, see footage of the world's most beautiful fishing spots or use a simulator to catch a marlin without getting wet. Kids love the Discovery Room where they can catch toy fish from a miniature boat and the marina where you can take pictures beside the world's largest broadbill swordfish. A boardwalk through a 4-acre wetland features learning stations. See Shopping: Specialty Shops. Gift shop; snack bar; Rr. $. 10-6 (300 Gulfstream Way, Dania; W of I-95 & S of Griffin Rd; 954-922-4212)

International Swimming Hall of Fame highlights the achievements of notable swimmers from Esther Williams to Greg Louganis. In the museum, recorded messages explain displays and a theater carries interesting videos. In another building is a gallery (wkdy 9-5) of aquatic art and a research library. See Pools. Gift shop; Rr. $. 9-7 (1 Hall of Fame Dr; just W of SR A1A; 954-462-6536)

Museum of Art features rotating exhibits and permanent art collections of 20th century America, the CoBrA (Copenhagen, Brussels and Amsterdam) movement and Africa, South Pacific and contemporary Cuba. Street parking; Rr. $. Tue-Sat 10-5; Fri - 8; Sun 12-5 (1 E Las Olas Blvd; downtown at Andrews Ave; 954-525-5500)

Museum of Discovery & Science is a learning center with plenty of themed interactive displays. Florida EcoScapes features a coral reef, shark tank and walk-in beehive. The Discovery Center has hands-on activities for kids such as wacky block building and a water play area. The Hammock Theater features anything from animal shows to science demonstrations. The 2nd floor includes Gizmo City with machines that enable you to play virtual volleyball, use a pulley to lift a car engine and play computer games. Space Base features 2 rides that require transfers from your WC into seats: Vista Voyager to the moon, a motion simulator, and the MMU or, Manned Maneuvering Unit, from which you repair a remote satellite. No Place Like Home has a ramp onto the back patio so you can explore a house that reveals its infrastructure and the inner workings of home appliances. The Sound Exhibit includes sound and light games, some of which are inaccessible. Choose Health examines the human body and the impact of lifestyle choices. The WC entrance to the IMAX Theater is on the 2nd floor; call for the schedule of these riveting, 5-story, 3D movies. Elevator; gift shop; snack bar; Rr. $. Mon-Sat 10-5, Sun 12-6 (401 SW 2 St; downtown between SW 4 Ave & Brook Ave; 954-467-6637)

Okalee Indian Village & Museum is a place to learn about the original Florida natives. The Okalee Museum covers current art and history of Seminole patchwork and genre paintings. A video explores tribal traditions. At the village, with sidewalks throughout, you can view demonstrations of cooking and crafts such as making dolls. Watch alligator wrestling and a snake show. The snack bar sells traditional foods such as fry bread and pumpkin bread. The Arts & Crafts Gift Shop has authentic handmade items. Guided tours; Rr. $. Tue-Sun 9-5 (Stirling Rd/SR 848 & US 441, Hollywood; 954-792-0745)

South Florida Museum of Natural History, formerly the Graves Museum, is a huge exhibition hall with lifelike dinosaurs, fossils, minerals and crystals, including a 6000-lb chunk of quartz. Marvel at antiquities from the Americas, Near East, ancient Egypt, historic Florida and beneath the sea. Gift shop; Rr. $. Tue-Fri 10-4; Sat -6; Sun noon-6 (481 S US 1, Dania; between Stirling Rd/ SR 848 & Sheridan St; 954-925-7770)

Young at Art Children's Museum offers hands-on art and multicultural activities in rotating and permanent displays. In the Global Village, you can take part in an archeological dig in Israel, fax a message to the Western Wall, explore a Mayan pyramid and a Native American pueblo, or learn to write your name in Japanese. Earthworks explores solid waste management, from recycling and minimizing to burning waste and using landfills. Gift shop; vending machines; Rr. $. Mon-Sat 10-5; Sun 12-5 (11584 SR 84, Davie; 954-424-0085)

■ **PARI-MUTUELS**

Dania Jai Alai has live jai alai, with WC seating in the rear of each section, and simulcasts for jai alai, harness and thoroughbred racing. Cafeteria; clubhouse dining (by reservation); Rr. $. Tue-Sat 12 & 7:15; Sun 1 (301 E Dania Beach Blvd, Dania; 4 blks E of US 1; 954-927-2841)

Gulfstream Park Horse Racing features live racing and full-card simulcasts Jan-Apr. The best WC seating is on the 1st level and in the Clubhouse apron. In the outdoor Terrace Restaurant and in the Royal Palm Restaurant, WC seating is on the 1st level. ADA betting windows; Rr. $. Wed-Mon races 1-5; simulcasts - mdnt (901 S US 1, Hallandale; S of Hallandale Bch Blvd/SR 858; 954-454-7000; 800-771-8873)

Hollywood Greyhound Dog Track offers live racing Dec-May and simulcasts year round. WC seating on all levels; ADA betting windows; free admission with dining reservations; poker room; billiard room; Rr. $. Races nightly 7:30; Tue, Thu & Sat 12:30. Simulcasts daily 12:30 (831 US 1, Hallandale; S of Moffett St/SR 824; 954-454-9400)

Pompano Park Racway features live harness racing Oct-Jul and year-round poker and simulcasts of thoroughbreds and jai alai. WC seating is throughout the grandstand and in the clubhouse box seats. Make reservations for the Top of the Park Restaurant where WC seating is on the top level with tabletop monitors and a view of the finish line. Playground; gift shop; Rr. $. Races Mon, Wed, Fri-Sat 7:30pm; simulcasts daily noon; poker 5:30pm (1800 SW 3 St, Pompano Bch; S of Atlantic Blvd/SR 814, E of Powerline Rd/SR 845; 954-972-2000)

■ **PARKS**

Boaters Park is a 6.5-acre, landscaped linear park, accessible only by private boat (under 30') from the Dania Cutoff Canal, just W of the Intracoastal. On the N side of the canal, at the W end of the park, #8 is a ramped, floating dock near ADA picnic tables, grills and Rr. Winter 8-6; summer 8-7:30 (W of Port Everglades, S of the Ft Lauderdale Airport; 954-985-1980)

*CB Smith Park is a 320-acre park with a beach WC (removable arms) for the beach on an 80-acre, man-made lake. The swim area is open and staffed with lifeguards Apr-Aug and on weekends Mar, Sep and Oct. The water slides are inaccessible. Sidewalks lead to the beach, ADA picnic shelters with grills and an ADA playground. You can fish off piers throughout the park and enjoy a 3.2-mi, paved bike trail. WC-tennis tournaments are held here; see WC Events. Special events are frequently held at Concert Green, an open grassy hill. See Campgrounds. Locker rooms. $/ wknd. Winter 8-6; summer 8-7:30 (900 N Flamingo Rd, Pembroke Pines; I-75 exit 9, E on Pines Blvd/SR 820 for 1 mi; 954-437-2650)

Deerfield Island Park is a 56-acre mangrove preserve that's become an important gopher tortoise habitat. Reach the island park by private boat or a free shuttle on a pontoon boat that is accessible at high tides (staff can time your trip accordingly). The shuttle departs from a floating dock in Sullivan Park, at the end of Riverview Rd; call for reservations and directions (954-360-1320). From the island marina, a boardwalk leads to 2 ADA picnic areas and Rr. Across a sandy stretch, is a 1600' boardwalk through wetlands. The .5-mi Coquina Trail generally requires an all-terrain WC. Guided tours and other programs are available by reservation and for a fee. Wed-Sun 9-5 (1720 Deerfield Island Park; in Intracoastal at Hillsboro Canal; 954-360-1320)

Easterlin Park is a 47-acre oasis of dense cypress forest in an urban area. Nine acres of clearing in the interior offer a family respite. A sidewalk leads to lovely cove on a small lake where you can fish. The 1-mi Woodland Nature Trail has a rough natural terrain. See Campgrounds. ADA picnic shelter; ADA playground; Rr by picnic area. $/wknd. Winter 8-6; summer 8-7:30 (1000 NW 38 St, Oakland Park; I-95 exit 32, W 1 blk on Commercial Blvd/SR 870, S on Powerline Rd, then W; 954-938-0610)

Fern Forest Nature Center is set on 244 wooded acres. The center has rotating nature displays and an elevator to the top floor where frequent programs are offered. Pick up a self-guiding booklet to enjoy the .5-mi Cypress Creek Trail boardwalk through a hardwood hammock. Near the picnic area, is a paved path with interpretative signs by particularly aromatic plants. The Prairie Overlook Trail is inaccessible. Various programs, from concerts with audience participation to storytelling, are held in the covered amphitheater; call for schedule. ADA picnic shelter; Rr at center. 8-6 (201 Lyons Rd S, Coconut Creek; 954-970-0150)

Hollywood North Beach Park occupies 56 acres between the Atlantic and Intracoastal and is next to Hollywood's public beach with a beach WC; see Beaches. An elevated concession stand, with ADA tables and Rr, overlooks the beach and ocean. On the Intracoastal side, you'll find ADA picnic shelters, Rr and a 1600' boardwalk from which you can fish. Broadwalk passes the park; see Bike Trails. $/parking. Winter 8-6; summer -7:30 (3501 N SR A1A, Hollywood; 954-926-2444)

John Lloyd Beach State Park is a 280-acre beach with boardwalks from parking to a canoe concession, marina, picnic area and onto the beach. With advance notice, rangers are happy to escort your vehicle to sites in the park. The canoe launch is a ramp into the 1.5-mi Whiskey Creek where you can paddle through mangrove and return to the put-in. Staff can help with transfers that are easiest at high tides; call to schedule your rental accordingly (954-923-6711). The marina has a boat ramp into the Intracoastal and a 300' fixed dock where you can fish. At the N end of the park near Port Everglades Inlet, a rock jetty (with an asphalt surface) is another good fishing spot. ADA picnic tables; grills; Rr at beach & marina. $. 8-dusk (6503 N SR A1A, Dania; 954-923-2833)

Markham Park is a 666-acre park with a diverse range of accessible fun. A large pool with a lift (fixed seat) is open all summer and weekends in spring and fall; lifeguards can help with transfers; locker rooms have Rr. You can fish from the shores of several, interlocking, man-made lakes, although some are designated for jet skiing or water skiing. Next to the canoe/boat rental dock is a narrow sandy stretch where you can transfer to a canoe; or you may be able to transfer from the fixed dock into a rowboat for touring the chain of lakes. Park staff cannot help with transfers. The boat ramp has a fixed dock; the launch leads to the New River and the L-35A canal and closes at dusk. Try the 150' and 100-meter rifle/pistol ranges and skeet field. The 1-mi automated clays course runs through the woods and is not readily accessible. The range clubhouse has a Rr and snack bar open during special events. The Fox Observatory offers presentations Sat at dusk (outside on a paved pad, if weather permits; otherwise inside the ramped building). You can learn to use computers to explore the universe and, if you can stand, star gaze through portable telescopes. The model airplane field is an open area with a 500' paved runway. The rigorous mountain bike trail and the wood-chip nature trails are inaccessible for most WCs but the paved roads throughout the park offer good cycling. See Campgrounds. ADA picnic shelters; grills; ADA playground; bike rentals; camps; tennis; Rr. $/wknd (16001 W SR 84, Sunrise; I-595 exit 1, W on SR 84; 954-389-2000)

Plantation Heritage Park is a lovely, passive 90-acre place to enjoy a 1.25-mi paved trail with universal fitness stations. A sidewalk leads to a historic gazebo by a duck pond with a waterfall. You can fish off the grassy banks of a 7-acre lake. The marina, where paddleboats are rented, has a short, steep ramp to the docks. The Anne Kolb Trail through 3 acres of nature is surfaced with wood chips. ADA picnic shelters; grills; ADA playground; Rr. $/wknd. Winter 8-6; summer 8-7:30 (1100 S Fig Tree Ln, Plantation; 954-791-1025)

*Quiet Waters Park is a misnomer for this 430-acre aquatic park! Sidewalks lead throughout the park, including to a water playground. You can borrow a beach WC (removable arms) to enjoy the beach around a freshwater swim lagoon that is staffed by lifeguards and open all summer (weekends in spring and fall). You can fish from the grassy shores of man-made lakes or board a rental canoe or solo kayak from the flat sandy shore. One lake is designated for cable water skiing and wake boarding. Locker rooms; ADA playground; ADA picnic shelters; grills; snack bars; Rr. See Campgrounds. $/wknd. Winter 8:30-6; summer 8-7:30 (401 S Powerline Rd, Deerfield Bch; from I-95, go W on Hillsboro Blvd 2.8 mi, then S; 954-360-1315)

Secret Woods Nature Center sits on 56 acres along the New River. This active center offers many varied programs from environmental talks and self-improvement classes to concerts and camps for kids. Off the parking lot is a Butterfly Garden where specially selected plants attract droves of butterflies. The New River Trail is a 3200' boardwalk through hammock and wetlands. The outdoor amphitheater has WC seating on the first level. Call for schedule. 8-6 (2701 W SR 84, Dania; 954-791-1030)

Snyder Park has 93 acres for family fun. The former rock quarry is open for swimming and staffed by lifeguards daily in summer and weekends at other times. From parking, a sidewalk crosses the man-made beach and ramps to the water's edge. Staff can help with transfers into the water and into a paddleboat or canoe (for rent 12-5 on weekends and daily in summer). ADA picnic shelter #16 has a grill and water. Nearby is a short boardwalk through wetlands and forest. Fish for bass off the flat grassy banks of the quarry and enjoy up to 3 mi of cycling on the paved roads through this woodsy park. For an extra fee, try the monthly nature programs (2nd Sat 10-12) and guided nature tours. ADA playground at beach; Rr. $. Wkdy 9-5; wknd -closing varies (3299 SW 4 Ave; 954-468-1586)

Tradewinds Park is a 600-acre park with some unusual opportunities. You can fish from the flat shores of several lakes. The shore by the boat rental area is flat and hard-packed for transfers from a WC to a rental canoe or paddleboat. Bring a Frisbee to play the 18-hole disc golf course on turf and natural terrain. The 1-mi Cypress Boardwalk offers a shady roll. Two paved bike paths (a 2-mi trail on the N side of the park and a 1-mi trail on the S) offer little shade but nearby Rr have ADA water fountains. The 3rd weekend of each month, you can ride a model steam train that requires a transfer onto a bench seat about 2.5' high and chugs around a 3-mi track. The same weekend features 1-hr guided tours through an old time barn, farmhouse and barnyard with animals. The ramped farmhouse has only 1 floor but some rooms are tight for a WC; the outside areas are hard packed. Frequently, you can watch softball and flag football games, or try out the Home Run Batting Cages. At the riding stable, on weekends, pony rides are offered for kids (over 51" tall). Kids can use a ramp to board the ponies; parents lead. See Horseback Riding. The Holiday Fantasy of Lights (mid Nov-Jan 1) starts with 5-K Runs and a 5-K Walk through roads lighted by candles. Under Attractions, see Butterfly Gardens. Snack bar on wknd; ADA picnic shelters; Rr. $/wknd. Winter 8-6; summer 8-7:30 (3600 Sample Rd, Coconut Creek; 954-968-3880)

Tree Tops Park is a lovely, 356-acre, suburban park. From parking, a sidewalk leads to a 1000' boardwalk above a marsh. The 1-mi Marsh Trail is mostly paved (with a hard-packed stretch) and leads to a beautiful overlook of a 23-acre marsh. The 1.5-mi Ridge Trail and a 1-mi bike path are both paved. You can fish in a 17-acre lake from flat areas along the shore or from a fixed dock that can be used to board rental canoes and paddleboats. Nearby is a flat area on the shore where WC paddlers may prefer to transfer to a canoe. Call for schedule of naturalist programs and special events. ADA playground; snack bar at marina on wknd; ADA shelters; grills; Rr. $/wknd. Apr-Sep 8-7:30; Oct-Apr 8-6 (3900 SW 100 Ave, Davie; 954-370-3750)

*TY Park, or Topeekeegee Yugnee Park, is a 150-acre, oak-shaded park in an urban setting. You can borrow a beach WC (removable arms) for the beach around a man-made swim lagoon with lifeguards (summer 9-5; Apr-Jun and Sep weekends). The shallow waters in

Castaway Island's water playground are accessible for some awesome water play. A 2-mi paved trail leads from parking to the beach, around the lake and through ADA picnic areas. You can fish in the stocked lake from a small dock off a gazebo. Several steps lead to the marina that rents canoes, paddleboats and johnboats. Call for schedule of programs that range from foreign languages to karate. See Campgrounds. Outdoor showers at swim lagoon & Castaway Island; snack bar; bike rentals; Rr. $/wknd. Summer 6:30am-7:30pm; winter -6 (3300 N Park Rd, Hollywood; I-95 exit 21, W for .5 mi on Sheridan St, then N; 954-985-1980)

West Lake Park and the Anne Kolb Nature Center include more than 1500 acres of recreation and nature. *West Lake Park South*, the area S of Sheridan St, has a sidewalk to a marina where you can rent solo/tandem kayaks, canoes and johnboats. The marina's boat ramp has a fixed dock; staff cannot help lift you, but can take your boat to a nearby floating dock for easier boarding. Canoe trails meander through narrow mangrove canals to the open waters of the 1400-acre West Lake. Snack bar at marina; tennis; basketball courts; ADA picnic shelters with water/elec; grills; ADA playground; accessible water play area. On the N side of Sheridan St is *West Lake North*. The Anne Kolb Center has hands-on nature displays, a 3500-gal aquarium and a 10-min video on local ecology - a great orientation before you hit the trails that are composed of recycled plastic. Lake Observation Trail leads 1374' to a 5-level observation tower with an elevator. The short Mud Flats Trail meanders along mangroves ending at a gazebo on the lake. Another trail leads to a 783' fishing pier on the Intracoastal. You can also take 40-min guided tours of West Lake on a 42-passenger boat that has a raised platform for WC riders. You can roll aboard from the fixed dock beside the visitor center. Generally, tours leave hourly 10-4, but low tides can alter the schedule. Next to the center is an outdoor amphitheater (WC seating on the top row) that occasionally offers programs. Call for outdoor and indoor naturalist programs. On the E side of the Intracoastal (access it from SR A1A), the park has a lighted, 870' fishing pier (24 hrs). ADA picnic tables; Rr. $/wknd for West Lake South. Winter 8-6; summer -7:30 (Sheridan St; E of I-95 & US 1, before Intracoastal; 954-926-2480)

■ PERFORMING ARTS

Bailey Concert Hall hosts drama, dance and concerts, including the Miami City Ballet and the Florida Philharmonic. WC seating 1st row center; Rr. Oct-Jun (3501 SW Davie Rd, Davie; 954-475-6884)

Broward Center for the Performing Arts, in downtown, offers Broadway musicals, drama, dance and comedies. The Concert Association, Florida Philharmonic, Miami City Ballet, Florida Grand Opera and Symphony of the Americas perform here. WC seating behind front & rear orchestra sections & mezzanine level; garage parking with skywalk to upper orchestra lobby; CRr. Mon-Sat 10-6; Sun 12-5 (201 SW 5 Ave; at Himmarshee St; 954-462-0222)

Cocoa Village Playhouse is a small community theater for musicals and concerts Sep-May. WC seating left of front row; street parking (30 Brevard Ave, Cocoa; 321-636-5050)

Coral Springs City Centre features Broadway shows, jazz/pop, variety/vaudeville, comedy and children's programs. The Florida Philharmonic, Gold Coast Opera and Coral Springs Pop perform here. WC seating is behind the orchestra section with folding chairs for companions. Rr (2855 Coral Springs Dr, Coral Springs; 954-344-5990)

Ft Lauderdale Children's Theater has productions by children (age 3-18) for children. WC seating throughout; classes; summer camps; Rr. Oct-May (640 N Andrews Ave; just N of Sistrunk

Blvd NE; 727-763-6882)

Hollywood Playhouse, a professional theater, features Broadway and off-Broadway favorites, premieres and children's musicals. Fri at 10:30pm is Late-Night Improv. WC seating in 10th row; Rr. Sep-Jun (2640 Washington St, Hollywood; 954-922-0404)

Parker Playhouse offers a Broadway series and various community shows Sep-Apr (954-763-2444). Story Theater features touring companies in children's shows Oct-Mar (954-763-8813). WC seating midway (row N) on ground floor (707 NE 8 St)

Sunrise Musical Theater is a 4000-seat auditorium with concerts by big-name, 80-90's era, rock groups. Use the E entrance. WC seating mid-center & on right main level; Rr (5555 NW 95 Ave, Sunrise; at Commercial Blvd; 954-741-7300)

Theater Under the Stars is an open-air band shell with free 90-min music and dance performances. WC riders can remain on the sidewalk or pull up on the grass next to one of the benches. Mon-Wed 7:30 (Broadwalk, Johnson St & SR A1A, Hollywood; 954-921-3404)

■ POOLS

Parks: Markham. Motels: Sheraton Yankee Clipper/Yankee Trader

Aquatic Center, in Community Park, has a heated, 25-meter pool and a lift (fixed seat); lifeguards can help with transfers. Aqua therapy; aerobic classes. $. Hrs vary (820 N 18 Ave, Pompano Bch; 954-786-4128)

Civic Center Pool is a heated 50-meter pool with a lift (fixed seat); staff can help with transfers. The ramped wading pool has a gentle fountain under which you can roll. Adult lap swim wkdy 6:30-8:30am, wknd 8-9:30am; locker rooms with roll-in showers & Rr; outdoor showers; snack bar. $. Winter 6:30am-6pm; summer -8pm (10610 W Oakland Park Blvd, Sunrise; 954-747-4636)

Coral Springs Aquatic Center has a heated 50-meter pool with a lift (fixed seat); staff can help with transfers. Water aerobics classes; locker rooms with roll-in showers & Rr; outdoor showers; snack bar. $. Wknd 10-6. Wkdy winter 9-6; summer 12-8 (12441 Royal Palm Blvd, Coral Springs; 954-345-2121)

Cyress Park Pool is a large, clover-shaped, heated pool with a lift (fixed seat). Water exercise classes; locker rooms with Rr; outdoor showers; snack bar. $. Sep-May Wed-Mon 10-6; Jun-Aug -8 (1300 Coral Spring Dr, Coral Springs; 954-345-2109)

Hallandale Beach City Pool is a heated, T-shaped pool with a lift (fixed seat); staff can help with transfers. Lap swimming; locker rooms with roll-in showers; snack bar (hrs vary). $. Winter wkdy 11:30-6; wknd 12-5. Summer 9-6 (202 SE 5 St, Hallandale; 954-457-1458)

Hall of Fame Pools are 2 heated, Olympic lap pools with a lift (sling seat). Staff can help with transfers (250-lb limit). See Museums: International Swimming Hall of Fame. Water aerobics wkdy 9-10; locker rooms with roll-in showers & Rr. $. 8-4; wkdy also 6pm-8pm; pool closed to public during competitions (501 SR A1A; 954-468-1580)

Jerry Resnick Aquatic Center has a 75' pool with a lift (fixed seat). Adult-only lap lane; picnic tables; outdoor showers; locker rooms with roll-in showers & Rr. Apr-Sep hrs vary (701 SW 71 Ave, N Lauderdale; 954-724-7063)

Mitchell/Moore Pool is a heated 75' pool with a lift (fixed seat); lifeguards can help with transfers. $. Spring-fall 11-4 (12-1 adults only); winter closed Wed & Fri (901 NW 10 St, Pompano Bch; 954-786-4116)

Pine Island Park Pool is a heated 50-meter pool with a ramp and submersible WC; staff can help with transfers. Both lap and recreational swimming are offered all day. Locker rooms with roll-in showers & Rr. $. Wkdy noon-7:45 (summer 9am-); wknd 10-5:45 (3800 SW 92 Ave, Davie; 954-423-5107)

Plantation Central Park has 2 heated, Olympic pools with lifts (sling seats); one also has a ramp and submersible

WC. Lifeguards can help with transfers. Aquatic programs are offered for children and adults with disabilities. The 103-acre park (wkdy 7am-11pm; wknd 8-dusk) also has 2 ADA playgrounds, one for tots and one for older children. Accessible water play area; ADA picnic tables; showers; vending machines; Rr. $. Hrs vary (9151 NW 2 St, Plantation; 954-452-2525)

Veterans Park has a ramped, heated, 25-meter pool; staff can help you enter the pool in your own WC. Snack bar in summer; locker rooms with roll-in showers & Rr. $. Wknd 9-6; wkdy 9-6; summer -8 (7600 NW 50 St, Lauderhill; 954-730-2985)

Village Pool is a heated 90' pool with a lift (fixed seat); staff can help with transfers. Take the sidewalk through the man-made beach to the pool. Try water aerobics Mon-Thu 9-9:45am; bring a companion if you need assistance. Outdoor showers; Rr. $. Winter wknd 10-5. Summer wkdy 11-7; wknd 10-7 (6767 NW 24 St, Sunrise; 954-572-2480)

■ **SCUBA/SNORKELING**

Anchor Scuba offers resort courses, private lessons for certification and guided private dive trips (day or night) with Bob Sheridan, an HSA instructor. The resort course takes 4 hrs (classroom and pool instruction) and enables you to dive, with a dive master, in open water down to 50'. Should you decide to become certified, the fee can be applied to classes that can be scheduled as convenient. Staff can help lift you into the pool. On the dives, staff can lift you from your WC and back to your WC onboard the 30' dive boat and onto the large dive platform level with the water. (37 N SR A1A, Pompano Bch; 954-788-3483; 800-374-9792)

Pro Dive offers snorkel and dive trips aboard a 60' glass-bottom boat. Roll aboard from the floating dock onto the dive platform where staff can help you up a step to the boat deck. Staff can also help lift you in and out of the water from the dive platform. Two-hr snorkel trips stop at the Twin Ledges coral reef, about .5 mi offshore and 10-20' deep. Four-hr dive trips stop at 2 reef sites, one 60-120' deep and the other 30' deep. Four-hr resort dive classes begin with classroom instruction, pool sessions next door (where staff lifts you into the pool) and then an open water dive at a 30' deep reef. Book in advance; equipment included; Pro Diver II has snack bar & Rr onboard. Snorkel trips Tue-Sat 9:30; Sun 2. Dive trips Mon-Sat 1 & Sun 9:30. Resort dives Tue-Sat 7:30am (Hall of Fame Marina, 515 SR A1A, Ft Lauderdale Bch; 954-467-6030; 800-776-3483)

■ SHOOTING RANGES

Parks: Markham

Outdoor World Bass Pro Shop has 75' rifle, pistol and archery ranges for marksmen age 14 and older. The pistol range has a lane with a lowered rest for WC riders. See Shopping: Specialty Shops. Rr. $. Mon-Sat 10-9; Sun 11-7 (IGFA Fishing Hall of Fame, 200 Gulf Stream Way, Dania; 954-929-7710)

Revere Gun Range is an indoor, 50' pistol range, including a lane without a built-in gun rest. Rentals available; hearing & eye protectors supplied; gun store; vending machines. $. Mon-Sat 10-9; Sun 12-6 (601 NE 28 St, Pompano Bch; 954-942-3777)

■ SHOPPING

Antiques: Check out downtown Dania along US 1. (800-903-2642)

Boutiques: Beach Place has beach shops, restaurants and entertainment (SR A1A; between Castillo & Cortez Sts; 954-764-3460). Downtown Hollywood is an historic area with boutiques, galleries and restaurants along tree-lined, brick sidewalks (Hollywood Blvd, near Young Circle Park). Las Olas Riverfront (Las Olas Blvd & SW 1 Ave; 954-522-6556) and further W, the Shops of Las Olas (954-480-4942) have chic shops, antiques, dining and entertainment. Riverwalk is a 1-mi promenade past downtown shops, cafes and entertain-

ment (SW 7 Ave to SW 2 Ave; 954-468-1541).

Flea Markets: Festival Flea Market is an indoor mall with 600 vendors with new merchandise. Valet parking on wknd; CRr. Tue-Fri 9:30-5; wknd -6 (2900 W Sample Rd, Pompano; 954-979-4555; 800-353-2627). Hollywood Greyhound Dog Track Flea Market has some 200 vendors with new and old merchandise, inside and outside on pavement. Food concessions; Rr. Summer wknd & winter Fri-Sun 8-3 (831 US 1, Hallandale; 954-454-8666). Swap Shop has 80 acres with more than 2000 vendors, new and used merchandise, arcade, food court, drive-in movie complex and inaccessible amusement rides. Canopy Concepts, in the main building, (954-581-7262) rents and repairs manual/power WCs. Some vendors on grass; elevator in main building; Rr. Wkdy 7-5:30, wknd -6:30 (3291 W Sunrise Blvd; W of I-95; 954-791-7927)

Malls: Broward Mall (University Dr & Broward Blvd, Plantation; 954-473-5550); Coral Square Mall (9469 Atlantic Blvd/SR 814, Coral Springs; 954-755-5550); Fashion Mall (321 N University Dr, Plantation; 954-370-1884); Galleria (2414 E Sunrise Blvd; 954-564-1015); Lauderhill Mall (US 441 & NW 40 Ave, Lauderhill; 954-581-5186); Pembroke Lake Mall (11401 Pines Blvd, Pembroke Pines; 954-436-5575); Pompano Square (US 1 & Copans Rd, Pompano Bch; 954-943-4683); Sawgrass Mills (12801 W Sunrise Blvd, Sunrise; 954-846-2350)

Specialty Shops: Anhinga Indian Museum features Seminole clothing and jewelry (5791 S US 441; 954-581-0416). Outdoor World Bass Pro Shop, with outdoors sporting goods, also has an aquarium where fishing demonstrations and classes are held, a children's activity area and a restaurant. See Museums and Shooting Ranges. Rr. Mon-Sat 9am-10pm; Sun 10-8 (IGFA Fishing Hall of Fame, 200 Gulf Stream Way, Dania; 954-929-7710). Ron Jon Surf Shop is as enticing for its funky beach ambience as its beachwear and sports equipment (Sawgrass Mills Mall, 12801 W Sunrise Blvd, Sunrise; 954-846-1880).

■ SOCCER

Dynamites Soccer is for kids (age 6-18) with mental and/or physical challenges. Kids are placed in age groups to work on soccer skills and then scrimmage. Call Christine Bowen 954-236-0654. Sep-Nov Sat 3-5 (Pine Island Park, 320 SW Pine Island Rd, Plantation)

■ SPECTATOR SPORTS

Football Miami Dolphins hold training camp mid-Jul to Aug. WC spectators can roll up to the fence or take the ramp to the 1st level of the bleachers where WC seating is in front. Limited HC parking; pro shop; Rr (Nova Southeastern University, 7500 SW 30 St, Davie; 954-954-452-7004)

Ice Hockey Florida Panthers, an NHL team, plays Oct-Apr. Easy WC entrances are at the plaza level entry gates, N and S of the main entrance. WC seating throughout; CRr (National Car Rental Center, 1 Panther Pkwy, Sunrise; Sunrise Blvd & NW 136 Ave; 954-835-8000)

Rodeo Five Star Pro Rodeo showcases championship events from bareback bronco riding and calf roping to steer wrestling and barrel racing. WC seating is in front of the bleachers; companions should bring folding chairs. Paved & grass parking. Jan-Nov last Fri-Sat 8pm; gates open 6:30 (Bergeron Rodeo Grounds, 4271 Davie Rd, Davie; 954-384-7075)

Soccer Miami Fusion plays Mar-Oct. WC seating is in the NW and SE corners, however you can sit anywhere on the ground level if you don't mind watching through a fence. Rr (Lockhart Stadium, 5201 NW 12 Ave; 954-717-2200; 888-387-4664)

■ TENNIS

USTA Wheelchair-Tennis clinics are held weekly for adults and kids, beginning through advanced, at 3 locations in Pembroke Pines. You must be able to push your WC and swing a racquet (that can be taped to your hand). One sports WC is available for loan, if needed. Clinics are held Wed 7:30-9:30pm and during some seasons, additional nights. For information call 954-435-6759. (Town Gate Tennis Center, 901 NW 155 Ave; 954-450-6917. Maxwell Park, 1200 SW 72 Ave; 954-986-5021. Rose Price Park, 901 NW 208 Ave; 954-437-1143)

■ TOURS

Lolly the Trolley has lift-equipped trolleys for 2-hr narrated excursions around Ft Lauderdale. See ritzy estates, historic landmarks, shops and restaurants. If you wish to eat, shop or sightsee, you can get off and pick up another trolley later. Reservations. Wkdy 9-5 (Las Olas Riverfront, Andrews Ave & Las Olas Blvd; 954-946-7320)

■ WAVERUNNERS

Hollywood Jet Skiing rents 2-person waverunners by the hour for those over age 19 to enjoy on the Intracoastal. Staff can help pull your WC across the sand to the water's edge and help lift you onto the waverunner. Rr. 10-dusk (4510 SR A1A, Hollywood; 954-921-8343)

ACCOMMODATIONS

■ CAMPGROUNDS

Easterlin Park has 56 campsites, 7 are ADA sites (RVs: #A-10, B-11 & -13 , C-3 & -8; tents: #D-2 & -4) with water/elec, ADA picnic tables, grills and paved areas. Sidewalks lead from the sites to the ADA bathhouse on Road D that has roll-under sinks and roll-in showers. See Parks. (1000 NW 38 St, Oakland Park; I-95 exit 32, W on Commercial Blvd, S on Powerline Rd, W on NW 38 St; 954-938-0610)

*Lakeside Campground, at CB Smith Park, has 60 RV sites with paved pads, water/elec, grills and picnic tables and 11 tent sites with grills, fire pits and picnic tables. Ask for a site with an ADA table. Sidewalks lead to a bathhouses with raised toilets, roll-under sinks and roll-in showers. You can borrow a beach WC for the park beach; see Parks. Laundry (900 N Flamingo Rd, Pembroke Pines; I-75 exit 9, 1 mi E on Pines Blvd; 954-437-2650)

Markham Park has 86 spacious, wooded, RV/tent sites; 5 are ADA (#A-1, B-5, C-1, D-2 & E-6) with large pads, water/elec, ADA picnic tables, grills and hard-packed paths to the ADA bathhouse with raised toilets, roll-under sinks and roll-in showers with hand-held sprayers and seats. The park has pool with a lift and lots of accessible fun; see Parks. Reservations; laundry (16001 W SR 84, Sunrise; I-595 exit 1 W; 954-389-2000)

*Quiet Waters Park has 16 shady sites with permanent canvas tents on ramped, wood platforms overlooking a beautiful, quiet lake, but close to a noisy, popular aquatic park. The 2 ADA sites (#11 & 14) have water, ADA picnic tables, grills, fire pits and sidewalks to the ADA bathhouse with raised toilets, roll-under sinks and roll-in showers with hand-held sprayers. Go ahead and enjoy the park, including the beach WC; see Parks. Camp store (401 S Powerline Rd, Deerfield Bch; from I-95, go W on Hillsboro Blvd 2.8 mi, then S; 954-360-1315)

*TY Park has 48 RV and 12 tent sites on flat terrain overlooking a well-stocked lake. All sites have grills; RV sites are paved and have water/elec; tent sites are hard-packed terrain. Sidewalks lead to a bathhouse with a large stall, roll-under sinks and a roll-in shower with a bench. Reserve a site with an ADA picnic table. Be aware that a train runs by this campground. The park has a swim lagoon and beach WC; see Parks. Laundry (3300 N Park Rd, Hollywood; I-95 exit 21, W for .5 mi on Sheridan St, N on N Park Rd; 954-985-1980)

■ HOUSES

Medical Travel rents a 2BR house with an interior designed by the Paralyzed Veterans of America to ADA specifications. The master bedroom has a queen bed; the 2nd bedroom has 1 twin bed and a hospital bed with a Hoyer lift. The half bath is not modified, but the full bath has a raised toilet, roll-under sink and roll-in shower with a seat. The house has a private patio and is 10 min from Haulover Beach where you can borrow a beach WC (see Miami: Beaches). Full kitchen; linens provided. Other similar houses may be available. $$$ (800 SW 9 St, Hallandale; 561-361-9384; 800-778-7953)

■ MOTELS

Amerisuites has 7 ADA 1BR suites, each with 2 full beds (22" high/open frames), a living room with a full sofa bed and kitchenette with a microwave and refrigerator. Bathrooms have raised toilets and tub/showers with seats. Pool; laundry. $$-$$$ (1851 SE 10 Ave; 954-763-7670)

Baymont Inn & Suites has 6 ADA rooms, each with a full bed (21" high/platform) and coffeepot. Bathrooms have raised toilets and roll-under sinks; rooms 109 and 111 have roll-in showers with hand-held sprayers; others have tubs. Free brkfst; pool; laundry; kids stay free. $$ (13651 NW 2 St, Sunrise; I-595 exit 1; 954-846-1200)

Comfort Suites has 5 ADA 1BR junior suites, each with a king bed (22" high/open frame), queen sofa bed, refrigerator and coffeepot. Bathrooms have raised toilets and roll-under sinks; rooms 101, 105 and 107 have roll-in showers with hand-held sprayers and seats; others have tubs. Free brkfst; pool; bar; full restaurant. $$-$$$ (1040 E Newport Center Dr, Deerfield Bch; 954-570-8887; 800-538-2777)

Diplomat Country Club & Spa, on the Intracoastal, has 3 luxury ADA units. Two rooms have a king or 2 full beds (open frames); a 2BR suite has a king and 2 full beds and a living room. All units have coffeepots and bathrooms with raised toilets, roll-under sinks and roll-in showers with hand-held sprayers and seats. Pool; bar; entertainment; full restaurant. $$$ (501 Diplomat Pkwy, Hallandale; I-95 exit 18, E 2.5 mi on Hallandale Bch Blvd/SR 858, N on Diplomat Pkwy, W of Intracoastal; 954-457-2000)

Holiday Inn has 3 ADA rooms, each with a king bed (23" high/open frame), refrigerator and coffeepot. Bathrooms have raised toilets, roll-under sinks and roll-in showers with hand-held sprayers and seats. Pool; bar; full restaurant. $$-$$$ (999 Ft Lauderdale Bch Blvd, Ft Lauderdale Bch; 954-563-5961)

Homestead Village Guest Studios has 5 ADA rooms, each with a king or 2 queen beds (22" high/open frames), kitchenettes and bathrooms with roll-under sinks. Rooms 123 and 125 have roll-in showers; others have tubs. Laundry. $$-$$$ (3873 W Commercial Blvd, Tamarac; 954-733-6644)

La Quinta has 4 ADA rooms and 3 ADA 1BR suites. Each unit has a king or 2 full beds (open frames). Suites also have a sofa bed, refrigerator, microwave, coffeepot and 2 TVs. Bathrooms have roll-under sinks; rooms 106 & 133 have roll-in showers with hand-held sprayers and seats; others have tubs. Free brkfst; pool; laundry. $$-$$$ (8101 Peters Rd, Plantation; 954-476-6047)

Ocean Terrace Suites has 1 ADA and 29 WC-friendly suites, all oceanfront and next to Deerfield Beach with a beach WC. All units have full kitchens, queen sofa beds and recliners in the living rooms and bathrooms with tubs/showers. The 1BR/2BA, ADA unit (#104) has 2 full beds (23" high/platforms) and a poolside terrace. Each 3BR/3BA suite has a king, 2 full and 2 twin beds (23" high/platforms) and large balconies overlooking the Atlantic. You can request a portable ramp, toilet extender, hand-held sprayer and shower seat. Restaurants, shopping and the Deerfield Fishing Pier are nearby. Pool;

laundry. $$$ (2080 E Hillsboro Blvd, Deerfield Bch; 954-427-8400)

Radisson Bahia Mar has 10 ADA rooms with either a king or 2 full beds (open frames) and coffeepots. Bathrooms have raised toilets, roll-under sinks and tubs with seats. The Bahia Mar Yachting Center is adjacent to the hotel; see Boat Rentals, Boat Tours and Fishing Charters. Pool; laundry; full restaurant. $$$ (801 SR A1A; 954-764-2233)

Riverside Hotel, along the New River, has 5 ADA rooms with a king or 2 full beds (open frames), refrigerators and bathrooms with raised toilets and roll-under sinks. Rooms 103 and 105 have roll-in showers with hand-held sprayers and seats; other rooms have tubs. Pool; bar; entertainment; full restaurant. $$-$$$ (620 E Las Olas Blvd; 954-467-0671; 800-325-3280)

Sheraton Suites has 8 ADA suites, each with a king bed (22" high/open frame), queen sofa bed in the living room, refrigerator, mini-bar, microwave, coffeepot and bathroom with a raised toilet and roll-under sink. Rooms 214, 632 and 732 have roll-in showers with hand-held sprayers and seats; others have tubs. The lobby adjoins the Fashion Mall; the beach is 8 mi to the east. Pool; bar; full restaurant. $$$ (311 N University Dr, Plantation; 954-424-3300)

+Sheraton Yankee Clipper has 16 ADA rooms with a king or 2 full beds (22" high/open frames), coffeepots and bathrooms with raised toilets and roll-under sinks. Six of these rooms have roll-in showers with hand-held sprayers and seats as well as tubs; others have only tubs. The hotel security desk loans an all-terrain WC (removable arms) to enjoy the ramped beach in back. The heated main pool has a lift (sling seat). Laundry; bar; entertainment; full restaurant. $$-$$$ (1140 SR A1A; 954-524-5551; 800-958-5551)

+Sheraton Yankee Trader has 16 ADA rooms with a king (21" high) or 2 full beds (22" high/open frames), coffeepots and bathrooms with raised toilets and roll-under sinks. Six of these rooms have roll-in showers with hand-held sprayers and seats as well as tubs; others have only tubs. The hotel security desk loans an all-terrain WC (removable arms) to enjoy the ramped beach in back. The heated main pool has a lift (sling seat). Laundry; bar; entertainment; full restaurant. $$-$$$ (321 N SR A1A; 954-467-1111; 800-958-5551)

Villas by the Sea Resort & Beach Club has 2 ADA rooms each with 2 full beds (open frames), a refrigerator and bathroom with a raised toilet, roll-under sink and roll-in shower with a hand-held sprayer and seat. Nearby is Anglin's Fishing Pier; see Fishing Piers. Children's programs; pool; laundry; bar; entertainment; full restaurant. $$-$$$ (4456 El Mar Dr, Lauderdale-by-the-Sea; 954-772-3550)

Wellesley Inn & Suites has 5 ADA rooms, each with a king bed (22" high/platform), refrigerator and coffeepot. Bathrooms have raised toilets and roll-under sinks; rooms 102 and 106 have roll-in showers with hand-held sprayers and seats; others have tubs. Free brkfst; pool. $-$$$ (3100 N University Dr, Coral Springs; 954-344-2200)

■ **RECREATIONAL VEHICLES**

Palm RV Centers rents a lift-equipped 27' RV that can sleep 3 with a foldout twin bed and a full sofa bed in the rear. The RV has a full kitchen, TV and roll-in shower. To drive, you must transfer into the 6-way power driver's seat; staff can install hand controls. Or, ride in your WC with tie downs in the center behind the front seats. 3-day minimum (2441 S SR 7; I-595 exit 8B, N on SR 441, W on SW 20 St, S on next street; 954-745-1778)

MIAMI

Bal Harbour, Coconut Grove, Coral Gables, Cutler Ridge, Florida City, Goulds, Hialeah, Homestead, Kendall, Key Biscayne, Miami Beach, Redlands, South Beach, Sunny Isles

Miami has all the glitz, attractions and cultural excitement you'd expect in a big city born of tourism. It also comes with some surprises: the country's largest urban park, an Art Deco historic district and topless beaches. Much of it is accessible. You can rent power and beach WCs at one source or borrow beach WCs at 8 of the glorious beaches here. A premier sailing operation, Shake-A-Leg, offers disabled sailors everything from an introductory sail to competitive racing. Try one of the WC-tennis clinics, pools with lifts and fun tours in the area. A catamaran with a lift to get you into the water is available for charter. In addition to an array of motels, the only downtown B&B and a primitive cabin in Oleta State Park meet ADA standards. US 1 is also called Biscayne Blvd and SR A1A is Collins Ave.

Tourist Info

Miami Visitors Bureau: 701 Brickell Ave, Ste 2700, 33131; 305-539-3000; 800-283-2707

Visitors Centers: Aventura Mall (19501 US 1; 935-3836); Bayside Marketplace (401 US 1; 539-8070); Coral Gables (3655 SW 22 St; Coral Way at Douglas Rd; 460-3477); International Mall (1625 NW 107 Ave; 470-7863); Westland Mall (1625 W 49 St, Hialeah; 364-3827)

Hotlines: Events: 305-375-4634; Arts Calendar: 800-283-2707

Web sites: www.tropicoolmiami.com; www.miamiandbeaches.com

Transportation

Metro-Dade Bus Service has buses with lifts on some routes. Wkdy 6am-10pm; wknd 9-5 (305-770-3131)

Metromover, a monorail, covers a 2-mi radius of downtown Miami, linking hotels, attractions, offices and shopping areas. Stations have elevators; roll-aboard cars have no lockdowns. Rr at Government Center Station. 6am-midnight (305-770-3131)

Metrorail, an elevated train, runs from downtown 21 mi into the suburbs, N to Hialeah and S along US 1 to Dadeland. You can connect to the Metromover at Government Center Station. Stations have elevators; roll-aboard cars have no lockdowns. 5:30am-midnight (305-770-3131)

Special Transportation Services offers door-to-door van service anywhere in the county for those who can't use public buses. Call for an application and pass. (305-263-5400)

Super Shuttle, a lift-equipped van, runs from the Miami Airport, Port Everglades and the Port of Miami to any location in Dade, Broward or Monroe Counties. Reserve 5 days in advance. (305-871-2000; 954-764-1700)

Tri-Rail Commuter Train runs from Miami Airport N to West Palm Beach. Cars have WC lockdowns. At some stops, you can connect to buses with lifts; call for information. Sun-Fri 4:30am-7:30pm; Sat 6am-10pm (305-836-0986; 800-874-7245)

WC Resources

Miami-Dade Disability Services & Independent Living can send you a Directory of Services for the Disabled that lists relevant programs, recreation and other helpful resources. (1335 NW 14 St, #200; 305-547-5444)

DMR rents and repairs (and delivers) manual and power WCs, scooters and beach WCs. Reservations are needed. Wkdy 9-6 (1051 NW 14 St; 7367 Coral Way; 7456 SW 48 St; 305-666-9911)

ACTIVITIES

■ ATTRACTIONS

Coral Castle took 28 yrs for Ed Leedskalnin to carve from 1000 tons of coral in tribute to the fiancee who jilted him just before the wedding. Note the 9-ton gate that swings open at touch, solar-heated bathtubs and the coral telescope fixed on the North Star. The living quarters on the top floor are inaccessible and gravel paths lead through the grounds. You can rent audio boxes for self-guided tours or call for the schedule of guided tours. Snacks; gift shop; Rr. 7am-8pm (28655 S Dixie Hwy, Homestead; 305-248-6345)

Everglades Alligator Farm features gator shows, snake demonstrations and wildlife lectures. A 30-min airboat tour in the Everglades begins as a slow narrative ride enjoying wildlife and ends

fast and thrilling. Staff can lift you down 1' onto the airboat's bench seat with a back and armrests but no seat belts. Woodchip paths; WC loaners; gift shop; snack bar; Rr. $. 9-6 (40351 SW 192 Ave, Homestead; 305-247-2628)

Fairchild Tropical Garden, a world-renown botanical garden, is 83 acres with 2.5 mi of sidewalks through rare palms, flowering trees and vines. Take a 45-min, guided walking tour (Nov-Apr; hrs vary) or a narrated, 40-min, roll-aboard tram tour that leaves hourly. Enjoy the museum of plant exploration or one of the frequent shows hosted by various plant societies. WC loaners; garden bookstore; cafe; CRr. $. 9:30-4:30 (10901 Old Cutler Rd, Coral Gables; 305-667-1651)

Gameworks contains state-of-the art

video and virtual reality games that require transfers into the ride vehicles. Bar/restaurant; Rr. $. 11am-closing varies (5701 Sunset Dr, S Miami; 305-667-4263)

Holocaust Memorial includes a 42' bronze arm rising from the ground, a memorial wall etched with names of victims and vignettes of victims helping victims. Take sidewalks through the meditation garden and the Dome of Contemplation with its eternal flame. Rr. 9-9 (1933 Meridian Ave; 305-538-1663)

Metrozoo is a 295-acre cageless home to 900 plus animals, from giant monitors and white tigers to wart hogs and wallabies. Sidewalks lead through waterfalls and various habitats. Tour the zoo on an elevated monorail (the last car in each train has a lift) or take a 45-min, behind-the-scenes tour on a roll-aboard tram. Private 90-min tours for up to 4 are also offered on a golf cart; staff can help with transfers. Ecology Theater, on Florida's native animals, occurs twice daily and the Wildlife Show on birds of prey, reptiles and mammals occurs 3 times daily. Each venue offers WC seating in the front row. Animal feedings are scheduled throughout the day at major exhibits and present a chance to talk with the animal keepers. Snuggle sheep and pot-bellied pigs in the paved petting zoo. Staff can help transfer a child from a WC for a pony ride; parents can walk along. WC/ECV rentals; ADA playground; gift shop; concession stands; Rr. $. 9:30-5:30 (12400 SW 152 St, S Miami; 305-251-0400)

Miami Beach Botanical Garden, a lush green respite from its urban setting, has sidewalks through an acre of exotic plants. Guided tours are by request. A small auditorium holds frequent shows and lectures on orchids, herbs and other green things. Gift shop; Rr. 9-4:30 (2000 Convention Center Dr, Miami Bch; 305-673-7256/993-2024)

Miami Seaquarium is a 38-acre park with marine exhibits, shows and an interactive dolphin program. The 750,000-gal Main Reef Aquarium has a narrated program as divers hand-feed tropical fish, cobia, loggerhead turtles and moray eels. Check out the ramped manatee viewing area, the gator exhibit and aviary. Take a boardwalk through Discover Bay, an endangered mangrove habitat, where guides feed and describe crocodiles, flamingos, rays and other wildlife. The Rainforest Exhibit features poisonous frogs, toucans and tropical creatures. Shows with a killer whale, sea lions, sharks and dolphins occur throughout the day. Only the Top Deck Dolphin Show is not accessible. For an extra fee, you can participate in WADEing, a 2-hr dolphin program that starts with a park tour and class on dolphin behavior. Next you spend 30 mins in Flipper Lagoon (site of the 1960's TV series) for a 1-on-1 encounter with a dolphin. If you need assistance, your companion must help you from your WC onto the dock and into the water. You may also need your companion's help to wait on a platform 4' underwater until you hang onto a dolphin's fin for a tow across the lagoon. Wet (suits are provided. WC rentals; gift shop; snack bars; Rr. $. 9:30-6 (last shows begin at 3pm) (4400 Rickenbacker Cswy; 305-361-5705)

Miccosukee Indian Village features demonstrations of doll making, basket weaving, alligator wrestling and other traditional customs. A 30-min guided tour on sidewalks covers Miccosukee history and culture. A museum houses Indian artifacts, films, exhibits and photos. A 30-min airboat ride goes to an authentic hammock village on island. Depending upon your size, staff can help lift you onto the airboat's bench seat with a back and armrests. Restaurant; gift shop; Rr. $. 9-5 (US 41; 25 mi W of Miami; 305/223-8380)

Monkey Jungle puts visitors in a cage to view monkeys that roam freely in their natural habitat; all paths are mulch.

Three shows — on rain forest monkeys, orangutans and swimming monkeys — run every 45 min. All-terrain WC loaners; snack bar; Rr; CRr in gift shop. $. 9:30-5 (14805 SW 216 St/Hainlin Mill Dr, Goulds; 22 mi S of Miami off US 1; 305-235-1611)

Parrot Jungle is a 22-acre sanctuary to more than 1100 birds that fly free, eat from your hand and even pose for photographs. The Jungle is a natural subtropical hammock of flowering trees and plants with sidewalks throughout. Shows occur every 45 min and include trained birds, monkeys, nocturnal animals, exotic reptiles and an albino alligator. Flamingo Lake is home to 100 flamingos. The petting zoo is on sand. WC loaner; gift shop; cafe opens at 8am; Rr. $. 9:30-6 (11000 SW 57 Ave, S Miami; 2.5 mi E of US 1; 305-666-7834)

■ BASKETBALL

Parks: Tropical

Miami Heat Wheels is a NWBA team with players age 18 and older. The Miami Sparks is a recreational team for players age 8-18. Men, women and kids with any lower-extremity disability are eligible to play. Contact Lisa McCahill (305-234-4948) for the game schedule, to try out for the team or just to shoot hoops with the group. Practices Sep-Apr Sun 10-1; Wed 7-9 (Goulds High School Gym, 11350 SW 216 St, Cutler Ridge)

■ BEACHES

+Bill Baggs Cape Florida State Park, at the S tip of Key Biscayne, offers spectacular views of Miami and Biscayne Bay, particularly at sunset. Ask at the entrance to borrow a beach WC (fixed arms); rangers can bring it to you at the beach area of your choice. Parking areas A-C have sidewalks and boardwalks down to the sand. At parking area D, take a sidewalk to the 1825 lighthouse and learn its history from the video and interpretive signage. Park at the Harbor or area D to enjoy fishing off the 8 platforms along the seawall on the Biscayne Bay. A 1.3-mi bike trail

runs from the entrance to area D, with access to the fishing platforms and seawall. Oceanfront & bayfront restaurants; bait shop; gift shop; outdoor showers; picnic shelters; grills; Rr near Lighthouse Cafe & in area D. $. 8-dusk (1200 S Crandon Blvd, Key Biscayne; off Rickenbacker Cswy; 305-361-5811)

+Crandon Park has a 2-mi beach with an offshore sandbar that calms the surf. Call ahead to borrow a beach WC (removable arms) and arrange for pick up. With an HC permit, you can be dropped off close to the sand; your vehicle must be returned to parking. At the S end of the beach, a paved ramp extends midway to the water. When water clarity is good (best in summers), lifeguards offer free, 1-hr, guided, in-water explorations of marine life for swimmers; call for reservations and to discuss any special needs (305-361-7373). Park in lots 3 and 4 for the beach. This park offers an enormous range of other activities; see Boat Ramps and Parks. Lifeguards; cabanas for rent; outdoor showers; snack bar located next to the ADA picnic shelter by parking lot 4; Rr. Dawn-dusk (4000 Crandon Blvd, Key Biscayne; off Rickenbacker Cswy; 305-361-7385/5421)

+Haulover Beach occupies 177 acres between the Intracoastal and Atlantic with a 1.5-mi stretch of ocean beach. Call ahead to borrow a beach WC (PVC with fixed arms; or, stainless steel with removable arms) available Apr-Oct 9-6 and Nov-Mar 9-4. The WCs are kept at 2 sites: the Main Lifeguard Headquarters (a 2-story building) along a boardwalk to beach; and the lifeguard tower in the *clothing-optional* area, N end of the beach, where you take a dune crossover. A paved bike trail runs the length of the beach. Kite flying for fun and competition is popular on a large grassy field near HC parking and a kite vendor. At the N end of the park is a boat ramp with fixed docks on the bay and fishing off the seawall on the 150' wide canal. The marina has fishing charters and a restaurant. Lifeguards;

ADA picnic tables; tennis courts & a teaching pro; 9-hole golf course; snack bar at N beach open seasonally; Rr. $. Dawn-dusk (10800 SR A1A, N Miami Bch; 305-944-3040/947-3525)

+Homestead Bayfront Park resembles a tropical island with an atoll pool surrounded by white beach dotted with palms. Much of the sand is fairly hard-packed; a sidewalk leads from the parking, past outdoor showers, to a concrete pad near the shoreline. Call to reserve a beach WC (fixed arms) 48 hrs in advance. The marina has a boat ramp, a hoist for up to 25' boats and fixed docks. Fish in the canal or the Biscayne Bay along the hard-packed shoreline, from the seawall or from a deck by the boat ramp. ADA picnic tables & grills on grass; bait shop/snacks; small playground with some ADA features; lifeguards; Rr at beach & marina. $ parking/free with HC permit. Dawn-dusk (9698 SW North Canal Dr, Homestead; 328 St ends in park; 305-230-3033)

+Lummus Park, in the Art Deco District, is a perpetual happy hour, with popular bars and restaurants across the street. The city loans a beach WC (fixed arms) at lifeguard headquarters (9:30-4:30) behind the Oceanfront Auditorium. Only 1 HC parking space is in front of headquarters; ask inside and you may be permitted to park in the lifeguards' lot. ADA playgrounds (at 6 & 14 Sts); umbrella & chair concessions; Rr (1001 Ocean Dr, South Bch; 305-673-7714)

North Shore Open Space Park is the city's last natural hammock and beach with 8 blocks of soft sand on the ocean. A nature center has interactive displays, live reptiles and indoor/outdoor programs with a focus on sea turtles. A sidewalk runs through the park and connects to what will become the North South Corridor, an 8-mi paved trail to South Beach. A hard-packed path ramps to the edge of the broad beach. ADA picnic tables; ADA playground; Rr. Dawn-dusk (79-87 Sts & SR A1A, Miami Bch; 305-993-2032)

+73 Street Beach loans a beach WC (fixed arms) 9:30-4:30; call the city lifeguard office 305-673-7714 beforehand. This beach can be windy and sometimes sand covers the sidewalk. Street parking; umbrella & chair concessions; lifeguards; Rr (73 St & SR A1A, Miami Bch; just N of JFK Cswy; 305-993-2020)

■ **BIKE TRAILS**
Beaches: Bill Baggs, Haulover, North Shore. Boat Ramps: Black Point. Parks: AD Barnes, Crandon, L & P Thompson For more information on bike trails in Dade County, call 305-375-4507.
The following trails are paved and flat:
Black Creek Path runs roughly 7 mi along the Black Creek Canal in S Miami Heights, from the L&P Thompson Park (12451 SW 184 St; 305-232-1049; see Parks) to Black Point Park on the Biscayne Bay (24775 SW 87 Ave; 305-258-4092; see Boat Ramps). Parking & Rr at both parks

M-Path is an 8-mi trail that runs under the elevated Metrorail S of downtown Miami. You can use this path between several attractions such as Vizcaya and the Museum of Science; see Museums. (SW 7-80 Sts)

Old Cutler Path starts at Cocoplum Cir (at SW 72 St) in Coconut Grove and runs about 12 mi by some very gracious, bayfront estates terminating at Goulds Park (SW 114 Ave). You also pass Matheson Hammock Park (9610 Old Cutler Rd, Coral Gables), where the trail takes a jog through a neighborhood and Deering Estate Park (16701 SW 72 Ave; see Parks). Parking at all sites; Rr & water fountains in parks.

Snake Creek Path runs about 2 mi along the Snake Creek Canal in N Miami Beach from Sierra Park (at NE 195 St and 1 Pl) to Miami Gardens Dr/183 St, just past I-95. Watch the low columns at the I-95 overpass. No facilities; limited parking only at Sierra Park (Greynolds Park; 305-945-3425)

Snapper Creek Bikeway, in S Miami, runs from SW 117 Ave (at SW 16 St) through residential areas along the

Snapper Creek Canal to SW 107 Ave. You use the sidewalk for a short gap in the bike path. No facilities or public parking (305-596-9324)

■ **BOAT RAMPS**

Beaches: Haulover, Homestead, Bayfront. Parks: Crandon, Matheson **Black Point Park** has a marina with a boat ramp and floating dock on a channel to Biscayne Bay. A bike path leads through the park and onto a jetty to a wood fishing deck. Bait shop; restaurant; shady ADA picnic table near Rr. $. 6-6 (24775 SW 87 Ave; 305-258-4092)

■ **BOAT RENTALS**

Club Nautico rents 19' bow riders and 25' open fisherman for half/full days on Biscayne Bay. With advance notice, staff can help lift you aboard from the floating dock. Bait shop; deli; restaurant; Rr. 9-5 (Miami Bch Marina, 300 Alton Rd, South Bch; 305-673-2502) **Fantasy Watersports** rents center consoles and bow riders for 6 on the Intracoastal. Floating dock; bait shop nearby; Bimini tops; 1-hr minimum. Wkdy 10-5; wknd 9-5 (163 St & SR A1A, N Miami Bch; 305-940-2628)

■ **BOAT TOURS**

Attractions: Everglades Alligator Farm, Miccosukee Indian Village **Fastrack Charters & Tours** offers custom private charters on a 40' catamaran with a lift to lower you in and out of the water. Choose a guided adventure: snorkeling (equipment provided), diving, fishing (the capt can clean and grill your catch onboard; bait/tackle included), ecotours and bird watching in Biscayne Bay. You may also choose a sunset cruise or a secluded beach party where you can enjoy tandem sit-on kayaks, waverunners or water volleyball (equipment provided). The catamaran holds up to 40, can go in the bay or ocean and has tie-downs for WCs. Depending on tides, you can roll aboard or use a ramp. A platform lift can be raised with your WC for a lateral transfer and then you can be lowered into the water or onto a kayak or waverunner; crew

can help with transfers. 2-hr minimum; Rr onboard (Bayside Marina, 400 US 1, Pier 5/Slip 21; 305-223-3488; 888-449-0697)

Island Queen Cruises offers 90-min sightseeing tours of the Port of Miami, Miami Beach and homes of the rich and famous. Or, try moonlight or 1-hr evening dance cruises. Take the ramp up to the 72' yacht where staff can lift your WC down to the deck. The upper deck is inaccessible. Cash bar & snacks. Hourly tours 11am-7pm. Dance cruises Mon-Thu 9pm; Fri-Sun 8pm (Bayside Marketplace, 401 US 1; 305-379-5119)

■ **BOWLING**

Scott Rakow Youth Center, a city facility, has a bowling alley with bowling ball ramps. Lanes are open to kids after school and Sat 11-7; and to adults only Sun 8:30am-7pm. Rr. See Pools. (2700 Sheridan Ave, Miami Bch; 305-673-7767)

■ **CANOEING/KAYAKKING**

Boat Tours: Fastrack. Parks: Crandon, Deering, Oleta **Metro-Dade Park Service** offers naturalist-guided canoe trips in the area, the Everglades and the Keys. Call for schedule and to explain any special needs. (305-662-4124)

■ **CASINOS**

Casino Princesa, a 200' ship, offers 4 1/2-hr trips with Vegas-style gambling, including poker tables on the 1st deck, and goes out 4 mi. Crew can help you up the boarding ramp. The upper 3 decks, including the dining room, are not accessible but you can be served on the 1st deck. Rr. 12:30pm, 7:30pm; Fri-Sat also 1am (Bayside Marketplace, 401 N US 1; 305-379-5825) **Miccosukee Indian Gaming** features poker, lotto, high-stakes bingo and more than 520 video pull-tab machines. Nightly entertainment can include anything from professional boxing to concerts. Childcare; restaurant; bar; Rr. 24 hrs (500 SW 177 Ave; at SW 8 St & Krome Ave/SR 997; 305-222-4600)

■ **DISC GOLF**

Parks: Kendall Indian Hammocks

■ **FISHING CHARTERS**

Blue Water Charters offer half/full-day, deep-sea sport fishing trips on a 45' Hatteras. Charters price for 6 but you can split charters on request. Crew can lift you in your WC aboard the back of the boat. Catering available. 8 & 1 (Bayside Marina, 5 St & US 1; 305-944-4531)

Bouncer's Dusky Charters has a 25' boat with a large back deck big enough for 3 anglers. From the floating dock, crew can lift you aboard in your WC. Inshore and offshore day trips run 8 or 12 hrs; evening trips run 4 hrs. Light tackle sport fishing or flyfishing is available. Restaurants at marina (Miami Beach Marina, 300 Alton Rd, Miami Bch 305-945-5114)

Capt Dave Sutton offers flats and backcountry fishing with a fly rod or light tackle on a 20' flats boat. He can help you board at a dock that best suits your needs. Half/full-day trips and, in summers, night trips go to Biscayne Bay or into the Everglades. Let him know the dimensions of your WC and he will provide tie-downs. (305-248-6126)

Capt Doug Lillard specializes in flats and backcountry fishing with a fly rod or light tackle in Biscayne Bay, the Everglades or local freshwater lakes. He can help you board the 18' flats boat at a dock that best fits your needs. Night tarpon trips and day trips for 2 run a minimum of 4 hrs. (954-894-9865)

Capt Mike Haines offers half/full-day flats and backcountry fishing for 3 with a fly rod or light tackle. From a floating dock, he can roll you aboard the 20' flats boat. Trips can range from Biscayne Bay to the Everglades. (305-248-8859)

■ **FISHING-PARTY BOATS**

Kelly Fleet offers 3 1/2-hr and, in the summer, 8-hr drift trips. Gangplanks lead aboard but at different tides, crew may need to help. All boats have shaded decks; one has an AC cabin with a lip at the entry. Drinks sold on board.

Half days 9, 1:45 & 8pm; Jun-Sep full-day trips on Wed & Sun 9-5 (Haulover Park Marina, 10800 SR A1A, Miami Bch; 305-945-3801)

Reward Fishing Fleet offers 4-hr, deep-sea fishing trips. Take the ramp onto the boat; crew can lift you in your WC onto the deck. Crew can also help you over the lip at the AC cabin. Snacks sold onboard. 9am; 1:45 & 8pm (Miami Bch Marina, 300 Alton Rd, Miami Bch; 305-372-9470)

■ **FISHING PIERS**

Beaches: Bill Baggs, Homestead. Boat Ramps: Black Point. Parks: L & P Thompson, Matheson, Oleta

Newport Beach Pier is a private, 1080' wood pier on the ocean rebuilt 4 times since 1936. A ramp leads to the Sunny Isles Beach. Bait shop; restaurant 10-7; Rr. $. 24 hrs (16701 SR A1A, Sunny Isles; at 170 St; 305-949-1300)

South Pointe Park is a 17-acre park at the S tip of Miami Bch with sidewalks throughout. The ADA 300', cement fishing pier is lighted and open until midnight and is a good spot to watch cruise ships heading in and out of the Port of Miami. Picnic shelters; Rr. Dawn-dusk (1 Washington Ave, Miami Bch; 305-673-7224)

■ **FITNESS TRAILS**

Parks: AD Barnes, Kendall

■ **HANG GLIDING**

Miami Hang Gliding uses a boat to launch hang gliders, which works well for folks with mobility impairments. First, take lessons on the ground; then, an instructor accompanies you throughout the flight. From the floating dock, staff can lift you aboard the boat and into a seat (no armrests). A friend may ride on the boat at no charge. Since you fly from a prone position, staff can lay you on the deck and attach the harness; then staff lifts you about 2' and attaches you to the hang glider. The glider is tethered to the boat during takeoff and disconnected at roughly 1200' where you fly free for 10 min over Biscayne Bay. You land in the water where a hydraulic lift returns you to the boat. Classes for certification are offered. Call to discuss your needs. Rr. Introductory flight wknd 9, 12:30 & 3:30; wkdy by appointment (Monty's Marina, 2550 S Bayshore Dr; 305-285-8978)

■ HORSEBACK RIDING

Good Hope Equestrian Center, NARHA-accredited, offers therapeutic and occupational horse training for adults over 21 with disabilities. The long-term program includes riding lessons as well as daily feeding and grooming of horses and cleaning stables, with the possible goal of preparation for future employment. Board horses via a mounting block with a lift; equipment is adapted as needed. Rr. Wkdy 9-3 (22155 SW 147 Ave, Redlands; 305-258-3188)

Kiwanis Horses & Handicapped offers 1-hr, recreational and therapeutic riding for anyone over age 4. A waiting list is typical for this free program. To enter, you must complete an application, provide a physician's approval and be evaluated by staff. A physical therapist works with the riding instructor to establish goals and volunteers work closely with riders. You can board horses by a WC ramp or mounting block. Rr. Oct-May Sat 8:30-1 (Circle T Ranch, 18350 SW 264 St; 305-271-2210)

■ KAYAKING

Parks: Haulover

■ MISC

City of Miami Beach offers a range of accessible recreation programs at various locations for kids, adults and seniors; visitors are welcome. Therapeutic Rec programs include ceramics, sailing, Special Olympic training in various sports and much more. After-school programs are available for able-bodied and disabled kids at several rec centers. A Social Club for adults with developmental disabilities sponsors different functions (dances, field trips, art classes) every Sat night. Ballroom and Latino dances are held weekly for seniors. (305-673-7224/993-2001)

Junior Sports programs, sponsored by Metro-Dade County Parks, provide a chance for kids with mobility impairments to try out and learn the fundamentals of various sports. Visitors are welcome. (Tropical Park, 7900 SW 40 St; 305-857-6680/665-5319)

Leisure Access Center offers after-school programs, sports programs every other Sat and seasonal camps for kids over age 5 with disabilities. Sports, exercise and recreational programs are also for adults with disabilities. Visitors are welcome. (AD Barnes Park, 3401 SW 70 Ave; 305-665-5319)

■ MUSEUMS

American Police Hall of Fame has more than 10,000 displays on law enforcement, including a mock crime scene (where successful detectives get certificates), a jail cell, gas chamber and guillotine. A memorial lists US officers killed in the line of duty since 1960. Elevator; gift shop; CRr. $. 10-5:30 (3801 US 1; 305-573-0070)

Bass Museum of Art features rotating exhibits of contemporary European and American art along with a permanent collection of period furniture and sculpture. Street parking; gift shop; cafeteria; Rr. $. Tue-Sat 10-5; Sun 1-5 (2121 Park Ave, Miami Bch; 305-673-7530)

Coral Gables Merrick House is the magnificent, turn-of-the-century, coral rock home of George Merrick, the imaginative founder of Coral Gables. Sidewalks lead from parking to a ramp on the W side of the house and offer vistas of the lovely 2-acre grounds. While the 2nd floor is not accessible, a 10-min video covers the upstairs. Rr on grounds. $. Wed & Sun tours 1-4 or by appt (907 Coral Way, Coral Gables; 305-460-5361)

Gold Coast Railroad Museum is a train shed housing antique railroad cars and memorabilia including the Pullman car used by Presidents Roosevelt, Truman, Eisenhower and Reagan. The train cars are inaccessible (President Roosevelt got up the steps and used a narrow WC). Gift shop; Rr. Wkdy 11-3; wknd 11-

4 (12450 SW 152 St, S Miami; 305-253-0063)

Historical Museum of Southern Florida dedicates 40,000 sq feet to the last 10,000 yrs in south Florida and the Caribbean. Learn about those who shaped this region, from the Tequesta Indians and pirates to cowboys, calypso musicians and land scammers. Temporary exhibits focus on current events, ethnic interests and folk life. See Tours. Parking garage with 2nd floor walkway; gift shop; Rr. $. Wkdy 10-5; Thu -9pm; Sun 12-5 (Miami-Dade Cultural Center, 101 W Flagler St; 305-375-1492)

Lowe Art Museum has permanent collections of Italian Renaissance art, Greco-Roman antiquities and Native American artifacts. Traveling exhibits include local and international artists. Tours for 5 or more can be arranged 3 days in advance. WC loaners; gift shop; CRr. $. Tue-Sun hrs vary (University of Miami, 1301 Stanford Dr; 305-284-3535)

Miami Museum of Art features a permanent collection and outstanding rotating exhibits of contemporary Western art. Parking garage with 2nd floor walkway; elevators; gift shop; Rr. $/free Thu 5-9 & 2nd Sat. Tue-Fri 10-5; wknd 12-5 (Miami-Dade Cultural Center, 101 W Flagler St; 305-375-3000)

Miami Museum of Science & Space Transit Planetarium is a chance to trek the path of early scientists in an Indiana Jones-style exhibit, surf the web at lightning speed and play virtual basketball. Tots can play in Gravity Playground. Interactive traveling and permanent exhibits offer educational fun. The planetarium is accessible; the observatory is not. Call for the schedule of daily laser and star shows. Outside, sidewalks lead to a ramped wildlife center housing rare birds and reptiles. Gift shop; vending machines; Rr. $/half price wkdy after 4:30. 10-6 (3280 S Miami Ave; 2 mi from downtown; 305-646-4200)

Vizcaya Museum is a 16th century Italian Renaissance villa with 10 acres of formal gardens on Biscayne Bay. A sidewalk leads from parking to the house. A lift takes you to the 1st floor with rooms of Renaissance, Baroque, Rococo and Neoclassic decorative arts. Via a service elevator, you can access the kitchen on the 2nd floor. A video and photo albums portray the rest of the 2nd floor, tower rooms and casino. Ask for the map of WC access through gardens with hard-packed gravel paths. Occasionally guided tours, some by moonlight, are offered. WC loaners; gift shop; cafe; Rr in cafe. $. 9:30-4:30 (3251 S Miami Ave, Coconut Grove; 305-250-9133)

Wings over Miami is an actual hangar with a large variety of vintage aircraft. Planes are roped off, but you can get close. Video booths feature footage of warplanes in action. Gift shop; drinks; Rr. $. Thu-Sun 10-5 (Tamiami Airport, 14710 SW 128 St; 305-233-5197)

Wolfsonian-FIU, a renovated 1927 warehouse in the Art Deco District, is home to over 70,000 objects-arts-moderns from furniture and machines to rare books and posters. Exhibits cover 19th and 20th century themes of nationalism, politics, industrialization, architecture, consumerism and world's fairs. Call for reservations to tour the building and for programs and workshops. Valet parking at Hotel Astor (956 Washington Ave); parking in street or nearby garages; Rr. $/D Thu 6-9pm. Mon-Sat 11-6; Sun 12-5 (Florida International University, 1001 Washington Ave, Miami Bch; 305-531-1001)

Ziff Jewish Museum: Home of Mosaic, in an exquisite, restored, 1936 synagogue, depicts 235 yrs of Jewish history and traditions in Florida through photos and artifacts. Enjoy rotating exhibits and a video on the restoration of the synagogue. Park on 3 St and use the ramp on E side of building (ring the bell). Guided tours on occasion; gift shop; CRr. $/Sat free. Tue-Sun 10-5 (301 Washington Ave; 305-672-5044)

■ **PARI-MUTUELS**
Calder Race Course features live horse

racing Jun-Dec at 11am and simulcasts every evening and some afternoons. WC seating is in the grandstand, clubhouse and restaurants (reservations advised). Valet parking; Rr (21001 NW 27 Ave; 305-625-1311)

Flagler Greyhound Track offers live dog racing Jun-Dec and simulcasts all year. At the clubhouse entrance, take the elevator to the clubhouse, restaurant and/or grandstand. WC seating on the restaurant's top tier; Rr. $. Races: 8pm; Tue, Thu & Sat also 1pm. Simulcasts noon-2:30am (401 NW 38 Ct; 305-649-3000)

Hialeah Park is currently not open for business, but hopes to reopen by 2004. Built in 1925, it is one of the country's most beautiful racetracks with 400 flamingos making it home. WC seating at all levels. Elevators; restaurant by reservation; playground; Rr (2200 E 4 Ave, Hialeah; 305-885-8000)

Miami Jai-Alai has WC seating in the rear of the main auditorium and in the restaurant. Rr. $. Wed-Mon noon; Wed-Sat also 7pm (3500 NW 37 Ave; E of airport; 305-633-6400)

■ **PARKS**

AD Barnes Park has a 2.5-mi paved trail with a tree house that is ramped to the treetops. You can fish on a lake from the pier by an ADA picnic shelter. The Leisure Access Center here offers a variety of fun for kids and adults with mobility impairments; see Misc and Pools. Paved jogging trail; ADA playground; Rr. 7-dusk (3401 SW 70 Ave; 305-666-5883)

Amelia Earhart Park is a 515-acre park with a chain of stocked fishing lakes where you can fish from mostly flat, grassy banks or from a fishing bridge. The Bill Graham Farm Village is a ramped, 1900 homestead with farm areas where you can pet animals; the country store is inaccessible. Tom Sawyer Island, a natural play area for kids, has no adaptive equipment. Picnic shelters (401 E 65 St, Hialeah; 305-769-2693)

Bill Sadowski Park is a 30-acre park with a nature center that, upon request, offers a range of environmental programs. The deck behind the center is a fine bird-watching site in early evening. Down a short hard-packed trail, you can fish off the grassy banks of a canal. The narrow, hilly nature trails are rough limestone. Every Sat night (8-10), weather permitting, the Southern Cross Astronomical Society offers stargazing programs with a variety of telescopes on a paved pad; call for schedule of lectures and slide shows (305-661-1375). ADA picnic shelters; playground. Center hrs vary; park 9-5 (17555 SW 79 Ave; 305-255-4767)

Crandon Park is the 960 acres on the N half of Key Biscayne with a beach, wooded preserve, tennis center, golf course and marina. The 2-mi ocean beach loans beach WCs; see Beaches. At the N end of the park (parking lots 1 and 2), the nature center offers displays and films on beach and bay issues. Call (305-361-6767) for the schedule and reservations for workshops and naturalist-led walks; discuss any special needs because the staff is anxious to be helpful. A ramped tram takes 45-min historic tours between the center and the S end of the park. Or, take one of the many paved hike/bike trails that run through the park and connect to bike paths beyond park borders. Near parking lots 3 and 4, toward the S end of the park are several other activities. Check out the 20-station fitness course with several accessible stations, an amusement area with a carousel (staff can lift a child from a WC to one of the stationary bench seats with backs) and an accessible splash fountain. Sidewalks lead throughout Crandon Gardens, formerly a zoo, which encompasses 30 acres of tropical gardens with exotic birds and lakes with swans afloat. Rent a canoe or sit-on kayak; call 305-365-3018 if you need adaptive equipment and/or staff to lift you into the craft. The marina (305-361-1281) has a lighted boat ramp and floating dock (open 24 hrs) on Biscayne Bay as well as a bait shop (8-6) and restaurants. ADA picnic tables; Rr. $/parking & tram. Dawn-dusk (4000 Crandon Blvd, Key Biscayne; off Rickenbacker Cswy; 305-361-5421)

Deering Estate is a 420-acre Biscayne Bay park of archaeological, environmental and historical significance. On 1-hr, guided nature tours, you can see an early Indian burial mound. These walking tours (at 10:30, 12:45 and 3) cover 1.5 miles along hard limestone trails and a viewing boardwalk by the mound. Guided 45-min tours (at 11:45, 2 and 4:15) explore 2 historic homes restored to their 1896 and 1922 eras; both have ramps and elevators. Guided 3-hr canoe trips on weekends go to Chicken Key, a nearby salt marsh. The launch site is level and hard-packed; staff cannot lift. A 30-45 min paddle takes you to the island where you can remain or transfer into your WC; a steep ledge on the rim of the island and certain parts of the trails are tough to navigate. When making reservations, discuss any special needs. Call for schedule of special events, and nature and history programs. The main entrance has HC parking on grass; a block further, the visitor center has paved parking. ADA picnic tables; Rr. $. 10-5 (16701 SW 72 Ave; 305-235-1668)

Kendall Indian Hammocks Park, a 115-acre nature park, is a great spot for family picnics. Sidewalks lead throughout the park; hard-packed nature trails with some tree roots lead through 40 acres of woods; and a paved fitness trail has several accessible stations. Bring your Frisbee to try out the 18-hole disc golf course on grass; staff can teach you the fundamentals. ADA picnic shelters; grills; Rr. 7am-dusk (11395 SW 79 St; between Kendall Dr & Sunset Dr; 305-596-9324)

Larry & Penny Thompson Park is a 270-acre park whose pine forest is still recovering from Hurricane Andrew in 1992. A 20-acre lake, with a sandy beach, lifeguards and water slides, is open for swimming in summers; the 30' slide has a ramp. Fish in the lake from a ramped, 50' cement dock or from the grassy flat banks. A paved bike path runs 1.5 mi through the park and around the lake. Snack bar in swim season; ADA picnic shelters; playground on sand; Rr. $/swimming & slides. Dawn-dusk (12451 SW 184 St; 305-232-1049)

Matheson Hammock Park, a small scenic park, has a sidewalk from the parking lot across a sandy beach (8-dusk) to an atoll pool where you can roll into the water on a very gradual slope. An atoll is a ring-shaped coral reef around a shallow lagoon; this one is saltwater and subject to tides from the Biscayne Bay. Coral was used to construct the historic structures that now house a restaurant and park office. You can fish under a bridge past the entry gate. Turn right from the gate, park beside the bridge, and then take the hard-packed path down to the embankment underneath. The marina has a boat ramp with floating docks on Biscayne Bay. Before the entry gate is a hard-packed nature trail with interpretive signage. The marina has a boat ramp, floating dock and fishing pier on Biscayne Bay. Picnic shelters; bait shop; lifeguards; Rr. $/free with HC permit. 6am-dusk (9610 Old Cutler Rd, Coral Gables; 305-665-5475)

Oleta River State Park, with 1040 acres sitting in the midst of N Miami, is the country's largest urban park. Dense mangrove opens to a 1200' man-made beach with a gradual drop into the calm waters of Biscayne Bay. From HC parking take the sidewalk to the beach or to a 90', T-shaped, ADA pier for fishing or viewing dolphin and manatee that visit here in winter. A sunny bike trail runs 2 mi. You must cross a 20' stretch of soft dirt down to the canoe/kayak launch. If not busy, concession staff can help carry you over that stretch. Canoes and solo/tandem kayaks are rented by the hour or day; call 305-947-0302. See Cabins. Bait shop; 1 step up to the snack bar; picnic tables; playground; outdoor showers; Rr. $. 8-dusk (3400 NE 163 St, N Miami; 305-919-1846)

Pine Tree Park is a lovely spot with a sidewalk along the Intracoastal. A hard-surfaced path leads to a fenced dog park where pets can run off leash. Doggie bag dispensers (45 St & Pine Tree Dr, Miami Bch)

Stillwater Park, a small city park, has an ADA playground and ADA picnic tables. Rr. Dawn-dusk (8440 Hawthorne Ave, Miami Bch; 305-993-2000)

Tropical Park is a 275-acre sports park with some great fishing and a nature preserve. Check out a pick-up game of WC basketball on Sun winter afternoons. WC-tennis events are held here as well; see WC Events. Ask rangers for accessible spots along the banks of the 4 fishing lakes; the 12-acre North Lake is stocked with largemouth bass and others. A scenic sidewalk leads to a peninsula on North Lake and the preserve has miles of paved trails. On weekend mornings, enthusiasts race remote control cars around a special racetrack. The stable sometimes hosts horse shows in a covered arena here; WC seating is beside the bleachers; call 305-554-7334 for the schedule. ADA picnic shelters; grills; ADA water fountains; snack bars; Rr. 7am-dusk (7900 SW 40 St; 305-226-8315)

■ **PERFORMING ARTS**

Actors Playhouse features comedies, musicals, dramas and children's productions. WC seating in aisles in front & center balcony; parking behind theater; elevator; Rr (Miracle Theater, 280 Miracle Mile, Coral Gables; 305-444-9293)

African Heritage Cultural Arts Center hosts performances in the 200-seat Narcisse Theater as well as offers performing and visual arts training for youth. Club Night, with cafe-style seating, features emerging artists in jazz and comedy. Rr (6161 NW 22 Ave; 305-638-6771)

Coconut Grove Playhouse offers dramas and musicals. WC seating at ends of rows 1, 6 and 7; Rr. Oct-May (3500 Main Hwy, Coconut Grove; 305-442-4000)

Colony Theater is a 465-seat, art deco masterpiece featuring Ballet Flamenco La Rosa, off-off Broadway productions and concerts. WC seating in center aisle; street parking; Rr (1040 Lincoln Rd, Miami Bch; 305-674-1026)

Dade County Auditorium is the 2400-seat, art deco home to the Greater Miami Opera and other performing artists. WC seating on aisle in back 1st floor; Rr (2901 W Flagler St; 305-547-5414)

Gusman Center, an ornate movie palace built in 1925, serves as a 1700-seat concert hall for the Florida Philharmonic, gospel music, international shows and, in Feb, the Miami Film Festival. WC seating in front; companions sit behind; Rr. Sep-Jun (174 E Flagler St; 305-374-2444)

Jackie Gleason Theater, once the set for its namesake's TV series, now hosts the Miami City Ballet, other dance groups, international orchestras and touring Broadway shows. In front of the building, encased in cement, are footprints and signatures of the theater's stars since 1984. WC seating at end of row N in orchestra section; street & valet parking; Rr (1700 Washington Ave; 305-673-7300)

James L Knight Center presents popular Latino, jazz and rock concerts. Take the elevator up to this 5000-seat, modernist hall. WC seating at ends of last row; Rr (400 SE 2 Ave; 305-372-4633)

Joseph Caleb Auditorium features the City Cultural Arts Series, local dance companies, Shakespeare performances and children's programs throughout the year. A resident troupe, the M Ensemble Company, presents an exciting dramatic series each year. WC seating in front & rear; Rr (5500 NW 22 Ave; N of downtown; 305-636-2350)

Lincoln Theatre is home to the New World and the Florida Symphonies and hosts other musical performances and plays. WC seating at end of row Q in center; Rr (541 Lincoln Rd, Miami Bch; 305-673-3330)

Miami Arena, a 16,500-seat facility, hosts large concerts, family shows and sports events. WC seating is in the rear of the lower level with only 1 companion but the box office can make exceptions for family shows. Rr (721 NW 1 Ave; 305-530-4400)

University of Miami School of Music offers free concerts during the school year in 2 venues. The Gusman Concert Hall (1314 Miller Dr) has WC seating on the aisle in the front row. The Clark Recital Hall (in the Weeks Center at 5501 San Amaro) has WC seating on the aisles in the center. Rr (Coral Gables; 305-284-6477)

■ **POOLS**

The following pools are heated and have lifts (fixed seats); staff can help with transfers. Changing rooms have Rr and roll-in showers with hand-held sprayers. Call for hours and the schedule of exercise and swim classes for folks with physical disabilities. **AD Barnes** also has a ramped pool, adapted aquatics and a submersible WC (3701 SW 72 Ave; 305-665-1626). **Flamingo Park** also has a water play area ramped to 18" (11 St at Jefferson Ave; 305-673-7750). **Helen Sands Pool** (S Dade Park, 16350 SW 280 St; 305-248-1386). **Norwood** (19401 NW 14 Ave; 305-653-1511). **Scott Rakow Youth Center** (2700 Sheridan Ave, Miami Bch; 305-673-7767). **Tamiami** (11202 SW 48 St; 305-223-7077). These pools are open in summer only: **Cutler Ridge** (10100 SW 200 St; 305-238-4166); **Marva Bannerman** (4829 NW 24 Ave; 305-635-2461); **Naranja** (14150 SW 264; 305-258-1945); **Palm Springs** (7901 NW 176 St; 305-558-3762); and **Richmond** (14375 Boggs Dr; 305-238-5692).

Venetian Pool is a private, historic, spring-fed pool sculpted from a rock quarry complete with waterfalls and caves. A hydraulic lift lowers you in your WC into the 78-degree water. Outdoor cafe on wknds; locker room; Rr. $. Days & hrs vary (2701 DeSoto Blvd, Coral Gables; 3 blocks S of Coral Way; 305-460-5356)

■ **SAILING**

Shake-A-Leg is a chance for folks with disabilities to try out sailing or become a recreational or competitive sailor. Make an appointment for a free, 1-hr, introductory sail. You may then choose a basic class (4 sessions Sat 9:30-1:30), intermediate classes, private instruction and even a racing clinic. Shake-a-Leg has universally accessible, self-righting, 20' sailboats, with 2 special seats for WC sailors and all lines into the cockpit for control. Staff lifts you from your WC into the boat from a ramped floating dock. Races every Wed evening during the summer and camps for kids age 5-15, with and without disabilities, run mid-Jun to mid-Aug from 9-4. 9-5 (Monty's Marina, 2600 S Bayshore Dr; 305-858-5550)

■ **SCUBA**

Bubble's Dive Center has experience with WC divers. Take either private or group lessons. Pool sessions occur in a pool with a ramp; on open water dives, staff can lift you in your WC onto the boat and into the water. Certified divers can take night dives and 2-site, half-day dives to explore wrecks and reefs. Day dives 8 & 1:30 (2671 SW 27 Ave; 305-856-0565; 800-622-0565)

■ **SHOOTING RANGES**

Trail Glades Gun Range offers the public a 69-position pistol/rifle range up to 300', 5 skeet and 6 trap fields and a 12-station sporting clays course. Sign up for classes in basic pistol safety, rifle safety and trap & skeet. Rr. Hrs vary (17601 SW 8 St; 305-226-1823)

■ **SHOPPING**

Boutiques abound in Bal Harbour Shops (9700 SR A1A, Bal Harbour; 305-866-0311); Bayside Marketplace, a large outside waterfront mall with street performers and the Pier 5 Market that showcases artisans and inventors (401 US 1; 305-577-3344); Coconut Grove's Main Hwy, the Grenwich Village of Florida; Cocowalk, a multilevel open mall (3015 Grand Ave, Coconut Grove; 305-444-0777); downtown Coral Gables along Coral Way (between 37 Ave & 42 Ave); historic Main Street in Homestead (41 N Krome Ave; 305-242-4814); downtown Miami on US 1 (3 Ave to NE 3 St; 305-379-7070); Streets of Mayfair (2911 Grand Ave, Coconut Grove; 305-448-1770); and South Beach with upscale boutiques and vintage shops (Ocean Dr & Collins Ave & Washington Ave).

Flea Markets: Opalocka/Hialeah Flea Market has over 1200 vendors along paved paths indoors and out. Rr. 7-7 daily (12705 LeJeune Rd; 305-688-8080)

Malls: Aventura Mall (19501 US 1, Aventura; 305-935-1110); Cutler Ridge Mall (20505 S Dixie Hwy, Cutler Ridge; 305-235-8562); Dadeland Mall (7535 N Kendall Dr; 305-665-6226); Mall of the Americas (7795 W Flagler St; 305-261-8772); Miami International Mall (1455 NW 107 Ave; 305-593-1775); Omni International Mall (1601 US 1; 305-374-6664); Prime Outlets (250 SW 344 St, Florida City; 305-248-4727); Westland Mall (1675 W 49 St; Hialeah; 305-823-9310)

Specialty Shops can be found in Little Haiti (Miami Ave to NE 2 Ave); Little Havana (Calle Ocho/SW 8 St, between SW 12 Ave & SW 27 Ave); the Miami Fashion District with outlet stores (E of I-95 along 5 Ave between 25 St & 29 St); Miami International Arts & Design District, open wkdy (NE 36 St to NE 41 St between NE 2 Ave & N Miami Ave)

■ **SPECTATOR SPORTS**
Baseball: Florida Marlins, a major league team, plays in the Pro Player Stadium with WC seating on all levels and at all prices. Rr. Apr-Sep (2269 NW 199 St; 305-626-7400)
Basketball: Miami Heat, an NBA team,

plays Nov-Apr and Miami Sol, a WBA team, plays May-Sep. WC seating & elevators on all levels. Use the drop-off area on the E extension of NE 8 St or the on-site garage on Heat Blvd. Rr. (American Airlines Arena, 601 US 1; 786-777-1250)
Football: Miami Dolphins, an NFL team, plays in the Pro Player Stadium with WC seating on all levels and at all prices. Rr. Aug-Dec (2269 NW 199 St; 305-626-7400)
■ **TENNIS**
WC-Tennis clinics, sponsored by Metro-Dade Parks, are free for residents and visitors. The Big Five Tennis Club holds adult clinics (age 18 and over) for novices from 9-10 and for intermediate players from 10-11 on Sat mornings (SW 92 Ave, Miami; just N of US 41/SW 8 St). Crandon and Tropical Parks (see Parks) hold clinics for kids (age 10-18) on various days and hrs. For registration and information, call Lisa MaCahill, Leisure Services 305-234-4948.
■ **TOURS**
Historical Museum of South Florida offers an array of historical tours led by Professor George on foot, Metrorail, bus, boat or a combination. The focus ranges from local historic crimes to downtown and interesting individual communities. He can also customize a tour to your interests and abilities. Overnight tours stay at historic B&Bs, some of which are WC friendly. (101 W Flagler St; 305-375-1621)
Miami Design Preservation League sponsors 90-min walking tours of the Art Deco district in South Beach, covering about 1 mi. Learn about the history and early 20th century architecture in this fascinating neighborhood. You can rent an audiotape or sign up for a guided tour (Thu 6:30pm; Sat 10:30am). Rr. $. 11-4 (Art Deco Welcome Center, 1001 Ocean Dr, Miami Bch; 305-672-2014)
WAVERUNNERS
Boat Tours: Fastrack

ACCOMMODATIONS

■ B&Bs
Miami River Inn, reportedly the only B&B in the city, has 3 ADA guestrooms with either a king, queen or 2 twin beds (28" high/open frames) and private bathrooms with roll-under sinks and tubs with a seat. The early 1900's house and cottages offer 40 rooms, views of the Miami River and a full breakfast in the palm-bedecked courtyard around the pool. $$-$$$ (118 SW South River Dr; at SW 2 St & SW 4 Ave; 305-325-0045; 800-468-3589)

■ CABINS/CAMPGROUNDS
†Larry & Penny Thompson Park has 240 wooded sites; RV sites have paved pads and water/elec hookups; tent sites are in a grassy field; not all sites have grills. Ask staff for a site near a bathhouse and to bring you an ADA picnic table. The ADA bathhouses have raised toilets and roll-in showers; bathhouse #4 also has roll-under sinks. Reservations are suggested from mid-Nov to Mar. The park has a freshwater lake for swimming and fishing and loans beach WCs; see Parks. Laundry; camp store (12451 SW 184 St; near Metrozoo; 305-232-1049)

Oleta River State Park has 14 primitive, 1-room cabins; 1 is ADA with AC, a full bed and set of bunks. The only furnishings are a swing lamp, small fold-down shelf/table and, on the ramped porch, a swing and bench. Outside you'll find a raised ground grill and an ADA picnic table on cement. No kitchen or linens! The ADA bathhouse next door has a raised toilet, roll-under sink and roll-in shower with a fold-down bench and a lowered showerhead. See Parks. Reservations suggested (3400 NE 163 St, N Miami; 305-919-1846; 800-326-3521)

■ CONDOS
Private oceanfront condos, in Miami's South Beach district, are WC friendly and rented by the month or less. One, on the 12th floor with an awesome view of Miami, has 1 BR with a king bed (open frame) and a queen sofa bed in the living room. The other, on the 9th floor with an ocean view, is a studio with a king-size Murphy bed and a queen sofa bed. Both have full kitchens and roll-in showers. Pool; laundry in building (Jason Colling, 69 Low Willington Crook, Durham, England D1150BG; Roney Palace, 2301 SR A1A, Miami Bch, 33139; myst1fy@hotmail.com; 305-673-3704)

■ MOTELS
Amerisuites has 5 ADA 1BR suites, each with a kitchenette, full bed (23" high/platform) and sofa bed in the living room. Each bathroom has a raised toilet, roll-under sink and roll-in shower with a hand-held sprayer and seat. Free brkfst; pool; laundry. $$$ (11520 SW 88 St, Kendall; just E of FL Tpke exit 20; 305-279-8688)

Baymont Inn has 5 ADA rooms, each with a full bed (23" high/platform) and bathroom with a raised toilet and roll-under sink; rooms 109 and 111 have roll-in showers with hand-held sprayers; others have tubs. Free brkfst; laundry. $$ (10821 Caribbean Blvd, Cutler Ridge; 305-278-001)

Best Western has 5 ADA 1BR suites, each with a queen bed (22" high/open frame), refrigerator and coffeepot. Bathrooms have raised toilets, roll-under sinks, roll-in showers with hand-held sprayers and seats. Free brkfst; pool; laundry. $$ (411 S Krome Ave/SR 997, Florida City; 305-246-5100; 888-981-5100)

Comfort Suites has 8 ADA 1 BR suites, each with a king bed (24" high/open frame), queen sofa bed in the living room, refrigerator, microwave and coffeepot. Bathrooms have roll-under sinks; rooms 109 and 123 have roll-in showers; others have tubs. Free brkfst; pool; laundry. $$ (3901 SW 117 Ave, Kendall; 305-220-3901)

Hampton Inn has 7 ADA rooms with a king or 2 full beds (23" high/platforms), coffeepots and bathrooms with raised toilets. Two rooms have refrigerators and microwaves. Five rooms have roll-under sinks; rooms 204 and 221 have roll-in showers with hand-held sprayers and seats; others have tubs. Free brkfst; pool; laundry; fitness room; across from MetroRail station. $$-$$$ (2800 SW 28 Ter, Coconut Grove; at US 1 & 27 Ave; 305-448-2800)

Hampton Inn/Airport has 6 ADA rooms and a 1BR suite, each with a king, queen or 2 full beds (23" high/platforms). The suite has a full sofa bed in the living room, a refrigerator and microwave; all units have coffeepots. Bathrooms have raised toilets; five units have roll-under sinks. Rooms 203 and 301 have roll-in showers with hand-held sprayers and seats; others have tubs. Free brkfst; pool; laundry; fitness room. $$-$$$ (777 NW 57 Ave; 305-262-5400)

Holiday Inn, along the Intracoastal, has 5 ADA rooms, each with a king bed (open frame) and coffeepot. Bathrooms have raised toilets, roll-under sinks and roll-in showers with hand-held sprayers and seats. Pool; bar; restaurant for breakfast & dinner. $$-$$$ (6060 Indian Creek Dr, Miami Bch; 305-865-2565)

Homestead Studio Suites has 7 ADA 1BR suites with a king, queen or 2 full beds (22" high/open frames), queen sofa beds in the living rooms and full kitchens. Bathrooms have roll-under sinks; rooms 118 and 120 have roll-in showers; others have tubs or showers. Pool; laundry; bar; entertainment; full restaurant. $-$$ (8720 NW 33 St; 305-436-1811)

Hyatt Regency has 17 ADA rooms and an ADA 1BR suite with a king or 2 full beds (open frames) and coffeepots. The suite has a queen sofa bed in the living room. Bathrooms have roll-under sinks; rooms 523, 525, 623, 625, 723, and 725 have roll-in showers with hand-held sprayers and seats; other rooms and the suite have tubs. A sidewalk leads to a dock on the Miami River. Free brkfst;

pool; laundry; bar; entertainment. $$$ (400 SE 2 Ave; 305-358-1234)

Marriott, on the Biscayne Bay, has 18 ADA rooms and suites with a choice of a king or 2 full beds (open frames) and coffeepots. Suites have queen sofa beds in the living rooms and refrigerators. Bathrooms have raised toilets and roll-under sinks; rooms 2117, 2217, 2317, 2417, 2517, and 2617 have roll-in showers; others have tubs. A marina on the premises has boat rentals and charter fishing. Pool; laundry; bar; entertainment; full restaurant. $$-$$$ (1633 N Bayshore Dr; 305-374-3900)

Miccosukee Resort, where gaming is the primary attraction, has 13 ADA rooms and 2 ADA 1BR suites with a choice of king or 2 full beds (open frames) and coffeepots. Suites also have refrigerators and microwaves. Bathrooms have raised toilets, roll-under sinks and roll-in showers with hand-held sprayers and seats. Pool; laundry; bar; entertainment; full restaurant. $$ (500 SW 177 Ave; 305-925-2555; 877-242-6464)

Ocean Surf Hotel is a charming renovated Art Deco structure with 2 ADA rooms, each with 2 full beds (21" high/open frames) and a bathroom with a raised toilet, roll-under sink and roll-in shower with a hand-held sprayer and seat. At 73 St, less than 2 blocks from this oceanfront hotel, is a ramped access to a beach with beach WCs; see Beaches. Free brkfst; electronic door locks. $$ (7436 Ocean Ter, Miami Bch; 305-866-1648; 800-555-0411)

Silver Sands Beach Resort has 3 ADA rooms, each with 2 full beds (open frames) and a kitchenette. Bathrooms have raised toilets, roll-under sinks and roll-in showers. This resort is 2 mi from Crandon Park where you can borrow a beach WC; see Beaches. Pool; laundry. $$$ (301 Ocean Dr, Key Biscayne; 305-361-5441)

Sonesta Beach Resort has 8 ADA rooms with a choice of a king or 2 queen beds (22.5" high/open frames), balconies and coffeepots. Bathrooms have raised toilets and roll-under sinks; rooms 203, 304, 325 and 705 have roll-in showers with hand-held sprayers and seats; others have tubs. This beachfront hotel is 2 mi from Crandon Park with beach WCs; see Beaches. Pool; bar; entertainment; full restaurant; fitness center & spa; tennis courts; children's programs. $$$ (350 Ocean Dr, Key Biscayne; 305-361-2021; 800-766-3782)

The Tides has 2 ADA rooms, each with 2 queen beds (20" high/open frames) and a bathroom with a roll-under sink and tub with a hand-held sprayer and seat. Pool; bar; entertainment; full restaurant. $$$ (1220 Ocean Dr, Miami Bch; 305-604-5070)

Westgate has 4 ADA 1BR suites, each with a king bed, queen sofa bed in the living room and kitchenette with a microwave, refrigerator and coffeepot. Bathrooms have raised toilets, roll-under sinks and tubs. This beachfront hotel has a fishing pier in back. Pool, laundry, full restaurant. $$-$$$ (16701 SR A1A, N Miami Bch; 305-949-1300; 800-894-8777)

Wyndham Resort has 23 ADA rooms with a choice of a king or 2 full beds (open frames) and bathrooms with raised toilets and roll-under sinks. Rooms 514, 516, 614 and 616 have roll-in showers with hand-held sprayers and seats; others have tub/showers. Pool; bar; full restaurant. $$$ (4833 SR A1A, Miami Bch; 305-532-3600)

WEST PALM BEACH

Juno Beach, Jupiter, Lake Worth, Loxahatchee, Pahokee, Palm Beach, Palm Beach Gardens, Palm Beach Shores, Riviera Beach, Tequesta, Wellington

West Palm Beach is the northernmost glitter on the Gold Coast. Beyond watching polo and croquet, there's plenty to do at the beaches (three with beach wheelchairs), a golf course with an adaptive golf cart, a water park with above average access and places to fly and glide. The county loans out a handcycle and a sports wheelchair to use in active tennis, quad rugby and basketball programs here. Six public pools have lifts.

Tourist Info

Palm Beach County Tourist Information: 8020 W Indian Town Rd, Jupiter, 33478; 561-575-4636

Palm Beach County Visitors Bureau: 1555 Palm Beach Lakes Blvd, #204, 33401; 800-833-5733

Arts Line: 561-471-2901; 800-882-2787

Web sites: www.palmbeachfl.com; www.pbccc.org; www.see-palmbeach.com

Transportation

Palm-Tran Bus Service has lifts on all buses throughout the county. (561-233-4287)

Palm-Tran Connections offers door-to-door van service for those who cannot use public buses. Complete an application to be pre-approved. (561-649-9848/649-9838)

Molly's Trolleys are ramped, 1920's-style trolleys (with lockdowns) that operate from City Place, in front of the FAO Schwartz bear, to various locations along Clematis St. (561-838-9511)

Tri-Rail Commuter Train runs from Miami Airport with stops all the way to West Palm Beach. All trains are equipped for WCs and at some stops, with 48-hr notice, staff can arrange for accessible courtesy buses to your destination. (305-

836-0986; 800-874-7245)

WC Resources
Coalition for Independent Living Options loans adaptive equipment and offers an after-school program and a teen summer camp. (6800 Forest Hill Blvd; 561-966-4288; 800-683-7337)

ACTIVITIES

■ ATTRACTIONS

Bethesda-by-the-Sea is an exquisite 15th century, Gothic-style Episcopal church. The formal Cluett Gardens have paved paths past fountains and unusual botanical specimens. Rr. 8-5 (141 S County Rd, Palm Bch; at Barton Ave; 561-655-4554)

Centennial Fountain is an accessible interactive water play feature in the heart of downtown that has become so popular the city brings in lifeguards during the summer (9-6). Clematis by Night is a street festival every Thu evening at 5:30 with free concerts, craft shows, you name it! (Clematis St; at Flagler Dr & Narcissus Ave)

Lion Country Safari is a chance to drive your own vehicle (no convertibles!) through 4 mi of African, Asian and North American habitats for a close up of 1200 free-roaming animals, from elephants and ostriches to lions and llamas. The walk-through areas include animal shows, aviaries, a nursery, petting zoo and living quarters for reptiles and primates. Roll aboard the Safari Queen pontoon boat for 10-min ride past islands of birds, monkeys and other creatures. The carousel and paddleboats are not accessible. Restaurant; gift shop; picnic area; Rr. $. 9:30-5:30; last car at 4:30 (2003 Lion Country Safari Rd, Loxahatchee; off Southern Blvd/US 98, 18 mi W of I-95; 561-793-1084)

Marinelife Center celebrates endangered sea turtles with live exhibits, touch tanks, an interactive audiovisual show and a restored, life-size, leatherback sea turtle. A mulched path passes turtle tanks with interpretive signage.

The center is located at Loggerhead Park (dawn-dusk), a 17-acre county park with a paved path running along the dunes over the beach. Tennis; ADA picnic tables; grills; outdoor showers; Rr. Tue-Sat 10-4; Sun 12-3 (14200 US 1, Juno Bch; at SR A1A, N of Donald Ross Rd; 561-627-8280)

Mounts Botanical Garden has paved paths through most of the 13 acres of exotic and native trees and plants, rainforest habitat, butterfly and water gardens. One-hr tours start on Sat at 11 and Sun at 2:30. Picnic shelter; Rr. $/D. Mon-Sat 8:30-4:30; Sun 1-5 (531 N Military Trail; between Belvedere Rd & Southern Blvd/US 98; 561-233-1749)

Palm Beach Zoo is a 23-acre tropical home to more than 400 animals, including a komodo dragon, Florida panther and a 100-lb rodent! Shaded paved paths lead throughout the zoo, including a petting zoo and reptile house. Shows, animal encounters and feedings occur daily. Adult strollers for rent; gift shop; cafe; Rr. 9-5 (Dreher Park, 1301 Summit Blvd; 561-533-0887)

■ BASKETBALL

Palm Beach County offers weekly WC-basketball clinics for kids up to age 18. The county also loans a sports WC that you can pick up at John Prince Park. While the wheels come off, it is bulky to transport; you must leave a deposit and copy of your driver's license. Call for location, time and registration and to borrow the sports WC. $. Sep-May (Special Populations Office, John Prince Park, 2700 6 Ave S, Lake Worth; 1st stop sign in park turn right, next stop sign turn left; 561-963-7379)

■ BEACHES

*Carlin Park is a 118-acre county park with a 3000' beachfront. A boardwalk leads from HC parking to a dune cross-over ramped to the rock-strewn beach. A friend can ask at the lifeguard tower on the sand to borrow the beach WC (no arms; drink and umbrella holders); guards will bring it to you. A cafe offers indoor and outdoor WC seating for breakfast and lunch (561-747-1134). An amphitheater, with open seating on the grass, hosts musicals and other types of performances. Lifeguards 9-5; ADA picnic tables; grills; outdoor showers; tennis; playgrounds; Rr. Dawn-dusk (400 S SR A1A, Jupiter; S of Indiantown Rd)

*John D MacArthur Beach State Park is a barrier island with 2 mi of secluded ocean beach lined by a tropical hammock. Ask at the ranger station or nature center to borrow a self-propelled beach WC (removable arms) so staff can bring it to you at the parking lot. From there, a ramped boardwalk leads over an estuary and dunes onto the white sand. Or, if you can transfer, a tram (with room to store a folding WC) can take you to the beach. At low tide the sand is hard packed; at high tide the beach is very narrow. While the estuary is quite natural, you may find spots open and hard packed enough to fish or surf cast. The nature center (Wed-Mon 9-5) features a 14-min video on the park's habitats, live exhibits of loggerhead sea turtles, fish and seahorses and numerous ecology programs, even concerts. ADA picnic shelters on grass in wooded areas; vending machines in nature center; ADA playground; Rr. $. 8-dusk (10900 SR A1A, N Palm Bch; 561-624-6950)

Lake Worth Beach stretches 1200' along the Atlantic with 2 ramps from parking: one at the N end and the other just S of the pier (see Fishing Piers). Lifeguards can help you in and out of the water. Across the street is Barton Park with a playground on grass, picnic

tables and grills. Cabana & umbrella rentals; shops; restaurant at pier; lifeguards; Rr across street. $/parking. 9-5 (SR A1A & SR 802, Lake Worth; 561-533-7367)

Ocean Reef Park, sandwiched by hotels, has a dune crossover from HC parking to an overlook of the county's 700' beachfront. Lifeguards 9-5; picnic tables; grills; outdoor showers; Rr. Dawn-dusk (3860 N SR A1A, Riviera Bch; just N of Blue Heron Blvd Bridge/SR 703)

*Palm Beach Municipal Beach, hidden by a seawall for 1 mi along SR A1A, loans a beach WC (removable arms). From the sidewalk by parking, take the ramp to the lifeguard tower to get the WC. If someone is waiting, 2-hr limits apply. Lifeguards summer 9-5; winter 8:30-4:30. $/parking. Dawn-dusk (Use S entrance at Chilean Rd & S SR A1A; 561-838-5483)

RG Kreusler Park is a 2-acre county beach where a dune crossover ramps to the sand. Lifeguards 9-5; outdoor showers; Rr. $/parking. Dawn-dusk (2695 S SR A1A, Palm Bch)

Riviera Municipal Beach has a 600' sidewalk from parking through the dunes to the edge of the hard-packed sand. If you can transfer into a 4-wheel vehicle, lifeguards can drive you the additional 600' to the shoreline. Lifeguards 9-5; cabana rentals; restaurants nearby; outdoor showers; Rr. Dawn-dusk (SR A1A, Riviera Bch; parking behind Ocean Mall; 561-845-4079)

■ BIKE TRAILS

Parks: Howard, John Prince, Okeeheelee

Flagler Dr in West Palm Beach has a palm-lined, sidewalk along the Intracoastal that is popular with joggers and skaters. A grassy median separates you from the road. This 7-mi trail runs the length of the city through lovely residential areas at the N end, past Currie Park and ends at Summa Beach Park where sailboats dot the shore.

Palm Beach has a 5-mi paved path,

much of it along the Intracoastal, from Worth Ave to the N end of the island at Palm Beach Inlet. Roll by some stunning mansions.

■ BOAT RAMPS

Fishing Piers: Currie. Parks: John Prince, Okeeheelee. Campgrounds: South Bay
Bert Winters Park has boat ramps with fixed docks on the Intracoastal. Picnic tables; playground; ball fields; Rr. Dawn-11pm (13425 Ellison Wilson Rd, Juno Bch; .5 mi S of Donald Ross Rd)
Burt Reynolds Park has boat ramps and fixed docks on the Intracoastal. This 36-acre county park (open dawn-dusk) is home to the Florida History Center; see Museums. ADA picnic tables; grills. 24 hrs (800 N US 1, Jupiter; N of Indiantown Rd)
Juno Park has a boat ramp and fixed dock on the Intracoastal. This 18-acre county park also has ball fields and lighted tennis. Picnic tables; Rr. Dawn-11pm (2090 Juno Rd, Juno Bch)
Phil Foster Park has boat ramps, fixed docks and a swim area on the Intracoastal. This park (open dawn-dusk) has the closest ramp to Peanut Island (see Parks). Lifeguards 9-5:20; picnic tables; grills; outdoor showers; Rr. 24 hrs (900 E Blue Heron Blvd/SR 703, Riviera Bch)

■ BOAT RENTALS

Club Nautico rents 24' pontoon boats (30" entry) for half/full days on the Intracoastal for up to 12. The ramp to the floating dock can be steep at low tide but staff can help. Bait shop. 9-5 (Sea Sport Marina, 1095 A N SR A1A, Jupiter)
Jupiter Hills Lighthouse Marina rents a pontoon boat (30" entry) for up to 12 on the Intracoastal. Staff can lift you aboard in your WC. 2-hr minimum (18261 SE US 1, Tequesta; 561-744-0727)

■ BOAT TOURS

Museums: Palm Beach Maritime. Parks: Peanut Island
Mariah is a 47' catamaran sailboat offering 3-hr sightseeing cruises in the Atlantic and the Lake Worth Lagoon. Crew can help you board via the wide gangplank then ease you down a few steps onto the bridge deck. Private charters are available. Call for schedule. Drinks & snacks included; Rr, not ADA, with steep ramp at marina office (N Palm Bch Marina, 1037 Marina Dr, N Palm Bch; 561-844-3297/329-4122)
Palm Beach Water Taxi offers 90-min, narrated, sightseeing tours covering local history, wildlife and mansions of the rich and famous. Arrange in advance with Chip (561-844-1724 x1009) to use the large accessible boat; if the tide is low, crew can lift you aboard from your WC. Tours 10, 2, 4 & sunset (98 Lake Dr, Palm Bch Shores; 561-683-8294; 800-446-4577)

■ BOWLING

Jupiter Lanes has ramped lanes and bowling ball ramps. Lounges; game room; food court; Rr. Sun-Thu 9am-11pm; Fri-Sat -1am (350 Maplewood Dr, Jupiter; 561-743-9200)

■ CANOEING/KAYAKING

Canoe Outfitters of Florida rents canoes and solo/tandem sit-in or sit-on kayaks for the Loxahatchee River. The 2.5-mi round trip on the upper stretch of the river to Riverbend Park is very scenic. Try a 3 1/2-hr, guided trip. With advance notice, crew can help you down the steep, sandy bank to the river and lift you in and out of your boat. 8-5 (8900 W Indiantown Rd, Jupiter; 1 mi W of I-95; 561-746-7053; 888-272-1257)
Lake Mangonia is a large, pristine inland lake with a launch for non-motorized boats. Next to the ramp is a short fixed pier for fishing or boarding, but you can also transfer from the gently sloping ramp into a canoe. Rr. Dawn-dusk (N Australian Ave & 30 St)

■ CASINOS

Palm Beach Princess has 7 decks of casino games, live music, nightclubs, floorshows, lounges and an all-you-can-eat buffet. Boarding is easy on the gently sloped gangway; elevators take you to all decks for the 5-hr trip; only the outside decks have stairs. Call for the schedule and route of the free bus with a lift that can take you to the day cruises. Rr. Mon-Sat 12:30 & 7; Sun 11 & 6 (777 E Port Rd, Riviera Bch; in Port of Palm Bch off MLK Blvd; 561-845-2101; 800-841-7447)

■ FISHING-CHARTERS

Blue Hole Fishing Adventures offer fly and light-tackle fishing offshore around the inlet and inshore on the Loxahatchee River. Capt Scott enjoys WC anglers and can roll you into his 24' flats boat from a floating dock for half/full-day or night fishing. (1111 Love St, Jupiter; 561-747-2101/747-0277)

Coastal Charters offers half/full-day inshore light tackle fishing trips on a 20' flats boat for up to 3 anglers. With advance notice, Capt Jeff Sacks can arrange for help to board you from a floating dock near where fish are running. (561-335-3055)

Seacret Spot Charters offers inshore, offshore and backcountry trips on a 24' boat for 2 anglers. The capt specializes in flyfishing, light tackle and sport fishing and can help your buddy lift you aboard in your WC for a half/full-day trip. (Sea Sport Marina, 1095 N SR A1A, Jupiter; 561-745-9178)

■ FISHING-PARTY BOATS

Blue Heron Fleet offers half-day drift trips in the Gulf Stream. The ramp is narrow, but with advance notice, crew can carry you aboard in your WC. Crew can also help you over the lip into the cabin. Drinks for sale; BYO food. Wed-Mon 8:30 & 1:30 (389 E Blue Heron Blvd/SR 703, Riviera Bch; 561-844-3573)

Capt Bob's Drift Fishing offers 4-hr trips in the Gulf Stream just off the coast. The ramp is narrow, but crew can carry you aboard in your WC; when the tide is low, crew can carry you down steps to a ramp. Crew can also help you over the lip to the cabin. Drinks for sale; BYO food. Thu-Tue 8:30am & 1:30pm (Municipal Marina, E 13 St, Riviera Bch; off US 1; 561-842-8823)

■ FISHING PIERS

Canoeing: Lake Mangonia. Parks: Howard, John Prince, Lake Ida, Okeeheelee, Pahokee

Currie Park has a lighted 150' pier, boat ramps with fixed docks and an overlook on the Intracoastal, all open 24 hrs. This city park also features a stunning MLK Memorial. Tours of the Maritime Museum start here; see Boat Tours. Tennis; picnic tables under trees. Dawn-dusk (2400 N Flagler Dr)

Gettler & **Poinsietta Parks** are both small city parks with short piers for fishing on the Intracoastal. Dawn-dusk (N Flager Dr, at 45 St & at 54 St)

Juno Beach Pier is a lighted, wood, 990' pier on the Atlantic. Snack bar; bait shop; outdoor showers; Rr across street in park. Nov-Feb 24 hrs (14775 SR A1A, Juno Bch; N of Donald Ross Rd; 561-799-0185)

Lake Worth Pier, a lighted 900' pier, is the closest you can get (without a boat) to the Gulf Stream in the Atlantic. See Beaches. Bait shop; restaurant; Rr across Beach Rd. $. 6am-mdnt (SR A1A & Lake Worth Rd/SR 802, Lake Worth; 561-533-7367)

■ FITNESS TRAILS

Parks: Dreher, John Prince, Okeeheelee

■ FLYING

North American Top-Gun offers a range of experiences in WW II fighter aircraft: introductory 15-min rides, aerobatics flights and 3- or 5-hr air-to-air combat. If you can grasp the control stick, you can be the pilot. Depending on the program you choose, an instructor sits in the front or back cockpit with dual controls. Staff lifts you from your WC onto the wing and then over into the cockpit. The weight limit is 350 lbs; the height limit is 6'8". All flights require a cockpit briefing; aerobatic and combat flights also require a classroom session. Be prepared to travel up to 200 mph! In the combat mission, the original M-2 machine guns have been replaced by a radar targeting system that delivers and senses hits. You can purchase a video of your ride, shot onboard from the wings and cockpit. Call for schedule at this site. (General Aviation Airport; W of Palm Bch off SR

710/Bee Line Hwy, just W of I-95; 904-823-3505)

■ GLIDING

Barry Aviation can take you for an introductory 20-min glider ride, a 40-min, mile high ride, or for the more serious, a 1-hr ride with 3 separate take-offs to 3 different altitudes. If you like, you can take over the controls, with a pilot right behind you. One of the sail-planes sits lower (24" off the ground), and with advance notice, staff can lift you into it. The weight limit for all passengers is 240 lbs; call ahead if you need to be lifted. Rr. Wed-Sun by appt (North County Airport, 11600 Aviation Blvd; at SR 710/Beeline Hwy & PGA Blvd; 561-624-3000)

■ GOLF

Okeeheelee Park has an adaptive golf cart (reserve 4 days ahead) for its 27-hole public course. The 1-person cart has hand controls, a bag carrier in front and a swivel seat from which you take your swing. You can ride the cart on the greens but not through deeper sand traps. Before use, you must be trained or assessed by the pro on a 4-hole loop. Staff can help with transfers. Non-peak hrs are suggested. Beverage carts with sandwiches; driving range; putting green; Rr at clubhouse & on course (7715 Forest Hill Blvd; 561-964-4653)

Palm Beach County sponsors WC-golf lessons on Sat mornings for 4-wk sessions in the fall and winter. Lessons are held at Okeeheelee (see above) where you can borrow an adaptive golf cart. $ (Schedule & registration 561-963-7379; golf info 561-964-4653)

■ HANDCYCLES

Palm Beach County loans a handcycle that attaches to your WC. Staff can help you attach the handcycle when you pick it up at John Prince Park where you can also test it out. You must transport it and leave a deposit and copy of your driver's license. Call ahead to schedule. (Special Populations Office, John Prince Park, 2700 6 Ave S, Lake Worth; at 1st stop sign in park

turn right, then at next stop sign turn left; 561-963-7379)

■ MISC

VSA Arts-Palm Beach County offers 4- to 8-wk sessions of graphic arts classes, from photography to painting. Classes are taught by professional artists and assisted by professionals who can adapt equipment or technique for participants with different disabilities. For information, schedule and locations, call 561-964-4822. $. Usually Sat

■ MUSEUMS

Ann Norton Sculpture Gardens and historic home sits on 2.5 acres of natural Florida gardens along the Intracoastal with over 300 varieties of palm trees. View more than 100 sculptures in her studio, home and grounds where paths are grass or crushed stone (some hard-packed and some loose). Rr. $. Nov-May Wed-Sun 11-4 (253 Barcelona Rd; 561-832-5328)

Flagler Museum is the Gilded Age mansion of railroad magnate Henry Flagler, built for his bride in 1902. Only the 1st floor of the 55-room mansion is open; it houses original furnishings and family memorabilia. Ongoing tours last 45 minutes; a brochure for self-guided tours is available. Paved paths lead through the gardens and to Flagler's private railroad car from 1886. Nov-Mar enjoy a music series, and in Feb, a lecture series. Gift shop; Rr. $. Tue-Sat 10-5; Sun 12-5 (Coconut Row & Whitehall Way, Palm Bch; 561-655-2833)

Florida History Center & Museum is jam-packed with 10,000 yrs of artifacts, memorabilia and photos of old Florida. The 1860 Jupiter Inlet Lighthouse and the 1896 DuBois Pioneer Home are inaccessible, although you can roll into the gift/book shop where you can catch a 13-min video on the lighthouse. Tours of the lighthouse occur Sun-Wed 10-4; the pioneer home is open Wed and Sun (1-5). Rr. $. Tue-Fri 10-5; wknd 12-5 (Burt Reynolds Park, 801 N US 1, Jupiter; 561-747-6639)

Hibel Museum of Art houses Edna Hibel's lithographs, paintings and porcelains. Gift Shop. Mon-Sat hrs vary (701 Lake Ave, Lake Worth; 561-533-1583; 800-771-3362) Hibel's work is also on display at a smaller gallery where Nov-May you can attend monthly concerts hosted by the Guild for International Piano Competitions (561-833-8817). Rr; gift shop. Tue-Sun hrs vary (1200 Town Center Dr, #108, Jupiter; 561-622-1380) In 2003, a third site will offer classes and rotating exhibits by other artists.

Museum of Polo & Hall of Fame celebrates the history of polo with exhibits and film. Rr. $D. Wkdy 10-4; Jan-Apr Sat 10-2 (9011 Lake Worth Rd, Lake Worth; 561-969-3210)

Norton Gallery features fine collections of 20th century American work, French impressionism and Chinese art as well as traveling exhibits and programs for children and adults. Tue-Sat 30-min tours start at 11:30 and 12:30 and Tue-Sun 1-hr tours start at 2. Gift shop; Rr. $. Tue-Sat 10-5; Sun 12-5 (1451 S Olive Ave; 561-832-5196)

Palm Beach Maritime Museum offers a 2-hr tour that includes a 1-hr, round-trip boat ride to Peanut Island and a tour of the island's bunker (once a bomb shelter for President Kennedy when at his Palm Beach home) and the boathouse museum. The museum features nationally touring exhibits from such sponsors as the Smithsonian. Boarding and disembarking the pontoon boat is easier from the fixed docks at high tide; staff can advise you of the times. Crew can help guests in manual WCs board the canopied boat. Rr. $. Thu-Sun 9, 11, 1 & 3 (Education Center at Currie Park, Flagler Dr; .5 mi N of Palm Bch Lake Blvd; 561-842-6287/662-1415)

Society of the Four Arts consists of exquisite sculpture and botanical gardens, a children's and adult's library and, Dec to mid-Apr, an art gallery and auditorium. Call for the schedule of special events including concerts, films, children's art shows and lectures by authors and noted speakers. Paths through the gardens are brick, pavers or grass. The auditorium has WC seating in front on both sides. Rr. $D. Gallery Dec-mid-Apr Mon-Sat 10-5; Sun 2-5. Garden & libraries wkdy 10-5; Sat 9-1 (Four Arts Plaza off Royal Palm Way, Palm Bch; 1 blk E of Intracoastal; 561-655-7227)

South Florida Science Museum is an excellent hands-on, science center with indoor and outdoor interactive exhibits including dozens of aquariums and touch tanks with a diverse range of sea life. The Science Trail, mostly on mulch with some boardwalk, passes whisper dishes, a fossil dig and nature's kaleidoscopes. The Aldrin Planetarium has daily shows (at 1, 2 & 3) and Fri nights. The telescope in the Gibson Observatory, open Fri until 10pm, is up a spiral staircase but, with advance notice, staff can set up a telescope on the observation deck so you can witness the night skies and special cosmic phenomena. Live science shows on weekends. Gift shop; vending machine; Rr by the entrance ramp to bldg. $. Mon-Thu 10-5; Fri -10; Sat -6; Sun 12-6 (Dreher Park, 4801 Dreher Trail N; 561-832-1988)

■ **PARI-MUTUELS**

Palm Beach Kennel Club holds year-round greyhound races and simulcasts of greyhounds, thoroughbreds, harness racing and jai alai. WC seating is on the 1st floor and in the dining room. The poker room opens 2 hrs before races. Rr. Mon, Wed & Fri-Sat 12:40pm; Sun 1pm; Wed-Sat 7:30pm (1111 N Congress Ave; across from Palm Bch Intl Airport; 561-683-2222)

■ **PARKS**

Blowing Rock Nature Preserve includes 73 acres of plants native to beachfront dunes, coastal strand, mangrove and tropical forest. From parking, take the ramp to a fairly level trail with some short, gravelly spots. The trail leads to a ramped deck where, at some high tides, you can see the ocean blown through

holes eroded into the exposed limestone. From here, a 15-min stroll takes
you through canopies of sea grapes
with some wonderful ocean views.
Across Beach Rd is the Education Center with rotating exhibits on local geology, ecology or even art. A boardwalk
N of the center takes you to a lagoon;
the trail from the S end is sandy. Picnic
in Coral Cove Park, 1 m S of the preserve. Guided, 1-hr tours; Rr in center. $.
9-5 (SR 707/Beach Rd; S end of Jupiter
Island; 561-747-3113)

Dreher Park is a 50-acre city park housing the South Florida Science Museum
(see Museums) and the Palm Beach
Zoo (see Attractions). Enjoy a 1.5-mi,
hard-packed fitness trail and observation piers on a small pond. Picnic shelters; grills; Rr. Dawn-dusk (1301 Summit Blvd; between Southern Blvd/US
98 & Forest Hill Blvd, just W of Parker
Ave)

Grassy Water Preserve Nature Center
has a short boardwalk through woods
and a swamp where you might encounter alligators, snakes and birds, including the rare snail kite. The center has
exhibits of indigenous wildlife. Call for
evening schedule. Guided tours Sun
3:30-5; Rr. 8-4:30; Apr-May at 6am for
birders (8624 Northlake Blvd; 561-627-
8831)

Howard Park is a 14-acre city park, just
S of downtown, with an ADA playground, shuffleboard and a community
center with activities from ping-pong
to literary discussions. The fitness trail
is on mulch. Picnic tables; tennis;
lighted basketball courts; Rr. 9-6:30;
during special events -9; Sat -3 (901
Parker Ave; at Okeechobee Blvd, across
from CityPlace; 561-835-7055)

John Prince Park is a 726-acre nature
and sports park with ball fields, tennis,
cricket field and petanque court. The
stocked 338-acre Lake Osborne has 3
small fishing piers and, at the N end, a
boat ramp with a fixed dock. More than
5 mi of paved bike trail run the perimeter of the park and lake. Try out the

shady .5-mi, 15-station WC-fitness trail;
another fitness trail runs 1.2 mi with 20
stations on a mulch path. A .5-mi nature trail, just N of the campground,
has interpretive signage. See Campgrounds. Playgrounds; picnic shelters;
grills; driving range, miniature golf &
irons course; Rr. Dawn-dusk (2700 6
Ave S; 4759 S Congress Ave; 2520 Lake
Worth Rd, Lake Worth; N of the Lantana Airport; 561-582-7992)

Okeeheelee Park is a 900-acre recreation area and nature park. Ball fields,
lighted tennis courts, a BMX track and
a lake for competitive and recreational
water skiing - all have viewing areas to
watch the fun. Cyclists enjoy the 8-mi
paved path that skirts the lakes and picnic areas. A 1.25-mi fitness trail is
mulched. The 111-acre stocked fishing
lake has a 50' fishing pier and a boat
ramp with a fixed dock for trolling and
non-motorized boats. Picnic areas are
throughout the park; some with shelters, most with grills and ADA tables. A
nature center has 2.5 mi of mostly
paved trails meandering through 90
acres of pine forest and wetlands. The
ramped center (hrs vary; 561-233-1400)
features hands-on exhibits about the
park's habitats and various ecological issues. The public golf courses here have
an adaptive cart; see Golf. Playgrounds;
gift shop; workshops; Rr. Dawn-dusk
(7715 Forest Hills Blvd; between Jog Rd
& FL Tpke)

Pahokee State Park, operated by the
city of Pahokee, extends 1 mi on the
shores of Lake Okeechobee. The marina
has boat ramps with fixed and floating
docks. If you didn't bring a boat, try the
2400' fishing pier that angles onto the
lake or the shorter, T-shaped pier. Bait
shop; snacks; picnic tables; Rr. 8-8 (US
441, Pahokee; 3.5 mi S of US 98; 561-
924-7832)

Peanut Island is an 86-acre, man-made
island in the Intracoastal with a palm-
lined park accessible only by boat. The
island has a fixed and a floating dock. A
lighted, 1.25-mi paved path circles the

island, passing the campground, a lighted 170' fishing pier, plenty of ADA picnic tables, grills and shelters. If using your own boat, Phil Foster Park offers a nearby launch; see Boat Ramps. A private water taxi can take you to the park. Water Tours Inc (561-339-2504) uses a 40' Navy launch out of Currie Park where, depending on the tides, the crew can lift you aboard and into a seat, then lift your WC aboard. The Palm Beach Maritime Museum offers transport and tours at the island; see Museums. Rr. Dawn-dusk (in the Intracoastal at the Lake Worth Inlet; 561-845-4445)

■ PERFORMING ARTS

Comedy Corner hosts nationally known stand-up comics. Thu and Sat shows at 7pm are smoke-free. WC seating throughout; Rr. Wed-Sun 8; Fri 10:15; Sat 7 & 9:15 (2000 S Dixie Hwy; 561-833-1812)

Cuillo Centre for the Arts is a professional theater in downtown featuring award winning off-Broadway shows and productions prior to their NY debuts. WC seating in front row; street parking; Rr. Nov-May (201 Clematis St; 561-835-9226)

Kravis Center has 3 venues for a variety of events including comedy, music, theater and dance by internationally renowned performers. The 2200-seat Dreyfoos Hall has WC seating in the front section on the aisles and in box seats. Some aisle seats have swing-away armrests for ease in transferring. The 320-seat Rinker Playhouse has WC seating in front on the aisles. The outdoor Gosman Amphitheater has bench style seats; WC seating is along the front and sides. The center is home to the following: Ballet Florida (659-2000); Florida Philharmonic (930-1812); Miami City Ballet (930-3262); Bob Lappin & the Palm Beach Pops (832-7677); Masterworks Chorus of the Palm Beaches (242-0817); Palm Beach Broadway Series (800-647-6877); and the Palm Beach Opera (833-7888). Va-

let parking available; Rr (701 Okeechobee Blvd; 561-832-7469)

Lake Worth Playhouse is a community theater for musicals and plays. The Mainstage Theater has WC seating in the rear, right of orchestra seating; or ushers can help you transfer into a front row seat. The Black Box Theater has movable seating; call in advance so staff can accommodate you. Street parking or unload in front and park in back; Rr. Sep-Jun (713 Lake Ave, Lake Worth; 561-586-6410)

Royal Poinciana Playhouse presents nationally touring Broadway musicals with top stars. WC seating center aisle & in boxes; valet parking available; Rr (70 Royal Poinciana Plaza, Palm Bch; 561-659-3310)

■ POOLS

Water Parks: Calypso Bay

Gaines Park has a lift (fixed seat) into its 25-meter heated pool; lifeguards can help with transfers. This city sports park also has ball fields, tennis, a gym, picnic shelters and grills. Lap lanes; aerobics sessions; outdoor showers; Rr. ₲. Hrs vary (1501 N Australian Ave; W of Palm Bch Mall, just N of Palm Bch Lakes Blvd; 561-835-7095)

Lake Lytal Park has a 50-meter heated pool with a lift (fixed seat); lifeguards can help with transfers. This 70-acre county park also has ball fields, tennis (see Tennis), picnic tables and grills. Aquacise classes; wading pool; roll-in showers in locker rooms; vending machines; lap swimming 2 hrs before opening; Rr. ₲. Hrs vary (3645 Gun Club Rd; off Congress Ave; 561-233-1426)

Lake Worth Beach has a heated Olympic pool where lifeguards can help you into the water. See Beaches. Summer lap swim 8-8:45 & aerobic sessions; vending machines; locker rooms with roll-in showers & Rr. ₲. 9-5 (SR A1A & Lake Worth Rd/SR 802, Lake Worth; 561-533-7367)

North County Aquatic Complex has a 50-meter heated pool with a lift (fixed seat); lifeguards can help with transfers. Aquacise classes; wading pool; roll-in showers in locker rooms; vending machines; lap swimming 1 hr before opening in summer; Rr. $. Hrs vary (861 Toney Penna Dr, Jupiter; off Military Tr; 561-745-0241)

Palm Beach Gardens has a lift (fixed seat) to its 75' heated/chilled pool. Lifeguards cannot lift you but can operate the lift. The pool is set back in a community park with a sidewalk from parking. Lap lanes; aquacise classes; Rr. $. Hrs vary (4404 Burns Rd, Palm Bch Gardens; 561-775-8270)

Santaluces High School has a 75' heated pool that is open to the public in summer. Lifeguards can help with transfers to the lift (fixed seat). Aquacise classes after hrs; lap lanes; wading pool; roll-in showers in locker rooms; vending machines; Rr. $. Wkdy & Sun 12-6; Sat 10-6 (6750 Lawrence Rd, Lantana; off Hypoluxo Rd; 561-641-9301)

■ **QUAD RUGBY**

South Florida Rattlers are a quad rugby team with players from SE Florida playing Oct-Apr. Practices are usually Sun 12-4 at the Lake Worth Community Center Gym. Spectators and players are welcome, but should call ahead to confirm. Visitors can borrow a rugby chair from the team if needed. (Dave Harrison 954-523-3567; John Bishop 561-964-1712)

■ **SCUBA**

With the strong currents of the nearby Gulf Stream, you can drift dive and cover more ground with less effort and in less time. The Stream also brings clear blue water with 70-100' visibility and marine creatures not found elsewhere in the state. Dive with sea turtles (especially in their mating season Apr-Jun), moray eels, nurse sharks, lobsters, tropical and sport fish.

Bob Sheridan, who is HSA-certified and teaches in Pompano Beach, can provide private lessons toward certification in the West Palm area. Class work can be done at your place, pool sessions can be done at one of the public pools with a

lift and he can arrange for open dives through a local shop. (954-788-3483; 800-374-3792)

SS Minnow has experience with WC divers and has a 40' custom boat with a large dive platform that eases getting in and out of the water. Try a 1- or 2-tank drift dive, or a weekend night dive. Crew lifts you aboard in your WC and from your WC onto the dive platform and into the water. Reserve in advance so extra staff can be arranged. Drinks/snacks included; Rr at dock. Wkdy 10am; Wed 5pm; wknd 8 & 1 (Phil Foster Park, Blue Heron Blvd/SR 703, Riviera Bch; 561-848-6860; 800-261-8468)

■ **SHOPPING**

Boutiques par excellence are at: CityPlace with restaurants and a 20-screen theater modeled after the Paris Opera House in an elegant open-air plaza (222 Lakeview Ave; 561-366-1000); Clematis Street District also with theaters, restaurants, live entertainment and a street festival every Thursday at 5:30 (downtown West Palm Bch; 561-833-8873); and Worth Ave with 4 tree-lined blocks of exclusive stores and salons from all over the world (Palm Bch).

Flea Markets: Dr Flea's International Flea Market is indoors with over 100 vendors. Thu-Sun 10-6 (1200 S Congress Ave; 561-965-1500). Uptown Downtown Flea Market & Outlet Mall has over 350 vendors under one roof. Wed-Sat 10-5; Sun 12-5; mall open daily (5700 Okeechobee Blvd; 561-684-5700)

Malls: Gardens of the Palm Beaches (3101 PGA Blvd, Palm Bch Gardens; 561-775-7750); Shoppes of Oakbrook (11594 US 1, N Palm Bch; 561-624-9500); Palm Beach Mall (1801 Palm Bch Lakes Blvd; 561-683-9187); Wellington Green (10300 E Forest Hill Blvd, Wellington; 248-258-6800)

■ **SKYDIVING**

Skydive America Palm Beach has experience with paraplegics on tandem dives over the gorgeous Lake

Okeechobee area. You must be fit, weigh less than 200 lbs and have good motor skills, upper body strength and balance. After 20-min instruction, staff lifts you about 5' into the plane where you are geared up, perhaps including a special harness for your legs. The flight takes about 12 min, and then you slide down to the opening and move out of the plane with your instructor. After 1 min of free-fall, the parachute takes over for the last 5 min. Extra staff catch you during landing, lift you back into your WC and then from your WC into the van to return to the airport. Weather conditions must be ideal. Speak to Karen or Larry to schedule your dive. Rr. Summer Wed-Sun, winter daily 9-dusk (Palm Bch County Glades Airport, 3597 Airport Rd, Pahokee; off SR 715, 15 mi NE of SR 80; 3.5 mi S of Pahokee; 561-924-2020; 877-258-3759)

■ **SPECTATOR SPORTS**

Auto Racing Moroso Motorsports Park features a 2.25-mi, 10-turn road course, a NHRA .25-mi drag strip and a skid pad. From along the fence, WC riders can watch drag and road races, motorcycle races and special events. Rr. Wed & Fri 6pm; Sat 5:30 (17047 Beeline Hwy, Palm Bch Gardens; 561-622-1400)

Baseball Roger Dean Stadium is the spring training home for the Montreal Expos and the St Louis Cardinals and home base for the class A Jupiter Hammerheads. WC seating with 1 companion is in all ticket categories. An elevator takes you to the suites on the 2nd floor. HC parking often gets full during spring training games; if so, use general parking and, if you can transfer, ask an attendant to send the golf cart to take you into the stadium. Call for schedule. Rr (4751 Main St, Jupiter, 561-775-1818)

Croquet The National Croquet Center has 12 lush acres devoted to the sport. WCs are not permitted on the pristine game lawns, but you can watch from

a veranda that features fine dining. Free introductory lessons are offered. (700 Florida Mango; at Summit Blvd; 561-478-2300)

Polo Gulf Stream Polo Club hosts matches Dec-Apr on Fri and Sun from 10-5. Parking & spectator areas on grass; no facilities (4550 Polo Rd, Lake Worth; off Lake Worth Rd, .5-mi W of FL Tpke; 561-965-2057). Palm Beach Polo, Golf and Country Club hosts polo matches Jan-Apr, with major games played in a stadium each Sat at 3. WC seating is on the ground level. Grass parking lot; snack bars; Rr. $ (13420 S Shore Blvd, Wellinton; 561-793-1440)

■ **TENNIS**

Palm Beach County sponsors weekly WC-tennis clinics at 2 locations. The county also loans a sports WC that you can pick up at John Prince Park; see Basketball. Call ahead for schedule and registration. $ (Lake Lytal Park, Joan Hutchinson, 3645 Gun Club Rd; 561-963-7379; South Olive Park, Rhonda Barona, 345 Summa St; 561-835-7025)

■ **TOURS**

Historical Society of Palm Beach County has brochures and maps you can use for a self-guided driving tour of historic sites. Rr. Tue-Fri 10-3 (139 N County Rd, Palm Bch; 561-832-4164)

■ **WATER PARKS**

Calypso Bay has an Olympic pool, with a lift (fixed seat) and 4 lap lanes. You can also use a lift to board an inner tube for a relaxing float down an 870' lazy river. Staff can help with transfers. The water playground slopes gently from zero depth to 18" where water guns and fountains offer accessible fun. Large umbrellas shade ADA picnic tables on the deck. The 30' waterslides have many steps. Snack bar; no outside food/drinks; inside roll-in showers; Rr. $. Spring & fall wknd 10-5; summer daily 9:30-6 (Seminole Palms Park, 151 Lamstein Ln, Royal Palm Bch; off Southern Blvd/US 98, 1 mi W of US 441; 561-790-6160)

ACCOMMODATIONS

■ B&Bs

Royal Palm House B&B is a 1925 home set in the historic Northwood District, minutes from CityPlace. The WC-friendly Date Palm Cottage has a double French door entrance with 1 step; staff can install a portable ramp. The cottage has a kitchenette, a queen bed (open frame) and a queen sofa bed in the sitting room. The standard private bath has a Jacuzzi, tub and shower. A gourmet breakfast is served in the morning room or on the tropical pool deck right outside your door. A free shuttle (without a lift) goes to the airport and downtown. 2-night minimum. $$$ (3215 Spruce Ave; 561-863-9836; 800-655-3196)

■ CABINS/CAMPGROUNDS

John Prince Park has 265 RV/tent sites with picnic tables, fire rings, grills and water/elec hookups. You can request a site near the ADA bathhouse, on the shady lakefront and/or with a paved pad. The ADA bathhouse has a raised toilet, roll-under sink and step-in showers. See Parks, because this one has plenty to do; the boat ramp in the campground has a fixed dock. Playground on sand; reserve up to 90 days ahead (2700 6 Ave S; 4759 S Congress Ave; 2520 Lake Worth Rd, Lake Worth; N of the Lantana Airport; 561-582-7992; 877-992-9925)

Lion Country Safari KOA is a 20-acre campground with 22 tent and 211 RV sites, all on flat, hard-packed, natural terrain. Sites 2 and 3 have ADA picnic tables; RV sites have paved pads and full hookups. Four one-room cabins are ramped, have a full bed (open frame) and a set of bunk beds; no linens, pillows, kitchens or bath facilities. The ADA bathhouse has raised toilets, roll-under sinks and roll-in showers with hand-held sprayers and seats. Specials in summers include tickets to the Lion Country Safari. Heated pool; laundry; camp store; playground on grass. Make reservations for Jan-Mar 6 months ahead. (2003 Lion Country Safari Rd, Loxahatchee; off Southern Blvd/US 98, 15 mi W of I-95; 561-793-9797)

Pahokee State Park has 100 RV/tent sites on flat, grassy terrain with picnic tables and ground grills; 64 have full hookups; the rest have water/elec. ADA bathhouses have raised toilets, roll-under sinks and roll-in showers with seats. (US 441, Pahokee; 3.5 mi S of US 98; 561-924-7832)

Peanut Island, to which you must take a private boat or water taxi (see Parks), has 20 tent sites. Each has a tent pad and grill; 5 sites have ADA picnic tables. Paved paths lead throughout the island; see Parks. The bathhouse has raised toilets, roll-under sinks and roll-in showers. Reservations (Intracoastal at Lake Worth Inlet; 561-845-4445)

South Bay RV Park, with some 35 acres along the shores of Lake Okeechobee, has 72 RV/tent sites; 17 have ADA picnic tables, ADA grills, paved pads and water/elec/cable; some sites are in shade. Sidewalks lead to the ADA bathhouses with raised toilets, roll-under sinks, roll-in showers and laundry facilities. The banks to the small Shiner Lake have flat, open spots for fishing. Or, use the nearby city boat ramp, with floating docks, to access Lake Ockeechobee. Game room; screened porch; bait shop nearby (100 Levee Rd, South Bay; off US 27, 2.5 mi NW of SR 80; 561-992-9045)

■ MOTELS

The Breakers, located on the ocean, has 16 ADA rooms and a 1BR suite (#1060). The rooms have a king or 2 full beds (23" high/open frames). Bathrooms have raised toilets, roll-under sinks; the suite and some rooms have roll-in showers with hand–held sprayers and seats; others have tubs. The suite has a king bed, sofa bed in the living room, mini-bar and refrigerator (extra fee). Walkway to the water; pool; bar; entertainment; full restaurant. $$$ (1 S Country Rd, Palm Bch; 561-655-6611; 888-273-2537)

Courtyard by Marriott has 8 ADA rooms with a king or 2 full beds (21" high/open frames) and full kitchenettes. Bathrooms have raised toilets and roll-under sinks; rooms 141 and 147 have roll-in showers with hand-held sprayers and seats; others have tubs. Pool; restaurant for brkfst; laundry. $$$ (600 Northpoint Pkwy; 561-640-9000)

Embassy Suites has 5 ADA 1BR suites, each with a king bed (platform), a microwave, refrigerator and a full sofa bed in the living room. Bathrooms have raised toilets and roll-under sinks; rooms 103 & 104 have roll-in showers with a seat; others have tubs with seats. Free brkfst; full restaurant; pool; laundry. $$-$$$ (4350 PGA Blvd, Palm Bch Gardens; 561-622-1000)

Hilton Oceanfront Resort, located on Singer Island, has 14 ADA rooms, each with a king bed (open frame), refrig-erator, coffeepot and bathroom with a roll-under sink. One bathroom has a roll-in shower with a seat; others have tubs. Pool; full restaurant; bar with entertainment; laundry; exercise room; socials; children's programs; bike rentals. $$$ (3700 N SR A1A, Palm Bch Shores; 561-848-3888)

Marriott has 4 ADA rooms, each with a king or 2 full beds (24" high/open frames), a full sofa bed and coffeepot. Bathrooms have raised toilets and roll-under sinks; room 211 has a roll-in shower with a hand-held sprayer and seat; others have tubs. Pool; laundry. $$-$$$ (4000 RCA Blvd, Palm Bch Gardens; 561-622-8888)

Studio 6 has 6 ADA studios, each with a king, queen or 2 full beds (22" high/platforms) and full kitchen. Bathrooms have raised toilets and roll-under sinks; 2 have roll-in showers with hand-held sprayers and seats; others have tubs. Laundry. $-$$$ (1535 Centrepark Dr N; 561-640-3335)

DON'T BE DISAPPOINTED, CALL FIRST!

Owners change, staff change, conditions change, hours change, even addresses change!

Please call beforehand.
Make sure the business can
still accommodate you.

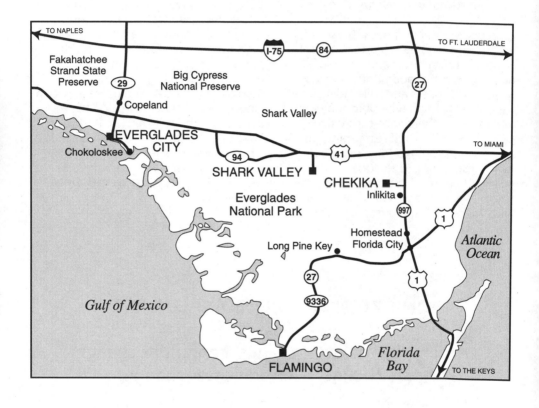

EVERGLADES NATIONAL PARK

The 1.5 million-acre Everglades National Park encompasses only one-fifth of Mother Nature's design for the Everglades. The Everglades' watershed begins at the Kissimmee River in central Florida and its only source is rainfall as it flows in a shallow, 50-mi wide River of Grass to the Gulf of Mexico and Atlantic Ocean. Development, agriculture and pollution threaten this unique and fragile habitat.

The best time to visit is December to March when it's cooler, trails are dryer and there are more activities, more migratory birds and fewer mosquitoes. We cannot overstate the mosquito infestation, especially in summer. Even in winter, wear long pants, long sleeves, closed shoes and plenty of bug repellent! Check at each visitor center for the current schedule of ranger-led activities. Canoes and boats offer the best way to experience the Everglades.

Tourist Info
Chamber: US 41 & Rte 29, Box 130, Everglades City, 33929; 239-695-3941
Everglades National Park: 40001 SR 9336, Homestead, 33034: 305-242-7700
Homestead-Florida City Chamber: 550 US 1, Homestead, 33030; 305-247-2332
Tropical Everglades Visitors Association: 160 US 1, Florida City, 33034; 305-245-
Web Sites: www.nps.gov/ever

WC Resources
The following rent manual WCs:
My Pharmacy (806 N Krome Ave, Homestead; 305-247-6949)
First Care Medical Supply (25 US 41 N, Naples; 239-262-7772)
Palm Medical (411 4 Ave N, Naples; at US 41; 239-262-2348)

EVERGLADES CITY
Chokoloskee, Copeland

Gulf Coast Visitor Center at the Everglades National Park, is 1 mi S of Everglades City, 80 mi W of Miami and 92 mi from the Park's main entrance. There is no entry fee in this part of the Park since most of it is underwater, usually at depths of 2 feet or less (but tides can range 3 feet or more). The Visitor Center has an elevator to the information desk and exhibits on the 2nd floor. The gift/snack shop, canoe rentals and Rr are on the ground floor. Ranger-led activities include boat tours, interpretive talks and, on winter weekends, canoe trips. ADA picnic shelters. May-Nov 8:30-5; Dec-Apr 7:30-5 (SR 29; 3 mi S of US 41; 239-695-3311)

ACTIVITIES

■ **ATTRACTIONS**
Wooten's Everglades Experience includes an animal park and, for additional fees, an airboat ride and swamp buggy tour. Take a 20-min roll along rough, mostly hard-packed, gravel paths past Florida panthers, jaguars, emus and a range of local wildlife. A 15-min gator show runs throughout the day. Next door is Wooten's airboat ride that can accommodate WCs. Staff can lower you aboard in front of an I-beam to which you can strap your WC or, if you prefer, staff can lift you into a boat seat. The 1/2-hr tours go 5 mi into the Glades. Across US 41 is Wooten's narrated swamp buggy ride through the brush past a gator breeding pond and old Indian site for a slow, bumpy 1/2 hr. The smaller, 16-passenger swamp buggy can be ramped for you to roll aboard in your WC, then staff can help you transfer to a seat (no seat belts available). Call to make sure that particular buggy is working! $. 8:30-5 (32330 US 41; 239-695-2781; 800-282-2781)

■ **BIKE TRAILS**
A 4-mi paved trail runs parallel to SR 29 from downtown Everglades City, past the Park Visitor Center to Chokoloskee. In winter, the 3-mi stretch from the Visitor Center to the island of Chokoloskee is especially pretty.

■ **BOAT RAMPS**
Barron River Marina has ramps and floating docks on the Barron River, 2 mi N of the Chokoloskee Bay. $. 24 hrs (803 Collier Ave; 239-695-3591)
Chokoloskee, at the mouth of the Turner River, has a ramp and a fixed dock. (S end of SR 29, Chokoloskee)
Glades Haven Marina has a ramp and fixed docks at several levels to ease WC boarding at different tides on the Wilderness Waterway. Staff can help. Restaurant; convenience store; picnic tables; Rr. $. 7-5 (800 Copeland Ave; 239-695-2579)

■ **BOAT TOURS**
Attractions: Wooten's
Chokoloskee Charters has a 26' Bayliner with an open cockpit that can accommodate up to 2 WC and 4 able-bodied passengers for morning or evening champagne ecotours in the 10,000 Islands and Florida Bay. At Parkway Marina, environmental engineer Charles Wright, has access to a manual lift for you to board from the dock and back into your WC onboard. Tours can be tailored but generally run 3 1/2 hrs and include great birding and hors d'oeuvres. (1180 Chokoloskee Dr, Chokoloskee; end of SR 29; 239-695-9107)
Eden's Jungle Boat Tour is a 1-hr, pontoon boat trip through the 10,000 Islands. Usually you can roll aboard but, if tides are low, staff can lower you aboard in your WC. Included in your ticket is a chance to roll along a ramped, elevated, .5-mi boardwalk through a mangrove. 9-5 (SR 29 at Dupont Rd; 239-695-2800; 800-543-3367)
Everglades National Park Boat Tours offers 1 1/2-hr, 10,000 Island tours on boats with accessible 1st decks. The capt or a ranger narrates on the 2nd deck making it tough to hear from below. The Manatee II is larger and more readily accessible than the Manatee I. Both have ramped entrances and WC tie-downs, but the Manatee II has Rr and WC seating inside and on the back deck. Snacks onboard. Manatee II trips at 10:30am, 12:30, 2:30 & 5 (Gulf Coast Visitor Center; 239-695-2591; in FL 800-445-7724)
North American Canoe Tours features half/full-day trips with a naturalist touring the backcountry and the 10,000 Islands aboard a deck boat for up to 6 people. At low tide, staff can help lower you in your WC from the fixed dock. Full-day trips include

lunch. Reservations; Rr at office, 2 blocks from launch site (Ivey House, 107 Camelia St; off SR 29, 3 mi S of US 41; 239-695-3299/695-4666)

■ CANOEING/KAYAKING

Everglades National Park Boat Tours rents 17' canoes for half/full days. The launch site at the Ranger Station is a paved ramp where the canoe must be near the bottom to sit in enough water to launch. Staff can help you transfer. Rr (941-695-2591; in FL 800-445-7724)

North American Canoe Tours rents canoes, kayaks and camping gear, provides guided trips and offers shuttle service. Canoes (17'), solo/tandem kayaks and flat-backed canoes (where you can attach your own 4hp motor) are rented by the half/full day or overnight. Guided tours with naturalists run from 3 hrs to overnight in the backcountry, 10,000 Islands or open Gulf waters. Staff can help lift you into the boat. There are several launch sites, depending on the trail or tour you choose; staff can advise you about relative access at the different sites and you can follow the shuttle van in your own vehicle. Full-day tours include lunch. Shuttle service for day and overnight trips can use a van or powerboat; transfers are not easy for either. Reservations; Rr at office, 1 mi from usual launch site (Ivey House, 107 Camelia St; off SR 29, 3 mi S of US 41; 239-695-3299/695-4666)

Trails include the 99-mi Wilderness Waterway through the 10,000 Islands, the shoreline along the Islands and Turner River Trail. Talk with rangers about day paddles. Most of the primitive campsites are platforms under thatched roofs, or chickees, above the water that, depending on the tides, can be several feet above the water's surface. The few ground sites are clearings on muddy terrain or beaches for which all-terrain WCs are advised. Backcountry overnight permits are required; ask at the Visitor Center.

Wilderness Inquiry, a non-profit group based in Minnesota, specializes in wilderness trips across the country for folks of all abilities. Paddling and camping experience is not required for the 6-day canoe trip through the 10,000 Islands to Gullivan Bay and the Gulf. Guides are specifically trained and experienced with disabled paddlers. Reservations; camping & canoeing gear included. Jan-Mar (800-728-0719)

■ FISHING CHARTERS

Chokoloskee Charters has a 26' Bayliner with an open cockpit that can accommodate up to 2 WC anglers for inshore and offshore trips for half, full or split days. At Parkway Marina, Capt Wright can use a manual lift to lower you from the dock and back into your WC onboard. (1180 Chokoloskee Dr, Chokoloskee; end of SR 29; 239-695-9107)

Thompson's Guide Service can take you fishing on a 19' flats boat along the 10,000 Islands for half/full days. The capt is experienced with disabled anglers, certified as a fishing guide by the National Park and an Emergency Medical Technician. To board, he can help transfer you onto the seawall, board your WC and then lift you back into your WC. (941-695-4102)

■ MUSEUMS

Museum of the Everglades has artifacts, displays and photos on local history and pursuits such as fishing. Ramped entrance; CRr. $D. Tue-Sat 11-4 (Broadway; 239-695-0008)

■ PARKS

Big Cypress National Preserve covers 730,000 acres of the 2400-sq-mi Big Cypress Swamp that is an imperiled water source for the Everglades and SW Florida. The visitor center (8:30-4:30) has exhibits and a film about the swamp. Hiking trails are inaccessible but you can drive a car on 3 scenic routes. Just W of SR 29 off US 41, take the 17-mi Birdon Rd/Turner River Rd loop or simply take the 16-mi Turner Rd; both roads are limestone. The 26-mi Loop Rd is paved for 8 mi and then becomes a rough dirt road full of potholes. Picnic tables; Rr. 24-hrs (US 41; E of Everglades City; 239-695-4111) **Fakahatchee Strand State Preserve** is a unique habitat with strands that look like islands of swamp forest marking the otherwise flat horizon. The preserve also has the only royal palm and cypress forest in N America. An 800' limerock path leads to a 1500' board-walk that takes you through an old growth cypress forest with trees 300-500 yrs old. If you cannot negotiate the path, call the office and a ranger will open the gate so you can drive to the boardwalk. You can also drive along the 11-mi dirt road in the interior strand. Picnic tables; Rr at office. 8-dusk (137 Coastline Dr; W of Copeland on SR 29; 239-695-4593)

■ **TOURS**
Attractions: Wooten's

ACCOMMODATIONS

■ **B&B/INNS**
Ivey House Inn is a new structure adjoining a B&B from 1928. The Inn has an ADA guestroom with 2 queen beds (25" high/open frames) and a small refrigerator. The room overlooks a lovely, screened courtyard with a shallow conversation pool. The private bath has a raised toilet, roll-under sink and roll-in shower with a hand-held sprayer and seat. Breakfast is served in the great room or the courtyard. Guests receive discounts on canoe/kayak rentals; see Boat Tours and Canoeing. Laundry; lounge; full restaurant. $$-$$$ (107 Camelia St; off SR 29, 3 mi S of US 41; 239-695-3299/695-4666)

■ **CAMPGROUNDS**
Canoeing: Trails
Barron River Resort has 67 RV sites, some on cement, some on grass, all with full hookups and about half on the river. Sidewalks lead to the bathhouse with an ADA stall with a toilet, sink and roll-in shower. A very steep ramp leads to fixed docks by a boat ramp. Marina; fishing charters; restaurant (803 Collier Ave; 3 mi S of US 41 & SR 29; 239-695-3591; 800-535-4961)
Glen Haven has 51 RV/tent sites on flat, grassy terrain with full hookups and picnic tables. ADA bathhouses have roll-under sinks and roll-in showers. Marina (see Boat Ramps); restaurant; deli; game room; pool; reservations for Oct-Apr (800 Copeland Ave; across from Gulf Coast Visitor Center; 239-695-2746)

■ **MOTELS**
Naples: Accommodations

SHARK VALLEY/CHEKIKA
Homestead

Shark Valley Visitor Center, in the Everglades National Park, is 42 mi E of Everglades City and 40 mi W of Miami. The center has rotating environmental exhibits and a bookshop. Ranger-led activities in winter include 1/2-hr talks, themed hikes and 3-hr bike hikes on which guests are encouraged to bring their own handcycles. WC loaner; vending machine; manual doors; Rr at center & parking lot. $. Nov-Apr 8:30-5; May-Oct 9-4:30 (US 41; 305-221-8776)

ACTIVITIES

■ **BIKES**
The tram tour concession rents bikes by the hr for the 15-mi long tram trail.

■ **TOURS**
Tram tours are 2 hrs along a 15-mi loop road through sawgrass prairie. The canopied, open-air trams are ramped and have tie-downs and room for 4 WCs. Midway is a 1/2-hr stop at an observation tower, reached by a circular, somewhat steep, 1200' ramp. Rangers narrate some tours; concession staff narrate others. Reservations (305-221-8455); Rr at Visitor Center & observation tower. May-Dec 9:30, 11, 1 & 3; Jan-Apr hrly (305-221-8776)

■ **TRAILS**
Bobcat Boardwalk runs a shady .5 mi through tropical vegetation with interpretive signs.
Shark River Slough is the sunny, flat, 15-mi, paved loop road used by trams, hikers and bicyclists. When the tram passes, you need to get onto the soft grassy, slightly sloping shoulders.

Chekika, in the Everglades National Park, is currently only a day-use area because of damage by Hurricane Irene in 1999. A boardwalk leads from parking to a grassy area that you must cross to ADA picnic shelters. The boardwalk meanders through a freshwater glade and stops about 4' from a fishing pond popular with bluegill, largemouth bass and alligators. Big rocks line the banks, but if the water level is up, you can fish from the boardwalk. An unimproved hiking trail is rough with tree roots and rocks. The Park plans to build a small campground and paved bike trails across the sawgrass prairie and along freshwater canals brimming with wildlife. Rr port-o-lets. $. Wkdy 8-5; wknd 8-6 (W end of SW 168 St/Richmond Dr, Homestead; W off Krome Ave/SR 997, just N of Inlikita; 305-242-7700)

FLAMINGO
Long Pine Key

Just beyond the Ernest Coe Visitor Center is the Everglades National Park's main entrance, open 24 hrs. It is 11 mi W of Homestead on SR 9336/SR 27 that continues as Main Park Rd. Pay your admission here to reach Flamingo.
Ernest Coe Visitor Center, with a ramped entrance, features a 15-min video and nature displays, including an overview of each area within the Park. Bookstore; Rr; CRr. 8-5 (305-242-7700)
Royal Palm Visitor Center, 4 mi past the main entrance, has a ramp to an information station and bookstore. Borrow audiotape guides for the Anhinga and Gumbo-Limbo Trails that start from the parking lot. Loaner WCs; vending machines; Rr (305-242-7700)
Flamingo Visitor Center, 38 mi SW of the entrance, has a WC lift to the 2nd floor breezeway where you can enter the museum/gift shop, restaurant (open Nov-Apr for breakfast, lunch and dinner) and Rr (29 3/4" entry). On the ground level are a CRr and a lounge that serves sandwiches. Flamingo Lodge is nearby and the campground is .5 mi away; see Accommodations. The nearby marina has a gas station and convenience store with groceries, camping and fishing supplies. Dec-Mar ranger-led, mostly accessible activities include canoe trips, talks, walks, kids' activities and campfire programs at the campground amphitheater. WC loaner; pay phones at marina & lodge. 7:30-5; May-Nov open, but often not staffed (941-695-2945)

ACTIVITIES

■ BIKES
Flamingo Marina rents bikes by the hour for the park road and trails; see Trails. (941-695-3101)

■ BOAT RAMPS
Flamingo Marina has a boat ramp, floating docks and ramped fixed docks on the Florida Bay. If your boat has a motor larger than 6hp, you must stay in the channel through the Bay. (941-695-3101)

West Lake has a ramp for canoes and boats with motors up to 6hp. A fixed dock is down steps. See Trails.

■ BOAT RENTALS
Flamingo Marina rents 16' skiffs with 15hp motors, 19' skiffs with 25hp motors, canoes and solo/tandem kayaks by the hour and half/full days. Canoes and kayaks are also available overnight. Skiffs are not allowed on the Florida Bay because of shallow waters. Staff is happy to help lower you aboard from your WC on the fixed dock; or you may choose to board from the floating docks by the boat ramp. (941-695-3101)

■ BOAT TOURS
Flamingo Marina offers a variety of tours with naturalists, from 90-min Bald Eagle cruises on the Florida Bay and 2-hr Pelican backcountry cruises to 4-hr Dolphin cruises on Whitewater Bay. Florida Bay and backcountry cruises are aboard canopied pontoon boats; crew can either lift you aboard in your WC or you can roll aboard on a ramp. Whitewater Bay cruises (intermittent in summer) are on a 6-passenger boat where the crew can lift you from your WC into a boat seat with a back. Reservations; Bald Eagle cruise boats have Rr (941-695-3101)

■ CANOEING/KAYAKING
Flamingo rangers lead canoe tours frequently Dec-Apr. You pay for the canoe/kayak rental at the marina then meet the ranger at the launch site.

Call for the schedule and access of various launch sites. Reservations (941-695-2945)

7 Canoe trails near here offer plenty of variety, from a 1.6-mi jaunt along the shady Bear Lake Canal or a 7.7-mi trek between West Lake and Alligator Creek to a paddle on the open waters of the Florida Bay. For an overnight trip, check out the well marked, 5.5-mi Hells Bay Canoe Trail (9.5 mi N of Flamingo) that has a somewhat accessible primitive camp 3.5 mi downstream at Pearl Bay Chickee; see Campgrounds. Backcountry overnight permits are required. Trailheads are marked on Main Park Rd. Check at the Visitor Center for trail maps, permits and advice about tides, winds and level of paddle involved.

■ FISHING
Long Pine Key fishing pond has some open flat grassy spots on the bank where you can fish for bass. No facilities (Marked turn is 5 mi past entrance)

■ FISHING CHARTERS
Capt Haines offers half/full-day flats and backcountry fishing for 3 with a fly rod or light tackle. From a floating dock, he can roll you aboard the 20' flats boat. Trips can range from the Everglades to Biscayne Bay. (305-248-8859)

Capt Sutton offers flats and backcountry fishing with a fly rod or light tackle on a 20' flats boat. He can help you board at a dock that best suits your needs. Half/full-day trips and, in summer, night trips go to the Everglades or Biscayne Bay. Let him know the dimensions of your WC and he can provide tie-downs. (305-248-6126)

Florida Bay Charters offers half/full-day trips on an 18' flats boat for 2 with Capt Chris Humphrey, a marine biologist. He can help roll you aboard from a fixed dock. (305-852-3111)

■ PICNIC AREAS
Trails: West Lake

Flamingo Campground and **Nine Mile Pond** (11.7 mi NE of Flamingo) have grassy clearings that make for nice picnics.

Long Pine Key has ADA picnic tables on hard-packed terrain in a lovely pine forest. Grills; water fountain; Rr (Marked turn is 5 mi past entrance)

■ **TRAILS**

The following are N to S:

Anhinga is a level, .5-mi trail of asphalt and boardwalk skirting a wooded hammock and several ponds where you surely will find gators, plenty of birds and interpretive signs. Park at the Royal Palm Visitor Center.

Gumbo-Limbo is a paved, level .5-mi trail through a jungle-like hammock with interpretive signs. Tree roots narrow the trail in spots. Park at the Royal Palm Visitor Center.

Long Pine Key Trail, 6 mi from the entrance, winds on a hard-packed bike trail for 5.5 mi through pines still recovering from Hurricane Andrew in 1992. Park at the Long Pine Key Campground.

Pinelands Trail starts 7 mi from the entrance. This .5-mi asphalt trail through a pine forest can get bumpy and narrow with tree roots. Park just off Main Park Rd.

Pahayokee, 13 mi from the entrance, is a short, U-shaped boardwalk with interpretive signs and a ramped observation tower midway from which you can see an endless horizon of sawgrass studded by cypress strands. Park 1 mi off Main Park Rd.

Mahogany Hammock Trail, 22.5 mi from the entrance, is a .5-mi boardwalk loop through a massive tropical mahogany jungle with interpretive signs. Take it counter-clockwise so you can take the 2 small inclines downhill. Park just off Main Park Rd.

West Lake, 7.3 mi NE of Flamingo, has a short boardwalk through mangrove. ADA picnic shelter; parking & Rr at the marked trailhead off Main Park Rd.

Snake Bight, 5.5 mi NE of Flamingo, is a 3.2-mi (round trip) shady, wide, hard-packed trail through a tropical forest with wild orchids, ending at the bay. The Park plans to restore the boardwalk at the end of the trail, a great spot to watch birds at high tide. The trail is only recommended when weather is dry and cool. Park off the road at marked trailhead.

Bear Lake has a 1.6-mi, hard-packed trail from the Main Park Rd through a dense forest ending at the lake. Park off the road at marked trailhead.

Eco Pond, between the Visitor Center and the campground, has a short, grassy, sloping trail to a ramped observation deck from where you'll see birds of all sorts of feather. Park at trailhead.

Guy Bradley is a 1-mi, paved trail along the Florida Bay between the Visitor Center and the campground's amphitheater where ranger programs are frequently featured in winter.

Coastal Prairie Trail begins at the campground's Loop C and runs 7.5 mi to Clubhouse Beach. This natural trail through salt marsh and buttonwood forest is overgrown, popular with mosquitoes and can be very muddy in stretches; recommended only when weather has been dry and cool.

ACCOMMODATIONS

■ **CAMPGROUNDS**

Flamingo has 235 RV sites on concrete pads in mangrove or on coastal prairie. The 18 ADA sites have ADA picnic tables, grills and access on the paved loop roads to ADA bathhouses with roll-under sinks and roll-in, unheated showers. Sixty-five walk-in only sites are on flat, natural terrain, some 600' from the road and, during much of the year, too muddy for WCs. You can rent a hot shower behind the marina store through the Lodge. The campground is .5 mi from the lodge and marina. You can camp here free among mosquitoes Jun-Sep. Amphitheater with program Nov-Apr; dump stations; reserve up to 5 mos in advance for Nov-Apr (800-365-2267); May-Oct self-registration (941-695-2945)

Long Pine Key, 7 mi from the entrance, has 108 drive-up RV/ tent sites with no hookups. Two ADA sites are flat and grassy with ADA picnic tables and raised fire pits. The nearby Rr has grab bars at the toilet, roll-under sinks, no shower and a utility sink outside for washing dishes. You can camp here free Jun-Sep, if you don't mind being mosquito bait! Amphitheater with program Nov-Apr; dump stations; phones; reservations accepted up to 5 mos in advance for Nov-Apr (800-365-2267); May-Oct self registration (305-242-7700)

Pearl Bay Chickee is the only backcountry canoe/boat campsite with accessible features. It's an elevated, roofed platform on the water (where two tents can be pitched and tied, not staked) with handrails, a canoe/boat dock and a chemical toilet. Pearl Bay is a 4-hr paddle from Hell's Bay Canoe Trailhead; by powerboat from the Whitewater Bay take the East River. Bring potable water, a portable stove and something to carry out all trash. You must get an overnight permit at the Flamingo or Gulf Coast Visitor Center.

■ **COTTAGES**

Flamingo Lodge offers 2 adjacent, ADA, 1BR cottages in the woods, just off the Florida Bay. The large door between the 2 units can be opened for easy access between. Each cottage has a queen bed (platform), full sofa bed in the living room, full kitchenette and bathroom with a raised toilet and roll-under sink. Cottage O has a roll-in shower; Cottage P has a large step-in shower with a bench; both have handheld sprayers. The pool deck is accessible from the lawn. Free brkfst in summer; step-into laundry; lounge; no TVs. $$-$$$ (941-695-3101; 800-600-3813)

■ **HOUSEBOATS**

Flamingo Marina rents a roomy 40' pontoon houseboat with a full kitchen that sleeps up to 8. Staff can lift you in your WC from the fixed dock onto the boat where you can roll into the galley through a sliding door. The bedroom and bathroom doors are too narrow for WCs. You can access the 2 sofa beds in the galley; 2 full beds are in the bedroom. Reserve 6 mos in advance; 2-night minimum (941-695-3101)

Rr means ADA or handicapped restrooms;
CRr stands for companion or unisex restrooms.

Look for ADA picnic tables
which have the bench cut away
or an elongated top at one end
so you can roll underneath
instead of sitting sideways.

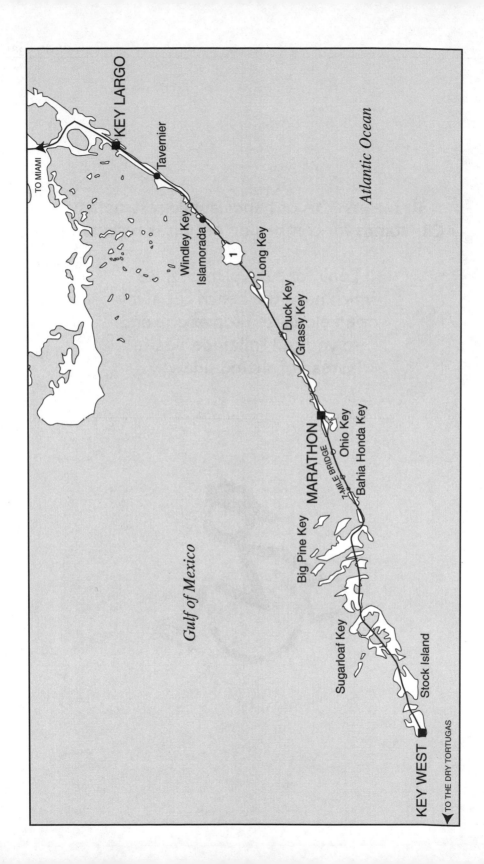

THE KEYS

The Florida Keys make a 156-mile hopscotch from the mainland toward Cuba. Along these islands are many definitions of paradise: sleepy seaside retreats, incomparable fishing and diving, fabulous tropical resorts and the high-powered excitement of Key West.

A few advisories: You will not find miles of white beaches in the Keys. There are some lovely beaches but seawalls, mangroves or hard coral more frequently line the shore. For anglers, many restaurants will cook the fish you catch and serve it with all the trimmings. The Overseas Highway or US 1 binds the islands and is studded with green Mile Markers (MM), from MM126, just S of Florida City, to MM0 in Key West. Except in Key West, addresses and directions are usually noted by MM.

Tourist Info
Florida Visitors Bureau: Mallory Square, 402 Wall St, Key West; 305-294-2587; 800-352-5397
Web sites: www.insiders.com/florida-keys; www.fla-keys.com; www.flkinfo.com; www.keysdirectory.com; www.thefloridakeys.com; www.gotothekeys.com
Lodging: 800-916-2030; 800-403-2154/www.warmingsun.com; www.askforkeywest.com

Transportation
Super Shuttle, a lift-equipped van, provides service to and from the Miami Airport, Port Everglades, the Port of Miami and any location in Dade, Broward or Monroe Counties, including the Keys. 5 days advance reservations (305-871-2000; 954-764-1700)

KEY LARGO
MM107-79: Islamorada, Long Key, Plantation Key, Tavernier, Windley Key

The upper Keys offer a mellow atmosphere but plenty of action. You can swim with dolphins, snorkel in the world-renowned John Pennekamp, snuba down to 20' or go even deeper by learning scuba from an instructor certified by the Handicapped Scuba Association. Enjoy the tropical scenery from a kayak or a catamaran with a lift. Fishing is awesome here. And, three public pools and one hotel pool has WC lifts; the Jacobs Aquatic Center also has a therapeutic pool.

Tourist Info
Key Largo Chamber: MM106; 106000 US 1, 33037; 800-822-1088

Islamorada Visitor Center: (in a train caboose that has a steep ramp and is cramped) MM82.5; Box 915, 33036; 305-664-4503; 800-322-5397

ACTIVITIES

■ ATTRACTIONS

African Queen, the actual boat from Bogey and Hepburn's classic film, can be viewed from the dock. For its history, check the gift shop next door. (Key Largo Harbor Marina, MM100; 305-451-3426)

Dolphins Plus offers both recreational and therapeutic swims with dolphins. Recreational swims include non-structured and structured programs; call 7 days in advance to discuss any special needs and determine which program best suits you. Both take 2 hrs and begin with a briefing on dolphins and how to be a polite guest. Staff can help you transfer from your WC to a sitting position on a platform that is lowered into the water; or, if you can use the ladder, enter the water from the floating dock. You must not be pregnant and be able to swim and speak English. Mask and fins are required and provided for the non-structured program; wetsuits can be rented. The non-structured program, at 9 and 1:30, is a 30-min or 1-hr swim with no guarantee of physical contact with dolphins. Children must be 10 years old; a guardian must accompany kids age 10-17. The structured program, at 8:45, noon and 3, enables you to interact with dolphins on a platform and in the water. A guardian must accompany kids age 7-17. Multiple-day courses and 2-day kids' summer camps are also options. Island Dolphin Care offers 1- and 5-day therapeutic programs for children (with various diagnoses) and their families. Children must be at least 3-yrs old, be able to swallow and control their heads and not be aggressive or afraid of water or animals. For information on this program, call 305-451-5884. Sidewalks throughout; ramp to registration, gift shop, Rr & shower on 2nd floor. 8-5 (31 Corrine Pl; from US 1,

E at traffic light just S of MM100, take first right then left onto Ocean Bay Dr, turn right before bridge; 305-451-1993)

Florida Keys Wild Bird Center is a 5-acre rehab center for injured birds. With a self-guiding brochure, take the boardwalk to learn about spoonbills, pelicans, ospreys and other feathered friends as they are nursed back to health. Another boardwalk reveals the importance of mangrove wetlands. $D. Dawn-dusk (MM93.6, Tavernier; 305-852-4486)

Robbies is a funky marina on the bay where you can feed a school of 50 to 100 tarpon that visit daily for hours. Rr. $. 8-5 (MM77.5, Islamorada; 305-664-9814; 877-664-8498)

Theater of the Sea provides a unique opportunity to observe and even interact with marine life. Admission includes dolphin and sea lion performances, each about 25 min, in an outdoor stadium with WC seating on the sides. A 1-hr, guided tour goes through various marine exhibits, all along brick or paved paths. The 5-min bottomless boat ride is not accessible. For additional fees, you can swim with dolphins, sea lions or stingrays (minimum age 5) or be a Trainer-for-the-Day (minimum age 10). The swim programs include a 15- or 30-min class and a 1/2 hr in the water. To swim with dolphins or sea lions, pull your WC up to the lagoon, where staff can lift you from your WC to the wide, wood steps and you can work your way into the 15' deep saltwater. Stingray swims take place at the far end of the park but you must traverse about 300' of sand and coral to the sandy lagoon that goes from 0-12' deep. The 3-hr Trainer-for-A-Day program involves much moving about, including getting up and down from floats in the water. Beyond a class and a behind-the-scenes tour, you help feed and train dolphins and sea lions and learn about their care. Call far in advance to make reservations for the special programs and to discuss any special needs. Gift shop; snacks; Rr. $. 9:30-5 (MM84.5, Islamorada; 305-664-2431)

■ **BEACHES**

Parks: John Pennekamp

Anne's Beach is a narrow strip of hard-packed, coral rock and sand along the Atlantic. You can park close to this beach and take a short boardwalk through mangrove to some picnic tables and cabanas. Rr at N end of boardwalk. Dawn-dusk (MM73.5 oceanside, Islamorada)

Founders Park has parking along a narrow strip of hard-packed beach on the bay and sidewalks throughout the park. The marina has a boat ramp with a fixed dock. The heated pool has a lift (fixed seat); lifeguards can help with transfers. ADA picnic tables; ADA showers; ball fields; Rr. $/non-residents. Dawn-dusk (MM87, Islamorada; marina 305-852-2381; pool 305-853-1685)

Harry Harris Park is roughly 15 acres with a 200' long strip of county beach and swim area along the Atlantic. You can park at the edge of the sand and take a sidewalk around the grassy park. Boat ramp to ocean; picnic tables & playground on sand; ball fields; vending machines; Rr. $/wknds for non-residents. 8-dusk (MM93.5, Tavernier; E on Burton Rd for .25 mi)

■ **BIKE TRAILS**

Florida Keys Overseas Heritage Trail will be a paved trail running 106 mi from Key Largo to Key West. Planned for completion in 2010, it will be separated from the busy US 1 by either landscaped median, boardwalk over the shoreline or alternative back roads and will include catwalks on US 1's many bridges or separate pedestrian bridges. Designated parking, rest stops, Rr and ADA water fountains are all part of the plan. Thirty-six mi exist with varying degrees of access; all bike trails in the Keys described below are part of the

Heritage Trail. For up-to-date information, call Florida Park Service 305-451-3005 or Monroe County 305-289-2500. **Islamorada** has a 6' wide, 10-mi trail/sidewalk from Founders Park to Snake Creek Bridge at MM85.5. After the bridge, the trail continues from Whale Harbor Channel at MM83.7 through a business district to MM73.7 on Lower Matecumbe Key.

Key Largo-Tavernier has 14 mi of trail along US 1 that should be resurfaced in 2003. The trail starts oceanside at MM106 where US 1 heads NW to the mainland; park at the Key Largo Chamber of Commerce or start at MM 103 and park at John Pennekamp State Park (see Parks). The trail crosses to bayside at a traffic signal at MM99, then back to oceanside at MM94 (with no traffic signal). As it goes through historic Tavernier, the trail uses a sidewalk with ramped curbs.

■ **BOAT RAMPS**

Beaches: Founders, Harry Harris

Sea Bird Marina has a boat ramp and concrete docks on the bay. With advance notice, staff can help lift you aboard. Bait; snacks. $. 7:30am-varies (MM69.5, Long Key; 305-664-2871; 888-640-3303)

■ **BOAT RENTALS**

Parks: John Pennekamp

Bud n Mary's Marina rents 21' center consoles and 18' run-abouts for half/full days in the Atlantic or Florida Bay. Park near the dock and, with advance notice, staff can lift you aboard in your WC. Bait shop; snack bar. 8-5 (MM79.8, Islamorada; 305-664-0091; 800-742-7945)

It's A Dive rents 17' and 18' center consoles with roomy cockpits for half/full days on the Florida Bay. Crew can lift you aboard in your WC from the fixed dock. Rr at dock. 8-5 (Marriott Beach Resort, MM103.8; 305-453-9881; 800-809-9881)

Robbies rents pontoon boats (30" entry) for up to 10 passengers for fishing, touring or bird watching in the Florida

Bay or mangrove channels. The marina also rents a variety of boats (14'-27' long) for the Atlantic or Florida Bay. All boats are available with convertible canopies and can be delivered to your hotel; all have hand-held radios and color charts of the local waters. Check out the video and satellite photos in the shop to familiarize yourself with the area. Because the ramp is narrow, staff can lift you aboard in your WC from the fixed dock. 2-hr minimum; bait shop; snacks; Rr at dock. 8-5 (MM77.5, Islamorada; behind the Hungry Tarpon Restaurant; 305-664-9814; 877-664-8498)

Sea Bird Marina rents 18' center consoles for half/full days up to 1 wk for use in the Atlantic or Florida Bay. With advance notice, staff can help lift you aboard in your WC or into a boat seat from the fixed docks. Bait shop; snacks. 7:30am-varies (MM69.5, Long Key; 305-664-2871; 888-640-3303)

■ **BOAT TOURS**
Parks: John Pennekamp
Everglade EcoTours are offered on a 54' boat that resembles a paddleboat. Daytime 90-min tours, 1-hr sunset champagne cruises and 90-min evening crocodile hunts (with cameras!) are narrated journeys in the Florida Bay and Everglades National Park. Ask for the Bay Princess because usually you can roll aboard by ramp; in extreme tides, crew can lift you aboard in your WC. Parking lot is fine gravel; Rr at dock. 8-dusk (Dolphin Cove, MM102; 305-853-5161; 888-224-6044)

Key Largo Princess is a 70' glass-bottom boat that goes out to Molasses Reef for 2-hr, narrated tours. Crew can help you on the steep ramp to the dock and across another ramp to the boat. Only the enclosed, 1st deck (with AC) is accessible. Send a friend to get service from the bar on the upper deck. 10, 1 & 4 (Holiday Inn, MM100; 305-451-4655; 877-648-8129)

Robbies offers 2- to 3-hr, guided tours into the Everglades aboard a 27' Open

Fisherman with a wide cockpit. Because the ramp is narrow, staff can lift you aboard in your WC from the fixed dock. You can design your own trip, including sunset cruises. Rr at dock (MM77.5, Islamorada; 305-664-9814; 877-664-8498)

■ **CANOEING**
Parks: John Pennekamp

■ **FISHING CHARTERS**
Bud n Mary's Marina can hook you up with a guide for either a backcountry trip for up to 2 anglers (using light tackle or fly rods and live bait) or an offshore spin fishing trip for up to 6. Park near the fixed dock and staff can lift you aboard in your WC. Ask for the name and phone number of your guide so you can discuss any special needs. (MM79.8, Islamorada; 305-664-2461; 800-742-7945)

Fins & Feathers offers half/full-day, deep-sea trips for up to 6 aboard a roomy, 36' sports fisherman. Crew can lift you in your WC down the 4 steps to the dock and aboard; in very low tides, crew can arrange for you to board by the ramp at the glass-bottom boat dock in the marina. BYO food & drinks; snack bar; tiki bar & Rr at marina (Holiday Inn Marina, MM100; 305-453-0088/852-1571)

It's A Dive offers half/full-day backcountry trips on a 21' flats boat and offshore trips in a 35' Contender with Capt Dale. Crew can lift you aboard in your WC from the fixed dock. The flats boat can carry 1 WC angler and 2 others; the offshore boat can carry 2 WC anglers and 4 others. Food & beverages can be arranged; Rr at dock (Marriott Beach Resort, MM103.8; 305-453-9881; 800-809-9881; capt 305-451-2442)

Robbies offers offshore trips on a 27' Open Fisherman with a wide cockpit for a half/full day. The capt and mate know where to catch fish but can also entertain and educate anglers. Crew can lift you aboard in your WC from the fixed dock. Ask about split charters to share expenses. Robbies can also hook you up with a guide for flats fishing. (S end of Holiday Isle docks, MM84.5, Islamorada; 305-664-8070; 877-664-8498)

Sea Horse Charters offers half/full-day offshore trips for up to 6 anglers aboard the 36' Sea Horse with a cabin and plenty of deck space. Charters use light spin tackle for game fish and specialize in sailfish. Crew can lift you in your WC aboard from the dock. BYO food & drinks; Rr at dock (Whale Harbor Dock, MM83.5, Islamorada; Capt Don Clark 305-664-5020)

■ FISHING-PARTY BOATS

Bud n Mary's Gulf Lady goes beyond the reefs for full-day trips (9:30-4:30). Roll onto the dock where, with advance notice, crew can lift you in your WC aboard the 65' boat. Crew can help you over the lip into the AC cabin. Coolers onboard; restaurants & Rr at marina (MM79.5, Islamorada; 305-664-2461; 800-742-7945)

Robbies offers 4-hr offshore trips day and night aboard a 65' party boat called Capt Michael. Crew can lift you aboard in your WC from the fixed dock. Cabin not accessible; drinks sold onboard. 9:30, 1:45 & 7:30pm (S end of Holiday Isle docks, MM84.5; 305-664-8070; 877-664-8498)

■ FISHING PIERS/BRIDGES

The following run parallel to the vehicular bridges and are just for fishing:
Craig Key Bridge bayside; park NE of bridge (MM 73)
Long Key Bridge bayside; park W of bridge (MM 70.5)
Long Key Channel oceanside (MM 65.2)

■ KAYAKING

Capt Slate's rents sit-on kayaks by the hour for touring the bay. Staff can help you across the gravel stretch and sandy beach to the water's edge and can lift you from your WC onto the kayak. 7:30-6 (Howard Johnson, MM102; 305-451-1325; 800-331-3483)

Kayakers of Key Largo offers 2-day kayak instruction and 3-hr tours of the bay or ocean. Instructor Jamie Jackson is certified in adaptive paddling and

meets beforehand with wannabee WC kayakers to assess abilities and any need for adaptive equipment. He can arrange for kayak rentals and meet you at a site where he can help lift you into a solo/tandem sit-in kayak. (305-451-9968)

Watersports rents sit-on kayaks by the hour for exploring nearby islands. Staff can lift you aboard. (Holiday Isle, MM 84, Islamorada; 305-664-5390)

■ PARASAILING

It's A Dive offers 10-min, solo/tandem flights 600' to 1000' high. You don the harness around your shoulders and legs before boarding the 29' powerboat. Staff can lift you aboard in your WC and then onto the platform for takeoff. Rr at dock. 10-5 (Marriott Beach Resort, MM103.8; 305-453-9881; 800-809-9881)

Watersports offers 10-min, solo/tandem flights 1000' above the Atlantic. Staff can lift you aboard in your WC from the fixed dock and onto the platform for takeoff. 9-5 (Holiday Isle, MM84, Islamorada; 305-664-5390)

■ PARKS

John Pennekamp Coral Reef State Park, one of Florida's finest parks, includes 53,661 acres of breathtaking, unique underwater coral reef and 2350 acres above water. Be aware, gates often close by noon when crowds reach capacity. Sidewalks or boardwalks lead to various activities, most within a very compact area. The visitor center, open 8-5, has a theater for scheduled nature videos and a 30,000-gal saltwater aquarium with huge viewing windows. The Tamarind Nature Trail is hard-packed with roots. The Mangrove Trail is an ADA boardwalk winding through mangrove swamp with a 30' stretch where you can fish along a creek; the observation tower on this trail is inaccessible. You can find accessible fishing areas throughout the park. Both beach areas are very close to parking and have Rr and outdoor showers. From Cannon Beach, you can snorkel over reefs and a reconstructed Spanish shipwreck 130' offshore. Roll aboard glass-bottom boats (snack bar and Rr aboard) for 2 1/2-hr tours over coral reefs at 9:15, 12:15 and 3 daily. Staff cannot help you board or make transfers for boating or diving. There are four-hr dive and 2-hr snorkel trips, however only the El Captain, which is a snorkel boat, is ramped so a WC can roll aboard from the fixed dock. You can rent a 19'-28' Open Fisherman by the hour for the bay and ocean. If you bring your own boat, use the boat ramp with a floating dock. To board rental canoes, kayaks and paddleboats, use the small sandy stretch by the rental dock or the boat ramp. Call for the schedule of guided walks and other ranger programs. See Campgrounds. Snack bar; souvenirs; ADA picnic tables & grills; Rr. $. 8-dusk (MM102.5; 305-451-1202; boat concession 305-451-1621; dive shop 305-451-6322)

Key Largo Hammocks State Botanical Site, once destined to be a housing development, is thankfully still 2300 acres of dense, tropical hardwood forest. A .5-mi paved trail leads to a picnic shelter; the other 6 mi of trails are hard-packed with roots. Rangers lead tours on Thu and Sun at 10am; with advance notice, special tours may be arranged. ADA picnic tables; CRr. 8-5 (CR 905; .5 mi N of US 1; 305-451-1202)

Lignumvitae Key State Botanical Site is a 280-acre virgin tropical forest on a remote island with limited WC access. A private shuttle service leaves Robbies (MM77.5, Islamorada; 305-664-9814; 877-664-8498) from a fixed dock where staff can help lift you aboard in your WC. Call ahead to schedule for high tides to ease boarding and disembarking from the 10-min shuttle. At the island, a boardwalk leads from the dock up a slope to the inaccessible, historic Matheson House that serves as a visitor center. You can only explore the woods on guided 1-hr tours at 10 and 2 but you must be able to transfer onto a 6-passenger golf cart. During the less

crowded but buggier summers, rangers may be able to time tours to accommodate your arrival relative to the tides. Snacks at marina. $/tour & shuttle. Thu-Mon 8-5 (305-664-2540)

Long Key State Park has 965 acres of rocky beachfront, mangrove and woods. The Golden Orb Trail starts near the inaccessible observation tower and has an 800' boardwalk along the shoreline of a mangrove-lined lagoon. The hard-packed, .5-mi Layton Trail, on NE side of the park, loops through a dense, tropical hardwood hammock. The canoe rental launch is not readily accessible but you can pull up near the dock and, with advance notice, rangers can help carry you (not in your WC) onto the dock and into a canoe. Enjoy a detailed, self-guiding brochure for the 1.25-mi canoe trail in the shallow lagoon. Along the ocean road are ADA picnic tables on hard-packed natural terrain. Near the observation tower are ADA picnic shelters with grills. Call for schedule of ranger walks and campfires. Rr. $. 8-dusk (MM67.5, Long Key; 305-664-4815)

Windley Key Fossil Reef State Park is the 32-acre quarry that once supplied rock for Flagler's Overseas Railroad in the early 1900's. The Education Center has displays and videos on local geology, nature and history. If you can transfer to a golf cart (the back seat has no armrests), you can enjoy a 1-hr tour at 10 or 2 on the short Flagler Quarry Trail. Call in advance to reserve the golf cart. All mulched trails; picnic tables; Rr. $/tours. Thu-Mon (MM85.5, Windley Key; 305-664-2540)

■ **POOLS**

Beaches: Founders. Motels: Howard Johnson

Jacob's Aquatic Center has 2 accessible pools. The multi-use pool has a ramp, submersible WC and grab bars around the edge; therapy and classes are held in this pool that can be heated as high as 88 degrees. The Jr Olympic pool, heated between 78 and 82 degrees, has a lift (sling seat) and lap lanes. Locker rooms with roll-in showers; picnic tables on grass; playground on sand; CRr. Hrs vary (MM100; 305-453-3422) **YMCA** operates an outdoor, heated public pool with a lift (sling seat); lifeguards can help you transfer. Depths range from 3' to 5', with one lane available. Aquacise sessions. $. Summer 8-8; other seasons hrs vary (MM104; by the Italian Fisherman Restaurant; 305-451-3122)

■ SCUBA/SNORKELING

Parks: John Pennekamp

Capt Slate's Atlantis Dive Center has staff, experienced with disabled folks, who offer snorkel and scuba trips as well as instruction. With 2-wk advance reservations, an HSA-certified instructor can teach a 1-day resort course or training for certification. Roll onto the snorkel and dive boats from the cement dock; in extreme tides, you can use a ramp. Only the snorkel boats have roofs, all have glass bottoms. Crew can lift you from your WC to the dive platform and help you in and out of the water. Daily snorkel trips take about 2 1/2 hrs and on Fri visit an area abundant with barracudas and moray eels tamed over the years. Daily 2-tank, 2-site dive trips take 4 hrs; 2 1/2-hr night dives make 1 stop. The 1-day resort course includes 2-3 hrs of poolside training in the morning and an open water dive in the afternoon. The 3- to 4-day course to become certified includes classroom, pool and 4 open-dive sessions. The pool is across the street from the shop; staff can lift you from your WC to the edge of the pool. You may need help over the gravel parking lot. Equipment rentals; vending machines; Rr in restaurant next door. Dive charters 8:30 & 1; snorkel 9:30, 12:30 & 3:30 (51 Garden Cove, MM106.5; 305-451-3020; 800-331-3483) **It's A Dive** offers 4-hr snorkel and dive trips to explore wrecks or fabulous coral reefs, as well as scuba instruction. Ask to take the 45' Corinthian Catamaran, as you can usually roll aboard from the fixed dock and, once you're on the deck, you can slide onto the dive platform; staff can help you in and out of the water. With a month's notice, an HSA-certified instructor can teach the 1-day resort or 3-day certification course. This short certification course requires advance home study and an 8-5:30 regimen. Pool sessions are held at the hotel pool where staff can lift you from your WC to the edge. Children too young to dive can power snorkel, using a buoyancy device with a small tank that has a regulator and pressure gauge. A photographer can video your underwater experience. Onboard freshwater showers & drinks; rental gear; Rr at dock. 8:30 & 1:30; night dives for 4 or more (Marriott Beach Resort, MM103.8; 305-453-9881; 800-809-9881)

■ SHOPPING

Boutiques and galleries dot US 1. In Islamorada, try Treasure Village (MM86.7) and Rain Barrel (MM86.7). **Specialty Shops**: World Wide Sportsman is more of a sporting goods theme park than a store! An elevator takes you to the 2nd floor cigar bar with music on weekends during store hours. Restaurant; Rr. 7am-8:30pm (MM81.5, Islamorada; 305-664-4615)

■ SNUBA

Snuba Key Largo features a new way to enjoy diving down to 20' without a tank on your back or certification. You use a mouthpiece connected by a long hose to an air source that sits on a raft above you. This operator offers 1- to 2-hr morning instruction in a local pool and a 3-hr reef trip in the afternoon. If you are certified for diving, the pool session is unnecessary. With advance reservations, the operator can schedule staff to help lift you (250-lb limit) in and out of the water, a dive boat that best suits your needs and a pool. Each disabled snuba diver is paired with a dive master. While gear is included, you are charged separately for instruction and dives. (305-451-6391)

ACCOMMODATIONS

■ CAMPGROUNDS
John Pennekamp Coral Reef State Park
has 47 RV/tent sites with water/elec,
grills and ADA picnic tables. If you are
tenting, bring sleeping pads because
sites are on pea rock and limestone. An
ADA bathhouse has raised toilets and
step-in showers. Sites nearest the bathhouse are #21-23 and #45-47. A new
ADA bathhouse is planned. See Parks.
(MM102.5; 305-451-1202)
Long Key State Park has 60 RV/tent
beachfront sites with water/elec, ADA
picnic tables and grills; some sites have
hard-packed terrain, others have sandy
soil. Ask in advance for a site near one
of the ADA bathhouses with raised toilets, roll-under sinks and roll-in showers
with hand-held sprayers. Sidewalks lead
from the paved road to the bathhouses.
Reserve 11 months in advance for Jan-
Mar; only 6 sites are kept for drop-ins.
See Parks. (MM67.5, Long Key; 305-
664-4815; 800-326-3521)

■ CONDOS/HOUSES
Freewheeler Realty may be able to
schedule WC-friendly condos and
homes for you to rent. (305-664-2075;
freewhel@aol.com)

■ COTTAGES
White Gate Court, on the Matecumbe
Bay, has a WC-friendly 1BR cottage
(#5) that sleeps up to 6. Two full beds
(open frames) are in the bedroom, another full bed is in the den and a queen
sofa bed is in the living room. The full
kitchen has a cook top and microwave,
but no oven. The otherwise standard
bathroom has grab bars and a step-in
shower with a seat. On a private, front
patio is a gas grill, table and chairs. Staff
can also put a portable ramp at studios
4 & 6 (each with a king bed and full
kitchen) and villa 7 (with 2 queen
beds). The 3-acre grounds include easy
access to a hard-packed, 220' beach
with about 50' to the water and a dock
for fishing. Snorkel gear, bikes &
paddleboats for loan; boat slips; coin

laundry; linens included; pets okay. $$$
(MM76 bayside, Islamorada; 305-664-
4136; 800-645-4283)

■ HOUSEBOATS
Houseboat Vacations rents 2 sizes of
houseboats, both with limited WC ac-
cess; ones with easier access may be-
come available in the future. All house-
boats currently have AC and bathrooms
with 22" wide doorways. Staff can lift
you in your WC down the 1' step to the
wide dock, down onto the front deck
and through a 30" wide gate. Depend-
ing on the tide, the drop from the dock
can be as much as 3'. From the deck,
you enter through a 26" wide, sliding
glass door. The 42' 1BR houseboat
sleeps up to 6; the bedroom has a 23"
doorway and a full bed is 23"; the
roomy living area has 2 full futons and
a dining table that seats 4. The en-
trance to the kitchen is 23". The 44' 2BR
houseboat sleeps up to 8. The 2 bed-
rooms each have 23" wide doorways
and a full bed; the living area has a full
futon and the accessible kitchen has a
table that converts to a full bed. 3-day
minimum (MM85.9, Windley Key; 305-
664-4009)

■ MOTELS
Cheeca Lodge has 5 ADA rooms and 5
ADA 1BR suites. In either rooms or
suites, choose a king or 2 full beds
(open frames). Suites have kitchenettes
and living rooms with queen sofa beds.
Bathrooms in both types of units have
raised toilets and roll-under sinks; units
110, 236 and 628 have roll-in showers
with hand-held sprayers and seats; oth-
ers have tubs. Fish off a lighted 525' pier
on the Atlantic or the concierge can ar-
range for accessible fishing charters.
Children's programs; pool; lounge; spa;
full restaurants. $$$ (MM82,
Islamorada; 305-664-4651; 800-327-
2888)
Hampton Inn has 4 ADA rooms on the
ocean, each with a king bed (24" high/
open frame) and a coffeepot. Bath-

rooms have raised toilets and roll-under sinks; room 101 has a roll-in shower with a hand-held sprayer; others have tubs. Take a paved path to a boat ramp and fixed dock where you can fish. Free brkfst; full restaurant; pool. $$$ (MM80, Islamorada; 305-664-0073)

Howard Johnson has 5 large ADA rooms on the bay, each with a patio and 2 full beds. Bathrooms have raised toilets; room 101 has a roll-in shower with a hand-held sprayer and seat; others have tubs. The heated pool has a lift (fixed seat) and staff can help with transfers. There's also a ramp onto the beach in back. Restaurant for brkfst; Tiki bar; small beach. $$$ (MM102; 305-451-1400)

Marriott Key Largo Bay Beach Resort has 12 ADA rooms with 2 queen beds (24" high/platforms), queen sofa beds and coffeepots. Bathrooms have raised toilets and step-in showers with hand-held sprayers and seats. The marina at this 17-acre resort offers boat rentals, backcountry fishing trips, parasailing, dive and snorkel trips; see It's a Dive.

Children's programs; pool; laundry; lounge; entertainment; full restaurant; fitness center; spa; putting green. $$$ (MM103.8; 305-453-0093; 800-843-5397)

Sands of Islamorada has an ADA room (#11) with 3 full beds (34" high/open frames), a kitchenette and bathroom with a raised toilet, roll-under sink and roll-in shower. The grounds include a boat ramp on the ocean, a fixed dock from where you can fish, a soft sand beach and picnic tables along the seawall. $$$ (MM80, Islamorada; 305-664-2791; 888-741-4518)

Weston Beach Resort has 6 ADA rooms with either a king or 2 queen beds (25" high/platforms), a queen sofa bed and coffeepot. Bathrooms have roll-under sinks; rooms 102 and 128 have roll-in showers with hand-held sprayers and seats; others have tubs. A boardwalk leads to a soft sand beach on the Florida Bay, as well as a dock from which you can fish. Pool; lounge; entertainment; full restaurant. $$$ (MM97; 305-852-5553)

MARATHON
MM 78-46: Conch Key, Duck Key, Grassy Key, Little Duck Key

For a quiet getaway and plenty of fishing, check out the Middle Keys. Marathon is the largest town here and has one of two airports in the Keys; the other is in Key West. Check out the two accessible opportunities to interact with live dolphins; one has programs specifically geared to persons with special needs. An ADA townhouse is available on Duck Key.

Tourist Info
Marathon Chamber: MM53.5, 12222 US 1, 33050; 305-743-5417; 800-262-7284

ACTIVITIES

■ **ATTRACTIONS**

Capt Hook's Marina is the place to be at 4 when staff feed the nurse sharks, eels, rays and other creatures residing in the pond. The dock is ramped and WC riders are allowed through the gate for a close view. Snacks (MM53; 305-743-2444; 800-278-4665)

Dolphin Connection offers 3 in-water wade programs to enjoy and learn about dolphins. A ramp from the classroom leads to a saltwater lagoon where the dolphins reside. You must speak and read English. The 45-min Dolphin

Discovery (at 10, 1 and 4) begins with a 15-min class. Then staff lifts you from your WC to the dock and onto a platform that is submerged in 3' water for 20 min of feeding and snuggling dolphins; participants must be 4'6" or taller. In the 30-min Dockside Dolphin (at 11:30), you help train these intelligent creatures; adults must accompany anyone 5 or younger. The 30-min Dolphin Detective (at 2:30) offers hands-on dockside activities for children age 5 and older. At least 3 months in advance, call Gina Wood, Special Needs Coordinator, for an evaluation. Rr in hotel (Hawk's Cay Resort, E at MM61, Duck Key; 305-289-9975; reservations 888-814-9154)

Dolphin Research Center is home to a family of Atlantic bottlenose dolphins and California sea lions where you can take a guided tour and, if you choose, participate in recreational or therapeutic sessions in the 30' deep lagoon. On the 45-min tour (at 10, 11, 12:30, 2:00, and 3:30), you watch staff train and conduct research with these fascinating animals. On the 2 1/2-hr Special Needs Recreational Swim, you and 2 companions take a tour, participate in a workshop on dolphin communications and meet your hosts from a floating dock. Staff can help you transfer from your WC to a lift (fixed seat) that lowers you into the water and are in the water with you for a 20-min swim. In Dolphin Assisted Therapy, dolphins can actually motivate participants (age 5 and older) to expand their skills. Time and frequency depends on the individualized therapy program; your therapist needs to contact the center. Make reservations 1 to 2 months ahead. The 1 1/2-hr Tips-On-Training Program, limited to the first 12 people who sign up each day, allows you to watch the training process from behind the scenes. You discover the animals' personalities and relationships with trainers. You can sit down on a floating dock and touch the dolphins. In winter, you may want to rent a wetsuit at a nearby dive shop. For an extra charge, staff can video your swim. Special life jackets provided; Rr. 9-4:30 (MM 59, Grassy Key; 305-289-1121)

■ **BEACHES**

Sombrero Beach, the largest county beach in Marathon, has a narrow strip of sand along the ocean, a shallow swim area and accessible observation pier (no fishing). Picnic tables; grills; Rr. 8-dusk (S at MM50 on Sombrero Bch Dr)

Veteran's Memorial Park is a small county beach with a shallow swim area at the W end of the Seven Mile Bridge. Picnic tables; Rr. 8-dusk (MM40, Little Duck Key)

■ **BIKE TRAILS**

Key Largo: Bike Trails

Marathon has a 7-mi bike path from MM58 by the Key Colony Beach community on Grassy Key. At MM50, you can take a trail that leads S to Sombrero Beach and to Pigeon Key (MM45) at the E end of the old 7 Mile Bridge, which is now a VERY long fishing pier.

■ **BOAT RENTALS**

Watersports rents a pontoon boat (25" entry) for up to 10 people. The fixed dock is ramped; staff can lift you aboard. Captain services are also available. Unenclosed port-o-let onboard; 2-hr minimum; Rr at marina (Hawk's Cay Resort, MM 61, Duck Key; 305-743-0145)

■ **BOAT TOURS**

Hoot Mon Sailing Charters offers 2 trips on a 38' sailboat for 2-6 people. The capt can help lift you aboard from your WC onto a boat seat in the shade or sun. The 1pm trip is 2 hrs; if you can get yourself in and out of the water, you can enjoy a swim or snorkel. The 1 1/2-hr sunset sail includes champagne. Bring refreshments if you like. Rr in hotel (Banana Bay Resort, MM49.5; 305-289-1433)

Keylypso is a powered catamaran offering 2-hr sunset cruises in the ocean or Gulf. At most tides, you can roll aboard from the dock; crew helps if needed. Wine, champagne, cheese and crackers are included. If you can get yourself in and out the water, snorkeling trips are available. (The Island, MM54; 305-743-7655)

■ **FISHING CHARTERS**
Endless Summer offers half/full-day, offshore and reef fishing trips for 1 WC and 5 able-bodied anglers in or near the Gulf Stream. The fixed dock is ramped; Capt Laurino and crew can lift you aboard the 42' Sportfish in your WC. (Hawk's Cay Marina, MM61, Duck Key; 305-289-9282)
Jerry's Charters offers half/full-day, sports fishing, deep-sea, backcountry, reef and wreck fishing aboard a 31' Sportsfisherman for up to 6. The parking lot is gravel near the boat but it is flat to the dock where crew can lift you aboard in your WC or into a fighting chair. Snacks & drinks provided; lunch can be arranged; Rr at hotel (Banana Bay Resort, MM49.5; 305-289-7298; 800-775-2646)

■ **FISHING-PARTY BOATS**
Marathon Lady offers 4-hr fishing trips out to the reef. Call ahead so staff can reserve a space for you at the rail. Mates can lift you aboard in your WC. Snacks onboard; Rr at dive shop. 8:30am daily; other times vary (MM53; 305-743-5580)

■ **FISHING PIERS/BRIDGES**
The following run parallel to the vehicular bridges and are just for fishing:
Conch Key oceanside; park W of bridge (MM63)
Duck Key oceanside; park W of bridge (MM61.5)
Grassy Key oceanside; park either end of bridge (MM60.5)
Seven Mile Bridge bayside; park E of bridge (MM46.5)

■ **MUSEUMS**
Parks: Pigeon Key
Museums of Crane Point Hammock sit in a lovely 63-acre, thatch-palm woods. The Museum of Natural History covers local geology, wildlife and history, in-

cluding shipwrecks along the Keys. The Children's Museum contains a shell exhibit, touch tank, tropical fish lagoon and an iguana habitat. Boardwalks and crushed-shell paths take you between the museums, over a lagoon and through a shady picnic area. Take the short hard-packed path or a trolley (staff can help with transfers) to the 1900 conch-style Adderly House. The Wild Bird Rescue Center has a somewhat hilly path by the aviaries, but through a large window, you can watch staff caring for injured birds. Some nature trails are narrow and mulched; the hard-packed shell road is a fine way to tour the grounds. Gift shop; Rr. $ Mon-Sat 10-5; Sun 12-5 (MM50.5; 305-743-9100)

■ **PARKS**
Pigeon Key National Historic Site sits on a 5.3-acre island below the Old Seven Mile Bridge, now a 2-mi pedestrian pier due to the devastating hurricane of 1935. Pigeon Key is a marine education center with an interesting history. Send someone to purchase tickets at the visitor center/gift shop (in an inaccessible train car from Henry Flagler's times) at MM47 on Knight's Key (oceanside). Because the hourly trolley onto Pigeon Key (bayside) is inaccessible, staff will direct you to drive to the island; HC parking is paved but staff allows you to park next to any of the buildings. The museum, with a WC lift, has photographs and postcards that reveal the island's history since before the railroad opened the Keys to tourism. Watch a 30-min film and then a guide leads you outside for a 30-min briefing before you tour the island on your own. Roads are hard-packed gravel and may be easier to navigate than the uneven sidewalks. Most of the 7 buildings, restored from Pigeon Key's days as a fishing village in the early 1900's, are used for administration, education and student lodging. Picnic tables on grass; Rr in the Gang Section Quarters. 10-4 (MM45, Pigeon Key;

305-289-0025/743-5999)

■ **PERFORMING ARTS**

Marathon Community Theater has performances Nov-Jun and a 1-screen movie theater. The building is ramped and removable seats allow for WC seating up front. Rr (MM50; plays 305-743-0994; movies 305-743-0288)

■ **SCUBA/SNORKELING**

Capt Hook's caters to snorkelers and divers, from novice to certified. Park by the dock where crew can lift you aboard in your WC at the open stern of the 30' boat with a roof. Crew can lift you from your WC to the dive platform. The boat goes out daily at 8:30 and 1 for 2-tank, 2-site dives. In the 1-day Discover Scuba program, you spend the morning in class and at a nearby hotel pool. In the afternoon you take 2 dives to 40' with an instructor. For the 5-day certification program, you spend mornings in class and 3 afternoons in the pool, then 4 open-water dives with an instructor. Advanced open water certification courses are also available. Call 72 hrs in advance so additional crew can be scheduled to help lift. Water, cooler space & ice onboard; all snorkel/dive gear is rented (MM53; 305-743-2444; 800-278-4665)

Tilden's Dive Center can accommodate snorkelers, beginning to experienced divers and *bubble-watchers,* or folks who watch from the boat. Crew can lift you in your WC from the fixed dock, aboard the 40' boat and later to the dive platform. Snorkelers can go on any of the shallow dive trips. Certified divers can choose 1-tank night dives or 2-tank, 2-site dives to explore the coral reefs and, for those certified to dive to 120' depths, wreck dives. In the 1-day resort course, morning combines class and pool instruction (staff can lift you in) and afternoon entails a 50' reef dive with a dive master. Full certification takes 5 days: 3 in class and the pool, and 2 on full-day shallow reef dives with a dive master. Snorkel/dive gear is available (Hawk's Cay Resort, MM61, Duck Key; 305-289-4931; 877-386-3483)

■ **SHOPPING**

Boutiques: Quay Shops include several fun spots, from an upscale kids' shop to a hot sauce and cigar shop! (MM54)

Specialty: For truly fresh seafood, try the afternoon market on the wharves at the end of 11 and 15 Sts. (MM48 oceanside)

■ **SNUBA**

Tilden Dive Center offers a new way to enjoy diving down to 15' without a tank on your back or certification. You use a mouthpiece connected by a long hose to an air source that sits on a raft above you. Crew can lift you in your WC aboard the 40' boat from the fixed dock. On 4-hr snuba trips, a dive master instructs you in snuba on the way out to the reef. At the 1st site, you snorkel just to get your water skills honed. At the 2nd site, each snuba diver is paired with a dive master. (Hawk's Cay Resort, MM61, Duck Key; 305-289-4931; 877-386-3483)

ACCOMMODATIONS

■ **CONDOS**

Duck Key Condo is a privately owned, 2-story, ADA townhouse (with an elevator) that overlooks the harbor. The home has 2 bedrooms, each with a queen bed (23" high/open frame), full kitchen with a roll-under sink, laundry room, queen sofa bed and porches off the living room and bedroom. The bathroom has a roll-under sink and roll-in shower with a hand-held sprayer and seat. The waterfront resort has tennis, a playground, sauna, steam and weight rooms and pools, including a kiddie pool with a pirate ship and water slide. You can use the boat ramp and, down a few steps, a fixed dock for boarding a boat or fishing on Tom's Harbor. $$$ (Jeff Tiffany; 561-627-1941)

■ MOTELS

Banana Bay Resort has 2 ADA rooms, each with 2 full beds (24" high/platforms) and a refrigerator. Bathrooms have raised toilets, roll-under sinks and tubs with hand-held sprayers and seats. This intimate bayside resort sits on 10 acres of landscaped tropical jungle and is near shops, restaurants and a cinema. Docks lead to a small, sugar-sand beach with picnic tables. See Boat Charters, Boat Tours and Fishing Charters. Free brkfst; pool; laundry; lounge; restaurant for lnch & dnr; 50-slip marina; boat ramp & fixed docks. $$$ (MM49.5; 305-743-2690; 800-226-2621)

Hampton Inn has 2 ADA rooms and 2 1BR suites. Both rooms have 2 queen beds (24" high/open frames) and coffeepots. Each suite has a king bed, kitchenette and queen sofa bed in the living room. Bathrooms have raised toilets and roll-under sinks. Room 112 and suite 104 have roll-in showers; others have tubs. Free brkfst; pool; laundry; lounge; fitness center. $$$ (MM48; 305-743-9009)

Hawk's Cay Resort is a 60-acre, tropical island playground with 10 ADA rooms and an ADA 2BR villa. Rooms have a range of bed sizes (22" high/platforms), refrigerators, coffeepots and balconies. The villa has an elevator to the 2nd floor, a queen bed (22" high/platform) in each bedroom, full kitchen, sofa bed in the living room, balcony, washer/dryer and grocery delivery service. Bathrooms have roll-under sinks; rooms 335 and 340 have roll-in showers; others have tubs. This resort has plenty of accessible fun, including the Dolphin Encounter; see Attractions, Boat Rentals, Fishing Charters and Scuba/Snorkeling. Children's programs; fitness center; boat ramp; pool; laundry; lounge; entertainment; full restaurants; marina. $$$ (MM61, Duck Key; 305-743-7000; 800-237-3329)

Wellesley Inn has 4 ADA rooms, each with a queen bed (21" high/platform), sofa bed and coffeepot. Bathrooms have roll-under sinks and roll-in showers with hand-held sprayers and seats. Free brkfst. $-$$ (MM54; 305-743-8550)

KEY WEST

MM39-0: Bahia Honda Key, Big Pine Key, Cudjoe Key, Dry Tortugas, Missouri Key, Ohio Key, Stock Island, Sugarloaf Key

The lower Keys have something for everyone: history, sightseeing, nightlife, shopping, art and, of course, fun in the water. You can take guided tours by myriad kinds of boats, trolley or strolling. Bahia Honda State Park loans out a beach wheelchair. One of the dive boats has a lift to enter the water. One hotel has a lift for its heated pool; another has a zero-depth pool. And you can choose from plenty of interesting B&Bs and inns. Be aware that US 1 is also Roosevelt Blvd as you enter Key West and thenTruman Ave as you enter downtown.

Street parking is usually hard to find in popular Old Town Key West. Try any of the 3 public facilities: a lot on Wall Street by Mallory Square; a garage on Front Street by the Hilton Hotel; and the Park n' Ride Garage on Caroline & Grinnel Streets (305-293-6426). With a disabled permit, you can park free at meters and garages.

Tourist Info

Lower Keys Chamber: MM31, Big Pine Key, 33043; 305-872-2411; 800-872-3722
Key West Chamber: 402 Wall St, 33040; 305-294-2587; 800-527-8539
Key West Welcome Center: MM4, 3840 N US 1; 305-296-4444

Web sites: www.key-west.com; www.keyexposure.com; www.keywest.com
Lodging: 800-916-2030

ACTIVITIES

■ ATTRACTIONS
City Cemetery is a surprisingly fun site with aboveground caskets and epitaphs such as *At Least I Know Where He's Sleeping Tonight*. A memorial honors 22 sailors killed on the USS Maine. Make reservations for the 1-hr guided tour along the paved roads, on Tue and Thu at 9:30am. $/tour. Dawn-6pm (Margaret & Angela Sts; 305-292-6718)
Hemingway House, built in 1851, is where Hemingway lived and wrote from 1931 onward. It is also home to some 50 descendents of his 6-toed felines. Guided 30-min tours occur every 10 min. The 2nd floor is not accessible but a video and photo album give you the picture. Sidewalks by pool & grounds; parking across street; WC entrance in backyard; gift shop; Rr. $/free for WC users. 9-5 (907 Whitehead St; 305-294-1575)
Key Encounter, an upstairs theater and museum with a ramp, features a giant 3-screen movie of the under- and above-water natural wonders of the Keys. The jungle walk has animated creatures and live exotic birds. The mirrored, infinity nature tunnel reflects images such as the magnificent Iguacu Falls in Brazil. The nature museum has a 22.5' skin of an anaconda snake that ate a woman. Art gallery; gift shop; Rr. $. Sun-Fri 11-5; shows every 30-min (Clinton Square Mall, 291 Front St; 305-292-2070)
Key West Aquarium, opened in 1934, has a turtle pool, shark tank and 50,000-gal Atlantic Shores exhibit with tarpon, barracuda, tropical fish, lobsters and birds. The touch tank has conchs, horseshoe and hermit crabs, sea urchins and baby nurse sharks. Guided 30-min tours (at 11, 1, 3 and 4:30) include stingray and shark feeding. Street parking; Rr in the square. $. 10-6 (Mallory Sq, 1

Whitehead St; 305-296-2051)
Mallory Square is the focal point of Old Town Key West where shops and museums abound and sunset celebrations include jugglers and fire-eaters. (NW end of Duval St)
Ripley's Believe It or Not is an *odditorium* with 10,000 sq ft of uniquities and gimmicks in video, illusion, artifact and interactive exhibits. Street parking; elevator to all 3 floors; Rr. $. 9am-11pm (527 Duval St; 305-293-9694)
Southernmost Point, only 90 mi from Cuba, is where almost every tourist snaps a photo. (Whitehead & South Sts)
■ BEACHES
Parks: Bahia Honda
CB Harvey Rest Beach has a paved bike path that skirts the usually quiet, 300' beach and passes picnic areas, a restaurant and the White St Pier. From parking at the E end, take the ramp with a step down to the sand. At the W end, close to pier parking, is a flat access to the sand. Picnic tables; Rr (White St & Atlantic Blvd)
Higgs Beach is a popular, 300' stretch of county beach on the ocean with a picnic area across the street and a short, paved nature trail. You can park on the street by the soft sand. Restaurant; vending machines; picnic tables; grills; playground; tennis; Rr. Dawn-10pm (S end of White St at Atlantic Blvd)
Simonton St Beach is a lovely, quiet spot for catching sunsets and dinner at nearby restaurants. This little city beach on the Gulf has a short fishing pier and parking next to the sand. The small boat ramp along the beach has no dock but works well for canoes. Rr (N end of Simonton St)
Smathers Beach, one of the longest and most popular city beaches in Key West,

has a central ramp from parking to a boardwalk that leads to the sand and picnic shelters. Concessions sell snacks, rent chairs, rent kayaks and more until sunset. A boat ramp with a cement dock on the Atlantic is at the S end of the beach. Outdoor showers; Rr (W of airport along S US 1/Roosevelt Blvd S)

■ BIKE TRAILS

Key Largo: Bike Trails

Key West has a trail from MM5.3 on Cow Key that forks when it comes to Roosevelt Blvd on Key West. From this point onward, both trails are wide sidewalks, adjacent to the water, heavily traveled and to be under renovations through 2005. The N fork runs along the bay on N Roosevelt Blvd to Bayview Park, just N of MM1. The S fork runs along South Roosevelt Blvd, past Smathers Beach, the White St Fishing Pier and Mc Coy Indigenous Park to Higgs Beach; see Beaches.

Saddlebunch Keys Trail runs from MM15 to MM11, starting at Bay Point Park, crossing 4 historic Flagler railroad bridges to Shark Key. Bring plenty of water and wear a hat because no shade or facilities are yet available along the way.

■ BOAT RAMPS

Beaches: Simonton St, Smathers

City Marina has a ramp and 2 steps down to a floating dock on Garrison Bight. Restaurant; Rr. $ (1801 N US 1/ Roosevelt Blvd N; 305-292 8167)

Oceanside Marina has a ramp and floating dock. Bait shop; restaurant; Rr. $ (5950 Peninsula Ave, Stock Island; 305-294-4676)

Old Wooden Bridge Fishing Camp has a boat ramp and several fixed docks of varying heights that ease boarding at different tides in the Florida Bay. Bait shop. $. 7:30-5 (1791 Bogie Dr, Big Pine Key; E at light by MM30, S at stop sign; 305-872-2241)

Sugarloaf Marina has a ramp and floating dock next to the marina. Bait shop; full restaurant; country store. $ (MM17, Sugarloaf Key; 305-745-3135)

Sunshine Marina has a ramp and floating dock on the Florida Bay. Restaurant; convenience store; gas; bait shop. $ (MM39, Ohio Key; 305-872-2217; 800-852-0348)

■ BOAT RENTALS

Bud's Boats rents 15'-25' center consoles for full days in the bay and backcountry. Arrange your rental at this location and, with prior notice, crew can bring your boat here and help lift you aboard in your WC. Bait shop (Old Wooden Bridge Fishing Camp, 1791 Bogie Dr, Big Pine Key; 305-743-6316)

Club Nautico rents a 20' and 24' center console for a minimum of 2 hrs. Call ahead so staff can arrange extra help to lift you aboard in your WC from the floating dock. 8-6 (Hilton Marina, 245 Front St; 305-451-4120)

Island Tranquility rents a deck boat (28" entry) for up to 8 on the ocean, 2-hr minimum. With advance notice, staff can help lift you aboard in your WC from the fixed dock. Bait shop; restaurant; small grocery. 8-6 (Garrison Bight Marina, 711 Eisenhower Dr; 305-294-3093)

Sunshine Marina rents pontoon boats (29" entry) for use on the Gulf by the half/full day for up to 10 people. Staff can help you board from the floating dock. 7-5 (MM39, Ohio Key; 305-872-2217; 800-852-0348)

■ BOAT TOURS

Adventure Charters offers full-day, private or split charters, for up to 14 on a 42' catamaran that you can roll aboard by ramp. Simply enjoy the scenic ride through the Great White Heron National Wildlife Refuge or, if you have good upper body strength, kayak, snorkel or swim off the boat. Crew can help lift you (200-lb limit) to a rear platform level with the water from which you can swim or board a solo/tandem sit-on kayak. In the morning, the catamaran stops at Snipe Key for a 2-hr guided kayak tour through a maze of tidal creeks. After lunch, fish, swim or snorkel. On the return trip, you can stop for a guided kayak tour of the Mud Keys. Reservations; gear included (wetsuits extra); Rr at the marina. Mon-Sat 9:30-5 (Safe Harbour Marina, MM5, 6810 Front St, Stock Island; 305-296-0362; 888-817-0841)

Pride of Key West is a glass-bottom catamaran that makes 2-hr narrated trips to a coral reef 6 mi offshore where you can see hundreds of species of fish. Roll up the ramp from the dock; crew helps, if needed. On the AC main deck, you can get right up to the viewing area. Snack bar onboard; park in lot by Mallory Square; Rr next door. 12, 2 & sunset (2 Duval St; 305-296-6293)

Safari Charters offers half/full-day and sunset private charters for up to 6 aboard a 36' catamaran to the Great White Heron National Wildlife Refuge. Roll onto the fixed dock and crew can lift you aboard in your WC; choose a sunny or shady spot under the awning. To snorkel, swim or kayak off the catamaran on day trips, crew can lift you from your WC to a ramp that is lowered/raised by pulley. From the ramp, slide across and into the tandem sit-in kayak as others stabilize it in the water. The 4 1/2-hr trips include snacks, beer and soda. A total of 6 are needed for the 7-hr trip that includes lunch. Or, take a 2-hr sail in the glorious, Key West sunset. Gear included; freshwater shower; wetsuits extra (Banana Bay Resort, 2319 N US 1; 305-296-4691; 888-672-3274)

Schooner Western Union, a 130' tall ship, has sailed the Caribbean and South Atlantic since 1939. Hear of her adventures and help hoist the sails, heave the lines and maybe, take the helm on a 2-hr cruise of the harbor. Crew can help you roll aboard by the gang plank. Then find your way between the main hold and the main mast where you can sit and see the action on both sides of the ship. Day, sunset and starlight sails offer free beer, wine, champagne and soda. Sunset sails

also include live music, homing doves and cannon fire. Park in the city lot behind Waterfront Market (near the dock) where you can find Rr. (Schooner Wharf, 202 William St; 305-292-1766)

■ **CASINOS**

Vegas West Casino Cruise offers gambling from slots to poker and roulette on a 4 1/2-hr cruise. Board by ramp to the top level where you'll find an outside deck, slot machines, cash bar and sandwiches. Crew can carry you in your WC down to the lower deck where the tables and Rr are located. 6:30pm (Hilton Marina, 237 Front St; 305-295-7775)

■ **FISHING CHARTERS**

Amity Charters offers flats fishing trips for 2 aboard a relatively roomy skiff, 4-hr minimum. Capt Ferguson can help you up the 10" curb from parking to the dock and lift you aboard in your WC. Rr in marina (Banana Bay Resort, 2319 N US 1; 305-304-6699)

RamerEzi offers half/full-day, deep-sea trips on a 34' sport fishing boat for up to 6 anglers. Capt Steve Magee and crew can lift you aboard in your WC. (City Marina, 1801 N US 1; 305-294-0803)

Wayward offers half/full-day, backcountry trips on an 18' flats boat. Capt Ron Ward can help you aboard. Fly or light tackle provided (Sugarloaf Marina, MM17, Sugarloaf Key; 305-872-0290)

■ **FISHING-PARTY BOATS**

Gulf Stream III has full-day trips Sep-Jun and night trips Jul-Aug. Take the ramp up to the boat and crew can lift you down into the boat in your WC. The cabin has a lip at the entrance and a snack bar. Rr at marina. Sep-Jun 9:30-4:30; Jul-Aug 6:30pm-1am (City Marina, 1801 N US 1; 305-296-8494; 888-745-3595)

■ **FISHING PIERS/BRIDGES**

The following run parallel to the vehicular bridges and are just for fishing: **Cudjoe Key** oceanside; park E of bridge (MM23.5)

Missouri Key bayside; park either end of bridge (MM39.5)

Niles Channel oceanside; park either end of bridge (MM26.5)

White St Pier extends 1000' over the Atlantic Ocean next to the CB Harvey Rest Beach. Curbs line the lighted pier until you get to the 450 sq ft landing at the end where a ramp leads to fishing spots at the rail. Rr at beach. 24 hrs (White St & Atlantic Blvd)

■ **KAYAKING**

Parks: Bahia Honda

Adventure Charters offers 2 1/2- and 4-hr, guided kayak tours in the Florida Keys' backcountry. Follow the guide in your vehicle to the launch site .5 mi from the shop. Take the ramp onto the floating dock where crew can help you from your WC to sit on the dock and aboard a solo/tandem kayak. After a 10-min paddle lesson, you can explore mangroves and flats. Reservations; BYO snacks; guide carries cooler; gear included; Rr at marina (Safe Harbour Marina, MM5, 6810 Front St, Stock Island; 305-296-0362; 888-817-0841)

Mosquito Coast Kayak offers 4-hr, guided trips island-hopping in the Gulf. Follow the group van in your vehicle to Sugarloaf Key, about 15 mi N. At the launch site, roll down the ramp to shallow water where staff can lift you into a solo sit-on or a tandem sit-in kayak. Most of the paddle is in shallow water at a slow pace. You can snorkel during short stops. Call ahead to discuss any special needs with Sue. Water, health bar & snorkel gear included. 9-5 (1107 Duval St; 305-294-7178)

■ **MUSEUMS**

Audubon House, once the home of a harbor pilot and master wrecker, was restored to commemorate Audubon's 1832 visit to the island. Staff shows you to the ramped rear of the house to access the 1st floor of the 3-story frame house. Enjoy Audubon's paintings of birds and nature as well as fine 18th and 19th century furnishings. Brick walkways lead through an acre of lush native and exotic plants. Guided tours are offered with advance notice. Street parking; gift shop; Rr. $. 9:30-5 (205 Whitehead St; 305-294-2116; 877-281-2473)

Curry Mansion is an 1869 20-room home suggesting a Parisian town house and filled with fine antiques, Audubon prints and Tiffany glass befitting Florida's first self-made millionaire. A lift gets you to the porch and 1st floor but narrow doorways make maneuvering tricky. At the entrance, get a self-guiding brochure. See B&Bs. Rr. $. 10-5 (511 Caroline St; 305-294-5349; 800-253-3466)

Little White House was the vacation retreat of Harry Truman and 12 other US presidents. Restored to its original 1940's condition, the 1st floor is accessible by ramp where you can peruse 2 exhibit rooms with presidential memorabilia and furnishings. A 10-min video and photo album cover the upstairs. A 45-min guided house tour starts every 15 min. Get the self-guiding brochure and use the paved paths through the 2-acre botanical garden around the house. Send someone into the gift shop (3 steps up) and staff will lead you to the WC entrance. Park a half block away at Hilton Hotel (245 Front St); Rr. $. 9-4:30 (111 Front St; through Truman Annex; 305-294-9911)

Mel Fisher Maritime Museum houses dazzling jewelry, artifacts, gold and silver brought up from sunken Spanish galleons. Learn about the causes of these shipwrecks and how today's treasure seekers operate. Parking garage next door; steep ramped entrance in rear; elevator; gift shop; Rr. $. 9:30-5:30 (200 Greene St; 305-294-2633)

Museum of Art & History, in the restored US Customs House of the 1890's, features local, national and international art, and history exhibits. WC parking; lift to the entry level in the rear; Rr. $. 9-5 (281 Front St; 305-295-6616)

■ PARASAILING

Sunset Watersports offers 12-min solo flights at 600' over the Atlantic. The dock is ramped; crew can lift you in your WC into the 28' powerboat. Don the harness and, with the chute already inflated, you can take off from, and back into, your WC. 10-5 (201 Williams St; 305-296-2554)

Tropical Dreams could be yours on a 15-min flight 300' above the Atlantic. Crew can lift you aboard the roomy, 31' powerboat in your WC or onto a boat seat. When it's your turn, crew can lift you to the platform where you are hooked to the harness for your flight. Rr in hotel. 10-6 (Windham Casa Marina, 714 Seminole St; 305-304-9022)

■ PARKS

⁺Bahia Honda State Park is 524 acres that emerged thousands of years ago from a prehistoric, underwater coral reef. The park is an environmental treasure that offers plenty of accessible fun. Ask at the entrance to borrow the beach WC (no armrests); you can pick it up at the SW end of the island at the rental concession. Across the road is Loggerhead Beach where, from parking, you can take a ramp onto the sand. The concession and marina are open 8-5; you can keep the WC until park closing as long as you return it to a ranger. At the concession (305-872-3954), sign up for daily 2 1/2-hr snorkel trips to the spectacular, 20' deep Looe Key National Marine Sanctuary (hrs vary). To board, roll onto the seawall dock where staff can lift you in your WC onto the 45' boat, however you must be able to use the ladders to get in and out of the water. Equipment is included; wetsuits are extra. Solo/tandem sit-on kayaks are rented by the hr to explore the lagoon and a nearby island; staff can help lift you into the kayak. Bikes are rented for the 3.5 mi of park roads. At the island's SW tip, an old railroad bridge offers a great overlook of nearby keys, but the path is bumpy and steep. The marina has 2 boat ramps with fixed docks; nor-mal to low tides make boarding in a WC easier. At Calusa Beach, on the Gulf, sidewalks lead to ADA picnic shelters and the soft sand (Rr; outdoor showers). The nature center at Calusa has displays on the local geology and wildlife. A hairpin left turn from the entrance takes you to Sandspur Beach on the Atlantic; a ramp from parking leads to a 30' deep stretch of soft sand (ADA picnic shelters; outdoor shower on grass; Rr). Beyond parking, a short nature trail is hard-packed but bumpy with tree roots. Call for the schedule of ranger programs in winter. At concession: gift shop; snack bar; small grocery; Rr. $. 8-dusk (MM36.5, Bahia Honda Key; 305-872-2353)

Dry Tortugas National Park includes 7 rugged islands, 70 mi W of Key West, that attract sooty terns and other rare birds including mosquitoes and hearty tourists. Fort Jefferson, on Garden Key, served as a Union army post in the Civil War before it became a prison for, among others, the alleged co-conspirators in Lincoln's assassination. Take a private boat or a 2-hr ferry (described below) to Fort Jefferson. The wood dock takes you to the Fort entrance and a fairly level brick path to the visitor center with a 10-min slide orientation and bookstore; the WC entrance is through the casemate to the left. The 6-sided Fort's first tier and parade grounds are bumpy and have descriptive signage. Intermittent ranger tours include the upper levels. Snorkelers and divers wade out from the soft sand beach to see sensational reefs and fish. But, you can see plenty of marine life beneath the crystal water from the 8' wide moat around most of the Fort. Primitive tent camping is available; you must bring in all supplies (including water) and carry out all trash. ADA picnic tables; Rr at dock. Dawn-dusk (305-242-7700) *Sunny Days* offers daily ferry service to Fort Jefferson. Board the catamaran by ramp for the 2-hr trip and a continental breakfast buffet.

Spend 4 1/2 hrs on the island and enjoy a guided tour and lunch buffet in the picnic area. Snorkel gear is included. Check in 7:30am; return 5pm (Sunny Days, Elizabeth & Greene Sts; 305-292-6100; 800-236-7937)

Fort Zachary Taylor State Historic Site, where the Atlantic meets the Gulf, has one of Key West's prettiest beaches and an 1845 fort. From beach parking, a path leads to the relatively hard-packed, coral rock beach where the waves can get choppy at times. The concession sells snacks and rents snorkel/water play equipment. Under the tree-lined edge of the beach are ADA picnic tables and grills. At the entrance station, ask to drive your vehicle to the Civil War fort. Or, take a footbridge into the parade grounds with some rough, broken areas. The lower level of the fort is masonry and eroded in spots; the upper level is not accessible. The nature trail through some of the park's 87 wooded acres is hilly and rugged. Guided tours occur at 12 and 2. Call for special events, including re-enactments. Beach: outdoor showers; Rr. Fort: Rr. $. 8-dusk (Southard St, through Truman Annex; 305-292-6713)

■ **PERFORMING ARTS**

Tennessee Williams Fine Arts Center hosts plays, concerts and ballets by visiting performers and presentations by the college chorus. WC seating in front on aisle; Rr. Nov-Apr (Florida Keys Community College, 5901 W College Rd; 305-296-1520)

Waterfront Playhouse is a community theater performing musicals, comedies and dramas. WC seating in aisles; street parking; Rr (Mallory Sq; 305-294-5015)

■ **SCUBA/SNORKELING**

Parks: Bahia Honda

Paradise Divers offers daily, 4 1/2-hr snorkel/dive trips to the Looe Key National Underwater Marine Sanctuary (at 9 and 1) and has capts experienced with disabled divers. At reduced rates, you can simply go for the ride. From the fixed dock, crew can lift you from

your WC aboard the 25' or 30' dive boat to a bench seat with a back. When it's time to dive, scoot to the dive platform in back where crew can help you in and out of the water. See Campgrounds. Rr at campground office (Sunshine Key Campground Resort, MM39, Ohio Key; 305-872-1114)

Sea Breeze Reef Raiders has a canopied catamaran adapted for WC snorkelers and divers with a ramp to the dock and boat and an onboard hoist (fixed seat) to get in and out of the water. Two site, 2-hr snorkel trips go out at 10 and 2:15 to reefs from 3' to 35' deep; certified divers in WCs are welcome. Call in advance for crew to set up the hoist. Snorkel gear included; free snacks and drinks, including beer/wine; warm freshwater shower onboard; Rr at (Galleon Marina, 617 Front St; E of Duval St; 305-292-7745; 800-370-7745)

Underseas offers 4-hr, 2-site snorkeling and scuba trips to the Looe Key National Underwater Marine Sanctuary and wrecks as well as diving instruction. At a reduced rate, you can just go along for the ride at 9 and 1:30. By ramp, roll aboard the 50' catamaran where you can ride in shade or sun. Crew can lift you in and out of the water from the dive platform. The 1-day resort course, for someone who wants to try diving, and PADI certification, for those who are more serious, are performance-based at a pace comfortable for you. You can get certified in less than a week. Private instruction is available. Pool sessions are held in a private pool (2 blocks from the shop) where you can roll to the edge and staff can lift you in and out of the water. (MM30.5, Big Pine Key; 305-872-2700; 800-446-5663)

■ **SHOPPING**

Boutiques: Key West downtown is lined with neat shops, galleries and restaurants, but be aware that many have steps at the entrance.

Specialty shops are infinite but consider these: At Key West Cigar Factory, you can watch cigars being hand-rolled; send someone in to open the WC door on Pirates Alley (3 Pirates Alley & Front St; 305-294-3470). At the Reef Relief Environmental Center, your purchases help protect the fragile reef system (201 William St; 305-294-3100). Sea Cloud Orchids sells and ships orchids, tropicals and all sorts of gardening gizmos (MM10; 305-294-3639).

■ TOURS
Ghost Tours are 1-mi, 1 1/2-hr walking tours on the island's mysterious haunted past. Learn about churchyard spirits, from pirates to forsaken lovers that lurk around town and end up in a haunted saloon. 8pm (La Concha Inn, 430 Duval St; 305-294-9255)

Island City Strolls are 1 1/2-hr private, appointment-only, walking tours that focus on your interests, such as the history of Old Key West, Secret Gardens, Literary Heritage and Art. All are accessible and, depending on the tour, your guide meets you at a chosen location and time. (305-294-8380)

Old Town Trolley Tours are 90-min narrated tours covering Key West, from colorful contemporary anecdotes to the history of Indians, pirates and Civil War soldiers. Call 24 hrs ahead to arrange for 1 of the 2 trolleys with lifts (boarding other trolleys requires climbing 3 steps). While able-bodied passengers can get off and reboard at any of the 14 stops in town, the WC lifts can only be used at Mallory Sq. 9-4:30; every 30 min (305-296-6688)

Trials of Margaritaville is a tour on the life of one-time resident, Jimmy Buffett. The 1 1/2-hr walking tour covers less than a mi and takes you by his first house, recording studio and favorite bars. 11 & 4 (Capt Tony's Bar, 426 Green St; 305-292-2040)

ACCOMMODATIONS

■ B&B/INNS
Blue Parrot Inn, built in 1884, has the ADA Maloney Room (#9) with 2 full beds (22" high/open frames), a refrigerator, ramp from the sidewalk to the entry and bathroom with a raised toilet, roll-under sink and roll-in shower with a hand-held sprayer and seat. Extraordinary gardens surround this 10-room inn. Free brkfst; pool; street parking extra. $$$ (916 Elizabeth St; 305-296-0033; 800-231-2473)

Casa Alante Guest Cottages include an ADA 1-room cottage with a queen bed (open frame), kitchenette and private bath with a raised toilet, roll-under sink and roll-in shower. From the terry cloth robe to the flower-bedecked breakfast tray served on your private terrace, this is a special place. Pool. $$-$$$ (1435 S US 1; 305-293-0702; 800-688-3942)

Center Court is a charming historic inn with an ADA cottage that has a king bed (28" high/open frame), kitchenette and porch with a pool and garden view. The bath has a raised toilet, roll-under sink and tub with a hand-held sprayer and seat. Free brkfst; pool; fitness room; pets at extra charge. $$$ (915 Center St; 305-296-9292; 800-797-8787)

Curry Mansion Inn, a historic museum and inn, has a WC-friendly guestroom. The room has a king bed (28" high/open frame), refrigerator and private bath with a 32" wide door, raised toilet, roll-under sink and step-in shower with a hand-held sprayer and seat. An outdoor lift takes you to the 1st floor of the 20-room mansion filled with fabulous antiques. Continental breakfast served in dining room; pool; laundry. $$$ (511 Caroline St; 305-294-5349; 800-253-3466)

Cypress House, circa 1888, is 1 block E of downtown and has an ADA guest studio room (not in the main house) with a ramp. The room has a queen bed (24" high/open frame) and a shaded patio with a hot tub. The bathroom has a pedestal sink, raised toilet and roll-in shower (25" entry) with a seat. Continental breakfast and happy hour is served in a covered area poolside or, if you prefer, in your room. $$$ (601 Caroline St; at Simonton St; 305-294-6969; 800-525-2488)

Frances Street Bottle Inn, a conch-style historic building, has an ADA guestroom with a queen bed (22" high/open frame) and bathroom with a raised toilet, roll-under sink and tub with a seat. Spa area; lounge; continental brkfst. $$-$$$ (535 Frances St; 305-294-8530; 800-294-8530)

Key Lime Inn, a Grand Bahamian style home in the historic district, has 2 ADA rooms, each with a refrigerator, coffeepot and private patio. Room 36 has a king bed (23" high) and room 37 has a queen bed (30" high), both on open frames. The private baths have raised toilets and roll-in showers with hand-held sprayers and seats. Enjoy fresh juice, croissants and a newspaper each morning. Pool. $$-$$$ (725 Truman Ave; 305-294-5229; 800-549-4430)

Paradise Inn is a luxurious intimate resort with an ADA room that has a king bed (24" high/open frame), sitting area and refrigerator. The private marble bath has a raised toilet, roll-under sink and roll-in shower with a hand-held sprayer and seat. The lush tropical courtyard contains a fountain-fed pool and a fishpond. Pool; laundry; lounge; continental brkfst. $$$ (819 Simonton St; 305-293-8007; 800-888-9648)

Pilot House Guest House is a lovely, Victorian 8-room house with an ADA poolside room with a full kitchen, king bed (18" high/open frame) and private bathroom with a raised toilet, roll-under sink and roll-in shower with a hand-held sprayer and seat. Pool. $$$ (414 Simonton St; 305-294-8719; 800-648-3780)

Weatherstation Inn is located 2 blocks from downtown and close to the Gulf. The ADA Backcountry Room has a queen bed (open frame) and bathroom

with a raised toilet, roll-under sink and roll-in shower with a hand-held sprayer. WC lift to the entrance; free brkfst; pool. $$$ (57 Front St; 305-294-7277; 800-815-2707)

■ **CAMPGROUNDS**
Parks: Dry Tortugas
Bahia Honda State Park has 80 level, hard-packed sites with either grills or fire rings and most with ADA picnic tables. The more shady Sandspur area is for tents. The Buttonwood area has 48 RV sites with water/elec. The ADA bathhouse in each area has raised toilets, roll-under sinks and roll-in showers. The park has a beach WC and more; see Parks. Cabins are not accessible. (MM36.5, Bahia Honda Key; 305-872-2353)

■ **CONDOS**
Sunrise Suites has small, designated WC-friendly, 2BR condos close to Smathers Beach and the airport. The master bedroom has a king bed (22" high/platform) and a bathroom with a wide door, grab bars, roll-under sink and tub with a seat. The second bedroom has a full bed and connects to a standard bathroom with a tub. Each condo has a full kitchen, queen sofa bed in the living room and the only dining table on the balcony. Heated pool; hot tub; tennis; exercise room; bike rental; concierge service. $$$ (3685 Seaside Dr; off S Roosevelt Blvd; 305-296-6661; 888-723-5200)

■ **MOTELS**
Banana Bay Resort is a romantic, adults-only getaway that has 2 ADA rooms, each with 2 full beds (24" high/platforms), a refrigerator, private veranda and bathroom with a raised toilet, roll-under sink and tub with a hand-held sprayer and seat. See Boat Charters & Fishing Charters. Free brkfst; marina; pool; laundry. $$$ (2319 N US 1; 305-296-6925; 800-226-2621)

Comfort Inn has 5 ADA rooms, each with a king or 2 full beds (27" high/open frames) and a bathroom with a raised toilet and roll-under sink. Room 101 has a roll-in shower, hand-held sprayer and seat; others have tubs. Free brkfst; pool; laundry. $$-$$$ (3824 N US 1; 305-294-3773)

Grand Key Resort has 10 ADA rooms, each with a king bed (24" high/open frame), mini-refrigerator, coffeepot and bathroom with a raised toilet and roll-under sink. Each ADA room can be opened to adjoin a standard room with 2 queen beds. Rooms 101, 179 and 317 have roll-in showers, hand-held sprayers and seats; others have tubs. This hotel has a zero-depth pool. Lounge; full restaurant. $$$ (3990 S US 1; 305-293-1818; 888-310-1540)

Hampton Inn has 6 ADA rooms, each with a king bed (22" high/platform), recliner, coffeepot and bathroom with a raised toilet and roll-under sink. Rooms 137, 151 and 153 have roll-in showers, hand-held sprayers and seats; others have tubs. Free brkfst; pool; poolside bar. $$-$$$ (2801 N US 1; 305-294-2917)

Hilton, right in downtown and with a marina on the Gulf, has 7 ADA rooms and an ADA 2BR suite. Each room has a king or 2 queen beds (open frames) and a refrigerator. Bathrooms have roll-under sinks; rooms 153 and 157 have roll-in showers; others have step-in showers with hand-held sprayers and seats or tubs. The suite has a parlor with a refrigerator and mini-bar, a king bed in both bedrooms and bathrooms with roll-under sinks and grab bars at the tubs. See Boat Rentals. Pool; tiki bar; lounge; full restaurant. $$$ (245 Front St; 305-294-4000)

Hyatt Key West, overlooking Mallory Square, has 5 ADA rooms, each with a king or 2 full beds (24" high/open frames), a sofa bed, coffeepot and, in some, a refrigerator. Bathrooms have raised toilets and roll-under sinks (room 1106 does not have grab bars). Rooms 2105 and 2106 have roll-in showers with seats; others have tubs. This resort also has a portable lift (with a fixed seat) that can be installed at the heated pool for guests in WCs; staff is happy to help with transfers. Neither the small beach nor the marina on the Gulf is accessible. Lounge; entertainment; full restaurant; fitness room. $$$ (601 Front St; 305-296-9900)

Radisson Hotel has 7 ADA rooms, each with a king or 2 full beds (open frames), a refrigerator and coffeepot. Bathrooms have raised toilets and roll-under sinks; rooms 101 and 102 have roll-in showers, others have step-in showers; all have hand-held sprayers and seats. Pool; full restaurant. $$$ (3820 N US 1; 305-294-5511)

Sheraton Suites Key West has 10 spacious ADA suites, each with a king or 2 full beds (18" high/platforms), a refrigerator, microwave, coffeepot and queen sofa bed in the living room. Bathrooms have raised toilets and roll-under sinks; rooms 142 and 154 have roll-in showers, others have step-in showers; all have hand-held sprayers and seats. Across from Smathers Beach; full restaurant; fitness room. $$$ (2001 S US 1; 305-292-9800; 800-452-3224)

Sugarloaf Lodge has 3 WC-friendly rooms, each with 2 full beds (open frames), a sofa bed and bathroom with grab bars. The next-door marina has a bait shop, fishing charters and a boat ramp with fixed docks (but you can use the floating dock behind the lodge). Pool; tiki bar; small beach; lounge; entertainment; full restaurant; country store. $$-$$$ (MM17, Sugarloaf Key; 305-745-3211; 800-553-6097)

We want to hear from you!
Your comments and suggestions
are important to us.
If you find something new,
please tell us about it.
If you've had a disappointing experence,
we'd like to know that too.

You can either e-mail us at:
wheelchairsonthego@yahoo.com

Or send your comments to:
Wheelchairs on the Go
14074 Egret Lane
Clearwater, FL 33762

As a service to our readers only,
you can access updates at
www.wheelchairsonthego.com/pages/2/updates

APPENDIX

TRAVEL RESOURCES

Specifically for Travelers with Disabilities

Access-able is a comprehensive web site and an on-line newsletter for WC travelers in the US and abroad and for WC riders in general. (303-232-2979; www.access-able.com)

The Enabled RVer features destinations and accessible RVs. (http://maxpages.com/enabledrver)

Handicapped Travel Club focuses on RV travel and campgrounds and sponsors rallies. (317-849-8019; www.handicappedtravelclub.com)

Guide to Outdoor Recreation explores different locations (many in Florida) with accessible outdoor opportunities. (www.gorp.com/gorp/eclectic/disabled.htm)

Moss Rehab Resource Net provides information and links to sites on travel such as different modes of transportation, cruises, tourism offices and more. (215-456-5995; www.mossresourcenet.org/travel.htm)

Scoot-Around North America locates and delivers rental scooters and WCs. (888-441-7575; www.scootaround.com)

Travelin' Talk Network is a worldwide network of persons with disabilities who share information and assist other members visiting their areas. A newsletter features accessible destinations, tips and resources. (303-232-2979; www.travelintalk.net)

TravlCare can arrange for medical equipment, wheelchairs, scooters, oxygen/respiratory care, nursing services, travel companions, IV/infusion therapies, interpretation services and transportation, including accessible van rentals. (407-566-1589; 800-700-4399; www.travlcare.net)

General Travel in Florida

Free Publications

Baseball Spring Training Guide: 850-488-8347; www.flasports.com
Great Florida Birding Trail: 850-922-0664; www.floridabirdingtrail.com
Camping Directory: 850-562-7151; www.floridacamping.com
Fishing & Boating: 850-488-8347; www.flasports.com
Play FLA Golf: 850-488-8347; www.flasports.com
RVers Guide to Florida: 813-684-7882; 800-330-7882; www.frvta.org
State Parks: 850-488-9872; www.dep.state.fl.us/parks
Vacation Guide: 850-488-5607; 888-735-2872; www.flausa.com/tools/index.php

Web Sites

Online visitor magazine: www.see-florida.com
Attractions: www.floridaattractions.org/cvb.asp
Dining, lodging, nightlife, shopping: www.floridavacationbeachguide.com
Festivals, events, sightseeing, outdoors: www.floridaexplorer.com
Florida tourism: www.funandsun.com
Orlando & Coastal accommodations, attractions: www.beachdirectory.com

SPORTS & RECREATION RESOURCES

Specifically for Persons with Disabilities

Also see the Index and Using this Guide, beginning on pg 10, for basketball, bowling, horseback riding, hunting, fishing, scuba, tennis, golf and quad rugby.

Access Outdoors features trips, destinations, products and services for enjoying the outdoors. (www.accessoutdoors.org)

Achilles Track Club encourages runners with crutches, in wheelchairs, on prostheses and without aids to participate with able-bodied runners. (212-354-0300; www.achillestrackclub.org/local/domestic.html#florida)

Buckmasters provides hunters information on adaptive equipment, state laws, hunting opportunities, organizations and more. (205-339-2800; www.badf.org/DisabledHunters.html)

Disabled Sports USA sponsors athletic programs that may include snow skiing, water skiing, sailing, kayaking, rafting, cycling, climbing, horseback riding, golf and social activities. (916-722-6447; www.dsusa.org)

Florida Disabled Outdoors promotes accessible outdoor recreational facilities and programs such as *Sportsability* clinics (see WC Events p 17) and hunts (see hunting p 13). (850-668-7323; fdoa@nettally.com; www.fdoa.org)

Golden Access Passport allows free entry to US National Parks, Monuments, Forests and Historic Sites for all permanent US residents eligible for (even if not receiving) federal benefits based on a disability. Apply in person at any National Park or Forest Service office.

Winners on Wheels are scouting groups for kids in wheelchairs. (800-969-8255; www.wowusa.com)

General

Bike/hike trails: www.traillink.com; www.railsfromtrails.com
Boating, fishing, hunting, licenses: 850-488-4676; www.floridaconservation.org
Cycling events, tours: www.floridacycling.com
Greyhounds, horse races: www.floridaracing.com
Florida outdoors: www8.myflorida.com/myflorida/tourism.htm

TRANSPORTATION

Specifically for Travelers with Disabilities

National companies renting lift-equipped vans: Accessible Vans of America (888-282-8267; www.accessiblevans.com); Wheelchair Getaways (800-642-2042; www.wheelchair-getaways.com); Wheelers Accessible Vans (800-456-1371; www.wheelerz.com)

Regional companies renting lift-equipped vans, most of whom deliver to nearby areas: in Orlando, Rainbow Wheels (800-910-8267; www.rainbowwheels.com); in Tampa Bay, Mobility Independent Transport System (727-518-8787; 800-868-6641); and, CEH (727-522-0364); on the Southeast Atlantic Coast, Medical Travel (561-361-9384; 800-778-7953)

National Car Rental Agencies offering hand controls in many locations are below. Some require a weeks notice; some can deliver the car to the airport terminal or provide accessible transportation to the rental lot. If you need a special make or model car, make your reservations through the central reservation number, then call the local agency to confirm with the manager one week prior to pick up. Alamo (800-327-9633); Avis (800-331-2221); Budget (800-527-0700); Dollar (800-800-4000); Enterprise (800-325-8007); Hertz (800-654-3131); National (800-227-7368)

Project Action Accessible Traveler's Database, National Easter Seal Society, provides information on public and private transportation including taxis and van rentals. (301-951-8660; www.projectaction.org/paweb/index.htm)

Fresh Air Transportation can arrange a driver and standard or lift-equipped vehicle anywhere in the US with 24-hour advance reservations. (888-472-8322)

Amtrak's stations are accessible and all trains have at least one car with WC seating and Rr. You cannot move between cars; meals can be delivered to WC passengers. Trains with sleeper coaches have an ADA compartment with a private bath on each car. On some routes, you can take your car. Request the publication, *Access Amtrak.* (customer service: 202-906-2121; auto train: 877-754-7495; reservations: 800-872-7245; www.amtrak.com)

Access Greyhound tries to meet the needs of all WC travelers with 48-hr notice. (800-752-4841)

Parking Fees, under Florida law, are waived at airports for vehicles with specialized equipment such as ramps, lifts or hand controls or with a Florida Toll Exemption Permit. Parking is free at parking meters for up to 4 hours and in state and municipal parking lots except when the lot is being used for an event.

TRAVEL AGENCIES & TOUR GROUPS

Specializing in Accessible Travel

Access Tours offers package tours of National Parks and other sites in the western USA. (208-787-2338; 800-929-4811; www.accesstours.org.)

Accessible Journeys plans individual travel and escorts groups. (800-846-4537; 610-521-0339)

Alaska Welcomes You! specializes in individual travel and group tours on lift-equipped buses through Alaska. (907-349-6301; 800-349-6301; www.alaskan.com/vendors/welcome.html)

Discovery Hills Travel specializes in cruises to Hawaii, Mexico and the Caribbean. (760-744-6536; 800-750-5975; www.discoveryhillstravel.com)

Easy Access Travel researches clients' vacation plans to minimize potential barriers. (909-372-9595; 800 920-8989; www.easyaccesstravel.com)

Elderhostel's educational tours are geared to persons age 55 and older, many are accessible. (877-426-8056; specialneeds@elderhostel.org; www.elderhostel.org)

Flying Wheels plans individual and group travel. (507-451-5005; 800-535-6790; www.flyingwheelstravel.com)

Handicapped Scuba Association leads dive vacations to exotic locations with HSA-certified dive instructors. (949-498-4540; www.hsascuba.com)

MedEscort arranges health care professionals throughout the USA for travelers needing attendants in particular sites. (215-791-3111; 800-255-7182)

Medical Travel plans US and overseas vacations for travelers needing medical services and supplies. (561-361-9384; 800-778-7953; www.medicaltravel.org)

Nautilus Tours & Cruises plans individual and group travel. (818-591-3159; 800-797-6004; www.nautilustours.com)

Search Beyond Adventures offers packaged and custom tours. (612-721-2800; 800-800-9979; www.searchbeyond.com)

TASC offers vacation packages, including medical assistance. (781-979-0400/

winter 407-522-8838; www.tascnet.org)
Travel Innovations specializes in individual travel. (800-321-8264; email: trvlinn@aol.com)
Travel Outlet plans individual and group travel. (740-928-0890; 800-708-6359; www.traveloutlet.org)
Turtle Tours plans guided tours. (520-204-1781; 800-453-9195)
Wheels Up! Travel plans individual and group travel. (888-389-4335; www.wheelsup.com)
Wilderness Inquiry leads outdoor adventures such as canoe, dogsled, sea kayak and raft trips. (612-676-9400; 800-728-0719; www.wildernessinquiry)

PUBLICATIONS

For Persons with Disabilities
Abilities is a lifestyle magazine published by the Canadian Abilities Foundation. 4/yr (416-923-1885; www.abilities.ca)
Ability Magazine features celebrity interviews, news and useful resources. 6/yr (949-854-8700; www.abilitymagazine.com)
Access to Recreation is a free catalog of products for indoor and outdoor recreation. (805-498-7535; 800-634-4351; www.accesstr.com)
Active Living focuses on health and fitness, travel, sports and recreation. 6/yr (905-309-1639; www.activelivingmagazine.com)
Challenge Magazine is published by Disabled Sports USA. 3/yr (301-217-9839; www.dsusa.org/challengemag.htm)
Disabled Dealer lists used wheelchairs, scooters, adaptive equipment, vans, RVs and homes for sale. 12/yr (800-554-6893; www.disableddealer.com)
Emerging Horizons focuses on travel. 4/yr (209-599-9409; www.EmergingHorizons.com)
Exceptional Parent is a magazine and annual resource guide for parents of children with disabilities. 12/yr (201-634-6550; www.eparent.com)
New Mobility covers a range of topics and resources for active lifestyles. 12/yr (215-675-9133; 888-850-0344; www.newmobility.com)
Open World magazine is published by the Society for the Advancement of Travel for the Handicapped. 4/yr (212-447-7284; www.sath.org)
Paraplegia News is published by the Paralyzed Veterans of America. 12/yr (602-224-0500x19; 888-888-2201; www.pn-magazine.com)
Quest is published by the Muscular Dystrophy Association. 6/yr (520-529-2000; www.mdausa.org/publications)
SpeciaLiving focuses on housing, products, travel, health issues and more. 4/yr (309- 825-8842; www.specialiving.com)
Spinal Network is a comprehensive book and directory (updated every few years) on health, technology, attendant services, employment, travel, sports, legal rights, government benefits and more. (888-850-0344x109)
Sports 'n Spokes, published by the Paralyzed Veterans of America, focuses on sports and recreation, including competitions. 8/yr (602-224-0500x19; 888-888-2201; www.sportsnspokes.com)
Travel 50 and Beyond features good travel values. 4/yr (713-974-6903; www.travel50andbeyond.com)
We Magazine is online and soon-to-be-again an in-print magazine. (212-931-6700; www.wemedia.com)

MISCELLANEOUS

Department of Justice ADA information and complaint line: 800-514-0301; www.usdoj.gov/crt/ada/adahom1.htm
Clearinghouse on Disability provides information and referrals to disability related services, programs, assistance and resources in Florida: 850-497-3423; 877-232-4968

ACCOMMODATIONS

General
Florida Room Reservations (800-847-4835)
Florida State Park Campground Reservations (800-326-3521)
KOA Campgrounds: www.koakampgrounds.com
Web Sites
Condos: www3.cyberrentals.com/FL/Florida.html
Discount lodging coupons: www.travelsaverguides.com
www.hotelcoupons.com; http://www.roomsavers.com/roomsaver
Swapping WC-accessible homes: www.independentliving.org/vacaswap.html
Bed & Breakfasts/Inns: www.1-888-inn-seek.com/regionsearch.htm
Bed & Breakfasts: www.bedandbreakfast.com/amenity/index.asp
Central Reservations for Chain Motels

Amerisuites	800-833-1516	La Quinta	800-531-5900
Baymont Inns & Suites	800-301-0200	Marriott	800-228-9290
Best Western	800-528-1234	Microtel Inn & Suites	888-771-7171
Budgetel	800-428-3438	Motel 6	800-437-7486
Candlewood Suites	888-226-3539	Park Inns	800-437-7275
Clarion	800-252-7466	Quality Inn	800-228-5151
Comfort Inns	800-228-5150	Radisson	800-333-3333
Country Inn & Suites	800-456-4000	Ramada	800-272-6232
Days Inn	800-325-2525	Red Carpet	800-251-1962
Doubletree	800-528-0444	Red Lion Inn	800-547-8010
Econo Lodge	800-553-2666	Red Roof Inn	800-843-7663
Embassy Suites	800-362-2779	Residence Inn	800-331-3131
Extended Stay Studios	800-398-7829	Rodeway	800-228-2000
Fairfield Inn	800-228-2800	Sheraton	800-325-3535
Hampton Inn	800-654-2000	Sleep Inn	800-221-2222
Hilton Hotels	800-445-8667	Super 8	800-848-8888
Holiday Inn	800-465-4329	Surburan Lodge	800-282-6827
Homestead Suites	888-782-9473	Travelodge	800-578-7878
Homewood Suites	800-225-5466	Wellesley Inn	800-444-8888
Howard Johnson	800-446-4656	Westin Hotels	800-228-3000
Hyatt	800-233-1234	Wyndham Hotels	800-228-3000

GENERAL INDEX

Certain Listings are identified by Region: **P**: Panhandle; **NW**: Northwest Gulf Coast; **TB**: Tampa Bay; **SW**: Southwest Gulf Coast; **NC**: North Central; **C**: Central; **O**: Orlando; **NE**: Northeast Atlantic Coast; **CA**: Central Atlantic Coast; **SE** Southeast Atlantic Coast; **E**: Everglades National Park; **K**: Keys.

ACCOMMODATIONS INDEX

Also see Appendix 410

Certain Listings are identified by Region: P: Panhandle; NW: Northwest Gulf Coast; TB: Tampa Bay; SW: Southwest Gulf Coast; NC: North Central; C: Central; O: Orlando; NE: Northeast Atlantic Coast; CA: Central Atlantic Coast; SE Southeast Atlantic Coast; E: Everglades National Park; K: Keys.

BEACHES & PARKS INDEX

Also see Nature Centers and Gardens in the General Index pg 413

*Denotes Bch WC; "/CG" denotes campground

CITIES INDEX

MUSEUMS INDEX

PERFORMING ARTS INDEX
HALLS, PLAYHOUSES AND THEATERS